# BUSINESS ETHICS

*Third Edition*

*Edited by*

# MILTON SNOEYENBOS
# ROBERT ALMEDER
# JAMES HUMBER

 **Prometheus Books**

59 John Glenn Drive
Amherst, New York 14228-2119

Published 2001 by Prometheus Books

Inquiries should be addressed to
Prometheus Books
59 John Glenn Drive
Amherst, New York 14228–2119
VOICE: 716–691–0133, ext. 210
FAX: 716–691–0137
WWW.PROMETHEUSBOOKS.COM

11 10 09 08 07    7 6 5 4 3

Library of Congress Cataloging-in-Publication Data

Business ethics / edited by Milton Snoeyenbos, Robert Almeder, James Humber.—3rd ed.
    p. cm.
    Includes bibliographical references.
    ISBN 978-1-57392-903-5 (alk. paper)
    1. Business ethics—Case studies. I. Snoeyenbos, Milton. II. Almeder, Robert F. III. Humber, James M.

HF5387 .B87 2001
174'.4—dc21                                                        2001031933

Printed in the United States of America on acid-free paper

# BUSINESS ETHICS

# CONTENTS

# PREFACE

Many of the job-related decisions corporate employees must make are moral in nature. Recognizing this fact, most institutions of higher learning now offer business ethics courses in an attempt to provide students with the tools necessary to make such decisions. As business ethics courses have proliferated, the number of texts designed for teaching such courses has increased as well. Unfortunately, however, many of these texts are flawed in one of two ways: (1) those that address issues of interest to business students are generally not philosophically sophisticated, and (2) philosophically sophisticated texts are often *too* sophisticated, concentrating on issues that appeal to philosophers rather than business students.

In designing this book a conscious attempt has been made to avoid both of these extremes. We began with the intuition that business ethics courses should be designed primarily for business students, and should therefore address the issues faced by business men and women in their professional lives. Furthermore, we felt that only "essential" elements of ethical theory need be considered; lengthy discourses on distributive justice, Kant's categorical imperative, metaethics, and similar topics would only bore students and leave them with the impression that moral philosophy is unintelligible to all but a few "eggheads," and totally irrelevant to "real life."

To achieve our goals we worked closely with the College of Business at Georgia State University in an effort to identify moral issues relevant to business men and women. We have taught a number of business ethics courses to students enrolled in the school of business, and, in the process, a wide variety of teaching materials have been evaluated. Sometimes the extant literature did not fill our needs; and where we found this to be the case we wrote essays ourselves or commissioned others to write them. All the essays included in this text have been chosen for their intelligibility and their potential to encourage classroom discussion. The essays are not intended to *solve* moral problems. Rather, they raise moral issues and propose "bold hypotheses" that invite further discussion. Additional discussion is encouraged by the inclusion of numerous case studies.

Business students who work through this text will learn some of the essentials of ethical theory, and will acquire the basic tools needed to deal with the types of moral problems they will face during their professional lives. Again, the case studies illustrate the types of situation people are likely to encounter in business. On the other hand, philosophy students will learn a great deal about the business world and the problems confronting corporate employees. Both philosophy and business have much to gain by a closer alliance; and if that alliance is strengthened in any way by our text, we will count it a success.

We wish to thank the faculty of the College of Business at Georgia State University for their advice and assistance in this project. Special thanks must also go to our wives, Peg Snoeyenbos, Virginia Almeder, and Helene Humber, whose patience and understanding make our work considerably easier than it might otherwise be.

It was our pleasure and good fortune to work with a highly skilled editor, Steven L. Mitchell of Prometheus Books, since the inception of this project. He brought not only diligence and editorial ability to his task, but philosophical acumen as well. We would also like to thank Christine Kramer, production manager, and Art Merchant, assistant editor, for their work on this edition.

Milton Snoeyenbos
Robert Almeder
James Humber

Georgia State University

# 1. INTRODUCTION

This collection of essays is about ethical issues that arise within the context of business practices. As such, it does not describe actual business practices; its primary concern is not with detailing how businesspersons actually finance an enterprise, market products, or handle labor negotiations. Instead, its focus is on such issues as whether businesspersons should give preferential treatment to disadvantaged individuals, whether managers have moral and social obligations other than maximizing profits for their firms' shareholders, and whether some advertising is deceptive and therefore should be restricted or banned. All of us have opinions on these issues, and the readings in this volume contain contrasting points of view; but in order to understand fully such controversies and to resolve them rationally some acquaintance with ethical theory is required. This introduction presents some of the fundamentals of ethical theory; it provides a framework for informed discussion of the specific ethical issues taken up in the rest of the book.

*Ethics* is a discipline involving inquiry into the moral judgments people make and the rules and principles upon which such judgments are based. All of us are able to recognize moral judgments; we know, for example, that the following sentences express moral judgments:

1. The insider trading practices of Ivan Boesky were morally wrong.
2. The Lockheed payoffs to Japanese government officials to obtain sales of the TriStar were reprehensible and should not have been made.
3. Price fixing is wrong.

The following sentences, however, do not typically express moral judgments:

4. Ivan Boesky engaged in insider trading.
5. Lockheed officials made payments to Japanese government officials to obtain sales of the TriStar.
6. Over 200 people were killed in rollover accidents involving Ford Explorers and Firestone tires in the late 1990s.

In examining these lists we can note that the sentences expressing moral judgments contain such *evaluative* terms as "good," "bad," "right," "wrong," "ought," and "should." The presence of these words frequently indicates that a moral judgment has been made. The presence of an evaluative word is not, however, sufficient for a judgment to be considered moral, for there are non-moral judgments that also contain evaluative terms. For example,

> 7. The Mona Lisa is a good painting.

makes an aesthetic, not a moral, judgment about the painting, and

> 8. If you want to get to Chicago in two hours, then you ought to take United flight 247.

makes a nonmoral, prudential claim; it tells you the best means to employ to achieve a practical goal. There is no connection with morality here whatsoever. Furthermore,

> 9. Most Americans believe price fixing is wrong.

does not express a moral judgment; it merely states a statistical fact about American opinion. It follows that we cannot simply say that a judgment containing an evaluative word is a moral judgment; nor is it the case that all moral judgments contain evaluative words, for there are contexts in which

> 10. Hooker Chemical polluted the Love Canal.

could be used to judge that Hooker's action was wrong. Although there do not seem to be hard and fast linguistic rules for marking off moral from non-moral judgments, it is the case that the former typically contain an evaluative term. Furthermore, most of us have a firm enough intuitive grasp of the moral/nonmoral distinction so that we can recognize moral judgments when they are made, and this is enough for our present purposes.

Having said that ethics involves the systematic study of moral judgments and the rules and principles upon which such judgments are based, we should note that there are two major types of systematic inquiry regarding moral judgments: *descriptive ethics* and *normative ethics*. The former is concerned with facts about the moral judgments or moral beliefs of a person or a group of persons; for example:

11. Jane Jones believes Ford Motor ought to have installed a safer gas tank on the early models of the Pinto.
12. Most Americans believe it was wrong of Ivan Boesky to trade stocks on the basis of insider information.

These are factual claims, the truth or falsity of which is determinable by empirical investigation. Research regarding such issues is conducted by social scientists with the aim of finding out what moral beliefs people actually hold or what judgments they make. Thus, we can ask Jones whether she believes Ford should have installed a safer gas tank on the early Pinto and receive a yes or no answer, and if we poll a large, representative sample of the American people and find that most of the sample believe Ivan Boesky was morally wrong in trading on insider information, then 12 can legitimately be inferred to be true.

Now as we have noted, there are differences between the factual claim made in 12, the truth of which is determinable by a poll, and the following moral judgment:

13. Ivan Boesky acted immorally in trading on insider information.

Some people allow that 12 is true, while claiming that what Boesky did was morally permissible. Descriptive ethics, however, is not primarily concerned with the correctness or adequacy of moral judgments such as 13; the scientist focuses on establishing what moral beliefs are actually held by an individual or group of persons.

*Normative ethics* is a second important branch of ethical inquiry. It is concerned primarily with two questions: (A) What kinds of things are good? (B) What kinds of acts are right and should be performed? The latter question is of primary interest in business ethics, and we shall return to it after a brief discussion of (A).

Since the time of the ancient Greeks normative ethical theorists have attempted to develop a defensible account of what kinds of things are good or valuable. In the course of their investigations they have sorted out three distinct senses of "value." In one sense, the *preference* sense, a person values something if he prefers, likes, or takes an interest in it; some people, for example, value their work while others value leisure time. In this sense, those who take an interest in smoking, or who like to smoke, can be said to value smoking. In another sense, something can be valuable to a person even though he does not take an interest in it. We say that a person's health is valuable to him even though he may neglect it, and, in this sense, smoking is not of value to a person even though he likes to smoke. In the first sense, then, what is valuable is what is liked or preferred, and in the second sense what is valuable is what serves as a means to some end independent of whether it is preferred. For example, milk is valuable as a means to a healthy body, irrespective of whether an individual likes milk. A thing valued because it serves as a means to some end independent of whether it is preferred is said to be *instrumentally valuable*. There are many things—such as money, food, and security—that would normally be considered of instrumental value for humans, but are there things that are good in and for themselves and not merely of instrumental value; that is, are there things that are good for their own sakes, or *intrinsically valuable*, without reference to a further end? Many normative theorists have argued that there are such intrinsically good things, but there is considerable disagreement as to what things possess this sort of value. Pleasure, happiness, goodwill, freedom, honesty, knowledge, benevolence, and self-development have all been proposed as being intrinsically good, and one task of normative ethics is to assess these proposals. Can it be shown, for example, that one of the above-mentioned things is intrinsically valuable whereas the others are merely instrumentally valuable, or should we allow that several or all of them are intrinsically valuable?

Without resolving this issue, we can note the relevance of the instrumental/ intrinsic value distinction to issues in business ethics. In a general sense the defenses of the capitalistic economic system rest on emphasizing either its instrumental or intrinsic value. Given that people have basic intrinsic wants, and that a modern society requires capital to satisfy those wants, the instrumental defense of capitalism rests on showing that it can accumulate and allocate capital more effectively than alternative economic systems, and therefore better satisfy those wants. The defender of capitalism may also stress its intrinsic values. Freedom, for example, is often regarded as having intrinsic value, and economic freedom, the freedom to buy, sell, and compete for profits, can be regarded as one aspect of that intrinsic good. The distinction between instrumental and intrinsic value is also important in discussing issues within the framework of capitalism. For example, if freedom of speech has intrinsic value, and justified uses of advertising involve an exercise of free speech, then advertising can be said to have intrinsic value. On the other hand, if promotion of the public good is regarded as intrinsically valuable, then advertising may or may not have instrumental value, depending on whether it is regarded as a successful means toward realizing the public good. Furthermore, ethical problems may emerge within a firm if a manager and her employees stress different values. If a manager regards profit as the sole value whereas a subordinate emphasizes family life, the latter may be pressured to acquiesce in an illegal or immoral business practice due to his family obligations and the fear that failure to cooperate could cost him his job. And the amount of work required of a subordinate for profit maximization may lead to a form of "corporate bigamy" leaving little time for the family. Similarly, a manager may value corporate loyalty while an employee believes that the public has a right to know about a potentially unsafe product. In such cases an awareness that the disputants are emphasizing different values is an important first step in resolving the conflict.

Having noted three distinct uses of "good" or "value," and their relevance for business contexts, we should also note that when we morally assess a person's acts we generally speak of "right" and "wrong." The second major branch of normative ethics, the branch that is perhaps most relevant to business ethics, is concerned with establishing standards for assessing acts as right or wrong, that is, with the development of a theory of right conduct. For purposes of illustration, suppose that a struggling minority firm submits the second lowest bid to supply a large corporation with a machine part, and suppose the corporation's purchasing agent, P, rejects the minority firm's bid; then consider the following conversation P has with her corporation's affirmative action officer, A:

$A_1$: Rejecting that minority firm's bid was wrong; although there is no law governing this sort of purchase, the rule we should adopt is to help those who have been disadvantaged, whenever it does not put our own company in serious economic jeopardy. Since the bids are so close, we should award the contract to the minority firm.

$P_2$: I disagree. We have an obligation to our company, and my act was right because, as a rule, the best course of action in these cases, the right thing to do, is to accept the lowest bid.

$A_3$: Wait a minute. We should treat our suppliers fairly; that's just an instance of the Golden Rule: treat others as you wish them to treat you. But in order to be fair to minority firms we must take past discriminatory practices into account in order to give them a fair shake.

$P_4$: I still think I am right. I think it is the case that economic efficiency—and that means accepting the lowest bid—leads to the best consequences for everyone, black and white, in the long run.

For our present purposes we need not extend this argument to try to determine who is right. What is noteworthy about this exchange is how one usually goes about justifying moral judgments. Ordinarily, moral disagreements occur within a context of action, and what one judges are *acts* (in this case P's act of rejecting the minority firm's bid). Furthermore, when a person judges an act, he usually appeals to some *moral rule* to justify his judgment: $A_1$ and $P_2$ both involve appeals to moral rules. But appeals of this type do not invariably settle a moral dispute, because, as $A_1$ and $P_2$ illustrate, moral rules may differ; and if two people accept different moral rules, their moral judgments may differ. To fully justify his moral judgments, then, a person must show why *his* moral rules are correct while his adversary's are not. To accomplish this a person appeals to a more general rule, a *moral principle* or standard. $A_3$ contains an appeal to the Golden Rule, while $P_4$ appeals to the principle that an act is right if and only if it has the best consequences for everyone.

Let us say that a set of moral rules justified by an appeal to a moral principle constitutes a moral theory. If a person has a *moral theory*, she makes moral judgments based on moral rules and she justifies her moral rules by appeal to a moral principle. When A judges P's act to be wrong he does so by appealing to the moral rule in $A_1$, and he justifies that rule in terms of the moral principle expressed in $A_3$. On the other hand, P justifies her act by appealing to the moral rule in $P_2$, and she justifies that rule by having recourse to the moral principle in $P_4$. Our example indicates that moral theories differ; distinct moral judgments may be based on different rules and principles. To adjudicate this dispute, then, A and P will have to assess the adequacy of the moral principles expressed in $A_3$ and $P_4$. Normative ethics involves the attempt to discover, formulate, and defend fundamental moral principles.

If the field of ethics has descriptive and normative domains, and if our primary concern in business ethics is with the normative domain, it would seem that our next task is to discuss and assess the various moral principles that normative ethical theorists have set forth. Before we can justifiably do so, however, we must take up two challenges that seem at the outset to undercut the relevance of the normative enterprise to the actions of businesspersons. First, it is often maintained that morals are relative. As we shall see, this claim can be interpreted in a variety of ways, but it is often taken to mean that, since all moral judgments, rules, and principles are relative to a particular cultural context, there can be no adequate universal normative theory, i.e., no normative moral theory that is binding on all people in all circumstances. It is claimed that if relativism is correct, there is simply no point in examining the various normative theories proposed as universal and hence asserted to be relevant within business contexts. Second, it is often claimed that the relation between morality and the law is such that, while businesspersons should obey the law, morality is in some fashion irrelevant in the context of business. If this view is defensible, there is surely no point in trying to formulate a normative ethical theory applicable within the business community. Let us examine these challenges in turn.

Many people believe that some form of moral relativism is acceptable—you have your moral rules and principle(s), I have mine, and that's that. In fact, however, there are different versions of relativism, and it is worthwhile to distinguish some of them to see whether they are acceptable and to note their relevance to issues in business ethics. In line with our previous discussion, let us focus on factual and normative versions of moral relativism.

It is often claimed that moral beliefs are in fact relative, that different people do make different moral judgments and advocate different moral rules and principles. Let us call this position *factual moral relativism* (FMR). As a factual matter, the truth of FMR can be decided by empirical investigation; the study of FMR falls within the domain of descriptive ethics. We can distinguish several specific claims within the domain of FMR; being factual claims, each is either true or false:

($R_1$) *Individual moral belief relativism*: the moral beliefs of one individual may differ from those of another.

($R_2$) *Societal moral belief relativism*: the moral beliefs widely accepted in one society may differ from the moral beliefs widely accepted in another society.

($R_3$) *Societal moral rule relativism*: the moral rules widely accepted in one society may differ from the moral rules widely accepted in another society.

($R_4$) *Societal moral principle relativism*: the moral principle(s) widely accepted in one society may differ from the moral principle(s) widely accepted in another society.

$R_1$ is true because one person may believe that Lockheed was morally right in making payoffs to Japanese officials to secure sales of its Tristar aircraft, while another person believes Lockheed's actions were wrong. $R_2$ and $R_3$ also seem to be true. In many areas of the Middle East, the Far East, and Africa, where a private-sector market economy governed by competitive pricing does not exist, the exchange of goods is governed by a complex network of tribal, social, and familial relations and obligations. In this context bribery is often regarded as a morally acceptable practice. In some cases it is governmentally sanctioned; civil servants' salaries, for example, may be kept low with the expectation that they will supplement their wages with bribe money. In America, on the other hand, bribery is widely acknowledged to be morally wrong. Lockheed's officials, for example, allowed that the bribes paid to Japanese officials were morally wrong; they defended the payoffs only as necessary for commercial success. It seems clear, therefore, that the specific moral beliefs widely accepted in one society may differ from those in another society, and the rules used to justify such acts may differ as well; $R_2$ and $R_3$ are true.

The truth or falsity of $R_4$ is not as easily established as the other forms of FMR. Certainly the truth of $R_1$, $R_2$, and $R_3$ does not establish the truth of $R_4$. Suppose that in society $S_1$ the judgment that a specific act of bribery is morally right and the belief that bribery is morally right are both widely accepted, while in society $S_2$ it is widely held that the act is wrong and that in general bribery is reprehensible. $R_2$ and $R_3$ are then true. But suppose the members of $S_1$ justify their moral rule by claiming that the practice of bribery has the best consequences for everyone concerned, while the members of $S_2$ justify their moral rule by maintaining that bribery does not have the best consequences for everyone. Both societies would then have justified incompatible moral rules by appeal to the same moral principle. Therefore, the truth of $R_1$, $R_2$, and $R_3$ does not substantiate $R_4$. Of course, the truth or falsity of $R_4$ is, as previously noted, a factual matter determinable by scientific investigation. The problem is that at present the anthropological evidence is not conclusive; there is data both for and against the truth of $R_4$.

Let us assume, however, that all the versions of FMR are true, including $R_4$, and proceed to raise the question of whether relativism's truth has any relevance for normative ethics. We have already noted that $R_1$, $R_2$, and $R_3$ do not necessarily conflict with the acceptance of one normative principle. Furthermore, even if $R_4$ is true, and societies do actually accept different normative moral principles, we still cannot conclusively infer that there is no single normative principle binding on all humans. If people in society $S_1$ accept moral principle $P_1$ while people in $S_2$ accept $P_2$, and $P_1$ and $P_2$ are incompatible, then the most we can infer is that one of the principles must be mistaken. In fact, both may be mistaken. But it does not follow that there is no true normative principle. Even if it could be shown that all the normative principles accepted by all societies to this point in time are, for one reason or another, inadequate, it would still not follow that there is no true normative principle; it may simply be the case that no person has discovered that principle. In short, the truth of the varieties of FMR does not preclude our finding a universally binding normative theory. The best that can be said for relativism is that if $R_4$ is, as a matter of fact, true, and if there is considerable disagreement on fundamental moral principles (a claim that anthropologists have yet to establish), then there is some inductive evidence for the claim that there is no such universal normative principle to be found.

Relativism is sometimes presented as a normative principle; *normative ethical relativism* (NER) is the claim that an act A in society S is right if and only if most people in S believe A is right. This is a universal normative principle insofar as it applies to any person in any society; it is relativistic insofar as it allows that an act that is right in one society may be wrong in another society. NER may be attractive to businesspersons, especially those doing business in the international arena. There is a democratic ring to NER, and it seems to capture the truth in the maxim "When in Rome do as the Romans do." Another advantage of NER is that it gives us a rather clear answer to whether a type of act is right or wrong. We simply take a poll in society S and if the majority in S believe the act is right then it is right. Since today we have sophisticated polling techniques, it is relatively easy to determine whether a type of act is morally right or wrong.

One argument against NER is that it may have morally objectionable consequences. If the majority of people in a society believe that owning slaves is an acceptable business practice, then it is morally right to own slaves in that society. Many people claim that the very possibility of allowing and sanctioning such practices is morally indefensible, and they reject NER on this basis alone. A second objection to NER is that it entails the infallibility of the majority, for what the majority believes to be right *is* right. Surely, we want to say, there are at least some cases in which the majority is wrong. A third criticism of NER is that it precludes the possibility of intersocietal comparisons. Suppose society $S_1$ regards slavery as right while $S_2$ regards it as wrong. Other things being equal, we would want to say the members of $S_2$ are more moral than the members of $S_1$. But if NER is true, we cannot justifiably say this. For the members of $S_1$ are right in following the majority's beliefs in $S_1$, and the same holds for $S_2$; both are performing right acts. We cannot fault the members of $S_1$ for not following the wishes of the members of $S_2$, because, according to NER, the members of $S_1$ are acting morally when they follow the majority opinion in $S_1$. Since NER is society-relative, there is no basis for condemning the members of $S_1$ for failing to adopt the majority opinion in $S_2$. Since we do want to make intersocietal moral comparisons, but NER precludes them, NER seems unacceptable.

In addition to these objections the arguments used to support NER are weak. First, it is sometimes claimed that the facts of factual moral relativism (FMR) provide evidence for NER. But even if it is true that individuals and societies have different moral beliefs, rules, and principles, as stated in $R_1$, $R_2$, $R_3$, and $R_4$, what people actually *believe* to be morally right cannot establish what *is* right, for, as we previously noted, some or even all of the individuals or groups may have mistaken beliefs. Hence, the facts of FMR seem irrelevant to the establishment of any normative principle, including NER. Second, it is argued that if we accept the principle of tolerance, namely, that we should not try to impose our moral beliefs on others, then we should accept NER because it is the only normative principle compatible with a commitment to tolerance. However, that conclusion does not follow. According to NER, if the majority believes in forcing a minority to accept some moral belief, then the act they are committing (an act of intolerance), is right. So NER need not foster tolerance. Furthermore, the denial of NER, and the acceptance of a nonrelativist normative principle, need not necessarily lead to intolerance, for the nonrelativist may accept the principle of tolerance as a moral rule. In general, then, the standard defenses of NER seem rather weak, and there do seem to be good arguments against its acceptability as a normative principle.

Let us now turn to the claim that although businesspersons should obey the law, if for none other than pragmatic reasons, ethical issues are in some sense irrelevant in the context of business, and hence, there is no point in attempting to formulate a normative theory that is applicable to business contexts.

One version of this position is that the jurisdictions of morality and the law are the same, so that the businessperson need not pay attention to moral rules or principles supposedly expressed independently of, or distinct from, the law—there are no such independent rules or principles. What is moral can be determined by simply examining the law. Furthermore, in following the law a businessperson is acting morally; to act morally is just to act in accordance with the law.

This view certainly simplifies moral matters; to check whether an act is morally wrong a businessperson need only check the legal statutes. But there are difficulties with this view of the relation between law and morality. First, if morality is synonymous with the law, then we cannot morally criticize the law. If act $x$ is morally wrong only because it is considered illegal, then a person cannot legitimately claim that $x$ is morally right even though it is illegal. So the view tends to entrench a form of societal conservatism; if slavery is legal in a society, and selling slaves an acceptable business practice, it cannot be legitimately claimed that the law should be changed because it is immoral. Furthermore, it should be noted that the law is coercive; enforcement is essential to the law, whereas, apart from societal pressures, our actions in the moral realm seem to be rooted in rational persuasion, conscience, and personal choice. These features of morality often serve as a basis for moral criticism of the law. The identification of law and morality, however, undercuts this voluntary or personal dimension and places considerable emphasis on enforcement. Individuals at odds with the public morality expressed in law are subjected to enforced penalties and at the same time are precluded from raising moral objections to the law, i.e., precluded from attempting to change the law by independent moral persuasion. In addition, on this view a change in law is a change in morality; so slavery is now illegal and immoral in America, yet in 1780 it was not only legal but also moral. Those who claim that slavery is always immoral must reject the identification of morality with the law.

A second version of the irrelevance of morality to business contexts rests on the claim that the law is totally independent of morality, and that although the law should be obeyed just because it is the law, moral considerations should not enter into the context of business.

This view seems partially correct insofar as it points out some differences between legality and morality. The law, as we noted, is coercive—it is connected with enforcement—whereas morality is not. Again, laws are made or enacted by humans, whereas it seems odd to say that moral rules or principles are *made* or *enacted*. But these differences do not entail a complete separation of law and morality. In fact, if we separate them completely, and claim that the law should be obeyed, then we once again seem to have no basis for failing to obey the law. If the law said slavery was legal, the question of its moral status would be irrelevant. On this view the law tends to be reduced to the domain of enforcement, and questions of the morality and justice of the law are simply set aside.

If moral rules are not synonymous with or reducible to positive law, and if legality is not totally independent of morality, it seems reasonable to say that legality often rests, in some sense, on morality. Legal obligation is not the basis of moral obligation, for the law is not as ultimate as fundamental moral principles. Laws are made and then repealed, but a genuine moral obligation is categorical and not repealable. For example, we should treat people with respect, not because of any legal considerations but because humans intrinsically ought to respect each other. And laws are often repealed on the basis of moral considerations. If a person argues that some laws are morally bad and ought to be changed, that the Constitution (morally) should be amended to preclude, say, abortion, or that a judge's decision ought to be reversed in the interest of justice, she is acknowledging the dependence of law on morality.

The upshot of our discussion is that normative ethics does seem relevant to the actions of businesspersons. We found that relativism does not undercut the attempt to find a universal normative theory, and we argued that the relation between law and morality is such that the former rests on the latter, and therefore it cannot be maintained that, although businesspersons should obey the law, morality is irrelevant in the business world. In light of our discussion, we can expand our notion of a moral theory to include legal rules or laws. Moral rules often serve as the justification for legal enactments, and moral rules, in turn, are justified on the basis of ultimate moral principles. This ordering of reasons reflects our claim that legality rests on morality.

If there were only one moral theory to which appeal could be made in making moral judgments, ethical disputes would be relatively easy to resolve. Unfortunately, things are not so simple in real life; and what we discover as we go about the process of living is that there are a number of competing moral theories from which we must choose. Although these theories can differ radically, some of them do have characteristics in common. The existence of these shared traits allows for the classification of moral theories into specific types. Traditionally, the broadest classification of moral theories is into one or the other of two classes: consequentialist and nonconsequentialist. Consequentialist theories hold that the rightness or wrongness of an act is ultimately determined by the act's *consequences*; i.e., an act is said to be morally right if it produces good consequences, and wrong if it produces bad results. Nonconsequentialists reject this view and claim that, ultimately, an act is right or wrong because of some factor independent of the act's consequences. In addition, most nonconsequentialists insist that an action cannot be judged morally unless one knows why the person who performed the action did what he did. In other words, nonconsequentialists tell us that a person's motives for acting are important, and that an action cannot be morally right unless the person (the agent) who performed it did what he did for the right reasons.

Many businesspersons and economists accept a moral theory that attempts to combine elements of both consequentialism and nonconsequentialism into one all-encompassing system. For reasons that will become apparent later, we have chosen to call this moral theory "restricted egoism." In what follows we shall examine restricted egoism in some detail. In addition, six other theories will be assessed. Three of these theories (ethical egoism, act utilitarianism, and rule utilitarianism) are consequentialist, and three (theologism, the Golden Rule and Kantianism) are nonconsequentialist. We should note that we have already discussed one nonconsequentialist theory, namely, normative ethical relativism. It says that an act A in society S is morally right if and only if most people in S believe A is right. This theory is a nonconsequentialist theory because according to it whatever most people believe is right (for whatever reason) is morally right. The people in S may believe A has the best consequences, but the majority may also believe A is right because a palm reader said A is right. Since on normative ethical relativisim the rightness of an act is not ultimately determined by the act's consequences, it is not a consequentialist theory.

Here is a chart of the theories discussed:

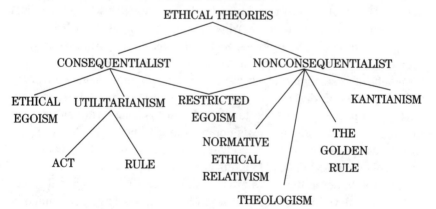

# CONSEQUENTIALISM

## *Ethical Egoism*

Ethical egoists claim that an act is morally right if and only if it tends, more than any alternative act open to the agent at the time, to promote the interests of the agent. That is to say, what is right, or what one ought to do, is to act in accordance with one's own self-interest.

Ethical egoism should be distinguished from psychological egoism, which is the claim that people do, as a matter of fact, always act in their own self-interest. Ethical egoism is an ethical theory that purports to tell us what people should do; psychological egoism, on the other hand, is a factual or empirical theory that makes a claim about what people actually do or what motivates them to act. Psychological egoism is sometimes used to support ethical egoism; the claim is that if people do invariably act in their own self-interest, then the only moral theory compatible with this fact is ethical egoism. If psychological egoism is true, though, ethics becomes pointless. This is so because a moral theory must tell us either that there are times when we ought to sacrifice our own self-interests or that we always ought to do what is in our own interests. If psychological egoism is true, it would make no sense to say that we *ought* to sacrifice our own interests (because we cannot, or as a matter of fact do not, do this), and it is pointless to tell us to maximize our self-interest (because we will do this anyway).

In discussing ethical egoism it is important to note that the theory advocates the long-term self-interest of the agent, and hence it is not a fair objection against ethical egoism to say that it favors short-term or immediate self-interest. In business, for example, an employee who is an ethical egoist may be very loyal and hard-working in the belief that these traits will promote the firm's interests, and that promotion of the firm's interests, e.g., profit maximization, is the best means to serve his own long-term self-interest. Similarly, an ethical egoist shareholder may advocate that the firm defer dividend payments and reinvest them in order to maximize capital gains, which he takes to be in his long-term self-interest. Acting in a self-sacrificing way is compatible with being an ethical egoist as long as the act leads to the long-term best interest of the agent. One advantage of ethical egoism in a business context, then, is that the egoist is obligated to act in the firm's interest so long as that interest is the best means to achieve his own long-term self-interest; in a large percentage of cases egoism is compatible with the firm's interests.

Although ethical egoism is a demanding theory in that it requires the agent to calculate very carefully her long-term self-interest, it is relatively simple in that she calculates only her own self-interest. So a second advantage of ethical egoism is that it is probable that each person best knows her own interests and knows relatively little about what is in the best interest of others. Ethical egoists claim that if we each consider just our own long-term self-interests, then each of us will likely be better off in the long run.

A third advantage of ethical egoism is that it provides a basis for the flexibility that seems to be needed in business decision-making. Normally a businessperson should keep his contracts, and the ethical egoist can explain why this is so; in most cases it is in his interest that contracts be kept. But the egoist claims that moral rules, e.g., "Always keep your contracts," are not inviolate. In fact, the principle of ethical egoism makes no reference to moral rules, for the rightness of an act is solely determined by whether it maximizes self-interest, and in certain cases strict adherence to a moral rule will not maximize self-interest. The egoist claims that business decision-making is too complex to be bound by strict rules and that the principle of ethical egoism provides the moral basis for both breaking and adhering to such rules.

In spite of these advantages, egoism has several weaknesses as an ethical theory in business contexts. First, if a businessperson believes that profit maximization is in her self-interest, then any means that she can employ and "get away with" to maximize profit are regarded as morally right. Thus, if in certain cases a businessperson can maximize profit by dumping a harmful pollutant or marketing an unsafe product, and the chances of her getting caught are slim, then she ought to commit such acts. In such cases the flexibility afforded the businessperson by ethical egoism allows her to commit acts that intuitively seem wrong.

More generally, one can argue that the ethical egoists' definition of "right act" does not reflect society's ordinary ways of speaking, and that, as a result, ethical egoists must be wrong when they say that we ought to pursue our own interests. Let us say, for instance, that we know a person, $P$, who acts only to further his own interests. Whenever $P$ helps others he does so only because this ultimately serves his own ends. At the same time, he never allows anyone to "get in his way." Furthermore, if it will ultimately benefit $P$ to lie about someone, or hurt someone, he will do so. Now would we ordinarily say that $P$ was a moral person, or that he was acting in morally right ways? It seems clear that we would not. Consequently, it seems that ethical egoists' understanding of what is right to do is mistaken and that their moral theory must be rejected.

Few ethical egoists would be convinced by the above criticism of their position. It might well be the case, they would say, that by "right act" most people do not mean "action which serves one's self-interest." Nevertheless, they would claim, this is what people should mean, and if they hold a contrary view they are mistaken. At this point, however, there is a second criticism that can be brought against the ethical egoists' position; namely, that the position is inconsistent. After all, ethical egoists claim that everyone should act to further his or her own interests. But how can business $X$ enjoin a competing firm $Y$ to seek only what is in $Y$'s best interest when there certainly will be competitive situations in which those acts serving $Y$'s interest will be detrimental to $X$'s interests? And in such cases $X$ seems to be telling $Y$ that it is morally right for $Y$ to work against $X$'s interests, that is, to do what $X$ considers to be morally wrong.

In conclusion, then, insofar as the calculation of interests and consequences enters into moral decision-making, it seems that impartiality is required of the agent; i.e., he should attempt to impartially consider the interests of all affected parties when calculating the consequences of an action. Ethical egoism's failure to meet the test of impartiality is a basic weakness of the theory.

## *Utilitarianism*

A consequentialist ethical theory that does attempt to take everyone into account is utilitarianism. There are a number of versions of utilitarianism, two of which we shall consider: act utilitarianism and rule utilitarianism.

According to the act utilitarian, an act is morally right if and only if it maximizes utility, i.e., if and only if the ratio of benefit to harm calculated by taking everyone affected by the act into consideration is greater than the ratio of benefit to harm resulting from any alternative act. In deciding to act, then, the act utilitarian will first set out the alternatives open to her. Second, she calculates the ratio of benefit to harm for each individual, including herself, affected by the alternative acts. Third, she adds up the ratios for each alternative act. Finally, she chooses the act that results in the greatest total ratio of benefit to harm. Assume, for example, that there are three alternative acts ($A_1$, $A_2$, $A_3$) open to person $P_1$, and that there are three people ($P_1$, $P_2$, $P_3$) affected by each alternative act. Assume, furthermore, that the ratio of benefit to harm for each person affected by each act can be expressed quantitatively, with a plus value indicating a benefit and a negative value indicating a harmful effect. Finally, assume a calculation yields the following result:

|       | $P_1$ | $P_2$ | $P_3$ | Totals |
|-------|-------|-------|-------|--------|
| $A_1$ | +4    | −5    | +8    | +7     |
| $A_2$ | +6    | +2    | −3    | +5     |
| $A_3$ | −2    | −5    | +4    | −3     |

In this situation the act utilitarian will choose act $A_1$ because it produces the greatest ratio of benefit to harm (+7) when everyone affected by the act is taken into consideration. Thus, the act utilitarian often recommends a course of action different from that recommended by the ethical egoist. In the above situation the ethical egoist as agent $P_1$ would choose $A_2$, for that act maximizes $P_1$'s self-interest.

In setting up our example we assumed that benefit/harm (or benefit/cost) ratios can be measured and compared, but these are assumptions that have been questioned. First, it is not altogether clear in some cases what is to count as a benefit or harm. In locating a plant, for example, what some people regard as a benefit others may see as a cost. Corporate managers may see the factory as providing beneficial jobs and profits, whereas environmentalists regard these as harmful because of a loss of wildlife habitat. Second, in some cases it may be difficult to assign quantitative values; for example, how does one measure the value of aesthetically pleasant surroundings or the value of a human life? Analogously, can something like aesthetic value ever be meaningfully compared with the value of a life? Third, the act utilitarian is concerned with the long-term consequences of acts, and in such contexts it may be very difficult to delimit the alternative acts available and to obtain reliable predictions as to the long-term consequences of performable acts.

If such difficulties could be overcome, however, act utilitarianism would have several advantages as an ethical theory in business contexts. First, unlike ethical egoism, act utilitarianism is impartial in that it takes each person's interests into account, and requires that act which maximizes utility irrespective of who benefits. Thus, the businessperson who accepts act utilitarianism has a basis for claiming that he is acting in a socially responsible manner in the sense that he takes everyone's interests, including employees, consumers, suppliers, etc., into account in decision-making. Second, the theory is able to account for why we typically hold certain business practices, e.g., contract-breaking, to be immoral; in most cases such practices do not maximize utility. But the act utilitarian denies that there are any unbreakable moral rules, e.g., "always keep your contracts," for in certain contexts breaking such a rule may maximize utility. A third advantage for the businessperson employing act utilitarianism is that it does not force him to accept binding rules; it allows for the flexibility that some people believe is necessary in today's complex business environment. In contrast with the egoist, however, such flexibility is based on overall utility considerations and not solely on self-interest. A fourth reason that act utilitarianism is attractive to businesspersons is that it provides a foundation for cost-benefit analysis, which in its purest form calculates benefits and costs in terms of money. Of course, the market itself places a monetary value on many goods, services, and activities; in addition utilitarians have devised ingenious methods of placing a price on such seeming unmeasurables as aesthetic value, health, and even human life. If we can legitimately make such calculations, the basic strategy of cost-benefit analysis is straightforwardly utilitarian. We choose that alternative act having the greatest benefit to cost ratio.

Act utilitarianism, however, is not free of problems. For example, let us assume that executive $X$ in company A has worked for months in order to bring about a contractual agreement between her company and another company, B. Whether or not the agreement actually does take place is dependent, in large part, upon what $X$ does, for negotiations are at a crucial stage. If the agreement is secured, both companies A and B will profit and many new jobs will be created. During the final negotiations the president of company A by chance discovers that $X$ has embezzled $5,000 from the corporation. The company's books are scheduled to be audited in a day or two, and the president of A knows that the accountants will discover $X$'s theft. The president of A confronts $X$ and tells her what he has learned. $X$ explains that she needed the money to pay for an operation for her husband, but that her husband has died and she never again will be pressed to steal money from the company. Also, $X$ says that if her theft is made known the people she is negotiating with in company B will no longer trust her, and the agreement between companies A and B will fall through. Since $X$'s theft will be detected by the impending audit, the president says there is very little he can do. As luck would have it, however, there is a low-level executive, $Y$, in company A who has had bad relations with all his supervisors and is about to be fired. $X$ suggests that the president make it appear as though $Y$ embezzled the $5,000. When $Y$ is fired, the company will not press charges, and $X$ quietly will repay the money she stole. The question then is this: should the president of A frame $Y$ for the embezzlement actually perpetrated by $X$? It appears as though an act utilitarian would have to say yes, but this violates our ordinary moral intuitions regarding justice and fair play. Furthermore, the following sort of utility calculation could be employed to justify an unjust act such as enslavement.

|       | $P_1$ | $P_2$ | $P_3$ | Totals |
|-------|-------|-------|-------|--------|
| $A_1$ | +22   | +22   | −25   | +19    |
| $A_3$ | + 6   | + 6   | + 6   | +18    |

It is conceivable that enslavement of $P_3$ via act $A_1$ would produce slightly greater total utility than act $A_2$, the other act open to the agent, even though $A_2$ results in a more equitable distribution. In that case the morally right act, according to the act utilitarian, is $A_1$. In such a case, however, act utilitarianism seems to clearly violate our ordinary perceptions of what is right.

Many utilitarians believe it is possible to avoid criticisms of the sort we have brought against act utilitarianism by reformulating the theory so that it has a place for moral rules. So reformulated, the position is known as *rule* utilitarianism. According to rule utilitarians, an act A in circumstance C is morally right if and only if the consequences of everyone acting on the rule "Do A in C" are better than the consequences of everyone acting on any alternative rule. The notion of "best consequences" here is specified in terms of utility maximization. Thus, an act is right if and only if it is in conformity with a particular moral rule, and that rule is chosen because, of all alternative rules, it maximizes utility. For example, a rule utilitarian might claim that "We must not hold a person accountable for a crime he has not committed" is a proper rule of conduct because if this rule were followed by everyone, it would maximize utility. Using this rule, the rule utilitarian could conclude that in our first counterexample to act utilitarianism it would be wrong for the president of company A to frame $Y$ for the crime committed by $X$. Since this result seems to accord with our moral intuitions, the rule utilitarian contends that his theory represents an advance over act utilitarianism.

Rule utilitarianism has several advantages as an ethical theory for businesspersons. First, as noted above, it seems to be able to handle many of the criticisms directed at act utilitarianism. Second, in any given situation it is much simpler to apply than act utilitarianism, since one need only apply the appropriate rule to justify an act. Third, there does seem to be a place for moral rules in an ethical theory, and rule utilitarianism gives us a way of allowing that while also acknowledging a place for the principle of utility.

Critics of rule utilitarianism, however, point out that if rule utilitarians are committed to the moral rule that maximizes utility, then they will have to allow that the acceptable rule in any case is one that allows exceptions that maximize utility. Thus, instead of the rule "We must not hold a person accountable for a crime he has not committed," the rule utilitarian must adopt the rule "We must not hold a person accountable for a crime he has not committed, unless doing so maximizes utility." In that case, rule utilitarianism collapses into the equivalent of act utilitarianism, and the objections we raised against act utilitarianism resurface. Analogously, in the enslavement counterexample to act utilitarianism, the rule utilitarian might argue that the rule "never enslave" maximizes utility. But he would have to allow that there are at least conceivable exceptions that maximize utility, and hence the rule he advocates is "Never enslave, except when utility is maximized by doing so." The result is that under certain circumstances rule utilitarianism, like act utilitarianism, does appear to sanction intuitively immoral practices such as slavery.

## Restricted Egoism

Ethical egoists advise us to act in our own self-interest whereas utilitarians advise us to maximize utility, and hence it might seem that these theories are incompatible. Interestingly, however, their incompatibility has been challenged by a number of economists and businesspersons (see, for example, the selections from Milton Friedman in this volume). Following Adam Smith, these people claim that the universal pursuit of self-interest is a process guided by an "invisible hand"—an invisible hand ultimately assuring that the public interest or total utility will be served. One qualification is needed here. Those who accept the invisible hand theory do not believe that it is morally right, in the pursuit of one's own self-interest, to break either the laws of the land or the established rules of competition. Thus, their moral theory is one that might be labeled "restricted egoism"; the theory is egoistic because it tells us that it is right to promote our own interests, yet this egoism is restricted by the demand that we obey certain laws and rules. On this view a corporation acts in a morally right manner if and only if it: (a) obeys the laws of the land as well as the accepted rules of competition, and within that context (b) pursues its own self-interest, thereby (c) by Adam Smith's invisible hand, automatically furthering the interests of society as a whole. For example, if an employee of a corporation can choose either act $A_1$ or $A_2$ or $A_3$ or $A_4$, and $A_2$ and $A_4$ are either illegal or violate the accepted rules of competition while $A_1$ and $A_3$ are not illegal and do not violate the accepted rules of competition, then the employee should select either $A_1$ or $A_3$. If $A_3$ maximizes the corporation's self-interest while $A_1$ does not, the employee should do $A_3$. According to restricted egoism, $A_3$ will then maximize social utility.

There are two major advantages with this theory. First, it commits businesspersons to conformity with the law, which can be looked up in the legal statutes. Second, it sanctions corporate self-interest, which typically means profit maximization, on the basis that pursuit of such self-interest in a competitive context will maximize utility, or further the overall interests of society. Whereas ethical egoism asserts that the pursuit of self-interest is moral, restricted egoism justifies the pursuit of self-interest in terms of utility.

If restricted egoism is represented in the above manner, the theory suffers from at least three difficulties. First, justification could be given for virtually *any* set of rules and laws. (Rules prohibiting competition or corporate activity could not be justified, but almost any other set of rules could be accepted as unbreakable guidelines for corporate conduct.) This being the case, restricted egoists could argue for the morality of many acts that we would ordinarily call immoral. For example, if some corporation was doing business in a country where bribes and kickbacks were accepted as part of the "competitive game," restricted egoists should argue that the company is morally bound to follow this established rule. But surely such a position is questionable. Or again, assume that a racist government is in power in a foreign country. It passes a law requiring all businesses to charge blacks more for goods and services than other citizens pay. Presumably, restricted egoists would now have to claim that it would be wrong for any corporation to break this law. But this runs counter to our ordinary moral intuitions. How, after all, can a corporation have a moral duty to further the ends of racism?

The second criticism is based on the fact that restricted egoists agree that a morally right act furthers both self-interest and the interests of society. Restricted egoists see no problem with this "dual consequence" theory, because they firmly believe in Adam Smith's invisible hand. That is to say, if they obey the law, corporate executives need worry about nothing but maximizing the interests of their own corporations; for if they are successful in this enterprise, Smith's "invisible hand" will see to it that society's interests are also served. But is this true? Certainly in *some* cases societal and business interests are in accord; but it is not at all clear that this is true in every case. For example, prior to the advent of child labor laws it was in the interest of business to have children work 12 to 14 hours a day at low wages. Given the amount of human suffering involved, however, it is not apparent that this served the public interest. Indeed, the fact that laws were passed prohibiting such practices tends to indicate that our society did not see child labor as fostering its best interests. Consider another counterexample. Suppose corporation A produces a chemical (C) it alone knows is a carcinogen. A produces C in a country which has no rules banning C. So it is legal to produce and sell C. The owners of A also know that cancers caused by C will only occur about 20 years after exposure, and they have reason to believe that no one else will find out that C is carcinogenic over that twenty-year period. In ten years A's owners plan to sell the plant, take profits and move to Switzerland. Suppose that in this context producing and selling C actually maximizes A's self-interest. In this case it looks like the invisible hand does not maximize utility.

Our third criticism is that cases could arise in which all three conditions of the restricted egoist theory are satisfied, but the act sanctioned by the theory is morally wrong. For example, suppose slavery is legal in a country and that slavery there is just one of the accepted rules of competition; every firm has some slaves. Furthermore, it is easy to imagine that having some slaves might well benefit a company. So suppose it turns out that having some slaves benefits a firm more than not having slaves, and, indeed, that having some slaves actually maximizes the corporation's self-interest. Suppose, further, that Adam Smith's invisible hand does work in this case, i.e., having corporate slaves maximizes social utility in that it produces more overall utility that any alternative act not having any corporate slaves. According to restricted egoism, in such a case it would be morally right to have some corporate slaves. However, the use of slaves in business seems clearly immoral.

Our criticisms of restricted egoism, ethical egoism, and utilitarianism are all limited in scope in that they call attention to specific problems within particular moral theories. We must, however, consider a much broader challenge to these moral theories. Some moral philosophers reject all forms of egoism and utilitarianism because these theories are consequentialist in nature. Moral theorists who reject consideration of consequences in ethics are called nonconsequentialists. In what follows we shall examine three nonconsequentialist moral theories and enumerate some of the problems faced by those who advocate them.

# NONCONSEQUENTIALISM

## *Theologism*

Although there are many different versions of theological ethics, theologism, as we shall use the term, asserts that an act is right if, more than any alternative open to the agent at the time, it is the one most consistent with what God wills, either directly or indirectly. Usually, theologism provides us with a set of rules (e.g., the Ten Commandments) thought to express God's will.

Whether or not an act is right or wrong, then, is determined in part by reference to these rules. We say that the rightness or wrongness of an action is partially determined by reference to moral rules because most theologians hold that an act may conform to the requirements specified by a legitimate rule of conduct and still not be morally proper. For example, let us say that a person accepts the Ten Commandments as specifying God's will, and refuses to steal when he has an opportunity to do so. In this case, then, he has followed one of God's commands. But if the individual refused to steal because he was afraid of being caught, or because he wanted to be rewarded in heaven for his good behavior, his action would not be truly right. The motives for action would be "impure," and this impurity would affect (perhaps "infect" is a better word) the moral character of his action. For his action to be truly right, God's command must be followed for the right reason, viz., stealing must be rejected, not out of concern for oneself, but rather out of love for God and fellow men. Given this motive, then, the action would be right. In short, most versions of theologism hold that God not only wants us to act in certain ways, but also to act in those ways for the right reasons.

One advantage of theologism, so understood, is that it commits us to a set of rules, such as the Ten Commandments, which can serve as a ready guide for determining whether acts are right or wrong. We do not have to engage in detailed consequential calculations, we simply apply the rules. Second, since most of the members of almost any society believe in God, and presumably God's rules, if we adopt such rules for a business context we would find many people who would not only agree with the rules but also be familiar with them. And, third, religion has always been a powerful motivating force. With a theory such as utilitarianism a person can make a calculation and determine what is morally right according to the theory, but still face the nagging question of why he or she should do what is morally right. Religion typically answers this question: you should do what God commands because of a love of God, or perhaps avoid what God prohibits to save your immortal soul. Religious support for moral rules makes many people take them seriously and act on them.

Theologism appeals only to one principle to justify its set of moral rules. Supposedly, the rules of theologism specify right action because these rules, and no others, express God's will. It is at this point, however, that a problem arises. Namely, do the theologians' moral rules express what is right because of God's command or not? If the theologian says that the rules express what is right because of God's command, two untoward consequences follow. First, it no longer makes any sense to say that God is good. (Since *anything* God wills is good, for God himself there is no difference between good and evil; and when we say God is good we assert nothing.) And second, theologians have to admit that if God commanded murder, theft, or cruelty, these actions would be right and morally obligatory. But few people—theologians included—want to admit that actions of this sort ever could be morally right. On the other hand, if the theologians were to claim that their set of moral rules specified right action independently of God's command, then they would have to find a new justification for their moral rules. This is so because the theologians' present position would then be that *regardless* of what God commands, their set of moral rules specifies right action. And in these circumstances it simply would be contradictory for the theologians to assert that it is because of God's command that their moral rules delineate right conduct.

Four other drawbacks of theologism deserve mention. Some people deny or question God's existence, and hence may find no basis for the stated rules. Then, too, there are different religions (Islam, Buddhism, Christianity, etc.) with different Gods and different rules—which set of rules should be obeyed? Even within one religion there will be different interpretations of one rule. The Bible says "Thou shall not kill," yet Christians disagree about the morality of war, capital punishment, abortion, and euthanasia. Finally, while religious rules are typically quite general, in business we want rather specific rules regarding conflicts of interest, hiring, privacy, gifts, sexual harassment, worker safety, and the environment. How these specific rules can be derived from theologism's more general rules is not at all clear.

## The Golden Rule

The Golden Rule, "Do unto others as you would have them do unto you," is perhaps the most widely accepted moral principle. It is found in most major religious traditions: Confucianism, "That which you do not want done to yourself, do not do to others" (*Analects*); Islam, "No one is a believer unless he loves for his brother what he loves for himself" (*Traditions*); and, Buddhism, "Hurt not others with what pains yourself" (*Udanavarga*). Furthermore, in surveys of businesspersons, the Golden Rule is cited more often than any other principle as the basis of proper ethical behavior.

According to the Golden Rule, one determines how he or she prefers to be treated and should in turn treat others the same way. You wish to be told the truth when you ask the salesperson the price of a product, so you should tell others the truth when they ask you for the price of your products. And you want others to pay their debts to you, so you should treat them the same way and pay your debts to them.

From the above, three advantages of employing the Golden Rule in business contexts can be seen. First, since you know how you want to be treated, in many cases it is quite straightforward to apply this principle. Second, since, as we have seen, the Golden Rule is advocated by so many people from different cultures, it would seem to be a good principle to adopt in our present global business environment. And third, it introduces a dimension of fairness into business decision-making, since you are committing yourself to acting toward any other individual in the same way you would want to be treated.

One criticism of the Golden Rule is summed up in a saying attributed to George Bernard Shaw: "Don't do unto others as you would that they should do unto you; their tastes may not be the same." For example, do not serve tripe to your guests just because you would like to be served tripe if you were a guest. Analogously, in the moral domain we cannot assume the similarity of wants or psychological makeup the Golden Rule seems to rest on, as the case of the masochist indicates. In business contexts, application of the Golden Rule often leads to counterintuitive results. If you work in computer design at company $C_1$ and a friend of yours has a similar job at company $C_2$, you may want her to give you $C_2$'s company secrets, but that hardly justifies you giving her $C_1$'s secrets. If you are in charge of purchasing and selling for $C_1$, you may want your counterpart at $C_2$ to sell its products to you below cost, yet that would not justify your selling $C_1$'s products below cost to $C_2$. In addition, in complex business transactions the Golden Rule often does not yield unambiguous advice. Suppose you invent a product which on balance will not satisfy consumers' wants, but which your boss wants you to market because it will result in many sales and thereby secure her a promotion. Since you would not wish to be sold a product that will not satisfy your wants, from the consumers' perspective you should not sell the product. By selling the product, however, you would probably satisfy a want you would have if you were to place yourself in your boss' shoes.

## Kantianism

To meet these types of objections to the Golden Rule, the German philosopher Immanuel Kant (1724–1804) developed his nonconsequentialist ethical theory. Let's introduce it with one of Kant's own type of example. Suppose a businessperson promises to keep a contract, but intends to break the promise if doing so serves his own self-interest. Is this businessperson's act, his promising, wrong? According to Kant, it is, but why? Kant says that whenever one acts, he or she does so in accordance with a *maxim*, a rule governing the individual's act. Here the maxim or rule is: "I keep my promises, but only if doing so serves my own self-interest." Now Kant's view is that to determine whether the businessman's act is right or wrong we must test the maxim of his act by what Kant called the Categorical Imperative: "Act only on that maxim according to which you can will that it should become a universal law." In effect, Kant asks whether the businessman's maxim can be universalized, where the universalization involves replacing "I" with "Everyone," in the maxim, i.e., "Everyone keep his or her promises, but only if doing so serves his or her own self-interest." Kant says that in this case the maxim cannot be universalized because it involves a contradiction. If one promises, this implies that one intends to keep the promise, for this is part of the meaning of "promise." But the maxim in effect then says: "I promise (i.e., I say so and so and intend to keep faith with what I said), but I do not intend to keep faith with what I said if breaking the promise is in my own self-interest." This is contradictory. So Kant's ethical theory is that an act is morally right only if the maxim of the act is universalizable, i.e., capable of being acted upon, or adopted, by everyone.

Consider another example, lining up (queuing). When you go to the bank you line up to see a teller and at the store you line up to pay your bill. Cutting into a line is unethical for Kant because the maxim of the line cutter (I line up, but cut-in if doing so serves my interests) cannot be universalized. If everyone cut-in there would be no concept of lining up.

Note that line cutting would be unethical for both rule utilitarians and Kantians, but for different reasons. Asked to choose between two rules (R1: Always line up, and R2: Line up only if it is in your self-interest), the rule utilitarian would select R1 because it would have more overall utility, whereas Kant would select R1 because only R1 is universalizable. The Categorical Imperative says we are ethically permitted to act only on maxims which are logically *capable* of being adopted by everyone; it is our duty to not act on those maxims which are not capable of being acted on by everyone. In one sense, the utilitarian and Kantian both ask: "What if everyone did that?" But the utilitarian focuses only on consequences; if a rule maximizes utility it is morally acceptable, if not it is morally unacceptable. For Kant, consequences are irrelevant to whether an act is moral. We should not act on maxims not capable of being acted upon by everyone, i.e., maxims which are logically impossible for everyone to act upon.

To generalize from our promising and queuing examples, we can note that business rests on various rules concerning property rights, employee obligations of loyalty to the firm, contract enforcement, protecting the firm's information, and so forth. An employee voluntarily agrees to follow these rules. However, maxims based on a person's agreeing to follow rules only if it is in his or her own self-interest to do so will not be universalizable because if the rules governing business were universally violated we would not have such rules. In fact, we would not have business.

Kant believes his Categorical Imperative allows us to derive a set of moral rules that must *always* be obeyed. In other words, to break one of these rules is always to do something wrong, regardless of the particular circumstances in which one acts. On the other hand, simply to act in the ways specified by these rules is not to guarantee that one's actions are morally right. Like theologism, Kant insists that an act cannot be counted as morally right unless the agent performs the act for the right reason. For Kant, however, one should not act from the motives specified by the theologian (i.e., love of God), rather, one must obey moral rules simply because this is the right thing to do. In short, one's motive for action must be respect for the moral law itself. And when one obeys a rule for this reason, one is doing what is morally right.

Kant offers a second formulation of his Categorical Imperative: "Act so that you treat humanity, whether in your own person or that of another, always as an end and never as a means only." This does not mean a business cannot legitimately employ a worker and use the worker to achieve the firm's goals; it means the firm cannot regard the worker *only* or merely as a means to its ends. Kant's point here seems to be that all persons deserve respect, and have dignity and a dimension of absolute worth simply because they are persons. If this principle is accepted, everyone has a moral duty to treat others fairly and equitably, to refrain from "using" humans as mere means for the procurement of one's own or others' ends, and so forth. Kant regarded these two formulations of his ethical theory to be equivalent; even though they seem quite distinct, Kant believed that use of either leads one to formulate the same set of rules that must be obeyed if one is to act in morally right ways.

One strength of Kantianism is that the Categorical Imperative provides a basis for the rules that actually guide business practices. In addition, the rules Kant derives from the Categorical Imperative are relatively simple and easy to comprehend: Keep your promises. Tell the truth. Do not steal. Help those in distress. Instead of making complex utility calculations, these rules tell you directly what to do. Third, Kant's Categorical Imperative has a fairness factor built into it. Fairness involves playing by the rules and not making an exception of yourself, and it is precisely those maxims that permit one to make an exception of himself that Kant's theory precludes. Fourth, according to Kant, his rules are absolute, unbreakable rules to which there are no exceptions, and this certainly seems to be a benefit to business, especially the rules governing employees' obligations to their employer. And fifth, the absolute nature of Kant's rules indicates a dignity and worth of humans which cannot be overridden by consequentialist appeals to self-interest or utility.

That rules are absolute, however, poses a problem for Kant's theory. For Kant lying is *always* wrong; there are no justifiable exceptions to this rule. But surely there are some circumstances in which we ordinarily would say it is morally right to lie. Consider this case. You are a security guard for a large company that you know does secret work for the CIA. One day while making your rounds you discover an old friend of yours planting a bomb on the premises. He pulls a gun, holds it to your head and says that he is bombing the building and its occupants because he suspects the company does work for the CIA. At the same time he says that because of your friendship he trusts you, and that if you swear on everything that you hold holy that the company does not work for the CIA, he will take his bomb and leave. Surely we believe that in these circumstances it would be morally right to lie, for to tell the truth would have truly disastrous consequences. This being the case, we must conclude that there is something incorrect with any moral theory which tells us to wholly disregard consequences and concern ourselves only with obeying unbreakable moral rules.

A second difficulty for Kant's theory is that it does not give us unambiguous guidance when rules conflict. One rule Kant explicitly discusses is that one should keep promises. Another is that one should help another person in distress. These are supposedly absolute — there are no exceptions to either rule. Suppose you agree to meet your boss at noon to sign an important contract which only you can sign and which must be signed by noon. However, on your way you encounter another employee who is hurt and needs help, and you are the only one around. If you help the person, you will be late and break your promise; but, if you keep your promise, you violate the rule requiring you to help one in distress. In either case, you break a supposedly absolute rule. And Kant's theory does not seem to tell us which rule we should obey when rules conflict. Kant's response to this difficulty is to claim that the Categorical Imperative is a necessary principle, and that two rules derivable from a necessary principle cannot, as a matter of logic, conflict. However, this begs the issue. We encounter such conflicts of rules all the time, which is evidence that the Categorical Imperative is not a necessary principle.

Our survey of ethical theories reveals weaknesses with both consequentialist and nonconsequentialist approaches. In focusing exclusively on consequences, egoism and utilitarianism overlook factors such as fairness and rights, which are important components of ethical decision-making. The nonconsequentialist theories we discussed take fairness and rights into consideration but exclude consequences, which also seems to be an important factor in ethical problem solving. In the next section we outline an approach to ethical decision-making which includes consideration of both consequentialist and nonconsequentialist factors.

# ETHICS RELATED DECISION-MAKING

Subsequent chapters in this text contain case studies, real or fictional situations having an ethical dimension of which you are asked to make an ethical assessment. This is the practical dimension of our text. Most of you reading it will be in business or other organizations and will face situations similar to these case studies. Our aim in this section is to review some of the decision-making skills you can use to arrive at ethical decisions.

The cases in this text typically involve an individual (or a group of people or an organization) facing an ethical problem in a particular setting, in which he or she must make a decision as to what to do. So the basic question in a case study typically is: "What should be done?" To answer this type of question, we discuss a method, an argument structure, that you can use in both real world contexts and the "paper" cases you will read in this text. Admittedly, the two are vastly different. In a real world situation you can talk with the people involved, gather additional facts and consult with experts, whereas the text cases are merely words on paper. So, as we discuss this method, we will need to address some major differences between actual cases and the paper cases you will be reading about and perhaps discussing in class.

The general decision-making argument structure is:

Individual X has problem P.
The alternative solutions to P are $S_1 \ldots S_n$.
$S_1$ is the best solution to P.

X should do $S_1$.

This is a good argument structure in that if you can establish all three reasons, i.e., show they are acceptable, then you will have established the acceptability of your conclusion. So let's examine each reason in turn to see how in general you can establish its acceptability.

## *The Problem*

The initial step in decision-making (or problem solving) is to determine the problem. To do so, keep six things in mind. First, gather the facts carefully to determine whether there is a problem. Suppose a security guard reports to you that an employee is stealing packaging material from the firm. Don't just assume this is true and try to find the best solution to the theft. A careful analysis of the facts may reveal that the packaging material has been used and is now unuseable to your company, that the employee has secured permission from his manager to take it, and that his doing so saves you removal costs. In other words, there is no problem to be solved.

Second, if there is a problem, try to state it as clearly as you can. Doing so will often enable you to specify the real problem rather than an apparent one. If your manager tells you to go to Boston for a 2 P.M. meeting tomorrow, you may identify the problem as how to get there in time for the meeting. But further thought may help you see that the real problem is a need for you to share information with others in Boston. Perhaps you can share this information equally well and with less expense through a teleconference. If so, your problem of how to get to Boston by 2 P.M. tomorrow disappears.

Third, determine whether the problem has an ethical dimension. Most problems managers face day in and day out do not; they involve purely technical or practical or administrative matters. Although such problems are important, our concern here is not with them. Look for situations involving: (1) violations of laws, (2) individuals who are treated unfairly, (3) individuals whose rights are being violated, and (4) negative overall consequences, or disutility. These often indicate an ethical dimension to a problem.

Fourth, identify those affected by the problem. Ethical problems usually involve consequences, in which case identifying those who benefit and those who are harmed will be important. If you believe that the actions of certain employees are unfair, try to determine those who are acting unfairly and those who are being unfairly treated.

Fifth, in many cases you will need to demonstrate the seriousness of your problem, since there is no need to deliberate at length about a trivial problem. There is no point in getting on your ethical high horse about an employee who inadvertently took home one of the company's pencils. So, if you think the members of your organization you are addressing will think the problem you mention is not serious enough, you will need to show that it indeed is.

And sixth, in many cases we are interested in determining what caused the problem. If we have demonstrated that a river is polluted, and this is a problem, we seek the cause. Perhaps natural causes rather than an upstream chemical plant are to blame. In problem solving, we are especially interested in causes because they often point us in the direction of finding the best solution. If we know only that a creek is polluted, then the best solution may be to build a purification plant. But if intentional dumping of waste from a manufacturer is causing the pollution, then the best solution will likely be simply to prevent the dumping. Often, then, identifying the cause of a problem points us toward a solution better than any we would arrive at if we knew only the nature of the problem, not its cause.

Although in real world situations individuals are often unaware there is an ethical dimension to a problem they face, this will rarely be true for the reader of a paper case. After all, the book you are reading is a business ethics text. So the cases included will be ethics cases. The "facts" of the case will essentially be given by the words you read. So read the case carefully. Then read it again. It will be important for you to cite the text accurately to support your argument. In addition to the text material, there are other factual resources you can use as evidence in case studies. You know a lot about human nature, and can say what people are likely to do in certain sorts of situations. If you are employed or are studying business courses, you know many facts about business which can be employed in case analyses.

In real world situations you will often know enough about the persons involved to be able to predict what they will do with a relatively high degree of probability. In paper cases you will not know those involved and, since you only have a few pages of text, you will have to make some inferences based on what you are given. This may incline you to claim merely that "A could occur" or "Person B might do V" or "D may lead to E." But you should avoid using these words in case analyses: "could," "might," "may," "possible," "can," and "perhaps." These excessive hedge words almost invariably make a sentence true; for example, "It is possible the theft will be discovered" will be true, but only because almost anything is possible. After all, it is possible a tiger will walk through the nearest door. But the real question is not whether it is possible, but rather whether it is likely a tiger will walk through the door, and whether it is likely the theft will be discovered. So, in many cases one of your tasks will be to argue for what is likely or probable based on what is given in the case. Avoid claiming that something is merely possible, since such a claim will not advance your argument.

In decision-making business ethics cases the key issue posed is typically what individual X should do, what course of action she should pursue. In such cases, the problem can often be stated simply as: "Person X has a decision to make as to what to do in this situation." If the ethical issue is relatively clear, you can briefly describe it and pose the problem as the decision facing X.

## *Alternative Solutions*

After establishing that a problem exists, your next step is to list alternative solutions to it. Here it is a good idea to brainstorm: think up solutions and write them down. Be creative—try to think of a wide range of solutions. Don't be too quick to criticize at this point, just use your imagination. Look at the case from different perspectives. If there are three individuals involved, role play, i.e., put yourself in place of one person, then another, and then the third. Doing so may help you to see new solutions. Talk with other people to get their take on the case. If you are examining a case as part of a class, come prepared to offer alternative solutions and encourage others to offer theirs.

It is very important to list all the important alternative solutions to a problem. If you say "The alternative solutions to problem P are $S_1$, $S_2$ and $S_3$," but you omit $S_4$, and $S_4$ is a good solution to P, then what you have said is simply false. Furthermore, if you omit $S_4$ from consideration, you cannot show that, say, $S_1$ is the best solution to P, for to do that you have to show $S_1$ is better than all the available alternative solutions, and you will not be able to do that without showing $S_1$ is better than $S_4$.

Having said that you should include the important or good alternative solutions in your considerations, it is also clear that you need to narrow your list, for if you have a dozen alternatives it will be very difficult to compare them all to determine which is the best. Not every product of brainstorming will be worth keeping on the list. So, examine the list and drop those which will not solve the problem. If you have to travel to Memphis tomorrow for a business meeting, and you think of your options as the train, plane, or car, but no train goes to Memphis, then scratch that alternative. Also, drop those solutions that are obviously poor. There often will be options which will solve a problem, but only minimally. If it is clear there are better options available, drop the poorer solutions from consideration. Your aim is to arrive at a relatively small set of good alternatives, say two to four, which are the best of the lot. Above all, avoid a list consisting of your preferred solution and others that are either not solutions or are very poor solutions. It will be easy for you to show your solution is better than these straw men, but by avoiding a comparison with other good solutions you cannot possibly show that your solution is the best of all the alternatives.

## *The Best Solution*

Suppose you have specified the moral problem, P, have narrowed the alternative solutions to $S_1$, $S_2$ and $S_3$, and intend to argue for $S_1$. You now have to establish the third reason of our problem solving argument structure:

Individual X has problem P.
The alternative solutions to P are $S_1$, $S_2$, and $S_3$.
$S_1$ is the best solution to P.

X should do $S_1$.

The third reason is often the core of your argument. In many cases the first two reasons are easily established, leaving only the third reason to argue. The most important thing to remember in arguing for the third reason is that your argument must be *comparative*; you must compare the alternative solutions and show yours is better than the others.

So, if there are three solutions, and you are arguing for $S_1$, your argument must be:

$S_1$ is a better solution to P than $S_2$.
$S_1$ is a better solution to P than $S_3$.

$S_1$ is the best solution to P.

Given that your argument must be comparative, the following structure will invariably provide insufficient evidence for its conclusion:

$S_1$ is a good solution to P.

X should do $S_1$.

---

If no solutions are compared, the writer cannot have established that $S_1$ is better than other alternatives and so cannot have proven that $S_1$ is P's best solution. $S_1$ may be a good solution to P, but $S_2$ or $S_3$ may be better than $S_1$, in which case X should not do $S_1$. Similarly, the following argument structure cannot prove its conclusion:

Individual X has problem P.
$S_2$ has some drawbacks as a solution to P.

---

X should do $S_1$.

Even if both reasons turn out to be true in a particular situation, $S_1$ may have many more significant disadvantages than $S_2$, in which case X should probably not do $S_1$. Unless you compare $S_1$ with $S_2$ and $S_3$, you cannot establish the third reason in our argument structure.

How, then, do we compare solutions? Consider an oversimplified example. You have determined that you must be in Boston for a 2:00 P.M. sales meeting tomorrow (P). Your only alternatives for getting there are: $S_1$, automobile; $S_2$, train; $S_3$, plane. To compare these alternatives you have to find some features of a solution that form the basis of the comparison. Here the features might be:

$F_1$: cost
$F_2$: comfort
$F_3$: time of arrival should enable you to discuss the agenda with subordinates before the meeting

You then compare $S_1$, $S_2$, and $S_3$ with respect to $F_1$, $F_2$, and $F_3$. Your argument might turn out something like:

$S_1$ is better than $S_2$ or $S_3$ with respect to $F_1$.
$S_1$ is better than $S_2$ or $S_3$ with respect to $F_2$.
$S_1$ is better than $S_2$ or $S_3$ with respect to $F_3$.

---

$S_1$ is the best solution to P.

In many cases $S_1$ will be the best solution with respect to one feature whereas $S_2$ is the best with respect to another feature. It may be less expensive to drive to Boston than the other options, but the plane may be more comfortable than either the auto or the train. If this occurs, you must consider the *number* and *weight* of the relevant features. If the features are of equal importance (or weight) in solving P, then you may argue:

> $F_1$, $F_2$, and $F_3$ are of equal importance in solving P.
> $S_1$ is better than $S_2$ or $S_3$ in solving P with respect to $F_1$.
> $S_1$ is better than $S_2$ or $S_3$ in solving P with respect to $F_2$.
> $S_2$ is better than $S_1$ or $S_3$ in solving P with respect to $F_3$.
> _____
> $S_1$ is the best solution to P.

$S_1$ has more advantages than any other competitor and, since the Fs count equally, is the best solution to P.

You will also have to consider whether some of the Fs should be weighted as being more important than other Fs in solving P. For example, if $F_1$ (cost) is the most important feature, then your argument might be:

> $F_1$ is the most important of the three features in solving P.
> $S_1$ is better than $S_2$ or $S_3$ in solving P with respect to $F_1$.
> $S_2$ is better than $S_1$ or $S_3$ in solving P with respect to $F_2$.
> $S_3$ is better than $S_1$ or $S_2$ in solving P with respect to $F_3$.
> _____
> $S_1$ is the best solution to P.

Although each solution has an advantage, since $F_1$ counts more toward the solution of P than the other Fs, $S_1$ is the best solution.

Of course, in many cases it will be difficult to establish one solution as the best. For one thing, if weighting is involved, it is often difficult to assign the proper weight to various features. The ideal here, a quantitative weighting (e.g., 60% to $F_1$, 25% to $F_2$, and 15% to $F_3$), is rarely attainable. But, if we use vaguer measures, it is often very difficult to say which solution is the best. For example, if $F_1$ is a "more important" feature than either $F_2$ or $F_3$, and $S_1$ is better than $S_2$ with respect to $F_1$ but $S_2$ is better than $S_1$ with respect to $F_2$ and also $F_3$, then we have no clear idea whether $S_1$ is better than $S_2$.

In comparing solutions, be thorough in making the comparisons. The following argument structure in the Boston trip example will invariably leave you with a poor argument:

$S_1$ has some advantages over $S_2$ in solving P.

$S_1$ is the best solution to P.

The argument will be incomplete for three reasons: (1) $S_3$ is not mentioned, hence this reason cannot possibly establish the conclusion; (2) $S_1$ may be better than $S_2$ with respect to "some" features, e.g., $F_3$, without being better with respect to $F_1$ and $F_2$, in which case the reason is true but the conclusion may be false; (3) to be complete, the comparison must mention the disadvantages as well as the advantages of all three solutions. By the same reasoning, the following argument will be poor:

There are some disadvantages to $S_2$ when compared to $S_1$ in solving P.

$S_1$ is the best solution to P.

In failing to include $S_3$, not including all Fs, and not discussing the advantages of all the solutions, the writer guarantees her argument will be poor, even though it may be fairly easy to show that this reason is true. So be sure to be thorough in making your comparisons.

Although many problems are purely practical, such as our Boston trip example, our interest here is with moral problems and (assuming we have specified a problem P with a moral dimension and have listed alternative solutions $S_1$, $S_2$, and $S_3$) our comparison of the alternatives will require us to specify features (Fs) to make the comparison. Depending on the case, a number of such features might be considered: motives or intentions, friendship, respect, loyalty, the law, and the nature of the business relationships among those persons involved, to list just a few. However, to simplify our discussion here, we focus just on two general features that are almost always factors in ethical decision-making, one, drawn from the consequentialist tradition, namely, utility, and the other drawn from the nonconsequentialist tradition, namely, rights.

## *Utility*

The overall structure of a utility argument is:

$R_1$     Individual X has moral problem P.

$R_2$     The alternative solutions available to X are $S_1$, $S_2 \ldots S_n$.

$R_3$     The individuals affected by $S_1$, $S_2 \ldots S_n$ are $I_1$, $I_2 \ldots I_n$.

$R_4$      $S_1$ has more utility than $S_2$.

• 

• 

• 

$R_n$      $S_1$ has more utility than $S_n$.

        $S_1$ maximizes utility.

We assume the person faced with the problem may be one of those $(I_1 \ldots I_n)$ affected by a solution. And we have discussed reasons $R_1$ and $R_2$ in previous sections. So now consider $R_3$. To establish $R_3$ you must list all those affected by the various acts enumerated in $R_2$. In some cases this may be very easy to do, for example, you and your boss may be the only people affected. In other cases, especially those involving a large number of people, it may be easier to divide the individuals affected into a limited number of groups $(G_1 \ldots G_n)$. For example, if you are considering implementing an affirmative action program at your firm, instead of considering every person affected you might focus on three groups: white males $(G_1)$; members of groups previously disadvantaged $(G_2)$; and society $(G_3)$. You could then restrict your discussion of consequences to these three groups.

The remaining reasons $(R_4 \ldots R_n)$ are all comparative utility calculations, in which your aim is to show that $S_1$ has more utility than each of $S_2 \ldots S_n$. To do so keep three things in mind: (1) In considering any solution you must calculate both benefits and harms. It is tempting just to calculate the benefits of your proposal $(S_1)$ and then compare it to just the harmful effects of $S_2 \ldots S_n$. However, this will leave you with a slanted, hence poor, argument which will be detected easily by fair-minded people. (2) Make sure you include in your comparisons all the individuals $(I_1 \ldots I_n)$ affected by the acts. Anything less will again leave you with a biased, hence poor, argument. Your aim is to show that the overall consequences of $S_1$ are better than the overall consequences of the other alternatives when everyone affected by the alternatives is considered. (3) Make sure you compare all the solutions $(S_1 \ldots S_n)$ mentioned in your statement of alternative solutions $(R_2)$. You have to show that $S_1$ has more utility than each of the other alternatives.

## Rights

Many moral disputes involve rights claims. For instance, management claims the right to gather information about employees, while employees claim a right to privacy. Having a right to Q is to be entitled to Q, as the six-teen year old who has a right to take the drivers' examination is entitled to take it and the student who has a right to a review of an assigned grade is entitled to a review. To say that someone has a right to Q, that she is enti-tled to Q, is to make a claim stronger than saying she has permission to Q. For example, the student who has a right to a review of an assigned grade has a claim to a review that is not based on the faculty granting her per-mission for a review. Furthermore, the student's claim to a review is not based on faculty good will. The student entitled to a review has, on the face of it, a justified claim to a review. In this case, the right to a review implies an obligation on the part of faculty members to provide such a review.

Now that we have some idea of what a right is, we can examine the different types of rights. For our purposes they fit on this map:

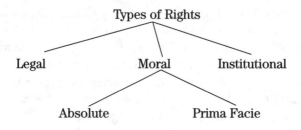

Some rights are legal rights. For example, for some charges a person has a legal right to a trial by jury. The person is legally entitled to a jury trial and the entitlement is supported by legal principles and cases. Other rights are in the moral domain. For example, prior to the Civil War slaves had no legal right to be free, but many people claimed everyone has a moral right to freedom. Today, some people claim there is a moral right to "blow the whistle" on what they consider to be corporate misdeeds, even though in their particular state there may be no law permitting whistle-blowing for the activities they regard as immoral. Of course, whether there is such a moral whistle-blowing right is contested, but at least it is true that some people claim there is such a right in the absence of a whistle-blowing law. Just as we can have a moral right without a corresponding legal right, so we may have a legal right without a corresponding moral right. A teacher has a legal right to tell a student "You will never amount to anything," but this is hardly a moral right. And corporations in many states have a legal right to terminate employees without offering a reason, even though many claim they have no moral right to do so. Of course, even though legal and moral rights are distinct, they often overlap. We no longer have slavery today, which reflects our belief in the moral right to freedom. Other rights are neither legal nor moral, but arise within institutional contexts. The right to eat in the executive dining room in a corporation, for example, is neither legal nor moral; it is an institutional right. Institutional rights differ from legal rights in that they are not part of the law. Since they are specific to a particular institution, they differ from moral rights, which are independent from any institution. Having differentiated institutional, legal, and moral rights, we can now focus primarily on moral rights.

*Absolute Moral Rights.* It is often claimed that some moral rights are absolute in the sense that there are no circumstances under which others can justifiably override those rights. So, if there is an absolute right to life, then there are no circumstances in which a person can justifiably take a life. A number of rights have been proposed as absolute: life, happiness, liberty, self-development, and so forth. Of course, it is very controversial as to whether any such rights are absolute. Take the right to life. The mere assertion that the right to life is absolute will be met by the claim that we are sometimes justified in killing in self-defense, that there are some just wars, etc. The point is that you will have to argue that a particular right is absolute, and such an argument will be very difficult to make. Furthermore, the moral rights frequently discussed in business are not properly construed as absolute rights. Businesses do have a right to gather information about employees, but there are moral limitations on the means they can employ, and employees do have a moral right to privacy, but it can in some cases be overridden by an organization's right to gather information. In general, then, the moral rights we encounter in organizational contexts are best not thought of as absolute.

*Prima Facie Rights.* A supervisor has a right to hear his workers' grievances before they take them to top management, but the right is not absolute, for in certain circumstances the workers would be justified in bypassing their supervisor. Rights that are not absolute, but can be justifiably overridden in certain cases, are called prima facie rights. Almost invariably, having a right is correlated with or corresponds to an obligation or duty on the part of others. Often this obligation is to not interfere with the proper exercise of the right. Consider the right to property. Others have a duty or obligation to not deprive you of what you have earned or the possessions you have obtained through legitimate means. But the right is prima facie, not absolute, for if the state has a good argument for taking your property and it compensates you fairly for it, then it may justifiably take your property. So, two main types of argument can be based on such rights:

1. Individual X has a prima facie right to Q.
2. Others may legitimately interfere with X's exercise of his right to Q if and only if adequate justification for doing so is provided.
3. No adequate justification for interfering with X's exercise of his right to Q has been provided.

Others may not interfere (legitimately) with X's exercise of his right to Q.

Stating Q as a prima facie right rather than absolute will often make 1 acceptable without argument, and 2 is acceptable as it stands, so 3 is often the only reason you will need to establish. And note that it puts the burden of proof on the other side to justify interference. The other argument structure based on prima facie rights is:

1. Individual X has a prima facie right to Q.
2. Others may legitimately interfere with X's exercise of her right to Q if and only if adequate justification for doing so is provided.
3. Adequate justification exists to legitimately interfere with X's exercise of her right to Q.

Those who have an adequate justification may legitimately interfere with X's exercise of her right to Q.

Again, in most cases 3 will be the main part of the argument.

In organizational contexts the right to be treated fairly is an important right. The basic idea here is that if two people or acts are similar in relevant ways, then they ought to be treated the same. If they are not treated the same, the situation is unfair. So the basic argument structure is:

1. People have a right to be treated fairly.
2. To be fair, similar cases ought to be treated similarly.
3. Persons $X_1$ and $X_2$ are similar with respect to properties $P_1 \ldots P_n$, which are relevant to being treated in manner T.
4. $X_1$ has been treated in manner T.
5. $X_2$ has not been treated in manner T.

This situation is unfair.

If Sam and Sarah have the same work records $P_1 \ldots P_n$ (i.e., hours, productivity, seniority, etc.), then if Sam got a raise (T) but Sarah did not the situation is unfair. Here 1 and 2 will be acceptable as they stand, and 4 and 5 are often easy to prove, leaving 3 as the difficult claim to establish.

Rights often conflict, although in many argumentative contexts the conflict is more apparent than real. If one person claims a right to something which another denies, the two are not necessarily inconsistent, for different types of rights may be involved. Legal and moral rights are often confused. You may not have a legal right to blow the whistle on what you take to be a corporate misdeed in the state of Alabama, yet you may have a moral right to do so. It may be legally permissible to quit your job and walk off without giving notice, yet you may have no moral right to do so. So a person saying she had a right to walk off may be correct in one sense but incorrect in another. All such disputes are resolved by clarifying the use(s) of "right." However, many rights disputes are not so easily resolvable. People have a right to financial privacy, but the government claims a right to access financial records in order to reduce money laundering. Workers may claim a right to not be monitored by television on the job, while management claims the right to protect its assets. In such rights disputes, three strategies for resolving the disputes should be considered.

First, you can try to dissolve the dispute by showing that the conflict is only apparent and that both rights ($R_1$ and $R_2$) can be satisfied. For instance, you might devise a plan in which the firm can protect its assets without using television monitoring; the rights of both parties are thereby protected.

Second, if $R_1$ and $R_2$ cannot both be achieved, you can rank rights; you argue that $R_1$ takes precedence over $R_2$, or vice versa. So, you might argue that in a particular situation the firm's right to protect its assets outweighs the employees' right not to be monitored. In ranking rights, it is important to remember that most rights in organizational contexts are best construed as prima facie rights. Accordingly, examination of the context, the setting of the particular case being considered, will often help in defending a ranking. Employees at a nuclear warhead production facility have privacy rights and the firm has a right to gather information about its employees, but in this particular context the employer's right to inspect the briefcases and files of employees takes precedence over the employees' privacy rights. In other contexts, the right to privacy should be ranked higher. If there is no reason to suspect employee theft in a Caterpillar distributorship, employee privacy rights will take precedence over the firm's right to install a television monitor in the bathrooms.

Third, you may argue for a compromise, i.e., you show that part of $R_1$ can be achieved and part of $R_2$ can be achieved. For example, instead of constant television monitoring which does fully protect the firm's assets, you might argue for an honesty test for each person hired. If such a test enables the company to select employees less inclined to steal, it may represent a good compromise: constant monitoring may not be needed, though the employees will be tested once; and, assets will be preserved, although not as well as by continuous monitoring.

## *The Best Solution to a Moral Problem*

Now that we have a basic idea of how to construct utility and rights arguments, we can return to our ethical decision-making structure.

> 1. Individual X faces moral problem P.
> 2. The alternative solutions to P are $S_1 \ldots S_n$.
> 3. $S_1$ is the best solution to P.
> _____
> X should do $S_1$.

Our focus is on 3. We know we have to compare $S_1 \ldots S_n$ and show that $S_1$ is better than the other solutions. The moral factors we use to make the comparison will include utility and rights. Depending on the particulars of a case, there may be other factors involved, but these two factors will typically be relevant and will typically be the most general features to use in case analyses. So our defense of 3 may be:

> $S_1$ has more utility than $S_2 \ldots S_n$ .
> $S_2$ better protects rights than $S_2 \ldots S_n$.
> _____
> $S_1$ is the best solution to P.

In many argumentative contexts one act $S_1$ will maximize utility while another best preserves the rights of those involved, e.g., perhaps $S_2$ is fairer than $S_1$. To see this, let's introduce another sense of the term "fair," namely, distributional fairness, i.e., the notion that different acts bring about similar benefit/harm ratios for those affected by the acts. For example, two acts ($S_1$ and $S_2$) may affect three people ($P_1$, $P_2$, $P_3$) as follows:

|       | $P_1$ | $P_2$ | $P_3$ | Totals |
|-------|-------|-------|-------|--------|
| $S_1$ | +163  | −51   | −51   | +61    |
| $S_2$ | + 20  | +20   | +20   | +60    |

$S_1$ produces more overall utility than $S_2$, even though $S_1$ significantly harms $P_2$ and $P_3$. $S_2$ is distributionally fairer than $S_1$; it provides equal benefits to everyone affected, and also doesn't harm any individual. In such a case you have to argue that in the particular situation being considered one factor (utility or fairness) should take precedence over the other, or be weighted more than the other. Here fairness would take precedence, since the utility calculation is very close (+61 vs +60). $S_2$ benefits everyone significantly, and equally, and $S_1$ harms $P_2$ and $P_3$ severely. These reasons would be used to claim that fairness takes precedence over utility in this case, from which it follows that $S_2$ is the best solution to P. In other contexts, utility could be shown to take precedence over distributional fairness, for example:

|       | $P_1$ | $P_2$ | $P_3$ | Totals |
|-------|-------|-------|-------|--------|
| $S_3$ | +36   | +25   | +22   | +83    |
| $S_4$ | +21   | +21   | +21   | +63    |

Here $S_4$ is distributionally fairer than $S_3$, yet $S_3$ would be preferred because it not only maximizes utility, it also benefits everyone affected more than anyone is benefitted by $S_4$. These reasons would be stated to show that in this case utility ranks higher than distributional fairness, which would then form the basis for concluding that $S_3$ is the best solution to P.

Utility and rights considerations often conflict in business contexts. Of two manufacturing plans, $S_1$ may maximize utility in the form of profits, dividends and wages but also violate workers' rights to a safe workplace, whereas $S_2$ results in a safer workplace than $S_1$ but has diminished utility. Again, the particular situation must be considered in weighing utility and rights factors. Examine the facts of the case carefully to answer these questions: (1) How wide is the utility disparity between $S_1$ and $S_2$? (2) How serious is $S_1$'s rights violation? (3) How extensive is the gap between the safety violation in $S_1$ and satisfaction of the right in $S_2$? Such considerations often will enable you to establish which moral factor should take precedence.

If it is difficult to determine which moral factor should take precedence in deciding between two acts ($S_1$ and $S_2$), as in

|       | $P_1$ | $P_2$ | $P_3$ | Totals |
|-------|-------|-------|-------|--------|
| $S_1$ | +35   | +2    | +3    | +40    |
| $S_2$ | +8    | +8    | +8    | +24    |

you may be able to rethink the entire situation and come up with another alternative solution to consider:

| | $P_1$ | $P_2$ | $P_3$ | Totals |
|---|---|---|---|---|
| $S_3$ | +13 | +12 | +13 | +38 |

Even though $S_1$ maximizes utility and $S_2$ is the fairest distributionally, you might argue that in this case $S_3$ is the best compromise that can be obtained between the utility and fairness factors.

In many cases, however, it will be very difficult to show that one solution is the best. The utility calculations comparing $S_1$ with $S_2$ may be so close that neither alternative has a definite advantage. Your rights analysis might not provide a conclusive answer. The two alternatives may turn out to be equally fair. In such cases managers face very difficult decisions. However, if your analysis has been thorough, you will undoubtedly have eliminated some alternatives. ($S_3$, $S_4$, $S_5$) that are definitely not the best but which you might have considered to be the best had you not done the analysis. Furthermore, if two solutions tie in your analysis, then in selecting one you are not acting immorally. No other alternative is better than the one you select. Keep in mind, however, that in these cases some people will be harmed, e.g., if $S_1$ and $S_2$ tie for best and you select $S_1$, then Sarah, who is terminated by $S_1$ but not $S_2$, will be harmed.

As you read the cases, keep in mind that our model of ethical decision-making is oversimplified. A real case in a particular context will almost invariably introduce complexities we have not considered, and in many cases moral factors in addition to utility and rights will be relevant to reaching the best solution to an ethical problem.

# SELECT BIBLIOGRAPHY

Adams, D., and E. Maine. *Business Ethics for the 21st Century*. Mountain Views, Calif.: Mayfield, 1997.

Beauchamp, T., and N. Bowie, eds. *Ethical Theory and Business*. 5th ed. Upper Saddle River, N.J.: Prentice-Hall, 1997.

Boatright, J. *Ethics and the Conduct of Business*. 3d ed. Upper Saddle River, N.J.: Prentice-Hall, 2000.

Bowie, N. *Business Ethics: A Kantian Perspective*. Oxford: Blackwell, 1999.

DeGeorge, R. *Business Ethics*. 5th ed. Upper Saddle River, N.J.: Prentice-Hall, 1999.

DesJardins, J., and J. McCall, eds. *Contemporary Issues in Business Ethics*. 4th ed. Belmont, Calif.: Wadsworth, 2000.

Dienhart, J. *Business, Institutions, and Ethics*. New York: Oxford, 2000.

Donaldson, T., and P. Werhane, eds. *Ethical Issues in Business*. 6th ed. Upper Saddle River, N.J.: Prentice-Hall, 1999.

Feldman, F. *Introductory Ethics*. Englewood Cliffs, N.J.: Prentice-Hall, 1978.

Frankena, E. *Ethics*. 2nd ed. Englewood Cliffs, N.J.: Prentice-Hall, 1973.

Frederick, R., ed. *A Companion to Business Ethics*. Oxford: Blackwell, 1999.

Glenn, J. *Ethics in Decision Making*. New York: John Wiley & Sons, 1986.

Hoffman, W., R. Frederick, and M. Schwartz. *Business Ethics*. 4th ed. New York: McGraw-Hill, 2001.

McInerney, P., and G. Rainbolt. *Ethics*. New York: Harper Collins, 1994.

Mill, J. S. *Utilitarianism*. Indianapolis: Bobbs-Merrill, 1957.

Rachels, J. *The Elements of Moral Philosophy*. New York: Random House, 1986.

Shaw, W., and V. Barry. *Moral Issues in Business*. 8th ed. Belmont, Calif.: Wadsworth, 2001.

Sullivan, R. *Immanuel Kant's Moral Theory*. New York: Cambridge University Press, 1989.

Velasquez, M. *Business Ethics*. 4th ed. Upper Saddle River, N.J.: Prentice-Hall, 1998.

Werhane, P., and R. Freeman, eds. *Encyclopedic Dictionary of Business Ethics*. Oxford: Blackwell, 1997.

# ELECTRONIC SOURCES

Ethics on the World Wide Web  commfaculty.fullerton.edu/lester/ethics/ethics_list.html

The Council for Ethics in Economics  www.businessethics.org

Markkula Center for Applied Ethics  www.scu.edu/SCU/Centers/Ethics

Institute for Business and Professional Ethics  www.depaul.edu/ethics

International Society of Business, Economics and Ethics  www.synethos.org

# 2. ETHICS AND ORGANIZATIONS

## INTRODUCTION

Do corporations have responsibilities extending beyond that of making as much money as possible? In his two articles, Milton Friedman argues that corporations have only one social obligation, namely, to maximize profits within the constraint of the law and ethical custom. Friedman offers two primary arguments, one based on property rights, the other on utility. The rights argument is that shareholders who own the firm typically want profits maximized; managers, as the agents of the owners, should maximize profit. He also argues that if a manager acts other than to maximize profit, his act will probably have social disutility. Friedman sees institutions as having distinct functions; e.g., business should maximize profit and government should fulfill a separate set of social obligations. If businesses play a socially responsible role beyond that of profit maximization, they not only undercut shareholder rights and social utility, they actually encourage a blurring of institutional functions, which may lead to socialism. In response, Robert Almeder argues that Friedman's arguments are unsound. Furthermore, he claims that from a moral point of view there are certain acts a corporation should not perform even though those acts have utility and are not legally prohibited. Almeder goes on to argue that it is strict adherence to the Friedman position that will most likely lead to socialism; the only kind of capitalism that can survive in the long run is one that repudiates certain central tenets of Friedman's position. The case study in this section considers Ford Motor Company's rationale for placement of the gas tank in its early Pinto model, and provides a specific context for discussing the Friedman-Almeder debate.

Milton Friedman's theory is not the only one that has been proposed for use in determining corporations' social responsibilities. In "A Stakeholder Theory of the Modern Corporation," R. Edward Freeman offers an alternative to Friedman's theory. On Freeman's view, Friedman falsely assumes that corporate executives' primary moral duty is a fiduciary one to their stockholders and that in fulfilling this duty they act in socially responsible ways. Freeman takes issue with this contention and in opposition argues: (1) that corporate managers have duties to all those groups and individuals who have a stake in or claim on the firm (Freeman calls these groups and individuals 'stakeholders'), (2) that no group of stakeholders should be given primacy over any other when companies arbitrate stakeholders' competing claims, and (3) that the law of corporations should be changed so as to require executives to manage their firms in accordance with the principal tenets of stakeholder theory; that is to say, Freeman holds that executives should be told (legally) to manage their firms in the interests of their stakeholders. In "Why I Am Not a Normative Stakeholder Theorist," James Humber argues that Freeman's theory ought to be rejected. In support of this position Humber argues: (1) that Freeman provides no acceptable justification for legally requiring corporations to manage their firms in accordance with the tenets of stakeholder theory, (2) that Freeman's use of 'stakeholder' can be rejected, and if this is done stakeholder theory is cast into doubt, (3) that there is good reason to believe that various corporations should always give primacy to some stakeholder groups over others, and finally, (4) that stakeholder theorists must choose between accepting inconsistency or giving moral approval to virtually any behavior that firms choose to adopt relative to their stakeholders.

A discussion of ethics and organizations should take into account the ethical issues that managers themselves regard as central in corporate life. This is the focus of the article by Milton Snoeyenbos and Barbara Caley. They pay particular attention to industry-wide ethical issues and controversies that arise inside organizations due to their hierarchical structure. The ethical issues discussed generally in this paper are precisely those to be covered in more detail in the later chapters. The authors also suggest general strategies for improving ethical behavior in organizations.

# BUSINESS AND SOCIAL RESPONSIBILITY

*Case Study*

# Cost-Benefit Analysis and the Ford Pinto

In the late 1960s, American automakers were faced with serious competition from German and Japanese firms in the subcompact market. Some Detroit executives felt that they should concentrate on medium-size and large models and let foreign competitors with their lower costs have the small-car market. Others argued that the subcompact market was potentially lucrative and should be pursued. Semon Knudsen, President of Ford, opposed the idea of building a subcompact in the United States, but Ford Vice President Lee Iacocca, who had developed the Mustang, favored building a domestic subcompact. Henry Ford II, Ford's CEO, decided in favor of Iacocca, Knudsen resigned, and Iacocca subsequently became President. In 1968 Ford Motor decided to produce the Pinto.

Iacocca conceived the idea of building a car that would cost less than $2,000 and weigh less than 2,000 pounds. There is some controversy as to whether these specifications were rigid, as claimed by Ford critic Mark Dowie, or flexible, as claimed by Ford officials. Mr. Iacocca oversaw the project with Vice Presidents Robert Alexander and Harold MacDonald, all of whom were members of Ford's Product Planning Committee, which reviewed the Pinto project as it developed. It is not clear whether Iacocca had any direct input as to the Pinto's design. A *Chicago Tribune* article stated: "None of the documents obtained (internal Ford memos) shows any direct involvement by Iacocca in the design decision involving the car." Harley Copp, a Ford engineer who largely designed the Ford Capri, which had the gas tank over the axle, and who later resigned and testified against Ford in many court cases involving the Pinto, said that the highest level of Ford's management made the decision to produce the Pinto knowing the gas tank was vulnerable to puncture. However, there appears to be no direct evidence this is true.

Although production planning for a new model normally takes about three and a half years, Ford decided to shorten the time from conception to production; it wanted the Pinto ready for the 1971 model year. However, even here experts who have studied this case disagree about the facts. Dowie suggested that Ford tried to reduce the time frame from 43 to 25 months. Others have suggested that Ford aimed for 38 months.  In the normal time frame, design changes and quality assurance standards are in place largely before production line tooling. But tooling requires about a year and a half and hence, in the case of the Pinto, tooling and product development overlapped considerably. In large part because of the overlap, design decisions controlled engineering decisions to a degree greater than in normal planning. The Pinto's design required that its gas tank be located behind the rear axle, placing it tightly between the axle and rear bumper. Upon rear impact, the gas tank could be driven against the Pinto's differential housing, which was designed with a series of exposed bolt heads and a flange that were sufficient to puncture the gas tank. It should be noted that the gas tank was located behind the axle on most full-sized domestic cars and also on the Japanese subcompacts. However, Ford had another option. Its European-built Capri had a fuel tank located over the rear axle. Ford had a patent on this type of fuel tank. And the Capri performed well in rear-end collisions. However, there were several factors which inclined Ford engineers to go with the behind-the-axle gas tank: (1) data indicated the over-the-axle tank increased the risk of fuel leakage into the passenger compartment; (2) the over-the-axle placement raised the Pinto's center of gravity, and thereby led to increased auto control problems; and (3) placing the gas tank over the axle significantly reduced trunk space. One Ford engineer, when asked about the gas tank placement, noted: "Safety isn't the issue, trunk space is. You have no idea how stiff the competition is over trunk space. Do you realize that if we put a Capri-type tank in the Pinto, you could only get one set of golf clubs in the trunk?"

Prior to production of the Pinto, in 1969 Ford crash-tested several autos modified to resemble the rear-end structure of the Pinto. These tests were conducted in part with an eye to Federal Motor Vehicle Safety Standard 301, which was proposed for adoption by the National Highway Traffic Safety

Administration (NHTSA) in 1969. Standard 301 proposed that all autos be required to withstand an impact of 20 mph, with only a small fuel loss. Specifically, an auto struck by a 4,000 lb. object moving at 20 mph should leak less than one ounce of fuel per minute. Of four Pinto prototypes tested, one failed completely when the fuel tank ruptured at a poorly welded seam, and the other three leaked slightly more fuel than permitted under the proposed standard. Court testimony later described some of these tests: "Prototypes struck from the rear with a moving barrier at 21 mph caused the fuel tank to be driven forward and to be punctured, causing fuel leakage." It should be noted that in these court cases Ford denied that it crash tested Pintos prior to production. Ford said the 1969 tests were on other subcompact cars to which were added Pinto-type fuel stystems.

Ford proceeded to production of the Pinto in August 1970. After the Pinto was in production, Ford continued its crash-test program. All crash tests on production Pintos resulted in leakage in excess of that permitted by NHTSA's proposed Standard 301. As subsequent court testimony indicated: "A production Pinto crash tested at 21 mph into a fixed barrier caused the fuel neck to be torn from the gas tank and the tank to be punctured by a bolt head on the differential housing. In at least one test, spilled fuel entered the driver's compartment."

Ford also studied options for improving the Pinto's rear-end design in order to meet NHTSA's proposed standard. Ford modified the Pinto's gas tank design, and ran several crash tests on cars so modified. In one successful test, a plastic baffle was placed between the front of the gas tank and the differential housing. In a second successful test, a piece of steel was placed between the tank and rear bumper. The third successful test was of a Pinto with a rubber-lined gas tank. The rubber-lined tank, which would have increased the cost of a Pinto by $6, was seriously considered. But the liners failed in both very hot and very cold weather. Harley Copp, Ford's executive in charge of crash testing, said that all crash test results were forwarded to Ford's Product Planning Committee.

Other design changes which could have been considered were: (1) a shock absorbent "flak suit" to cover the tank at $4; (2) a tank within the tank at $6; (3) placing a protective shield between the differential housing and the tank at $2; (4) reinforcement of the bumper at $3; and (5) the addition of eight inches of crush space at $6. It is not known how effective these measures would have been on the Pinto. One expert said that equipping the Pinto with a reinforced rear structure, smooth axle, improved bumper, and additional crush space at a total cost of $15 would have made the fuel tank safe in the 34 to 38 mph range when hit in the rear end by a car the size of a Ford Galaxie. However, such tests were not conducted.

Ford decided to go ahead with its gas tank design, and not alter the tank in light of its crash-tests. It did so for several reasons. First, cost-benefit analysis, as detailed in a Ford memorandum titled "Fatalities Associated with Crash-Induced Fuel Leakage and Fires," suggested that there were no advantages in upgrading the Pinto's fuel tank. In the early 1970s, NHTSA decided that cost-benefit analysis was an appropriate basis for safety design standards. To make such an analysis some specific value had to be placed on a human life, and NHTSA decided on a figure of $200,725 as the estimated cost to society every time a person is killed in an auto accident:

| | |
|---|---:|
| Future Productivity Losses | |
| Direct | $132,000 |
| Indirect | 41,300 |
| Medical Costs | |
| Hospital | 700 |
| Other | 425 |
| Property Damage | 1,500 |
| Insurance Administration | 4,700 |
| Legal and Court | 3,000 |
| Employer Losses | 1,000 |
| Victim's Pain and Suffering | 10,000 |
| Funeral | 900 |
| Assets (Lost Consumption) | 5,000 |
| Miscellaneous Accident Cost | 200 |
| Total Per Fatality | $200,725 |

Using NHTSA's data, Ford calculated costs and benefits by considering the variables of lives saved by product redesign and the cost of the product. For example, a Ford internal memorandum gives the following calculation of an $11 gas tank improvement, which was estimated to save 180 lives:

### Benefits

Savings: 180 burn deaths, 180 serious burn injuries, 2,100 burned vehicles.
Unit Cost: $200,000 per death, $67,000 per injury, $700 per vehicle.
Total Benefit: $180 \times (\$200,000) + 180 \times (\$67,000)$
$+ 2,100 \times (\$700) = \$49.5$ million.

COSTS

Sales: 11 million cars, 1.5 million light trucks
Unit Cost: $11 per car, $11 per truck
Total Cost: 12,500,000 × ($11) = $137 million.

(This calculation was based on all of Ford's vehicles over an extended period of time, not just the Pinto.) Early in 1971 a Ford management committee reviewed the data discussed in "Fatalities Associated with Crash-Induced Fuel Leakage and Fires." Mr. MacDonald chaired the meeting and Mr. Alexander attended. Since the costs of the $11 safety improvement outweighed its benefits, Ford maintained it was not justified in making the improvement.

A 1998 court case in Broward County, Florida brought to light that General Motors utilized similar calculations. A cost-benefit analysis on fire-related fatalities was prepared in 1973 by Edward Ivey, a GM engineer. It puts a dollar value on a human life similar to that used by Ford ($200,000) and calculated the annual cost to GM of fuel-fed fire fatalities at $2.40 per car on the highways. It also calculated that it would be worth $2.20 per car to prevent such fires. In another memo revealed at the trial, Mr. Ivey was said by an outside GM lawyer to have said that he did the cost-benefit calculations "for Oldsmobile management" to assist them "in trying to figure out how much Olds could spend on fuel systems."

A second factor in Ford's decision was that the Pinto did meet all auto safety standards at the time. NHTSA Standard 301 was only a *proposed* rule. The rule was proposed early in 1969, and its objectives were initially supported publicly by Ford management. In fact, Ford voluntarily adopted the 20 mph standard as an objective for all its vehicles. In August, 1970, NHTSA specified the precise test method to meet Standard 301: all vehicles would be required to satisfy a 20 mph fixed-barrier test, i.e., the vehicle is towed backward into a fixed barrier at 20 mph. Ford and all other automakers objected to this test method. Ford favored a moving-barrier test, one in which an object impacts a stationary vehicle. Ford believed the moving-barrier test to be more realistic than the fixed-barrier test.

James Neal, speaking for Ford, said: "The Pinto met every fuel-system integrity standard of any Federal, State or Local Government." Neal also stressed that Ford was the only auto manufacturer in the world at that time to have set a 20 mph internal standard for rear collision without fuel leakage. Herbert Misch, Ford's Vice President of Environmental and Safety

Engineering, said that Ford set the 20 mph standard as a performance goal to be met by future autos. Misch conceded that the Pinto failed rear-impact tests at 20 mph, but defended Ford's testing procedures. He also said that the tests with rubber-lined tanks were conducted to determine how to satisfy the 20 mph standard sometime in the future. Misch added: "It is simply unreasonable and unfair to contend that a car is somehow unsafe if it does not meet standards proposed for future years or embody the technological improvements that are introduced in later model years."

Third, Ford contended that the Pinto was as safe as comparable subcompacts. It compared the Vega, Gremlin, Colt, and Toyota with the Pinto and argued that: (1) fuel tank metal thickness was above average on the Pinto; (2) only the Pinto had metal plates in the trunk to deflect impact; (3) all the subcompacts had puncture sources; and (4) bumpers were comparable on all five autos. In a 1980 trial Mr. Neal conceded the Pinto was not as safe as a Lincoln or Cadillac. He added: "If the public wanted it, and could pay for it . . . Detroit could build a tank of a car—a car that would withstand practically anything [but] only the rich could afford it and they would have to stop at every other gasoline station for a refill."

However, critics argued that the Pinto was not as safe as comparable subcompacts with respect to gas tank placement. Dr. Leslie Ball, head of safety for NASA's manned space program, said that all comparable Japanese and European subcompacts had safer gas tank positioning. Ball said the "production of the Pinto was the most reprehensible decision in the history of American engineering." Byron Block, auto safety expert, said Ford made an "extremely irresponsible decision when they placed such a weak tank in such a ridiculous location in such a soft rear end. It's almost designed to blow up premeditated."

A fourth factor was undoubtedly Ford's tight production schedule. When crash tests revealed the gas tank problem, Ford had $200 million worth of tools on line and in place. Redesign and retooling would have been very expensive.

A fifth factor was that Ford had to cut costs to be competitive. Ford wanted the Pinto to weigh less than 2,000 lbs. and cost less than $2,000. It felt that control of both variables was necessary to compete against Volkswagen and the Japanese imports. Within the scope of the law, it had to control both weight and cost. A 1969 memo from Ford's product development engineers indicated that the company could save 18 cents per auto and reduce weight by using a certain type of controller. They shaved 50 cents per car and reduced weight a bit by changing the Pinto's flooring.

When it debuted, the Pinto was priced at $1919, about $170 less than its American competitor the Vega, and just less than the $1999 a Volkswagen Beetle cost.

The sixth factor in Ford's decision was a belief that Americans were not primarily interested in safety. As Lee Iacocca was fond of saying, "Safety doesn't sell." Some reporters said Iacocca held this position because of a failed attempt to add costly safety features to 1950s Fords. But Harold Boles, who sold Ford products during this period, said Iacocca was simply telling the truth: "During the 60s people wanted power cars, and then, with the gas crisis in 73–74, they wanted fuel economy. Safety was definitely not Job 1 then. Iacocca knew marketing, knew the consumer—he just told the truth."

From 1968 until its adoption by NHTSA in 1977, Ford opposed Standard 301, claiming that its cost-benefit analysis indicated that it was not rational to make the change sooner. However, critics claimed that Ford's lobbying against 301 indicated that it was not really serious about rear-impact safety. They claimed that Ford lobbied against 301 to block higher, and therefore more costly, legal safety standards in order to continue to sell the Pinto for a lower price and thereby increase its market share and profits.

Considerable controversy has ensued as to whether the Pinto is a safe automobile. Mark Dowie, Pinto critic, claims that more than 400,000 autos burned every year during the early 1970s, that every year 3,000 people were burned to death in autos, and that 40 percent of auto burn deaths could have been prevented by adoption of Standard 301. Dowie states that although Ford made 24 percent of the autos on American roads, its autos were involved in 42 percent of the accidents that involved fuel leakage. Dowie claims that between 1971 and 1977 Pinto crashes caused at least 500 burn deaths of people who would not have been seriously injured if the auto had not burned. Dowie says the figure could go as high as 900.

Speaking for Ford, Mr. Misch cited statistics from NHTSA's Fatality Analysis Reporting System (FARS) to show that in 1975 there were 848 fire-related auto deaths, but only 13 involved Pintos. He claimed that in 1976, Pintos were involved in only 22 of 943 fire-related deaths. These data indicate that Pintos were involved in 1.9 percent of fire-related auto deaths, and Mr. Misch pointed out that Pintos constitute 1.9 percent of the autos in America. In addition, fewer than half of the Pintos mentioned in the FARS study were struck from the rear. Mr. Misch concluded the Pinto is a safe auto, and is not involved in 70 to 130 burn deaths annually, as Mr. Dowie claimed.

It is difficult to assess exactly how many people were killed in low-speed collisions in which Pintos were rear-ended. Dowie's figures do not seem to be based on verifiable evidence; in fact, in a phone conversation with Douglas Birsch, a neutral analyst of the case, Dowie "admitted that (based on new evidence) his number might be too high, but insisted that Ford's number was too low." Dowie is probably correct about Ford's FARS-based data. First of all, fire explosion is not a data element on most police reporting forms, unless a non-collision fire caused an accident. Second, FARS data do not include an auto fire's origin. And third, if a death due to burns occurs sometime after a crash, it will probably not be recorded on the police officer's accident report. Altogether, we can conclude that Dowie's figures are too high and Ford's too low.

Reactions to the Pinto case have been very divergent. An industry spokesman said: "We have to make cost-benefit analyses all the time. That's part of business. Everyone knows that some people will die in auto accidents, but people do accept risks and they do want us to hold down costs. We could build an absolutely safe car, but nobody could afford it." A Pinto critic said, "One wonders how long the Ford Motor Company would continue to market lethal cars were Henry Ford II and Lee Iacocca serving twenty-year terms in Leavenworth for consumer homicide."

## FOR DISCUSSION

Should Ford have produced the Pinto in the form that it did produce it? Why or why not? Is cost-benefit analysis the appropriate basis for safety design standards? Why or why not? If not, what other factors should be considered? Discuss NHTSA's figures regarding the estimated cost of an auto fatality. Analyze each factor in Ford's decision not to implement the $11 gas tank improvement. Do the reasons (individually or together) provide an adequate justification for Ford's decision? Discuss the moral basis of Ford's opposition to NHTSA Standard 301.

## SOURCES

*Grimshaw* v. *Ford Motor Co.*, App., 174 Cal. Rptr. 348, pp. 359–88; Ralph Drayton, "One Manufacturer's Approach to Automobile Safety Standards," *CLTA NEWS* 8, no. 2 (February 1968): 11 ff; "Magazine Claims Ford Ignored Pinto Fire Peril," *Automotive News* (August 15, 1977): 3; "Ford

Rebuts Pinto Criticisms and Says Article Is Distorted," *The National Underwriter* (Prop. Ed.) 81 (September 9, 1977): 36; Mark Dowie, "How Ford Put Two Million Firetraps on Wheels," *Business and Social Review* no. 23 (fall, 1977): 44–55; "Ford Fights Pinto Case: Jury Gives $128 Million," *Automotive News* (February 13, 1978): 3 ff; J. Gamlin, "Jury Slaps Massive Fine on Ford in 1972 Pinto Crash," *Business Insurance* 12 (February 20, 1978): 1 ff; "Ford Motor Is Indicted in Indiana Pinto Death," *Automotive News* (September 18, 1978): 2; *Reckless Homicide?: Ford's Pinto Trial*, Lee P. Strobel. South Bend, Ind.: And Books, 1980; "After Pinto," *U.S. News and World Report* 88 (March 24, 1980): 11; "Ford's Pinto: Not Guilty," *Newsweek* 95 (March 24, 1980): 74; "The Ford Motor Car," in Manuel Velasquez, *Business Ethics*, 2d ed. (Englewood Cliffs, N.J.: Prentice-Hall, 1988) pp. 119–23; *Taking Sides*, L. Newton and M. Ford, eds. (Guilford Conn.: Dushkin, 1990), pp. 130–47; *The Ford Pinto Case*, D. Birsch and J. Fielder, eds. (Albany: SUNY Press, 1994).

*Milton Friedman*

# The Social Responsibility of Business Is to Increase Its Profits

When I hear businessmen speak eloquently about the "social responsibilities of business in a free-enterprise system," I am reminded of the wonderful line about the Frenchman who discovered at the age of seventy that he had been speaking prose all his life. The businessmen believe that they are defending free enterprise when they declaim that business is not concerned "merely" with profit but also with promoting desirable "social" ends; that business has a "social conscience" and takes seriously its responsibilities for providing employment, eliminating discrimination, avoiding pollution, and whatever else may be the catchwords of the contemporary crop of reformers. In fact they are—or would be if they or anyone else took them seriously—preaching pure and unadulterated socialism. Businessmen who talk this way are unwitting puppets of the intellectual forces that have been undermining the basis of a free society these past decades.

The discussions of the "social responsibilities of business" are notable for their analytical looseness and lack of rigor. What does it mean to say that "business" has responsibilities? Only people can have responsibilities. A corporation is an artificial person and in this sense may have artificial reponsibilities, but "business" as a whole cannot be said to have responsibilities, even in this vague sense. The first step toward clarity in examining the doctrine of the social responsibility of business is to ask precisely what it implies for whom. Presumably, the individuals who are to be responsible are businessmen, which means individual proprietors or corporate executives. Most of the discussion of social responsibility is directed at corporations, so in what follows I shall mostly neglect the individual proprietor and speak of corporate executives.

*New York Times Magazine*, 13 September 1970, pp. 33, 122–26. Copyright © 1970 by the New York Times Co. Reprinted by permission.

*   *   *

In a free enterprise, private-property system, a corporate executive is an employee of the owners of the business. He has direct responsibility to his employers. That responsibility is to conduct the business in accordance with their desires, which generally will be to make as much money as possible while conforming to the basic rules of the society, both those embodied in law and those embodied in ethical custom. Of course, in some cases his employers may have a different objective. A group of persons might establish a corporation for an eleemosynary purpose—for example, a hospital or a school. The manager of such a corporation will not have money profit as his objective but the rendering of certain services.

In either case, the key point is that, in his capacity as a corporate executive, the manager is the agent of the individuals who own the corporation or establish the eleemosynary institution, and his primary responsibility is to them.

Needless to say, this does not mean that it is easy to judge how well he is performing his task. But at least the criterion of performance is straightforward, and the persons among whom a voluntary contractual arrangement exists are clearly defined.

Of course, the corporate executive is also a person in his own right. As a person, he may have many other responsibilities that he recognizes or assumes voluntarily—to his family, his conscience, his feelings of charity, his church, his clubs, his city, his country. He may feel impelled by these responsibilities to devote part of his income to causes he regards as worthy, to refuse to work for particular corporations, even to leave his job, for example, to join his country's armed forces. If we wish, we may refer to some of these responsibilities as "social responsibilities." But in these respects he is acting as a principal, not an agent; he is spending his own money or time or energy, not the money of his employers or the time or energy he has contracted to devote to their purposes. If these are "social responsibilities," they are the social responsibilities of individuals, not of business.

What does it mean to say that the corporate executive has a "social responsibility" in his capacity as businessman? If this statement is not pure rhetoric, it must mean that he is to act in some way that is not in the interest of his employers. For example, that he is to refrain from increasing the price of the product in order to contribute to the social objective of preventing inflation, even though a price increase would be in the best interests of the corporation. Or that he is to make expenditures on reducing pollution beyond the amount that is in the best interests of the corporation or that is required by law in order to contribute to the social objective of improving the environment. Or that, at the expense of corporate profits, he is to hire "hard-core" unemployed instead of better-qualified available workmen to contribute to the social objective of reducing poverty.

In each of these cases, the corporate executive would be spending someone else's money for a general social interest. Insofar as his actions in accord with his "social responsibility" reduce returns to stockholders, he is spending their money. Insofar as his actions raise the price to customers, he is spending the customers' money. Insofar as his actions lower the wages of some employees, he is spending their money.

The stockholders or the customers or the employees could separately spend their own money on the particular action if they wished to do so. The executive is exercising a distinct "social responsibility," rather than serving as an agent of the stockholders or the customers or the employees, only if he spends the money in a different way than they would have spent it.

But if he does this, he is in effect imposing taxes, on the one hand, and deciding how the tax proceeds shall be spent, on the other.

This process raises political questions on two levels: principle and consequences. On the level of political principle, the imposition of taxes and the expenditure of tax proceeds are governmental functions. We have established elaborate constitutional, parliamentary, and judicial provisions to control these functions, to assure that taxes are imposed so far as possible in accordance with the preferences and desires of the public—after all, "taxation without representation" was one of the battle cries of the American Revolution. We have a system of checks and balances to separate the legislative function of imposing taxes and enacting expenditures from the executive function of collecting taxes and administering expenditure programs and from the judicial function of mediating disputes and interpreting the law.

Here the businessman—self-selected or appointed directly or indirectly by stockholders—is to be simultaneously legislator, executive, and jurist. He is to decide whom to tax by how much and for what purpose, and he is to spend the proceeds—all this guided only by general exhortations from on high to restrain inflation, improve the environment, fight poverty and so on and on.

The whole justification for permitting the corporate executive to be selected by the stockholders is that the executive is an agent serving the interests of his principal. This justification disappears when the corporate executive imposes taxes and spends the proceeds for "social" purposes.

He becomes in effect a public employee, a civil servant, even though he remains in name an employee of a private enterprise. On grounds of political principle, it is intolerable that such civil servants—insofar as their actions in the name of social responsibility are real and not just window-dressing—should be selected as they are now. If they are to be civil servants, then they must be selected through a political process. If they are to impose taxes and make expenditures to foster "social objectives," then political machinery must be set up to guide the assessment of taxes and to determine through a political process the objectives to be served.

This is the basic reason why the doctrine of "social responsibility" involves the acceptance of the socialist view that political mechanisms, not market mechanisms, are the appropriate way to determine the allocation of scarce resources to alternative uses.

On the grounds of consequences, can the corporate executive in fact discharge his alleged "social responsibilities"? On the one hand, suppose he could get away with spending the stockholders' or customers' or employees' money. How is he to know how to spend it? He is told that he must contribute to fighting inflation. How is he to know what action of his will contribute to that end? He is presumably an expert in running his company—in producing a product or selling it or financing it. But nothing about his selection makes him an expert on inflation. Will his holding down the price of his product reduce inflationary pressure? Or, by leaving more spending power in the hands of his customers, simply divert it elsewhere? Or, by forcing him to produce less because of the low price, will it simply contribute to shortages? Even if he could answer these questions, how much cost is he justified in imposing on his stockholders, customers, and employees for this social purpose? What is his appropriate share and what is the appropriate share of others?

And, whether he wants to or not, can he get away with spending his stockholders', customers', or employees' money? Will not the stockholders fire him? (Either the present ones or those who take over when his actions in the name of social responsibility have reduced the corporation's profits and the price of its stock.) His customers and his employees can desert him for other producers and employers less scrupulous in exercising their social responsibilities.

This facet of "social responsibility" doctrine is brought into sharp relief when the doctrine is used to justify wage restraint by trade unions. The conflict of interest is naked and clear when union officials are asked to subordinate the interest of their members to some more general social purpose. If the union officials try to enforce wage restraint, the consequence is likely to be wildcat strikes, rank-and-file revolts, and the emergence of strong competitors for their jobs. We thus have the ironic phenomenon that union leaders—at least in the United States—have objected to government interference with the market far more consistently and courageously than have business leaders.

The difficulty of exercising "social responsibility" illustrates, of course, the great virtue of private competitive enterprise—it forces people to be responsible for their own actions and makes it difficult for them to "exploit" other people for either selfish or unselfish purposes. They can do good—but only at their own expense.

Many a reader who has followed the argument this far may be tempted to remonstrate that it is all well and good to speak of government's having the responsibility to impose taxes and determine expenditures for such "social" purposes as controlling pollution or training the hard-core unemployed, but that the problems are too urgent to wait on the slow course of political processes, that the exercise of social responsibility by businessmen is a quicker and surer way to solve pressing current problems.

Aside from the question of fact—I share Adam Smith's skepticism about the benefits that can be expected from "those who affected to trade for the public good"—this argument must be rejected on grounds of principle. What it amounts to is an assertion that those who favor the taxes and expenditures in question have failed to persuade a majority of their fellow citizens to be of like mind and that they are seeking to attain by undemocratic procedures what they cannot attain by democratic procedures. In a free society, it is hard for "good" people to do "good," but that is a small price to pay for making it hard for "evil" people to do "evil," especially since one man's good is another's evil.

I have, for simplicity, concentrated on the special case of the corporate executive, except only for the brief digression on trade unions. But precisely the same argument applies to the newer phenomenon of calling upon stockholders to require corporations to exercise social responsibility (the recent GM crusade, for example). In most of these cases, what is in effect involved is some stockholders trying to get other stockholders (or customers or employees) to contribute against their will to "social" causes favored by the activists. Insofar as they succeed, they are again imposing taxes and spending the proceeds.

The situation of the individual proprietor is somewhat different. If he acts to reduce the returns of his enterprise in order to exercise his "social responsibility," he is spending his own money, not someone else's. If he wishes to spend his money on such purposes, that is his right, and I cannot see that there is any objection to his doing so. In the process, he, too, may impose costs on employees and customers. However, because he is far less likely than a large corporation or union to have monopolistic power, any such side effects will tend to be minor.

Of course, in practice the doctrine of social responsibility is frequently a cloak for actions that are justified on other grounds rather than a reason for those actions.

To illustrate, it may well be in the long-run interest of a corporation that is a major employer in a small community to devote resources to providing amenities to that community or to improving its government. That may make it easier to attract desirable employees, it may reduce the wage bill or lessen losses from pilferage and sabotage or have other worthwhile effects. Or it may be that, given the laws about the deductibility of corporate charitable contributions, the stockholders can contribute more to charities they favor since they can in that way contribute an amount that would otherwise have been paid as corporate taxes.

In each of these—and many similar—cases, there is a strong temptation to rationalize these actions as an exercise of "social responsibility." In the present climate of opinion, with its widespread aversion to "capitalism," "profits," the "soulless corporation," and so on, this is one way for a corporation to generate good will as a by-product of expenditures that are entirely justified in its own self-interest.

It would be inconsistent of me to call on corporate executives to refrain from this hypocritical window-dressing because it harms the foundations of a free society. That would be to call on them to exercise a "social responsibility"! If our institutions, and the attitudes of the public, make it in their self-interest to cloak their actions in this way, I cannot summon much indignation to denounce them. At the same time, I can express admiration for those individual proprietors or owners of closely held corporations or stockholders of more broadly held corporations who disdain such tactics as approaching fraud.

Whether blameworthy or not, the use of the cloak of social responsibility, and the nonsense spoken in its name by influential and prestigious businessmen, does clearly harm the foundations of a free society. I have been impressed time and again by the schizophrenic character of many businessmen. They are capable of being extremely farsighted and clear-headed in matters that are internal to their businesses. They are incredibly short-sighted and muddleheaded in matters that are outside their businesses but affect the possible survival of business in general. This short-sightedness is strikingly exemplified in the calls from many businessmen for wage and price guidelines or controls or incomes policies. There is nothing that could do more in a brief period to destroy a market system and replace it by a centrally controlled system than effective governmental control of prices and wages.

The short-sightedness is also exemplified in speeches by businessmen on social responsibility. This may gain them kudos in the short run. But it helps to strengthen the already too prevalent view that the pursuit of profits is wicked and immoral and must be curbed and controlled by external forces. Once this view is adopted, the external forces that curb the market will not be the social consciences, however highly developed, of the pontificating executives; it will be the iron fist of Government bureaucrats. Here, as with price and wage controls, businessmen seem to me to reveal a suicidal impulse.

The political principle that underlies the market mechanism is unanimity. In an ideal free market resting on private property, no individual can coerce any other, all cooperation is voluntary, all parties to such cooperation benefit or they need not participate. There are no "social" values, no "social" responsibilities in any sense other than the shared values and responsibilities of individuals. Society is a collection of individuals and of the various groups they voluntarily form.

The political principle that underlies the political mechanism is conformity. The individual must serve a more general social interest—whether that be determined by a church or a dictator or a majority. The individual may have a vote and a say in what is to be done, but if he is overruled, he must conform. It is appropriate for some to require others to contribute to a general social purpose whether they wish to or not.

Unfortunately, unanimity is not always feasible. There are some respects in which conformity appears unavoidable, so I do not see how one can avoid the use of the political mechanism altogether.

But the doctrine of "social responsibility" taken seriously would extend the scope of the political mechanism to every human activity. It does not differ in philosophy from the most explicitly collectivist doctrine. It differs only by professing to believe that collectivist ends can be attained without collectivist means. That is why, in my book *Capitalism and Freedom*, I have called it a "fundamentally subversive doctrine" in a free society, and have said that in such a society, "there is one and only one social responsibility of business—to use its resources and engage in activities designed to increase its profits so long as it stays within the rules of the game, which is to say, engages in open and free competition without deception or fraud."

# Milton Friedman Responds

MCLAUGHRY: The question of environmental pollution is very much on the public's mind. There are various ways to approach this question. One is the completely laissez-faire approach; another is to tax pollution; another is to give tax incentives or subsidies to companies to encourage them to stop polluting; a fourth is to use police power to make pollution illegal and impose penalties. What would you view as the best way to attack the pollution problem in a free enterprise society?

FRIEDMAN: Well, there is a great deal of misunderstanding about the pollution problem in our society. First, it is often in the private interest not to pollute. That being said, we mustn't suppose that there are no mechanisms within the free enterprise society which lead to the "right" amount of pollution.

Let me stop here for a minute. An ideal of zero pollution is one of the fallacies mouthed about the problem. That is absurd. As in all these cases, you must balance returns with costs. People's breathing is one source of pollution. We breathe in oxygen and breathe out carbon dioxide. If too much carbon dioxide is breathed out, there is a lot of pollution. Now we can simply stop breathing, but most of us would consider the cost of eliminating that pollution greater than the return. We must decide upon the "right" amount of pollution, that amount at which the cost of reducing pollution to all the people concerned would be greater than the gain from reducing the level.

In many cases, the private market provides precisely that incentive. For example, consider a town that has been cited as a horror—Gary, Indiana, where the U.S. Steel Company is the major source of pollution. Let's assume for a moment that contrary to fact, none of the pollution spreads into Chicago. Instead, it's all concentrated in Gary. Now, if U.S.

Steel pollutes heavily in Gary, the Gary environment becomes unattractive. People don't want to live and work there. U.S. Steel has to pay higher wages to lure employees. You'll say to me that not all the people in Gary work for U.S. Steel. Some people run stores and gas stations. But exactly the same thing is true. If Gary is an unpleasant environment, nobody will run a grocery store there unless he can earn sufficiently more there than he can elsewhere to compensate for enduring the pollution. Consequently, food costs will be high and that again will raise the wages U.S. Steel will have to pay to attract a labor force. Under those circumstances, all the costs of pollution are borne by U.S. Steel, meaning a collection of its stockholders and customers.

MCLAUGHRY: Doesn't your argument depend on an assumption of perfect labor mobility?

FRIEDMAN: No, no. It depends on some labor mobility, but after all, there is labor mobility. It isn't necessary that every person be mobile. Wages are determined at the margin.

For example, the fact that 2 percent of the people are good shoppers makes it unnecessary for the other 98 percent to be good shoppers. Why is it that the prices are roughly the same in different stores? Doesn't that assume that every shopper is a good shopper? Not at all. It's a fact that because some people do compare prices and select the better buys, the rest of us don't have to pay such careful attention. The same is true here. Some people in the labor force will move in and out. The people in Gary will not live in Gary unless it offers better opportunity than they can get elsewhere. Maybe other things aren't very good; maybe by your standards and my standards these people are not very well off. But among the alternatives they have, that's best.

MCLAUGHRY: Don't the traditions and habits of people with lower income and lower education levels combine to frustrate that easy mobility of labor?

FRIEDMAN: On the contrary. There is enormous mobility of labor at the very lowest levels—not only in this country, but all over. How were Indians ever led from India to Africa, to Malaysia, to Indonesia, except for the fact that they heard of better opportunities? How was the United States settled? From the end of the Civil War to World War I, if I remember correctly, a third of the people in the United States had immigrated from abroad. The people who came here were not those who earned high wages; they were not the "jet set." They were poor, ignorant people who arrived with nothing but their hands. What encouraged them to migrate? The fact that they had heard at distances of five or six thousand miles that there were better jobs and better conditions in the United States than where they were. So it's absurd to say that because people in Gary, Indiana are in the low-income bracket, they can't migrate elsewhere. Look at the enormous migration to the West Coast. Look at the Okie migration. If you count the number of people in the low-income class who every year move back and forth, it is quite obvious that there is enormous mobility of labor.

MCLAUGHRY: How does your argument relate to another topic of current interest—safety?

FRIEDMAN: What's the "right" number of accidents for Consolidated Edison to have? Now that seems like a silly question. All accidents are bad. But let's suppose for a moment that Con Ed does have an accident. One of its trucks hits your car. You have a case against them and they will have to pay damages. Well, that's part of their operating expense, and it has to be recouped from their customers. Suppose it costs them less to avoid a certain number of accidents than it does to pay for damages in these accident suits. Well, that would reduce the price they have to charge their customers. Obviously it's in their interest—and their customers' as well—to avoid these accidents. On the other hand, suppose it costs Con Ed more to avoid additional accidents than it does to pay damages—and it well might. To avoid all accidents, they might have to do all their work at night, give instructions that their trucks should never go faster than 2 mph, and so on. You can see by this that Consolidated Edison must have the "right" number of accidents, that number where the cost of avoiding an additional accident would be more than the damages paid the victim.

Well now, what is the difference between this situation and the pollution case? There's only one: In the pollution case, it is often impossible to identify the individual victims and to require person-by-person compensation. In Consolidated Edison's case you can identify the victims easily. In the U.S. Steel case, you can identify the victims as a group, and all the costs fall back on U.S. Steel. Therefore, in a single-company town like Gary, U.S. Steel has a private interest in maintaining the right level of pollution, because an extra $100 spent to reduce pollution would add less than $100 to the welfare of all of the people in the city of Gary. Under the circumstances where you cannot identify the victim, however, it is highly desirable to take measures to see that costs are imposed on the consumer. There is only one person who can pay the costs, and that's the consumer. If the people whose shirts are dirtied by Consolidated Edison could bring suit, Con Ed would have to pay the cost of cleaning their shirts—which is to say, Con Ed's customers would. If it were cheaper to stop polluting than it was to pay those costs, Con Ed would do so.

In those cases where you can determine what costs are being imposed on people other than the customer, the least bad solution seems to me to be a tax. Let's consider an industrial enterprise which pollutes a river. If you can calculate roughly that by putting in the effluent, an industry is causing a certain amount of harm to people downstream, then the answer would seem to be to tax it, roughly equal to the amount of harm it has imposed. This provides the right incentive. If it's cheaper for the corporation to put the effluent in the water and pay the tax than it is not to pollute or to clean up the river, then that is what should be done.

*Robert Almeder*

# Morality in the Marketplace

## I. INTRODUCTION

In order to create a climate more favorable for corporate activity, International Telephone and Telegraph allegedly contributed large sums of money to "destabilize" the duly elected government of Chile. Even though advised by the scientific community that the practice is lethal, major chemical companies reportedly continue to dump large amounts of carcinogens into the water supply of various areas and, at the same time, lobby to prevent legislation against such practices. General Motors Corporation, other automobile manufacturers, and Firestone Tire and Rubber Corporation have frequently defended themselves against the charge that they knowingly and willingly marketed a product that, owing to defective design, had been reliably predicted to kill a certain percentage of its users and, moreover, refused to recall promptly the product even when government agencies documented the large incidence of death as a result of the defective product. Finally, people often say that numerous advertising companies happily accept, and earnestly solicit, accounts to advertise cigarettes knowing full well that as a direct result of their advertising activities a certain number of people will die considerably prematurely and painfully. We need not concern ourselves with whether these and other similar charges are true because our concern here is with what might count as a justification for such corporate conduct were it to occur. There can be no question that such behavior is frequently legal. The question is whether corporate behavior should be constrained by nonlegal or moral considerations. As things presently stand, it seems to be a dogma of contemporary capitalism that the sole responsibility of business is to make as much money as is

From "The Ethics of Profit: Reflections on Corporate Responsibility," *Business and Society* (winter 1980): 7–15. This is a revision of the essay that appeared in the first edition of this volume. Reprinted by permission.

legally possible. But the question is whether this view is rationally defensible.

Sometimes, although not very frequently, corporate executives will admit to the sort of behavior depicted above and then proceed proximately to justify such behavior in the name of their responsibility to the shareholders or owners to make as much profit as is legally possible. Thereafter, less proximately and more generally, they will proceed to urge the more general utilitarian point that the increase in profit engendered by such corporate behavior begets such an unquestionable overall good for society that the behavior in question is morally acceptable if not quite praiseworthy. More specifically, the justification in question can, and usually does, take two forms.

The first and most common form of justification consists in urging that, as long as one's corporate behavior is not illegal, the behavior will be morally acceptable because the sole purpose of being in business is to make a profit; and the rules of the marketplace are somewhat different from those in other places and must be followed if one is to make a profit. Moreover, proponents of this view hasten to add that, as Adam Smith has claimed, the greatest good for society is achieved not by corporations seeking to act morally, or with a sense of social responsibility in their pursuit of profit, but rather by each corporation seeking to maximize its own profit, unregulated in that endeavor except by the laws of supply and demand along with whatever other laws are inherent to the competition process. This, they say, is what has made capitalist societies the envy of the world while ideological socialisms sooner or later fail miserably to meet deep human needs. Smith's view, that there is an invisible hand, as it were, directing an economy governed solely by the profit motive to the greatest good for society,[1] is still the dominant motivation and justification for those who would want an economy unregulated by any moral concern that would, or could, tend to decrease profits for some *alleged* social or moral good.

Milton Friedman, for example, has frequently asserted that the sole moral responsibility of business is to make as much profit as is legally possible; and by that he means that attempts to regulate or restrain the pursuit of profit in accordance with what some people believe to be socially desirable ends are in fact *subversive* of the common good since the greatest good for the greatest number is achieved by an economy maximally competitive and unregulated by moral rules in its pursuit of profit.[2] So, on Friedman's view, the greatest good for society is achieved by corporations acting legally, but with no further regard for what may be morally desirable; and this view begets the paradox that, *in business*, the greatest good for society can be achieved only by acting without regard for morality. Moreover, adoption of this position constitutes a fairly conscious commitment to the view that while one's personal life may well need governance by moral considerations, when pursuing profit, it is necessary that one's corporate behavior be unregulated by any moral concern other than that of making as much money as is legally possible; curiously enough, it is only in this way that society achieves the greatest good. So viewed, it is not difficult to see how a corporate executive could consistently adopt rigorous standards of morality in his or her personal life and yet feel quite comfortable in abandoning those standards in the pursuit of profit. Albert Carr, for example, likens the conduct of business to that of playing poker.[3] As Carr would have it, moral busybodies who insist on corporations acting morally might do just as well to censure a good bluffer in poker for being deceitful. Society, of course, lacking a perspective such as Friedman's and Carr's, is only too willing to view such behavior as hypocritical and fostered by avarice.

The second way of justifying, or defending, corporate practices that may appear morally questionable consists in urging that even if corporations were to take seriously the idea of limiting profits because of a desire to be moral or more responsible to social needs, then corporations would be involved in the unwholesome business of selecting and implementing moral values that may not be shared by a large number of people. Besides, there is the overwhelming question of whether there can be any nonquestionable moral values or noncontroversial list of social priorities for corporations to adopt. After all, if ethical relativism is true, or if ethical nihilism is true (and philosophers can be counted upon to argue for both positions), then it would be fairly silly of corporations to limit profits for what may be a quite dubious reason, namely, for being moral, when there are no clear grounds for doing it, and when it is not too clear what would count for doing it. In short, business corporations could argue (as Friedman has done)[4] that corporate actions in behalf of society's interests would require of corporations an ability to clearly determine and rank in noncontroversial ways the major needs of society; and it would not appear that this could be done successfully.

Perhaps another, and somewhat easier, way of formulating this second argument consists in urging that because philosophers generally fail to agree on what are the proper moral rules (if any), as well as on whether we should be moral, it would be imprudent to sacrifice a clear profit for a dubious or controversial moral gain. To authorize such a sacrifice would be to abandon a clear responsibility for one that is unclear or questionable.

If there are any other basic ways of justifying the sort of corporate behavior noted at the outset, I cannot imagine what they might be. So, let us examine these two modes of justification. In doing this, I hope to show that neither argument is sound and, moreover, that corporate behavior of the sort in question is clearly immoral if anything is immoral—and if nothing is immoral, then such corporate behavior is clearly contrary to the long-term interest of a corporation. In the end, we will reflect on ways to prevent such behavior, and on what is philosophically implied by corporate willingness to act in clearly immoral ways.

## II. THE "INVISIBLE HAND"

Essentially, the first argument is that the greatest good for the greatest number will be, and can only be, achieved by corporations acting legally but unregulated by any moral concern in the pursuit of profit. As we saw earlier, the evidence for this argument rests on a fairly classical and unquestioning acceptance of Adam Smith's view that society achieves a greater good when each person is allowed to pursue her or his own self-interested ends than when each person's pursuit of self-interested ends is regulated in some way or another by moral rules or concern. But I know of no evidence Smith ever offered for this latter claim, although it seems clear that those who adopt it generally do so out of respect for the perceived good that has emerged for various modern societies as a direct result of the free enterprise system and its ability to raise the overall standard of living of all those under it.

However, there is nothing inevitable about the greatest good occurring in an unregulated economy. Indeed, we have good inductive evidence from the age of the Robber Barons that unless the profit motive is regulated in various ways (by statute or otherwise) untold social evil can (and some say *will*) occur because of the natural tendency of the system to place ever-increasing sums of money in ever-decreasing numbers of hands. If all this is so, then so much the worse for all philosophical attempts to justify what would appear to be morally questionable corporate behavior on the grounds that corporate behavior, unregulated by moral concern, is necessarily or even probably productive of the greatest good for the greatest number. Moreover, a rule utilitarian would not be very hard pressed to show the many unsavory implications to society as a whole if society were to take seriously a rule to the effect that, provided only that one acts legally, it is morally permissible to do whatever one wants to do to achieve a profit.

The second argument cited above asserts that even if we were to grant, for the sake of argument, that corporations have social responsibilities beyond that of making as much money as is legally possible for the shareholders, there would be no noncontroversial way for corporations to discover just what these responsibilities are in the order of their importance. Owing to the fact that even distinguished moral philosophers predictably disagree on what one's moral responsibilities are, if any, it would seem irresponsible to limit profits to satisfy dubious moral responsibilities.

For one thing, this argument unduly exaggerates our potential for moral disagreement. Admittedly, there might well be important disagreements among corporations (just as there could be among philosophers) as to a priority ranking of major social needs; but that does not mean that most of us could not, or would not, agree that certain things ought not be done in the name of profit even when there is no law prohibiting such acts. There will always be a few who would do anything for a profit; but that is hardly a good argument in favor of their having the moral right to do so rather than a good argument that they refuse to be moral. In sum, it is hard to see how this second argument favoring corporate moral nihilism is any better than the general argument for ethical nihilism based on the variability of ethical judgments or practices; and apart from the fact that it tacitly presupposes that morality is a matter of what we all in fact would, or should, accept, the argument is maximally counterintuitive (as I shall show) by way of suggesting that we cannot generally agree that corporations have certain clear social responsibilities to avoid certain practices. Accordingly, I would now like to argue that if anything is immoral, a certain kind of corporate behavior is quite immoral although it may not be illegal.

## III. MURDER FOR PROFIT

Without caring to enter into the reasons for the belief, I assume we all believe that it is wrong to kill an innocent human being for no other reason than that doing so would be more financially rewarding for the killer than if he were to earn his livelihood in some other way. Nor, I assume, should our moral feelings on this matter change depending on the amount of money involved. Killing an innocent baby for fifteen million dollars would not seem to be any less objectionable than killing it for twenty cents. It is possible, however, that some self-professing utilitarian might be tempted to argue that the killing of an innocent baby for fifteen million dollars would not be objectionable if the money were to be given to the poor; under these circumstances, greater good would be achieved by the killing of the innocent baby. But, I submit, if anybody were to argue in this fashion, his argument would be quite deficient because he has not established what he needs to establish to make his argument sound. What he needs is a clear, convincing argument that raising the standard of living of an indefinite number of poor persons by the killing of an innocent person is a greater good for all those affected by the act than if the standard of living were not raised by the killing of an innocent person. This is needed because part of what we mean by having a basic right to life is that a person's life cannot be taken from him or her without a good reason. If our utilitarian cannot provide a convincing justification for his claim that a greater good is served by killing an innocent person in order to raise the standard of living for a large number of poor people, then it is hard to see how he can have the good reason he needs to deprive an innocent person of his or her life. Now, it seems clear that there will be anything but unanimity in the moral community on the question of whether there is a greater good achieved in raising the standard of living by killing an innocent baby than in leaving the standard of living alone and not killing an innocent baby. Moreover, even if everybody were to agree that the greater good is achieved by the killing of the innocent baby, how could that be shown to be true? How does one compare the moral value of a human life with the moral value of raising the standard of living by the taking of that life? Indeed, the more one thinks about it, the more difficult it is to see just what would count as objective evidence for the claim that the greater good is achieved by the killing of the innocent baby. Accordingly, I can see nothing that would justify the utilitarian who might be tempted to argue that if the sum is large enough, and if the sum were to be used for raising the standard of living for an indefinite number of poor people, then it would be morally acceptable to kill an innocent person for money.

These reflections should not be taken to imply, however, that no utilitarian argument could justify the killing of an innocent person for money.

After all, if the sum were large enough to save the lives of a large number of people who would surely die if the innocent baby were not killed, then I think one would as a rule be justified in killing the innocent baby for the sum in question. But this situation is obviously quite different from the situation in which one would attempt to justify the killing of an innocent person in order to raise the standard of living for an indefinite number of poor people. It makes sense to kill one innocent person in order to save, say, twenty innocent persons; but it makes no sense at all to kill one innocent person to raise the standard of living of an indefinite number of people. In the latter case, but not in the former, a comparison is made between things that are incomparable.

Given these considerations, it is remarkable and somewhat perplexing that certain corporations should seek to defend practices that are in fact instances of killing innocent persons for profit. Take, for example, the corporate practice of dumping known carcinogens into rivers. On Milton Friedman's view, we should not regulate or prevent such companies from dumping their effluents into the environment. Rather we should, if we like, tax the company after the effluents are in the water and then have the tax money used to clean up the environment.[5] For Friedman, and others, the fact that so many people will die as a result of this practice seems to be just part of the cost of doing business and making a profit. If there is any moral difference between such corporate practices and murdering innocent human beings for money, it is hard to see what it is. It is even more difficult to see how anyone could justify the practice and see it as no more than a business practice not to be regulated by moral concern. And there are a host of other corporate activities that are morally equivalent to deliberate killing of innocent persons for money. Such practices number among them contributing funds to "destabilize" a foreign government, advertising cigarettes, knowingly to market children's clothing having a known cancer causing agent, and refusing to recall (for fear of financial loss) goods known to be sufficiently defective to directly maim or kill a certain percentage of their unsuspecting users because of the defect. On this latter item, we are all familiar, for example, with convincingly documented charges that certain prominent automobile and tire manufacturers will knowingly market equipment sufficiently defective to increase the likelihood of death as a direct result of the defect and yet refuse to recall the product because the cost of recalling and repairing would have a greater adverse impact on profit than if the product were not recalled and the company paid the projected number of predictably successful suits. Of course, if the projected cost of the predictably successful suits were to outweigh the cost of recall and repair, then the product would be recalled and repaired, but not otherwise. In cases of this sort, the companies involved may admit to having certain marketing problems or a design problem, and they may even admit to having made a mistake; but, interestingly enough, they do not view themselves as immoral or as murderers for keeping their product in the market place when they know people are dying from it, people who would not die if the defect were corrected.

The important point is not whether in fact these practices have occurred in the past, or occur even now; there can be no doubt that such practices have occurred and do occur. Rather the point is that when companies act in such ways as a matter of policy, they must either not know what they do is murder (i.e., unjustifiable killing of an innocent person), or knowing that it is murder, seek to justify it in terms of profit. And I have been arguing that it is difficult to see how any corporate manager could fail to see that these policies amount to murder for money, although there may be no civil statute against such corporate behavior. If so, then where such policies exist, we can only assume that they are designed and implemented by corporate managers who either see nothing wrong with murder for money (which is implausible) or recognize that what they do is wrong but simply refuse to act morally because it is more financially rewarding to act immorally.

Of course, it is possible that corporate executives would not recognize such acts as murder. They may, after all, view murder as a legal concept involving one noncorporate person or persons deliberately killing another noncorporate person or persons and prosecutable only under existing civil statute. If so, it is somewhat understandable how corporate executives might fail, at least psychologically, to see such corporate policies as murder rather than as, say, calculated risks, tradeoffs, or design errors. Still, for all that, the logic of the situation seems clear enough.

## IV.  CONCLUSION

In addition to the fact that the only two plausible arguments favoring the Friedman doctrine are unsatisfactory, a strong case can be made for the claim that corporations *do* have a clear and noncontroversial moral responsibility not to design or implement, for reasons of profit, policies that they know, or have good reason to believe, will kill or otherwise seriously injure innocent persons affected by those policies. Moreover, we have said nothing about wage discrimination, sexism, discrimination in hiring, price fixing, price gouging, questionable but not unlawful competition, or other similar practices that some will think businesses should avoid by virtue of responsibility to society. My main concern has been to show that since we all agree that murder for money is generally wrong, and since there is no discernible difference between that and certain corporate policies that are not in fact illegal, then these corporate practices are clearly immoral (that is, they ought not to be done) and incapable of being morally justified by appeal to the Friedman doctrine since that doctrine does not admit of adequate evidential support. In itself, it is sad that this argument needs to be made and, if it were not for what appears to be a fairly strong commitment within the business community to the Friedman doctrine in the name of the unquestionable success of the free enterprise system, the argument would not need to be stated.

The fact that such practices do exist—designed and implemented by corporate managers who, for all intents and purposes, appear to be upright members of the moral community—only heightens the need for effective social prevention. Presumably, of course, any company willing to put human lives into the profit and loss column is not likely to respond to moral censure. Accordingly, I submit that perhaps the most effective way to deal with the problem of preventing such corporate behavior would consist in structuring legislation such that senior corporate managers who knowingly concur in practices of the sort listed above can effectively be tried, at their own expense, for murder, rather than censured and fined a sum to be paid out of corporate profits. This may seem a somewhat extreme or unrealistic proposal. However, it seems more unrealistic to think that aggressively competitive corporations will respond to what is morally necessary if failure to do so could be very or even minimally profitable. In short, unless we take strong and appropriate steps to prevent such practices, society will be reinforcing a destructive mode of behavior that is maximally disrespectful of human life, just as society will be reinforcing a value system that so emphasizes monetary gain as a standard of human success that murder for profit could be a corporate policy if the penalty for being caught at it were not too dear.

Fortunately, a number of states in America have enacted legislation that makes corporations subject to the criminal code of that state. This practice began to emerge quite strongly after the famous Pinto case in which an Indiana superior court judge refused to dismiss a homicide indictment against the Ford Motor Company. The company was indicted on charges of reckless homicide stemming from a 1978 accident involving a 1973 Pinto in which three girls died when the car burst into flames after being slammed in the rear. This was the first case in which Ford, or any other automobile manufacturer, had been charged with a criminal offense. The indictment went forward because the state of Indiana adopted in 1977 a criminal code provision permitting corporations to be charged with criminal acts. At the time, incidentally, twenty-two other states had similar codes. At any rate, the judge, in refusing to set aside the indictment, agreed with the prosecutor's argument that the charge was based not on the Pinto design fault, but rather on the fact that Ford had permitted the car "to remain on Indiana highways knowing full well its defects." The fact that the Ford Motor company was ultimately found innocent of the charges by the jury is incidental to the point that the increasing number of states that allow corporations to fall under the criminal code is an example of social regulation that could have been avoided had corporations and corporate managers not followed so ardently the Friedman doctrine.

In the long run, of course, corporate and individual willingness to do what is clearly immoral for the sake of monetary gain is a patent commitment to a certain view about the nature of human happiness and success, a view that needs to be placed in the balance with Aristotle's reasoned argument and reflections to the effect that money and all that it brings is a means to an end, and not the sort of end in itself that will justify acting immorally to attain it. What that beautiful end is and why being moral allows us to achieve it, may well be the most rewarding and profitable subject a human being can think about. Properly understood and placed in perspective, Aristotle's view on the nature and attainment of human happiness could go a long way toward alleviating the temptation to kill for money.

In the meantime, any ardent supporter of the capitalistic system will want to see the system thrive and flourish; and this it cannot do if it invites and demands government regulation in the name of the public interest. A *strong* ideological commitment to what I have described above as the Friedman doctrine is counterproductive and not in anyone's long-range interest because it is most likely to beget an ever-increasing regulatory climate. The only way to avoid such encroaching regulation is to find ways to move the business community into the long-term view of what is in its interest, and effect ways of both determining and responding to social needs before society moves to regulate business to that end. To so move the business community is to ask business to regulate its own modes of competition in ways that may seem very difficult to achieve. Indeed, if what I have been suggesting is correct, the only kind of enduring capitalism is humane capitalism, one that is at least as socially responsible as society needs. By the same token, contrary to what is sometimes felt in the business community, the Friedman doctrine, ardently adopted for the dubious reasons generally given, will most likely undermine capitalism and motivate an economic socialism by assuring an erosive regulatory climate in a society that expects the business community to be socially responsible in ways that go beyond just making legal profits.

In sum, being socially responsible in ways that go beyond legal profit-making is by no means a dubious luxury for the capitalist in today's world. It is a necessity if capitalism is to survive at all; and, presumably, we shall all profit with the survival of a vibrant capitalism. If anything, then, rigid adherence to the Friedman doctrine is not only philosophically unjustified, and unjustifiable, it is also unprofitable in the long run, and therefore, downright subversive of the long-term common good. Unfortunately, taking the long-run view is difficult for everyone. After all, for each of us, tomorrow may not come. But living for today only does not seem to make much sense either, if that deprives us of any reasonable and happy tomorrow. Living for the future may not be the healthiest thing to do; but do it we must, if we have good reason to think that we will have a future. The trick is to provide for the future without living in it, and that just requires being moral.

## NOTES

1. Adam Smith, *The Wealth of Nations*, ed. Edwin Canaan (New York: Modern Library, 1937), p. 423.

2. See Milton Friedman, "The Social Responsibility of Business Is to Increase Its Profits," *New York Times Magazine*, 13 September, 1970, pp. 33, 122–26 and "Milton Friedman Responds," *Business and Society Review* no. 1 (spring 1972): 5ff.

3. Albert Z. Carr, "Is Business Bluffing Ethical?" *Harvard Business Review* (January-February 1968).

4. Milton Friedman, "Milton Friedman Responds," *Business and Society Review* no. 1 (spring 1972): 10.

5. Ibid.

# STAKEHOLDER THEORY

# EC Technology

With year 2000 sales of $184 million, EC Technology is the second largest manufacturer of suspension assemblies for magnetic hard-disk drives (HDD). It is essentially a one product company in a very fast moving industry. Harnish Inc., the industry leader, controls 55 percent of the market, while EC has about 20 percent. No other manufacturer has more than 10 percent. Formed in 1988, EC has grown in sales rapidly, from $5 million in 1988 to $16 million in 1990 to $46 million in 1995 to $184 million in 2000. However, earnings have been erratic: 1995 (+ $.80 per share), 1996 (–.46), 1997 (–.66), 1998 (+ 2.04), 1999 (+ .94), and 2000 (–1.09).

One major reason for EC's fluctuating earnings is that its larger competitor, Harnish, has a bigger R&D budget and consistently introduces the next generation product. Following a product innovation by Harnish, EC's market share drops until it can match Harnish's product, undercut its prices, and regain market share. Harnish has recently introduced a suspension assembly that integrates electrical conductors directly into the suspension unit, which represents a major advance over older suspension units, which have separate electrical wire connections to an HDD's electronic circuitry. Harnish's patented innovation has resulted in a dramatic increase in both suspension performance and reliability. EC's engineers can work around Harnish's patent, but it will take about one year. Furthermore, the new Harnish design will lead to a reduction in the number of suspensions needed in each HDD unit. So overall suspension demand will likely be flat for some time.

EC stock, which historically is very volatile, has recently plunged from $48 to $11, and Ed Ballard, EC's CEO and President, is aware that large institutions, which control 62 percent of EC's stock, are restless. Ballard ordered a workforce reduction from 2,000 to 1,450. He also cut several minor executive perks and reduced manufacturing costs as much as possible. However, Ballard had always run a tight ship at EC, and there wasn't much fat in the firm to trim. In fact, the recent breakthrough by Harnish convinced Ballard he needed to up EC's R&D budget from 4 percent of sales to 6 percent. Harnish spends about 4 percent on research, and Ballard figured that EC could remain competitive in the long run only by increasing R&D expenditures relative to Harnish. When EC's CFO Leon Berman ran all the projections, he told Ballard that EC's earnings would not begin to recover for at least a year and a half. He said that 2001 would probably come in at –$1.50/share. The year 2002 also looked like an overall loss, with some recovery in the second half. With no big surprises, 2003 would see positive earnings.

In spite of these problems, Ballard and Berman had devised a contingency plan they now had to consider carefully. In 1998 Ballard had dispatched Berman to Malaysia to analyze the option of moving EC's production facility to that country. At that time Malaysia, and all of Southeast Asia, was in a very serious economic downturn. Unlike most of its neighbors, Malaysia resisted suggestions by the World Bank and the International Monetary Fund to restructure large sections of its economy. Instead, the government tried to work out of the downturn by restricting capital flows, including a ban on foreigners' selling of their Malaysian stockholdings, and by cutting the costs of government. One result was that foreign capital investment dried up almost completely. Nevertheless, Berman was well received in Malaysia. He travelled to the capital, Kuala Lumpur, four times and had several informative meetings with the country's trade ministers and with businessmen who showed him several facilities for sale at rock-bottom prices due to the numerous bankruptcies the country had experienced. Ballard stopped by Berman's office on March 16, 2001. He respected Berman immensely, viewing him as an accurate bean counter who could also see the big picture and keep a secret. He asked Berman to review the situation once again, saying that he needed to have a plan by EC's annual meeting in August.

Berman said that EC was not large enough and competitive enough to afford two manufacturing plants, but could afford to move its manufacturing operation to Malaysia from Eau Claire, Wisconsin, and keep its present home office in Eau Claire. This would involve closing the Eau Claire manufacturing facility and moving 1,250 jobs overseas. About 200 administrative, marketing, and technical personnel would remain in Eau Claire. According to Berman, this would necessitate a significant write-off in 2001 and/or 2002 for plant closings and relocation costs. Although EC would have the expense of purchasing a new facility in Malaysia, Berman thought it was a good time to buy cheap Malaysian assets. He added that it was unlikely that EC could quickly sell the Eau Claire plant—that might take two to four years, but he thought that most of the Eau Claire plant's production lines could be moved to Malaysia. Berman said he thought the benefits of a move to EC's bottom line might begin in late 2004. It would probably be 2002 before a building could be purchased; he had been advised there would be some bureaucratic delays. The year 2003 would be needed to move, install machinery, and train workers. And this would all be complicated by the fact that 2002–2003 would involve a transition to a new product, which meant changes in the production line. However, overall employee benefits would be about one-sixth of those in Eau Claire, there would be no union to contend with, and by late 2004 earnings should begin to move to the plus side. The year 2005 should be in the black. Berman believed the wage differential would eventually add $1.25 to EC's bottom line each year. With solid sales advances the increase could be greater. He noted that the $1.25 could have more than covered EC's annual losses in 1996, 1997, and 2000.

Berman said that at present 65 percent of total suspension assembly sales were to U.S. HDD manufacturers, 25 percent to Asia, and 10 percent to Europe. However, he said that by 2010 the Asian market was projected to have 45 percent of the total, with the U.S. at 40 percent and Europe at 15 percent. At present EC had only 10 percent of the Asian market, but with a plant in Malaysia Berman thought EC could garner 30 percent of the Asian market by 2010. So the move would mean that EC would probably grow more rapidly than Harnish in the most rapidly growing area of the market. However, Berman cautioned that Harnish was technologically and financially stronger than EC, and might well follow EC to Asia. He also conceded that with EC's sole plant in Asia, Harnish would probably increase its share of the U.S. market. In addition, he said that Harnish could easily afford plants on two continents, and such a strategy would leave Harnish with an overall edge, even though it would be saddled with the higher cost of a U.S. plant.

Ballard inquired how stockholders were likely to react. Berman said that, although you couldn't predict the behavior of Wall Street, he thought the stock would not move lower in the short-term whatever the news. He thought that on any further bad news the stock would be kept near $10 by speculators betting on a takeover of EC. He believed a Malaysia announcement might move the stock from $11 to $15 in the short-term, as investors thought EC was taking action to correct its problems. Still, Berman said that with his 4 percent of stock, Ballard's 10 percent and other corporate insiders holding 8 percent, only about 22 percent of stock could be counted on in a takeover battle. The 62 percent in institutional portfolios and remaining 16 percent in the hands of individual traders was essentially short-term oriented. Berman had analyzed the turnover in EC stock and found an enormous turnover rate except for the insiders who held on to their shares. Berman thought there was about a 20 percent probability that a much larger electronics firm would make a buyout offer on any Malaysian announcement, reasoning that a purchaser might think that EC's stretching of profitability out to 2005 would exhaust the patience of the remaining EC holders who were in EC for the intermediate to long-term. He thought an offer might be around $22 per share. Overall, Berman thought the chances of a buyout offer in the short-term were greater on the Malaysian option than the option of staying in Eau Claire. Ballard agreed, but said they had a responsibility to generate long-term profit for shareholders. He said he couldn't worry about Wall Street speculators, but had to try to generate long-term value. Ballard added that the market priced all stocks rationally and that if there was long-term value in EC stock enough smart investors would support the stock to keep it from a takeover attempt.

Ballard had become EC's President in 1991 and CEO in 1994, and had hired Berman in 1994. They worked well together, socialized frequently, and both wanted to stay with EC in Eau Claire. Berman thought there was a very high probability that new top management would be brought in if EC were bought out. Ballard had two daughters in high school, both of whom loved Eau Claire, and Ballard and his wife had both grown up there. He was also concerned that the Malaysian move would mean many trips to Kuala Lumpur. Berman thought that in the first few years they would each have to spend a total of one-third of the year there, with each making four to five trips per year. Ballard dreaded that thought. Since his children were grown and his wife collected Asian artifacts, Berman was unconcerned about the travel. His only concern was that there seemed to be no Jewish community in Kuala Lumpur, which disappointed him.

Ballard was concerned about the Eau Claire employees. True, EC located in Eau Claire in large part because the area had both a skilled workforce and a low-wage structure. Of 315 metropolitan areas measured by the U.S. Bureau of Labor Statistics, Eau Claire ranked 270th in average wages. Nevertheless, EC paid the highest wages in the Eau Claire area and, although most of the 1,250 employees who would be terminated could probably find some work in the area, the vast majority would take a significant wage reduction. Ballard had already taken heat from his recent termination of 550 employees. Several had denounced him when the reduction was announced, his BMW had been keyed in the employee parking lot, several students acted rudely toward his daughters, and at a recent Lions Club meeting another member had spoken out openly against him. Still, Ballard was concerned for his employees, and worried about the effects of a plant closing on them. Berman said there was a tradeoff, since the Malaysian hires would benefit as much as the Eau Claire employees lost. Ballard agreed theoretically, but said he had lived in Eau Claire all his life. He noted that if he fired 1,800 people in a city of 55,000 he would run into some of them almost every day. He pointed out that he, not Berman, would be blamed.

Ballard inquired about the union situation. Berman said that Malaysia was a top-down, authoritarian society. There would be no union in Malaysia. Moreover, Malaysians had an excellent work ethic, and did not expect much in the way of health or retirement benefits. Overall employee expenditures, he reiterated, would be one-sixth of those in Eau Claire. Ballard said he had found the EC union to be very responsible; he said he didn't mind at all having someone stand up for workers' rights. Furthermore, the Eau Claire workforce was well educated and highly skilled; EC's employees routinely made significant productivity improvements. Berman allowed that the Malaysians were neither well educated nor technically skilled, and that they were used to taking orders, and hence would probably not offer the originality the U.S. workers brought to the plant each day. Still, he said that most of the EC assembly jobs were routine and that the Malaysians might prove to be more productive than their individualistic U.S. counterparts.

Ballard had some concerns about the impact of a move on the greater Eau Claire community. Having grown up there, he viewed himself as indebted to it. And EC was a socially responsible company. It donated 2 percent of pretax profits to local charities, and its employees were heavy contributors to the United Way. Ballard had a special interest in the Boy Scouts and many EC employees worked with that organization because of his influence. He also supported a local battered women's shelter, but since almost all the women employed at EC worked in assembly and would be terminated by a move to Malaysia, Ballard questioned how he could maintain a leadership role with a women's organization. In fact, Ballard wondered whether he could legitimately ask people in the community to follow him in any endeavor. Ballard had many good friends working at EC, some of whom he had known most of his life. Several had worked at the Uniroyal Goodrich Tire Co. plant in Eau Claire, which closed in 1992, leaving several thousand unemployed. Ballard had hired every friend he could from Uniroyal in 1992, knowing they were good workers and that he could count on them. He knew that friendship, true friendship, took time to build.

Having come from New York in 1994, Berman said he had no close ties to Eau Claire, yet he felt an overall obligation to his country. Berman's parents had been able to get out of Germany in 1941 and they had instilled in him a hard loyalty to the United States. The federal government had provided technical and financial assistance to EC in its start-up stage. In fact, some of the low interest loans had just been paid off; they were like free money, said Berman, who wondered how far EC would have gotten without them. Furthermore, he reminded Ballard that a government consortium had helped EC get an important contract in 1995, a contract with IBM, which subsequently became EC's largest customer. Ballard said he knew all that, but added that when you get to the level of government instead of people, from a certain perspective the whole thing becomes totally impersonal. When you are dealing with governments, he said, you look ahead, not behind. What concerned him, looking ahead, was the stability of Malaysia's government. Berman agreed this was a problem. Since independence in 1957, the country had been run by the party of the current leader, Mahathir bin Mohamad, a charismatic, but authoritarian figure, who controlled the country tightly. When critics of his regime mounted a strong political challenge during the recent economic turndown, Mahathir crushed the opposition, and many of his top opponents were sent to jail on what some thought were trumped up charges.

As for the business climate in Malaysia, many observers called the system "croney capitalism": those who funded the ruling party were recipients of government contracts, those who did not contribute were shut out. It had been this way since independence, when Mahathir's party took over and systematically began to favor Islamic business interests and not those of the Chinese who had controlled business in Malaysia for generations. Ballard said he could understand this attitude and did not think it would impact EC as long as croneyism was confined to core industries such as finance, utilities, infrastructure, and defense. As long as research was done in the United States and manufacturing in Malaysia, Ballard thought there would be no big problem there for EC. Berman said he tended to agree, although Malaysia was in no way as politically stable as Wisconsin. He said that, with the relatively high Islamic population there, you could not rule out the possibility of an Islamic revolution, with confiscation of the plant being a real possibility if that occurred. The more likely risk, Berman thought, was that Malaysia would fail to advance in education, and that EC might increasingly find it difficult to secure skilled workers. He wondered whether workers in a tropical country could ever come close in productivity to those in a northern climate.

The more he listened to Leon Berman, the more Ed Ballard realized that this was going to be a very difficult decision. At fifty-six, he thought, maybe he just lacked the fire to make the choice or to follow through once he made it. But Berman said that wasn't it. He said that in the past the decisions were relatively easy, that they were such that everyone else as well as stockholders could benefit, and that win-win solutions to problems could be worked out. Now, he added, the decision was not only much more complex, but that some people would inevitably win while others lost. Such decisions, he said, were why the CEO made three times as much as the CFO.

## FOR DISCUSSION

What should Ed Ballard do? Why?

*R. Edward Freeman*

# A Stakeholder Theory
# of the Modern Corporation

## INTRODUCTION

> Corporations have ceased to be merely legal devices through which the
> private business transactions of individuals may be carried on. Though
> still much used for this purpose, the corporate form has acquired a larger
> significance. The corporation has, in fact, become both a method of prop-
> erty tenure and a means of organizing economic life. Grown to tremen-
> dous proportions, there may be said to have evolved a "corporate
> system"—which has attracted to itself a combination of attributes and
> powers, and has attained a degree of prominence entitling it to be dealt
> with as a major social institution.[1]

Despite these prophetic words of Berle and Means (1932), scholars and
managers alike continue to hold sacred the view that managers bear a special relationship to the stockholders in the firm. Since stockholders own
shares in the firm, they have certain rights and privileges, which must be
granted to them by management, as well as by others. Sanctions, in the
form of "the law of corporations," and other protective mechanisms in the
form of social custom, accepted management practice, myth, and ritual,
are thought to reinforce the assumption of the primacy of the stockholder.

The purpose of this paper is to pose several challenges to this assumption, from within the framework of managerial capitalism, and to suggest
the bare bones of an alternative theory, *a stakeholder theory of the
modern corporation*. I do not seek the demise of the modern corporation,
either intellectually or in fact. Rather, I seek its transformation. In the

From R. Edward Freeman, "A Stakeholder Theory of the Modern Corporation," in *Ethical
Theory and Business*, 5th ed., ed. Tom L. Beauchamp and Norman E. Bowie (Upper Saddle
River, N.J.: Prentice-Hall, 1997), pp. 66–76. Reprinted with permission.

words of Neurath, we shall attempt to "rebuild the ship, plank by plank, while it remains afloat."[2]

My thesis is that I can revitalize the concept of managerial capitalism by replacing the notion that managers have a duty to stockholders with the concept that managers bear a fiduciary relationship to stakeholders. Stakeholders are those groups who have a stake in or claim on the firm. Specifically I include suppliers, customers, employees, stockholders, and the local community, as well as management in its role as agent for these groups. I argue that the legal, economic, political, and moral challenges to the currently received theory of the firm, as a nexus of contracts among the owners of the factors of production and customers, require us to revise this concept. That is, each of these stakeholder groups has a right not to be treated as a means to some end, and therefore must participate in determining the future direction of the firm in which they have a stake.

The crux of my argument is that we must reconceptualize the firm around the following question: For whose benefit and at whose expense should the firm be managed? I shall set forth such a reconceptualization in the form of a *stakeholder theory of the firm*. I shall then critically examine the stakeholder view and its implications for the future of the capitalist system.

## THE ATTACK ON MANAGERIAL CAPITALISM

### *The Legal Argument*

The basic idea of managerial capitalism is that in return for controlling the firm, management vigorously pursues the interests of stockholders. Central to the managerial view of the firm is the idea that management can pursue market transactions with suppliers and customers in an unconstrained manner.

The law of corporations gives a less clearcut answer to the question: In whose interest and for whose benefit should the modern corporation be governed? While it says that the corporations should be run primarily in the interests of the stockholders in the firm, it says further that the corporation exists "in contemplation of the law" and has personality as a "legal person," limited liability for its actions, and immortality, since its existence transcends that of its members. Therefore, directors and other officers of the firm have a fiduciary obligation to stockholders in the sense that the "affairs of the corporation" must be conducted in the interest of the stockholders. And stockholders can theoretically bring suit against those directors and managers for doing otherwise. But since the corporation is a legal person, existing in contemplation of the law, managers of the corporation are constrained by law.

Until recently, this was no constraint at all. In this century, however, the law has evolved to effectively constrain the pursuit of stockholder interests at the expense of other claimants on the firm. It has, in effect, required that the claims of customers, suppliers, local communities, and employees be taken into consideration, though in general they are subordinated to the claims of stockholders.

For instance, the doctrine of "privity of contract," as articulated in *Winterbottom* v. *Wright* in 1842, has been eroded by recent developments in products liability law. Indeed, *Greenman* v. *Yuba Power* gives the manufacturer strict liability for damage caused by its products, even though the seller has exercised all possible care in the preparation and sale of the product and the consumer has not bought the product from nor entered into any contractual arrangement with the manufacturer. Caveat emptor has been replaced, in large part, with caveat venditor.[3] The Consumer Product Safety Commission has the power to enact product recalls, and in 1980 one U.S. automobile company recalled more cars than it built. Some industries are required to provide information to customers about a product's ingredients, whether or not the customers want and are willing to pay for this information.[4]

The same argument is applicable to management's dealings with employees. The National Labor Relations Act gave employees the right to unionize and to bargain in good faith. It set up the National Labor Relations Board to enforce these rights with management. The Equal Pay Act of 1963 and Title VII of the Civil Rights Act of 1964 constrain management from discrimination in hiring practices; these have been followed with the Age Discrimination in Employment Act of 1967.[5] The emergence of a body of administrative case law arising from labor-management disputes and the historic settling of discrimination claims with large employers such as AT&T have caused the emergence of a body of practice in the corporation that is consistent with the legal guarantee of the rights of the employees. The law has protected the due process rights of those employees who enter into collective bargaining agreements with management. As of the present, however, only 30 percent of the labor force are participating in such agreements; this has prompted one labor law scholar to propose a statutory law prohibiting dismissals of the 70 percent of the work force not protected.[6]

The law has also protected the interests of local communities. The Clean Air Act and Clean Water Act have constrained management from "spoiling the commons." In an historic case, *Marsh* v. *Alabama*, the Supreme Court ruled that a company-owned town was subject to the provisions of the U.S. Constitution, thereby guaranteeing the rights of local citizens and negating the "property rights" of the firm. Some states and municipalities have gone further and passed laws preventing firms from moving plants or limiting when and how plants can be closed. In sum, there is much current legal activity in this area to constrain management's pursuit of stockholders' interests at the expense of the local communities in which the firm operates.

I have argued that the result of such changes in the legal system can be viewed as giving some rights to those groups that have a claim on the firm, for example, customers, suppliers, employees, local communities, stockholders, and management. It raises the question, at the core of a theory of the firm: In whose interest and for whose benefit should the firm be managed? The answer proposed by managerial capitalism is clearly "the stockholders," but I have argued that the law has been progressively circumscribing this answer.

## *The Economic Argument*

In its pure ideological form managerial capitalism seeks to maximize the interests of stockholders. In its perennial criticism of government regulation, management espouses the "invisible hand" doctrine. It contends that it creates the greatest good for the greatest number, and therefore government need not intervene. However, we know that externalities, moral hazards, and monopoly power exist in fact, whether or not they exist in theory. Further, some of the legal apparatus mentioned above has evolved to deal with just these issues.

The problem of the "tragedy of the commons" or the free-rider problem pervades the concept of public goods such as water and air. No one has an incentive to incur the cost of clean-up or the cost of nonpollution, since the marginal gain of one firm's action is small. Every firm reasons this way, and the result is pollution of water and air. Since the industrial revolution, firms have sought to internalize the benefits and externalize the costs of their actions. The cost must be borne by all, through taxation and regulation; hence we have the emergence of the environmental regulations of the 1970s.

Similarly, moral hazards arise when the purchaser of a good or service can pass along the cost of that good. There is no incentive to economize, on the part of either the producer or the consumer, and there is excessive use of the resources involved. The institutionalized practice of third-party payment in health care is a prime example.

Finally, we see the avoidance of competitive behavior on the part of firms, each seeking to monopolize a small portion of the market and not compete with one another. In a number of industries, oligopolies have emerged, and while there is questionable evidence that oligopolies are not the most efficient corporate form in some industries, suffice it to say that the potential for abuse of market power has again led to regulation of managerial activity. In the classic case, AT&T, arguably one of the great technological and managerial achievements of the century, was broken up into eight separate companies to prevent its abuse of monopoly power.

Externalities, moral hazards, and monopoly power have led to more external control on managerial capitalism. There are de facto constraints, due to these economic facts of life, on the ability of management to act in the interests of stockholders.

## A STAKEHOLDER THEORY OF THE FIRM

### *The Stakeholder Concept*

Corporations have stakeholders, that is, groups and individuals who benefit from or are harmed by, and whose rights are violated or respected by, corporate actions. The concept of stakeholders is a generalization of the notion of stockholders, who themselves have some special claim on the firm. Just as stockholders have a right to demand certain actions by management, so do other stakeholders have a right to make claims. The exact nature of these claims is a difficult question that I shall address, but the logic is identical to that of the stockholder theory. Stakes require action of a certain sort, and conflicting stakes require methods of resolution.

Freeman and Reed (1983)[7] distinguish two senses of *stakeholder*. The "narrow definition" includes those groups who are vital to the survival and success of the corporation. The "wide-definition" includes any group or individual who can affect or is affected by the corporation. I shall begin with a modest aim: to articulate a stakeholder theory using the narrow definition.

## Stakeholders in the Modern Corporation

Figure 1 depicts the stakeholders in a typical large corporation. The stakes of each are reciprocal, since each can affect the other in terms of harms and benefits as well as rights and duties. The stakes of each are not univocal and would vary by particular corporation. I merely set forth some general notions that seem to be common to many large firms.

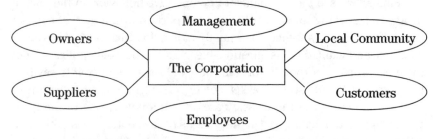

**Figure 1.  A Stakeholder Model of the Corporation**

Owners have a financial stake in the corporation in the form of stocks, bonds, and so on, and they expect some kind of financial return from them. Either they have given money directly to the firm, or they have some historical claim made through a series of morally justified exchanges. The firm affects their livelihood or, if a substantial portion of their retirement income is in stocks or bonds, their ability to care for themselves when they can no longer work. Of course, the stakes of owners will differ by type of owner, preferences for money, moral preferences, and so on, as well as by type of firm. The owners of AT&T are quite different from the owners of Ford Motor Company, with stock of the former company being widely dispersed among 3 million stockholders and that of the latter being held by a small family group as well as by a large group of public stockholders.

Employees have their jobs and usually their livelihood at stake; they often have specialized skills for which there is usually no perfectly elastic market. In return for their labor, they expect security, wages, benefits, and meaningful work. In return for their loyalty, the corporation is expected to provide for them and carry them through difficult times. Employees are expected to follow the instructions of management most of the time, to speak favorably about the company, and to be responsible citizens in the local communities in which the company operates. Where they are used as means to an end, they must participate in decisions affecting such use. The evidence that such policies and values as described here lead to productive company-employee relationships is compelling. It is equally compelling to realize that the opportunities for "bad faith" on the part of both management and employees are enormous. "Mock participation" in quality circles, singing the company song, and wearing the company uniform solely to please management all lead to distrust and unproductive work.

Suppliers, interpreted in a stakeholder sense, are vital to the success of the firm, for raw materials will determine the final product's quality and price. In turn the firm is a customer of the supplier and is therefore vital to the success and survival of the supplier. When the firm treats the supplier as a valued member of the stakeholder network, rather than simply as a source of materials, the supplier will respond when the firm is in need. Chrysler traditionally had very close ties to its suppliers, even to the extent that led some to suspect the transfer of illegal payments. And when Chrysler was on the brink of disaster, the suppliers responded with price cuts, accepting late payments, financing, and so on. Supplier and company can rise and fall together. Of course, again, the particular supplier relationships will depend on a number of variables such as the number of suppliers and whether the supplies are finished goods or raw materials.

Customers exchange resources for the products of the firm and in return receive the benefits of the products. Customers provide the lifeblood of the firm in the form of revenue. Given the level of reinvestment of earnings in large corporations, customers indirectly pay for the development of new products and services. Peters and Waterman (1982)[8] have argued that being close to the customer leads to success with other stakeholders and that a distinguishing characteristic of some companies that have performed well is their emphasis on the customer. By paying attention to customers' needs, management automatically addresses the needs of suppliers and owners. Moreover, it seems that the ethic of customer service carries over to the community. Almost without fail the "excellent companies" in Peters and Waterman's study have good reputations in the community. I would argue that Peters and Waterman have found multiple applications of Kant's dictum, "Treat persons as ends unto themselves," and it should come as no surprise that persons respond to such respectful treatment, be they customers, suppliers, owners, employees, or members of the local community. The real surprise is the novelty of the application of Kant's rule in a theory of good management practice.

The local community grants the firm the right to build facilities and, in turn, it benefits from the tax base and economic and social contributions of the firm. In return for the provision of local services, the firm is expected to be a good citizen, as is any person, either "natural or artificial." The firm cannot expose the community to unreasonable hazards in the form of pollution, toxic waste, and so on. If for some reason the firm must leave a community, it is expected to work with local leaders to make the transition as smoothly as possible. Of course, the firm does not have perfect knowledge, but when it discovers some danger or runs afoul of new competition, it is expected to inform the local community and to work with the community to overcome any problem. When the firm mismanages its relationship with the local community, it is in the same position as a citizen who commits a crime. It has violated the implicit social contract with the community and should expect to be distrusted and ostracized. It should not be surprised when punitive measures are invoked.

I have not included "competitors" as stakeholders in the narrow sense, since strictly speaking they are not necessary for the survival and success of the firm; the stakeholder theory works equally well in monopoly contexts. However, competitors and government would be the first to be included in an extension of this basic theory. It is simply not true that the interests of competitors in an industry are always in conflict. There is no reason why trade associations and other multiorganizational groups cannot band together to solve common problems that have little to do with how to restrain trade. Implementation of stakeholder management principles, in the long run, mitigates the need for industrial policy and an increasing role for government intervention and regulation.

## The Role of Management

Management plays a special role, for it too has a stake in the modern corporation. On the one hand, management's stake is like that of employees, with some kind of explicit or implicit employment contract. But, on the other hand, management has a duty of safeguarding the welfare of the abstract entity that is the corporation. In short, management, especially top management, must look after the health of the corporation, and this involves balancing the multiple claims of conflicting stakeholders. Owners want higher financial returns, while customers want more money spent on research and development. Employees want higher wages and better benefits, while the local community wants better parks and day-care facilities.

The task of management in today's corporation is akin to that of King Solomon. The stakeholder theory does not give primacy to one stakeholder group over another, though there will surely be times when one group will benefit at the expense of others. In general, however, management must keep the relationships among stakeholders in balance. When these relationships become imbalanced, the survival of the firm is in jeopardy.

When wages are too high and product quality is too low, customers leave, suppliers suffer, and owners sell their stocks and bonds, depressing the stock price and making it difficult to raise new capital at favorable rates. Note, however, that the reason for paying returns to owners is not that they "own" the firm, but that their support is necessary for the survival of the firm, and that they have a legitimate claim on the firm. Similar reasoning applies in turn to each stakeholder group.

A stakeholder theory of the firm must redefine the purpose of the firm. The stockholder theory claims that the purpose of the firm is to maximize the welfare of the stockholders, perhaps subject to some moral or social constraints, either because such maximization leads to the greatest good or because of property rights. The purpose of the firm is quite different in my view.

"The stakeholder theory" can be unpacked into a number of stakeholder theories, each of which has a "normative core," inextricably linked to the way that corporations should be governed and the way that managers should act. So, attempts to more fully define, or more carefully define, a stakeholder theory are misguided. Following Donaldson and Preston, I want to insist that the normative, descriptive, instrumental, and metaphorical (my addition to their framework) uses of 'stakeholder' are tied together in particular political constructions to yield a number of possible "stakeholder theories." "Stakeholder theory" is thus a genre of stories about how we could live. Let me be more specific.

A "normative core" of a theory is a set of sentences that includes among others, sentences like:

1. Corporations ought to be governed . . .
2. Managers ought to act to . . .

where we need arguments or further narratives which include business and moral terms to fill in the blanks. This normative core is not always reducible to a fundamental ground like the theory of property, but certain normative cores are consistent with modern understandings of property. Certain elaborations of the theory of private property plus the other institutions of political liberalism give rise to particular normative cores. But there are other institutions, other political conceptions of how society ought to be structured, so that there are different possible normative cores.

So, one normative core of a stakeholder theory might be a feminist standpoint one, rethinking how we would restructure "value-creating activity" along principles of caring and connection.[9] Another would be an ecological (or several ecological) normative cores. Mark Starik has argued that the very idea of a stakeholder theory of the *firm* ignores certain ecological necessities.[10] Exhibit 1 is suggestive of how these theories could be developed.

In the next section I shall sketch the normative core based on pragmatic liberalism. But, any normative core must address the questions in columns A or B, or explain why these questions may be irrelevant, as in the ecological view. In addition, each "theory," and I use the word hesitantly, must place the normative core within a more full-fledged account of how we could understand value-creating activity differently (column C). The only way to get on with this task is to see the stakeholder idea as a metaphor. The attempt to prescribe one and only one "normative core" and construct "a stakeholder theory" is at best a disguised attempt to smuggle a normative core past the unsophisticated noses of other unsuspecting academics who are just happy to see the end of the stockholder orthodoxy.

If we begin with the view that we can understand value-creation activity as a contractual process among those parties affected, and if for simplicity's sake we initially designate those parties as financiers, customers, suppliers, employees, and communities, then we can construct a normative core that reflects the liberal notions of autonomy, solidarity, and fairness as articulated by John Rawls, Richard Rorty, and others.[11] Notice that building these moral notions into the foundations of how we understand value creation and contracting requires that we eschew separating the "business" part of the process from the "ethical" part, and that we start with the presumption of equality among the contractors, rather than the presumption in favor of financier rights.

**EXHIBIT 1**: A Reasonable Pluralism

| | A. | B. | C. |
|---|---|---|---|
| | *Corporations ought to be governed . . .* | *Managers ought to act . . .* | *The background disciplines of "value creation" are . . .* |
| Doctrine of Fair Contracts | . . . in accordance with the six principles. | . . . in the interests of stakeholders. | —business theories —theories that explain stakeholder behavior |

| Feminist Standpoint Theory | . . . in accordance with the principles of caring/connection and relationships. | . . . to maintain and care for relationships and networks of stakeholders. | —business theories —feminist theory —social science understanding of networks |
| Ecological Principles | . . . in accordance with the principle of caring for the earth. | . . . to care for the earth. | —business theories —ecology —other |

The normative core for this redesigned contractual theory will capture the liberal idea of fairness if it ensures a basic equality among stakeholders in terms of their moral rights as these are realized in the firm, and if it recognizes that inequalities among stakeholders are justified if they raise the level of the least well-off stakeholder. The liberal ideal of autonomy is captured by the realization that each stakeholder must be free to enter agreements that create value for themselves, and solidarity is realized by the recognition of the mutuality of stakeholder interests.

One way to understand fairness in this context is to claim à la Rawls that a contract is fair if parties to the contract would agree to it in ignorance of their actual stakes. Thus, a contract is like a fair bet, if each party is willing to turn the tables and accept the other side. What would a fair contract among corporate stakeholders look like? If we can articulate this ideal, a sort of corporate constitution, we could then ask whether actual corporations measure up to this standard, and we also begin to design corporate structures which are consistent with this Doctrine of Fair Contracts.

Imagine if you will, representative stakeholders trying to decide on "the rules of the game." Each is rational in a straightforward sense, looking out for its own self-interest. At least *ex ante*, stakeholders are the relevant parties since they will be materially affected. Stakeholders know how economic activity is organized and could be organized. They know general facts about the way the corporate world works. They know that in the real world there are or could be transaction costs, externalities, and positive costs of contracting. Suppose they are uncertain about what other social institutions exist, but they know the range of those institutions. They do not know if government exists to pick up the tab for any externalities, or if they will exist in the nightwatchman state of libertarian theory. They know success and failure stories of businesses around the world. In short, they are behind a Rawls-like veil of ignorance, and they do not know what stake each will have when the veil is lifted. What ground rules would they choose to guide them?

The first ground rule is "The Principle of Entry and Exit." Any contract that is the corporation must have clearly defined entry, exit, and renegotiation conditions, or at least it must have methods or processes for so defining these conditions. The logic is straightforward: each stakeholder must be able to determine when an agreement exists and has a chance of fulfillment. This is not to imply that contracts cannot contain contingent claims or other methods for resolving uncertainty, but rather that it must contain methods for determining whether or not it is valid.

The second ground rule I shall call "The Principle of Governance," and it says that the procedure for changing the rules of the game must be agreed upon by unanimous consent. Think about the consequences of a majority of stakeholders systematically "selling out" a minority. Each stakeholder, in ignorance of its actual role, would seek to avoid such a situation. In reality this principle translates into each stakeholder never giving up its right to participate in the governance of the corporation, or perhaps into the existence of stakeholder governing boards.

The third ground rule I shall call "The Principle of Externalities," and it says that if a contract between A and B imposes a cost on C, then C has the option to become a party to the contract, and the terms are renegotiated. Once again the rationality of this condition is clear. Each stakeholder will want insurance that it does not become C.

The fourth ground rule is "The Principle of Contracting Costs," and it says that all parties to the contract must share in the cost of contracting. Once again the logic is straightforward. Any one stakeholder can get stuck.

A fifth ground rule is "The Agency Principle" that says that any agent must serve the interests of all stakeholders. It must adjudicate conflicts within the bounds of the other principals. Once again the logic is clear. Agents for any one group would have a privileged place.

A sixth and final ground rule we might call, "The Principle of Limited Immortality." The corporation shall be managed as if it can continue to serve the interests of stakeholders through time. Stakeholders are uncertain about the future but, subject to exit conditions, they realize that the continued existence of the corporation is in their interest. Therefore, it would be rational to hire managers who are fiduciaries to their interest and the interest of the collective. If it turns out the "collective interest" is the empty set, then this principle simply collapses into the Agency Principle.

Thus, the Doctrine of Fair Contracts consists of these six ground rules or principles:

1. The Principle of Entry and Exit
2. The Principle of Governance

3. The Principle of Externalities
4. The Principle of Contracting Costs
5. The Agency Principle
6. The Principle of Limited Immortality

Think of these ground rules as a doctrine which would guide actual stakeholders in devising a corporate constitution or charter. Think of management as having the duty to act in accordance with some specific constitution or charter.

Obviously, if the Doctrine of Fair Contracts and its accompanying background narratives are to effect real change, there must be requisite changes in the enabling laws of the land. I propose the following three principles to serve as constitutive elements of attempts to reform the law of corporations.

## The Stakeholder Enabling Principle

Corporations shall be managed in the interests of its stakeholders, defined as employees, financiers, customers, employees, and communities.

## The Principle of Director Responsibility

Directors of the corporation shall have a duty of care to use reasonable judgment to define and direct the affairs of the corporation in accordance with the Stakeholder Enabling Principle.

## The Principle of Stakeholder Recourse

Stakeholders may bring an action against the directors for failure to perform the required duty of care.

Obviously, there is more work to be done to spell out these principles in terms of model legislation. As they stand, they try to capture the intuitions that drive the liberal ideals. It is equally plain that corporate constitutions which meet a test like the doctrine of fair contracts are meant to enable directors and executives to manage the corporation in conjunction with these same liberal ideals.[12]

# NOTES

1. Cf. A. Berle and G. Means, *The Modern Corporation and Private Property* (New York: Commerce Clearing House, 1932), p. 1. For a reassessment of Berle and Means's argument after fifty years, see *Journal of Law and Economics* 26 (June 1983), especially G. Stigler and C. Friedland, "The Literature of Economics: The Case of Berle and Means," pp. 237–68; D. North, "Comment on Stigler and Friedland," pp. 269–72; and G. Means, "Corporate Power in the Marketplace," pp. 467–85.

2. The metaphor of rebuilding the ship while afloat is attributed to Neurath by W. Quine, *Word and Object* (Cambridge: Harvard University Press, 1960), and W. Quine and J. Ullian, *The Web of Belief* (New York: Random House, 1978). The point is that to keep the ship afloat during repairs we must replace a plank with one that will do a better job. Our argument is that stakeholder capitalism can so replace the current version of managerial capitalism.

3. See R. Charan and E. Freeman, "Planning for the Business Environment of the 1980s," *The Journal of Business Strategy* 1 (1980): 9–19, especially p. 15 for a brief account of the major developments in products liability law.

4. See S. Breyer, *Regulation and Its Reform* (Cambridge: Harvard University Press, 1983), p. 133, for an analysis of food additives.

5. See I. Millstein and S. Katsh, *The Limits of Corporate Power* (New York: Macmillan, 1981), chap. 4.

6. Cf. C. Summers, "Protecting All Employees Against Unjust Dismissal," *Harvard Business Review* 58 (1980): 136, for a careful statement of the argument.

7. See R. E. Freeman and D. Reed, "Stockholders and Stakeholders: A New Perspective on Corporate Governance," in *Corporate Governance: A Definitive Exploration of the Issues*, ed. C. Huizinga (Los Angeles: UCLA Extension Press, 1983).

8. See T. Peters and R. Waterman, *In Search of Excellence* (New York: Harper and Row, 1982).

9. See, for instance, A. Wicks, D. Gilbert, and R. E. Freeman, "A Feminist Reinterpretation of the Stakeholder Concept," *Business Ethics Quarterly* 4, no. 4, (October 1994); and R. E. Freeman and J. Liedtka, "Corporate Social Responsibility: A Critical Approach," *Business Horizons* 34, no. 4 (July-August 1991): 92–98.

10. At the Toronto workshop Mark Starik sketched how a theory would look if we took the environment to be a stakeholder. This fruitful line of work is one example of my main point about pluralism.

11. J. Rawls, *Political Liberalism* (New York: Columbia University Press, 1993); and R. Rorty, "The Priority of Democracy to Philosophy," in *Reading Rorty: Critical Responses to Philosophy and the Mirror of Nature (and Beyond)*, ed. Alan R. Malachowski (Cambridge, Mass.: Blackwell, 1990).

*James M. Humber*

# Why I Am Not a Normative Stakeholder Theorist

In order to assure that corporations act in socially responsible ways, some ethicists argue that firms should be required to act in accordance with the directives of a moral theory which they call "normative stakeholder theory" or "normative stakeholder analysis." In what follows, I argue against this view. The first step in my argument is to outline briefly the main tenets of normative stakeholder theory. Next, in section II, I offer my criticisms of the theory; here my argument is that normative stakeholder analysis is so beset by problems that it should be rejected by any corporate executive who wants to direct his/her firm in socially responsible ways.

## I. NORMATIVE STAKEHOLDER THEORY: A SYNOPSIS

In 1970 Milton Friedman argued that corporate executives act in a morally responsible way when they seek to maximize profits while obeying the law and following the accepted rules of competition. This theory, which came to be known as "restricted egoism," was repeatedly and severely criticized, and in 1988 R. Edward Freeman proposed an alternative theory for use by corporate managers who wish to direct their firms in socially responsible ways.[1] Basically, Freeman contended that restricted egoism overemphasized the importance of maximizing profits. As Freeman saw things, this overemphasis falsely assumed that corporate executives' primary moral duty was a fiduciary one to their stockholders and that in fulfilling this duty they would act in a socially responsible manner. In opposition to this view Freeman asserted that managers have duties to numerous groups and individuals, that these duties are all (at least *prima facie*)[2] of equal strength, and that to act in a socially responsible manner

115

the claims of all these groups and individuals must be dealt with fairly, i.e., fulfilled in a manner that maintains a proper "balance" among the competing claims. Moreover, Freeman argued that the law of corporations should be amended to require executives to manage their firms in accordance with the principal tenets of his theory; that is to say, Freeman held that corporate executives should be told (legally) to manage their firms in the interests of those groups and individuals to whom their firms bear legitimate obligations (F, p. 113).

As presented above, Freeman's theory seems straightforward enough. However, before any corporate manager could hope to put the theory into practice s/he would have to know at least two things. First, because Freeman's theory enjoins corporate executives to pursue the interests of all those who have legitimate claims upon the firm, managers must have some means for identifying those claimants. Freeman calls these individuals and groups *stakeholders* and he distinguishes two senses of the term "stakeholder":

> The "narrow definition" includes those groups who are vital to the survival and success of the corporation. The "wide-definition" includes any group or individual who can affect or is affected by the corporation. (F, p. 105)

Freeman identifies those groups vital to the survival and success of the firm as owners, management, the local community, customers, employees and suppliers. He does not really elaborate upon the notion of stakeholder in the wider sense and, as a result, when he says that "The stakeholder theory does not give primacy to one stakeholder group over another . . . "(F, pp. 108–109) it is not clear whether he takes this to mean that the claims of stakeholders in the wider sense are as legitimate as the claims of stakeholders in the narrow sense. What does seem clear, however, is that whenever Freeman uses "stakeholder" in the narrow sense, he believes that the claims of all groups denominated by the term should be considered *prima facie* equal.

The second thing a corporate executive must know before s/he could put Freeman's theory into practice is how to construe the firm's duties towards stakeholders, for without such knowledge the executive could not know how the corporation should act in order to treat its stakeholders in morally right ways. For example, if the method for construing the firm's duties were basically utilitarian, the firm would be morally required to maximize benefits among all its stakeholders; if it were Kantian the firm would be required to treat its stakeholders as ends and not as means only, i.e., to fulfill its duties the firm could never lie to its stakeholders, it would always keep its promises to them, etc. Now, when addressing this issue Freeman advocates a "reasonable pluralism."[3] As he puts it:

> "The stakeholder theory" can be unpacked into a number of stakeholder theories, each of which has a "normative core," inextricably linked to the way that corporations should be governed and the way that managers should act. (F, p. 109)

In essence, this allows corporations to construe their duties to stakeholders along virtually any line they wish. As examples of various "normative cores" Freeman cites pragmatic liberalism, feminist theory and ecological theory, and in one of his earliest articles on stakeholder theory—one co-authored with William Evan—he sought to provide stakeholder theory with a Kantian "normative core."[4] In the final analysis, then, Freeman seems to advocate passage of enabling legislation which will force corporations to be managed in the interests of stakeholders but which will permit corporations to define those interests (i.e., their duties to their stakeholders) in almost any way they wish.

## II. STAKEHOLDER THEORY: A CRITICAL ANALYSIS

Like restricted egoism, stakeholder theory has been criticized.[5] Most of the criticisms are practical in nature and concern problems that would arise with any attempt to implement the theory. However, the theory faces other problems as well—problems relating to justification and possible inconsistency. Moreover, these problems are more serious than those focusing on implementation of the theory, for if they remain unresolved we have no reason at all to accept normative stakeholder analysis and very good reasons for rejecting the theory. The following four examples are problems of the sort just mentioned—problems which, unless resolved, seem to require rejection of Freeman's normative theory.

*Problem #1.* Normative stakeholder analysis is not the only theory managers could use when attempting to direct their firms in socially responsible ways. Restricted egoism is one alternative, but there are others as well.[6] If this is so, however, the obvious question is this: Why should businesses be legally required to use stakeholder theory to fulfill their obligations to society rather than to employ some other possible theory? Freeman appears to give a variety of different answers to this question. At one point he offers what he calls the "legal argument." This asserts:

> . . . the law has evolved to effectively constrain the pursuit of stockholder interests at the expense of other claimants on the firm. It has, in effect, required that the claims of customers, suppliers, local communities and employees be taken into consideration. . . . (F, p. 103)

Here Freeman is saying that corporations are now recognized as having legal obligations to those groups that he has labeled "stakeholders." He then seems to assume that this serves as a justification for the claim that corporate managers should adopt normative stakeholder theory and view their firms as having moral obligations to those same groups. However, there are two problems with this view. First, this "legal argument" gives a corporate manager no reason at all to prefer stakeholder theory to restricted egoism. After all, restricted egoism is not totally egoistic; it tells managers to maximize profits for stockholders *within the constraints of the law*. Thus, if the law now requires managers to limit profit maximization somewhat in order to benefit stakeholders, restricted egoists would claim that this is the morally right thing for firms to do. And if this is so it is impossible for Freeman to argue that legal restrictions upon profit maximization provide any greater support for his normative theory than they do for restricted egoism. Quite apart from this fact, however, there is a second, and even more important reason for rejecting Freeman's "legal argument." That is, his argument simply assumes that because corporations are legally required to limit profit maximization and act in the interests of stakeholders, this action also must be viewed as morally right. But this view is absurd. Just as it was possible for business owners in Georgia in the 1940s to argue that it was morally wrong for the state to prohibit them from allowing Blacks and Whites to use the same restrooms and drinking fountains, so, too, it is possible for corporate executives to argue that it is wrong for the government to limit their pursuit of profit and force them instead to act in the interests of stakeholders.[7]

After presenting his legal argument in support of stakeholder analysis, Freeman offers what appears to be a second justification for his normative theory. Basically, the argument—which he calls an "economic argument"—proceeds as follows:[8] (1) Restricted egoists (or what Freeman calls "managerial capitalists") have only one argument for the claim that firms which employ their moral theory fulfill their responsibilities to society; specifically, they argue that maximizing profits produces the greatest good for society as a whole because Adam Smith's "invisible hand" is at work. However, (2) "externalities, moral hazards and monopoly exist in fact . . . " and these hinder the "invisible hand's" effectiveness. (Indeed, Freeman believes that it is because society recognizes this fact that it passed laws requiring corporations to serve the interests of stakeholders who are not stockholders. In effect, this legal action is viewed by Freeman as an attempt on society's part to force restricted egoists to be socially responsible.) (3) Normative stakeholder theory enjoins its adherents to operate in the interests of *stakeholders*, not just stockholders. Thus, (4) use of normative stakeholder theory for moral decision-making satisfies the interests of more people in society than does use of restricted egoism. Hence, (5) firms using stakeholder analysis for moral decision-making will be more socially responsible than firms using restricted egoism. Therefore, (6) corporations should use normative stakeholder theory for moral decision-making.

Freeman's economic argument is superior to his legal argument, for unlike the latter it does show that we have some reason for believing that use of stakeholder analysis has a better chance of fulfilling corporations' social responsibilities than does use of restricted egoism. However, the argument cannot serve as a justification for forcing corporations to appeal to stakeholder theory whenever they engage in moral decision-making. To justify action of this sort Freeman must show that normative stakeholder theory is *the one correct, or "true," moral theory* for use by business, and this he has not done. Indeed, if he has shown anything at all it is only that normative stakeholder analysis is superior to *one* alternative theory, viz., restricted egoism. Assuming this as true, alternative moral theories exist for use by corporate executives and it is possible that one or more of these theories is superior to stakeholder analysis. Moreover, no matter how many alternatives to stakeholder theory Freeman were to examine and invalidate, the possibility would always remain that there is some other theory which he failed to consider and which is, in fact, preferable to stakeholder analysis. To put the matter another way, Freeman cannot hope to justify acceptance of his moral theory as the "official" theory for use by corporate America if he does nothing more than attack competing theories and show that they are inferior to normative stakeholder analysis. And since all he does in his economic argument is to attack one competing moral theory, that argument cannot succeed as a justification for requiring corporations to use stakeholder analysis when they engage in moral decision-making.

When speaking of the role of management in the modern corporation Freeman offers what could be interpreted as a third attempt to justify his contention that normative stakeholder analysis ought to be the official moral theory for businesses. He says:

the reason for paying returns to owners is not that they "own" the firm, but that their support is necessary for the survival of the firm, and that they have a legitimate claim on the firm. *Similar reasoning applies in turn to each stakeholder group.* (F, p. 109, emphasis added)

If this is intended to be a justification for normative stakeholder analysis, it asserts that use of that theory should be imposed upon corporate executives because following that theory's injunctions (i.e., following the theory's commands to fairly balance the interests of all stakeholder groups) is both: (1) necessary for corporations to survive and thrive, and (2) requisite to satisfy legitimate moral obligations which firms have to their stakeholders. However, (1) is false and (2) begs the question. Indeed, Freeman has no choice but to acknowledge the falsity of (1). This is so because in both his legal and economic arguments Freeman claims that changes in the law were needed to force corporations to attend to the interests of those stakeholders who were not owners of stock, and if this is true it must be the case that *before* the law changed at least some firms were thriving while showing little or no concern for those stakeholders who were not stockholders. Finally, it should be clear that Freeman cannot claim that normative stakeholder analysis should be mandated for use by corporations because it is the only theory that satisfies the "legitimate claims" of stakeholders. Whether or not one thinks that the claims of stakeholders are legitimate will be determined by whether or not s/he thinks stakeholder theory is true (e.g., restricted egoists need not recognize the claims of all stakeholders as legitimate). Thus, if Freeman were to assert (2) as his justification of normative stakeholder theory his argument would be circular.

If our reasoning thus far is correct it seems we have no justification at all for requiring corporations to use normative stakeholder analysis for moral decision-making. But there are additional problems with stakeholder theory, and when these are taken into account they appear to provide firms with good reasons for *not* accepting stakeholder analysis as their "official" moral theory.

*Problem #2.* The second problem with stakeholder theory is this: there is no reason why corporate executives should accept Freeman's definitions of "stakeholder." Why, for example, shouldn't managers recognize *only* what Freeman calls the "narrow definition" of the term as legitimate and reject the wider definition as improper? After all, according to Freeman, groups denoted by the narrow definition are vital to the survival of the firm whereas groups and individuals designated by the wider definition are not.

Why shouldn't this difference be sufficient to qualify *only* members of the former class as true stakeholders? Or again, why should we not insist that "stakeholders," when properly understood, has an even broader scope than specified by Freeman's wide definition? In fact, the grounds for advocating such a view are supplied by Freeman himself in his "legal argument." If, as Freeman argues, recent changes in the law require corporations to take the claims of customers, employees, etc. into consideration and this is what qualifies members of these groups as stakeholders, why shouldn't recently enacted legal protections for owls, toads, endangered species of fish, and other organisms qualify these beings as stakeholders? Until Freeman resolves issues of this sort it seems premature on his part to urge that changes be made in the enabling laws of the land so as to force corporations to be managed in the interests of stakeholders.

*Problem #3.* Even if Freeman could show that his uses for the term "stakeholder" were the only correct uses his theory would still face problems. Assume, for example, that a corporate manager, C, were to resolve to direct her/his firm's affairs in the interests of stakeholders and that Freeman succeeded in showing her/him that in the circumstances at hand "stakeholder" designated only stockholders, employees, consumers, suppliers, local community and management. Why should C accept Freeman's command to not give primacy to one stakeholder group over another? After all, might not C reason that certain stakeholders were more "vital" to the firm's survival than others and hence that the firm's obligations to these stakeholders were stronger than its obligations to the other groups? If, for instance, C were the manager of a firm that could easily and cheaply move from one location to another, couldn't C justifiably argue that her/his firm duties to, say, its stockholders should always take precedence over its duties to the local community?

*Problem #4.* Finally, when all is said and done, normative stakeholder theory seems open to the objection that its adherents must choose between embracing inconsistency or giving moral approval to virtually any behavior that firms choose to adopt relative to their stakeholders. This problem arises because Freeman insists that stakeholder theory " . . . can be unpacked into a number of stakeholder theories, each of which has a 'normative core', inextricably linked to the way that corporations should be governed and the way that managers should act" (F, p. 109). To see why and how this view gives rise to problem #4, consider the following example.

Assume that Appletree City is a planned community with 15,000 citizens. The city owns many square miles of land that are not being used. All unused land outside the city's center is zoned residential. In January the Mayor and the City Council of Appletree City are contacted by the Directors of two small development companies (let us say companies X and Y). Both companies want to build child care facilities on unused Appletree City land; firm X wants to build east of the city, Y on the west. For X and Y to build, however, Appletree City must re-zone some of its unused land to "commercial." After discussion, the Mayor and the City Council agree that it definitely is in the best interests of their city to have the child care facilities built; consequently, they recommend the action to the Zoning Board. After appropriate public notice and discussion, Appletree City re-zones parcels of land on its east and west boundaries. The re-zoned land is purchased by companies X and Y, and the firms sign contracts agreeing to build child care facilities on the property within eighteen months. However, one week before X and Y are slated to begin clearing their sites, two discoveries are made. Specifically, the land owned by X is found to contain an endangered species of turtle, and Y's property is discovered to house an endangered species of frog. Now, firm X accepts a version of stakeholder theory that has Kantianism as its normative core. On this view, breaking promises is always wrong, and non-rational, non-autonomous organisms such as turtles are not considered to be members of the moral community. Appealing to this version of stakeholder theory, the managers of firm X reason that it is morally right for them to keep their promise to Appletree City and to abide by the terms of their contract; hence they clear their land and exterminate the endangered turtles. On the other hand, the directors of firm Y accept a version of stakeholder theory that embraces ecological principles as its normative core. On this view Y's principal moral duty is to care for the earth, and promise keeping—even contractual promise keeping—is not an inviolable moral obligation.[9] Given this moral stance the managers at company Y reason that they will best fulfill their obligation to their stakeholders if they break their contract and refuse to build on their newly acquired property, for in this way they will provide a habitat for the rare frogs and preserve them for the appreciation and enjoyment of all. Now, if we assume that the managers of X and Y acted in morally right ways as measured by their own versions of normative stakeholder theory, how would Freeman analyze the situation? Would he say that our example shows that it is both right and wrong for companies to break their promises whenever such action is necessary to save an endangered, non-human life form? If so, he would admit the theory is inconsistent. On the other hand, Freeman could avoid contradiction by asserting that it is morally right for ecological stakeholder theorists to break their promises to save endangered species but wrong for Kantian stakeholder theorists to do so. However, if he took this tack he would have to allow that virtually any kind of corporate activity must be accepted as moral; for in order to ensure that actions which they desired to pursue were proper, stakeholder theorists would have only to adopt the "normative core" for their theory that provided an ethical justification for their behavior. In effect, almost any activity that a firm chose to call proper would have to be accepted by Freeman stakeholder theorists as truly proper for that firm, and this seems absurd.

## NOTES

1. William E. Evan and R. Edward Freeman, "A Stakeholder Theory of the Modern Corporation: Kantian Capitalism," in Tom L. Beauchamp and Norman Bowie, eds., *Ethical Theory and Business*, 3d ed. (Englewood Cliffs, N.J.: Prentice Hall, 1988). Freeman's views are expressed in a more economical fashion in, "A Stakeholder Theory of the Modern Corporation," which first appeared in the 5th edition of the Beauchamp-Bowie text (1997). The latter article is reprinted in this volume, pp. 101–14; all references to this reprinting of the article are cited in my essay as F.

2. By "*prima facie* equal" I mean that all duties are considered equal unless particular circumstances present in an individual case of moral decision-making require that a firm's duties to one group or individual be weighed more heavily than its duties to other groups or individuals. This seems to be what Freeman means when he says: "The stakeholder theory does not give primacy to one stakeholder group over another, though there will surely be times when one group will benefit at the expense of others" (F, pp. 108–109).

3. This is the term Freeman uses to describe his view in "Stakeholder Theory," *The Blackwell Encyclopedic Dictionary of Business Ethics*, Patricia Werhane and R. Freeman, eds. (Oxford, UK: Blackwell Publishers, 1997), p. 606.

4. Evan and Freeman, "A Stakeholder Theory of the Modern Corporation."

5. For some of the best known criticisms see: Kenneth Goodpaster, "Business Ethics and Stakeholder Analysis," *Business Ethics Quarterly* 1, pp. 69–77; also, Alexei M. Marcoux, "Balancing Act," in Joseph Dejardins and John McCall, eds., *Contemporary Issues in Business Ethics*, 4th ed. (Wadsworth: Belmont, Calif.: 2000), pp. 92–100, and Norman Bowie, "New Directions in Corporate Social Responsibility," *Business Horizons* 34 (July-August 1991): 54–65.

6. For example, there is the theory which John Boatright calls the "managerial view." This theory combines the principle tenets of restricted egoism with an insistence that socially responsible corporations have a duty to be philanthropic and to promote charitable giving. See John Boatright, *Ethics and the Conduct of Business*, 2d ed. (Prentice-Hall: Upper Saddle River, N.J.: 1997), p. 359.

7. For a more complete discussion of why legal obligation cannot be the basis of moral obligation see the Introduction to this volume.

8. For Freeman's statement of the argument see F, pp. 104–105.

9. When Freeman discusses that version of stakeholder theory which has ecological principles as its normative core he says that this form of the theory directs corporations to be managed " . . . in accordance with the principle of caring for the earth," and that it tells corporate managers that they ought to act ". . . to care for the earth" (F, p. 111).

# Corporate Policy Statements

*Views on Corporate Responsibility:* The state provides a corporation with the opportunity to earn a profit if it meets society's needs. It follows inevitably that reported profits are the primary scorecard that tells the world how well a corporation is meeting its basic responsibility to society. This is all pretty simple and pretty elementary and I am sure you all studied it years ago in school. However, in recent times critics of our business structure seem to be losing sight of the primary purposes of the corporation and some want to blame the corporation for all of society's ills—real and imaginary. I have no quarrel with the citizenry, the bureaucrats, the legislators, or the educators who say that corporations have a responsibility to society beyond the obligation to generate a fair return or profit for the investor. The corporation—as I have said earlier—is a paper citizen, and every citizen has a responsibility to his fellow citizen. Democratic society is based on that fact. The corporation cannot ignore the truth any more than an individual human being can. However, I take real issue with the critics when they propose that corporations must put their other citizenship responsibilities ahead of their responsibility to earn a fair return for the owners. The only way in which corporations can carry their huge and increasing burden of obligations to society is for them to earn satisfactory profits. If we cannot earn a return on equity investment, which is more attractive than other forms of investment, we die. I am not aware of any bankrupt corporations which are making important social contributions.

. . . There are times when it is hard to define and quantify our responsibility. How much of our shareholders' money should the managers of the business give away in the interest of higher education, and to the United Way campaigns of our base communities? To the fostering of culture and the arts? How much should we spend in money and time attempting to persuade the public to adequately finance public schools, or to help reorganize local government? There is no charity for charity's sake in our handing out the company's money or in our asking the company's people to give of their time. Procter & Gamble's support of civic campaigns is now and always will be limited to what we believe represents the enlightened self-interest of the business. Here in the term self-interest we are back to the word "profit" again. Let's take our own home city of Cincinnati as an example. The future earnings of this company rest first and foremost on our ability to attract and hold bright, capable, dedicated, and concerned people as our employees. If one-quarter of those people are expected to spend their careers in Cincinnati, then it serves the interests of the stockholders for us to support soundly conceived efforts to maintain and enhance this community as a good place to live and raise families.

Procter and Gamble Co.

*Alcoa's Fundamental Objectives:* Aluminum Company of America, as a broadly owned multinational company, is committed to four fundamental, interdependent objectives, all of which are essential to its long-term success. The ideas behind these words have been part of Alcoa's success for many years—as has the company's intention to excel in all these objectives: (1) provide for shareholders a return superior to that available from other investments of equal risk, based on reliable long-term growth in earnings per share; (2) provide employees a rewarding and challenging employment environment with opportunity for economic and personal growth; (3) provide worldwide customers with products and services of quality; (4) direct its skills and resources to help solve the major problems of the societies and communities of which it is a part, while providing these societies with the benefits of its other fundamental objectives. Supporting Principles—in achieving its fundamental objectives, Alcoa endorses these supporting principles and pledges to: conduct its business in a legal and ethical manner ; provide leadership and support for the free market system through successfully achieving its corporate objectives, superiority in product development and production, integrity in its commercial dealings, active awareness of its role in society, and appropriate communication with all employees and with the public; maintain a working environment that will assure each employee the opportunity for growth, for achievement of his or her personal goals, and for contributing to the achievement of the corporate goals; without regard to race, color, national origin, handicap or sex, recruit, employ, and develop individuals of competence and skills commensurate with job requirements; make a positive contribution to the quality of life of the communities and societies in which it operates, always mindful of its economic obligations, as well as the environmental and economic impact of its activities in these communities; for the well-being of all employees at all locations, maintain safe and healthful working conditions, conducive to job satisfaction and high productivity.

Aluminum Co. of America

# MORALS, MANAGEMENT, AND CODES

*Case Study*

# Aero Products

Aero Products is the aerospace division of XYZ Corporation, a U.S. capital goods conglomerate. Aero is a major producer of subassemblies for the aerospace industry, and in 1967 it placed the low bid for an order of brake assemblies for an Air Force aircraft under contract to PQR Corporation. Aero's president, Jack Dale, assigned responsibilities as follows:

John Sunday: Chief Engineer, Aircraft Wheel Section

Tim Hart:
Manager, Design Engineering

Carl Sinclair: Production Manager

Earl Ward: Design Engineer

Jim Lauris: Production Engineer

Ed Link:
Manager, Technical Services

Stan Gove: Test Lab Supervisor

Ward designed the brake, called B-9. Ward was regarded as a brilliant design engineer ; he had an excellent track record of product innovation. He also had a nasty temper, which flared when his work was questioned. No one questioned his preliminary design for B-9 when it was submitted. Ward slected Lauris for the task of producing the final production design. Lauris, twenty-four, and one year out of Caltech, had shown great promise. However, all of his assignments to date had essentially been "paper" projects involving the assessment of previous brake designs and data regarding brake testing. This was his first major assignment; his task was to determine the best brake lining materials and make minor design adjustments in the brake. Lauris would work out the kinks prior to production and submit a brake assembly to the dynamometer qualification tests required by the government. These tests, which simulate the aircraft's weight and speed, must be passed prior to production. Lauris was told by Tim Hart, Design Manager, that PQR wanted to begin flight testing in mid-1968, hence Lauris had to work fast. Since Aero's suppliers had not delivered the housing and other parts, Lauris made a prototype using the disc brake Ward had designed and the suggested lining material.

In September 1967, Lauris tested the prototype for thermal build-up and wear. Normal aircraft brake lining temperatures run to 1,000 degrees but the test showed the B-9 prototype reached 1,500 degrees, and the lining disintegrated. After three more similar failures Lauris began to suspect the brake's design. He reworked the design computations, and it seemed to him that the brake was too small; five discs, he figured, should be used instead of four. Lauris's calculations indicated that the four-disc brake's total surface area was just too small to stop the plane without generating heat sufficient to disintegrate the linings.

Lauris then took his test results and computations to Ward, who said that it was a borderline case between the two computations. He indicated that Lauris could improve results by testing more materials. Ward said that theoretical calculations were one thing, actual testing quite another. He said that a five-disc brake might require one type of material while his four-disc design might require a totally different material to pass the tests. Ward said that on one brake project he had to test a dozen materials before he found one that worked. The four-disc brake, he noted, would be very cost effective, very light—which pleased the Air Force—and could help Aero land new contracts. Ward stressed that the four-disc design was a revolutionary advance of particular importance to the Air Force: the lighter the part, the greater the plane's payload. He informed Lauris that brake subassemblies designed for the four-disc assembly had begun arriving, that to redesign and reorder new subassemblies would be costly, and that flight testing was still scheduled for mid-1968. Ward was also aware, but did not inform Lauris, that his superior, Sinclair, had reported to PQR that initial tests of the B-9 were very successful. Sinclair had checked with Ward just prior to the second test, and asked how things were going. Ward said: "The kid has some problems, but he'll work them out. It will be okay. We have to give these smart kids a chance to show their stuff; we can't solve all their problems for them." On that basis Sinclair sent his optimistic report to PQR.

Lauris ran two more tests in mid-November. Both failed government specifications, but he did reduce the temperature to 1,300 degrees. Still unsatisfied, he decided to talk it over with Sinclair. As an MBA in industrial management, Sinclair was not an engineer. He said that he trusted Ward's experience and judgment, and noted that it would be a coup if the B-9 could be made to work. He told Lauris that Aero had many former military officers in its ranks and that the company operated top-down like the military, which meant operating through the chain of command. He said that Ward, in particular, did not like to be second-guessed. Sinclair said he would not tell Ward that Lauris had tried to bypass him, but he advised Lauris not to try to bypass Ward again. His advice was to retest. He pointed out that this was a big contract and that everyone was relying on Lauris to work out the bugs. Finally, Sinclair pointed out that PQR was the number one brake contractor and that some ten years earlier Aero had designed and built a brake for PQR that was not a success. For ten years PQR had eliminated Aero as a source of brakes. Aero needed a contract with PQR. This time around, Sinclair said, Aero had submitted a very low bid based on its new design— an offer that PQR had to accept. So a lot was riding on this contract.

Lauris said he was really uncomfortable talking with Ward. He said he had run and rerun theoretical calculations which established that a four-disc brake could not work on a plane of this size and type, and that no amount of working with other lining materials would work. He asked Sinclair whether Aero or XYZ had any type of review or appeal process in which upper-level managers reviewed the work of subordinates. Sinclair said that neither Aero nor XYZ had such a process. Lauris said he thought there was an ethical problem involved. Sinclair said the problems Lauris faced were practical, scientific problems. Either Lauris could get the brake to work, as Ward was convinced could be done, or he couldn't get it to work. Lauris asked whether Aero or XYZ had a code of ethics. Sinclair said that such problems hadn't arisen within XYZ and that Aero only employed about six hundred people. He said that problems were just worked out within the group. No formal document had ever been needed.

By this time the main housing had arrived, so Lauris built a production model. It was this model that had to pass formal qualifications tests for the military. Using a new lining, Lauris got the temperature down to 1,150 degrees, but this was still 150 degrees too high and there was still some disintegration beyond normal wear. Lauris ran a dozen tests between January and March 1968, with similar results. He reported to Ward that he didn't think the B-9 could qualify. He was convinced a five-disc brake was necessary.

Ward then met with Sinclair, who called in his boss, Tim Hart. Hart was aware of the problems, but said that John Sunday told him to "Get that brake qualified." Hart inquired as to the best strategy. Sinclair said they were close but needed more time. He suggested that Ward show Lauris how to run a controlled test and how to work up the data. Ward agreed.

When Lauris met with Ward he again stated that his theoretical calculations showed that the four-disc brake would not work. Ward said: "Jim, you're part of a big operation here—a small part. You're not in school now; it's no longer just theory. We have deadlines we have to hit, and to hit them you do what you are told. The big boys up above know more about the big picture than someone who isn't dry behind the ears. You take Sinclair; he's no engineer, but he knows how the game is played. Just do your job."

Ward and Lauris retested. The brake had to stand up under fifty simulated stops. Fans were employed as a cooling device. Instead of maintaining pressure on the brake until the wheel stopped, the pressure was reduced when the wheel decelerated to 15 mph. This meant the wheel had to "coast to a stop." In some cases it rolled over 16,000 feet, whereas normal stopping distance was 3,000 feet. These data were deleted. After each stop the brake was disassembled and parts were machined to reduce friction. In this way the disintegration was reduced to a satisfactory level, but the temperature was still too high. Some of the data recording instruments were then recalibrated to read lower temperatures than were actually recorded. Ward assured Lauris that there was no problem, that standards were always set too high, and the brake would perform well in flight tests. He said: "Sinclair and the big boys know what's going on. They'll back us up." Lauris then turned the data over to Stan Gove, Test Lab Supervisor, who would prepare the qualification report for the military.

In checking the data, Gove caught several errors and discrepancies, and consulted with Lauris. The latter readily allowed that there were calibration errors, but said he thought they were minor. Gove said he thought there were some serious problems; for example, a thermometer had been recalibrated so that while the actual test temperature was 1,100 degrees, the instrument recorded 1,000 degrees. Lauris said that this was the first qualification test he had ever conducted and that he wasn't exactly aware of the proper procedures, but he assured Gove that he followed the test procedures set out by Ward. And he said that Ward assured him that Sinclair wanted the tests done as they were performed. Gove then checked with Ed Link, Technical Services Manager. He told Link he could not sign a report that had errors. Link said he had talked with Sinclair and Hart; the two had indicated that testing was rushed because of the time factor, but that the data were basically all right and could be cleaned up. Link said that he would try to take Gove off the hook; if Gove would prepare the data, he would get someone upstairs to actually write the report. "After all," he said, "we're just filling in blanks and drawing curves, we're not responsible for it after it leaves here." Gove suggested that Link could discuss the issue with Sunday, but Link said: "Look, this is no big deal. Sunday probably already knows about it, but if he doesn't I'm not going to be the one to tell him." Gove asked Link if his conscience would bother him if the plane crashed on a test-flight landing. Link said: "I only worry about things I have control over. I have no control over this; neither do you, so why worry? Look, you've got five kids—worry about them and the wife. We'll take care of you; we'll get somebody to sign it."

Gove prepared the data and graphs. He was told by Ward to review the data and then deliver it to Sunday, who would assign someone in the engineering section to write the report and sign it. After this review, however, he was visited by Hart, Link, and Lauris. Hart said that no one was available to write it, and that the job fell to Lauris and Gove. Lauris protested that it would violate his professional code as an engineer. Hart said: "Look, there is always some latitude in experimental design and the data interpretation; professionals have to use judgment." Gove said that he knew there had been data manipulation and falsification—he could see it in the contradictory data he had been given. Link said: "You always have to rationalize the data when it comes in from a number of sources, that's part of engineering know-how. Besides, the military has a fudge factor built in—nobody will ever know the difference. Sure you changed the data, but only to make it consistent with the big picture." Lauris said he thought he should discuss the matter with Sunday. "Sunday won't touch this thing," said Hart. "Somebody's got to write and sign it, and you two are it. If the government checks us, well, Lauris did the tests and Gove drew the curves. You can defend it better than anyone. So you guys write it up and sign it, that's it. You'll get a big bonus for this, and we'll work out the kinks after the flight tests. We'll take care of you; write it up and sign it."

Lauris said he thought it was unfair to ask him to sign the document, since he had protested all along. Hart said: "Look, you've had some problems with this project. We all hoped you could get it to 1,000 degrees, but you fell short. This isn't all that unusual for a greenhorn. Still, we have a bit of time going forward. This is just paper. Your signature is just ink. We can work it out. But let's be clear about the facts here. (1) You did the testing. (2) You did the controlled tests. (3) You turned the controlled test data over to Stan Gove. Since your fingerprints are all over that data, you sign." Lauris asked if there was some review process at XYZ to which he could appeal. Hart said: "No. Sign it and get on with the job."

## FOR DISCUSSION

What should Lauris do? Why? If you were brought in to replace John Sunday would you take any steps to change decision-making procedures in your section? If "yes," what steps and why?

## SOURCE

This case is based on Kermit Vandiver's "Why Should My Conscience Bother Me?" in *In the Name of Profit*, ed. Robert L. Heilbroner et al. (New York: Doubleday, 1972), pp. 3–31.

*Milton Snoeyenbos*
*Barbara Caley*

# Managing Ethics

A number of surveys on ethics in business have been conducted that not only provide us with data regarding the ethical issues businesspersons actually consider to be most troublesome, but also indicate that top and middle managers have different perspectives regarding the source and nature of business disputes containing an ethical component. This article discusses the data and offers some suggestions for resolving the ethical problems revealed.

In 1961, Raymond Baumhart surveyed a large sample of subscribers to the *Harvard Business Review,* and in 1977, Steven Brenner and Earl Molander reported the results of a survey that repeated some of Baumhart's questions. These studies are not representative of businesspersons. Less than 30 percent of the readers queried actually replied, and it is known that subscribers are significantly above average in position, income, and education. In fact, 44 percent of the respondents were top managers, 35 percent were middle managers and 20 percent were either lower management or nonmanagement business personnel. Nevertheless, the large sample size (over 2,700 replies from 10,000 queried) gives us some indication of how businesspersons actually regard ethical issues and how their views have changed. In 1987, Vitell and Festervand extended the earlier surveys by analyzing the responses of 118 top managers from manufacturing firms located in the southeastern United States. Many of the same questions from the earlier surveys were employed.

Of those who responded to the Brenner-Molander survey 80 percent believe there are ethical absolutes and that ethical matters are not relative. Furthermore, in the 1961 and 1977 surveys 98 percent agreed that "in the long run, sound ethics is good business." However, about half of the respondents in both surveys agree that "the American business executive tends not to apply the great ethical laws immediately to work. He is preoccupied chiefly with gain." Evidently, then, for the businessperson, as for most of us, there frequently is a gap between what the person knows or believes that he ought to do and what he actually does; behavior fails to match a professed standard.

One reason for this gap may be that the manager finds herself in a context in which there is pressure to follow generally accepted *industry* practices that she regards as unethical. In all three surveys respondents were asked: "In your industry, are there any generally accepted business practices which you regard as unethical?" The results in percentages are:

|  | 1961 | 1977 | 1987 |
|---|---|---|---|
| None | 19 | 27 | 44 |
| Yes, a few | 59 | 49 | 47 |
| Yes, many | 9 | 6 | 3 |
| Don't know | 13 | 18 | 6 |

Although the differences could be largely due to the fact that the 1987 survey was regional in scope and the earlier surveys were national, businesspeople seem to believe that unethical practices are decreasing. But these results are difficult to interpret. The decrease may be due to a heightened sense of ethics by managers or increased law enforcement. On the other hand, it may reflect a greater ability to conceal unethical practices or an actual ethical decline, i.e., what was formerly viewed as unethical may presently be so commonplace that it is now regarded as ethically acceptable.

In all three surveys respondents were asked to indicate which industry practices they would most like to see eliminated. The results, in order of importance, are:

| 1961 | 1977 | 1987 |
|---|---|---|
| 1. Gifts, gratuities, bribes | 1. Gifts, gratuities, bribes | 1. Unfair pricing practices |
| 2. Unfair pricing practices | 2. Unfair competitive practices | 2. Gifts, gratuities, bribes |
| 3. Dishonest advertising | 3. Cheating of customers | 3. Cheating of customers |
| 4. Unfair competitive practices | 4. Unfairness to employees | 4. Competitors' pricing collusion |
| 5. Cheating of customers | 5. Unfair pricing practices | 5. Unfairness to employees |
| 6. Competitors' pricing collusion | 6. Dishonest advertising | 6. Contract dishonesty |
| 7. Contract dishonesty | 7. Competitors' pricing collusion | 7. Dishonest advertising |
| 8. Unfairness to employees | 8. Contract dishonesty | 8. Unfair credit practices |

Although it is difficult to discern trends here, it is clear that the respondents agree that they would most like to eliminate certain marketing practices they regard as unethical. Bribes often occur in selling or purchasing, and unfair pricing, cheating of customers, and dishonest advertising are all within the marketing orbit. Why managers would like to eliminate these particular practices is unclear. It may be that managers view these practices as the most serious ethical problems they face. Alternatively, as Vitell and Festervand suggest, these practices may be more conspicuous than others because of their proximity to the marketplace, and, therefore, managers may be more likely to receive public criticism when they occur.

Aside from the question of unethical industry practices, the 1961 and 1977 surveys asked managers whether they had ever *personally* experienced a role conflict between what was expected of them as efficient, profit-conscious managers and what was expected of them as ethical persons. In 1961, 75 percent reported such conflicts, compared with 59 percent in 1977. A 1990 survey that asked respondents whether they had personally experienced ethical dilemmas (rather than role conflicts) during their business careers revealed that over 80 percent had experienced such dilemmas (Delaney).

The types of role conflict most frequently experienced have changed:

| *1961* | *1977* | *1987* |
|---|---|---|
| 1. Firings and layoffs | 1. Honesty in communication | 1. Honesty in communication |
| 2. Honesty in communication | 2. Gifts, entertainment, kickbacks | 2. Gifts and kickbacks |
| 3. Price collusion | 3. Fairness and discrimination | 3. Fairness and discrimination |
| 4. Gifts, entertainment, kickbacks | 4. Contract honesty | 4. Price collusion |
| | 5. Firings and layoffs | 5. Firings and layoffs |

Honesty in communication is a more significant problem recently than in 1961, with a major increase in number manipulation in reports submitted to top management, governmental agencies, and clients. The decreased experience of role conflicts connected with firings and layoffs may indicate that such practices are becoming accepted as routine or that there is more equity built into firing decisions.

As noted, the three surveys studied are weighted toward the opinion of top management. The 1965 Evans survey, focusing on middle managers, reveals that their most important moral conflicts are:

1. Complying with superior's requirements when they conflict with one's own ethical code
2. Job demands infringing on home obligations
3. Methods employed in competition for advancement
4. Avoiding or hedging responsibility
5. Maintaining integrity when it conflicts with being well-liked
6. Impartial treatment of subordinates because of race, religion, or personal prejudice
7. Moral concern that your job does not fully utilize your capabilities

These data indicate that middle managers experience role conflicts primarily because of "pressure from the top," a conclusion reinforced by a survey by Archie Carroll. In Carroll's survey, 64 percent of the managers surveyed agreed that "managers today feel under pressure to compromise personal standards to achieve company goals," but of those agreeing 50 percent of top managers, 65 percent of middle managers, and 84 percent of lower managers agreed with the statement. A 1987 survey by Posner and Schmidt asked managers: "I find that sometimes I must compromise my personal principles to conform to my organization's expectations." Twenty-one percent of top managers, 29 percent of middle managers, and 46 percent of lower managers agreed. A 1998 survey by Petry et al. found that 56 percent of workers surveyed felt some pressure from above to act unethically or illegally on the job and 48 percent said that due to such pressure they had actually acted unethically or illegally during the past year. Twenty percent of middle managers in this survey said they experience a high level of pressure to commit unethical or illegal acts. The Petry survey also found that the most commonly reported sources of pressure were: balancing work and family; poor internal communications; work hours/work load; and poor leadership. Apparently, then, the lower one is in the managerial hierarchy the more one feels pressure to act unethically. Of course, pressure per se is not unethical; in a competitive, profit-oriented environment, pressure to produce is necessary for the efficiency that benefits both consumer and producer. But unethical pressure arises when top management sets a return on equity, sales quota, market share, etc., that cannot reasonably be achieved without a subordinate's engagement in unethical behavior. Unethical pressure may be either intentional or inadvertent. In other words, the manager may or may not be aware that he is pressuring a subordinate to the point that the latter is likely to commit an unethical or illegal act. Some unethical pressure is undoubtedly intentional. A manager may adopt a "produce or else" attitude toward subordinates, knowing it will probably result in unethical behavior, but believing that it will yield greater production or sales and that the subordinate can be held responsible for the unethical acts. A manager may require a subordinate to manipulate figures in a report that requires the latter's signature, believing that responsibility for wrongdoing will fall on the subordinate. Many people in business believe that advancement is open only to those individuals who are unethical, and a manager may intentionally encourage unethical behavior in intrafirm competition. A 1993 survey of middle managers by Altany concludes that "Engaging in what many would consider slightly unethical or deceptive behavior also appears to be correlated to advancement." When faced with scenarios and asked to choose between options Altany regards as "ethical" or "ethically questionable," a higher percentage of upper middle managers chose the ethically questionable options than lower middle managers.

On the other hand, some top managers are undoubtedly unaware that they are placing unethical pressure on their subordinates. This hypothesis is consistent with the results of Carroll's survey and the data from our three surveys. First, many of the industry-wide practices that top managers do not themselves condone and would most like to see eliminated (e.g., gratuities and bribes, unfair competitive and pricing practices, cheating customers, and contract dishonesty) may arise in large part because of inadvertent pressure from above. Second, the role conflicts actually experienced by managers, and prominently mentioned in the surveys (e.g., honesty in communication, gifts and kickbacks, fairness and discrimination, and contract honesty), may arise in part because of pressure superiors inadvertently place on subordinates. The surveys indicate that the role conflicts and industry practices that managers most want to see eliminated are those they have personally experienced, and, although some managers may be familiar with unethical acts they believe they can pressure subordinates into committing, others may simply not be well enough acquainted with lower-level operational details to recognize the unreasonableness of particular demands they make of subordinates. This may be especially significant in large diversified firms in which a manager with training and experience in one department may be transferred to the upper levels of a department in which he has little or no lower-level experience.

What steps can be taken to improve ethical behavior in business? It seems clear from the surveys that there must be greater awareness on the part of top managers that their leadership is essential. In one sense, managers should already be aware of this, since it is a principle of management theory that top management sets the standards of behavior and subordinates imitate the behavior that is expected for success within the organization. The 1977 survey, however, indicates that 65 percent of managers believe that society, not business, has the primary responsibility for setting ethical standards. Certainly there is some basis for this opinion; individuals are members of society long before they enter business, and the manager should be able to assume that the persons he or she hires are already ethical. Yet the surveys also reveal the importance of an organizational influence. Respondents to the 1961 survey ranked the following as factors that influence a person to make ethical decisions:

> An individual's personal code of behavior
> Behavior of a person's superiors in the firm
> Formal company policy
> Ethical climate of the industry
> Behavior of a person's equals in the company

The following were ranked as factors influencing a person to make unethical decisions:

> The behavior of a person's superiors in the company
> Ethical climate of the industry
> The behavior of a person's equals in the company
> Lack of company policy
> Personal financial needs

In the 1977 survey, the following factors were ranked as most influencing a person to make unethical decisions:

> Behavior of superiors
> Formal policy or lack thereof
> Industry ethical climate
> Behavior of one's equals in the company
>  Society's moral climate
> One's personal financial needs

We have already noted Evans's survey result that middle managers experience role conflicts primarily because of organizational pressure. Furthermore, that survey indicates that when middle managers are pressured to comply with a superior's directive that is contrary to their personal code of behavior, they most often comply rather than resign or object and leave themselves open to dismissal, demotion, or horizontal transfer. Similarly, the Carroll survey reveals that 61 percent of middle managers and 85 percent of lower managers would "go along with their bosses to show their loyalty" if asked to engage in behavior they personally believe to be unethical. Thus, the surveys unambiguously indicate that, although a person's socially acquired ethical beliefs may strongly influence his behavior, when faced with an ethical dilemma a person in a lower-level organizational position will typically seek guidance in his immediate organizational context and, in particular, will refer to his superiors' ethical behavior. Organizational factors are central both to a person's perception of an ethical dilemma and his subsequent behavior once a problem is recognized. And, since it is clear that pressure to commit unethical acts is in part traceable to the managerial hierarchy, it is unreasonable for a top manager to expect that a subordinate's decisions will be based solely or primarily on values acquired prior to and independent of his business experience. Unless top management sets the standards of behavior expected in the organization, the pressure to produce may well lead to unethical behavior of the sort revealed in the surveys. And top managers must not only exhibit leadership by professing high standards, they must clearly articulate them and see that they are enforced.

The importance of top management leadership is also stressed in two 1988 studies. A Touche Ross survey of top corporate executives, business school deans, and congressmen indicated that 73 percent believe the firm's chief executive officer plays the most significant role in setting ethical standards for employees, whereas 25 percent believe the employee's immediate supervisor plays the most significant role. A Business Roundtable study of ten firms considered leaders in ethics concluded that: "In the experience of these companies with regard to corporate ethics, no point emerges more clearly than the crucial role of top management. To achieve results, the Chief Executive Officer and those around the CEO need to be openly and strongly committed to ethical conduct, and give constant leadership in tending and renewing the values of the organization."

How can top management develop and enforce high ethical standards in business? We can begin to answer this question by addressing the trouble spots our surveys reveal. Since we have noted that a considerable amount of unethical behavior arises from questionable industry practices, one suggestion is that top managers take an active role in curbing such practices through the implementation of industry-wide ethical standards (or codes) that not only are clearly articulated but also have an adequate enforcement mechanism. Respondents to both the 1961 and 1977 surveys indicate that they favor industry-wide codes. In 1961, 71 percent favored codes, 19 percent were neutral, and 10 percent were opposed. In 1977, 55 percent were in favor, 20 percent neutral, and 25 percent opposed. In practice, however, industry-wide self-regulation has never been widely practiced in America. As Ian Maitland explains, self-regulation is potentially anti-competitive, i.e., the very power needed to prevent industry-wide ethical problems could well be used to restrain trade and result in industry protectionism.

Top management can, however, improve the ethical climate of business by institutionalizing ethics within the corporation. Of course, in the small firm there may not be a need for an elaborate formal structure, but in the large corporation there is a need for articulated objectives, relatively formal procedures and rules, and communication and enforcement mechanisms. If people want their organizations to be ethical as well as productive, then in complex firms there is a need to articulate and communicate ethical standards that are both equitable and effectively enforced. To accomplish these ends, the standards of expected behavior should be institutionalized, i.e., they should become a relatively permanent aspect of the organization. To institutionalize ethics we suggest that the firm: (a) adopt a corporate ethical code, (b) designate an ethics committee at a relatively high level in the organization, and (c) make ethics training part of its management development program.

The first step in institutionalizing ethics is to articulate the firm's values or goals. Many corporations do have general objectives; 3M Corporation, for example, has goals relating to profits, customers, employees, and society. With respect to profit, it states, "3M management will endeavor to maintain optimum profit margins in all product lines in order to finance 3M's future growth and to provide an adequate return to stockholders." The corporation also states that in pursuing its goals the firm will adhere to "uncompromising honesty and integrity . . . manifested in the commitment to the highest standards of ethics throughout the organization and in all aspects of 3M's operations." So 3M's code, developed by top management, has committed the firm's employees to ethical behavior in the achievement of general corporate goals. However, since our surveys reveal that the pressure to achieve goals can and does override ethics, the emphasis should be on setting reasonable goals and subgoals, i.e., goals should be set so that unethical pressure is not placed on subordinates. In addition to a general statement of goals and the means to implement them, a top management committed to ethics should: (a) extensively consult with personnel at all levels of the firm regarding goals and subgoals; (b) see to it that reasonable, specific subgoals are set; and (c) articulate a fine-grained ethical code that addresses ethical issues likely to arise at the level of subgoals.

A code, then, should be relatively *specific*. In addition to general policy statements mentioning overall corporate objectives and means, it should spell out in some detail policy regarding ethical issues that are liable to arise in the conduct of a particular corporation's business. It should detail the individual's obligations to the organization in areas such as: confidential information, trade secrets, bribes, gratuities, gifts, conflicts of interest, expense accounts, honesty, etc. But it should also mention employer obligations in areas such as: hiring, affirmative action, promotion, layoffs, termination, privacy, dissent, grievances, communication, worker and product safety, contributions, employee development, and job quality. In addition, specificity can be enhanced by integrating a firm's ethical concerns with its legal requirements. In the areas of safety and health, for example, specific ethical policy could be integrated with the law in areas such as: equipment, apparel, handling and testing of materials, testing of employees, treatment, compensation, and employment of the handicapped.

If a code is to be more than window dressing, it must be enforced, equitable, and effective; it must be a living document that organizational members are aware of, comprehend, and to which they are committed. If top management is genuine in its ethical commitment, there are a variety of ways to institutionalize a code; the "best" way will largely depend on the individual organizational context. In some cases, a board of directors' subcommittee comprised of inside and outside directors will be effective. In other cases, a committee comprised of managers and employees from different organizational strata will be successful. However it is constituted, the committee should have the authority and responsibility to: (1) communicate the code, pertinent changes, and decisions based on it to all members of the firm; (2) clarify the code and issues relating to its interpretation; (3) facilitate the code's use; (4) investigate grievances and possible code violations; (5) enforce the code by disciplining violators and rewarding those who comply with and uphold it; and (6) review, update, and upgrade the code.

If a code is specific, details obligations of both employer and employee, and is institutionalized and enforced, we can then meet the four main criticisms of codes, namely, that they are: (1) too general, (2) stated negatively, (3) slanted, and (4) mere window dressing. First, although many codes are too general and/or vague, enough so that employees often cannot tell which acts are permitted or prohibited, an extensive, balanced and specific code will meet this criticism. Second, codes are often stated in terms of negative rules: Employees should not do X. The criticism is that this type of code sets a mere moral minimum in which employees will scan the rules, and if the act contemplated is not explicity prohibited, will conclude that the act is morally permissible. However, a detailed code may contain positive as well as negative rules. You can (positively) tell your employees to act with integrity and also specify negative rules which identify types of situations that often arise but are unacceptable because they do not conform to acting with integrity. Third, some codes are slanted, almost invariably in favor of the firm. In part, this is due to the adoption in 1991 of Federal sentencing guidelines for organizations, which allow firms convicted of federal crimes to be given very reduced sentences if they have in place effective systems for the prevention and detection of violations. Accordingly, many firms have built into their ethics codes legal compliance programs which tell employees about the law, how to prevent violations, and the penalties for being in violation. However, a good ethics program allows that employees as well as the employer have rights, and a good code reflects the balance. Fourth, although some codes are mere window dressing, our suggestion is that they should be institutionalized and enforced. The main reason is that this is the ethical thing to do; the federal sentencing guidelines provide additional motivation.

In addition to an explicit ethical code and ethics committee, institutionalization can be aided by devoting part of the employee training program to ethics. Ideally this would embrace all employees, and could focus on the code, the ethics committee, and the responsibilities of employer and employee. At Chemical Bank, for example, new employees have a general orientation in which they receive and read the Code of Ethics and sign an agreement to abide by it. Training personnel discuss the code and answer questions. The new employees then view a film in which Chemical's Chairman emphasizes the importance of ethical behavior. Employees also receive instruction in ethical standards as part of their functional training and when they are promoted. Chemical Bank also utilizes a Decision Making and Corporate Values seminar to train managers in ethics. Held twice a year, the seminar articulates Chemical's values and helps managers recognize the ethical implications of their business decisions.

Within the firm, then, top management can create an ethical environment by: (1) articulating goals for the firm, and, in particular, by developing a two-way communicative process that sets realistic subgoals, such as sales quotas, for employees; (2) encouraging the development of an ethical code applicable to all members of the firm; (3) instituting an ethics committee to oversee, enforce, and develop the code; and (4) incorporating ethics training in the employee development program. Establishment of such internal programs, in the context of developing industry-wide codes of ethics to deal with issues that transcend a particular firm, would be a significant step in establishing an ethical climate in business.

Are corporations institutionalizing ethics? A 1986 survey by Michael Hoffman of Bentley College's Center for Business Ethics addresses this question. The center queried the Fortune 500 industrial firms and the Fortune 500 service firms, and received 279 responses (28 percent). The survey indicated that 223 (or 80 percent) of the firms responding have taken steps to incorporate ethical values in their organizations. Of the 223, 93 percent have written ethical codes and 44 percent have ethics training for employees, with a majority of those having training actually requiring it. As of 2000, virtually all the 500 companies in the Standard and Poors 500 have corporate ethics codes.

Many firms have comprehensive ethics programs. Boeing's strategy consists of five key elements. First, the company has an ethics code titled *Business Conduct Guidelines*. It covers: marketing practices; offering of business courtesies; conflicts of interest; acceptance of business courtesies; and use of company time, materials, and proprietary information. The code consists of brief statements of the company's basic principles, followed by interpretations of those principles. Second, each of Boeing's operating units has an Ethics Advisor to interpret the firm's ethics policies and provide clarification and advice before employees act. Third, Boeing's Corporate Headquarters has an Office of Business Practices, which can be contacted directly via telephone by any employee who believes the ethics code has been violated. Fourth, Boeing has an Ethics and Business Conduct Committee that reports to the company's Board of Directors, and is composed of board members and upper management. This committee oversees all of Boeing's ethics programs and handles any questions referred to it by Ethics Advisors or the Office of Business Practices. Fifth, Boeing has extensive ethics training programs throughout its operating divisions. Each division has developed its own three-hour ethics program centered on the ethics code. The programs utilize case studies and focus on techniques for ethical decision-making relating to the principles set forth in the code.

Is there any evidence that all this ethics apparatus actually works? Yes, there is considerable evidence that ethical behavior improves if an organization has: (1). a commitment to ethics by top management, (2). a code of ethics, (3). code enforcement, and (4). an ethics training program. Let us examine this evidence in these four key areas.

An early study by Newstorm and Ruch (1975) found top executives to be very important as a source of their managers' ethical standards, a finding confirmed by Weaver and Ferrell (1977). Hegarty and Sims (1979) indicate that top management leadership is positively related to ethical behavior. The research of Benson (1989) and Brooks (1989) indicates that top managers must support ethical codes in order for subordinates to follow them. Support for the claim that ethical codes have a positive impact on ethical behavior is found in the studies of Weaver and Ferrell (1977), Hegarty and Sims (1979), Rudelius and Bucholz (1979), Dubinsky (1985), Benson (1989), Brooks (1989), Singhapakdi and Vitell (1990), and Nwachukwu and Vitell (1997). That it is important to enforce the code is confirmed by the research of Weaver and Ferrell (1977), Laczniak and Murphy (1985), Singhapakdi and Vitell (1990) and Nwachukwu and Vitell (1997). Although the impact of ethical training programs on behavior has not been extensively studied, some recent research suggests the effect may be positive (Delaney and Sockell, 1992).

In addition to institutionalizing ethics in their organizations, managers can take personal steps to make their firms more ethical by learning more about the subject, recruiting ethical people, and encouraging ethical behavior.

Of course, we all know a lot about ethics; it is not an arcane subject like calculus. We all call certain acts right and others wrong. We know we should respect people, treat them fairly, and consider the consequences of our actions. But there are additional resources managers can use to learn more about ethics and, specifically, ethics in organizations. There are many books on organizational ethics. And courses are available at most universities. Some university professors will serve as ethics consultants to firms, and some universities have ethics centers that typically employ consultants.

You can also learn more about ethics by talking with people in your firm about the subject. As a manager, you want to create a context in which your employees feel free to discuss ethics with you. Talk with other managers, but also your employees. And talk with your customers and suppliers. What do they think about your firm? Have they spotted problems you have not experienced? Remember that the number one source of ethical problems in organizations is the failure to communicate. When you talk about ethics remember that good communication is two-way: listen as well as talk. Get to know the moral role-models in your firm, people known for integrity and high standards. You can learn a lot about the ethical environment in your firm from them. Finally, talking with people in other organizations may provide valuable insights. What ethics problems have they faced? What ethics structures do they have in place? Other firms are often willing to share their problems and strategies; use this resource to gain knowledge relevant to your situation. But keep in mind that your firm is distinct from every other. You cannot simply take another firm's ethics apparatus and impose it on yours. That apparatus reflects the specific values of the other firm, and it is focused on the problems that organization faces. So, borrow from others, but don't simply impose others' values and ethical structures on your own organization.

In one sense, ethical organizations consist of ethical employees. In part, we can make employees ethical by having codes, etc. But it also helps to recruit ethical people. So build ethics into your hiring procedures. We commonly screen for intelligence, ability, and motivation. Well and good, but we can also include ethics. Scenarios can be posed in the interview that have an ethical dimension. Tests can be structured to assess character and values.

You can also take steps to encourage ethical behavior. First, set a good example. As a manager you are a role model for better or worse. Set high standards and live up to them. Second, don't undercut your own standards by sending mixed messages when you communicate with employees. When you talk about ethics, try to state a clear and unambiguous message. Because ethics is a complex topic, this is not always easy to do. And some of the ethical problems you will face will be very difficult to resolve. Acknowledge the complexities, but try to work to a definite solution to the problem while providing reasons for your solution. Third, and this bears repeating, talk with employees about ethics and encourage them to talk with you. You have to devote some time to ethics, just as you devote time to every important part of your job. Most important, take specific steps to encourage the free flow of information both up and down the managerial hierarchy, including discussion of ethics. And fourth, when you discuss ethics avoid excessive abstractions and focus on the specifics of your firm. Perhaps there is an ethical dimension to a marketing plan which you notice when you review it. Raise the issue in that particular context at that time. Even if you do not notice an ethical problem with the marketing plan, ask others if they have any ethical concerns about it.

In addition to recruiting good people and encouraging ethical behavior, managers should reward employees who are ethical. Codes and committees are useful in deterring and punishing offenders, but good deeds should be rewarded. In some cases an acknowledgment is sufficient; after all, we expect good behavior. But there isn't any reason ethics cannot be factored into performance evaluations. And if you are serious about creating an ethical organization, then ethics should be a factor in promotion.

# REFERENCES

Altany, D. "Torn Between Halo and Horns." *Industry Week* 242 (1993): 14–20.

Baumhart, R. "How Ethical are Businessmen?" *Harvard Business Review* 39 (1961): 6ff.

Benson, G. "Codes of Ethics." *Journal of Business Ethics* 8 (1989): 305–19.

Brenner, S., and E. Molander. "Is the Ethics of Business Changing?" *Harvard Business Review* 55 (1977): 57–71.

Brooks, L. "Corporate Codes of Ethics." *Journal of Business Ethics* 8 (1989): 117–29.

Business Roundtable. *Corporate Ethics: A Prime Business Asset.* 1988.

Carroll, A. "Managerial Ethics: A Post-Watergate View." *Business Horizons* 18 (1975): 75–80.

Delaney, J., and D. Sockell. "Ethics in the Trenches." *Across the Board* 27 (1990): 15–26.

Dubinsky, A. "Studying Field Salespeople's Ethical Problems." In *Marketing Ethics.* Edited by Gene Laczniak and Patrick Murphy. Lexington, Mass.: Heath, 1985.

Evans, R. Appendix B to T. McMahon's "Moral Problems of Middle Management." *Proceedings of the Catholic Theological Society of America* 20 (1965): 23–49.

Hegarty, H., and H. Sims Jr. "Organizational Philosophy, Policies, and Objectives Related to Unethical Decision Behavior: A Laboratory Experiment." *Journal of Applied Psychology* 64 (1979): 331–38.

Hoffman, M., et al. "Are Corporations Institutionalizing Ethics?" *Journal of Business Ethics* 5 (1986): 85–91.

Laczniak, G., and P. Murphy. "Incorporating Marketing Ethics into the Organization." In *Marketing Ethics.* Edited by Gene Laczniak and Patrick Murphy. Lexington, Mass.: Heath, 1985.

Maitland, I. "The Limits of Business Self-Regulation." In *Ethical Theory and Business.* 4th ed. Edited by T. Beauchamp and N. Bowie. Englewood Cliffs, N.J.: Prentice-Hall, 1993, pp. 121–30.

Newstorm, J., and W. Ruch. "The Ethics of Management and the Management of Ethics." *MSU Business Topics* 23 (1975): 29–37.

Nwachukwu, S. and S. Vitell. "The Influence of Corporate Culture on Managerial Ethical Judgments." *Journal of Business Ethics* 16 (1997): 757–76.

Petry, E., et al. "Sources and Consequences of Workplace Pressure." *Business and Society Review* 99 (1998): 25–30.

Posner, B., and W. Schmidt. "Ethics in American Companies: A Managerial Perspective." *Journal of Business Ethics* 6 (1987): 383–91.

Rudelius, W., and R. Bucholz. "Ethical Problems of Purchasing Managers." *Harvard Business Review* 57 (1979): 8–17.

Singhapakdi, A., and S. Vitell. "Marketing Ethics: Factors Influencing Perceptions of Ethical Problems and Alternatives." *Journal of Macromarketing* 10 (1990): 4–18.

Touche Ross. *Ethics in American Business.* 1988.

Vitell, S., and T. Festervand. "Business Ethics: Conflicts, Practices, and Beliefs of Industrial Executives." *Journal of Business Ethics* 6 (1987): 111–22.

Weaver, K., and O. Ferrell. "The Impact of Corporate Policy on Reported Ethical Beliefs and Behavior of Marketing Practitioners." In *Contemporary Marketing Thought.* Edited by B. Greenberg and D. Bellenger. Chicago: American Marketing Association, 1977, pp. 477–81.

## SELECT BIBLIOGRAPHY

Aguilar, F. *Managing Corporate Ethics.* New York: Oxford University Press, 1994.

Beauchamp, T., and N. Bowie, eds. *Ethical Theory and Business.* 5th ed. Upper Saddle River, N.J.: Prentice-Hall, 1997, chap. 2 on social responsibility and stakeholder theory.

Carroll, A. *Business and Society: Ethics and Stakeholder Management.* 3d ed. Cincinnati: Southwestern, 1996.

Freeman, R. *Strategic Management: A Stakeholder Approach.* Boston: Pittman, 1984.

Friedman, M. *Capitalism and Freedom.* Chicago: University of Chicago Press, 1962.

———. *Free to Choose.* New York: Harcourt Brace Jovanovich, 1980.

Hesson, R. *In Defense of the Corporation.* Stanford: Hoover Institution Press, 1979.

Hoffman, W., J. Moore, and D. Fedo, eds. *Corporate Governance and Institutionalizing Ethics.* Lexington, Mass.: Lexington Books, 1984.

Humber, J. "Milton Friedman and the Corporate Executive's Conscience." *Philosophy in Context* 10 (1980): 71–80.

Nash, L. *Good Intentions Aside: A Manager's Guide to Resolving Ethical Problems.* Boston, Mass.: Harvard Business School Publishing, 1990.

Reeves-Ellington, R., and A. Anderson. *Business, Commerce, and Social Responsibility.* Lewiston, N.Y.: Edwin Mellen Press, 1997.

Snell, R. *Developing Skills for Ethical Management.* New York: Chapman & Hall, 1993.

Trevino, L., and K. Nelson. *Managing Business Ethics.* New York: John Wiley & Sons, 1995.

Weiss, J. *Business Ethics: A Managerial, Stakeholder Approach.* Belmont, Calif.: Southwestern, 1993.

## ELECTRONIC SOURCES

Business Ethics Organization   http://www.businessethics.org

Business Social Responsibility Organization   http://www.bsr.org

The Carol and Lawrence Zicklin Center for Business Ethics Research rider.wharton.upenn.edu/~ethics/zicklin/

Centre for Applied Ethics   www.ethics.ubc.ca/resources/

Essential Organization   http://essential.org

Ethics Officer Association   www.eoa.org/

Ethics Resource Center   www.ethics.org

International Society of Business, Economics and Ethics   www.synethos.org

Students for Responsible Business   http://net-impact.org

# 3. EMPLOYER RIGHTS

## INTRODUCTION

The work contract establishes employee obligations to the employer; in return for his wage and benefits the employee is expected to utilize his knowledge and skills for the benefit of the organization. Employees have clear, specific, and extensive legal obligations to their employers, and these are spelled out in C. G. Luckhardt's article "Duties of Agent to Principal." The rest of this chapter discusses employer rights in the areas of conflict of interest, gifts, payoffs, trade secrets, employee monitoring, downsizing, and honesty in organizational communication.

If employees have an obligation to adhere to their work contracts, the firm also has an obligation to be relatively specific about the details of the work contract. This point is clearly made in Robert E. Frederick's discussion of conflicts of interest. Although firms have a right to preclude conflicts of interest, Frederick's discussion of Inorganic Chemical's policy points up the fact that corporate policies are often excessively general and biased in favor of the organization. The need for specificity in corporate policy statements is echoed in Robert Almeder's discussion of bribes and gifts.

We commonly regard knowledge as a social good and value its dissemination, which raises the question of whether we should allow corporations to protect the information they generate. Robert E. Frederick and Milton Snoeyenbos argue that there is a moral basis for allowing patents and trade secrets, but they also argue that an individual has a right to use her skills and knowledge to better herself, and hence the firm has an obligation to make sure that its secrets are legitimate trade secrets. The case studies in this section points up the conflict between corporate and individual rights within the context of trade secrets.

Although technology now enables managers to monitor closely the productivity of their employees, the employees also have privacy rights. Moreover, productivity may slip if employees believe the monitoring is intrusive. Ernest Kallman's article offers suggestions that he believes allow corporations to monitor employees without either violating employees' rights or reducing their productivity.

Although the 1990s was a prosperous decade, it also saw massive layoffs as firms struggled with global competitive pressures. Businesses certainly have a legal and moral right to downsize due to factors such as automation, market shrinkage, product obsolescence, and lack of capital, but the effect on employees is often severe and should not be overlooked. Brian N. Bulger and Carolyn Curtis Gessner examine both voluntary and involuntary reductions in force, and stress the need for corporations to be fair to employees as well as effecting the needed cost reductions.

Surveys reveal that honesty in communication is a major problem in organizations, and the Von Products case study illustrates communication dilemmas that can arise. James M. Humber argues that employees have a *prima facie* responsibility to tell the truth, and he points out that it is very difficult to justify lying in corporate communications. Humber also discusses conditions under which the liar would legitimately be excused from responsibility for his act.

# AGENT'S DUTIES

*C. G. Luckhardt*

# Duties of Agent to Principal

Agency is defined as "the fiduciary relation which results from the manifestations of consent by one person to another that the other shall act on his behalf and subject to his control, and consent by the other so to act."[1] The person for whom action is taken is called the principal, and the person who takes the action is called the agent. In order to understand the extent of and rationale for the various duties agents have with regard to their principals, it is important to distinguish and understand four elements of this definition of agency. The first is the concept of acting on behalf of, or for, another. "Acting for another" implies that the agent is a kind of stand-in for the principal, for *were* the principal able to act, there would be no need for him to employ an agent. But since the principal is unable to act, perhaps because of constraints of time or ability, he deputizes another person to act in his place. This suggests that the agent is, in effect, a "mini"-principal, i.e., a person whose own identity is submerged, and who takes on the identity of the principal. Ideally, the agent would be identical with the principal, but obviously this is impossible in practice. As your agent, I cannot have *exactly* the same intentions, thoughts, desires, abilities you have; nor can I make the same decisions as you. But one of the guiding thoughts behind the law of agency is the idea that I should resemble you in as many ways as are relevantly possible. As we shall see, the ramifications of this idea for the duties of agents are vast, and the questions it raises legion. Must the agent, for example, have all of the interests of the principal at heart when he represents him? If not, then what kinds and how many? And if so, does that mean that he must have none of his own? And if he may have his own interests, may these conflict with those of the principal?

A second important element of the definition of agency given above is that of consent. The principal must consent to the agent's acting on his behalf, and the agent must consent to work for the principal. Intuitively, this requirement of an agency relationship is understandable: I can represent your interests only if you want me to, and you can't force me to represent your interests if I don't want to. But plausible though it may be, this requirement is fraught with many legal difficulties. What constitutes consent, for example? How may the principal and the agent manifest their respective consents? Can either consent tacitly or implicitly? And how may either revoke his consent? The general rule is that failure of the agent to perform his duties will constitute adequate grounds for the principal to revoke his consent, and so the requirement of consent is closely linked with the duties that the agent is determined to have.

A third aspect of this definition of agency is the notion of control. This element gives the principal the right to direct and control the agent's activities. But this means that the agent must be subject to that control, i.e., that he must obey the instructions and directions of the principal. The duty of obedience is, as we shall see, one of the most strictly enforced of all the duties agents bear.

The fourth important aspect of the definition of agency given above is that of a fiduciary relationship. For purposes of understanding the duties agents bear to principals, this is perhaps the most important aspect of agency. In general, a fiduciary relationship is one based on trust, or faith (from the Latin *fidere*), and in the case of agency the legal requirements stemming from this concept extend beyond mere obedience to those of care and loyalty. Even though we may have mutually consented for me to be your agent, the idea here is that you must be able to trust me in order for the relationship to persist. Therefore, if I show through my lack of care or loyalty that I cannot be trusted, you may unilaterally terminate my employment as your agent. In addition you may have further causes of action against me for violating this requirement of trust.

Care, loyalty, and obedience are the three major elements constituting the agent's duties towards his principal. But in the minds of the courts, they have far-reaching connotations and sometimes surprising applications. In what follows we shall examine how these requirements are commonly interpreted and applied.

# DUTIES OF CARE AND SKILL

The duties of care and skill arise from the courts' understanding that an agent who is paid for his services is required to act with "standard care and with the skill which is standard in the locality for the kind of work which he is employed to perform."[2] When the agent contracts with the principal, the former is ordinarily presumed to possess the skills standardly required for carrying out his agency. There are two exceptions to this, however. If the agent represents himself as possessing more than standard skills, he can be held liable if he does not possess them. And if the principal knows that the agent does not possess the standard skills, then he may not hold the agent liable for not possessing them. Suppose $P$ employs $A$ as his attorney to sue $T$. Ordinarily $A$ can be held liable only if he does not possess the skills and exercise the care of other attorneys in the locality in which he is employed. But if $A$ holds himself out as being a specialist in tax law, for example, then $P$ may reasonably expect him to possess the skills and exercise the care of a tax specialist. (These do not, of course, amount to his being expected to win every case he represents.) Conversely, if $P$ knows that $A$ is not a tax specialist when the latter is hired, he may not expect that $A$ should exercise the skills or care of a specialist. An interesting question arises when the agent possesses special skills not known to the principal, but fails to exercise them. Technically speaking, the principal cannot expect the agent to exercise them. Nevertheless, most holdings suggest that the agent may nevertheless be held liable for not exercising such special skills.

Furthermore, agents are under a general obligation to exercise a standard degree of care in their transactions and behavior. In other words, they should not act negligently. If an agent $A$ is hired to buy milk-cows for $P$ from $T$ and he discovers at the time of delivery that the cows are on the verge of death, normal discretion and care would dictate that he would not go through with the purchase. Failure to exercise such discretion would constitute a violation of his duties.

Nor would a person exercising a standard degree of care attempt to do the impossible or the impracticable. If the agent discovers that he cannot do what he has been told to do, or that it is impracticable to do so, it is his duty not to waste his time and effort (and possibly the prinicpal's money) attempting to do so. Thus if just before he sets out to buy $T$'s cows, $A$ discovers that they are dead, he is not only not under a duty to purchase them, but he also has a duty not to continue in his efforts, such as going to $T$'s place of business. The standard that is commonly used in determining whether he should continue his efforts is whether the agent could reasonably expect that the principal wanted him to do so. That is, he is to put himself in what he reasonably views as the principal's shoes. Of course, if he has been able to determine the principal's desires directly, then the agent is under a duty to do just that, even if this means that he continues his best efforts to attain what he, the agent, might regard as impracticable goals.

## DUTY TO GIVE INFORMATION

Closely related to the duty of care is the duty to give information. If the agent receives information bearing on the principal's interests, he has a duty to communicate this information to the principal. If $P$ instructs $A$, his agent, to sell some real estate to $T$, and $A$ meantime acquires the information that $F$ would be willing to pay more for the property than $T$, he is obliged to tell this to $P$. Or if the agent is unable to carry out the directions of his principal, because events make it impossible, impracticable, or illegal for him to do so, he should make that known to his principal. In the milk-cow examples above, the agent is also under an obligation to tell the principal that he has not bought the nearly dead or dead cows. Or again, an agent unable to obtain fire insurance for a principal must tell the principal that he has not been able to do so. Otherwise, in addition to being lawfully fired, he may be held liable for the amount of the insurance settlement that the principal might have received for his uninsured goods. The exceptions to this duty occur in cases where the agent has a superior duty to a person other than the principal. Thus, an attorney who acquires confidential information from one client is under no obligation to disclose it to another client whose interests it might affect.

## DUTY OF GOOD CONDUCT

The requirements of skill, care, and the giving of information on the part of the agent are all related to actions for which the agent is employed. But the agent may also be held liable for some actions that are clearly outside the ambit of his employment. Thus, the duty of good conduct is usually understood as part of the agent's duty to care for the principal's interests. Actions that bring disrepute upon the principal, although not within the scope of the agent's employment, may be grounds for dismissal. Thus in a famous McCarthy-era case, a Hollywood screenwriter was found to have been legitimately dismissed from his job when he was convicted of contempt of Congress for refusing to answer whether he was a communist.[3] Furthermore, the duty of good conduct requires that the agent not act towards the principal in such a way as to "make continued friendly relations" with him impossible.[4] Insubordination, either in speech or by other means which jeopardize the "friendly relations," may subject an agent to lawful dismissal.

## DUTY TO OBEY

All agents have a duty to refrain from knowingly violating the reasonable directions of the principal. This is an essential element of agency, stemming from the requirement of control. If the agent does violate the reasonable instructions of the principal, either as to acts to be performed, or the manner of performing them, he may lose his job and incur liability for any loss his violation has caused the principal. If, however, the principal's directions were unreasonable, then the agent may disobey, and may even have a valid claim against the principal for breach of his employment contract. Unreasonable directions include: (a) those which are illegal, unethical, or (according to a few holdings) contrary to public policy; (b) those which threaten the physical condition of the agent; (c) those which violate the ordinary customs of business with regard to such agency; (d) those which are impossible or impracticable for the agent to carry out; and (e) those which conflict with interests the agent is otherwise privileged to protect, whether such interests be his own or those of a third party. It is not proper for an agent to refuse to carry out orders solely on the grounds that doing so will harm the principal's interests. However, the agent may refuse to obey instructions if he stands directly to lose by doing so. Thus, if $A$ is on salary, he may not refuse to sell $P$'s goods at the price $P$ demands, even if the price is so low that $A$ knows that $P$ will lose money selling them at that rate. If, however, $A$ is working on commission, and knows that such a price will adversely affect his own income, he may refuse to sell at that price. Or, alternatively, if he knows that following the principal's directions will damage his own business reputation, he may refuse to follow them.

In the absence of instructions to the contrary the agent is ordinarily free to carry out the principal's orders in a manner customary to such undertakings. Thus real estate agents are free to advertise their clients' property in newspapers, unless the clients instruct them otherwise. If the principal's instructions are ambiguous and the agent is unable to receive clarification from the principal before the time to act, then his obligation is to act reasonably, in light of the facts of which he is aware.

## DUTY TO ACT ONLY AS AUTHORIZED

The duty to obey requires that the agent do what the principal tells him to do. The duty to act only as authorized is the other side of that coin, insofar as it requires the agent not to do what he has been told or should infer that he is not to do, except when he is privileged to protect his own or another's interests. The usual standard that is applied here is that the agent act in accordance with "reasonable customs or, if there are no customs, that he is to use good faith and discretion."[5] Ordinarily, if his actions are based on a misinterpretation of the principal's unambiguous instructions, the agent can be held liable for the costs of his actions. Thus, if $A$ is instructed to buy $T$'s milk-cows, and he buys a bull as well, he may then be held liable to $P$ for its value. Furthermore, the agent may be liable to the principal where he makes a mistake concerning the facts upon which his instructions depend. If $P$ directs A to deliver some goods to $T$, then $A$ may be liable for the cost of recovery of goods, or for the cost of the goods themselves, if they are delivered to $F$ and cannot be recovered. Factors determining whether an agent is liable for acting mistakenly include "the subject matter of the authorization, the language used in conferring it, the type of agent, and the kind of business done by him."[6]

## DUTY OF LOYALTY

The duty to obey is predicated on the view that the agent should not do anything the principal directs him not to do. The duty of loyalty extends beyond the doing of intentionally forbidden acts. It states that the agent has a duty to act solely for the interests of the principal. In its narrowest sense, the duty of loyalty requires that an agent not "act or speak disloyally in matters which are connected with his employment."[7] Outside his employment, however, the agent is not prevented from acting in good faith in a way that might injure his principal's business. Thus the agent for a soft drink company may not use his title as employee of that company, nor the special information he has acquired as an employee of the company, to advocate legislation banning the use of saccharine in soft drinks, when such legislation could harm his company's interests. However, as a citizen he may advocate such legislation, so long as he does not use the information he has acquired as an employee of the company. One important upshot of this rule is that employees are under a duty not to advise the public to buy elsewhere than from their employers, nor are they to suggest that their employers' products are inferior to those of a competitor.

## DUTY NOT TO ACQUIRE AN ADVERSE INTEREST

Closely related to the duty of loyalty (and often construed as one element of it) is the duty not to acquire an adverse interest. This requires that an agent not acquire any interest adverse to that of the principal unless the latter agrees that the agent may do so. Thus a buyer for a department store may not acquire an interest in a manufacturing business from which he purchases goods for the store, either directly or through a "straw." Neither may a seller purchase the principal's goods for himself, either directly or through a "straw." To act in either of these ways would put the agent in a position in which he would have an adverse interest: to buy for less insofar as he represents the principal, while at the same time buying for more in terms of self-interest, or selling for more in terms of the principal's interest, while selling for less in terms of his own interest. Such divided interest means that the agent is not being completely loyal to the principal, as the law requires, and it subjects the agent to liability, to discharge from his employment, breach of contract, loss of compensation, as well as tort liability for losses caused and for profits made. If the agent makes his potential adverse interests known to the principal, however, and takes no unfair advantage of him, then the agent is not liable if the principal agrees that he may act in this way.

## DUTY NOT TO COMPETE

In addition to acquiring an adverse interest, agents are also required not to compete with their principals, unless the principals consent to it. A real estate agent who represents a seller may not also show his own property to prospective buyers, in competition with that of the seller whom he represents. Nor may he buy property for himself which had originally been sought by the principal. Both of these actions would constitute a breach of duty during the time of the agent's employment. But during this time the agent is free to make plans to compete with the principal at the end of such employment, so long as he does not use confidential information in order to do so. After his employment has ended he may even hire the principal's employees for himself, as well as solicit customers for his competing business.

## DUTY OF CONFIDENTIALITY

The duty of confidentiality requires that an agent not use or communicate confidential information for anyone's benefit other than that of the principal. The use of such information, acquired as a result of a person's agency, is prohibited both for the agent's own benefit, as well as for the benefit of third parties, even though the information does not relate to the subject of his agency. Thus a dairy worker who overhears the owner discussing plans to buy adjacent land may not use this information for his own advantage, nor may he disclose it to others for their advantage. Included within this restriction are such matters as "unique business methods of the employer, trade secrets, lists of names, and all other matters which are peculiarly known in the employer's business."[8] After the termination of his employment the agent has a continuing duty not to reveal such information, with the exception of "the names and customers retained in his memory as the result of his work for the principal and also methods of doing business and processes which are but skillful variations of general processes known to the particular trade."[9]

## NOTES

1. *Restatement, Second, Agency* § 1.
2. Ibid., § 379.
3. *Twentieth-Century Fox Film Corp.*, v. *Lardner*, 216 F .2d 844.
4. *Restatement*, § 380.
5. Ibid., § 383, a.
6. Ibid., § 383, c.
7. Ibid., § 387.
8. Ibid., § 395, b.
9. Ibid., § 396, b.

# CONFLICT OF INTEREST

*Sorrel M. Mathes*
*G. Clark Thompson*

# Inorganic Chemicals Company's Conflict of Interest Policy

## GENERAL STATEMENT OF POLICY

The company expects and requires directors, officers, and employees (herein "employees") to be and remain free of interests or relationships and to refrain from acting in ways which are actually or potentially inimical or detrimental to the company's best interests.

## APPLICATION OF POLICY

### 1. *"Conflicts of Interests" Defined*

A conflict of interest exists where an employee:
    a.   has an outside interest which materially encroaches on time or attention which should be devoted to the company's affairs or so affects the employee's energies as to prevent his devoting his full abilities to the performance of his duties;
    b.   has a direct or indirect interest in or relationship with an

From Sorrel M. Mathes and G. Clark Thompson, "Ensuring Ethical Conduct in Business," in *The Conference Board Record* 1, no. 12 (December 1964): 22. Reprinted by permission of The Conference Board.

outsider such as a supplier (whether of goods or services), jobber, agent, customer, or competitor, or with a person in a position to influence the actions of such outsider, which is inherently unethical or which might be implied or construed to:

i.   make possible personal gain or favor to the employee involved, his family, or persons having special ties to him, due to the employee's actual or potential power to influence dealings between the company and the outsider;

ii.  render the employee partial toward the outsider for personal reasons, or otherwise inhibit the impartiality of the employee's business judgment or his desire to serve only the company's best interests in the performance of his functions as an employee;

iii. place the employee or the company in an equivocal, embarrassing, or ethically questionable position in the eyes of the public; or

iv.  reflect on the integrity of the employee or the company;

Practically, conflicts of interests of the types just mentioned are reprehensible to the degree that the authority of the employee's position makes it possible for him to influence the company's dealings with the outsider ; thus, for example, the situation of those who buy or sell for the company, or who can influence buying or selling, is particularly sensitive,

c.   has any direct or indirect interest or relationship or acts in a way which is actually or potentially inimical or detrimental to the company's best interests.

## 2. *Examples of Improper Conflicts*

There follow a few obvious examples of relationships which probably would run afoul of the foregoing definition, but any relationship covered by the definition is subject to this policy:

a.   Holding an outside position which affects the performance of the employee's work for the company.

b.  Relatively substantial (whether with reference to the enterprise invested in or to the employee's net worth) equity or other investment by the employee or members of his immediate family in a supplier, jobber, agent, customer, or competitor. Under normal circumstances, however, ownership of securities of a publicly held corporation is not likely to create a conflict of interests unless the ownership is so substantial as to give the employee a motive to promote the welfare of that corporation and unless the employee, through his position with the company or otherwise, is able to promote such welfare.

c.  The acquisition of an interest in a firm with which, to the employee's knowledge, the company is carrying on or contemplating negotiations for merger or purchase. In some cases, such an interest may create a conflict even though the interest was acquired prior to the time the company evinced any interest in merger or purchase. Similar considerations are applicable to real estate in which the company contemplates acquiring an interest.

d.  The receipt of remuneration as an employee or consultant of, or the acceptance of loans from, a supplier, jobber, agent, customer, or competitor of the company.

e.  The acceptance by the employee or members of his family from persons or firms having or seeking to have dealings with the company of any cash gifts, or of gifts or entertainment which go beyond common courtesies extended in accordance with accepted business practice or which are of such value as to raise any implication whatsoever of an obligation on the part of the recipient.

f.  Speculative dealing in the company's stock on the basis of information gained in the performance of the employee's duties and not available to the public, or other misuse of information available to or gained by the employee by reason of his employment.

*Robert E. Frederick*

# Conflict of Interest

The employee has legal obligations to the organization he works for via the law of agency. For example, an agent has a "duty to his principal to act solely for the benefit of the principal in all matters concerned with his agency" (*Restatement*, Sec. 385). Again, the agent is barred from acting for individuals whose "interests conflict with those of the principal in matters in which the agent is employed" (*Restatement*, Sec. 394). However, the agent's interests may conflict with those of his principal. Perhaps only the total "organization man" completely identifies his interests with those of his employer, but that individual is a caricature not found in reality. These differing interests can lead to conflicts unless the broad and nonspecific language of the law of agency is clarified by an explicit and detailed work contract between employer and employee.

A conflict of interests in the corporate setting arises when an agent has an interest that influences his judgment in his own behalf or in behalf of a third party, and which is contrary to the principal's interest. The moral and legal basis of conflicts of interest is relatively clear. Via the work contract the agent agrees to further the principal's interest. If the agent acts for himself or a third party in a manner contrary to the principal's interest, he breaks his contract with the principal. Contract breaking is unfair to the principal, and, if generally practiced, would undermine the institution of business, with attendant social disutility. Given the asymmetry in the law of agency, however, which places obligations of loyalty, obedience, and confidentiality on the agent, and given that the employer typically sets the majority of the provisions in the work contract, it seems morally, if not legally, incumbent on the employer to clearly specify in the contract what constitutes a conflict of interest.

In many cases there is little in the way of such specification. An example is 1(a) of Inorganic Chemicals' policy, which says that a conflict of interest occurs when an employee "has an outside interest which materially encroaches on time or attention which should be devoted to the company's affairs or so affects the employee's energies as to prevent his devoting his full abilities to the performance of his duties." As it stands, this is rather vague, particularly for the at-will employee whose work contract may not contain an explicit job description and clauses proscribing certain sorts of management directives. Thus, a sales manager might find that his "duty" is to maximize sales—a rather open-ended task. But that manager may have "outside interests," such as family interests and obligations, which may "prevent his devoting his full abilities to the performance of his duties."

We can begin to devise more specific guidelines by dividing employees' outside interests into the broad categories of those that the employer believes do not conflict with his interests, and those the employer believes do conflict with his interests. The latter category is divided into those interests of the employee that the employer *mistakenly* believes are in conflict with his interests, and interests of the employee that the employer *correctly* believes conflict with his. This last category is in turn divided into those areas in which the employer has a *legitimate* claim that the employee modify his activities, and those in which he does *not* have a legitimate claim. Our schema, then, looks like this:

Employee's outside interests (EOI)

A. EOI the employer believes do conflict with his interests.

B. EOI the employer does not believe conflict with his interests.

C. Employer has a mistaken belief.

D. Employer has a correct belief.

E. EOI the employer has a legitimate claim against.

F. EOI the employer does not have a legitimate claim against.

Let us say that Jones is Smith's employee. Then we can give the following examples of the various categories:

B. Jones collects stamps and Smith does not believe Jones's hobby conflicts with his interests. Nevertheless, Smith, in his capacity as Jones's employer, demands that Jones stop collecting stamps.

C. Jones collects stamps, and, for reasons we need not speculate on,

Smith mistakenly believes this conflicts with his interests, and demands that Jones stop collecting stamps.

E. Jones is a government civil rights lawyer and in his spare time is an organizer for the local Ku Klux Klan. Smith demands that Jones cease this activity.

F. Jones works for XYZ Publishing Company and in his spare time writes successful novels. Company rules prohibit Jones from publishing at XYZ. Smith correctly believes that Jones's novels detract from XYZ's sales and demands that Jones stop writing novels.

Each of the above examples follows the same pattern: the employee engages in certain outside activities that the employer attempts to interfere with or prevent. Typically, clauses in the work contract, e.g., Inorganic's 1(a), give the employer the right to interfere, in some cases, with the employees' outside activities. However, such clauses should not give the employer the right to interfere in all of the employee's outside activities since the employee has legitimate outside interests that are protected by his rights to privacy and freedom of action. For instance, example B is a clear case where Jones's rights to privacy and free action are violated by Smith. In order to prevent this sort of abuse the work contract should unequivocally state that employees have legitimate outside interests and that the employer has no right to regulate those interests either by design or suggestion. Another example is employees' interests in and duties to their families. We all know of firms that place undue burdens on employees to the detriment of family life. However, employees are properly interested in their families and have a right to act so as to satisfy those interests. Hence the work contract should not be such that it can be construed as giving the employer the right to interfere in all of the employees' outside activities.

But there are many cases where the interests of the employer and the employee genuinely conflict. And since each has a right, within legal limits, to serve those interests, the work contract should provide some mechanism for determining whose rights prevail in particular instances. Example C is a situation in which Jones's rights to privacy and free action prevail since Smith has no interests that are at stake, although he incorrectly believes he has. Example E is more difficult. In a free society such as ours, individuals have great latitude when engaging in activities that satisfy their interests. Indeed, many people would say that individuals have a right, providing they do not violate the law, to engage in any activity they please as long as it does not result in significant harm to others. Now, Jones has a legal right to organize for the Klan, but even if his outside activity does not impair his job performance, it is highly likely that his activities will severely damage the credibility of the organization for which he works. Thus Smith can legitimately demand that Jones cease this sort of activity. Similar considerations apply to example F, but it seems that in the circumstances in question Jones's rights should prevail rather than Smith's.

The issue of outside interests, then, is relatively clear. In E and F both the employer and the employee have interests that are protected by rights. Each can justify his position by appeal to those rights, but there has to be some determination of whose rights are overriding. There are two ways that work contracts can apply in such cases. First, if the contract specifically prohibits a certain activity, e.g., organizing for the Klan, then by entering into the contract the employee forfeits his right to engage in that activity. If he does so anyway, he breaks the contract and is thereby subject to the appropriate penalty. Second, since the contract cannot possibly deal specifically with all potential conflicts, it should provide a means for settling disputes. I will discuss both of these points more fully in a moment, but first there are some other difficulties with Inorganic's policy that should be noted.

Thus far I have not considered conflicts of interest that occur in the actual work setting. Most of these conflicts should be specifically dealt with by the work contract. But note that 1(c) of Inorganic's policy defines a conflict as any act that is "actually or potentially inimical or detrimental to the company's best interests." If we suppose the company's "best interest" is profit maximization, then in every situation there is only one proper act, and an indefinite number of acts which are, perhaps unbeknown to the agent, "potentially inimical or detrimental" to maximizing profit. If an employee performs an act that does not maximize profit, then, even though he is interested in maximizing profit and believes his act to be in the company's best interest, according to 1(c) there is a conflict of interest. However, it seems more reasonable to describe his act as a performance shortcoming rather than a conflict of interest, since the employee acted in what he believed was the company's interest. If the employee's performance continually exhibits such shortcomings, management has the right to take appropriate measures to correct it, but they cannot justify such measures by an appeal to conflict of interest. Thus, since Inorganic's policy applies to performance shortcomings as well as genuine conflicts of interest, it is too broad to serve as a useful guideline for identifying cases of conflict of interest.

Furthermore, Inorganic's 1(c) states that a conflict arises when an agent has an interest that is "potentially inimical or detrimental to the company's best interests." If an actual conflict arises when an agent's self-interest influences his act contrary to a principal's interest, then a potential conflict arises when an agent has not acted but does have a self-interest or motive contrary to the principal's interest. Now the *Restatement* (Sec. 385) says that an agent has a "duty to his principal to *act* solely for the benefit of the principal," not that he must have no self-interests. Some individuals, after all, are able to place self-interests aside; they do not act on them. So, a potential conflict of interest is not inherently unethical. The issue rests on how the agent acts.

Since the Inorganic policy is typical of corporate policy statements, the foregoing suggests that such policies are often too general and tend to be biased in favor of the organization, particularly where factors such as performance shortcomings can be regarded as conflicts of interest. The remedy would seem to be a list of more specific guidelines covering particular areas where conflicts arise. The hazard with this approach is that the scope of such conflicts is difficult to circumscribe solely with specific guidelines. There will always be exceptions or borderline cases.

This suggests the following strategy: (1) the firm should have a brief, general, but accurate conflict of interest policy statement; (2) it should establish specific guidelines to cover clear-cut interests; (3) it should establish a committee, officer, or procedure to: (a) handle borderline cases, and (b) set policy in new areas by articulating and developing specific guidelines; (4) new policies should be disseminated to employees; (5) employees should be required to consult with the conflict of interest body prior to acting in borderline or new but questionable areas; and (6) the firm should make clear the penalties for violation of corporate policy in conflicts cases.

The following should suffice as a general policy statement covering all conflict of interest cases:

> The law states that employees have a legal obligation to use their best judgment to act solely for the benefit of the company in all job related matters. The law also prohibits employees from acting for individuals (including themselves) and parties whose interests conflict with the firm's interests in matters related to the employee's employment. The company has established guidelines to cover company policy regarding situations in which conflicts of interest frequently arise. Managers have the responsibility to see that their employees understand these guide-

lines. The company has a Conflict of Interest Board that handles situations not clearly covered by the guidelines. If an employee is in doubt as to whether an act constitutes a conflict, he should consult with the board before he engages in the act. If at any time the company determines that an employee has acted in a way such that he has an interest in his act that influences his judgment in his own behalf or in the behalf of a third party, and which is contrary to the company's interest as spelled out in the following guidelines, the employee will be disciplined as deemed appropriate to the act(s) involved.

Now the key is the list of specifics delineating this policy statement. Fortunately, such specifics can be articulated in the four major areas in which most conflict of interest cases arise: bribes, gifts, external affiliations, and insider information.

Bribes, kickbacks, payoffs, etc., in a competitive context, are immoral for two reasons: (1) Kantian universalization of maxims allowing bribery would undermine the institution of business, which rests on competitive bidding based on price, and (2) although bribes may be advantageous to the few persons involved, they generally have disutility for the vast majority of society's members, and hence rule utilitarian considerations weigh against bribery. Since such practices are also illegal, a firm's conflict of interest policy should be very straightforward:

> Bribes, kickbacks, payoffs, etc., are illegal and immoral; any employee who engages in or encourages others to engage in such acts will be summarily fired and his acts will be reported to the appropriate legal authorities.

Specific, clear-cut policy statements can also be developed regarding gifts and entertainment. In some firms individuals cannot give any gift to, or receive any gift from, another party. Where specific sanctions are listed for violations, one has a clear-cut policy. If gifts are allowed, morally relevant variables can be specified, e.g., data on the value of the gift, the context in which it was given or received, the intent behind giving the gift, and the position of the giver or receiver in the organization. Borderline cases will invariably arise, but these can be handled by (3), (4), (5), and (6) of our suggested strategy for dealing with conflicts. That is, all gifts should be reported to the conflict of interest body in the firm. Consultation with the body should be required before a borderline case or a new but questionable case is acted upon by the gift giver or recipient in the firm. Finally, new guidelines should be disseminated to employees.

A similar strategy applies to external affiliations. Conflicts of interest frequently arise when an employee has a financial interest in another organization with which the firm does business. Such conflicts can be precluded by explicitly forbidding employees to invest in suppliers, distributors, or customers associated with their employer. If investments are allowed they may be limited in a variety of ways (e.g., percentage of stock limits), and the firm may also require disclosure of outside interests. Borderline cases can be handled by the firm's conflict of interest body.

A corporate policy on insider information can also be spelled out more completely than Inorganic's policy. Saying, with 1(c), that a conflict occurs when an employee "has any direct or indirect interest or relationship or acts in a way which is actually or potentially inimical or detrimental to the company's best interests" is simply too general. Employees should know that the law states that insider information must be disclosed to the public before anyone possessing it can trade in or recommend the purchase or sale of the securities involved. Disclosure of insider information should be done in strict accordance with company policy. Insider information is material, nonpublic information; the test of materiality being that the information itself would affect investment decisions of investors and, if generally known, affect the price of the security. The following have been held by the courts to involve insider information based investment decisions: (a) dividend change, (b) indication of a new discovery or product, (c) corporate projections indicating a change in rate of earnings, (d) a sharp drop in earnings, (e) a sharply downward revised projection of earnings, and (f) significant unexpected losses. Finally, if there is any question about whether an item is insider information, the company's Conflict of Interest Board should be consulted prior to acting on the information.

It should be stressed that each firm will have to articulate its own specific guidelines. For example, a privately held firm may not need a policy on insider information, and a bank may want to have very specific guidelines regarding lending officers who might have a personal financial interest in a business that makes loans with the bank. All in all, however, the strategy I have developed promises to diminish the conflict of interest problem if a firm is serious about its implementation.

# GIFTS AND ENTERTAINMENT

*Case Study*

# Corporate Gift Giving

Priority Parts, Inc. is a mid-sized corporation engaged in the manufacture of rivets, bolts, clamps, screws, latches, and other metal-fastening mechanisms. Early in 2000, Priority Parts was taken over by a much larger corporation, Universal Motors and Electric, Inc. (UME). Immediately after the takeover, UME replaced many of Priority's top-level managers, but retained others. Ronald Frump, Head of Purchasing, and Tim Pakker, Sales Manager, were among those retained.

Until the takeover by UME, Priority Parts had no corporate policy on gift giving. However, UME had a policy, and in less than a week after UME's acquisition of Priority, both Pakker and Frump received a copy of a memo which read, in part:

> No employee of Priority Parts shall (1) *offer* gifts, favors, gratuities, meals, or entertainment to others at company expense, or (2) *accept* gifts, favors, gratuities, meals, or entertainment from persons with whom they are doing business, unless the following three conditions are met. First, the offer (or acceptance) must be public, consistent with generally accepted business practices, and in accord with society's prevailing moral standards. Second, the value of the goods given (or received) must be small enough that the goods cannot reasonably be viewed as a bribe, kickback, or payoff. Third, all transfers of goods must be such that public knowledge of those transfers will not prove embarrassing to the company.

When Pakker received the company's memo on gift giving, he felt worried. For one thing, when UME took over Priority it created a new position— Assistant Sales Manager—and filled that position with a bright and extremely ambitious young man named Ed Rabbitt. Pakker felt that Rabbitt wanted his job, and with the new top-level management at Priority,

Pakker did not feel secure in his position. Pakker knew that he had been retained at Priority after the UME acquisition because of his many sales contacts. However, in a year or two Rabbitt would be familiar with most of those contacts, and Pakker's advantage over Rabbitt would be nullified. Furthermore, if Pakker somehow embarrassed Priority by violating the directives spelled out in the company's memo on gift giving, this might give Rabbitt the edge he needed to oust Pakker and take over his job as Sales Manager.

Feeling that his position at Priority was precarious, Pakker resolved to adhere strictly to the company's guidelines on gift giving. However, the more Pakker studied the memo he had received, the more confused he became. What *exactly* was prohibited by the company's new policy, and what *exactly* was permitted? Pakker was not sure, for he found the company's memo to be extremely unclear. In the end, Pakker decided that he needed help in interpreting Priority's new policy. Pakker knew that his long-time friend, Ronald Frump, had received a copy of the gift-giving memo; thus, he called Frump and arranged with him to discuss the issue over lunch.

When Pakker and Frump got together for lunch, Pakker soon discovered that Frump was as confused by the memo as he was. Frump said that he rarely received gifts that were valuable; but as it happened, just two weeks earlier he had been given something which was worth a fairly substantial sum. After receiving the company's memo on the receipt of gifts, Frump now wondered whether he should keep what he had been given. He related several facts to Pakker, and then asked for his opinion on the subject. The facts were as follows.

For over ten years Priority Parts sold all of its scrap metal to Triple S Salvage, Inc. Throughout the ten-year period, Frump's contact at Triple S was Tom Toonces. Over the years Frump and Toonces became close friends—they had family picnics together, played tennis together, etc. Recently, Toonces had a falling out with his co-workers at Triple S; as a result, Toonces left the company to take a new job out of state. When Toonces left he gave Frump his season tickets for the local professional football team. Toonces said that Triple S had given many of its executives tickets earlier in the year, and that he had been one of those receiving tickets. Toonces chose to give Frump his tickets because the two were close friends, and Toonces knew that Frump was an avid football fan. Also, Toonces was still angry at the people at Triple S, and he refused to give the tickets to anyone who worked at that company.

Frump told Pakker that he wanted to keep the football tickets. To be sure, the tickets were worth hundreds of dollars. However, the tickets were given to Frump by Toonces personally, and not by Toonces acting as a representative of Triple S. Also, Toonces was going out of state and it was extremely unlikely that he and Frump would be doing business in the future. How, then, could the tickets be viewed as a bribe? Furthermore, Frump pointed out that the tickets had to be classified as a *public* gift, for as soon as Frump attended a football game he'd be sitting among Triple S executives who also had been given season tickets.

When Frump asked for Pakker's view on the subject of the football tickets, he was disappointed by Pakker's response. Pakker advised Frump to return the tickets to Toonces because keeping them could place Frump in a compromising position. Each year Frump examined bids from various salvage companies to determine which firm would purchase Priority's scrap. What would happen, Pakker said, if, in the upcoming year, some company other than Triple S were to submit the high bid for Priority's scrap? If Frump awarded the contract to that company, might not the personnel at Triple S conclude that Toonces had given Frump the football tickets as an incentive to *stop* doing business with Triple S? And what if someone at Triple S were to voice such an opinion to top management at Priority? Even if the charge were wholly untrue, Priority Parts would be put in an embarrassing position.

Frump thought about Pakker's advice, but in the end decided to reject it. So far as Frump was concerned, Pakker was overly cautious because he had Ed Rabbitt breathing down his neck, seeking to usurp his job. Further, Frump was honestly convinced that the football tickets were a *personal* gift, given to him by a close friend, and that the tickets had nothing whatsoever to do with business. Also, Frump was sure that the tickets would have no influence on him when he awarded contracts for the sale of Priority's scrap; thus, he resolved to keep the tickets.

Apart from his questions concerning the football tickets, Frump raised one other issue for discussion with Pakker. Virtually all of the gifts Frump received were given to him at his office by salespersons. However, each year Frump was given a Christmas turkey and four bottles of domestic champagne by the chief sales representative at Bestwest Steel. The gifts invariably were delivered to Frump's house rather than to his office. Because the gifts were sent to his home, it was unlikely that anyone at Priority knew that he received them. However, Frump never tried to keep the receipt of these gifts secret; everyone in his family knew that the gifts came from Bestwest Steel. Were the gifts publicly received? Frump was not sure, and neither was Pakker. After some discussion, Pakker and Frump decided that the best course of action would be for Frump to inform people in his office whenever he received a gift at home. This could be done informally. For example, when Frump received his traditional gifts from Bestwest, he could make a point of mentioning to several of his coworkers and secretaries that he was happy to receive the turkey and champagne from the sales personnel at Bestwest Steel, because these gifts came in handy at Christmas.

Like Frump, Pakker had two questions relating to the memo on gift giving. First, Pakker had directed his sales personnel at Priority to give small gifts—pocket protectors, plastic pens, key chains, etc.—to all customers at other firms. All these gifts were embossed with Priority's *logo*, and all were imprinted with the company's name, address, and telephone number. Pakker had always viewed these gifts as advertisements, and assumed that any gift that had the company's name, address, and phone number on it was properly classified as an advertisement. Now, however, Pakker was beginning to have doubts. In the previous year, for example, Pakker noticed that Priority Parts had been doing business with China-Cabinets, Inc. for ten years. To commemorate the occasion, Pakker gave the purchasing agent at China-Cabinets a gift of two gold-plated pens. The pens were inset with diamond chips and set in a marble base. The base had a brass plate on which Pakker had engraved the names of both companies, together with the phrase, "1990–2000: A Decade of Togetherness." When Pakker gave the pen set to the purchasing agent at China-Cabinet, he thought of it as an ingenious advertisement. However, the pens cost almost $500. Was that sum so large that the set could "reasonably be viewed" as a bribe, kickback, or payoff rather than as an advertisement? Pakker was not sure, and he asked Frump for his opinion.

Frump took no time in responding to Pakker. So far as Frump was concerned, *anything* that had a company's name, address, and phone number permanently attached to it was an advertisement, and this held true regardless of the value of the object being given or received. On the other hand, Frump told Pakker that he would not classify the pen set as an advertisement, because the pens had nothing engraved on them, and they were able to be separated from their base and used in non-business contexts. At the same time, Frump was not sure whether the pens were valuable enough to be "reasonably" viewed as a bribe, kickback, or payoff. Frump thought that the memo's guideline on this issue was hopelessly vague because different people could be influenced by different amounts—one person might be swayed to do something wrong for $500 while another might not do the same thing for $5,000.

After thinking the matter over, Pakker decided that he would adopt a "play it safe" attitude and no longer give any gifts on behalf of the company that were worth more than $50. Frump, on the other hand, refused to set any specific limit on the value of gifts he would accept. He said that he would evaluate each gift individually, and reject those which he felt were sufficiently large to have an influence upon the objectivity of his decision making.

Pakker's final difficulty with the gift-giving memo concerned those portions of the memo that dealt with "accepted business practices" and "prevailing moral standards." What, Pakker asked Frump, was an "accepted" business practice? And how was he to determine society's "prevailing" moral standards? To illustrate his point, Pakker used two examples. The first concerned his dealings with a former business associate, Brooks Brothers. For years Pakker and Brothers did business together, and over the years they had formed a close friendship. In 1998, Brothers retired. Still, Pakker and Brothers got together occasionally for lunch or golf, and whenever they did get together Pakker treated Brothers at company expense. The Pakker-Brothers gatherings were purely for fun and reliving old times; business was never discussed. Now, Pakker asked, was this an "accepted" business practice? In one sense it was, for every salesperson Pakker had ever known had, at one time or another, used his or her expense account to pay for non-business-related expenses. Top-level management knew this sort of thing went on, but, as long as expenses of this kind occurred infrequently and were kept to a minimum, management tended to wink at the practice. Still, the company's official position was that expense accounts were for business-related expenses only. In this sense, then, Pakker's actions could not be classified as an "accepted" business practice.

Pakker's second example concerned his biggest account, Bluejay Aircraft, Inc. Bluejay's corporate headquarters was in Cincinnati, and Pakker's contact at Bluejay was Dion Y. Sius. Whenever Pakker was in Cincinnati to do business with Bluejay, Sius insisted that Pakker not take him out to dinner at company expense, but rather use his expense account to finance a trip to some of Kentucky's best strip bars—establishments such as the Leopard's Lair and the Kitty Kat Lounge. Places such as these were outlawed in Cincinnati, though they were perfectly legal in Kentucky.

When Pakker next did business with Sius, should he consider society's prevailing moral standards to be those established in Cincinnati, or those accepted in Kentucky? Indeed, should he look to the law at all? After all, though nude dancing was legal in Kentucky, this did not prove that it was commonly thought to be moral. In fact, the majority of Kentucky's citizens might well believe that the voyeurism and exhibitionism which occurred in nude dancing establishments was perverted and immoral.

When Pakker asked for Frump's opinion concerning his activities with Brothers and Sius, Frump said that he thought Priority's management was not so much interested in morality as in maximizing profits and strengthening Priority's position in the market. This being the case, he felt that Pakker would be treading on dangerous ground if he continued to use company funds to pay for Brothers' lunches and greens fees. On the other hand, if using company funds at Kentucky's strip joints was necessary to secure lucrative contacts with Bluejay Aircraft, Pakker should continue that practice. After all, Pakker was doing nothing illegal. How, then, could his actions embarrass Priority Parts?

After some thought, Pakker concluded that Frump's advice was sound. In the future, he would take "generally accepted business practices" to mean "practices which are officially sanctioned by the company," and not "commonly practiced business activities." Further, when considering the morality of his use of his corporate expense account, his only concern would be to obey the law in the jurisdiction where he was operating; he would not try to determine society's shared moral beliefs, or to adhere to those moral standards.

## FOR DISCUSSION

When Pakker and Frump reach different conclusions concerning gift giving, whose view do you think is closer to being correct? Explain why you believe as you do. When Pakker and Frump reach the same conclusion, do you agree with their position? Explain why you accept or reject their view. Many of the problems faced by Pakker and Frump arise because of vagueness and unclarity present in Priority Parts' gift-giving memo. Can you think of ways to reword the memo so as to eliminate, or at least reduce, that vagueness and unclarity?

*Robert Almeder*

# Morality and Gift Giving

A bribe is the offering of some good, service, or money to an appropriate person for the purpose of securing a privileged and favorable consideration (or purchase) of one's product or corporate project. Typically, but not necessarily, the person offering the bribe does so in secret and only when the person receiving the bribe antecedently agrees (either explicitly or implicitly) to accept the bribe under the conditions indicated by the briber. Understandably, the briber's business posture is enhanced by the successful bribe and it would not be otherwise enhanced, because, presumably, without the bribe the briber's product or project would not merit any special consideration as against the product or projects of the briber's competitors.

Few people in the business community are willing to defend the morality of the practice of bribery. Most businesspersons see the practice of bribery as one that, if adopted on a wide-scale basis, tends to undermine a free, competitive, and open economy by encouraging a lack of real competition for quality products. After all, where bribery is an acceptable practice, the briber gains unfair advantage because the briber's product secures preferential treatment not based upon the merits or price of the product. Even at its best, the practice of bribery, *as a rule*, tends to undermine open competition along with the usual efficiencies and quality-of-goods characteristic of the open economy. Thus, what is basically wrong with bribery is that, *as a rule*, it strikes at the heart of capitalism by undermining a free and competitive economy. If capitalism is to survive as the best of economic systems, it can do so only where there is open competition.

The practice of bribery can also be faulted for the reason that the briber violates the golden rule because the briber, presumably, would not want his product discriminated against for reasons that had nothing to do with the quality of his product.

---

I would like to thank James Humber for his comments on an earlier draft of this paper.

But what about the practice of giving gifts to persons with whom one is doing business? Is gift giving of this sort a clear case of bribery? If it is, then for the reasons just mentioned it, like bribery, should be considered immoral. In other words, if one gives a gift in order to secure a business advantage that would not otherwise occur, and if in the typical case the person receiving the gift accepts it under the conditions indicated by the giver, then this act of gift giving is in fact a bribe and should be considered a bribe. Many businesspersons, however, do not see *all* gift giving to one's clients as a clear case of bribery. They see nothing wrong with the practice of gift giving if it is done under certain circumstances.

Those who favor some form of gift giving in the marketplace do so because they think such a practice, unlike bribery, need not be an instance of deliberately intending to secure a decision that enhances one's business posture. A salesman, for example, may or may not intend his gift as a bribe. He may give a gift not for any special treatment, but only for fair treatment, or to insure equal treatment. He may even give the gift simply because in the years of doing business with someone he has become genuinely friendly with the person who just happens to be able to enhance the salesman's business posture and profit.

In response to this last line of reasoning, however, others are quick to note that what is wrong with bribery is not simply that those who offer bribes do so with the *intent* of securing special treatment, although certainly they do so. Rather, what is essentially wrong with bribery is that the practice has the effect of influencing the judgments of the bribed to provide special treatment not based on the merits or price of the product. This same effect can occur even when one merely offers a gift, that is, provides a service without intending or wishing that that service secure special treatment for the gift giver. The person who receives the gift may, consciously or otherwise, be disposed predictably to favor the interests of the gift giver. All that is needed to move a gift into the category of a bribe is that (a) the person receiving the gift be in a position to make a decision that enhances the assets of the giver and (b) the gift be of such a nontoken nature that it is reasonable to think that it may put the interests of the giver in a privileged status even when all else is equal.

As a result of these last considerations some corporations allow gift giving to their clients, or potential clients, only under the conditions that (a) the gift is not substantial enough to put the receiver into a conflict of interest position, and (b) the gift is given publicly and is not in any way a secret offering. Although these conditions seem sound in light of the reflections noted above, still we need to answer the question "Under what circumstances, if any, does an employee have a proportionate reason for running the risks involved in accepting gifts?" In answering this last question, Thomas Garrett urges that the basic question to be asked with regard to the practice of gift giving is this: "Will this gift, entertainment or service cause any reasonable person to suspect my independence of judgment?"[1] Garrett goes on to urge that it should

> be clear that infrequent gifts of only a nominal cost, ten dollars or less, and small advertisement gifts will be acceptable by policy or law. On the other hand, practically any cash gift is liable to raise eyebrows and create a suspicion of bias.[2]

These same considerations would, presumably, apply with respect to entertainment. So, then, as Garrett would have it, if the gift is nominal, publicly given, and not intended to secure any special advantage, the practice of gift giving would seem to be acceptable.

In spite of the reasonableness of Garrett's conclusion, however, some people still think that even a nominal gift could, all else being equal, secure an advantage not merited in terms of quality or price of product. Even an annual gift costing $10 has the *potential* for securing an advantage for the giver, an advantage not merited by the quality or price of the product. Accordingly, even though Garrett's proposal seems quite sensible, any gift, depending on the nature of the receiver and the circumstances involved *could* have the effect of a bribe, even when the gift is nominal and public.

Given these last reasons, it would appear that the only safe moral position to adopt is the one that prohibits all gift giving between corporate representatives and those with whom they would do business. In this latter regard, it is interesting to note that many major corporations now prohibit all gift giving, and those that allow it usually permit only nominal gifts. And, of course, some companies (perhaps too many) have perfectly ambiguous policy statements that provide no clear direction except to indicate that one should be "reasonable" and not do anything such that were it publicly disclosed it would embarrass the company.

In the end, the wisest policy to adopt would seem to be one of complete prohibition of any gift giving between companies (and their representatives) and persons with whom companies do (or wish to do) business either directly or indirectly.

## NOTES

1. Thomas Garrett, *Business Ethics* (New York: Appleton-Century Crofts, 1966), p. 78.
2. Ibid., p. 79.

# Corporate Policy Statements

Gifts, favors, and entertainment may be given to others at company expense only if they meet *all* of the following criteria: (a) they are consistent with accepted business practices, (b) they are of sufficiently limited value, and in a form that will not be construed as a bribe or payoff, (c) they are not in contravention of applicable law and generally accepted ethical standards, and (d) public disclosure of the facts will not embarrass the company. Secret commissions or other compensation to employees of customers (or their family members or associates) are contrary to company policy.

E. I. DuPont de Nemours & Co.

No IBM employee, or any member of his or her immediate family, can accept gratuities or gifts of money from a supplier, customer, or anyone in a business relationship. Nor can they accept a gift or consideration that could be perceived as having been offered because of the business relationship. "Perceived" simply means this: If you read about it in your local newspaper, would you wonder whether the gift just might have something to do with a business relationship? No IBM employee can give money or a gift of significant value to a supplier if it could reasonably be viewed as being done to gain a business advantage. If you are offered money or a gift of some value by a supplier or if one arrives at your home or office, let your manager know immediately. If the gift is perishable, your manager will arrange to donate it to a local charitable organization. Otherwise, it should be returned to the supplier. Whatever the circumstances, you or your manager should write the supplier a letter, explaining IBM's guidelines on the subject of gifts and gratuities. Of course, it is an accepted practice to talk business over a meal. So it is perfectly all right to occasionally allow a supplier or customer to pick up the check. Similarly, it frequently is necessary for a supplier, including IBM, to provide education and executive briefings for customers. It's all right to accept or provide some services in connection with this kind of activity—services such as transportation, food, or lodging. For instance, transportation in IBM or supplier planes to and from company locations, and lodging and food at company facilities are all right.

IBM

*Gifts.* Federal law restricts the extent of the deductibility of gifts to non-government clients, prospects, or suppliers to an amount not exceeding $25 per year to any individual. ARA strongly discourages gifts in excess of $25 per year to any individual, but in the event a gift is proposed to be made in excess of $25, approval must be secured in advance from both the General Counsel and the most senior Management Committee member to whom the operating component involved ultimately reports. Any gifts given must meet the following criteria: (a) gifts in the form of cash, stocks, bonds (or similar types of items) shall not be given regardless of amount; (b) gifts are in accord with normally accepted business practices, and comply with the policies of the organization employing the recipient; (c) such a practice would be considered legal and in accord with generally acceptable ethical practices in all governing jurisdictions; (d) subsequent public disclosure of all facts would not be embarrassing to ARA. *Entertainment:* Where entertainment of a nongovernment client, prospect, or supplier is involved, lavish expenditures are to be avoided. The cost and nature of the entertainment should be planned and carried out in a way which appropriately and reasonably furthers the conduct of the business of ARA. This, of course, does not mean that employees of prospective non-government clients may not be transported to, shown, and served at comparable service installations as part of the normal sales effort, at ARA expense.

ARA Services

# TRADE SECRETS AND PATENTS

*Case Study*

# Trade Secrets at Morris Computer

Carol Curtin graduated with a B.A. in Computer Science in 1993 from Purdue University. She was an exceptional student and was asked to stay on to do graduate work by her advisor, Dr. Chou Vue, who helped her secure a graduate research fellowship. Carol finished her Ph.D. in four years, and then stayed on at Purdue one more year in order to publish a paper from her dissertation. During that year she also coauthored two papers with Dr. Vue.

Carol thought she might eventually go into an academic career, but she wasn't totally convinced she wanted to be a teacher and so in 1998 she decided to take a job with Morris Computer Corporation in Indianapolis. Although Morris was not as attractive in terms of cutting-edge technology as some Silicon Valley firms, its focus was rather similar to Carol's research specialty. In fact, Dr. Vue had done some research for Morris in the 1980s that helped the firm achieve its first commercial success. Furthermore, Morris was only 60 miles from Purdue at West Lafayette. And Morris agreed to let Carol continue to collaborate with Dr. Vue on some research they had not been able to finish. This was important to Carol because she wanted to keep open her option of an academic appointment and she needed publications if she ever wanted a job in academia. Since Dr. Vue was an internationally known expert in the field, any publications she could coauthor with him would surely help her if she eventually wanted a scholarly career.

At the time she was hired, Morris Computer told Carol that it considered all information she generated while employed there to be proprietary. It said that all information had to be kept confidential until it was commercialized. Nevertheless, it permitted Carol to work with Dr. Vue as long as none of Morris's trade secrets were revealed to anyone. An attorney from Morris told Carol that the work she was doing with Dr. Vue had to be publishable, and nonpatentable, and hence open to use by Morris as well as other corporations and individuals. Carol agreed.

By May 2001 Carol was deep into chip design for Morris; she was head of the Chip Design Department. But things had not been going well for over a year. She simply had not been able to improve much on Morris's M-200 chip. The company was counting on her design team for its next generation product, but they had essentially made no progress in a year. She discussed her problem in a very general way with Dr. Vue, a way that she felt sure would not reveal any of Morris's trade secrets, but he was noncommittal and said he really hadn't even thought about things in that area of research for so many years that he would not be able to comment. Carol thought that was odd, since she had heard Dr. Vue talk about some of these issues with one of his new graduate students, but she let the matter pass without comment.

While working the next weekend in Dr. Vue's Purdue laboratory, Carol mistakenly punched in a wrong sequence on her computer and up popped a document prepared by Dr. Vue for one of Morris's competitors, Compuchip. Evidently, Dr. Vue had been doing contract work for Compuchip. The document specified a chip design that would enable Compuchip to leapfrog Morris's M-200. Furthermore, it was exactly what Carol had been looking for—it solved precisely the problem she had not been able to solve in over a year. Carol could not stop reading the document. It was Vue at his best, with an elegant, simple solution that had completely escaped her. She would never have thought of it. Carol absorbed the entire document in five minutes. As she hurriedly logged off and left Lafayette for Indianapolis, Carol began to sort out her options.

## FOR DISCUSSION

What should Carol Curtin do? Why?

# Trade Secrets at Atlas Chemical Corp.

Rudy Kern joined Atlas Chemical just after obtaining his master's degree in chemical engineering from Purdue University in 1985. His thesis was on the catalysis of heavy metal-chlorine reactions, and he was hired by Atlas to work on a chloride process for the production of titanium dioxide, $TiO_2$, an important ingredient in paints and paper. Kern took the position for several reasons. First, the job was based squarely on his area of expertise. Second, Kern was a born tinkerer, he wanted to get out of the laboratory and into the solving of large-scale production problems. Finally, he saw a good promotion opportunity in that the $TiO_2$ chloride process was relatively new; as Atlas moved from the research stage to production, some of the technical staff had a good chance to move into management slots.

Atlas encountered major problems in scaling up its $TiO_2$ process. It had begun experimental work in 1980, but did not get its first small plant into production until 1995, and it wasn't until 2000 that the firm's $TiO_2$ project broke even. From 1985 on, Kern was the major innovator in the project's development. He was responsible for most of the breakthroughs that enabled Atlas to move from the pilot-plant stage to full-scale production. Kern received excellent performance evaluations, above average salary increases, and by 1993 he applied for a management position, but was rejected on the grounds that he was too valuable as an engineer. Management explained that he was the only person aware of all the $TiO_2$ production technology and that he was needed on the plant floor. Kern did receive a significant raise that put him just a notch below the plant's manager on Atlas's pay scale, and he was titled Master Engineer, the top engineering title at Atlas. Nevertheless, by 2000, Kern was dissatisfied with his position at Atlas. He could see that from here on the project would be a moneymaker for Atlas. Most of the bugs had been worked out of the process, which didn't leave Kern with much to do that was not routine. It didn't look like Kern would make the management ranks. As

183

Kern saw it, his career had plateaued at Atlas. He began to read engineering publications with an eye on the help-wanted ads.

Finding a position with another firm was more difficult than Kern initially envisaged. He was narrowly specialized in a particular field of chloride chemistry, and furthermore, Atlas was the only firm using a chloride process to produce $TiO_2$; other firms used a sulfate process. This made it very difficult for Kern to utilize his skills for another $TiO_2$ producer. The fact that his expertise was narrowly based and highly technical seemed to preclude him from finding a new position.

In early 2000, however, Kern noticed the following ad:

Major, innovative, chemical firm seeks experienced $TiO_2$ process engineer. Excellent opportunity for a person presently at the senior process engineering or plant production foreman level. Must have extensive $TiO_2$ production process experience. Salary open. Title: Plant Engineer, Technical Services. Equal Opportunity Employer.

Kern applied, and soon was contacted by Vulcan Chemical Corporation, which informed him that it was interested in interviewing him, since it was planning to use a chloride process to produce $TiO_2$. Prior to the interview, however, and prior to contact with any Vulcan representatives, Vulcan asked Kern to sign and mail an agreement pledging that he would "not disclose to Vulcan Chemical Corp., either during pre-employment contacts or in the course of any subsequent employment with Vulcan, any information that I know to be the proprietary information, data, or trade secrets of any third party." Once Kern complied with the request, he was interviewed by Vulcan and got the job. He received a 25 percent salary boost, and a promise that he would be considered for a management position as the project developed.

When Atlas learned of Kern's plan to join Vulcan, it already knew of Vulcan's strategy to develop a $TiO_2$ chloride process. It immediately went to the State Court in New Jersey and obtained a restraining order blocking Kern from working for Vulcan in the $TiO_2$ position.

In subsequent court proceedings, Atlas allowed that there was nothing mysterious or secret about $TiO_2$ itself; any physical chemist could accurately enumerate its characteristics. Basically it is a white powder that has a high capacity for scattering light, and is hence opaque. This accounts for its ability to impart whiteness (or opacity) to paint, paper, rubber, etc.

About 92 percent of world $TiO_2$ production of roughly 3 million tons is produced by the sulfate process, which begins by dissolving titanium ore in sulfuric acid. The process is relatively uncomplicated, but it does use a lot of sulfuric acid, and it contaminates the acid to the extent that much of it cannot be recycled readily. The sulfate process leaves its producer a significant disposal problem, a distinct disadvantage in a highly competitive context and an era of environmental concern. The chlorine process involves simple chemistry. Titanium ore is reacted with chlorine to produce titanium tetrachloride, which is then oxidized to produce $TiO_2$ and chlorine. The advantage of the chlorine process is that chlorine, one of the initial reactants, can be recovered in relatively pure form and reused. Although any high school science student would understand the basic chemical reaction of the chlorine process, the production process is technologically complex. The oxidation of titanium tetrachloride must be accomplished at 2,200° F, at which temperature the tetrachloride is very corrosive. Furthermore, a complex catalyzing procedure must be employed to optimize reaction time. It had taken Atlas almost twenty years to work out the technical problems in its $TiO_2$ process.

Atlas is at present the only producer of $TiO_2$ via the chloride process. It produces 88 percent of $TiO_2$ worldwide. It started work on the process in 1980, along with three other firms, but Atlas was the only firm to move beyond the pilot plant to production. It began producing $TiO_2$ commercially via the process in 1995, encountered numerous problems, and only started to realize a profit on the process in 2000. Atlas calculates its research and development expenses for the process to be $42 million over twenty years. The process is reliably estimated to have a lower operating cost than the sulfate process.

In court proceedings, Atlas stated that its $TiO_2$ process was based on trade secrets. It maintained that none of its trade secrets were patentable; its success was based on innumerable tricks of the trade that would be readily understood by any process engineer but that were based on extensive trial and error research that would be very difficult to duplicate in total. Atlas stated that Kern had developed most of these secrets and that he knew more about them than anyone else in the firm. Atlas made available its Trade Secret Policy Statement, which all employees are required to read and sign in agreement. The policy requires that employees not disclose Atlas's trade secrets or use them for their own or others' advantage either while at Atlas or after they leave the company. Atlas also said that it requires each scientist to record his discoveries and sign a document stating that the discoveries so recorded were the sole property of Atlas. Furthermore, Atlas indicated that it has a policy to restrict access to research data. As its top engineer, Kern had to have access to all such data, but Atlas claimed that Kern was the only scientist with access to all its $TiO_2$ trade-secret research data irrespective of who developed the data. Atlas argued that it would be impossible for Kern, as Plant Engineer for Vulcan's $TiO_2$ project, to serve without making use of Atlas's extensive trade secrets. Atlas also pointed to its heavy research and development expense over many years, and the fact that it only recently had begun to cover these costs. Atlas admitted that sooner or later someone would solve the complex production problems and develop a similar chloride process to make $TiO_2$. But, having spent $42 million to develop its process, Atlas argued that it should be allowed to keep any competitor from solving the difficult engineering problems by illegitimately securing Atlas's trade secrets.

In its memorandum to the court, Vulcan declared that it had invented its own chloride process and now wanted to move to the pilot plant stage and then to production. Its new process, it asserted, was a trade secret. It added that it in no way was seeking, and would not seek, Atlas's trade secrets. Atlas responded by saying the basic chemistry has to be essentially the same, hence, Kern would almost of necessity encounter the same or very similar scale-up problems he had already encountered and solved at Atlas. Atlas said that it did not believe that Vulcan had developed a new process and that Vulcan had provided no evidence its process was new. Atlas added that it thought Vulcan's ad was directed at one and only one person: Rudy Kern.

In Kern's memorandum to the court, he acknowledged that Atlas had legitimate trade secrets in the $TiO_2$ area and that he knew the secrets, but he claimed he would not disclose or use such information. Vulcan, he stated, had not asked him to reveal Atlas's secrets, and he fully intended to abide by the document Vulcan asked him to sign saying he would safeguard Atlas's secrets. He noted that he had never signed a covenant with Atlas not to work with a competitor if he left Atlas. He asked the court to remember that Atlas was not alleging that he used Atlas's secrets, or that he took or copied Atlas's documents, or in any way actually violated Atlas's confidentiality. He reminded the court of his narrow background in $TiO_2$ chemistry, noted that Atlas and Vulcan were the only two firms currently experimenting with the chloride process, and argued that he had a legitimate right to change jobs and attempt to better himself as long as he did not violate his confidentiality pledge to Atlas.

In response, Atlas claimed the issue was not whether Kern intended to disclose or use Atlas's trade secrets, but, rather, whether he could avoid doing so. Atlas claimed that even if Kern had the best of intentions, the processes would be so similar that it would strain credulity to believe that Kern would: (1) not indicate to his employees when they were going into a blind alley, (2) fail to in fact point his employees down the trail that Atlas had successfully pursued, and hence (3) reveal Atlas's trade secrets. As project engineer for Vulcan, Kern's task is to maximize production efficiency. Since Kern had already attained that end for Atlas via its trade secrets, Atlas asked how Kern could do the same for Vulcan without violating Atlas's trade secrets. Atlas conceded it had never asked Kern to sign a covenant saying that Kern would not work for a competitor if he left Atlas. Atlas said it thought such covenants would not be held to be legal. However, Atlas maintained that if Kern joined Vulcan he should be required to work on an area other than $TiO_2$, and that he should not communicate with others at Vulcan anything about his $TiO_2$ knowledge developed at Atlas.

## FOR DISCUSSION

In your opinion is Atlas legally entitled to bar Kern from working as $TiO_2$ project engineer for Vulcan? Why or why not? Is Kern morally justified in accepting the position at Vulcan? Why or why not? Is Vulcan morally justified in hiring Kern? Why or why not?

*Robert E. Frederick*
*Milton Snoeyenbos*

# Trade Secrets, Patents, and Morality

Suppose that company M develops a super-computer that gives it a competitive advantage, but decides that, rather than marketing it, it will use the computer to provide services to users. In doing so, it keeps its technical information secret. If another company, N, were to steal the computer, N would be subject to moral blame as well as legal penalty. But suppose that, without M's consent, N obtained M's technical information, which thereby enabled N to copy M's computer. Should N then be subject to moral blame and legal penalty?

At first glance it seems that N should be held morally and legally accountable; but N has a line of defense which supports its position. Information, or knowledge, unlike a physical asset, can be possessed by more than one individual or firm at any one time. Thus, in obtaining M's information N did not diminish M's information; since M possesses exactly the same information it had before, N cannot be said to have stolen it. Furthermore, everyone regards the dissemination of knowledge as a good thing; it has obvious social utility. M's competitive advantage, moreover, was not a good thing, since it could have enabled M to drive other firms out of the computer service business; M might have established a monopoly. Thus, M has no right to keep the information to itself, and, in the interests of social utility, N had a right to obtain M's information. Hence, N should be praised rather than blamed for its act.

This defense of N raises the general question of whether a firm's use of trade secrets or patents to protect information is justifiable. If it is not, then N may at least be morally justified in using clandestine means to obtain M's information. If there is a justification for allowing trade secrets and patents, then, not only is N's act unjustifiable, but we also have a basis for saying that the release of certain information in certain contexts to N by an employee of M is unjustifiable. In this paper we argue that there are both consequentialist and nonconsequentialist reasons for allowing firms to protect *their* proprietary information via patents and trade secrets. On the other hand, an individual has a right to liberty and a right to use *his* knowledge and skills to better himself. These rights place certain constraints on what can qualify as a trade secret or patentable item of information. We begin with a discussion of present patent and trade secret law.

Patents differ significantly from trade secrets. A patent provides a legal safeguard of certain information itself, but the information must be novel. Some internal information generated by a firm may not meet the U.S. Patent Office's standards of inventiveness. Then, too, even if an item is patentable, there may be disadvantages to the firm in seeking and securing a patent on it and/or advantages to the firm in just trying to keep the information secret. There are legal costs in securing a patent, and patents have to be secured in every country in which one wishes to protect the information. In the U.S. a patent expires in seventeen years, and, since it is not renewable, the information then becomes public domain. Furthermore, since a patent is a public document, it both reveals research directions and encourages competitors to invent related products that are just dissimilar enough to avoid a patent infringement suit. So there are ample reasons for a firm to keep information secret and not attempt to secure a patent. If a firm can keep the information secret, it may have a long-term advantage over competitors. The disadvantage is that, unlike a patented device or information, the law provides no protection for a trade secret itself. A competitor can analyze an unpatented product in any way, and, if it discovers the trade secret, it is free to use that information or product. For example, if a firm analyzes Coca-Cola and uncovers the secret formula, it can market a product chemically identical to it, although, of course, it cannot use the name "Coca-Cola," since that is protected by trademark law.

It is, however, unlawful to employ "improper means" to secure another's trade secret. Legal protection of trade secrets is based on the agent's duty of confidentiality. Section 395 of the *Restatement of Agency* imposes a duty on the agent "not to use or communicate information confidentially given to him by the principal or acquired by him during the course of or on account of his agency . . . to the injury of the principal, on his own account or on behalf of another . . . unless the information is a matter of general knowledge." This duty extends beyond the length of the work contract; if the employee moves to a new job with another firm, his obligation to not disclose his previous principal's trade secrets is still in effect.

Since patents are granted by the U.S. Patent Office in accordance with the U.S. Patent Code, patent law cases are federal cases, whereas trade secrets cases are handled by state courts in accordance with state laws. There is no definition of "trade secret" adopted by every state. A few follow the definition in Section 757 of the *Restatement of Torts*, according to which a trade secret consists of a pattern, device, formula or compilation of information used in business and designed to give the employer an opportunity to obtain an advantage over his competitors who neither know nor use the information. On this definition virtually anything an employer prefers to keep confidential could count as a trade secret. Most states use the definition of "trade secret" found in the Uniform Trade Secrets Act:

> [a trade secret is any] information, including a formula, pattern, compilation, program, device, methods, technique, or process, that: (i) derives independent economic value, actual or potential, from not being generally known to, and not being readily ascertainable by proper means by, other persons who can obtain economic value from its disclosure or use, and (ii) is the subject of efforts that are reasonable under the circumstances to maintain its secrecy.[1]

With terms such as "actual or potential" in the definition, the UTSA definition is in that sense broader than that found in the *Restatement*.

In practice the *Restatement* specifies several factors it suggests that courts should consider in deciding whether information is legally protectable: (1) the extent to which the information is known outside the business, (2) the extent to which it is known to employees in the firm, (3) the extent to which the firm used measures to guard secrecy of the information, (4) the value of the information to the firm and to its competitors, (5) the amount of money the firm spent to develop the information, and (6) how easily the information may be developed or properly duplicated.

According to (1), (2), (4), (5), and (6), not all internally generated information will count legally as a trade secret. And, via (3), the firm must take measures to guard its secrets: " . . . a person entitled to a trade secret . . . must not fail to take all proper and reasonable steps to keep it secret. He cannot lie back and do nothing to preserve its essential secret quality, particularly when the subject matter of the process becomes known to a number of individuals involved in its use or is observed in the course of manufacturing in the plain view of others" (*Gallowhur Chemical Corp.* v. *Schwerdle*, 37 N. J. Super. 385, 397, 117 A2d 416, 423; *J. T. Healy & Son, Inc.*, v. *James Murphy & Son, Inc.*, 1970 Mass. Adv. Sheets 1051, 260 NE2d 723 [Ill. App. 1959]). In addition to attempting to keep its information secret, the firm must inform its employees as to what data are regarded as secret: there "must be a strong showing that the knowledge was gained in confidence," (*Wheelabrator Corp.* v. *Fogle*, 317 F. Supp. 633 [D. C. La. 1970]), and employees must be warned that certain information is regarded as a trade secret (*Gallo* v. *Norris Dispensers, Inc.*, 315 F. Supp. 38 [D. C. Mo. 1970]). Most firms have their employees sign a document that (a) specifies what its trade secrets or types of trade secrets are, and (b) informs them that improper use of the trade secrets violates confidentiality and subjects them to litigation.

If a firm has information that really is a legitimate trade secret, if it informs its employees that this information is regarded as secret, and informs them that improper use violates confidentiality, then it may be able to establish its case in court, in which case it is entitled to injunctive relief and damages. But the courts also typically examine how the defendant in a trade secret case obtained the information. For example, if an employee transfers from company M to company N, taking M's documents with him to N, then there is clear evidence of a breach of confidentiality (or "bad faith") if the evidence can be produced by M. But trade secret law is equity law, a basic principle of which is that bad faith cannot be presumed. In equity law the maxim "Every dog has one free bite" obtains, i.e., a dog cannot be presumed to be vicious until he bites someone. Thus, if the employee took no producible hard evidence in the form of objects or documents, but instead took what was "in her head" or what she could memorize, then M may have to wait for its former employee to overtly act. By then it may be very difficult to produce convincing evidence that would establish a breach of confidentiality.

In considering possible justifications of patents and trade secrets, we have to take into consideration the public good or social utility, the firm's rights and interests, and the individual's rights and interests. Our aim should be to maximize utility while safeguarding legitimate rights.

As Michael Baram has noted, "A major concern of our society is progress through the promotion and utilization of new technology. To sustain and enhance this form of progress, it is necessary to optimize the flow of information and innovation all the way from conception to public use."[2] Given the assumption that technological progress is conducive to social utility, and that the dissemination of technological information is a major means to progress, the key issue is how to maximize information generation and dissemination.

One answer is to require public disclosure of all important generated information, and allow unrestricted use of that information. In some cases this is appropriate, e.g., government sponsored research conducted by a private firm is disclosed and can be used by other firms. Within a capitalistic context, however, it is doubtful that a general disclosure requirement would maximize social utility. The innovative firm would develop information leading to a new product only to see that product manufactured and marketed by another firm at a lower price because the latter firm did not incur research costs. The proposal probably would also result in less competition; only firms with strong financial and marketing structures would survive. Small, innovative firms would not have the protection of their technological advantages necessary to establish a competitive position against industry giants. If both research effort and competition were diminished by this proposal, then the "progress" Baram mentions would not be maximized—at least not in the area of marketable products.

In a market economy, then, there are reasons grounded in social utility for allowing firms to have some proprietary information. The laws based on such a justification should, in part, be structured with an eye to overall utility, and in fact they are so structured. Patents, for example, expire in 17 years. While the patent is in force it allows the firm to recoup research expenses and generate a profit by charging monopolistic prices. Patent protection also encourages the generation of new knowledge. The firm holding the patent, and realizing profits because of it, is encouraged to channel some of those profits to research, since its patent is of limited duration. Given that its patent will expire, the firm needs to generate new, patentable information to maximize profits. Competitors are encouraged to develop competing products that are based on new, patentable information.

Patent protection should not, however, extend indefinitely; it would not only extend indefinitely the higher costs that consumers admittedly bear while a patent is in force, but in certain cases, it could also stifle innovation. A firm holding a basic patent might either "sit on" it or strengthen its monopoly position. A company like Cisco, for example, with the basic internet infrastructure patents, might use its profits to fund research until it had built up an impenetrable patent network, but then cut research drastically and rest relatively secure in the knowledge that its competitors were frozen out of the market. Patents allow monopoly profits for a limited period of time, but patent law should not be structured to forever legitimatize a monopoly.

Richard De George has recently offered another argument to the conclusion that the right to proprietary information is a limited right:

> Knowledge is not an object which one can keep locked up as long as one likes. . . . Whatever knowledge a company produces is always an increment to the knowledge developed by society or by previous people in society and passed from one generation to another. Any new invention is made by people who learned a great deal from the general store of knowledge before they could bring what they knew to bear on a particular problem. Though we can attribute them to particular efforts of individuals or teams, therefore, inventions and discoveries also are the result of those people who developed them and passed on their knowledge to others. In this way every advance in knowledge is social and belongs ultimately to society, even though for practical purposes we can assign it temporarily to a given individual or firm.[3]

Allowing the firm to use proprietary information has utility, but the right to such information is limited. In point of fact, although we have stressed the utility of allowing use of proprietary information, U.S. patent and copyright laws were enacted during the industrial revolution to reduce secrecy. Patent laws allow limited monopolies in return for public disclosure of the information on which the patent is based. Thus, patent laws provide information to competitors and encourage them to develop their own patentable information that not only generates new products, but also adds to the store of available knowledge.

If allowing limited use of proprietary information has utility, it is still an open question as to the proper limits of such use. Does the present seventeen-year patent limit maximize utility? This is an empirical question that we will not attempt to answer. Although most experts and industry representatives believe the present limit is about right, U.S. drug firms have recently argued that research and development time and Federal Drug Administration (FDA) testing and licensing requirements are so extensive that social disutility results, as well as disutility for innovative firms.

Although patents expire and the information protected can then be used by anyone, trade secrets can extend indefinitely according to present law. In 1623, the Zildjian family in Turkey developed a metallurgical process for making excellent cymbals. Now centered in Massachusetts, the family has maintained their secret to the present day, and they still produce excellent cymbals. Preservation of such secrets may well have utility for firms holding the secrets, but does it have social utility? Not necessarily, as the following case illustrates. Suppose that Jones, a shadetree mechanic, develops a number of small unpatentable improvements in the internal combustion engine's basic design. The result is an engine that is cheap, reliable, and gets 120 miles per gallon. With no resources to mass produce and market his engine, Jones decides to sell to the highest bidder. XYZ oil company, with immense oil reserves, buys the information. To protect its oil interests, it keeps the information secret. Now suppose it is in fact against XYZ's interests to divulge the information. Then, to calculate overall utility we have to weigh the social disutility of keeping the information secret against the social utility of keeping the existing oil industry intact. Although utility calculations are difficult, it seems clear that disutility would arise from allowing the information to be kept secret.

If the preservation of *some* secrets has social disutility, it also seems clear that requiring immediate disclosure of *all* trade secrets in a capitalistic context would have disutility as well. The arguments here parallel those we developed in discussing patents. Again, specification of the appropriate duration of a trade secret is a utility calculation. The calculation will, however, have to take into consideration the fact that the law provides no protection for the secret itself. The firm with a significant investment in a trade secret always runs the risk that a competitor may legitimately uncover and use the secret.

Allowing patents and trade secrets has obvious utility for the firm that possesses them, but the firm also has a *right* to at least the limited protection of its information. It has a *legal* right to expect that its employees will live up to their work contracts, and employees have a correlative duty to abide by their contracts. The work contract is entered into voluntarily by employer and employee; if a prospective employee does not like the terms of a (legitimate) trade secret provision of a contract, she does not have to take the job. The normal employment contract specifies that the firm owns all employee-generated information. Even if the employee transfers from firm M to firm N, M still owns the information produced when he was employed there, and the employee is obligated not to reveal that information.

The moral basis of contract enforceability, including contractual provisions for the protection of proprietary information, is twofold. First, as argued, allowing trade secrets has social utility in addition to utility for the firm. The institution of contract compliance is necessary for the systematic and orderly functioning of business, and a sound business environment is essential to general social utility. However, if only a few people broke their contracts, business would continue to survive. This leads to the second moral basis for adhering to the provisions of one's contract.

If an individual breaks his contract, then he must either regard himself as an exception to the rule banning contract-breaking, or he must believe, in Kant's terms, that a maxim concerning contract-breaking is universalizable. But if we agree that in moral matters everyone ought to adopt the moral point of view, and that point of view requires that one not make himself an exception to the rule, it follows that the person in question is not justified in breaking the rule. On the other hand, if he claims that breaking the contract is in accordance with a maxim, then we can properly demand to have the maxim specified. Clearly the maxim cannot be something like: "I will keep my promises, except on those occasions where it is not to my advantage to keep the promises." For if everyone followed this maxim, there would be no institution of promising or promise-keeping. Since the maxim is not universalizable, it cannot legitimately be appealed to as a sanction for action. Of course, other maxims are available, and the contract-breaker may claim that his act is in accordance with one of these maxims. But note that this reply at least tacitly commits the person to the moral point of view; he is agreeing that everyone ought to act only on universalizable maxims. The only dispute, then, is whether his maxim is in fact universalizable. If we can show him that it is not, he is bound to admit that he is not morally justified in breaking the contract. As a standard, then, contracts should be kept, and where an individual breaks, or contemplates breaking, a contract, the burden is on him to produce a universalizable maxim for his action.

Our analysis does not, however, imply that a person is morally obligated to abide by all contracts; some contracts, or provisions of certain contracts, may be morally and/or legally unacceptable. A person does have a right to liberty and a right to use her knowledge and skills to earn a living. Thus, firm M cannot legitimately specify that *all* knowledge an employee gains while at M is proprietary. This would prohibit the person from obtaining employment at another firm; in effect the work contract would amount to a master-slave relationship. As the *Restatement of Torts* appropriately specifies, only certain information qualifies as a legitimate trade secret. Furthermore, the employee brings to her job certain knowledge and skills that typically are matters of public domain, and, on the job, the good employee develops her capacities. As the court noted in *Donohue* v. *Permacil Tape Corporation*: an ex-employee's general knowledge and capabilities "belong to him as an individual for the transaction of any business in which he may engage, just the same as any part of the skill, knowledge, information or education which was received by him before entering the employment. . . . On terminating his employment, he has a right to take them with him."[4]

Given that an individual's rights to liberty and to use his knowledge and skills to better himself are primary rights, and hence cannot be overriden by utility considerations, the burden clearly is on the firm to: (1) specify to employees what it regards as its trade secrets, and (2) make sure the secrets are legitimate trade secrets. In addition, a company can employ certain pragmatic tactics to protect its trade secrets. It can fragment research activities so that only a few employees know all the secrets. It can restrict access to research data and operational areas. It can develop pension and consulting policies for ex-employees that motivate them not to join competitors for a period of time. More importantly, it can develop a corporate atmosphere that motivates the individual to remain with the firm.

We began by sketching an argument that company N was justified in obtaining information about company M's computer without M's consent. Our conclusion is that N's argument is specious. Utility considerations justify allowing M to keep its information secret for a period of time, and any employee of M who divulges M's secret information to N is morally blameworthy because she violates her contractual obligations to M.

## NOTES

1. *Uniform Trade Secrets Act* §§ 1–12, 14 U.L.A. 437–467 (1990 & Supp. 1993).

2. Michael Baram, "Trade Secrets: What Price Loyalty," *Harvard Business Review* 46, no. 6 (November-December 1968): 64–74.

3. Richard T. DeGeorge, *Business Ethics* (New York: Macmillan, 1982), p. 207.

4. Cited in Baram, "Trade Secrets," p. 71.

# EMPLOYEE PRODUCTIVITY MONITORING

# Monitoring Electronic Mail

In 1990 SRI International posed computer related scenarios having a possible ethical dimension to a number of individuals identified as "experts in computer ethics." Here is one of the scenarios:

> The information security manager in a large company was also the access control administrator of a large electronic mail system operated for "company business" among its employees. The security manager routinely monitored the contents of electronic correspondence among employees. He discovered that a number of employees were using the system for personal purposes; the correspondence included love letters, disagreements between married partners, plans for homosexual liaisons, and a football betting pool. The security manager routinely informed the human resources department director and the corporate security officer about these communications and gave them printed listings of them. In some cases, managers punished employees on the basis of the content of the electronic mail messages. Employees objected to the monitoring of their electronic mail, claiming they had the same right of privacy as they had using the company's telephone system or internal paper interoffice mail system.

The experts assessing the scenarios were asked to judge issues related to the scenarios as "unethical" (meaning not conforming to an appropriate

From Donn B. Parker, Susan Swope, and Bruce N. Baker, *Electronic Conflicts in Information and Computer Science, Technology, and Business* (Wellesley, Mass.: QED Information Sciences, Inc., 1992).

197

personal standard of conduct), "not unethical" (meaning not violating an appropriate personal standard of conduct), and "no ethics issue" (meaning no appropriate personal standard of conduct was involved or the action was clearly illegal). For the above scenario, vote as to whether the following actions are unethical, not unethical, or no ethics issue as defined above: (1) information security manager—monitoring electronic correspondence of employees; (2) information security manager—informing manager of abuse; (3) employees—using electronic mail system for personal communications; (4) information security manager—failing to ask for rules on personal e-mail use from management; (5) top management—punishing some employees based on the content of their e-mail messages. Once you have voted go on to read how the "experts" voted and the summaries of their opinions.

### Information Security Manager: Monitoring Electronic Correspondence of Employees

|  | Total | Unethical | Not Unethical | No Ethics Issue |
|---|---|---|---|---|
| General Vote | 25 | 14 | 11 | 0 |

## OPINIONS

Monitoring e-mail was unethical according to a narrow majority of group members because the employees apparently had no warning that they might be monitored or that their use of the system was restricted. They were thus less likely to send discreet messages. Under the circumstances, management was taking unfair advantage of the employees. Furthermore, some participants argued that e-mail should be given the same rights to privacy as postal mail.

The sizeable minority who voted that the information security manager did not act unethically noted the considerable differences between U.S. postal mail and e-mail. E-mail, as well as telephone systems and internal mail in the workplace, are company property and resources. No rights of privacy extend to individuals using property or resources supplied for company (as opposed to personal) business. E-mail is also by its nature more accessible than other forms of communication. Finally, they argued, monitoring all communication forms is necessary for management control of its resources, particularly when a company has trade secrets or classified information to protect.

**Information Security Manager: Informing Management of Abuse**

|  | Total | Unethical | Not Unethical | No Ethics Issue |
|---|---|---|---|---|
| General Vote | 24 | 22 | 2 | 0 |

## OPINIONS

Giving management printouts of the actual messages is quite different. Although a summary of the types of calls made would be acceptable, all but two of the general group considered it highly unethical to provide others with the detailed content of clearly personal messages. The right to privacy is the central ethical principle. Material security considerations do override privacy considerations, but what the security manager is reporting has nothing to do with security (unless the relationships make individuals vulnerable to blackmail). Even then, in the absence of a prohibition on the personal use of the e-mail system, providing the messages verbatim to management is unethical.

The two individuals who did not consider the action unethical reiterated that employees have no right to expect privacy in e-mail. The facility is meant for business communications and is subject to management scrutiny.

**Employees: Using Electronic Mail System
for Personal Communications**

|  | Total | Unethical | Not Unethical | No Ethics Issue |
|---|---|---|---|---|
| General Vote | 25 | 10 | 11 | 4 |

## OPINIONS

The general group was divided on the ethicality of using e-mail for personal purposes. More than half the group believed that type of use was not unethical or not an ethics issue based on the absence of a clearly stated company policy forbidding the use of e-mail for other than company business. Several participants asserted that if the company explicitly prohibited personal use, the employees would be acting unethically. Such use would also be unethical if it interfered with the employees' job performance. Otherwise, according to some, personal use of e-mail might be indiscreet or unwise, but not unethical. Employees should realize that the system can be monitored and, if security considerations are involved, probably is. Some participants characterized betting information as not personal or private, particularly given its illegality.

A sizeable minority of the general group contended that employees' personal use of corporate resources was unethical prima facie. It is a misuse of corporate facilities and could reduce system effectiveness. One participant believed this use could constitute petty larceny or even a felony. Unless a clear policy permits personal use, employees should treat e-mail resources the same as petty cash or a company car.

### Information Security Manager: Failing to Ask for Rules on Personal E-mail Use from Management

|  | Total | Unethical | Not Unethical | No Ethics Issue |
|---|---|---|---|---|
| General Vote | 24 | 11 | 3 | 10 |

### Top Management: Failing to Set Rules and Inform Employees

|  | Total | Unethical | Not Unethical | No Ethics Issue |
|---|---|---|---|---|
| General Vote | 23 | 20 | 2 | 1 |

## OPINIONS

The majority opinions on rule setting reflect the relative obligations and responsibilities of the information security manager and top management. These participants argued that management is responsible for setting clear policies, defining the consequences of violating them, and ensuring that each employee understands them. Depending on a policy's importance, management may even insist that employees sign an acknowledgment that they have been briefed and understand the policy. The policy should then be applied consistently. Therefore, most group members believed enforcing an unstated or fuzzy policy that violates employees' apparent expectations of privacy is unethical. Those who disagreed iterated that e-mail by its nature is not private and cannot be compared to the U.S. Postal Service.

Conversely, a majority argued the information security manager is not responsible for ensuring that policies are set or promulgated, but only for carrying them out. For this reason, a majority of the general group decided that his failure to ask for a rule on personal e-mail use was either not unethical or no ethical issue was involved. A significant minority did think the information security manager was ethically obliged to ask for a clear, publicized policy from management. In its absence, however, he is acting unethically by monitoring the e-mail because the lack of a policy infers that the employees' privacy will be respected.

### Top Management: Punishing Some Employees Based on the Content of Their E-mail Messages

|  | Total | Unethical | Not Unethical | No Ethics Issue |
| --- | --- | --- | --- | --- |
| General Vote | 25 | 23 | 0 | 2 |

## OPINIONS

Almost everyone contended that imposing a penalty based on message content was unethical, for several reasons. First, employees apparently did not know that their e-mail would be monitored. It would be appropriate to punish employees for violations of a clearly stated, and well-promulgated company policy, but not for one they were unaware existed.

Second, because management knew the actual contents of the messages, they seemed to be applying employee sanctions based on behavior indicated by the message content rather than for misuse of e-mail. Management acted improperly in disciplining employees for non-job-related aspects of their personal lives. This was a violation of the employees' right to privacy and freedom of action in their personal lives.

Third, because employees were punished "in some cases," management again appeared to be acting on the content of the message rather than the unauthorized use of company resources. Such disciplinary actions are also arbitrary. Management should be consistent in applying sanctions.

If the information security manager had given management a simple list of those who were using e-mail for personal reasons, if the employees knew such use was against company policy, and if penalties were applied consistently, then according to the participants, management would be acting well within its authority. Otherwise, management acted unethically.

## GENERAL PRINCIPLES

Employers have a right to limit or prohibit employees' use of company resources. However, these limits must be clear, must be made known to all employees in advance, and must be consistently enforced.

In the absence of a policy forbidding use of e-mail or other intraoffice communications, reading communications intended for others is a violation of privacy.

It is wrong to monitor employee's personal communications without their knowing that monitoring is at least a possibility. It is an invasion of privacy. However, employees' consent, beyond their deciding to continue their employment with the company, is not necessary.

When using company e-mail, individuals should realize that by nature it is not private. It is inherently more accessible, more open to others' perusal than other intraoffice mail.

Employers have no right to impose sanctions on employees for non-job related behavior.

When personal habits interfere with job performance, they become legitimate management concerns. Otherwise, employees have the right to privacy and freedom of action in their personal lives.

A company has the right to engage in surveillance of employees when suspicions of explicit wrongdoings cannot prudently be ignored.

Unauthorized use of company resources may be construed as petty larceny or even a felony, e.g., California Penal Code Section 502—unauthorized use by an employee of over $100 of computer services.

A security officer has a right and duty to act on information clearly inimical to his employer's legitimate and ethical business interests.

*Ernest Kallman*

# Electronic Monitoring of Employees: Issues and Guidelines

## INTRODUCTION

Considerable controversy surrounds the use of computers by management for electronic monitoring [EM] of employee productivity. The central issue is whether or not the amount of control that this technology places in management's possession is so intrusive that it constitutes an invasion of employee privacy. A more practical issue from management's perspective is the negative effect on productivity when employees believe that their privacy is being violated. This paper evaluates these issues and proposes a balance between control and privacy that can enable management to successfully utilize electronic monitoring to achieve increased productivity without invading privacy.

Electronic monitoring means the use of specialized computer software for the capture and analysis of data to measure the quantity of work being done by employees using computer terminals. Examples include the counting of keystrokes by data entry clerks or the number of calls taken by a telephone operator or an airline reservationist. EM results in the ability of management to use computers to monitor, supervise and evaluate employee performances electronically. It is a major step toward the automation of employee control.

The scope of EM systems is large and increasing rapidly. In 1987, the Office of Technology Assessment (OTA) estimated that 20 to 35 percent of terminal users are being monitored (27, p. 40), and that this represents several million employees being monitored in 60,000 companies. Michael Smith at the University of Wisconsin estimates that "by the year 2000, there will be 30 to 40 million terminal users and as many as 50 to 75 per-

From *Journal of Systems Managment* 44, no. 6 (June 1993): 17–21.

cent of them will be monitored" (4). This trend will definitely change the way supervision is performed. It is, therefore, critically important that today's management understand how to deal with the issue of EM technology and privacy.

## ARGUMENTS IN FAVOR OF EM

Authorities (courts, legislatures, etc.) have historically allowed employers broad rights of observation and record keeping when monitoring workers in the factory or office (27, p. 13). These rights are based on the employer ownership of the premises at which the work is done and on the basic right to control the business.

Management's primary argument for installing EM is to increase productivity (23, 26, p. 128, 27, p. 34). The large capital investments for computer systems are frequently justified on promised productivity increases. EM is often viewed as a control to help ensure that these increases are achieved.

Henriques (11) cites more accurate cost accounting as a second management argument for EM. More exact measurement and control of employee output enables companies to do a better job in pricing of goods and services. In some cases, Sherizen (23) found that this can also be an internal company practice as when companies are using chargeback systems to monitor costs within their own company.

The third major argument for EM is that it allows management to do a better job of personnel management (9, 12). First, they reason no bias is involved because this approach is an impartial method of collecting performance data. The computer records results with absolute accuracy regardless of race, age, gender, or any other characteristic of the employee (11). Secondly, it helps establish fair performance expectations because the computer fairly and accurately records individual productivity figures. An advantage of accurate work quantity measurements is that it enhances the ability of management to reward high-achieving employees through incentive pay for exceeding work quotas (12). Finally, Grant and Higgins (9) contend that this approach improves the performance appraisal process. The consistency and objectivity of EM performance measurement provides an improvement over traditional evaluations based on subjective and intermittent data collected by human supervisors. EM performance data is also available more quickly and frequently, thus increasing the employee's awareness of individual productivity. In addition, the ability to provide negative feedback in a nonthreatening manner may be better with these systems because the data is not subjective.

## CRITICISMS OF EM

The primary criticism of monitoring is that it is an invasion of worker privacy. Other criticisms are derived from the privacy issue and include concerns such as the creation of employee stress, and the "fairness" in the application of the approach.

Unions and some authors have compared the use of EM with George Orwell's Big Brother in the workplace (5, 9). The fear is that overzealous employers will get carried away with information gathering to the point of exceeding the boundary between work performance and privacy. As an AT&T telephone operator explains: "I can't even go to the bathroom without being watched. I have to put up a flag at my terminal, wait until the restroom is empty, sign out, sign back in and remove my flag" (19).

Two aspects of this monitoring make it different from traditional work supervision and reinforce the big brother perception. First, it is continuous, whereas the traditional approach is intermittent (26, p. 130). This means that everything that the employee does, from taking regular rest breaks to restroom breaks, is timed to the second. In addition, the worker has no control over (or, in some cases, even knowledge of) when monitoring occurs and how the information is to be used. This contrasts with traditional monitoring which is easy for a worker to detect since it usually entails the physical presence of the supervisor. According to Brown (5), EM is, therefore, perceived by employees as being covert and conveys a lack of trust by management. This perception erodes mutual trust and loyalty, and thus demotivates employees rather than encouraging them toward more conscientious effort.

Opponents of EM have made very limited progress with the privacy issue in persuading government authorities to support their opposition to EM systems. The OTA (26, p. 181) says that the privacy argument isn't appropriate because the work is done on the employer's premises in a group setting. In addition, supervision has traditionally been an aspect of the employer-employee relationship and the collection of quantitative data has been used for a long time in evaluating and compensating performance.

As a result of their inability to make progress with the privacy argument, opponents of EM have shifted their focus to the effects on employees of continuous monitoring and the resultant lack of personal privacy. One of the primary effects cited is mental stress. Sheridan (22) believes that job stress could emerge as the most important public health problem related to office automation. Continual monitoring puts pressure on the employee to work at a machine-established pace. This leads to anxiety, fatigue, and apprehension from knowing that he or she will be expected to work at a machine-paced level for the whole day.

The effects of stress on health include musculoskeletal aches and pains, visual difficulties, and psychological complaints (22). At AT&T, where monitoring is widely used, stress-related emotional disorders have resulted in job counseling for approximately 25 percent of the monitored workforce (19). This leads to increased absenteeism and turnover, decreases in performance, and even acts of sabotage (26, p. 128), all of which subverts management's goal of higher productivity.

According to Nussbaum and duRivage (19), stress is also caused by excessive production quotas and work speedups. The ability of management to count keystrokes down to the split second enables managers to increase production and piece rate standards. This causes work speedups that result in lower pay for more work, or even dismissal for those employees who are unable to keep up with the new standards. This stress is further compounded by the posting of individual scores in an effort to promote competition.

In the traditional office, the OTA (26, p. 135) found that the social environment of the office helped act as a buffer to help reduce stress. However, when EM is introduced, a higher level of stress is produced and because there is a tendency for workers to spend more time at a computer terminal, there is less opportunity for social interaction and stress reduction. Thus, stress is not only increased but also intensified.

Katon (14) and Nussbaum and duRivage (19) believe that EM leads to poor management. They say that employers who install EM also tend to adopt scientific management principles which support the concept of breaking a task into greatly simplified units. They contend that this approach is not appropriate for designing office work. Instead of learning from the now discredited experiences in the factory, office managers are embracing the worst abuses of the assembly line and imposing them on office workers. This leads to an overdependence on "the numbers" as the sole measure of an employee's performance. Human assessments of an employee's performance, based on a supervisor's opinion of non-quantifiable aspects of a job, are practically eliminated. This results in a very narrow and incomplete appraisal of an employee's total contribution to the company.

Susser (25) says that EM systems can cause lower morale, increased turnover, and absenteeism, as well as lower product quality and poor customer service. According to Nussbaum and duRivage (19), some workers, when forced to meet unrealistic production goals, cut off customers, enter incomplete data, and even drop paper clips into equipment to slow it down. In view of its potential disadvantages and their consequences, it is apparent that management must carefully evaluate EM prior to proceeding with its implementation.

## LEGAL CONSIDERATIONS

As noted above, critics of EM have increasingly linked it with workplace stress. In the last ten years, worker's compensation claims for mental and emotional stress have grown dramatically as have the number of lawsuits seeking damages under various tort theories (24, p. 579). As a result, the cost of providing financial compensation to employees for stress related disabilities and injuries has increased dramatically.

While the issue of privacy invasion is frequently addressed in these cases, Susser says that the real issue relates to the fairness with which the EM systems are applied in the work place (24). Since workers are usually not included in the design and implementation of EM systems, they don't perceive any fairness and are thus generally hostile toward them.

The OTA (27, p. 111) proposes that fairness involves three considerations: (1) the work standards, (2) the measurement process, and (3) the methods of applying measurements to the evaluation of employees. Work standards should reflect the average capacities of the specific work force and indicate whether the standards will create unhealthy stress for the employees. The measurement process relates to whether or not workers are told and, if so, whether they understand how the measurements are being done. The third area of employee evaluation concerns the inclusion of quality as well as quantity criteria and whether there is a way to adjust expectations when unusual conditions arise such as system downtime or other problems. The OTA research suggests that agreement between employers and employees on these issues helps workers accept EM and reduce stress. . . .

## MANAGEMENT GUIDELINES

Research suggests that there are some very specific guidelines that management can follow that will greatly enhance the probability of success.

*Seek worker involvement:* According to Nath and Gilmore (18), employees' resistance will be greatly reduced if they are provided with an opportunity for personal input in two critical areas. First, active employee input should be encouraged during the systems planning and design. Baetz (2) recommends that an effective way to achieve this is with some or all employees being involved with participative design and evaluation teams. By using this approach, companies have found that employee understanding and cooperation are very greatly increased. Secondly, after the system has been implemented, a "quality circle" consisting of employees should be formed. The purpose of the group is to provide management with feedback on the operational equity within the system. This helps to reduce the perception that the system is "too invasive" and enhances the belief that it is an equitable representation of individual performance.

*Decide what information is really needed:* EM provides management with an unparalleled capability relative to the scope and quantity of information it is able to collect on workers. Because of a "more is better" mentality, Nath and Gilmore (18) believe many managers are tempted to gather more information than they really need. However, it is not necessarily the quantity, but the quality and relevancy of information that is really important.

Nath and Gillmore (18) also say that humans need a certain amount of privacy. Having a computer record on how often they go to the restroom, take medicine, or attend to personal needs is demeaning and insulting. Workers who feel their privacy is invaded will leave if they can. This increases turnover. Ironically, in high turnover situations, it's often the best and most productive employees who will leave because they are better able to find alternative employment. Thus, the quality of the work force could decline over time. By collecting only needed data, the chances of offending workers and spurring unwanted turnover are reduced.

*Employee notification:* Make sure that all employees understand when and how their work is being monitored and why measurement is necessary (6, 8, 27).

*Strive for fairness:* The OTA (27, p. 111) found that the major difference between employee protests over invasion of privacy and acceptance of EM depended on the level of agreement between employees and employers on the issue of fairness. Three key aspects of this issue are involved. The fairness of standards, the measurement process employed, and the way in which measurements are used in employee evaluations.

*Employee data access:* Provide employees with access to their records and regular, supportive feedback. Access can either be on-line or through weekly or monthly reports. There should be a procedure for error discovery and correction.

*Implement a reward-for-performance policy:* Reward individuals appropriately though either incentive pay, public recognition or promotions. Make sure that the performance measurements include quality or subjective factors if applicable to the position (18, 24).

*Use statistics to inspire group competition:* Be very careful about using statistics to motivate individual competition. Posting all individual scores can backfire by making those employees who score below average angry and stressed. If handled sensitively, group competition will not only increase productivity, but also morale and camaraderie (24, 27).

*Don't "inch up" production standards:* Employees resent managers who "inch up" production standards so that employees have to work harder and harder to achieve the same rate of pay. This is a very poor management technique that leads employees to feel that they are working under "sweat shop" conditions (19, 24).

*Provide facilities for social interaction:* According to the OTA (26, p. 135), the office is a social environment and can be an important factor in worker job satisfaction. Because they are electronically monitored, workers may spend so much time at a terminal that social isolation results from a lack of opportunity to interact with others. Social isolation has been shown to be associated with depression, anxiety, job dissatisfaction, and muscular fatigue and psychosomatic symptoms. As a result, management needs to provide lounges and discussion rooms to break the routine of social isolation.

*Provide supervisory training on performance feedback:* Chalykoff and Kochan (6) found that managers can have substantial control over employees' responses to electronic monitoring. Those managers who use principles of good performance appraisal and feedback can minimize the negative effects of EM. As a result, there can be a significant return in terms of employee satisfaction and reduced turnover for supervisory training pertaining to characteristics of good performance feedback.

## SUMMARY

As computer use continues to increase so will the appeal of electronic monitoring. The trend will be driven by management's desire to achieve increased productivity based on the perception that electronic monitoring will provide an element of control which will contribute to higher employee outputs. EM will be further spurred by new applications of technology which lend themselves to monitoring and measurement. These include the increased use of retail point of sale systems and the trend toward working at home via remote computer terminals.

However, imposing an EM system without proper planning can cause a number of undesirable results. Among these are employee resistance to what they see as an invasion of their privacy by the EM system. Their reaction to this may be merely low morale and griping or may take more active forms like sabotage. EM can cause stress levels to rise significantly, sometimes causing illnesses for which the company could be held financially liable. And finally, there is the threat from restrictive legislation which will at least require employers to notify those affected about the EM system and its use.

The burden is clearly on management to balance these conflicting perceptions and objectives. The key is in how management does its job. The same EM technology has been a success and a failure depending on the organization in which it was applied. In many instances success seems to be related to situations where management shared the responsibility for the planning and implementation of the EM system with those who were affected by it. The guidelines offered in this paper provide management with a fuller framework within which to plan and build their EM systems. These, together with good management practice, should go a long way to resolving the issues surrounding electronic monitoring.

## REFERENCES

1. N. Faye Angel, "Evaluating Employees By Computer," *Personnel Administrator* (November 1989): 67–72.

2. Mary L. Baetz, *Planning for People in the Electronic Office* (Homewood, Ill: Dow Jones-Irvin, 1985).

3. Mitch Betts, "VDT Monitoring Under Stress," *Computerworld*, 21 January 1991, pp. 1, 14.

4. Beth Brophy, "New Technology, High Anxiety," *U.S. News & World Report*, 29 September 1986, pp. 54–55.

5. Tom Brown, "We Need Managers, not Big Brothers," *Industry Week*, 29 September 1986, p. 13.

6. John Chalykoff, and T. A. Kochan, "Computer-aided Monitoring: Its Influence on Employee Job Satisfaction and Turnover," *Personnel Psychology* (winter 1989): 807–29.

7. Joseph E. Collins, "OTA Report on Electronic Monitoring," *Data Management* (December 1987): 7.

8. T. M. Dworkin, "Protecting Private Employees from Enhanced Monitoring: Legislative Approaches," *American Business Law Journal* (spring, 1990): 59–85.

9. R. Grant and C. Higgins, "Monitoring Service Workers via Computer: The Effect on Employees, Productivity and Service," *National Productivity Review* (spring 1989): 101–12.

10. R. Grant, "Computerized Performance Monitors: Are They Costing You Customers?" *Sloan Management Review* (spring 1988): 39–45.

11. Vico E. Henriques, "In Defense of Computer Monitoring," *Industry Week*, 7 July 1986, p. 14

12. Vico E. Henriques, "Hallmark of a Computer's Measurement Is Fairness," *The Office* (May 1987): 40–44.

13. John Hoer, "Privacy," *Business Week*, 28 March 1988, pp. 61–68.

14. Paul Karon, "In Pursuit of Productivity: Computer Monitoring of PC Workers," *PC Week*, 2 June 1987, p. 77.

15. Robert E. Kraut, and Susan Dumais, "Computerization and the Quality of Working Life: The Role of Control," *Proceedings of the ACM Conference on Office Information Systems* (Cambridge, Mass., 1990), pp. 56–68.

16. Richard J. Long, *New Office Information Technology: Human and Managerial Implications* (London: Croom Helm, 1987).

17. Massachusetts Coalition on New Office Technology, "H4457-Bill Summary, Electronic Monitoring: Supervision or Surveillance," March 1991.

18. R. Nath and B. Gilmore, "Managing Computerized Supervisory Systems," *Management Solutions* (July 1987): 4–11.

19. Karen Nussbaum and V. duRivage, "Computer Monitoring: Mis-management by Remote Control," *Business and Society Review* (November 1985): 16–20.

20. Marlene Piturro, "Employee Performance Monitoring or Meddling," *Management Review* (May 1989): 31–33.

21. Marlene Piturro, "Electronic Monitoring," *Information Center* (July 1990): 26–31.

22. Peter Sheridan, "Electronic Monitoring: Stress Producer for VDT Operators," *Occupational Hazards* (April 1986): 39–53.

23. Sanford Sherizen, "Work Monitoring: Productivity at what cost to privacy?" *Computerworld* 7 July 1986, p. 55.

24. Peter Susser, "Electronic Monitoring in the Private Sector," *Employee Relations* (spring 1988): 575–95.

25. Peter Susser, "Modern Office Technology and Employee Relations," *Employment Relations Today* (spring 1988): 9–17.

26. U.S. Congress, Office of Technology Assessment, *Automation of Americas Offices*, OTA-CIT-287 (Washington, D.C.: U.S. Government Printing Office, December, 1985).

27. U.S. Congress, Office of Technology Assessment, *The Electronic Supervisor: New Technology, New Tensions*, OTA-CIT-333, 2 vol. (Washington, D.C.: U.S. Government Printing Office, September, 1987).

# DOWNSIZING

*Case Study*

# Layoffs at Alexo Plastics

Bill Armbruster shook his head and read the memo again. He'd been with Alexo Plastics for fifteen years and had served as head of the Technical Support Group (TSG) in the firm's marketing department for the past four years. Several times in the past year there had been rumors of large-scale layoffs, but none had been carried out to date. But Mike Ross's memo left no room for doubt that layoffs were imminent. Current business conditions and competitive pressures within the industry meant that Alexo needed to reduce its staff positions by as much as 33 percent. Consequently, Bill was told via memo to reduce his six-person group by two.

## BILL ARMBRUSTER AND THE LAYOFFS

In Bill's eight years in the marketing department, he had been promoted twice, most recently to his present job as TSG department head. He had started as a marketing analyst and had been promoted to product development manager prior to his present assignment. TSG's mandate was to provide a wide range of consulting services to Alexo customers who were attempting to develop new products from materials supplied by Alexo. Thus, TSG played a key role in developing or solidifying several strategic alliances involving Alexo and its major customers.

The company had grown steadily over the past five years, and some talented people had been added to marketing and TSG to handle the increased workload. Thinking about these people and their many contributions to Alexo saddened Bill. Adding to his concern was the way in which he had learned of the layoffs—a "surprise" memo from someone with whom he interacted daily. Bill would have expected Mike to come to him and discuss the layoffs in person before sending an official memo.

Early in the day after he received the memo, Bill arranged a meeting with Mike. Bill expressed surprise that the news about the layoffs came to him in a formal letter. Because he and Mike had been friends for many years, Bill didn't hesitate to tell him that he was more than a little annoyed that he hadn't learned about the layoffs sooner, and in a less formal manner. Bill explained that he did not think his department could perform its important mission with only four people. Bill asked if there was any way that TSG could be exempted from the cuts. Mike told him in an uncharacteristically abrupt way that Bill had no choice but to lay off two people. Bill left Mike's office more annoyed and frustrated than when he went in. Mike had been no help at all in easing the stress Bill felt. It wasn't like Mike to be so secretive or so abrupt with his department heads.

## THE TECHNICAL SUPPORT GROUP

Bill was upset with the prospect of laying off two people from his department. His six-person department was effective and reasonably close-knit. There were many projects with larger customers in which the entire Technical Support Group needed to work together. They often consulted with one another. They interacted well and were able to generate creative ideas to solve difficult problems brought to them by customers. Bill considered the impact of the layoffs on his group's functioning and thought about each member of his department. He didn't want those laid off to feel resentful towards him, and he hated the idea of being the "bad guy." Bill also wanted to do his best to preserve the positive work environment that had developed since he became department head. He knew that this would be difficult to manage.

## NANCY O'COIN

His train of thought was interrupted when his de facto second-in-command, Nancy O'Coin, stopped in to remind him that he had a meeting with the head of new product development in fifteen minutes. Bill admired Nancy's efficiency and had often remarked how much more smoothly the department functioned in the three years since Nancy had joined TSG. He had recommended her for two extraordinary salary increases, both of which had been approved, one just two months ago. Alexo had few women in managerial positions, and Nancy was clearly on a "fast track" to join that small group.

Nancy was a hard worker with an outgoing personality. She worked well with Bill. She was not afraid to voice her opinions to him if she had a different viewpoint, though she was very tactful. Bill had come to rely on Nancy's memory and organization, as well. She was also very highly regarded by Alexo customers. Would he even consider laying off Nancy? He'd often wondered how the department had gotten along without her. But it *had*, though less effectively.

Returning to his office after the meeting, he didn't stop to talk with people as he usually did. He went directly to his desk and began reviewing the other people in his department. Whom would he lay off?

## PHIL ESPOSITO

Phil Esposito, fifty-eight years old, had been with the company for twenty-eight years. Phil had the longest tenure and the highest salary of the six-member staff. He had lost some of his enthusiasm, and his job performance had slipped slightly in the past year. Phil always received excellent reviews from customers, not just for his work ethic but because he was a veteran in the industry. No one would ever think of questioning Phil's loyalty, integrity, or professionalism. In addition, he was highly respected by his co-workers. Bill remembered how Phil had taught him the ropes when he was new to the firm and how supportive he had been when Bill was promoted to department head. On the other hand, Phil's age and length of service qualified him for Alexo's early retirement plan, which would not be available to anyone else in the department. However, Bill didn't know if Phil was interested in early retirement.

Bill was concerned that Phil might not adapt well to "life after layoffs" in TSG. Another employee in the department had mentioned that Phil had been talking a lot recently about how much Alexo had changed from the good old days when he had first joined the firm. It just wasn't the same company it used to be, Phil had stated. Phil had even submitted a some-what bitter memo to Mike Ross expressing his opinion that the company was going downhill.

## AL JENSEN

Bill's thoughts then turned to Al Jensen. At forty-eight, he was ten years younger than Esposito but had been with the company nearly as long, starting during his college years. A conscientious worker, he lacked Phil's savvy but brought more energy to the job. About the only thing Bill could fault him for was a "prickly attitude," which made him, on occasion, difficult to work with. Al was moody and often kept to himself. But no one could dispute his competence. Al's real passion was in the technical challenge of the job itself. He was not a people person and not the most socially adept individual Bill had ever met. Bill was certain that, if Al was one of the four "survivors" in TSG, he would continue to do his job with the enthusiasm he had always shown.

## ALICE FORD

Bill didn't "connect well" with Alice Ford. Alice was thirty and had been at Alexo for five years. She was intelligent and knew Alexo's products, as well as the manufacturing technologies and processes of Alexo's customers, better than anyone in the department. She was perceived as abrasive by co-workers and as arrogant by customers. Bill had discussed these perceptions with Alice, and recently she was getting higher marks from both groups. She had mentioned to Bill on several occasions that she was under a great deal of stress, as a single mother with two young children. She often needed to leave early to pick up one of her children from preschool or music lessons. Recently, she had met with Bill to discuss the possibility of rearranging her work schedule so that she could spend more time with her children. Should she be one of the ones to go? Her technical skills were superb, and, with the proper coaching, she could develop into a great asset to the company.

## RICH TIEDLINGER

Bill had hired Rich Tiedlinger, twenty-four years old, just over a year ago. Rich's technical abilities were strong though not as strong as Alice's. He was clearly the most energetic and likeable member of the department. He was working toward his MBA in a well regarded university's evening program. He still made mistakes, but his attitude almost made up for them. His gung-

ho approach did not wear well with the older members of the group, especially Al, though even he thought that Rich contributed to the *esprit de
corps* of the department. His enthusiasm seemed to be an intangible asset to
the group. To some, Rich seemed a born leader of the "rah rah" variety.
Would he fine-tune his leadership skills at Alexo or elsewhere?

He was clearly ambitious and Bill wondered how long he was likely to
stay at Alexo. Bill was willing to bet that Rich would go on to bigger and
better things in the years to come, maybe even Bill's position if given the
right opportunity.

## PHIL GONZALES

The sixth member of his group was Phil Gonzales, thirty-three years old.
Bill genuinely admired Phil. He had worked his way up through the blue-
collar ranks at Alexo, had taken night courses at a local community college, and had been in his present job for two years.

Bill knew that Phil had moved up in the company at least in part due
to a conscious Alexo strategy to improve relations with the city's growing
Hispanic community, who made up an increasing percentage of Alexo's
work force. More new Hispanic managers had been appointed last year
than ever before. And Bill knew that the company's policy on providing
opportunities for minorities was as important as its policy on opportunities for women. Phil was a role model for other Hispanic workers in the
firm. He knew everyone from the shop floor to the executive offices and
was respected for the high quality of his work in TSG.

## DECISION TIME

There is no way around it, Bill thought. This is going to be awful, but I have
to do it. Since he could not avoid laying off two workers, he wanted to
make sure that what he did was done professionally, with a fairness and
sensitivity that these people deserved. Bill knew also that it would make
his job a lot easier if one or two of them would leave voluntarily, either
taking early retirement or pursuing other opportunities—inside or outside
the firm. Of course, there were possible negatives in this approach; maybe
the wrong people would leave. Would that be right from the perspective of
the firm and the effectiveness of TSG? He picked up a blank pad of paper
and began to write down his thoughts.

*Brian W. Bulger*
*Carolyn Curtis Gessner*

# Sign of the Times: Implementing Reductions in Force

In the past few years, the increasing uncertainty and instability of doing business in the United States have forced many companies to reduce their work forces dramatically. The need to cut employees can arise from a variety of factors, including economic and competitive pressures on in-house costs, mergers or acquisitions that result in duplicative staffing, or perceptions that the company should become "lean and mean" to be an aggressive presence in the marketplace. Whatever the reasons, reductions in force may bring about the desired results. However, such drastic actions carry problematic consequences that employers must recognize and evaluate before making reductions.

In particular, reductions in force (RIFs) frequently lead to litigation against the company by its terminated employees. Such suits are not limited to employees who were "formally" discharged; constructive discharge claims have been brought by individuals who left their jobs under the auspices of ostensibly "voluntary" early retirement or incentive plans. Management personnel over the age of forty often bring suits under federal and/or state age discrimination laws. These lawsuits can be difficult for employers to win and extremely expensive to lose, as age discrimination claimants are generally entitled to jury trials and may receive back pay, front pay, and liquidated damages.

For these reasons, as well as the more fundamental priorities of fairness and employee morale, an employer considering an RIF should move cautiously. Its decisions must be based on demonstrable, objective factors. This article examines the steps employers should follow in implementing RIFs. . . .

---

From *Employee Relations Law Journal* 17, no. 3 (winter 1991–1992): 431–48.

## EVALUATING THE EMPLOYER'S OPTIONS

As a preliminary step, employers should strongly consider whether actions other than RIFs will have the desired effects on business strength. Such a self-examination works both prospectively and retrospectively: it gives the employer a clearer understanding of its needs before drastic actions are taken, and it may serve as evidence of the employer's good faith should RIF decisions ever be challenged. In order to maintain employee morale and forestall future liability, the employer should endeavor to show that it did not want to terminate employees, but that it, in fact, had no other reasonable options.

Such a self-examination begins with pinpointing the business needs that drive the inclination to make cuts. By targeting problem areas, alternatives may be more effectively developed and evaluated, and narrowly tailored decisions may be more easily defended.

Alternatives to drastic reductions can be contemplated in a series of stages. The first stage includes steps that may generate some improvement in the employer's financial picture, such as:

- *Implementing nonemployment cost reductions*—Trimming waste in the company's overhead is a logical first step in controlling costs, although a well-managed company will likely find the actual savings generated by such cuts to be limited.
- *Exploring methods to increase productivity and/or profitability*— Although most companies seek to improve these factors continually, the pressure of potential staff reductions may act as an added incentive to change traditional performance patterns.
- *Examining whether usual attrition rates will yield sufficient vacancies to meet reduction needs*—In a workplace with significant turnover and relatively interchangeable job responsibilities, leaving jobs open after employees depart may remove some economic pressure. Realistically, though, fewer employees are likely to leave voluntarily during periods of declining opportunity in the job market, so historic attrition rates may not provide an accurate picture of the future.

Unfortunately, these tactics will not usually lead to sufficient improvement in an employer's economic position. If this is the case, the employer may opt to move on to the second stage of alternatives. These options have a first-hand economic impact on employees, but are less financially devastating than involuntary RIFs. In addition, this class of options includes creative opportunities for job restructuring or early retirement, options that may appeal to some employees while saving the employer money at the same time. Such options include:

- Pay freezes or reductions
- Shorter work hours or weeks
- Short-term temporary shutdowns or layoffs
- Job sharing
- Voluntary leaves of absence
- Incentive or early retirement programs

Again, these types of actions may not lead to the dramatic cost savings the employer requires. However, the consideration and implementation of such programs demonstrate the employer's good faith and may decrease the number of involuntary terminations to be made later. In most cases, therefore, employers will want to attempt some form of voluntary reduction before deciding whether to move on to the third stage, involuntary terminations.

## Voluntary Separations

Voluntary separations, either through a job "buy-out" program or an early retirement incentive "window," have significant advantages over involuntary terminations. Foremost among these advantages is the mutual satisfaction engendered by truly voluntary programs, especially when the program eliminates the need for involuntary RIFs: the employee chooses the path he or she wishes to follow, and the employer is not forced to make—and defend—often painful decisions about cutting individual employees. The resulting sense of certainty and increased morale can significantly help the company weather economically difficult periods.

Obviously, however, these programs have their downsides. On the most basic level, incentives are expensive in the short term and potentially impractical for employers strapped for cash. Even more troubling in the long run, the employer lacks firm control over who will leave the company if the program is truly voluntary. Although the employer may limit its incentive offer to specified classes of employees, such distinctions need to be based on objective, verifiable business needs. . . .

# INVOLUNTARY REDUCTIONS

Unfortunately, even after all other voluntary means have been exhausted, it may still be necessary to conduct an involuntary reduction in force to meet the business needs of the company. The potential for legal action by employees who are involuntarily terminated is, of course, much higher. Therefore, the employer must be prepared to defend each individual non-retention decision as well as the overall impact of its reduction upon various protected groups.

## *Designing the RIF Plan*

Whether or not a proposed RIF follows a voluntary program, the company should conduct an analysis of the need for and size of the RIF. This study should be performed by senior management, particularly if the RIF is large. The involvement of senior management serves both internal and external purposes: lower-level officials may have personal interests in the RIF, and juries expect involvement of senior management in decisions of this importance.

At the outset, the pre-RIF work force should be analyzed in terms of protected groups (that is, race, sex, and age). Age studies should not simply categorize employees as over/under forty, but should cover various age brackets. This study can and should be undertaken pursuant to a directive from senior management that the company's policy is to conduct the RIF in the fairest, most objective manner it can and avoid any significant adverse impact upon protected groups. From this overall picture, smaller segments can be studied to determine the employment picture by division, department, job classification, and so on. Ultimately, these materials will be used for an impact study of the effects of the RIF.

At the next step, management will lay out a plan for determining who is to be retained or let go. This plan should be written with assistance of counsel and with the determination that following the plan strictly is the best way to defend against litigation.

Formulating the plan consists primarily of determining the best means for deciding retention issues. To the extent possible, the first focus of any plan is on what jobs or job functions generally need to be eliminated or retained. This may be easy, as, for example, when an entire product line has suffered a serious drop in sales, necessitating large cutbacks for that line. In most cases, however, the employer is looking for across-the-board cuts of the work force, often coupled with a redesigned organization. The plan should designate management committees to study and then apply the plan's imperatives.

## Conducting Job Studies

Following development of the RIF general plan, management should undertake an intensive study of job functions, without regard to the identities of incumbents. Normally, the plan will designate a committee to handle this task. Written instructions should be provided to the committee, detailing the factors to be considered in whether to consolidate or eliminate jobs or job functions. The committee should not consider the individual strengths and weaknesses of the employer's incumbent personnel in reaching these decisions. Rather, factors that should be studied include types of duties performed and time spent on performance, overlaps among jobs or departments, availability of qualified personnel for such positions, and so on. A caveat is necessary here because an analysis of cost considerations may be used to suggest age discrimination, as more highly paid employees generally are older and more senior.

The committee should be instructed to determine which jobs or tasks can be eliminated, consolidated, or reduced, and which should be retained. An analysis can be made of the likelihood of meeting the business goals through the proposed changes, which can be used by senior management to decide whether further study and cuts are necessary before proceeding to the next step. The committee also should be instructed to prepare detailed job descriptions that include necessary and preferred qualifications. These descriptions can then be used to evaluate the fitness of particular employees for the remaining jobs.

## Evaluating Individual Employees

Once a new structure has been decided upon after a study of job functions, management can move to the next step—determining which individuals are to be retained to fill the remaining jobs. Most often, the initial evaluation is done by the manager of a particular area. However, many companies have used committees to evaluate personnel or to pass on initial recommendations, whereas others have experimented with peer review systems.

Whether an evaluation is conducted by an individual or a committee, the standards of evaluation must be clear and documented in writing. Similarly, evaluations should be written or otherwise documented. Of course, written evaluations will be important issues in subsequent litigation, so evaluators must be thoroughly trained in evaluation procedures. "Smoking gun" memoranda are common at this stage—for example, "This is really a young man's game, and Joe's not cut out for it anymore." Even otherwise neutral words like "dynamic" or "aggressive" can be deemed code words for youthfulness in the context of an age discrimination lawsuit.

An important question to be faced is whether evaluators will consult previous performance evaluations or if a whole new system is to be used for the RIF. It is a simple fact that because most managers are not completely candid in the yearly appraisals, "grade inflation" inevitably creeps into the system. Moreover, the previous evaluation system may be so vague or subjective that it has little value in defending against discrimination claims. There are advantages to using existing appraisals, however, because not only do they lend some historical perspective to the differences among employees, but perhaps even more importantly, employees generally will have failed to contest past adverse comments. Additionally, failure to consult existing evaluations may be held against the company.

Whether or not previous evaluations are consulted, employers should consider also adopting a special RIF evaluation system. The goal of this system is to rank employees relative to one another, and numerical rating systems are used frequently. Inconsistencies with previous ratings, however, may be difficult to explain.

Instructions as to factors for consideration, and their relative weights, should be given to evaluators. These factors should include performance ratings, particular skills, and other objective criteria. Additionally, consideration of seniority will serve to negate any implication of discrimination, such as years of service.

## Reviewing the Proposed RIFS Impact on Protected Groups

Once the initial evaluator has finished ranking employees and made retention/nonretention recommendations, a review must be conducted to determine whether adverse impact or some other form of discrimination is operating. This review should be conducted by senior personnel familiar with the legal definitions and implications of discrimination. The review may be conducted by a committee, balanced to ensure representation of protected groups.

The reviewing committee should be instructed, first, to evaluate the rankings by cross-checking evaluations against the instructions, job descriptions, and relevant performance documents. Next, retention decisions should be evaluated against the pre-RIF work force makeup to determine if protected groups are adversely affected. If adverse impact is found, it may be necessary to check each individual decision and evaluator carefully for indications of bias, and to review job descriptions and evaluation criteria to ensure that they are nondiscriminatory.

## *Separations*

Once the review process is completed, the employer may proceed with implementation of separations. Practices will vary among employers, but every effort should be made to respect the dignity of individuals and to reduce feelings of anger toward the company.

If individual managers are to announce separations, they should be trained to do so. Separation should be accompanied by explanation of company benefits available, and outplacement assistance is a virtual requirement in these situations. Exit interviews should be required, and the employer may want to establish a formal appeal process for separation decisions. All interview sessions should be documented so that a record of statements made to the employee is available in the event of litigation.

## *Communications*

At *all* steps in the RIF process the employer should be communicating with employees. At the outset the reasons for cuts, together with the need for a certain number of cuts, should be communicated. Once a plan is adopted, it should be publicized. The employer may even want to solicit suggestions about the plan from employees. Criteria to be used in decisions should be published, and an appeal process may be instituted and employees so advised.

Although an active, communications program contains the risk of communicating improper statements, a well-developed program can reduce employee anxiety and anger by demonstrating the necessity and fairness of the RIF. When coupled with significant severance benefits, effective communication may reduce the chance of RIF litigation by many employees. . . .

# HONESTY IN COMMUNICATION

*Case Study*

# A Communication Decision at Von Products, Inc.

Gerald Fowler inherited some money in 1969 and he used it to found Von Products, a company that manufactured air driers for use in refrigeration and air conditioning equipment. In 1969, Fowler was convinced that air conditioning was the new wave of the future. Fowler was right, and Von Products prospered. In 1973 and 1982, Fowler expanded his operations, each time selling stock in the corporation. In 2001, Von Products employed 406 people, with Fowler retaining ownership of 51 percent of the corporation's stock. The organization of Von Products' top-level management was as follows:

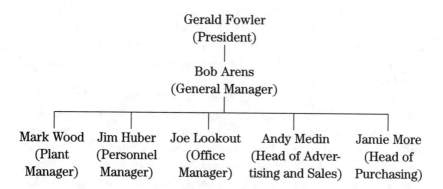

Gerald Fowler
(President)

Bob Arens
(General Manager)

| Mark Wood (Plant Manager) | Jim Huber (Personnel Manager) | Joe Lookout (Office Manager) | Andy Medin (Head of Advertising and Sales) | Jamie More (Head of Purchasing) |

Fowler felt that Von Products was "his baby," and he strictly reviewed most management decisions in the corporation. One of the things Fowler insisted upon was that he personally make all management-level appointments and promotions. Below the level of management, the personnel manager was empowered to make all decisions regarding hiring, firing, and promotion. When management positions were to be filled, however, Bob Arens, the general manager, made recommendations to Fowler, who then made the ultimate decision.

On July 10, 2001, Jim Huber was called into Fowler's office. Fowler told him that Andy Medin was leaving the corporation, and that he, Fowler, was going to appoint a new head of advertising and sales. At present no one except Medin, Fowler, Arens, and Huber knew of Medin's upcoming resignation, and Fowler said that he wanted the information to be kept confidential. Fowler further told Huber that the list of candidates for promotion to Medin's position had been narrowed to two: Milt Snobiski, currently manager of the advertising department, and Bob Allen, sales manager. Fowler asked Huber to go over the files of both men and make a recommendation for promotion. The request was unusual; however, Fowler explained that Arens had strongly recommended one person for promotion, while he favored the other. Before he made his final decision, then, Fowler wanted a third opinion. And since Huber was personnel manager, he was selected for the task. Fowler refused to tell Huber whom Arens had recommended or whom he, Fowler, favored, because he did not want to prejudice Huber's judgment.

From the outset Huber felt uneasy about making the decision requested of him. He knew both Snobiski and Allen well, for all three men had grown up together and had gone to the same high school. Still, Huber was not familiar with the dossiers of either man. Huber had joined Von Products only two years ago; and both Allen and Snobiski had been hired over twelve years ago by Huber's predecessor, a man who recently had died of a heart attack.

Even before he looked at the résumés of the two men, Huber knew whom he favored for promotion. Huber felt that Snobiski was hard working, loyal, and competent. Furthermore, Huber and Snobiski were good friends. On the other hand, Huber knew that Allen had been made sales manager by Fowler on the recommendation of Arens, even though Andy Medin, a competent department head, had not favored the decision. In Huber's opinion, Allen had risen high in the corporation only because he constantly "buttered up" Arens. Furthermore, Huber knew that Allen had assumed Andy Medin's duties for two months in 2000 while Medin was sick, and that during that time advertising and sales suffered.

When Huber examined Allen's file he found that the subject had a slightly better than average record. At the same time, there was nothing outstanding about it. Snobiski's file, on the other hand, was, with one exception, truly impressive. Great leaps in sales were recorded in 1993, 1995, and 1999, and all were traceable to aggressive advertising campaigns masterminded by Snobiski. Furthermore, the file was replete with complimentary evaluations by Medin. Yet there was a problem with Snobiski's record. When Huber examined data concerning Snobiski's educational background, he found that Snobiski claimed to have a bachelor's degree in business from Ohio State and a master's in business administration from Indiana University. The dates of the degrees accorded with times when Huber felt sure Snobiski was serving in the Navy. To check, Huber called both Ohio State and Indiana and found that his friend had no degree from either university.

Huber knew Fowler very well. If Fowler found out that Snobiski had falsified his employment application, not only would Snobiski be fired, Fowler would do his best to see that he was not hired anywhere else. Furthermore, Fowler would make Allen head of advertising and sales, a move that Huber honestly felt would be disadvantageous for the corporation. With this in mind, Huber considered the various options that he felt were open to him:

1. He could tell Fowler all that he had found, and argue for Snobiski's promotion. But Huber knew that Fowler felt that falsification of records was among the worst of all evils. Thus, choice of this course of action probably would do little more than cause Fowler to doubt Huber's trustworthiness. Furthermore, Huber's report would cause Snobiski to be fired, and a truly productive person would be lost to Von Products.

2. He could tell Fowler that he favored Allen, justify the recommendation by some strained arguments, and omit any mention of Snobiski's educational record.

3. He could argue for Snobiski's promotion, withholding all information concerning Snobiski's educational background.

4. He could give all the information at his disposal to Fowler, and then argue against the promotion of either man. Once again, however, Snobiski would be fired. Further, Huber felt sure that if Snobiski was removed from consideration, Allen would be promoted regardless of what he had to say in opposition to the appointment.

As Huber considered the various alternatives available to him, he felt caught between a rock and a hard place. To tell all he knew would bring about dismissal of a valuable employee and a good friend, and almost certainly put Allen in a position Huber felt he did not deserve. However, the alternative was to withhold information, and this made Huber feel uncomfortable.

## FOR DISCUSSION

What should Huber do? Why?

*James M. Humber*

# Honesty in Organizational Communication

Top corporate executives consistently complain of problems involving communications within the organization.[1] In one study of 100 businesses and industries it was found that only 20 percent of the information downward from the level of the board of directors was understood at the worker level.[2] And if anything, problems with upward communications are even more severe than those encountered in downward transmissions of information.[3]

There are a variety of reasons to explain why communication problems arise within corporate structures. Upward communication is hampered by the very structure of the corporation itself. Top managers insulate themselves from all but a few key employees to avoid undue interruptions and embarrassing encounters. Pressures of time and the routine demands of jobs also hinder the upward flow of information. The chain of command in most companies makes it impossible for employees to talk to decision makers in their organizations without first presenting their messages to each higher management echelon. Then, too, some workers are not able to communicate clearly, either orally or in writing; and those who receive information sometimes misinterpret. In addition, subordinates are reluctant to pass on "bad" information to their superiors; and employees claim to feel pressures (sometimes real, sometimes imagined) to tell their bosses "only what they want to hear." With all of these impediments to upward communication, it is amazing that any undistorted information gets to the top.

There are at least as many factors operating to distort downward communication in corporations as there are factors working to hamper the upward flow of information. For example, some executives withhold bad news from their employees for fear of upsetting morale. In a large international or multinational corporation, top management and local management rarely come into contact. Furthermore, it is sometimes difficult, in a very large company, to identify the person or persons to whom information should be sent. Then, too, managers, like their subordinates, are often burdened by routine tasks. Sometimes persons in executive positions are incapable of communicating clearly; and oftentimes those below top-level management misunderstand the messages they receive. Overarching all of this, of course, is the problem of the "authoritarian" executive. A person of this sort does not feel that company information is any of the worker's business. And naturally, in these circumstances very little information is communicated downward.

There are a host of books and studies in management theory that attempt to provide employers with the means for improving internal corporate communications. My purpose in this essay is not to add to that body of literature, but rather to assess the moral quality of certain kinds of intentional distortions in the flow of information within business and industry. The following three cases will help to illustrate the kinds of communicative distortions I want to examine.

*Case #1*. Joe Doe and Sue Roe are coworkers competing for a promotion. Doe purposely passes on false information to Roe. As Doe expects, Roe acts on the false information and so "looks bad" in the eyes of her superiors.

*Case #2*. A department manager (DM) must write a report evaluating the work of four employees in his department. The first three employees are good friends of his, but he does not like the fourth employee. In writing his report the DM does not omit any pertinent information, but goes out of his way to stress his friends' strengths while emphasizing the weaknesses of the employee he does not like.

*Case #3*. A regional manager (RM) must report to top level executives concerning the operations of the various districts for which she has responsibility within the organization. The RM instructs an assistant, *A*, to collect data and prepare a report, telling *A* in the process that it is very important for his region to "look good" to the bosses. *A* prepares a report that makes no mention of the problems plaguing various districts in the RM's region.

In case #1 above, one employee straightforwardly tells another something that he knows to be false. In case #2, the truthfulness of communication is distorted by emphasis or "coloring." And in the final example, important information is withheld. What all three cases have in common, of course, is that in each instance an intentional deception or lie has been perpetrated.[4] Distortions of all three sorts occur in all organizations with varying degrees of frequency. But are such deceptions morally wrong? And if they are morally wrong, are the deceivers morally blameworthy? These are the questions that will serve as the focus of this essay. Before we can attempt to answer these questions, however, we first must decide whether employees in business and industry have any moral obligation to tell the truth in their corporate communications.

Ethicists and moral philosophers differ widely in their views concerning whether there is a moral duty to tell the truth. At one extreme we find people like Kant and St. Augustine claiming that there is an absolute, unconditional, or unbreakable moral obligation to tell the truth. Since an unbreakable moral duty is one that holds in all circumstances without exception, acceptance of this view would force the conclusion that all lies are morally wrong. But there are good reasons to believe that this theory, which we could call nonconsequentialist extremism, is not correct.[5] For example, nonconsequentialist extremists claim that there are other inviolable moral duties in addition to the absolute moral obligation to tell the truth. How is one to act if two or more of these unbreakable moral duties conflict? Kant took note of the problem; but in the end claimed that there was no real difficulty because "a conflict of duties and obligations is inconceivable."[6] This "solution," however, is far too facile. For instance, let us assume that we have only two absolute moral duties—one is to keep our promises, and the other is to tell the truth. Let us say further that S is a soldier who promises faithfully to do all in his power to confuse the enemy and protect his comrades. During one battle S is captured, imprisoned, and repeatedly interrogated regarding troop placements. Though S is tortured, he gives the enemy no information. One day, however, S learns that the enemy is planning to attack his army's headquarters. S knows that he is due to be questioned the next day, and that if he pretends to "break" under pressure, he may lie convincingly concerning the location of his army's headquarters and so cause the enemy's attack to be misdirected. What should S do? If he deceives his captors, he breaks his absolute moral duty to tell the truth. If he does not lie, he fails to keep his unbreakable promise to protect his comrades and confuse the enemy. In this case, at least, absolute moral duties do seem to conflict, and nonconsequentialist extremism would appear to make it impossible for S to act in a morally right way.

Another problem with nonconsequentialist extremism is that we ordinarily believe moral duties may be broken when the consequences of not violating those duties would be disastrous. For example, assume that the captain of a fishing boat is smuggling innocent political prisoners out of a country ruled by a corrupt dictator. Just before the captain is about to leave port with his surreptitious cargo, his vessel is boarded by the police. The police chief is a good friend of the captain, and will believe whatever the captain tells him. Thus, if the captain lies about the location of the prisoners he will save all of their lives. On the other hand, if the captain tells the truth or refuses to say anything, the boat will be searched and all the innocent prisoners killed. Now if the captain were to lie in these circumstances would he really do something wrong? Kant and St. Augustine would have to answer affirmatively, but a judgment of this sort violates our most basic moral intuitions.

Although the above two criticisms of nonconsequentialist extremism proceed along different lines, they make essentially the same point, i.e., even if we believe there is a moral duty to tell the truth, we ordinarily do not think that this obligation must *always* be obeyed if we are to act in morally right ways. Indeed, this belief is held so strongly by the vast majority of mankind that, historically, nonconsequentialist extremism proved unworkable. For example, discontent with St. Augustine's absolute rejection of all lies gave birth to a theory known as the doctrine of mental reservations.[7] In its most extreme form this doctrine holds that it is not wrong for one person to say something misleading to another, just so long as the speaker is careful to add a qualifier to the statement in his or her mind so as to make the verbal statement true. For instance, let us say that I am at Dick's house and that I pocket a $5.00 bill which I find on the floor. Dick enters the room and asks me if I have seen $5.00. According to the doctrine of mental reservations I would not be lying if I said, "I did not see $5.00," and then silently completed the statement by saying something to myself like "yesterday" or "on the table."

Although those who accept the doctrine of mental reservations insist that we have an absolute moral duty to tell the truth, they allow us to "mentally qualify" any false statement so as to make it true. Hence the actual effect of the doctrine is to deny that we have any moral duty at all to communicate truthfully. The reason this is so is that there can be no such thing as a private language. That is to say, if I tell Dick (x) "I did not see $5.00," what I communicate to Dick is nothing more or less than the meaning of (x), for the "mental addition" to (x), which I make in my mind, is no communication at all. In reality, then, when I assert (x)—albeit a "mentally qualified" (x)—I lie to Dick; for what I have actually communicated [viz., the meaning of (x)], is something that I know to be false. And if the doctrine of mental reservations allows me to do this with any statement, at any time, without fear of doing something wrong, it effectively denies that there is any moral duty to tell the truth.

Those who accept the doctrine of mental reservations leap from dissatisfaction with St. Augustine's absolute injunction against lying to a position that denies there is any moral duty at all to tell the truth. Proponents of the mental reservations doctrine make no attempt to justify this "leap," because they do not understand the true nature of their own position. That is, they believe there is an absolute duty of veracity, but that they do not violate this duty when they assert mentally qualified statements because all such statements are true. We now know that this view of things is wrong. But this still leaves one question unanswered; specifically, is it possible to justify the mental reservationists' true position? Or to put it another way, can we construct an argument showing that there is no moral duty to tell the truth? Perhaps the best known attempt to provide such a justification has been made by a group of moral philosophers whom we may call consequentialist extremists.[8] Consequentialist extremists believe that we have one and only one moral duty, and that is to maximize good consequences. Thus stealing, lying, killing, etc. cannot be said to be wrong because they violate moral injunctions against such actions. If actions of this sort are wrong, they are wrong only because they produce bad consequences. And of course, consequentialist extremists insist that there may be cases where it would be morally right to steal, lie, or kill. Specifically, it would be right whenever such action maximized good consequences. For example, consequentialist extremists might well claim that it would be right for the fishing boat captain to lie to the police chief in our earlier example because lying in this instance would save many innocent lives.

Insofar as consequentialist extremists claim that it sometimes may be morally permissible to lie, cheat, steal, etc., they no doubt are correct. On the other hand, there seems to be no reason to agree that we have no moral duties other than the duty to maximize good consequences. If this truly were the case, we would feel no moral qualms whatsoever about a person lying, stealing, cheating, etc., whenever it was clear that good consequences were produced by such action. But in fact, we often do feel morally troubled when such actions are performed and justified by an appeal to good consequences. For example, if I steal $50,000 from a millionaire who will never miss the money, and then give that money to charity, have I done something morally right? Or again, if I tell a dying friend on his deathbed that I will use his fortune to care for his pet cats, but after his death use his money to relieve human misery, is my lie justified? In cases such as these we do not feel that the moral issues are as clear-cut and simple as consequentialist extremists would have us believe. And we feel this way because we think there are many moral duties, and not just one as consequentialist extremists would have us believe.

We have rejected nonconsequentialist extremism because it imposes *absolute* moral obligations upon us. On the other hand, consequentialist extremism goes too far in the opposite direction when it asserts that there are no moral obligations other than the duty to maximize good consequences. In the end, then, the truth would seem to lie somewhere between these extremes. And indeed, if the examples given throughout the text of this essay indicate anything, it is that we ordinarily acknowledge the existence of many moral duties (including the duty to tell the truth), but that we do not hold these duties to be absolute or unbreakable. Duties that are not absolute are called *prima facie* moral duties. *Prima facie* moral duties are so-called because violating them constitutes *prima facie* evidence of moral wrongdoing. That is to say, unless the person violating a *prima facie* duty can *justify* his or her violation, the person performing the action will be said to have done something morally wrong. Of course, what counts as an adequate justification for breaking a *prima facie* moral duty is the subject of much dispute; and more will be said of this later. For now, however, we need only note that our inquiries thus far would seem to require that we acknowledge the existence of a *prima facie* moral duty to tell the truth.

Having determined that there is a *prima facie* moral duty to tell the truth, it might appear that we now should try to specify those conditions under which violation of that duty would be justified. Before we can approach this task, however, there is another issue to be faced. There are some who allow that we ordinarily have a *prima facie* duty of veracity, but they go on to argue that the actions of employees in business and industry must be judged by a special moral theory. If this claim is true, and if this "special" moral theory imposes no duty on employees to tell the truth with respect to their internal corporate communications, we need not worry about seeking a justification for deceptive corporate communiques. Before we proceed further, then, we need to examine the major tenets of this "special" moral theory.

Milton Friedman is the propounder and chief advocate of a special moral theory that he feels must be used to judge the actions of employees in business and industry.[9] Admittedly, Friedman says, all persons have ordinary moral responsibilities. However, when individuals become employees of a company, they assume two duties that supersede their ordinary moral obligations. For Friedman, all employees must: (1) do their best to maximize profits for the corporation, and (2) obey the law and follow the rules of ethical custom.

Friedman's theory has been criticized from a number of quarters. Elsewhere, for example, I have argued that Friedman's theory is so beset by theoretical and conceptual difficulties that it must be rejected out of hand.[10] Also, Alan Goldman rejects the view that, as a general rule, professional obligations override or supersede ordinary moral obligations.[11] For the purposes of this paper, however, we may ignore these challenges to Friedman's position; even if we accept Friedman's theory we still must admit that employees in business and industry have a *prima facie* duty to communicate truthfully. There are two reasons for saying this. First, if our earlier reasonings are accepted, the *prima facie* moral duty to tell the truth is one of our society's "ordinary rules of ethical custom." Thus, insofar as Friedman imposes a moral duty upon employees to follow these rules, he also enjoins them to tell the truth. And second, virtually no one would dispute the claim that, generally, truthfulness in internal corporate communications is an aid to maximizing corporate profits. Indeed, recognition of this fact has spawned the many books, articles, and studies intended to provide employers with the means for improving the quality of information flow within their companies. If we accept Friedman's theory, then, we can say that corporate employees have a moral duty to be truthful in their communications because this helps to maximize company profits. On the other hand, this duty cannot be absolute, because we can imagine situations in which deception might be required for maximization of profits. For instance, one employee may have to lie in order to catch another who is stealing trade secrets.

No matter which way we turn it seems we must admit that company employees have a *prima facie* moral obligation not to distort the truth in their corporate communications. But if the duty to tell the truth is only *prima facie*, under what conditions would it be morally permissible for an employee to lie? Or, to put it another way, how could an employee morally justify lying in a corporate communication? In an essay of this length we cannot hope to take individual note of all the various cases in which lying might be justified. Nevertheless, we can say something in general about the process of justification, and so provide a means for testing the acceptability of moral justifications as they arise in actual practice. If nothing else, this examination should illustrate how very difficult it is to justify distorting the truth in corporate communications.

First, there seems to be agreement among many philosophers that a justification, if it is to be adequate, must be capable of being made public.[12] That is to say, appeals to personal conscience, secret moral knowledge, intuitions not shared by mankind in general, etc., will not do. Thus, if a moral view is to be adequately justified, the person doing the justifying must be able to present reasons and arguments capable of supporting the reasonableness of his or her position.

Second, because justifications must be capable of being made public, we would seem to have no alternative but to appeal to *consequences* in our justifications. For example, if an employee, $E$, were to lie in a corporate communication and then attempt to justify that lie by telling us that her lie was necessary to increase corporate profits, $E$'s "justification" could not be accepted; as it stands it tells us nothing more than that, in this particular instance, $E$ feels that her duty to maximize profits supersedes her duty to tell the truth. But why should we accept this belief? It is hardly self-evident. To fully justify her position, $E$ must appeal to some publicly accessible facts supporting her contention that the duty of veracity is outweighed by the duty to increase profits. And the only facts that would appear to be publicly accessible are the probable consequences of the two alternative courses of action. That is to say, if $E$ is to justify her contention that she did not act wrongly when she lied, she must at the very least show that lying probably produced a greater balance of benefits over harms than not lying. If $E$ cannot produce such factual support for her position, she cannot be said to have justified her belief that the duty to maximize profits outweighed her duty to tell the truth. And so long as this state of affairs remains, $E$'s action must be counted as morally wrong.

We have seen that we must appeal to the consequences of our actions whenever we attempt to justify lying in corporate communications. And this fact makes it so very difficult to justify deceptive communications in business and industry. The collective experience of mankind testifies to the fact that lying usually, if not always, produces harmful consequences. The individual who lies must worry about getting caught. If she is caught, her reputation suffers. If she is not caught, she oftentimes must continue to lie in order to conceal the original deception. Furthermore, trust is essential for the success of any cooperative venture; and lying, if it occurs frequently, undermines trust. In the corporate context an atmosphere of mistrust can have especially deleterious consequences: for if lying is continually expected, employees will tend to act on their own, oftentimes at cross purposes. In addition, when false information is passed on, decisions at various levels in the organization are made on the basis of incorrect data. And in these circumstances it is highly unlikely that decisions will be correct. Finally, if lying in internal corporate communications hurts business and industry, it also hurts society as a whole; for the more efficient and economically viable are our corporations, the stronger our economy.

Lying in corporate communications usually has harmful consequences for the liar, the corporation, and society. From past experience we *know* these effects customarily attend deceit; and it is from these negative consequences that this *prima facie* obligation not to lie in corporate communications derives its force. And this force is considerable. Of course, it is conceivable that an employee could show that some competing moral obligation superseded his duty not to lie; but this is quite unlikely. The reason this is so is that an employee who contemplates passing on false information is seldom in possession of the facts necessary to justify a deceptive communication. Even top-level executives do not have a complete and true picture of the organization's operations. As a result, they cannot predict the ultimate consequences of their actions with a high degree of certainty. On the other hand, they know perfectly well that lying will most likely produce the negative results noted previously. If it is difficult for persons at this level in the organization to justify deception, how much more so for individuals in middle-level management and below.[13]

We have seen that deceiving fellow employees in corporate communications is, in virtually all instances, morally wrong. But one question remains: are all those who lie in corporate communications morally blameworthy? Or, to put it another way, are there any conditions that would excuse a liar from responsibility for a wrongful act? In an essay of this length we cannot consider all possible excusing conditions. Nevertheless, we can consider the three most often appealed to, and see whether any succeeds in relieving the liar of responsibility.

First, we do not hold persons responsible for their actions when those actions are compulsory. For example, if we believe a murderer is mentally ill and unable to control his or her actions, we do not think the crime warrants punishment. Similarly, an employee could be a compulsive liar, and so not morally blameworthy if he or she were to lie. Cases such as this will be very rare, however, and if such an individual were discovered in an organization, he or she should be relieved of all responsibilities, at least until the illness has been corrected by proper medical attention.

Second, persons who act wrongfully out of ignorance are usually excused for their wrongdoing. I say "usually," because mere appeal to ignorance will not suffice to relieve one of responsibility. For instance, if an employee, $E$, purposely withholds information because of a mistaken belief that information is privileged, $E$ is *not* excused if any reasonable person in the same position would have known that the information was not privileged. In every instance, the test is that of the "reasonable person," i.e., would a reasonable person have known what the person who passes on misinformation claims not to have known? If we believe a reasonable person would have known, we hold the employee who passes on distorted data responsible for his or her action. If we hold the contrary view, we do not blame. The difficulty, of course, is that the "reasonable person" test is very vague, and so difficult to apply in particular instances of wrongdoing. (How, after all, can we be sure what a reasonable person would have known in any given set of circumstances?) Thus, if an employee errs once or twice and then attempts to excuse his or her action by appealing to ignorance, it may be best to give the employee the benefit of the doubt. On the other hand, if an employee repeatedly passes on incorrect information, continued appeals to the excuse of ignorance cannot persist without placing the employee in a "no win" situation. Reasonable persons do not make the same mistake over and over again. Hence, if $E$ continually misinforms coworkers, and then attempts to excuse these actions by appealing to ignorance, we must conclude: (a) that $E$ is a reasonable person who is lying about being ignorant (in which case $E$ is a liar), or (b) that $E$ is a reasonable person who is purposely ignorant (in which case $E$ is responsible for his or her false communication), or (c) that $E$ is not a reasonable person (in which case $E$ is incompetent).

Finally, Aristotle long ago realized that all persons have a breaking point, and that when this point is reached wrongdoers are not held responsible for their actions. For instance, a prisoner of war (POW) may "break" under torture and divulge information leading to the death of many of his comrades. In this case we would ordinarily say that the POW has done something wrong (after all, his action has caused the deaths of many fellow soldiers); at the same time, we would not blame the POW for breaking under torture. Similarly, employee $E$ may be subjected to great pressures by his or her superior to "color" reports, cover up damaging information, etc. If $E$ is caught in such a situation, if the pressures are severe (e.g., loss of job, permanently damaged reputation, etc.), and if there is no way for $E$ to escape the situation by appealing to authorities in the organization above the level of his or her immediate superiors, then $E$ may well have an excuse for forwarding deceptive information. Indeed, the person immediately responsible for $E$'s wrongful action would appear to be $E$'s superior. At the same time, one well might want to ask why responsibility for $E$'s wrongful act should not extend further up in the organization. That is to say, one could claim that top-level executives have a duty to do their best to ensure truthful communications within their organizations, and that as a result, these individuals have an obligation to provide means for persons such as $E$ to take action against superiors who pressure them to distort company communications. If these claims are true, and if an organization does not take steps to provide protection for employees who are pressured to deceive, does this mean that top-level management must assume some (or all) of the responsibility for lies prompted by pressure from above? The question is an interesting one; and it is one I will, quite happily, allow readers the freedom to answer for themselves.

## NOTES

1. Throughout, I will be using "communications" to refer to all messages internal to the occupations of the organization. For example, all employees' oral, written, formal, and informal comments concerning business will be covered, while discussions among workers concerning football games or parties will not be counted as communications. Also excluded will be different communications of all sorts between and among corporations.

2. R. P. Cort, *Communicating with Employees* (Prentice-Hall, 1963), p. 10.

3. R. M. D'Aprix, *How's That Again?* (Dow Jones-Irwin, 1971), p. 10.

4. The term "lie" has a variety of different uses in our language. In one use, "lie" and "deception" are synonymous. On the other hand, there are some philosophers who believe it is important to distinguish between lying and deception [see, for example, J. Ellin, "The Solution to a Dilemma in Medical Ethics," *Westminster Institute Review* 1 (1980): 3ff.] I do not wish to become embroiled in this conflict; and throughout, I will use "lie" to mean "intentionally deceptive statement." For all intents and purposes, this is the definition accepted by Sissela Bok in her classic work on lying. [See S. Bok, *Lying* (Vintage Books, 1979), p. 14.]

5. For a discussion of nonconsequentialism in ethics see the introduction to this text.

6. I. Kant, *The Doctrine of Virtue*, trans. M. J. Gregor (Harper & Row, 1964), p. 23.

7. For an excellent discussion of this doctrine see Bok, *Lying*, pp. 37ff.

8. For a detailed discussion of consequentialism in ethics see the introduction to this text.

9. For a statement of Friedman's views see M. Friedman, "The Social Respon-

sibility of Business Is to Increase Its Profits,"*New York Times*, 13 September 1970, pp. 33, 122–126, and "Milton Friedman Responds," *Business and Society Review* (spring 1972): 5–16.

10. J. Humber, "Milton Friedman and the Corporate Executive's Conscience," *Philosophy in Context* 10 (1980): 71–80.

11. A. H. Goldman, *The Moral Foundations of Professional Ethics* (Littlefield, Adams and Co., 1980).

12. This view is accepted by philosophers who disagree about almost everything else. For example, Bok notes that Hume, Wittgenstein, and Rawls all agree that moral justification needs to have the capability of being made public (see Bok, *Lying*, p. 97).

13. There are numerous studies which show, as R. Cort says, that "the divergence between what the employee thinks and what the supervisor thinks he thinks is nothing less than astounding" (see Cort, *Communicating with Employees*, p. 11.) If misunderstanding in the corporation is this widespread, how can anyone predict, with any degree of certainty, the beneficial effects which a deceptive communication will have?

# SELECT BIBLIOGRAPHY

Bacon, M. *The Moral Status of Loyalty*. Module Series in Applied Ethics. Dubuque, Ia.: Kendall/Hunt, 1984.

Boatright, J. *Ethics and the Conduct of Business*. 2d ed. Upper Saddle River, N.J.: Prentice-Hall, 1997, chap. 6, trade secrets and conflict of interest.

Bok, S. "Trade and Corporate Secrecy." In *Secrets*. New York: Random House, 1983.

Conrad, C., and B. Dervin, eds. *The Ethical Nexus: Communication, Values, and Organizational Decisions*. Stamford, Conn.: Ablex, 1993.

Dietz, G. *In Defense of Property*. Baltimore: The Johns Hopkins Press, 1971.

Fielder, J. "Organizational Loyalty." *Business and Professional Ethics Journal* 11 (1992): 71–90.

Friedman, M. *Capitalism and Freedom*. Chicago: University of Chicago Press, 1962.

———. *Free to Choose*. New York: Harcourt Brace Jovanovich, 1980.

Garrett, T. *Business Ethics*. Englewood Cliffs, N.J.: Prentice-Hall, 1966, chap. 3.

Langford, D. *Business Computer Ethics*. Reading, Mass.: Addison Wesley Longman, 1998.

Machan, T., ed. *Commerce and Morality*. Lanham, Md.: Rowman & Littlefield, 1988.

Murphy, K. *Honesty in the Workplace*. Pacific Grove, Calif.: Brooks Cole, 1992.

Oz, E. *Ethics for an Information Age*. Business and Educational Technologies. ISBN: 0-697204626.

Parker, D., S. Swope, and B. Baker. *Ethical Conflicts in Information and Computer Science, Technology, and Business*. Wellesley, Mass.: QED Information Systems, 1990.

Rothbard, M. *For a New Liberty*. New York: Collier Books, 1978.

Seavey, W. *Agency*. St. Paul, Minn.: West Publishing Co, 1964.

Weckert, J., and D. Adney. *Computer and Information Ethics*. Westport, Conn.: Greenwood, 1997.

# ELECTRONIC SOURCES

The Carol and Lawrence Zicklin Center for Business Ethics Research rider.wharton.upenn.edu/~ethics/zicklin/

Centre for Applied Ethics   www.ethics.ubc.ca/resources/

Ethics Officer Association   www.eoa.org/

Institute for Business and Professional Ethics   www.depaul.edu/ethics

# 4. EMPLOYEE RIGHTS

## INTRODUCTION

Corporations are goal oriented and often hierarchically organized, which places a premium on efficiency and the attendant employee obligations of loyalty, obedience, and confidentiality. In recent years it has been argued that employees have certain rights that cannot morally be overridden on grounds of efficiency. This chapter explores some of the moral rights that have been proposed in the areas of hiring, reverse discrimination, diversity, sexual harassment, termination, privacy, worker safety, and whistleblowing.

In their article on hiring practices, Snoeyenbos and Almeder offer what they believe to be fair suggestions having utility across the scope of the hiring procedure: job analysis, job description, job specification, recruitment, testing, and interviewing. The case study in this section provides a specific context for discussing hiring practices.

Although there is no doubt that women, blacks, and members of certain other minority groups have been discriminated against in business practices in our society, there is considerable disagreement as to whether they are entitled to preferential employment treatment. Anita Gonsalves argues that reverse discrimination is both unfair and has disutility. In response, James Humber develops a specific proposal for preferential treatment of disadvantaged individuals, which he claims not only has overall utility but is fair to all. In the first of her two articles, Barbara Hall argues that consequence, fairness and rights considerations favor employers developing a diverse workforce. Her second article, on sexual harassment, summarizes recent legal cases and offers suggestions as to how firms can deal with sexual harassment cases.

The trauma of being fired has been compared to that attending divorce or the death of a loved one. In their articles, Patricia Werhane examines the present "employment at will" legal doctrine that governs discharge, John McCall discusses whether employers should provide reasons in termination cases, and James Kiersky examines whether employees should be permitted due process in such cases. The case study invites discussion regarding a specific discharge and the way it is handled.

John Boatright analyzes the various sorts of privacy and recent threats to privacy, and then discusses three factors which must be considered when corporations collect information that may threaten an employee's right to privacy: relevance, consent, and method. The case studies in this section explore two areas of concern with respect to privacy: a general moral issue concerning the kinds of employee data firms should be allowed to gather and retain, and the issue of specifying the morally permissible means used to gather such data.

In their article on worker safety, Robert Almeder and J. D. Millar argue that the worker has a *prima facie* moral right to know about any materially harmful working condition. The case in this section focuses on the issue of whether employees working under certain conditions have a right to know whether fellow employees have tested HIV positive.

If a firm is engaged in immoral or illegal activity, does an employee have a right or obligation to blow the whistle? Alan Westin lists certain complexities that should be considered in framing whistleblowing policies. Ronald Duska specifies several conditions an employee must meet before he or she can justifiably blow the whistle on the firm. He then considers whether an employee is ever obligated to blow the whistle on his or her firm.

*Ronald Duska*

# Employee Rights

Let us look at what specific rights have been claimed for employees in recent times. Such a list, of course, will not be exhaustive; no list of rights is. Nor will this list attempt to order the rights in terms of which are derived from which. To do that would require settling an issue in ethical theory of whether rights are derived from basic necessities for the good life or from the basic requirements necessary to achieve human dignity. In either case, as society changes and life adapts to new circumstances, newly perceived necessities will become candidates for rights. As the employer-employee relationship evolves, new rights will be asserted.

## THE RIGHT TO WORK

Clearly, one cannot be an employee unless one is employed, so it seems somewhat odd to talk about the right to work as an employee's right. One can talk of a potential employee's right, but even, in that case, since there is no actual employer, who would have the corresponding obligation to provide a job? However, since having a job is currently an "essential need" or requirement for most people, it can be argued that all able-bodied individuals have a right to a job. So, the right to work would be a right of recipients that leaves it unspecified who has the obligation to provide the work. We cannot require a particular employer to provide a job for a particular individual. What can be claimed is that, if a particular employer has a job to offer, prospective employees, with proper qualifications, have a right to an equal opportunity to attain the job.

Does the person who is "most qualified" have a right to the job? The condition of qualified has force only within the context of a business which has as one of its primary goals, the maximization of productivity. In

From: *A Companion to Business Ethics*, ed. Robert E. Frederick (Oxford: Blackwell Publishers, 1999). Reprinted with permission of Blackwell Publishers Ltd.

a family-owned private business, set up for the security of the family, the owner is perfectly within his or her rights to hire any of the children they wish without regard to qualifications, since the owner may have started the business for the specific purpose of providing jobs and financial security for members of the family.

Hence, if there are rights to work, they seem to be delimited by circumstances. It seems the claim that every able-bodied person has a right to work can only make sense if a consequent obligation to provide jobs falls primarily on the state to set up an environment that encourages job creation, and enforces equal opportunity for hiring. This would mean there would seem to be more force to the claim of a right to work within the context of a more socialist state than in a more free-market oriented state. Certainly, one of the motivations behind socialism is the feeling of the necessity of providing jobs to the unemployed based on a belief that everyone who is able has a right to a job.

## THE RIGHT TO MEANINGFUL WORK

A corollary to the right to work, is the claim of some that there is a right to meaningful work, i.e., a moral claim that tedious, repetitive, and boring work is dehumanizing. As John Ruskin said, "It is a good and desirable thing, truly, to make many pins in a day; but if we could only see with what crystal sand their points were polished—sand of human soul, much to be magnified before it can be discerned for what it is—we should think there might be some loss in it also." All agree it is a good thing to create jobs that do not alienate or dehumanize, but is the creation of jobs, that have meaning and purpose (whatever that might mean beyond the fact that they provide, through the division of labor a desired good for society), really an obligation of anyone? Is it even possible? There are some jobs that are tedious and distasteful by their very nature. Yet they need to be done.

There is an analogy here with the right to property. Most people want to claim property as their own, as long as it is beneficial for them, but any right to property should carry with it an obligation to protect the rest of society from that property which turns obnoxious. Not all property is beneficial. There is garbage, old cars, junk, and old deserted buildings. Does the right to property entail a right to dispose of it without any obligation, if it is undesirable property? One would think not. There needs to be more attention paid to the downside of property.

Just as there is undesirable property, similarly there are tedious jobs in the world. Society needs someone to do them. The issue of distributive justice must focus on how this burden of the world is to be distributed, as well as the goods of the world. Since some jobs are burdensome, a view that claims a right to meaningful work and equates meaningful work only with jobs that are not burdensome, is seriously flawed in facing reality. At most, what can be claimed is a right of a worker to a job which is made as meaningful as possible. The correlative duty would be for the employers to do what they can to alleviate tedious, burdensome, and dehumanizing working conditions.

## THE RIGHTS OF THE EMPLOYEE

Once hired, an employee certainly can claim rights such as:

- The right to a safe and healthy work environment
- The right to job security and due process in firing and promoting
- The right to privacy
- The right to compensation for injury
- The right to participation or voice in matters affecting workers
- The right to equal treatment without regard to race or gender
- The right to pension protection
- The rights to collective bargaining such as those established by the National Labor Relations Board
- The right to be free from harassment
- The right to a living wage

We will examine each to see what the claim is based on and to what extent it is justified.

*The right to a safe and healthy work environment.* One can defend the claim that employees have a right to a safe and healthy environment on the grounds that an employer like everyone else is obliged to do no harm. However, such a claim is challenged by some defenders of a free market view which sees the employment relationship as simply a contractual arrangement, wherein both parties are free to accept or reject the terms of the contract. From such a perspective, the worker is seen as free to choose to do the job under whatever circumstances it occurs. If workers desire a safe and healthy environment, then they can refuse to work under those unsafe conditions. If enough workers refuse, there will be a short supply of workers and the employer will be forced either to develop safer work environments or to pay higher wages to reflect the higher safety risk. Defenders of the right to a safe work environment counter that the employment relationship must be seen in a more realistic light. It is clear that in an urbanized market economy where there are more workers than desirable jobs, there are severe asymmetries of power between employer and employee. Given that fact, the employee is forced to take certain jobs to survive, so that the conditions of a contract—two free and autonomous individuals making an uncoerced choice—are difficult to meet. Consequently, a claim that it is not incumbent on an employer to provide a safe and healthy work environment if the worker chooses to accept a job under such circumstances is disingenuous. Such an attitude justified the sweatshops of the late nineteenth and early twentieth centuries, but it seems no longer tenable.

Even if the free market contractual approach were tenable, the requirements of the free contract would make it imperative that the prospective employee knows the safety and health risks before going into the situation. So, the prospective employee could claim a right to the knowledge of the *conditions* of the job, as well as a right to some later choice if new and unforeseen health and safety factors come to light. There seems to be no way under either model that an employer can justify withholding such vital information from employees.

Given the realities of the asymmetries of power in the employer-employee relationship, it seems reasonable to assume that there should be a right to a safe and healthy work environment. Further, such a right would necessarily override the right of shareholders to profit maximization. All profit maximization is trumped by other stakeholder rights so the goal of business which is to maximize profits becomes limited to as much profit as possible while respecting the rights of other stakeholders.

*The right to job security and due process in disciplining, demoting, promoting, and firing.* It was long held that the employer had a right to fire employees at will—the core of the doctrine euphemistically named, "employment at will." The arguments were: for the sake of efficiency (a utilitarian argument) and to respect the property rights of owners (a deontological argument), owners were free to fire workers as they wished. The business was the owner's property and the owner had the right to do what he or she willed with that property, including firing employees for whatever reason or no reason.

This view, of course, fails to recognize that the employment relationship is a reciprocal relationship which involves interdependencies between an employer and an employee. Implied or explicit agreements and promises are entered into when a job is offered and accepted. No prospective employees, in their right mind, would *freely* accept a job on the condition that they could be let go on the whim of the employer. The operative word here is *freely*. If one has little or no choice, one accepts to work under conditions that would not otherwise be endured. Reasonable people expect that others have justifiable reasons for what they do. Hence, there is a right to job security which means the person, once hired, has a right to hold that job as long as there are no good reasons for terminating the employment.

Given the right to job security, it is incumbent on the employer to give the employee the right to due process when decisions are made concerning his or her welfare. Such decisions involve a renegotiation of the implied understanding. The insistence on due process is made because employers who hold power over the employee are analogous to the U.S. government which holds power over its citizens. Since, to avoid the abuse of power, governments cannot act against their citizens without giving due process and since the employee is in the same subservient relationship to the employer, as the citizen to the government, similar protections need to be given. Hence, there should be a right to due process, a right to procedures, including notice and a hearing or process where good reasons for firing or demotion need to be presented. Of course, given that most states in the U.S. are still employment-at-will states, the right to due process can be no more than a moral right, since it is not recognized as a legal right, except, of course, where it was negotiated into a contract. However, as we know, provisions in contracts that give power to one or the other party are only negotiated from strength.

*The right to privacy.* The right to privacy is also argued for by drawing an analogy of the employee to the citizen. The right to privacy is not specifically mentioned in the U.S. constitution, but is asserted in the rulings of supreme court justices. Justice Brandeis (1890), one of the first to assert privacy rights, maintained that the right to privacy was "the right to be let alone." The claim to a right to privacy springs from an individualism which asserts that no one has the right to tell another what to do in his or her personal and private life, and also asserts that other people do not have the right to know what goes on in a person's private life if that person does not wish to disclose it. A derivative of the general right to privacy, is of course, the right to freedom in one's off hours, as long as what one does does not hurt the employer. Privacy rights, of course, are negative rights. The employer need not do anything except respect an employee's privacy.

There are arguments against privacy rights or, at least, arguments that there are times when those rights can be overridden. Specifically, privacy rights can be overridden when private action *harms* others. That, of course, means the actions are no longer private. Such a stance, however, respects privacy rights much more than an earlier view which held an employer had a right to tell an employee what they could or could not do in his or her private life. Here, we have the question of how much an employer is entitled to demand from an employee which is not job relevant. What are the rights of the employer vis-á-vis the employee?

Defenders of procedures which seem to violate privacy, such as polygraphs and drug testing, defend this invasion of privacy on the grounds that it conflicts with others' rights to a safe workplace. However, that would not be a denial of the right to privacy, only a claim that it conflicts with other rights.

The right to privacy, of course, implies a right to freedom in one's off hours and relates to a different and more controversial rights' claim, the claim that employees have a right to freedom of speech. Now, few contest the right to free expression of opinions, but what if those opinions, possibly gained in working for a company, when publicly expressed, are harmful to that company? The complexity of such issues indicate that a great deal of work needs to be done in resolving the public/private distinction and how it relates to the employer-employee relationship.

*The right to compensation for injury.* A rather compelling case can be made for a right to compensation for injury, on the basis of economic harm. There are good reasons to believe in compensatory justice. When one person suffers economic harm from another person's activity, the injured party is entitled to compensation. It is the principle that makes parents tell their child to fix or pay for the neighbor's window that the child broke. If I suffer harm in your service, fairness would seem to dictate that you reimburse me for that harm. There is, of course, an exception in the case where the harm was expected and compensation initially took the risk of harm into account, so that the employee was paid more for participating in a high-risk job. As in other cases we have seen, the strength of the rights' claim here will rest on the characteristics of the contract or agreement, explicit or implied, between the employer and employee.

*The right to participation or voice in matters affecting workers.* This is a recently articulated and much more controversial right, but it is a right that flows out of the temper of the times that call for solidarity and total quality control management. As the view of the relationships between owners, managers and employees changes, and as the notion of stakeholder gains ascendancy, the employee is seen as a more and more important player in the corporate culture. Accordingly, in those matters which seriously affect workers, participation in deciding their own fate is seen not so much as a desideratum, but more as a right. The existence of such a right becomes tenable, if one recognizes the asymmetry of power between employer and employee, and how that affects employment agreements. The right is asserted as a foil to ward off the potential abuse of power that can arise from such asymmetry. Existing agreements, to be morally binding, need to be the result of informed mutual consent. If existing implied and explicit contracts or established relationships need to be changed, those affected by the result of the changes ought to have a voice in renegotiating the revisions.

*The right to equal treatment without regard to race or gender.* Since violations of equal treatment occur in the workplace, it seems obvious that one assert a right to equal treatment without regard to race or gender, where race or gender are irrelevant, as they usually are. This is a general human right, derived from the principle of justice which can be applied to workers specifically.

*The right to pension protection.* This right is a much more specific right and does not seem too problematic. Given the beliefs in a right to one's own property, or to what one worked for, and granting that the pension is the property of the workers, promised by the employer, it would seem that good stewardship would oblige the companies to protect the pension and not to put it at risk in speculative business projects.

*The right to organization bargaining and the right to strike.* These are, of course, legal rights and established by legislation and regulation in the United States by the NLRB, but there is a moral basis for the NLRB regulations. The U.S. bishops remind us that human nature being what it is, one way to overcome power is to confront it with equal power. In modern industrialized societies with most of the power on the side of corporations, organizations of workers or consumers are indispensable to redress the balance of power. Hence, to gain the power to secure their rights, workers need to be able to organize. To attack the ability to organize is to attack a right essential to human dignity.

*The right to be free from harassment.* This right, like the right to equal treatment, is a human right that should not be violated anywhere, let alone in the workplace. Emphasis lately has been on the right to be free from *sexual* harassment, but it is imperative to note that there are other forms of harassment.

*The right to a living wage.* This is the last employee right we wish to consider. As far back as 1891, Pope Leo XIII, in an encyclical entitled *Rerum Novarum* (Of New Things), articulated a number of employee rights. Among these was the right to a living wage. For him, a living wage was enough to support a family with children, so that the children were adequately cared for. It is debatable how many jobs today pay a living wage. At any rate, the Pope's call for rights was reiterated by the U.S. bishops in 1986. The bishops not only argued for a living wage, they articulated a set of rights. The argument was simple and familiar.

According to the bishops, asymmetry of power presses workers into choosing between an inadequate wage and no wage at all. Justice demands minimum guarantees. "The provision of wages and other benefits sufficient to support a family adequately is a basic necessity to prevent (the) exploitation of workers. The dignity of workers requires adequate health care, security for old age or disability, unemployment compensation, healthful working conditions, weekly rest, periodic holidays for leisure and reasonable security against arbitrary dismissal" (National Council of Catholic Bishops, 1986).

We do not claim that this list is exhaustive, even if it is exhausting. For, if we ground rights on necessity, then as society articulates the new necessities required for living well in a new technologically advanced age, it will also articulate newly discovered goods which will become candidates for rights.

# REFERENCES

Brandeis, Justice, and S. Warren. 1890. *Harvard Law Review.*
National Council of Catholic Bishops. 1986. Economic Justice for all. *Origins* 16, no. 24 (November 27). Washington, D.C.: U.S. Catholic Conference.
Ruskin, J. 1968. "Stones of Venice." In M. Abrams et al. (eds). *The Norton Anthology of English Literature.* vol. 2. New York: W. W. Norton.

# HIRING

# Hiring Procedures at
# World Imports, Inc.

World Imports, Inc. purchases a variety of unassembled chandeliers and lamps from foreign producers for assembly at its manufacturing facility in Philadelphia and for sale through ten local outlets. The company also manufactures a variety of electrical items: fixtures, wall receptacles, plugs, switches, etc., for use in its own products and for sale to other assemblers of more complex electrical equipment. The company, privately owned and an employer of 550 people, has the following organizational structure:

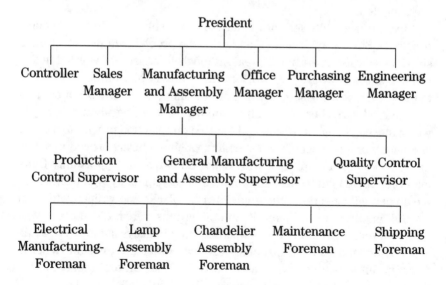

In 1992, World Imports's President Tom Naylor became concerned with quality-control problems. A disturbing percentage of electrical items the company manufactured were defective and rejected by quality-control testing. Most of these items had to be scrapped, which cut directly into profits. Naylor was very concerned that defective electrical items would bypass quality control, be shipped, cause accidents, and subject the company to product liability lawsuits. Rejection ratios were also increasing in the two assembly divisions. Discussions with his top managers indicated that the firm had a high personnel turnover ratio and significant personnel problems; absenteeism, for example, was on the rise, and more employee complaints were percolating upward. Naylor concluded that personnel problems were a big factor in World Imports's quality problems.

In the past, World Imports's personnel relations were handled by the office manager, but this manager had no formal training in personnel management and little experience with, or knowledge of, manufacturing or assembly work. These facts, coupled with strong growth in recent years, led Naylor to conclude that the time had arrived to create a personnel department at the manager level. Naylor knew just who he wanted to hire—Joan Miller, the daughter of his controller, a recent masters-level graduate in management, and a part-time office worker in the firm for several years. Naylor took Ms. Miller to lunch, offered her the position, and she accepted.

Joan immediately set out to analyze and resolve the firm's personnel problems. Since Naylor had clued her to the problems in manufacturing, she decided to start with that area. Although Joan had not worked in this division she was aware that work of this sort can be routine and boring, but also that exacting standards must be maintained in the production of consumer electrical products. Since she was a bit uneasy about the way in which she had been hired, and had focused on selection procedures in her graduate work, she decided to start by examining hiring procedures. She first checked for compliance with Equal Employment Opportunity Commission (EEOC) guidelines, and found that the company was well within the 80 percent selection ratio guidelines for blacks and women, although she did find that the vast majority of both groups were hired at the lowest level and remained there. She noted that no job analysis data were available for positions in the manufacturing and assembly division. When a foreman felt a new position was needed, he made an oral request to his supervisor and the latter's manager, who then made the decision. If approved, the foreman and office manager discussed the issue, and the latter wrote up a brief job description and specification, which also served as an ad in the local newspaper. A recent ad ran as follows:

### ELECTRICIAN TECHNICIAN

Electrician for supervising the mfgr. and testing of electrical products. Responsible for equipment maintenance. Supervises 12 helpers. Reports to Electrical Manufacturing Foreman. Experience required. Good benefits. Day shift. 634-0297.

Candidates for the position were asked to submit two references, and the office manager selected one to be queried about facts of previous employment. To facilitate the process, an informal telephone reference check was conducted by the office manager. After undesirable candidates were eliminated, the remaining candidates were given the Wonderlic Personnel Test. This is a 12 minute, 50 question general intelligence test that contains items relating to verbal, arithmetical, clerical, and judgmental abilities, and is used as a quick means of estimating the general mental ability of adults in industrial situations. Standard questions are:

1. The eleventh month of the year is _____.
2. SEVERE is the opposite of:
   (1) harsh (2) stern (3) tender (4) rigid (5) unyielding
3. Which word is different from the others?
   (1) certainty (2) dubiousness (3) assuredness (4) confidence (5) sureness
4. Answer yes or no. Does B.C. mean "before Christ?" _____.

In order to be considered for hiring, a candidate's scores must exceed the norm on this test. The remaining candidates are interviewed by the general supervisor and the foreman. The interview is unstructured, but it is understood among the foremen that the following items are to be considered (even if they are not explicitly discussed in the interview) and subsequently discussed: appearance, mannerisms, home and family background, education, motivation, work history, personality, and health.

After the interviews are complete, the foreman, his general supervisor, and the division manager review reference checks, test results, and interviews, and then make a joint selection.

## FOR DISCUSSION

Are World Imports's selection procedures acceptable? Why or why not? If you believe the firm's selection procedures can be improved, state specifically what improvements should be made and why.

*Milton Snoeyenbos*
*Robert Almeder*

# Hiring Ethics

Whether one owns a firm, manages it, invests in it, works for it, purchases its products, or relies on others who purchase its products, in some way we all have an important stake in a company's hiring practices. The firm seeks to hire those individuals who will contribute to its goals of efficiency and profitability. The individual seeks a position that is commensurate with her skills and will reward her efforts. Consumers want a quality product at the lowest possible cost, and this is, in part, a function of the quality of labor hired. In addition, our society also has an interest in hiring practices; since passage of the 1964 Civil Rights Act, we have attempted to ensure that candidates will not be discriminated against on the basis of race, color, religion, sex, or national origin. An important question, then, is whether the stated interests of the firm, the prospective employee, and the larger society can all be met successfully and simultaneously. In this article we argue for an affirmative answer to this question. Keeping these interests in balanced perspective we discuss ethical dimensions of the employee hiring procedure: job analysis, job description, job specification, recruitment, testing, and interviewing.

In the initial stages of the hiring process, a job opening is identified and the personnel manager performs a *job analysis*. Relevant information is collected and written up as a *job description* that details the job's main features and activities necessary for effective performance; it lists what the worker does and how he is to do it. In turn, the job description is used to develop a *job specification* which lists the necessary qualifications, i.e., knowledge, abilities, and experience needed to successfully perform the job. The organization then develops a pool of candidates by *recruiting*, and selects a person, primarily on the basis of *tests*, *interviews*, and reference checks. Although there can be other dimensions to the hiring process, the aspects denoted by the italicized terms above are the most important and the most commonly used, and on them our discussion will focus.

## JOB ANALYSIS

From an ethical and practical standpoint, it is important for the personnel manager to conduct an accurate and thorough job analysis, an account of whether a position is actually needed and, if so, of what it should consist. The firm is interested in effective and efficient job performance that will enable it to maximize its goals. An accurate job description and job specification rest on having a detailed analysis of the position to be filled, and testing and interviewing should focus on those factors mentioned in the job description and specification, i.e., factors relevant to job performance. Utility for the firm thus requires a thorough analysis of the position to be filled. Fairness to the prospective employee also entails a thorough, accurate job analysis. The applicant should seek placement in a position where he can be rewarded commensurate with his ability, motivation, and output. If a job far exceeds or falls far short of a person's potential, these aims will not be realized. Since an individual typically seeks a position on the basis of a job description and job specification, and these rest on a job analysis, a person cannot seek a position commensurate with what he has to offer unless the employer conducts an accurate, thorough job analysis. Job analysis is also important in securing compliance with society's equal employment legislation. As we shall see, the law and federal guidelines require that personnel selection procedures must have validity, i.e., such procedures must represent actual, relevant aspects of job behavior. Since an accurate account of such behavior is typically developed in a job analysis, the law mandates that an employer conduct a thorough job analysis.

Let us now focus on the specifics of job analysis. If we assume we are dealing with an existing position to be filled, the personnel manager should not merely rely on the existing job description and job specification. A thorough job analysis requires a detailed understanding of the position as seen by its present jobholder and his supervisors. To acquire this understanding, the personnel manager can conduct interviews, observe the present employee on the job, or utilize questionnaires.

Questionnaires are frequently used to analyze a job. The employee is given a list of questions relating to various tasks and is asked to check whether she performs them and, if so, how long it takes. Other questions may be more open-ended, and simply ask the person to describe in writing the nature of some aspect of the job. But it is doubtful that a questionnaire can itself provide a thorough job analysis, since it places emphasis on the jobholder's ability to report accurately on her job's functions. In practice this ability is often lacking, and hence information secured by a questionnaire is often incomplete or inconsistent. Questionnaires can, however, provide background information for a more thorough interview.

Observation of the incumbent jobholder can provide relevant information if the job involves routine or repetitive physical skills, but it is hardly sufficient for jobs requiring the exercise of judgment (e.g., paramedic) or those requiring a considerable amount of unquantifiable mental activity (e.g., draftsman). In these cases, observation must be coupled with an interview to obtain a thorough job analysis.

Interviews with the job incumbent and her supervisors are perhaps the common way of conducting a job analysis. In many cases the utility of an interview is strengthened if it is used in conjunction with a questionnaire and direct observation of the incumbent jobholder. The interview can reveal information not obtainable by observation and can be used to confirm and clarify data gathered by both observation and the questionnaire. Since job incumbents frequently view the job analysis interview as an evaluation procedure, the most serious problem with such interviews is that the information received may be distorted. To avoid distortion, the interviewer should prepare carefully for the interview, be objective, gather information accurately, and verify the information obtained.

## JOB DESCRIPTION

Assuming the personnel manager has a thorough, accurate job analysis, the next step is to write up a job description. This typically includes: (1) a job identification, which lists items such as the job title, department, division, plant location, and pay range; (2) a job summary detailing the position's procedures and responsibilities; it describes the duties performed, how they are to be performed, and the purpose of each duty, and (3) an account of working conditions.

Some management theorists argue for a detailed account of tasks, duties, and working conditions, whereas others favor a more unstructured or general job description. It is difficult to resolve this issue in a comprehensive manner because the nature of the job plays an important part in selecting the proper approach, e.g., managerial positions will typically require a more general description than a job on a factory line. In most cases, however, we favor a relatively specific job description. Arguments against a detailed job description are that it: (1) limits the jobholder's initiative and creativity, (2) is easily dated with job changes, and (3) can be used by the employee to avoid additional duties. But (3) is a motivational issue; the unmotivated employee could also seek to avoid additional duties by appeal to the vagueness of a nonspecific job description, in which case changes as mentioned in (2) would also have to be addressed and the job description made more specific. And, against (1), the employee with initiative might be able to develop responsibilities in addition to those already specified in some detail, which might lead to a job description revision that increases the productivity of other employees holding the same type of job. An additional factor related directly to hiring is that if the job description is used to help train new workers how to perform their jobs, it should contain specifics.

There are two major reasons favoring a specific, complete job description. The pragmatic reason is that the law requires it. In the case of hiring, selection tests are based on the job description; one tests for the ability to perform tasks specified in the job description. In *Griggs* v. *Duke Power Co.* (1971), the Supreme Court held that selection tests must have validity, i.e., they must accurately represent actual on-the-job activities. In *Albemarle Paper* v. *Moody* (1975), the Supreme Court held that if tests are used to screen candidates for a job, then the duties and responsibilities of that job must be carefully analyzed and described prior to testing. More fundamentally, utility for the firm and fairness to the prospective employee are enhanced when the employee knows what is expected of him. Turnover costs relating to mismatched employees who resign, and the long range consequences of retaining mismatched employees, favor having the employer provide a relatively specific and complete job description.

## JOB SPECIFICATION

A job specification lists qualifications needed to perform the job. In some cases this may seem straightforward, as in law or accounting, where specific training is required and professional standards are well articulated. Where the firm intends to hire an untrained person and train her for a job, careful consideration must be given to developing a set of qualifications. In either case, however, morality requires that the employer use only those qualifying criteria that relate directly to success on the job. The morality of employing only qualifying criteria that relate to job success rests on both consequentialist and nonconsequentialist grounds. If job qualifications are set too high for the actual job, the individual hired may not be able to work to potential; and if they are set too low, the individual hired may not be able to perform successfully. In either case, job satisfaction is not liable to be achieved and the firm's efficiency and profitability are liable to be impaired, with consequent disutility to the firm and society. In addition, those individuals not hired have been denied fair access to the market.

## RECRUITMENT

In recruiting candidates a firm typically attempts to obtain a large selection ratio, i.e., a large number of applicants relative to the positions open. In this way the company has a better chance of selecting the best person for the job. However, fairness to the job seeker and utility for the firm both require that the personnel manager seek to attract only relevant candidates. Interviewing and testing are expensive activities for the firm, and a considerable amount of applicants' time and money can be wasted if an overzealous recruiter, intent on maximizing his selection ratio, fails to recruit only relevant candidates who can fill the job description and specification. Also, we should not overlook the psychological damage to an otherwise qualified applicant who is rejected in the early stages of the screening process (perhaps with no subsequent explanation) because of a recruiting mismatch.

A recruiting device, such as an advertisement, should therefore be relatively complete. It should contain items such as the job title, duties, qualifications and experience required, working conditions, salary, and fringe benefits. It should also be somewhat detailed, if that is possible; relevant portions of the job description and specification could in certain cases be included. Of course, the amount of information included must be balanced with the cost of the advertisement. In addition, fairness requires that the employer reveal his identity if he expects the job seeker to provide detailed biographical data. It also requires that the advertisement portray the firm in a realistic manner. Hiring is only one aspect of personnel management; retaining good employees is another important function. Job satisfaction is a key element in attaining a high retention ratio, and a considerable amount of job dissatisfaction is traceable to unrealistic recruitment efforts that attempt to make a firm "look good" to applicants. Thus, utility to the firm and fairness to the applicant necessitate realistic recruiting techniques.

## TESTING

The hiring process through the recruitment stage involves gathering applicants. Subsequent steps involve the rejection of candidates until available positions are filled. While the actual selection process may involve many stages, including application blanks and reference checks, we will discuss only the testing and interviewing steps.

Psychological testing became an important tool in the hiring process in the 1920s. It held the promise of bringing scientific objectivity to selection procedures, and this promise has certainly been partially realized. The psychologists' intelligence, physical, achievement, aptitude, and personality tests have enabled many people to make better career selections and have helped firms to better match employees and available job, both of which lead to increased employee job satisfaction, productivity, and profitability. More recently, however, scientists have restudied tests because a high percentage of minorities were failing them. Critics of such tests argued that they were culture bound, and reflected the majority culture. Also, the predictive ability of such tests was questioned; some researchers claimed that most industrial occupations tests had little validity. Other studies indicated that many workers who could not pass commonly used tests could, nevertheless, perform tasks the tests were designed to measure as well as individuals who did pass.

If an employer uses a test as a hiring selection procedure, it should be *validated,* i.e., it should demonstrably measure what it proposes to measure which, in the case of a selection test, means the test must bear a predictive relationship to *actual* job performance regarding a particular job or type of work. There are both consequentialist and nonconsequentialist grounds for the validation requirement. The firm's aim is to staff positions with people who can best enable it to attain its goals, and validation requires the employer to show that his test is actually related to job performance. This should lead to greater efficiency and profitability for the company. The consequences for the jobholder, in terms of success and satisfaction, should be better for the person whose qualifications fit the position than for a person who is mismatched with a job via an invalid test. Also, society not only benefits from the avoidance of mismatches, but also from the lessening of social unrest resulting from awareness that selection tests must be based on merit rather than factors unrelated to job performance. On the nonconsequentialist side, a test that is not valid can hardly be fair to an otherwise qualified candidate who is rejected via the test. And not only does the decision help ensure fairness in selection, it also reinforces the private enterprise, free market conception of the economy by helping to provide equal employment opportunity and fair access to the market. Hence, the decision promotes both social justice and economic efficiency.

Special care must be taken to ensure the validity of certain sorts of tests that may be used in screening candidates. Personality tests, used to measure stability, motivation, and other aspects of character, are frequently problematic. They may invade privacy and are difficult to evaluate properly. In many cases the relationship between personality traits and job success is tenuous. Where such a relationship can be established, however, it can both help the employee to better himself and his placement in the organization, and also enable the employer to provide the applicant more adequate placement.

## INTERVIEWING

Many personnel managers base their selection decisions primarily on interviews. But there are major problems with this approach to hiring. Interviewers frequently: (1) base decisions on initial impressions; (2) judge applicants on the basis of features irrelevant to job performance; and (3) judge applicants based on an ideal stereotype. As a result, interviewers often overlook or suppress relevant information and frequently make hiring decisions which are inadequate. Fairness and utility regarding the person hired, the firm, and members of society require that interviews, and indeed any selection procedure, have validity.

To help ensure an ethical interviewing process, interviewers should: (1) be chosen carefully and trained adequately; (2) be thoroughly acquainted with the job based on a detailed job analysis, job description, and job specification; (3) use a structured interviewing process in which only job related questions are asked; and (4) determine whether their decisions are validated. Furthermore, given the problems with interviews, recruiters should probably not rely on them alone, but should use them in conjunction with other selection procedures, such as reference checks and tests.

Apart from its place in the hiring process, interviews also are used to give job candidates a preview of life in the firm. In many cases a preview is used to make the firm "look good" and "sell" it to the candidate. But there are reasons why a preview should be realistic, i.e., why it should balance the positive and negative aspects of the job and organization. If the candidate has unrealistic expectations, he may become dissatisfied and resign, with attendant turnover costs to the firm and himself; or he may stay on as a dissatisfied employee who affects the firm's productivity and other workers' morale.

# REVERSE DISCRIMINATION

*Case Study*

# A Promotion Decision
# at Ballentyne International

Wygand Motors, an auto parts supplier, almost slid into bankruptcy during the 1990 recession. Its stock fell to $2 and Wygand was bought out by Frank Ballentyne, a dynamic leader, who renamed the company Ballentyne International (BI). Ballentyne cut debt, invested in research, and focused on engineering high-quality, high-margin parts. He encouraged managerial autonomy at BI's three plants and promoted profit sharing, which enabled BI to attract top talent and kept the plants free of unions.

When Tamika Jackson graduated with a MBA from Duke University in 1998 she went to Atlanta and became Assistant Personnel Manager at Universal South, a small African-American owned insurance firm. By 2001 she was ready for the challenge of a larger firm, and took the job as Personnel Manager at BI's Cary plant. She hoped she would not have to make any significant decisions for a few months while she put in place a new set of employee selection procedures. Unfortunately, Don Strach, Production Manager, became ill suddenly and took early retirement, so two weeks into her new job the task fell to Tamika to make a recommendation to Art Lloyd, Plant Manager, who would make the final selection to replace Strach. Lloyd said the decision needed to be made soon, and that he would consider only three internal candidates, each of whom was the Production Foreman of one of BI's three production lines at Cary. He said all three candidates wanted the job, all were qualified, and that he wanted one name with reasons in five days. As she turned to her task, Tamika felt a certain foreboding; the only female and only African-American on a management committee of seven at Cary, she thought that Lloyd, who knew all three very well, could have made the decision himself and taken her off the hook. She felt she was being tested early in the game.

Tamika started with the most objective of the factors she would consider, seniority. Mary Santoli, thirty-seven, had been with BI for fourteen years, the last seven as Production Foreman on line A. Bill Larson, forty-nine, a thirteen-year BI veteran, had headed up line B as Production Foreman for the last eight years. And Jim Sims, thirty-nine, had been employed at BI for twelve years, six as Production Foreman of line C. Since Cary was a non-union plant, seniority was not as important a promotion criterion as it would be at a unionized plant. Nevertheless, production line employees viewed it as a very significant factor in promotions. Also, Tamika remembered that Art Lloyd had discussed the importance of seniority in their first meeting two weeks ago. Lloyd said the auto makers were requiring their suppliers to be flexible and that BI would have an edge in being flexible if it could remain union-free. Those advocating a union wanted a seniority-based promotion system. Lloyd said that by paying some attention to seniority BI could claim that it was important to the firm, and hence argue that the union was not needed. However, Lloyd had not spelled out how the seniority factor was to be weighted in the decision. Furthermore, Tamika was not clear about what Lloyd and BI meant by seniority, since one candidate had been at BI the longest time and another had seniority as a Production Foreman.

Next, Tamika reviewed performance records of the three candidates. Fortunately, BI had a point system of 10 (top) to 1 recorded annually and based solely on production output on the line. The scores were as follows, with the numbers in parentheses recording the person's supervisory role as a Production Foreman and the other (previous) scores as individual workers on a production line:

|         |   |   |   |   |   |    |    |     |   |   |   |   |   | last year |
|---------|---|---|---|---|---|----|----|-----|---|---|---|---|---|-----------|
| Santoli | 7 | 7 | 8 | 8 | 9 | 9  | 10 | (7  | 7 | 7 | 8 | 8 | 8 | 9)        |
| Larson  |   | 7 | 8 | 8 | 8 | 10 | (6 | 7   | 8 | 8 | 8 | 9 | 9 | 10)       |
| Sims    |   |   | 7 | 8 | 7 | 8  | 9  | 9   | (7 | 7 | 7 | 8 | 8 | 8)        |

Tamika then considered affirmative action. BI had an affirmative action program and everyone knew Frank Ballentyne was committed to it; he called it The Ballentyne Way. Yet it was not easy to hire women to work for an auto parts manufacturer; many worked in BI's general offices, but these were not located at Cary, which was a production plant and ran a very lean office staff. Furthermore, Cary line work was physically strenuous. The year 2000 demographic figures were:

| | % white male | % white female | % African- Am. male | % African- Am. fem. | % Other |
|---|---|---|---|---|---|
| Residents in areas of BI facilities | 39 | 41 | 6 | 7 | 7 |
| Applicants for BI positions | 51 | 28 | 11 | 6 | 4 |
| BI employees | 49 | 31 | 9 | 6 | 5 |
| 100 top paid BI employees | 74 | 17 | 5 | 2 | 2 |
| Cary area residents | 37 | 41 | 9 | 10 | 3 |
| Applicants for Cary positions | 47 | 31 | 13 | 6 | 3 |
| Cary employees | 56 | 25 | 7 | 6 | 6 |
| 100 top paid Cary employees | 80 | 12 | 4 | 2 | 2 |

Mary Santoli, as a woman, and Jim Sims, as an African-American, would get special consideration under BI's affirmative action plan. But how much this factor was to count was unclear to Tamika; it had never been quantified at BI.

Tamika also considered leadership potential. She thought that potential in a new, higher ranking job was hard to gauge, but in this case it should reflect two major factors: (1) past performance as a Production Foreman, to which she assigned one-third weight, and, (2) the input of line employees. She weighted this factor two-thirds of her leadership potential score because she herself did not really know the candidates, (1) had been factored into the performance criterion, and none of the other criteria included input from employees. She was unsure how to use (1) to assess potential, but decided to interview employees to measure (2). The interviews revealed that employees ranked the candidates: (1) Jim Sims, (2) Mary Santoli, (3) Bill Larson. Several who ranked Bill lowest thought he was too set in his ways. Some of the younger line workers said that Bill knew how to pressure people into producing, but they wondered how that approach would work in the long run. However, one line veteran said that, although Bill would never be popular, he knew how to get what could be gotten out of unmotivated workers. Mary Santoli was uniformly thought to be very professional in handling employees and leading her line; as one veteran of her line observed, there were very few complaints about her as a Production Foreman. She was regarded as a fine problem-solver who could work through situations to make good decisions. Jim Sims ranked highest among the employees on leadership potential. Several said that harmony was the key to excellence at Cary, and that Jim best knew how to bring people together. A number said that the key to leadership at Cary was to bring together the pro-union and anti-union factions, and that Jim could best do that. One said that only Jim really understood how boring line work was to the average worker. Several mentioned that Jim organized a weekend volleyball league for his line crew that was very popular and that he led the drive to organize a benefit which raised over $110,000 when the son of a Cary employee on another line was severely injured in a skiing accident.

Tamika felt she had enough factual information, but now came the hard part, deciding how to weight the criteria she was using. Once that was done she could work toward the decision.

## FOR DISCUSSION

Who should Tamika recommend? Why?

# Wage Differences at Robert Hall

Robert Hall Clothes, Inc., owned a chain of retail stores that specialized in clothing for the family.[1] One of the chain's stores was located in Wilmington, Delaware.

The Robert Hall store in Wilmington had a department for men's and boy's clothing and another department for women's and girl's clothing. The departments were physically separated and were staffed by different personnel. Only men were allowed to work in the men's department and only women in the women's department. The personnel of the store were sexually segregated because years of experience had taught the store's managers that unless clerks and customers were of the same sex, the frequent physical contact between clerks and customers would embarrass both and would inhibit sales.

The clothing in the men's department was generally of a higher and more expensive quality than the clothing in the women's department. Competitive factors accounted for this: There were few other men's stores in Wilmington so the store could stock expensive men's clothes and still do a thriving business, while women's clothing had to be lower priced to compete with the many other women's stores in Wilmington. Because of these differences in merchandise, the store's profit margins on the men's clothing was higher than its margins on the women's clothing. As a result, the men's department consistently showed a larger dollar volume in gross sales and a greater gross profit, as is indicated in Table 1.

Because of the differences shown in Table 1, women personnel brought in lower sales and profits per hour. In fact, male salespersons brought in substantially more than the females did (Tables 2 and 3).

As a result of these differences in the income produced by the two departments, the management of Robert Hall paid their male salespersons more than their female personnel. Management learned after a Supreme

From Manuel G. Velasquez, *Business Ethics: Concepts and Cases*, 4th ed. (Upper Saddle River, N.J.: Prentice-Hall, Inc., 1998), pp. 419–22. Reprinted with persmission of Pearson Education, Inc.

Court ruling in their favor in 1973 that it was entirely legal for them to do this if they wanted. Wages in the store were set on the basis of profits per hour per department, with some slight adjustments upward to ensure wages were comparable and competitive to what other stores in the area were paying. Over the years, Robert Hall set the wages given in Table 4. Although the wage differences between males and females were substantial, they were not as large as the percentage differences between male and female sales and profits. The management of Robert Hall argued that their female clerks were paid less because the commodities they sold could not bear the same selling costs that the commodities sold in the men's department could bear. On the other hand, the female clerks argued, the skills, sales efforts, and responsibilities required of male and female clerks were "substantially" the same.

## TABLE 1

|  | Men's Department | | | Women's Department | | |
|  | Sales ($) | Gross Profit ($) | Percent Profit (%) | Sales ($) | Gross Profit ($) | Percent Profit (%) |
| Year | | | | | | |
|---|---|---|---|---|---|---|
| 1963 | 210,639 | 85,328 | 40.5 | 177,742 | 58,547 | 32.9 |
| 1964 | 178,867 | 73,608 | 41.2 | 142,788 | 44,612 | 31.2 |
| 1965 | 206,472 | 89,930 | 43.6 | 148,252 | 49,608 | 33.5 |
| 1966 | 217,765 | 97,447 | 44.7 | 166,479 | 55,463 | 33.3 |
| 1967 | 244,922 | 111,498 | 45.5 | 206,680 | 69,190 | 33.5 |
| 1968 | 263,663 | 123,681 | 46.9 | 230,156 | 79,846 | 34.7 |
| 1969 | 316,242 | 248,001 | 46.8 | 254,379 | 91,687 | 36.4 |

## TABLE 2

| Year | Male Sales Per Hour ($) | Female Sales Per Hour ($) | Excess M Over F (%) |
|---|---|---|---|
| 1963 | 38.31 | 27.31 | 40 |
| 1964 | 40.22 | 30.36 | 32 |
| 1965 | 54.77 | 33.30 | 64 |
| 1966 | 59.58 | 34.31 | 73 |
| 1967 | 63.14 | 36.92 | 71 |
| 1968 | 62.27 | 37.20 | 70 |
| 1969 | 73.00 | 41.26 | 77 |

**TABLE 3**

| Year | Male Gross Profits Per Hour ($) | Female Gross Profits Per Hour ($) | Excess M Over F (%) |
|------|------|------|------|
| 1963 | 15.52 | 9.00 | 72 |
| 1964 | 16.55 | 9.49 | 74 |
| 1965 | 23.85 | 11.14 | 114 |
| 1966 | 26.66 | 11.43 | 134 |
| 1967 | 28.74 | 12.36 | 133 |
| 1968 | 29.21 | 12.91 | 127 |
| 1969 | 34.16 | 15.03 | 127 |

**TABLE 4**

| Year | Male Earnings Per Hour ($) | Female Earnings Per Hour ($) | Excess M Over F (%) |
|------|------|------|------|
| 1963 | 2.18 | 1.75 | 25 |
| 1964 | 2.46 | 1.86 | 32 |
| 1965 | 2.67 | 1.80 | 48 |
| 1966 | 2.92 | 1.95 | 50 |
| 1967 | 2.88 | 1.98 | 45 |
| 1968 | 2.97 | 2.02 | 47 |
| 1969 | 3.13 | 2.16 | 45 |

## FOR DISCUSSION

How should the managers of the Robert Hall store in Wilmington compensate their employees? Why?

## NOTE

1. Information for this case is drawn entirely from *Hodgson* v. *Robert Hall Clothes, Inc.*, 473 F. 2nd 589, cert. denied, 42 U.S.L.W. 3198 (9 October 1973) and 326 F. Supp. 1264 (D. Del. 1971).

*Anita Gonsalves*

# Reverse Discrimination

I wish to thank our Association for inviting me to address you at the millennium. Together we enter a bright era with tremendous prospects to which we can all look forward. To move ahead we need to tackle our most difficult problems, and my topic tonight is reverse discrimination (or preferential treatment), as controversial an issue as any we face. I'm going to give you my take on this topic, I'm against it, while allowing there is another side to which I promise to be fair-minded.

On the slide you see three terms which are sometimes run together but are best kept distinct. (1) *Equal Opportunity.* Although this expression may have different meanings in other contexts, its meaning in a business context is that the company adopts policies which give people equal consideration in selection procedures such as hiring and promotion. It means that people who meet the basic qualifications for a position are given a fair chance to compete for it. The 1964 Civil Rights Act is a good example; it prohibits discriminatory selection procedures based on an individual's race, color, religion, sex or national origin, thereby allowing all qualified candidates to be considered. This is unquestionably good for businesses, since selection procedures based solely on performance-related factors, qualifications, and merit tend to maximize profits. Furthermore, it is fair to all prospective candidates, since no person who is discriminating against others would want to be treated as that person is treating him or her. I think this is a policy the vast majority of Americans believe in. I accept it. It is the traditional promise of America. (2) *Affirmative Action.* As I will use this expression, it involves programs which go beyond merely granting equality of opportunity to everyone who happens to apply for a job. Although affirmative action encompasses a commitment to equality of opportunity, it means the firm takes additional measures to enlarge its recruiting pool to include those previously disadvantaged. For example, a firm takes affirmative action by advertising positions in minority newspapers, by participating in minority job fairs, and so forth. Once hired, it means that individ-

272

uals from the group previously discriminated against are mentored properly and encouraged through corporate support programs. Furthermore, and this I think is very important, it means that in the broader social arena the corporation takes an active role in addressing those issues which cause people to be disadvantaged in the first place. In particular, I believe the social responsibility dollar should be sliced strongly toward lower level education in order to give every child a true shot at overall equal opportunity. I believe that a concerted effort by American corporations to address the serious problems and inequities we have in lower-level education would benefit our corporations as well as those who are disadvantaged, and would be applauded by the vast majority of Americans. Of course, we cannot do it all, but I think we can and should do more. I certainly am committed to affirmative action. (3) *Reverse Discrimination.* This notion, also called preferential treatment, involves a preference for members of a disadvantaged group in selection procedures and discrimination against members of the advantaged group, in our society white males. On this approach there will be some occasions in which an Hispanic female will be selected over a white male even though she is less qualified. She gets preferential treatment while he is subject to reverse discrimination. We have practiced reverse discrimination in the United States since President Johnson signed Executive Order No. 11,246 in 1965, and the Office of Federal Contract Compliance initiated enforcement programs and numerical goals and timetables around 1969. My view, and one I believe is shared by a broad majority of Americans, is that, although equal opportunity and affirmative action are justified, reverse discrimination is not morally justified. Let me explain why.

Let us first examine the consequences of reverse discrimination. We have to acknowledge that it has done some good for many people. A very large number of people have gotten jobs (rather than people who were better qualified) and these jobholders and their families have certainly benefitted. Moreover, some of those hired became role models for some members of the disadvantaged group, who may in turn have become more motivated to prepare for the selection process in the belief they can get a job or promotion. Considering the corporation, the Civil Rights Act certainly has encouraged managers to examine selection procedures more carefully, which can only benefit employers. And many consultants claim the diversity which results from reverse discrimination is probably beneficial to corporations. In addition, some commentators suggest that at the societal level reverse discrimination has fostered racial harmony.

On balance, nonetheless, I think reverse discrimination has had overall negative consequences. The other day I had a promotion opening at $36,000. It came down to two men, one white and the other African-American. Both were qualified, but the white applicant was more qualified. And he seemed to me to have the best attitude toward the position, as objectively measured and also based on my own intuition. If I hired the African-American, it would surely benefit him, but that would be completely offset by the harm to the white applicant. Furthermore, since both applicants were internal, and there was some likelihood they both may have thought the white candidate was better qualified, there was some chance that both would come to think that discrimination was practiced, which could negatively impact both since the African-American might come to see himself as a quota-filler. Although some of my employees probably would realize role-model benefits from my hiring the African-American, it does seem odd for one to select as a role-model a person who is not as good at the job as one who could have been doing it. This seems to be the wrong type of role-modeling. In fact, some people might think that in selection procedures you do not have to be the best qualified if you are an African-American. I certainly do not want to send that message to my employees.

Furthermore, our firm will not maximally benefit if I hire the African-American. Our task is to maximize profits—that is why we are in business. To achieve it we need the best performer in every slot, and I mean the best, not the merely adequate. From this perspective, race and sex are simply not relevant to selection decisions. In emphasizing an irrelevant feature, reverse discrimination harms the corporation. Although it is sometimes argued that diversity based on reverse discrimination will benefit a corporation, this is doubtful, since it would have to be shown that it offsets the decreased profitability resulting from not selecting the most qualified candidate. I know of no study showing this. If it is claimed that having different viewpoints in the firm is better in a complex global environment, I certainly agree that having different viewpoints has some advantages, but this can be an argument for reverse discrimination only if it is assumed that African-Americans as such have a different or distinct viewpoint or that women, as a group, have, say, a distinct way of thinking or considering things, assumptions which certainly have not been proven. In fact, it seems to me that such assumptions stereotype African-Americans or women, and hence are themselves symptomatic of the very type of thinking we need to overcome.

Many people outside of business do not realize that if a corporation gets maximum performance from its employees it benefits society. It can pay its employees more, and reward shareholders with higher dividends. Furthermore, it can lower prices, thereby benefitting consumers. And increased profitability means a higher tax take for society. So reverse discrimination, which I believe undercuts performance maximization, has negative overall consequences for society as well as a business.

As far as consequences go, then, my own view is that reverse discrimination, in spite of some benefits, is on the whole a harmful practice at the individual, corporate, and social levels.

Before I turn to my second type of arguments, those based on rights, I would like to take a brief detour to address one criticism of my arguments based on consequences, a criticism raised mainly by academics in the humanities who claim that selection procedures in business are not today based on qualifications or merit. So the view is that the merit-based arguments against reverse discrimination are actually based on hypocrisy. However, I never have seen any of these critics provide evidence for their position. Do these critics believe Ms. Carly Fiorina, CEO at Hewlett-Packard, was selected by an executive search firm based on something other than merit? Meg Whitman, CEO at eBay— was she hired based on something other than her qualifications? How about Ken Chenault, CEO of American Express; was this African-American hired based on something other than merit? Make no mistake about this: in today's business world you produce or you are gone, and this means you better select the best candidate going in. It is especially vital for our young people today to understand that you either produce or your job is given to someone else, perhaps someone in India or Malaysia where we pay someone one-tenth of what you make in the United States. In today's global marketplace and workplace, there is no place for bringing irrelevant factors into selection procedures; only merit counts.

Let us now consider the rights arguments concerning reverse discrimination. These are also called fairness, justice, or entitlement arguments.

First off, if we believe in equal opportunity, that is, if we believe in giving every person a chance to compete under fair conditions, then reverse discrimination is unjustified, since it is incompatible with equal opportunity. You cannot give everyone equal consideration if you discriminate against anyone, white or black, male or female. So, if you believe individuals have a moral right to equal consideration, reverse discrimination is not morally justified.

Advocates of reverse discrimination often argue that members of groups who have been discriminated against by white males should be compensated by white males. They infer that reverse discrimination is the best way to compensate the victims. However, the compensation argument is not a good argument. Our standard model of compensation is between individuals. If you sell me a product with a warranty, but the product fails to satisfy the warranty, then I can sue you for compensation and if I win you have to pay me. This model is quite understandable. We can identify the individual harmed and identify the individual who caused the damage. We can also assess how much the injured person was damaged, and in terms of that we can determine the amount to penalize the injurer. However, reverse discrimination compensates a person because that person is a member of a group—the group of African-Americans or the group of women. In some cases group compensation is permissible; for example, a particular German corporation might compensate a group, say, the group of Jews who were used by the firm as slave laborers in WW II. In this case one individual, the German firm, is compensating all individual Jews imprisoned there, justifiably so, since each Jew there was injured badly. However, with reverse discrimination every group member is compensated irrespective of whether he or she has actually been injured and only certain members of the advantaged group have to pay compensation irrespective of whether those particular people caused any injury. This is not fair. A wealthy Hispanic female who may be a racist and whose father is a physician and her mother a lawyer is to be compensated, whereas a poor white male who may never have discriminated is being asked to pay the compensation. There seems to be no way to sort out those individual members of the group of white males who should be doing the compensating and no easy way to sort out those in the disadvantaged group who really deserve compensation.

Furthermore, reverse discrimination will only magnify the disparities within the two groups. If you require a company to have a quota of Puerto Ricans, it will select only the most qualified Puerto Ricans. However, these are probably not the Puerto Ricans who deserve compensation. The less qualified Puerto Ricans, the ones who really have been discriminated against, the ones from homeless families, those who attended the worse schools until they dropped out, these will not be benefitted in this competition. The really advantaged white males, the Yale graduates, do not have to worry. They will not be displaced; they have it made. So the one who pays the compensation will in all probability be the white male who is poor. The one among the white males who can least afford to pay compensation is the one asked to pay it by this system, and he often pays it to one who neither deserves nor needs it.

In addition, there is a real question of whether our standard model of compensation is applicable at all to our present situation. On that model individual A injures B and then A compensates B for the injury A caused. According to the reverse discrimination model, C in the past injured D, but now E in the present compensates F for an injury (?) caused by whom? How can this be justified if E is an innocent, young white male? It would seem that the innocent should not have to pay for the sins of their forefathers. The response is likely to be that today's young white males either are actually discriminating or are benefitting from an economic system which continues to favor them and disadvantage members of other groups. I believe this is false. Let's consider the evidence.

In today's society it is undeniably true that African-Americans earn less than whites. Why? Economists try to answer this question scientifically. Two plausible causes of the wage gap are (1) a difference in human capital, e.g., differences in school quality, measured by teachers' salaries, student/teacher ratio, etc., and (2) discrimination in the labor market. Recent research by Neal and Johnson indicates that the wage gap difference is almost all accounted for by differences in human capital, which means that none of the wage gap difference is due to discrimination in the labor market.[1] These authors studied a sample of males who took an ability test at age thirteen and they then compared these scores with the individuals' wages measured roughly ten years later. The differences in test scores explained almost all the differences in wages ten years later. This is true for the subset of whites and it is true of white and African-American comparisons. Generalizing, we can say that whites with less early human capital than other whites will earn less than those whites with more early human capital. We can also say that African-Americans with less early human capital will earn less than whites with more early human capital *and* that the difference in wages is due almost entirely to the lack of human capital and not to discrimination in the labor market.

So the compensation argument: (1) rests on an unclear notion of group compensation; (2) magnifies disparities within groups; and (3) incorrectly assumes there is present labor market discrimination.

Neal and Johnson allow that human capital investment can affect a student's ability test score. They are not claiming that a person's test score is wired in and cannot be improved. This means that our focus should be on investment in early human capital, rather than on reverse discrimination. The research suggests we should abandon reverse discrimination in the labor market and focus on affirmative action, specifically on early childhood education, on vocational training, and on methods to motivate our young people to learn and excel. Reverse discrimination certainly is not a solution to these sorts of problems. In fact, it looks like it is a solution with no problem to solve. If so, and if we are committed to equal opportunity for all, then we should remove race and gender from selection decisions and shift our focus to affirmative action. For business this means: (1) a commitment to true affirmative action in business practices, and (2) a willingness to use corporate resources in the social responsibility arena to foster the development of early human capital.

## NOTE

1. D. Neal and W. Johnson, "The Role of Premarket Factors in Black-White Wage Differences," *Journal of Political Economy* 104, no. 5 (1996): 869–95; W. Johnson and D. Neal, "Basic Skills and the Black-White Earnings Gaps," in *The Black-White Test Score Gap*, ed. C. Jencks and M. Phillips (Washington, D.C.: Brookings, 1998).

*James M. Humber*

# In Defense of
# Reverse Discrimination

Generally, those who attack reverse discrimination do so by arguing that the practice is both unjust and produces bad consequences.[1] If these attacks are taken as being directed against programs of reverse discrimination which are now in place throughout the United States, I believe they are sound. However, reverse discrimination can be practiced in a variety of different ways, and in what follows I intend to argue that properly restructuring our programs of reverse discrimination would not only allow defenders of the practice to meet the force of their critics' attacks, but also provide them with the means for demonstrating that reverse discrimination is both just and beneficial to society. I shall begin my analysis by first considering arguments offered in support of the claim that reverse discrimination is unjust. After disposing of these arguments and showing that a properly constructed program of preferential treatment can be defended as just, I shall then demonstrate that practicing reverse discrimination in the manner that I envision would also benefit society.

## I. REVERSE DISCRIMINATION AS JUST

One charge often leveled by critics of reverse discrimination is that it denies jobs to today's white males, thus unjustly holding these individuals responsible for the sins of their fathers. For this objection to have force, however, one must assume that discrimination is not being practiced in our society today, and this assumption is false. To see why this is the case, consider the following analogy.

Let us say we have two fighters, X and Y. Two months prior to their meeting in the ring X is given the best exercise, training, advice, food, etc., by the Fighting Commission. On the other hand the Fighting Commission does not allow Y to sleep, forces him to live on a subsistence diet, and does not permit him to train. Now, if on the day of the fight the rules of the game are enforced "impartially" by the Fighting Commission, would we say that the fight is fair? I think not. Indeed, I believe we would say, not merely that Y *had been* discriminated against, but that he *is* being discriminated against because he is forced to fight under rules favoring X. To make the fight fair, and so not to discriminate against Y, X needs to be handicapped in some way (e.g., he could be made to wear oversized gloves and wear a heavy weight belt). Now today, blacks and women are in a situation that is entirely similar to that of our mistreated boxer.[2] Blacks were once enslaved in our society, and after emancipation were treated as second-class citizens. Sometimes the government actively promoted the view that blacks were less than fully human (consider, for example, laws enforcing segregation and prohibiting miscegenation), and at other times it merely tolerated wrongdoing directed specifically at blacks (e.g., it often allowed realtors and loan officers the freedom to ensure that blacks did not move into all white neighborhoods). Regardless of whether the discrimination was practiced overtly or covertly, however, it gave rise to a pernicious legacy.[3] Today, many young blacks believe that achieving intellectually is somehow to "sell out" their race and "become white" (or at least "Oreo"); young black males comprise a much larger proportion of the prison population than would be expected based on their numbers in our society; black families are often in disarray; the wages and educational levels of blacks are far lower than those of whites, etc. Moreover, what is true of blacks is also true (albeit, perhaps, to a somewhat lesser extent) of women. Women were not allowed to vote until well into the twentieth century, and until the early 1970s were given only four realistic career choices: nurse, stewardess (i.e., flight attendant), school teacher or secretary. They were taught to be submissive and to eschew the study of math and science for home economics and typing. Behind every successful man, they were told, stands a good woman, still, it was the *man* who was successful and the *woman* who "stood behind." The legacy of this history is as well known as that of blacks: men still dominate in the sciences and in the boardroom; women's salaries, overall, are less than men's, and working women who are married still shoulder the major burdens of childcare and housework. Now, given these circumstances it seems clear that if we were to practice reverse discrimination for women and blacks we would not necessarily be "punishing sons for the sins of their fathers." If blacks and women today suffer because of past discrimination that either has been perpetrated by or acquiesced to by our government, they are in a position analogous to a boxer who has been denied proper training by the Fighting Commission. And just as it would be discriminatory to force such a boxer to fight without somehow handicapping his opponent, so too it would be discriminatory to use the same standards for evaluating blacks' and womens' applications for employment and school admission as we use for white males' applications.[4]

At this point some may wish to object to our argument. What we have failed to notice, they will say, is that reverse discrimination operates on an *individual* level whereas our defense of the practice deals with group characteristics. It may well be the case, for example, that many blacks and women suffer from the effects of past discrimination, but this is not true of all members of these groups (e.g., if Oprah Winfrey had daughters, it is not at all clear that past discrimination against blacks and women would effect *them* in deleterious ways). Moreover, many white males would claim to have never practiced discrimination. For a program of reverse discrimination to be just, however, it must operate just as handicapping operates in our boxing example; that is to say, it must compensate those who suffer from discrimination and do so at the expense of those who unjustly benefit from the practice. But, critics assert, this is precisely the problem. We cannot identify either those individuals in minority groups who are discriminated against or those in the majority who unjustly benefit from the practice; thus when we practice reverse discrimination we really do nothing more than reward blacks and women at the expense of white males, and this may well give unwarranted advantages to many who have *not* suffered from discrimination while, at the same time, unjustly penalizing numerous white males. Indeed, it is actually *very likely* that practicing reverse discrimination will produce more instances of injustice than justice, for the minority group members who will serve as the principle beneficiaries of the practice will be the highest achievers in those groups (i.e., they will be those who have suffered the least from past discrimination and so least deserve a handicap), while those who will be penalized will be those who lack the highest qualifications (i.e., they will be those white males who are the least likely to have unjustly benefited from discrimination). And if this is true—if reversing discrimination will likely produce more instances of injustice than justice—the practice should be condemned and proscribed.

If, as critics assert, reversing discrimination produces more instances of injustice than justice, then those who oppose the practice would be correct in insisting that preferential treatment of blacks and women ought to be prohibited as unjust. However, I do not think that critics are correct when they say that injustice is the likely effect of practicing reverse discrimination. Indeed, if a program of reverse discrimination were properly constructed and administered I believe things would be quite otherwise than they assert. As a first step towards seeing why this is the case it will be helpful to consider a second example.

Let us say that two people are being considered for a job—a black woman, *BW*, who has been discriminated against, and a white male, *WM*, who knows *BW* has been the victim of discrimination. *WM* has a more impressive dossier than *BW* and so insists that he be hired. What should be our reaction? Remember our earlier example of the fighters. What would we think if fighter *X* were to balk at having to wear a weight belt and extra-large gloves, even though he knew how *Y* had been treated before the fight? Would we not say that he was seeking an unfair advantage? Similarly, if *WM* knew *BW* had been the subject of discrimination but insisted nevertheless that he be hired because his qualifications were superior to hers would he not be endorsing the past discrimination against *BW* by seeking to perpetuate it? It does not matter that *WM* had not himself discriminated against *BW* in the past. Fighter *X* did not starve fighter *Y* or refuse to allow him to sleep either, but if *X* refuses to handicap himself in his fight with *Y*, he is approving of those past practices and attempting to take unfair advantage of *Y*. In the same way, if *WM* knows that *BW* has been the victim of discrimination, and yet insists that he rather than *BW* deserves the job they both seek, *WM* is condoning the earlier discrimination against *BW* and trying his best to treat her unfairly. And in this case it would be in the interest of justice to employ *BW* rather than *WM*, for this action would compensate a victim of discrimination and penalize one whom we knew condoned discriminatory practices.

At this point our argument may seem subject to a criticism. Throughout our *WM/BW* example we assumed that *WM* knew *BW* had been the victim of past discrimination. The assumption is important; for if *WM* had no reason to believe that *BW* had been discriminated against, it would be proper for him to demand that he rather than *BW* be given the sought-after job. And, our critics will insist, this is precisely the point: it is impossible for white males to know that individual minority group members with whom they are competing for jobs have been the victims of past discrimination. But is this true? Surely it is so if by "to know" we mean "to be absolutely certain," for we cannot be absolutely certain about any matter of fact. But do we not have evidence that most blacks and women have been subject to discrimination? Surely we do. I suggest then, that whenever a woman or minority group member applies for employment or school admission, the initial assumption ought to be that this individual has been discriminated against. Furthermore, I do not think it would take much effort for an employer or school admissions officer to find evidence tending to support or disconfirm this initial assumption. Indeed, such an employer or admissions officer would only need information of the following two sorts: (1) relevant autobiographical information concerning the minority job candidate or school applicant (e.g., where the applicant lived from birth until eighteen years of age, what the candidate's family income had been during her/his formative years, what level of education the applicant's parents had attained, what the parents did for a living, etc.), and (2) a brief psychological profile of the applicant. If information of these sorts were appended to the applications of all those candidates for school admission and employment who wished to be considered for reverse discrimination handicap, employers and admissions officers could determine, with a high degree of probability, whether or not a particular applicant had been the subject of discrimination.[5] For example, consider the following two cases.[6]

*Case #1.* Three persons are applying for a job—a white male (*WM*), and two white women (*WW1* and *WW2*). All three candidates meet the minimum requirements for employment, but according to all "objective" criteria, *WM* is best qualified for the job, *WW1* next best qualified, and *WW2* least qualified. The fact that *WW2* seems least qualified to compete in a "man's domain" gives some evidence of her having been subject to the psychological "conditioning forces" so often brought to bear upon women in our society. It is hardly overwhelming evidence; but what if we assume that it is supplemented by psychological data indicating that *WW2*, unlike *WW1* and *WM*, lacks aggressiveness and assertiveness, and is somewhat unsure of herself in her role as a businessperson? Further, *WW2* (again unlike *WW1* and *WM*) scores much higher on her verbal tests than on her mathematical examinations. All else being equal, I believe the employer then could say that it was highly probable that *WW2* had been subjected to stronger "conditioning" forces than either *WM* or *WW1*. At this point it would not be improper for the employer to tell *WM* and *WW1* that although *WW2* did not score as high as they did on "objective" tests, she was being hired because she was qualified and most likely the subject of discriminatory pressures far more severe than those experienced by either of them. If either *WM* or

*WW1* protested, they would be advocating continued discrimination against *WW2* and so justly denied employment. If neither protested, both would recognize what was in fact the case, namely, that they had competed fairly with *WW2* for a position of employment and had lost.

*Case #2.* A white male (*WM*) and a black male (*BM*) are applying for admission to a school with one remaining opening. Although *BM* scores lower than *WM* on all examinations he nevertheless meets all the minimum requirements for admission. Furthermore, while the autobiographical history of *WM* shows that he comes from a solid middle class background, *BM*'s history indicates that he grew up in a ghetto, did not know his father, etc. Given these facts, it would be proper for the admissions officer to reason that in all probability, one of the principal reasons *BM* suffered as he did in his early life was that he and his family, being black, were victims of discrimination. And at this juncture *BM* could be admitted to school, and *WM* told why he was being rejected. Specifically, *WM* would be told that although his examination scores were better than *BM*'s, he was judged not to be as qualified an admissions candidate as *BM* in a fair competition, i.e., in a competition in which *BM* was given an advantage so as to offset the debilitating effects of probable past discrimination. And at this stage *WM* could react in either of two ways. He could accept the admissions officer's judgment, admit that he had lost in fair competition with *BM*, and so acknowledge that no injustice had been done. Or, he could claim that he should not be handicapped in his competition with *BM* even though *BM* probably had been the victim of discrimination. In the latter case, however, *WM* would be demanding that the past discrimination of *BM* be perpetuated. And in this circumstance it would be proper to tell *WM* that it was in the interest of justice to admit *BM* because this action compensated a victim of discrimination by taking away from one who condoned discriminatory practices.

At this point one might wish to object to both of our examples. What we have failed to notice, the critic could say, is that there is a third option open to those who believe they have been victimized by reverse discrimination. Namely (to use case #2 as an example) *WM* could object to the admissions officer's decision by claiming that he had been handicapped too severely in his competition with *BM*. And if this were the basis for *WM*'s protest he would not be condoning the past discrimination against *BM*. Indeed, *WM*'s point simply would be that his competition with *BM* had not been fair because of the degree of handicap. But what gives *WM* the authority to make such a judgment? Consider, once again, our earlier example of the fighters. Fighter $X$ is handicapped in his bout with $Y$; the fight goes the distance and $Y$ is declared the winner. What would we think if $X$ objected to the decision, claiming that he had been overly penalized, e.g., his weight belt should have been ten pounds instead of twenty? Would we say, "Yes, $X$ is right, the fighter who is being handicapped should be the one to determine the type and degree of handicap"? Surely this would be absurd. Rather, we would tell $X$ that he was a sore loser, and that the best means we have been able to devise for guaranteeing fair fights is to let an impartial panel of judges determine handicaps and make judgments concerning victory. And the same rules should apply in the marketplace. *WM* cannot be allowed to determine the degree to which he should be handicapped in his competition with *BM*—indeed, to let him do so would virtually assure an *unfair* competition.

We have considered the major arguments for the injustice of reverse discrimination and concluded that none carries the day. Thus, if we were to practice reverse discrimination we would not necessarily be "punishing the sons for the sins of their fathers." Furthermore, if the right information were made available to employers and admissions officers, victims of discrimination could be identified with a high degree of probability. And in these circumstances, reverse discrimination could be used to rectify many of the injustices of discrimination without harming anyone.

Before discussing the utilitarian claim that it would be harmful to society to practice reverse discrimination, I would like to say a few words about how programs of preferential treatment might actually function in practice. If we assume that all minority applicants for employment and school admission were allowed to file autobiographies and take psychological tests, there are five general rules or guidelines which, if followed, might go a long way toward assuring justice in hiring and admissions.

First, whenever two or more *equally qualified individuals*[7] apply for a job or school admission, and only one of these candidates (say candidate $C$) is a member of a disadvantaged class, preference ought to be given to $C$. And this holds true regardless of whether or not $C$ has been the victim of discrimination. If $C$ has suffered discrimination, he or she deserves to be preferentially treated as compensation for past injuries. If, on the other hand, $C$ has not been a discrimination victim, he or she should be preferred because (as we shall see in the next section) such action would benefit society.

Second, an employer who practices reverse discrimination ought to consider only those candidates judged to be minimally qualified when evaluated according to "ordinary" standards (e.g., examinations, school grades, on-the-job experience, etc.). This is because nonqualified candidates probably would fail in their endeavors and, as critics of reverse discrimination quite rightly point out, such failures would be detrimental both to society as a whole and to the persons who failed.

Third, employers and school admissions officers (like impartial fight judges) should determine the degree of handicap in any competition for jobs and school admission. Furthermore, the handicap should increase as does the evidence of discrimination. Under this rule, of course, white males need not always "lose out" in competitions with individuals who have been victimized by discrimination. It is quite possible, for instance, that a white male's qualifications could be so outstanding that he would be selected over all candidates who had been given a preferential advantage due to past discrimination.

Fourth, in order to ensure that employers and school admissions officers do their best to practice reverse discrimination fairly, their applications for admission and employment should be reviewed periodically by officials of the government. And where differences of opinion arise, employers and admissions officers should be required to *justify* their decisions. If they could not justify their decisions, they should be required to make amends to the wronged parties.

Finally, critics of reverse discrimination often point out that reversing discrimination would be unfair to disadvantaged group members themselves because the most likely beneficiaries of such a practice would be the best qualified (and hence least discriminated against) minority group members. The assumption upon which this argument depends, namely, that the least qualified individuals will, in general, be those who have suffered the most from discrimination, seems plausible if not probable. Thus we are led to formulate a fifth "guideline": whenever an employer or admissions officer is deciding between two or more disadvantaged group members, he should select the least qualified person unless the autobiographies and/or psychological test *clearly indicate* that a better qualified individual has suffered more from discrimination.

I do not want to claim that the above five guidelines for practicing reverse discrimination are exhaustive. Nor am I so idealistic as to believe that it would be easy for employers and admissions officers to make judgments of merit using these guidelines. Injustices would be done, and honest mistakes would be made. However, if reverse discrimination were practiced in the manner broadly specified above it seems highly probable that more instances of injustice would be corrected than would be produced. And this is all the supporter of reverse discrimination need show in order to make the case that reverse discrimination is a just procedure. Indeed, it would be illegitimate to demand that the advocate of reverse discrimination show more than this, for there can be no such thing as certainty in the practical affairs of human life.

## II. REVERSE DISCRIMINATION AS BENEFICIAL

In order to fully defend reverse discrimination it is necessary to show not only that this practice serves the interests of justice, but also that it benefits the entire society. As a first step toward achieving this goal I will show why we must reject the major arguments in support of the view that reverse discrimination produces more harm than good.

(i) The first utilitarian objection to reverse discrimination recognizes that equality of opportunity is a good to be achieved in our society, but then claims that reversing discrimination is inconsistent with that goal. Given our earlier example of the fighters we can now see that this argument is plainly wrong. A boxer who has been starved and kept awake can have an equal opportunity to win a fight against one who has been well-fed and trained, only if the healthy fighter is handicapped in some way. Similarly, in order to give individuals who have been discriminated against a truly equal opportunity, those who have not been discriminated against must be handicapped.[8] Far from inhibiting equality of opportunity, then, reverse discrimination actually fosters that goal.

(ii) The second argument against reverse discrimination is that this procedure may well harm society by causing it to be served by the less able. Because I advocate hiring the least qualified individuals in some circumstances, it may seem that my defense of reverse discrimination is particularly susceptible to this criticism. But this is not so. On my view, every individual hired (or accepted in school) would be qualified. And to ensure that the persons who are given employment or accepted in school do a good job, we need only insist that it be made easy to dismiss those who fail to perform their tasks properly. Cases of incompetence could be documented, I think, with relative ease. An if incompetents could be dismissed without undue encumbrance, society would not suffer in the least.

(iii) The third objection to practicing reverse discrimination is that this procedure would have harmful effects for two classes of blacks and women. First, some critics claim that persons who were hired or given school admission under a program of reverse discrimination could never be sure whether or not they were "objectively" qualified for their positions, and as a result they could not take pride in their accomplishments. Second, others claim that if blacks and women knew that they would be given preferential treatment when they applied for jobs and school admissions they would have no incentive to push themselves to achieve at their highest potentials. It should be clear, however, that neither of these arguments is telling as against a program of reverse discrimination such as we have outlined. First, under the program we have outlined, those hired or accepted in school would know that they were qualified. And if they were not dismissed they would know that they were performing their tasks well. Thus, they could take pride in their achievements. And similar considerations also apply to minority group members seeking employment or school admission. These individuals would know that in order to be considered for a job or an opening in school, they would have to achieve at a certain level. But, the critic will assert, might not members of disadvantaged groups see the advantages of being disadvantaged and so do their utmost to appear "disadvantaged" and "minimally qualified" in order to obtain employment? I think not. After all, how does one prepare to be "disadvantaged" and "minimally qualified"? And even if this were possible, what difference would it make? Those hired or admitted to school would be qualified. And to keep their positions, these qualified individuals would have to perform adequately. In the end, absolutely no one would suffer.

Given our brief examination of the utilitarian arguments against reverse discrimination certain conclusions seem mandated. First, rather than being at odds with equality of opportunity reverse discrimination is really a means for achieving that goal. Second, so long as it is relatively easy to dismiss incompetents hired under reverse discrimination programs, society will not suffer. And third, practicing reverse discrimination will give those who perform well a sense of pride, while at the same time providing other minority group members with truly inspiring "role models." To this we can add two further benefits. First, we have seen that practicing reverse discrimination will further the interests of justice. And although the demands of justice and the demands of utility may not always be in accord, in this instance, at least, they appear to be. Finally, once minority group members understand that they really are being given an equal opportunity to succeed in our society a giant step will have been taken toward achieving true harmony in our relations with one another. I am aware that there are those who would disagree with this assessment, and insist that reversing discrimination will do nothing but incite a white-male "backlash," thus ultimately making things worse. Of course, these pessimists may be right. For my own part, however, I much prefer the counsel of Hume, who tells us that men are motivated not only by self-interest, but also by humanity, fellow-feeling, and a desire for justice.

## NOTES

1. For arguments in opposition to reverse discrimination see: Alan Goldman, "Limits to the Justification of Reverse Discrimination," *Social Theory and Practice* vol. 3, no. 2, and "Reparations to Individuals or Groups?" *Analysis* vol. 33, no. 5; E. van den Haag, "Reverse Discrimination: A Brief Against It," *National Review* (April 1977); W. Blackstone, "Reverse Discrimination and Compensatory Justice," *Social Theory and Practice* (spring 1975) and Anita Gonsalves, "Reverse Discrimination" (this volume).

2. Throughout my discussion I consider only blacks and women as being the subjects of discrimination. This should not be taken to imply that I believe members of these two groups are the only ones who suffer from the effects of past discrimination. Quite the contrary; I think there are members of some groups (e.g., native Americans) who have perhaps an even greater claim to being discriminated against than do women and blacks. However, I have limited my discussion to blacks and women for three reasons: (1) Doing so aids economy of discussion; (2) I believe blacks and women currently serve as the main focus of today's debate over reverse discrimination; and (3) whatever I say in support of practicing reverse discrimination for blacks and women can be extended, *mutatis mutandis*, to members of other groups who suffer today from the effects of past discrimination.

3. Sometimes opponents of reverse discrimination point out that there are studies which show that the wage gap between blacks and whites is almost totally explained by differences in human capital. (See for example, Gonsalves, "Reverse Discrimination" in this volume). The intent in offering these studies' results is to show that there is no marked discrimination present in today's labor market. In the studies cited, the authors compare the ability test scores of black and white males at age thirteen to their salaries ten years later; the conclusion drawn is that virtually all differences in wages are explicable in terms of variances in ability. It should be clear that if my argument is correct, using these studies to demonstrate the non-discriminatory character of today's labor market misses the point completely. My contention is that many of the blacks that score low on the ability test do so because of the effects of past discrimination and that virtually none of the low scores of whites can be explained in this way. To be more explicit: my claim is that many of the low scores of the young black males are explained by the fact that

they were given poor pre-natal care, raised in poverty by uneducated parents, reared without a male role model, taught to speak black English, given poor nutrition, sent to poor, inner-city public schools, etc., *and that these conditions obtained because of the effects of past discrimination.* Moreover, I maintain that few if any of these conditions obtain for low scoring white males, and when they do, *they are not due to the effects of past, systematic discrimination.* Thus, on my view, to claim that today's labor market is not discriminatory because wage differences between blacks and whites can be explained in terms of differences in ability is essentially the same as claiming that boxing matches between fighters who had been mistreated by the Boxing Commission and those who had been given the best training were fair because the high incidence of victories by the best trained fighters is explicable in terms of their being stronger and better prepared at the time of the weighing in ceremony. Both claims are ludicrous.

4. I want to make it perfectly clear at this point that I am not arguing that reverse discrimination should be used to *compensate* for every instance of disadvantage (or even every minority disadvantage), but only for those disadvantages that are due to the effects of past, *systemic* discrimination, i.e., discrimination in our society that the government has, at some time, either fostered or permitted to exist. For example, I would use reverse discrimination to help a black person whose illiterate grandparents migrated to Chicago in the 1940s, who grew up in public housing in a gang ridden section of southside Chicago, who never knew his mother or father, etc. On the other hand I would not use reverse discrimination to compensate a black who dropped out of school and had disciplinary problems because his parents, both of whom were well-paid professionals, had experienced a traumatic and acrimonious divorce.

5. Here I want to stress that my position is not that all women and blacks should be required to submit autobiographical and psychological data when applying for jobs and school admissions. To impose such a requirement would be wrong because some candidates might feel that providing such information would violate their right to privacy, and others might not want to be considered as a candidate for preferential treatment. Thus, my position is that information of sorts (1) and (2) should be required only of those women and blacks who voluntarily choose to be considered for reverse discrimination handicap when applying for jobs and school admissions.

6. Case #1 illustrates how psychological tests could be used to determine a person's "discrimination status"; case #2 makes the same point with regard to autobiographical data.

7. When I say "equally qualified" here I mean equally qualified before the imposition of any handicap to offset the debilitating effects of past discrimination.

8. Sometimes critics of reverse discrimination attack the practice by claiming it "changes the rules" in the middle of the game. Put most simply, the claim is that employers practicing reverse discrimination will hire members of disadvantaged groups, and in many cases these individuals will not be as highly qualified as the

white males who were denied employment. But this changes the rules of the game because we have all been led to believe that the person who is best qualified for a job should be the one hired. Given what I have said above, it should be clear that I do not think this criticism is sound. I agree that today in our society we believe that highly qualified persons deserve to be employed before those who are not as well qualified. But we accept this "informal rule" only because we tacitly assume that all individuals competing for a job or admission to school have been given an equal opportunity to develop their talents. More accurately, then, the "informal rule" accepted in our society today is: *"Where equality of opportunity obtains*, the best qualified individual ought to be selected for employment or school admission." This being so, employers or school admissions officers who practice reverse discrimination do not change the rules in the middle of the game. In fact, they abide by them; for what they do is handicap white males in their competition with disadvantaged group members so as to assure equality of opportunity, and then, given this adjustment, hire or admit the individual whom they consider to be best qualified.

# DIVERSITY

*Case Study*

# Texaco: The Jelly Bean Diversity Fiasco

In November, 1996, Texaco, Inc., was rocked by the disclosure of tape-recorded conversations among three executives about a racial discrimination suit pending against the company. The suit, seeking $71 million, had been brought by 6 employees, on behalf of 1,500 other employees, who alleged the following forms of discrimination:

> I have had KKK printed on my car. I have had my tires slashed and racial slurs written about me on bathroom walls. One co-worker blatantly called me a racial epithet to my face.

> Throughout my employment, three supervisors in my department openly discussed their view that African-Americans are ignorant and incompetent, and, specifically, that Thurgood Marshall was the most incompetent person they had ever seen.

> Sheryl Joseph, formerly a Texaco secretary in Harvey, Louisiana, was given a cake for her birthday which occurred shortly after she announced that she was pregnant. The cake depicted a black pregnant woman and read, "Happy Birthday, Sheryl. It must have been those watermelon seeds."

The suit also included data on Texaco's workforce:

---

From Marianne M. Jennings, *Business Ethics: Case Studies and Selected Readings*, 3d ed. (Cincinnati, Ohio: West Educational Publishing Company, 1999). Copyright © 1999. Reprinted with permission of South-Western College Publishing, a division of Thomas Learning.

| 1989 | Minorities as a percentage of Texaco's workforce | 15.2% |
|---|---|---|
| 1994 | Minorities as a percentage of Texaco's workforce | 19.4% |

### # of Years to Promotion by Job Classification

| Minority Employees | Job | Other Employees |
|---|---|---|
| 6.1 | Accountant | 4.6 |
| 6.4 | Senior Accountant | 5.4 |
| 12.5 | Analyst | 6.3 |
| 14.2 | Financial Analyst | 13.9 |
| 15.0 | Assistant Accounting Supervisor | 9.8 |

### Senior Managers

| | White | Black |
|---|---|---|
| 1991 | 1,887 | 19 |
| 1992 | 2,001 | 21 |
| 1993 | 2,000 | 23 |
| 1994 | 2,029 | 23 |

### Racial Composition (% of blacks) by Pay Range

| Salary | Texaco | Other Oil Companies |
|---|---|---|
| $ 51,100 | 5.9% | 7.2% |
| $ 56,900 | 4.7% | 6.5% |
| $ 63,000 | 4.1% | 4.7% |
| $ 69,900 | 2.3% | 5.1% |
| $ 77,600 | 1.8% | 3.2% |
| $ 88,100 | 1.9% | 2.3% |
| $ 95,600 | 1.4% | 2.6% |
| $106,100 | 1.2% | 2.3% |
| $117,600 | 0.8% | 2.3% |
| $128,800 | 0.4% | 1.8% |

(African-Americans make up 12% of the U.S. population)

The acting head of the EEOC wrote in 1995, "Deficiencies in the affirmative-action programs suggest that Texaco is not committed to insuring comprehensive, facility by facility, compliance with the company's affirmative-action responsibilities."

Faced with the lawsuit, Texaco's former treasurer, Robert Ulrich, senior assistant treasurer, J. David Keough, and senior coordinator for personnel services, Richard A. Lundwall, met and discussed the suit. A tape transcript follows:

*They look through evidence, deciding what to turn over to the plaintiffs.*

**Lundwall**. Here, look at this chart. You know, I'm not really quite sure what it means. This chart is not mentioned in the agency, so it's not important that we even have it in there. . . . They would never know it was here.

**Keough**. They'll find it when they look through it.

**Lundwall**. Not if I take it out they won't.

*The executives decide to leave out certain pages of a document; they worry that another version will turn up.*

**Ulrich**. We're gonna purge the [expletive deleted] out of these books, though. We're not going to have any damn thing that we don't need to be in them—

**Lundwall**. As a matter of fact, I just want to be reminded of what we discussed. You take your data and . . .

**Keough**. You look and make sure it's consistent to what we've given them already for minutes. Two versions with the restricted and that's marked clearly on top—

**Ulrich**. But I don't want to be caught up in a cover-up. I don't want to be my own Watergate.

**Lundwall**. We've been doing pretty much two versions, too. This one here, this is strictly my book, your book . . .

**Ulrich**. Boy, I'll tell you, that one, you would put that and you would have the only copy. Nobody else ought to have copies of that.

**Lundwall**. O.K.?

**Ulrich**. You have that someplace and it doesn't exist.

**Lundwall**. Yeah, O.K.

**Ulrich**. I just don't want anybody to have a copy of that.

**Lundwall**. Good. No problem.

**Ulrich**. You know, there is no point in even keeping the restricted version anymore. All it could do is get us in trouble. That's the way I feel. I would not keep anything.

**Lundwall**. Let me shred this thing and any other restricted version like it.

**Ulrich**. Why do we have to keep the minutes of the meeting anymore?

**Lundwall**. You don't, you don't.

**Ulrich**. We don't?

**Lundwall**. Because we don't, no, we don't because it comes back to haunt us like right now—

**Ulrich**. I mean, the pendulum is swinging the other way, guys.

*The executives discuss the minority employees who brought the suit.*

**Lundwall**. They are perpetuating an us/them atmosphere. Last week or last Friday I told . . .

**Ulrich**. [Inaudible.]

**Lundwall** Yeah, that's what I said to you, you want to frag grenade? You know, duck, I'm going to throw one. Well, that's what I was alluding to. But the point is not, that's not bad in itself but it does perpetuate us/them. And if you're trying to get away and get to the we . . . you can't do that kind of stuff.

**Ulrich**. [Inaudible.] I agree. This diversity thing. You know how black jelly beans agree. . . .

**Lundwall**. That's funny. All the black jelly beans seem to be glued to the bottom of the bag.

**Ulrich**. You can't have just we and them. You can't just have black jelly beans and other jelly beans. It doesn't work.

**Lundwall**. Yeah. But they're perpetuating the black jelly beans.

**Ulrich**. I'm still having trouble with Hanukkah. Now, we have Kwanza (laughter).

The release of the tape prompted the Reverend Jesse Jackson to call for a nationwide boycott of Texaco. Sales fell 8 percent, Texaco's stock fell 2 percent, and several institutional investors were preparing to sell their stock.

Texaco did have a minority recruiting effort in place and the "jelly bean" remark was tied to a diversity trainer the company had hired. The following are excerpts from Texaco's statement of vision and values:

> **Respect for the Individual**
> Our employees are our most important resource. Each person deserves to be treated with respect and dignity in appropriate work environments, without regard to race, religion, sex, age, national origin, disability or position in the company. Each employee has the responsibility to demonstrate respect for others.
> The company believes that a work environment that reflects a diverse workforce, values diversity, and is free of all forms of discrimination, intimidation, and harassment is essential for a productive and efficient workforce. Accordingly, conduct directed toward any employee that is unwelcome, hostile, offensive, degrading, or abusive is unacceptable and will not be tolerated.

A federal grand jury began an investigation at Texaco to determine whether there had been obstruction of justice in the withholding of documents.

Within days of the release of the tape, Texaco settled its bias suit for $176.1 million, the largest sum ever allowed in a discrimination case. The money will allow a 11 percent pay raise for blacks and other minorities who joined in the law suit.

Texaco's chairman and CEO, Peter I. Bijur, issued the following statement after agreeing to a settlement:

> Texaco is facing a difficult but vital challenge. It's broader than any specific words and larger than any lawsuit. It is one we must and are attacking head-on.
>
> We are a company of 27,000 people worldwide. In any organization of that size, unfortunately, there are bound to be people with unacceptable, biased attitudes toward race, gender and religion.
>
> Our goal, and our responsibility, is to eradicate this kind of thinking wherever and however it is found in our company. And our challenge is to make Texaco a company of limitless opportunity for all men and women.
>
> We are committed to begin meeting this challenge immediately through programs with concrete goals and measurable timetables.
>
> I've already announced certain specific steps, including a redoubling of efforts within Texaco to focus on the paramount value of respect for the individual and a comprehensive review of our diversity programs at every level of our company.
>
> We also want to broaden economic access to Texaco for minority firms and increase the positive impact our investments can have in the minority community. This includes areas such as hiring and promotion; professional services such as advertising, banking, investment management and legal services; and wholesale and retail station ownership.
>
> To assist us, we are reaching out to leaders of minority and religious organizations and others for ideas and perspectives that will help Texaco succeed in our mission of becoming a model of diversity and workplace equality.
>
> It is essential to this urgent mission that Texaco and African-Americans and other minority community leaders work together to help solve the problems we face as a company—which, after all, echo the problems faced in society as a whole.
>
> Discrimination will be extinguished only if we tackle it together, only if we join in a unified, common effort.
>
> Working together, I believe we can take Texaco into the 21st century as a model of diversity. We can make Texaco a company of limitless opportunity. We can make Texaco a leader in according respect to every man and woman.

Even after the announcement, Texaco stock was down $3 per share, a loss of $800 million total, and the boycott was continued. Texaco's proposed merger with Shell Oil began to unravel as Shell's CEO expressed concern about Texaco's integrity. However, after the settlement, additional information about the case began to emerge. Holman W. Jenkins Jr. wrote the following piece for the *Wall Street Journal*:

Quietly, corporate America is debating whether Texaco's Peter Bijur did the right thing.*

Mr. Bijur gets paid to make the hard calls, and with the airwaves aflame over "nigger" and "black jelly beans," Texaco took a battering in the stock and political markets. He had every reason for wanting to put a stop-loss on the media frenzy. "Once the taped conversations were revealed," he says, settling was "reasonable and honorable." So now Texaco is betting $176 million that paying off minority employees and their lawyers is the quickest way out of the news.

But as the company's own investigation showed, the truly inflammatory comments reported in the media never took place. They were purely a fabrication by opposing lawyers, and trumpeted by a credulous *New York Times*. And some digging would have shown this problem cropping up before in the career of Mike Hausfeld, lead attorney for the plaintiffs.

In an antitrust case years ago, he presented a secret recording that he claimed showed oil executives conspiring to threaten gasoline dealers. But a check by the same expert who handled the Nixon Watergate tapes showed no such thing. Says Larry Sharp, the Washington antitrust lawyer who opposed Mr. Hausfeld: "To put it generously, he gave himself the benefit of the doubt in making the transcript."

But this time the lie has been rewarded, and the broader public, unschooled in legal cynicism, heads home believing Texaco an admitted racist.

The catechism of corporate crisis management says you can't fight the media. Mr. Bijur had to consider that Jesse Jackson was threatening a boycott if Texaco failed to "regret, repent and seek renewal." Mr. Jackson pointedly added that "any attempt to shift to denial would add insult to injury"—a warning against trying to spread some egg to the faces of those who were fooled by the fake transcript.

There may have been wisdom, if not valor, in Mr. Bijur's decision to run up the white flag. But he also evinced symptoms of Stockholm Syndrome, telling CNN that Texaco was just the "tip of the iceberg" of corporate racism. Ducking this fight so ignominiously may yet prove a penny-wise, pound-foolish strategy. The City of Philadelphia has decided to dump its Texaco holdings anyway, partly out of fear of more litigation.

What else could Texaco have done? It could have apologized for any offense, but stuck up for its former treasurer Bob Ulrich, who was wronged by the phony transcript and stripped of his medical benefits by Texaco. And the company could have vowed to fight the lawsuit like the dickens, arguing that Texaco is not the cause of society's racial troubles but has tried to be part of the solution.

Start with the tapes: A fair listening does not necessarily reveal a "racist" conversation by executives at Texaco, but certainly a candid conversation about the problems of race at Texaco. They spoke of "jelly beans" dividing into camps of "us" and "them," an honest representation of life at many companies, not just in the oil patch.

Mr. Bijur could have made this point, starting with the *New York Times*, which has been embroiled in its own discrimination lawsuit with Angela Dodson, once its topranking black female. In a complaint filed with New York City's Human Rights Commission, she claims the paper was "engaged in gender-based harassment and disability-based discrimination . . . because the *Times* no longer wanted me, as a black person, to occupy a position as Senior Editor."

Her deepest ire is reserved for Times veteran Carolyn Lee, who is white and more accustomed to being lauded as a champion of women and minorities. Ms. Dodson told the Village Voice: "It got to the point that whenever I was in her presence or earshot she made remarks [about other black people] that could only be taken as negative."

This sounds remarkably like the anecdotes filed in the Texaco complaint. All an outsider can safely conclude is that race makes everything more complicated, as sensitivity begets sensitivity. Mr. Bijur would have done more for racial understanding had he used his platform to open up this subject.

Yes, the cartoonist racists are out there, he might have said, but the *Times* coverage of Texaco only found cartoonist racists. The paper could have looked to its own experience for another story—a story about how garden-variety interpersonal conflict can land even decent people in the snares of racial mistrust.

This is what affirmative action, by throwing people together, was supposed to get us past. And it may be no accident that our most quota-ridden newspaper, *USA Today*, jumped off the bandwagon on the Texaco tapes, noting the ambiguity of whether the "jelly bean" remarks were meant to be hostile or friendly to blacks.

And McPaper kept on asking intelligent questions, like whether the *New York Times* had been "used by plaintiffs in the case to promote a faulty but more inflammatory transcript?" ("Not unless the court was used," answered *Times* Business Editor John Geddes, sounding like a lawyer himself.)

So Mr. Bijur was not facing a uniformly hopeless media torrent. The truth, even a complicated truth, catches up with the headlines eventually.

In time, he might have found surprising allies drifting to his side. The *New Republic* and the *New Yorker* have run thoughtful articles arguing that businesses should be allowed to use quotas but shouldn't be subject to harassment litigation if they don't. Right now, we do the opposite: Forbid companies to promote by quota, then sue them under federal "adverse impact" rules when they don't.

In effect, liberal voices are arguing that business could do more for minorities with less conflict if freedom of contract were restored. The world is changing, and companies have their own reasons nowadays for wanting minorities around. They need input from different kinds of people on how to deal with different kinds of people. No doubt this is why McPaper feels free to thumb its nose at the conformity crowd on stories like Texaco and church-burnings. (See September's *Harvard Business Review* for what business is thinking about diversity now.)

If companies were set free to assemble the work forces most useful to them, they could sweep away a heap of excuses for recrimination. Whites couldn't feel cheated out of jobs. Blacks wouldn't end up at companies that want them only for windowdressing. And the world could go back to feeling OK about being an interesting place. We might even allow that cultural patterns other than racism may explain why so many rednecks, and so few blacks, become petroleum engineers.

Mr. Bijur may have made the best of a bad deal for his shareholders. Whether it was best for America is a different judgment.

Richard Lundwall, the executive who taped the sessions with the other executives, was charged with one count of obstruction of justice. Lundwall had turned over the tapes of the conversations to lawyers for the plaintiffs in the discrimination suit on October 25, 1996. Lundwall had been terminated.

Texaco hired attorney Michael Armstrong to investigate the underlying allegations. Mr. Armstrong found the tapes had not been transcribed correctly.

As part of its settlement, Texaco agreed to, at a cost of $55 million, assign a task force to police hiring and promotion as well as requiring mentors for black employees and sensitivity training for white employees.

The following interview with CEO Bijur appeared in *Business Week*:

**Q**: *How did your legal strategy change once the news of the tapes was printed?**

**A**: When I saw [the story], I knew that this lawsuit was pending and moving forward. I made the judgment that we needed to accelerate the settlement process. And those discussions on settlement commenced almost immediately.

**Q**: *It has been reported that you didn't get the board of directors involved with the settlement talks and other issues. Why not?*

**A**: You're drawing conclusions that are erroneous. The board was fully involved throughout the entire process. I talked to numerous directors personally. We had several board and executive committee meetings. The board was fully supportive of our actions.

**Q**: *Have you met with shareholders?*

**A**: Yes, of course. I went down to [New York] and met with the Interfaith Center on Corporate Responsibility, which is a group of religious shareholders. I expressed our position on this and listened carefully to their position and got some good counsel and guidance. But I wanted to provide our side of the issue as well. I have met with [New York State Comptroller] Carl McCall and [New York City Comptroller] Alan Hevesi about concerns that they had, and I will continue to meet with other shareholders as I normally do.

**Q**: *Why do you think the oil industry has such a poor reputation on issues of racial diversity and gender equality? How does Texaco stack up against the others?*

**A**: The percentage of minorities within Texaco is just about average for the petroleum industry. We have made really significant progress in the last several years in improving the percentage. But there are some very interesting points that need to be examined to place in context what may be going on in this industry. I just read a study that showed that in 1995, there were only nine petroleum engineering minority graduates that came out of all engi-

*Smart, Tim. "Texaco: Lessons From A Crisis-in-Progress." Reprinted from December 2, 1996, issue of *Business Week* by special permission. Copyright © 1997 by McGraw-Hill, Inc.

neering schools in the United States—only nine. That's not an excuse. But it is indicative of why it is difficult for this industry to have a lot of people in the pipeline. Now, of course, that does not apply to accountants, finance people, and anybody else. But we are a very technically oriented industry.

**Q:** *Have you personally witnessed discrimination at Texaco?*

**A:** In the nearly 31 years I have been with Texaco, I have never witnessed an incident of racial bias or prejudice. And had I seen it, I would have taken disciplinary action. I've never seen it.

**Q:** *Is there a widespread culture of insensitivity at Texaco?*

**A:** I do not think there is a culture of institutional bias within Texaco. I think we've got a great many very good and decent human beings, but that unfortunately we mirror society. There is bigotry in society. There is prejudice and injustice in society. I am sorry to say that, and I am sorry to say that probably does exist within Texaco. I can't do much about society, but I certainly can do something about Texaco.

**Q:** *What are your views on affirmative action?*

**A:** Texaco's views on affirmative action have not changed a bit. We have supported affirmative action, and we will continue to support affirmative action.

**Q:** *This is your first big trial since taking over. What have you learned?*

**A:** I've learned that as good as our programs are in the company—and they really are quite good, even in this area—there's always more we can do. We've got to really drill down into the programs. We've got to make certain that they're meeting the objectives and goals we've set for them.

**Q:** *Are there other lessons in terms of your style of management?*

**A:** I don't think I would do anything different the next time than what I did this time.

**Q:** *How will you make sure the spirit as well as the letter of the policy is followed at Texaco?*

**A:** We're going to put more and more and more emphasis on it until we get it through everybody's head: Bigotry is not going to be tolerated here.

Robert W. Ulrich was indicted in 1997. Mr. Lundwall entered a "not guilty" plea on July 8, 1997, and J. David Keough has sued Texaco for libel. Texaco named Mary Bush, a financial consultant, as its first black female board member.

As Lundwall's prosecution has proceeded, new discoveries have been made. For example, "Purposeful erasures" have been found on the tapes.

In an interim report on its progress toward the settlement goals, Texaco revealed the following:

**Polishing the Star**. As part of its settlement of a discrimination lawsuit brought by black employees, Texaco has moved on a half-dozen fronts to alter its business practices.

**Hiring**. Asked search firms to identify wider arrays of candidates. Expanded recruiting at historically minority colleges. Gave 50 scholarships and paid internships to minority students seeking engineering or technical degrees.

**Career Advancement**. Wrote objective standards for promotions. Developing training program for new managers. Developing a mentoring program.

**Diversity Initiatives**. Conducted two-day diversity training for more than 8,000 of 20,000 U.S. employees. Tied management bonuses to diversity goals. Developing alternative dispute resolution and ombudsman programs.

**Purchasing**. Nearly doubled purchases from minority- or women-owned businesses. Asking suppliers to report their purchases from such companies.

**Financial Services**. Substantially increased banking, investment management and insurance business with minority- and women-owned firms. A group of such firms underwrote a $150 million public financing.

**Retailing**. Added three black independent retailers, 18 black managers of company-owned service stations, 12 minority or female wholesalers, 13 minority- or women-owned Xpress Lube outlets and 6 minority- or women-owned lubricant distributors.

In May 1998, the Texaco executives were acquitted of all criminal charges.

## FOR DISCUSSION

1. Provide a summary of the players and their concerns.
2. Discuss the ethics of the recording.
3. Why do you think the executives discussed document destruction?
4. What ethical issues surround diversity training and affirmative action?

*Barbara Hall*

# Diversity at Work

The United States is essentially a country of immigrants. From the moment the first European immigrants set foot in the New World to the present, many divergent groups of people have made America their home. The fabric of this country is a tapestry woven of a diverse mixture of peoples and cultures. Our society's diversity, however, has not always been reflected in the hiring and advancement practices of much of corporate America. In recent years, efforts have been made to remedy the homogeneity in American business. Many companies are beginning to recognize the importance of having a diversified workforce.

To facilitate our discussion of diversity and its effects in the workplace, let's start with a definition of the term. Most of us know the ordinary meaning of "diversity." A group is diverse when its members have significant characteristics differentiating them from one another, yet they must also share sufficiently similar characteristics in order to be recognized as a part of the group. Is this the sense of "diversity" we can use in business contexts?

*Case Study:* Corporation DIV is a small company with fewer than 100 employees. Mr. Terrell, the president of DIV, has made a concerted effort to hire a diverse group of individuals. Of his employees 15 percent are gay, 10 percent are convicted drug addicts seeking to rehabilitate, 5 percent are Buddhist, 20 percent are Christian, 30 percent have college degrees, 12 percent are high school drop-outs, and 21 percent are vegetarians. His employees are also all white males. Regina Lowes, a black woman, believes that she was unfairly denied a job for which she had excellent qualifications because she is the "wrong" color and gender. She is suing under Federal Anti-Discrimination laws. Mr. Terrell says that he is not breaking the law and that his employees are more diverse than at any other company in town.

Corporation JKL is somewhat larger than DIV. JKL corporation has an equal proportion of women to men, and blacks and other minorities constitute 30 percent of the employees. The CEO of JKL Mary Foster, believes that a truly diverse workforce is essential to the success of her company. Foster hires all of JKL's employees from Mead College located in a neighboring town. Students of all ethnic backgrounds attend Mead. The school, however, only admits individuals who share its conservative ideals.

Which company, DIV or JKL, would be considered to have more diversity among its employees? Using our definition above, most people would say that DIV has a more diverse workforce than JKL. While JKL appears to have a more varied group of employees, in actuality its workers all have similar values and perspectives. Although DIV's employees are all white males, the variety of their backgrounds suggests there will be a variety of perspectives—a key goal of our ordinary notion of diversity. A person using the term "diversity" in the context of U.S. hiring and employment practices would, however, conclude that JKL had the more diverse workforce. Diversity, in this sense is assessed primarily in terms of race, gender, ethnicity, national origin, sexual orientation, religion, physical ability and age. The qualities that constitute diversity are, for the most part, qualities over which individuals have no control. Principles of fairness dictate that no person should be denied employment merely because of certain fundamental and inalterable attributes she possesses.[1]

Now that we have a general idea of what constitutes diversity in the context of the workplace, we can explore reasons why a company should want to have a diverse group of employees. Perhaps the most obvious reason for supporting diversity is that any company which does not have a diverse workforce is more likely to be charged with violating the Civil Rights Act, which prohibits discrimination based on race, gender, etc. Certainly a company with relatively little diversity would at least be suspect. This rationale for maintaining a diversified workforce, while legally tenable, does not provide positive reasons in favor of diversity.

Does diversity make good business sense? Many people are suggesting that it does. R. Roosevelt Thomas Jr., founder of the American Institute for Managing Diversity, says that an increasing number of companies are beginning to look at diversity as a business issue as opposed to a legal compliance issue, a moral issue or a social responsibility issue.[2]

Allstate Insurance is the No. 1 life and auto insurer among African-Americans and the No. 1 homeowner and life insurance firm among Hispanic Americans, according to a study done by an independent firm, The Simmons Research Group.[3] Why does Allstate have such a strong client base in these communities? Since 1993 the company has made diversity a priority strongly connected to its overall corporate objectives. Recognizing the growing diversity of the overall population, it became apparent to Allstate that good community and consumer relations lead to an overall increase in the customer base. A key factor in developing good relations is having a workforce that reflects the make-up of the community.

> Because the community's immigrant population is constantly changing [Allstate] says it is important to recruit as diverse a group of sales reps as possible. [They] constantly scout for potential candidates from within the community because these prospects best understand their people's needs. . . . They are also excited about dealing with their own people and putting them at ease.[4]

According to Thomas: "This is no longer simply a question of common decency, it is a question of business survival."[5] Diversity makes good business sense because of the diversity in the overall society. A company that does not or cannot understand and meet the needs of a diverse customer base is less likely to prosper than a company that is more attuned to the needs of both potential and actual customers. One key way to accomplish this is to hire employees who are members of the diverse segments of the population.

A related benefit of diversity hiring is that companies whose success depends upon their ability to develop new ideas are more likely to benefit by having a diverse workforce than one that is homogeneous and stagnant. Diversity "infuses new blood" into the corporate body.

Many advocates of diversity suggest that the problem is not that women and minorities are not being hired in greater numbers. The declining percentage of white males, along with the increasing percentages of women and minorities in the overall population, virtually guarantees an increased presence of women and minorities in the workplace. The problem is not in achieving diversity, they argue, but in managing it. Given the variety of cultures, nationalities, races, etc. a corporation has or eventually will have, how can such a hodgepodge group be effectively managed in order to achieve optimal productivity?

Effective management of any group of workers entails creating the kind of environment in which the employees are able to develop to their fullest potentials. People who view their jobs as stagnant and uninteresting tend to be less productive than are those whose talents are more fully utilized. Diversity is problematic for many corporations not because these companies are failing to hire women and minorities, rather, the problem is that the women and minorities hired often "plateau and lose their drive and quit or get fired."[6]

Women and minorities have often been relegated to lower-level positions, thereby, creating a "glass ceiling" that restricts their upward mobility while maintaining a disproportionately high number of white males in senior managerial positions. The following tables list the percentage of minorities employed at ten of the top corporations in a major U.S. city, and the percentages of minorities holding upper level positions at those corporations.[7]

Racial Makeup of Top Ten Major Atlanta Companies

ALL U.S. EMPLOYEES

| Company | Employees | White | Black | Hispanic | Asian/ Pacific Islander | American Indian/ Alaskan Native |
|---|---|---|---|---|---|---|
| United Parcel Service | 311,876 | 65 % | 21.9% | 10.2% | 2.2% | 0.7% |
| Home Depot | 184,894 | 74.7% | 25.3% | | | |
| BellSouth | 88,308 | 70 % | 24 % | 4 % | 1 % | 1 % |
| Georgia-Pacific | 53,415 | 73 % | 22 % | 4 % | <1 % | <1 % |
| Coca-Cola Enterprises | 50,168 | 64.3% | 18 % | 15 % | 2 % | 0.5% |
| Southern Co. | 26,823 | 82.4% | 16.2% | 0.4% | 0.8% | 0.2% |
| First Data | 26,500 | 70 % | 15 % | 10 % | 4 % | 1 % |
| Genuine Parts | 25,642 | 83 % | 8.8% | 6.6% | 1 % | 0.6% |
| AFC Enterprises | 16,861 | 18.6% | 52.9% | 20.6% | 1.3% | <1 % |
| National Service Ind. | 14,648 | 54.1% | 33.8% | 9.1% | 2.8% | 0.3% |
| Metro Area | 837,355 | 63.1% | 30.2% | 3.8% | 2.6% | 0.3% |
| United States | 41,886,106 | 72.6% | 13.7% | 9.1% | 3.9% | 0.6% |

MANAGEMENT (officials and managers)

| Company | White | Black | Hispanic | Asian/ Pacific Islander | American Indian/ Alaska Native |
|---|---|---|---|---|---|
| United Parcel Service | 73.6% | 15.7% | 7.3% | 2.9% | 0.5% |
| Home Depot | 84.8% | 15.2% | | | |
| BellSouth | 73 % | 20 % | 5 % | < 1 % | > 1 % |
| Georgia-Pacific | 91 % | 7 % | 1 % | < 1 % | < 1 % |

| | | | | |
|---|---|---|---|---|
| Coca-Cola Enterprises | 82.3% | 8.3% | 7.5% | 1.5% | 0.4 % |
| Southern Co. | 91.9% | 7.3% | 0.3% | 0.4% | 0.1% |
| First Data | 87 % | 6 % | 5% | 1 % | 1 % |
| Genuine Parts | 91.3% | 3.3% | 4.3% | 0.5% | 0.6% |
| AFC Enterprises | 74 % | 13.6% | 5.7% | 3.3% | <1 % |
| National Service Ind. | 84.1% | 10.6% | 4.2% | 0.8% | 0.2% |
| Metro Area | 83.3% | 13.2% | 1.7% | 1.5% | 0.2% |
| United States | 87 % | 5.9% | 3.9% | 2.8% | 0.4% |

Growing numbers of minority workers are filing lawsuits against their employers over issues of promotion and advancement. As long as the statistics continue to indicate the relative absence of minorities and women from high-level corporate positions, this trend will likely continue. Hopefully, though, the courts will not be the final venue for resolving this issue. How can diversity be gained and managed at all levels of the corporate world? R. R. Thomas offers some guidelines for corporations seeking to manage diversity:

1. *Clarify Your Motivation*—A lot of executives are not sure why they should want to learn to manage diversity. [Only] business reasons will supply the necessary long-term motivation.
2. *Clarify Your Vision*—When managers think about a diverse work force, what do they picture? Not publicly, but in the privacy of their minds?
3. *Expand Your Focus*—Managers usually see affirmative action and equal employment opportunity as centering on minorities and women, with very little to offer white males. [Diversity] includes not only race, gender, creed, and ethnicity but also age, background, education, function, and personality differences. The object is not to assimilate minorities and women into a dominant white male culture but to create a dominant heterogeneous culture.
4. *Audit Your Corporate Culture*—If the goal is not to assimilate diversity into the dominant culture but rather to build a culture that can digest un-assimilated diversity, then you had better start by figuring out what your present culture looks like.
5. *Modify Your Assumptions*—The real problem with [the] corporate culture tree is that every time you go to make changes in the roots, you run into terrible opposition. Every culture, including corporate culture, has root guards that turn out in force every time you threaten a basic assumption.

6. *Modify Your Systems*—The first purpose of examining and modifying assumptions is to modify systems. Promotion, mentoring and sponsorship comprise one such system, and the unexamined "cream [rises] to the top" assumption . . . can tend to keep minorities and women from climbing the corporate ladder.
7. *Modify Your Models*—The second purpose of modifying assumptions is to modify [inefficient] models of managerial and employee behavior.
8. *Help Your People Pioneer*—Learning to manage diversity is a change process, and the managers involved are change agents. There is no single tried and tested "solution" to diversity and no fixed right way to manage it.[8]

To this point we have argued that diversity typically makes business sense; it has beneficial consequences for the corporation and those working for it. Yet this may not be true in some cases. A small U.S. food company owned by a Vietnamese-American family that intends to market Vietnamese food exclusively to the Vietnamese-American community, and is not interested in expanding into other food categories, may benefit from having only Vietnamese-American salespersons. This raises the question of whether there are moral reasons other than utility for advocating diversity. One argument for diversity is based on fairness. If we assume that candidates for a position are equally qualified, and will be equally successful on the job, then exclusive hiring of one group, white males, is based on a factor irrelevant to job success, and hence is unfair. Even in the case of the Vietnamese-Americans who hire only Vietnamese-American salespersons based on business utility reasons, there will be other positions in the firm (accountants, warehouse workers, clerks, computer operators, etc.) that could just as well be staffed using a diversity strategy.

Rights considerations can also be employed in favor of diversity. One basic moral right people have is a right to equal consideration with regard to selection procedures. If you are qualified for a position, then you ought to be at least considered for it. Yet, as our case of JKL corporation reveals, a firm which hires only individuals who have been educated at a local college and who have the conservative ideals and values taught at that college fails to consider at all those who have not been educated there and do not share these ideals and values.

Our conclusion is that although diversity does not make business sense for some corporations, in the large majority of cases a diversity program has utility (i.e., it benefits the firm and those employed by it), is fair, and also protects the right of individuals to equal consideration in selection procedures.

## NOTES

1. It is debatable whether the categories of religion and perhaps sexual orientation are less immutable than the others. However, these are still fundamental aspects of a person's being and, thus, deserving of legal protection.

2. Louisa Wah, "Diversity at Allstate—A Competitive Weapon," *Management Review* 88 (1999): 24–28.

3. Ibid.

4. Ibid.

5. R. Roosevelt Thomas Jr., "From Affirmative Action to Affirming Diversity," *Harvard Business Review* 68 (1990): 108.

6. Ibid.

7. *The Atlanta Journal-Constitution*, 2 July 2000, p. F9.

8. Thomas, "From Affirmative Action to Affirming Diversity," pp. 112–17.

# SEXUAL HARASSMENT

*Barbara Hall*

# A Summary of Sexual Harassment

What is sexual harassment? Is a solicitation for sexual favor a necessary condition? A sufficient condition? Must the victim be in a subordinate employment position vis-à-vis the perpetrator, or might they be peers? Is it possible to be guilty of sexual harassment without ever having had any physical or verbal contact with the victim? These are but a few of the questions that need to be addressed in coming to a proper understanding of sexual harassment.

## THE HISTORY OF SEXUAL HARASSMENT LEGISLATION

Allegations of sexual harassment are handled by the Equal Employment Opportunity Commission (EEOC) which was created to enforce Title VII of the 1964 Civil Rights Act. Title VII prohibits employment discrimination based on race, color, sex, ethnicity, or religion. The Act was originally intended to provide individuals protection against being fired, not hired, overlooked for promotion, or paid less because of their race, ethnicity, sex, color, or religion. Initially, most of the complaints were based on gender or racial discrimination in selection procedures. However, starting in the late 1970s, some individuals began complaining about sexual harassment. In 1980 the EEOC published its "Guidelines on Sexual Harassment." The guidelines specify that sexual harassment is a form of sexual

312

discrimination, and, therefore, proscribed by Title VII. According to the guidelines:

> Unwelcome sexual advances, requests for sexual favors, and other verbal or physical conduct of a sexual nature constitute sexual harassment when (1) submission to such conduct is made either explicitly or implicitly a term or condition of an individual's employment, (2) submission to or rejection of such conduct by an individual is used as the basis for employment decisions affecting such individual, or (3) such conduct has the purpose or effect of substantially interfering with an individual's work performance or creating an intimidating, hostile, or offensive working environment.[1]

When the alleged misconduct falls into either the first or second category it is commonly referred to as *quid pro quo* sexual harassment (literally meaning something for something) and an employer is strictly liable for such behavior. *Quid pro quo* is the classical form of sexual harassment. It is what comes to mind when most people think of the subject. The basic elements are: an unwanted sexual solicitation; the solicitation is directed at an employee by the employer or a person in a senior position (usually a supervisor, etc.); and there is either an explicit or implicit promise of benefit or threat of detriment to the employee's job or compensation depending on whether the solicitation is accepted or rejected.

The first judgment in favor of a plaintiff charging *quid pro quo* sexual harassment was *Williams* v. *Saxbe*, 413 F. Supp 654 (1976). In that case the plaintiff had worked at the Community Relations Service of the Department of Justice. While there, her supervisor made sexual advances toward her. She refused and was discharged. The defense argued that she was fired because she turned down her supervisor, not because she was a woman. The judge noted that the defendant's behavior was directed at the woman precisely because she was a woman.[2]

*Case Study:* Darlene has been working as a sales agent at company TUV for about eleven months. The manager of her department, Thomas, seems to be a friendly, family guy type person. He has pictures of his wife and children all over his desk and office walls. Once, when Darlene was walking past Thomas in the hall he playfully pinched her on the buttocks. She was stunned and offended but managed to maintain her composure and laugh it off. She decided not to mention the incident to anyone, out of fear her coworkers might think she was overreacting to a "playful little pinch." She did, however, try to avoid Thomas as much as possible.

One morning Darlene arrived at work an hour early in order to catch up on some work. She believed herself to be alone in the office until she saw Thomas walking towards her. He said to her, "You know, Darlene, you are a really dedicated employee. I would love to see you get promoted to the district sales position I am trying to fill. If you'll be nice to me, I'll make sure you are at the top of the list." Darlene knew she was more qualified for the position than any of the other candidates being considered. If she got the job she would get a substantial raise in pay and have her own office and secretary. Since Thomas was her immediate supervisor, and knew her excellent work record, she was confident that she was already at the top of the list. Thomas then walked over to her and started to caress her shoulders. He said, "I am, you'll learn, not very nice to people who aren't nice to me." He then suggested that she join him for drinks and "whatever" after work that day. He grinned at her when he said "whatever." Darlene could not disguise her revulsion. She was so upset that she went home and called in sick.

The next morning she decided that she would go to work and report Thomas' conduct to the head of the human resources department, having been told in her orientation that this was the proper procedure. When she arrived at work, she saw one of her coworkers, David. He was smiling broadly and said to her, "Aren't you going to congratulate me? I just found out that I got the district sales position!" Darlene's disappointment showed. She wanted to be happy for David, but she suddenly felt ill and decided to go home and call in sick again.

Darlene is a victim of *quid pro quo* sexual harassment. Her supervisor, the person with the power to determine the fate of her employment at TUV, made it known to her in a not so subtle manner that if she wished to get the promotion she'd desired, she would have to "be nice" to him. She did not accept his proposition and now someone else has gotten the promotion. Darlene plans to sue TUV because of this incident. The company will thus incur costly legal fees or reach a costly out of court settlement with Darlene.

The other distinct type of sexual harassment mentioned in the EEOC Guidelines concerns a hostile working environment. These cases are usually less clear cut than are the *quid pro quo* cases. In these types of cases the proscribed acts or behavior need not be aimed at a specific victim but do have a negative effect on the general working environment because they are disproportionally more demeaning to one sex than the other.

The seminal case in this area is *Meritor Savings Bank* v. *Vinson* 477

U.S. 57 (1986). Michelle Vinson started working as a teller at The Meritor Savings Bank of New Jersey in 1974. During the next four years she received promotions to head teller and then assistant branch manager. Throughout this period her supervisor, Sidney Taylor, vice president of Meritor, propositioned her for sex. Eventually she agreed, fearing that she would lose her job otherwise. She stated that she had sex with him forty to fifty times during her four years at Meritor. He raped her several different times and fondled her in front of coworkers. Once he followed her into the restroom and exposed himself to her. In 1978 Vinson took a total of two months of sick leave. The bank thought this excessive and fired her.

Vinson filed a suit against the bank and charged it with sexual harassment in violation of Title VII. The bank was eventually found guilty of sexual harassment by creating a "hostile working environment." How did this case differ from a case of *quid pro quo* sexual harassment? First, there was no contention that Ms. Vinson's job was threatened in any manner (though she stated that she eventually acquiesced to Taylor's demands out of a fear of losing her job). Second, not only did Ms. Vinson's employment suffer no detriment, but she actually received two promotions. Thus, there was no evidence that Ms. Vinson's employment opportunities with the bank were either threatened or adversely affected. Thus none of the conditions for *quid pro quo* obtained. The Supreme Court held, however, that it is not necessary that the employee suffer an economic detriment as long as the employer's conduct "has the purpose or effect of unreasonably interfering with an individual's work performance or creating an intimidating, hostile, or offensive working environment."

Another major case dealing with hostile working environment sexual harassment is *Robinson* v. *Jacksonville Shipyards, Inc.* 760 F. Supp 1586 (1991). Lora Robinson worked as a welder at Jacksonville Florida Shipyards, Inc. She had been there for more than ten years. She testified that during her tenure there she almost daily encountered sexually graphic posters, calendars, and drawings showing nude and partially clothed women in a variety of sexually suggestive poses. These sorts of materials colored the atmosphere throughout the shipyard. For many years Robinson said nothing. Then she began to complain, first to her immediate supervisors and then to the shipyard superintendent. She said the pictures were "degrading, humiliating, nauseating" and that she wanted them removed. When the supervisor refused to do so, she complained to the vice president of the shipyard, who also refused to do anything. She filed a lawsuit against the shipyard in 1986.

Robinson was successful in her suit. The judge in the case applied the five-pronged test articulated in another case, *Henson* v. *City of Dundee*, 682 F. 2d 897 (11th Cir. 1982). In that case the judge gave the following five criteria as a test for a hostile working environment:

1. The employee is a member of the protected class (all humans)
2. The employee experiences unwelcome sexual overtures, namely, those that are neither solicited nor invited, and are undesired or offensive
3. The harassment is based on sex, that is, but for her or his sex, the individual would not have been tormented
4. The harassment is so chronic that it disrupts the working conditions and creates an abusive environment
5. The employer is liable for the offense when the employer knew or should have known about the offense

The judge found that: (1)Robinson belonged to a protected class; (2) she was subject to unwelcome and unsolicited harassment because of the pictures, (which were taken to be sexual overtures by the court); (3) the harassment was directed at her as a woman; (4) her ability to perform on the job was significantly affected; and (5) the shipyard not only knew about the harassing conduct, but endorsed it. *Robinson* is important because it shows that behavior does not have to be blatantly or specifically directed at the employee affected.

## RECENT CHANGES TO THE LAW ON SEXUAL HARASSMENT

The Supreme Court decided two cases in its 1998 term which brought about important changes in the law on sexual harassment. In its opinions in the two cases, *Burlington Industries Inc.* v. *Ellerth*, 118 S. Ct. 2257 (1998) and *Faragher* v. *City of Boca Raton*, 118 S. Ct. 2275 (1998), the Court expanded the liability of employers for harassing conduct by supervisors, but also specified the elements necessary for an employer to provide an affirmative defense in harassment cases.[3]

The first case, *Burlington Industries* v. *Ellerth*, outlined the circumstances under which "an employee who refuses the unwelcome and threatening sexual advances of a supervisor, yet suffers no adverse, tangible job consequences, can recover against the employer without showing the employer is negligent or otherwise at fault for the supervisor's actions." The facts in the case were that while Ellerth was an employee at Burlington Industries her supervisor (T. Slowik) made obscene and offensive gestures and remarks in an attempt to get her to submit to his sexual demands. He also threatened to "make her life very hard" if she rejected him. She refused his advances. Her position with Burlington did not suffer impairment. She even received a promotion. Ellerth later quit her job. She did so having made no complaints about her supervisor even though she knew that Burlington had a policy prohibiting sexual harassment.

Thus, when Ellerth sued Burlington for sexual harassment, she had suffered no negative economic consequences for refusing the sexual advances of her supervisor (she was even promoted), and she had quit her job without making use of the company's policy against sexual harassment. Ellerth filed suit in the U.S. District Court in Illinois. The court dismissed her claim and granted judgement to Burlington. In the opinion of this court, Slowik's behavior was "severe and pervasive enough to create a hostile work environment"; however, because Burlington did not know "nor should have known" about the behavior, Ellerth had no legal basis for suing.

The Court of Appeals reversed the decision of the lower court, ruling that Burlington did have vicarious liability for it's supervisor's actions. Burlington sought a reversal of the decision in the U.S. Supreme Court, which agreed to hear the case. The Supreme Court ruled that an employee *can* seek legal redress via a sexual harassment suit even though she may have failed to make any complaints to the employer and even though she may not have sustained any detrimental economic effects to her employment. In certain cases, an employer does have vicarious liability for the intentional wrongdoings of an employee. The liability exists when the employee "uses apparent authority" or when the employee "was aided in [the wrongdoing]" given his position as an agent of the employer.

The justices held that in those cases in which there is no negative effect to the plaintiff's employment opportunities or benefits but the actions of the supervisor are "severe and pervasive," they amount to a non-tangible employment action against the plaintiff. The sexually harassing actions of the supervisor, in essence, amount to what was previously termed a "hostile work environment." A company could be found liable provided it has no affirmative defense to offer.

A company may present an affirmative defense under the following conditions: (1) the company can establish that it acted with "reasonable care" to prevent and straightaway correct any sexual harassment; and (2) the plaintiff "unreasonably" failed to utilize the preventative or corrective options offered by the employer or to in any way evade harm.[4]

Further, the Court held that when there is a "tangible employment action" (i.e., the employee *does* actually suffer economic harm) due to a supervisor's sexual harassment, the company's legal responsibility is a matter of *strict liability*.[5] What constitutes a "tangible employment action"? The Court stated:

> [a] tangible employment action constitutes a significant change in employment status, such as hiring, firing, failing to promote, reassignment with significantly different responsibilities, or a decision causing a significant change in benefits.

In the majority of cases, the injury the employee sustains from the supervisor's action must "inflict direct economic harm" in order to be considered a tangible employment action.

The Court remanded the case back to the District Court for trial to determine if Ellerth had a claim which would result in vicarious liability for Burlington. Since Ellerth suffered no tangible employment action, Burlington would be allowed to present an affirmative defense.

The other sexual harassment case decided by the 1998 Supreme Court was *Faragher* v. *City of Boca Raton*. In this case, the Court upheld its decision in *Ellerth* that an employer could be liable for sexual harassment by a supervisor even if the employer had no actual notice of the supervisor's conduct. In *Faragher*, the plaintiff had been a lifeguard for the city of Boca Raton for a number of years. During this period she was repeatedly subjected to salacious and offensive remarks and inappropriate touching by her supervisors. When she quit her job, she did so without informing her employer (the city of Boca Raton) of the harassment she had undergone.

The Supreme Court reversed the appellate court's ruling that the city had no liability. Given *Ellerth*, the fact that an employer may not be directly aware of the harassing behavior of its supervisors will not absolve it from responsibility for those actions. *Faragher* is important, however, because it provides some clarification on the "reasonable care" standard that an employer must use in order to be allowed to present an affirmative defense. As stated above, *Ellerth* established that an employer can provide an affirmative defense to a hostile work environment charge if it can show that it has acted with "reasonable care" to detect, correct, and thwart sexually harassing behavior and that the employee "unreasonably" failed to utilize these measures. Whereas, in *Ellerth*, Burlington would be allowed to present an affirmative defense at trial, the defendant in *Faragher* would not be allowed to do so.

The Court in *Faragher* found that "reasonable care" can be interpreted to mean that an employer must do more than simply have a policy against sexual harassment. Its policy must be on the books, and all employees should be made aware of the rules and procedures for reporting violations of the policy. The employer must give more than just "lip service" to promulgate the policy. A record of prompt and effective eradication of such behavior would certainly be indicative of an employer's dedication to the policy. Given that the employer has used reasonable care in handling sexual harassment complaints, it is incumbent upon the plaintiff to exercise his/her rights as articulated in the employer's policy.

An employer may only offer an affirmative defense in cases in which the employee has suffered no economic deprivation as a result of the harassment. Then it must be shown that the employer has exercised "reasonable care" in promulgating its policy and that the plaintiff unreasonably failed to utilize the employer's sexual harassment policy. The court in *Faragher* stated that while the plaintiff suffered no economic deprivation (tangible employment action) due to the harassment, the defendant, City of Boca Raton, did not use reasonable care in informing employees of its policy.[6] (The Coast Guard claimed it never received the notice.)

When the harassment has led to a "tangible employment action" by the supervisor, then the employer has *strict liability* and no defense is applicable. Cases involving non-tangible employment actions are tantamount to "hostile environment" cases. The categories of *quid pro quo* and "hostile environment" have not been abandoned by the Court in the *Ellerth* and *Faragher* decisions, rather, what constitutes *quid pro quo* harassment has been changed. Previously, the mere threat of retaliation by the supervisor, even if it was not acted upon, was considered *quid pro quo* harassment and, so, carried with it a strict liability. Now, the threat of retaliation, if it is not acted upon by the supervisor and, therefore, no actual economic harm occurs, will be considered a hostile work environment case, which will be amenable to an affirmative defense by the employer. Strict liability or *quid pro quo* harassment cases require a plaintiff's tangible economic loss.

## SAMPLE CASE

Ron proudly considers himself to be a fairly secure and liberal thinking guy when it comes to tolerating people's differences. So, he always mentions to acquaintances that, even though he is "straight," he is a copy editor for a gay men's magazine. There are both men and women working at the magazine. His immediate supervisor (Lydia) is a woman. Ron isn't sure which of the male employees is gay, though he knows that a large percentage of them are.

Last week Ron had lunch with Lydia. While they were seated she reached under the table and placed her hand on his thigh. She then winked and asked him if he would like to engage in some "after work activities" with her. Ron, who was practically stunned, had the presence of mind to refuse the offer and to inform her that he was engaged to be married. Since that incident Lydia has been rather brusque to him whenever he needs her advice on a project. Ron is disturbed by the change in Lydia's attitude and also worried about receiving a negative annual review from her. These reviews (which determine salary) are scheduled for the end of the month. Ron isn't sure how to handle the matter. He vaguely remembers a paragraph or two in the employee manual stating the company's intolerance of discrimination and sexual harassment. There was no procedure outlined for reporting such matters, but even if there had been Ron would not have filed a complaint because he did not want to stir up trouble.

He decides to speak with the section supervisor, Bill, the person to whom Lydia reports. Ron requests a private meeting with Bill at which he plans to discuss the problem and, if at all possible, to leave Lydia's name out of it. Bill suggests that he and Ron meet after work at a bar not too far from the building in which they work.

Ron enters the bar and sees Bill seated in a booth waiting for him. He goes over to the booth. Bill seems excited to see Ron and, before he has a chance to sit down, Bill stands and gives him a kiss on the cheek. He then says how he'd always thought Ron was very attractive, but never dared approach him while at work. He expresses his appreciation and pleasure at the fact that Ron had made the "first move." Ron is taken aback and not sure what his appropriate response should be. He decides to leave the bar and tender his resignation from the magazine in the morning.

# FOR DISCUSSION

Does Ron have a viable suit for sexual harassment? Why or why not?

# NOTES

1. Karen A. Crain and Kenneth A. Heischmidt, "Implementing Business Ethics: Sexual Harassment," *Journal of Business Ethics* 14 (1995): 299–308.

2. John W. Dienhart and Jordan Curnott, *Business Ethics: A Reference Handbook* (Santa Barbara, Calif.: ABC-CLIO, Inc., 1998).

3. An affirmative defense involves the defendant claiming not only his innocence, but also offering positive evidence of some malfeasance on the part of the plaintiff which actually led to plaintiff's harm rather than any act or omission by the defendant.

4. A plaintiff may be "unreasonable" if the plaintiff fails to complain to the employer of harassing incidents when the plaintiff is aware of the company's willing and effective efforts to eliminate such occurrences.

5. When a defendant has strict liability that defendant is precluded from offering any defense whatsoever against the allegation.

6. The District Court found that the city had entirely failed to disseminate its policy on sexual harassment among beach employees and the policy itself was very inadequate.

7. Note: The Supreme Court just recently (October 2000) rejected an appeal by a married couple who claimed they were sexually harassed at work by the same supervisor. A lower court ruled that the couple cannot sue under the federal law banning sexual discrimination at work because someone who harasses people of both sexes is treating them equally.

# DISCHARGE

# A Termination at Pacemakers, Inc.

When he took the job as manager of the circuit department in the technology division of Pacemakers, Inc. four years ago, Jack Rice knew he was on a hot seat. Pacemakers, in business just twelve years, had achieved second place in sales in the industry in the short span of seven years. Then, a two-year series of product recalls based on circuit failures severely damaged the company's reputation and earnings. Sales slipped to fourth place in the industry and there were rumors that Pacemakers was a stockmarket takeover candidate. Top management, convinced there would be only two or three ultimate survivors in this business, and determined to be among them while also remaining independent, decided to clean house in the circuit department. To head the department they brought in Jack, largely because Stan Drew wanted him. Stan, manager of the technology division, had been Jack's old boss when they worked at Circuit Technology, Inc., the leading U.S. firm in integrated circuits. Although he had never had management responsibilities, Jack had a reputation as an excellent new product man and he was hired to lead the development of a new series of pacemakers based on the latest work in integrated circuits.

Jack looked on the position as a real challenge. He was responsible for one of the three basic technological ingredients in a pacemaker: circuitry, battery, and pacing leads to the heart. And technology is the key to this business; doctors want the best pacemaker for their patients, and quality, not cost, is the primary factor. This was the challenge Jack desired; he'd had enough of designing circuits for products like electronic games, where cost factors dominated. Jack also got along well with his boss; he believed that Stan Drew knew what applied science was all about—hire creative people, increase the research and development budget, and quality products will emerge.

At first it was rough; Jack had to upgrade his staff—hire several new scientists, reorient others, and discharge a few. He also had to acquaint himself with battery technology, the basic aspects of biophysics, and his competitors' products. It took him two years to see clearly what sort of a product he wanted. And then he had to motivate his staff to pull with him, often by spending long hours with them working on design and materials problems.

About that time, Jack's boss, Stan Drew, was fired. Stan said little about his dismissal except that he had taken the long-range view and both sales and earnings were still unimpressive and erratic. Stan was replaced by Mark Burns, who had a finance background. There was some grumbling about this among members of the circuit department, but top management explained that the firm's condition was still precarious and attention had to be focused on the present bottom line as well as the long range.

Mark Burns met with Jack to discuss the problems at Pacemakers. Mark said he was uncomfortable with the way Stan Drew was terminated and was aware there was some discontent among the research personnel. Jack replied: "People are nervous. We are on track with the product. Our team knows that. But medical technology takes time. We have to cross the FDA's hurdles and their standards are tough. The main point from our end is that we are gaining even though our research budget is lower than our competitors'. So we are optimistic. Then we see our boss, the guy responsible overall for our progress, get clipped. You know, there are no golden parachutes at our level; most of our team isn't even vested in the pension plan. It's scary. You work hard, you produce, but you've got the mortgage to pay and college bills, and if you get cut you have little or nothing to fall back on. You're right. The troops are anxious." Mark said that a little fear was a good motivator, and added that the volatility in technological businesses meant there could be no job guarantees. He added: "We do need to provide more security, particularly for our managers. I'm going to see that you get a salary increase. I'm also going to do my best to get you a productivity incentive bonus. I also think managers at your level should be in on our profit-sharing plan. I'll discuss this with top management. Finally, I know that at age fifty-eight vesting in our pension plan is important to you, and I'll work on that. Do your job and don't worry. I'm behind you."

Over the next year, Jack's relations with Mark became strained. Jack had talked with Stan Drew as one inventor to another. Management, to them, meant a deep involvement with and interest in the actual process of invention, a process that involved creativity and one not reducible to strict control, prediction or rationalization. In contrast, Mark talked of management by objective and cost-benefit analysis; his vocabulary, to Jack, seemed textbook and unrelated to the unpredictability of inventive work. Jack also did not like the extended business lunches and group meetings that Mark favored; they seemed to be personnel relations ploys and unrelated to the job. Mark felt he was in charge of a bunch of wild horses which needed to be shaped into a team. He held meetings to develop lines of communication and a clearer sense of direction. Mark brought in several organizational consultants to talk to Jack's department but felt undercut when word got back to him that in response to an employee who brought up a circuit problem to Jack, the latter said: "Let's do it like Mark wants—sit down, hold hands, and meditate." Jack was also upset that, although his salary was increased, Mark said no more about bonuses, profit-sharing, or vesting in the pension plan. Finally, Jack felt that although Mark talked long term he really had his eye on the quarterly earnings report. Technology, Jack thought, takes time. But Jack also knew the company was now tracked on his product and he was confident that in time it, or a successor based upon it, would be a big winner.

Three and a half years into his job, a pacemaker with Jack's circuits hit the market. It had a good reception in tests, but market acceptance was mixed. Jack believed that this was largely due to the company's tarnished reputation, but he allowed that competitors had not stood still and that their recent products were still a bit ahead of Pacemakers.' As he entered the office of Bill Smith, executive vice president for manufacturing, to attend his quarterly meeting, Jack felt secure in the knowledge that Pacemakers was at least competitive and that they could gain the edge with the next generation of pacemakers he had on the drawing board.

Bill Smith informed Jack that recent sales figures were disappointing and that it did not seem to him that a turnaround was near. He added that top management had been disappointed with Jack's performance for some time and that he was being terminated effective at the end of the day. Jack was stunned. He protested that he clearly had turned his department around and asked Bill to bring in Jack's immediate boss, Mark Burns, to discuss the issue. Bill said the decision was his, not Mark's, and that it was final. Jack asked for some reasons. Bill said they were in the sales figures. He added that a new circuit department manager had already been hired from outside the firm, and he would be reporting in two days. Allowing that the termination was abrupt, Bill offered Jack two months severance pay and told him he would provide him with a good recommendation.

A few days later, in discussing Jack with the firm's personnel manager, Bill Smith said:

> Jack Rice and Mark Burns just didn't see eye to eye. There was some personality conflict that I could not put my finger on. Maybe I should have canned Mark; he couldn't explain the problem to Jack, and Jack wasn't really aware of it—he was too concerned with his tinkering in the lab. But I couldn't fire Mark; he's ticketed for a top-level managerial slot. And I couldn't transfer Jack—there's no other slot in the organization where he would fit. Instead of demoting him in his own department, I thought it was best to just let him go. He'll catch on as a new product man somewhere, but I won't recommend him for a managerial position.

Mark Burns said, in commenting privately on Jack's dismissal:

> Jack was not on top of things; he was too unorganized. He was a brilliant Lone Ranger from Silicon Valley with a narrow, inventor's mentality, who was always jumping ahead of his staff to the next, vaguely thought out project. He had to do everything himself on the technical side of things, but he could not delegate or understand other aspects of the business. His product is okay, it'll help us survive. But as we grow we need more coordination and long-term planning, and Jack was uncomfortable with that approach. He thought it inhibited him. And he never understood that top management wanted at least a show of social responsibility. I found out that he did not even pass out the United Fund cards, and, as for affirmative action, Jack refused to hire on the basis of anything but merit; he'd just laugh and say, "Put 'em in your steno pool." He just did not have a feel for the human side of things. I talked with him about these matters, but it did not seem to have an impact. When I told Bill Smith that I thought we should dump Jack, I offered to do it and give reasons, but Bill said that he would take care of it. Sales, he said, were not that good, which was sufficient.

One of the supervisors formerly under Jack made these observations, three months after Jack's termination:

Things have changed some around here; we are not quite as free-wheeling as we used to be under Jack. The R and D budget has been cut a bit, and some of us are wondering who is next to go. In many ways I think Jack was a fall-guy for Burns and Smith. They are not innovators and this is a risk business. They got a good product out of him and solid ideas for future products. Sales are slow now, but they'll pick up and Burns and Smith will look good. The new boss has some good ideas. But that will mean he has to make changes to leave his mark. That might set us back a year or so. I'm just not sure what games are being played here.

Jack went to see Martha Hargett, a labor law attorney. She informed Jack that he got fired in the wrong state, that Georgia was the strongest "at-will" state, meaning that an employer can fire an employee at any time for a good reason, a bad reason, or no reason at all. The only exceptions in Georgia are that you cannot be fired because you receive a subpoena for a court appearance or because your wages are garnisheed one time. Hargett mentioned several federal statutes that restrict terminations, and, after hearing Jack's case, said he might have a basis for a lawsuit. Given his age, he might be able to bring an age discrimination action because a much younger man replaced Jack. Hargett also explained it is illegal to fire someone to deprive him of employee benefits. But she noted that Jack had a relatively brief period of employment at Pacemakers. Hargett also though that a fraud action might be brought because of the compensation promises made by Mark Burns. She cited a former IBM executive who was lured to another firm in 1998 with compensation promises that were not honored, and who won a $10 million case for breach of contract and fraud. However, she noted that Jack had nothing in writing. Hargett also said that lawsuits are painful, expensive, and often take five years to resolve. She said her fee for a case this questionable was fifty percent of a judgment and the client pays all expenses off the top. These include Xerox copies, $4 per-page court reporter's records, and fees charged by professional "expert witnesses."

Jack had this comment after reflecting on his dismissal and his three months of trying unsuccessfully to secure a similar position:

I'm still bitter and baffled about this whole thing. I'm baffled because I put up the product that will eventually save this company. I'm bitter because I got the shaft. Mark and Bill Smith know that, and there's nothing I can do about it. Oh, I sent a zinger letter to the company's top dog, but I didn't even get a reply. I lie awake at night thinking about how those two toads above me will benefit from my work. Smith even had the gall to warn me not to take Pacemaker's trade secrets with me. Their secrets? Hah! In this business the next new product is in somebody's head—mine! I'll take that with me to a competitor and bury these clowns. So far though, I'll admit I haven't had any takers.

## FOR DISCUSSION

Was Pacemakers justified in firing Jack Rice? Why or why not? Discuss and evaluate the context of Jack's termination and the way it was handled. Could steps be taken to improve termination procedures at Pacemakers, Inc.? If so, what steps would you take?

*Patricia H. Werhane*

# Employment at Will

The principle of Employment at Will (EAW) is a common-law doctrine stating that, in the absence of law or contract, employers have the right to hire, promote, demote, and fire whomever and whenever they please. The principle was stated explicitly in 1887 by H. G. Wood, who wrote, "a general or indefinite hiring is prima facie a hiring at will" (Wood, 1887).

In the United States EAW has been interpreted as the rule that when employees are not specifically covered by union agreement, legal statute, public policy, or contract, an employer "may dismiss their employees at will . . . for good cause, for no cause, *or even for causes morally wrong*, without being thereby guilty of legal wrong" (Blades, 1967, p. 1405). Today at least 60 percent of all employees in the private sector of the economy, from part-time or temporary workers to corporate presidents, are "at will" employees.

EAW has been widely interpreted as allowing employees to be demoted, transferred, or dismissed without having a hearing and without requirement of good reasons, or "cause" for the employment decision. This is not to say that employers do not have reasons, usually good reasons, for their decisions. But there is no legal obligation to state or defend their decisions. Thus EAW sidesteps the requirement of due process or grievance procedures in the workplace, although it does not preclude the institution of such procedures.

As a recognized common-law principle, traditionally EAW has been upheld in the U.S. state and federal courts. However, in the last fifteen years legal statutes have increased the number of employees who are protected from EAW, including those protected by equal opportunity and age discrimination legislation. Moreover, what is meant by "public policy" has been expanded. For example, cases in which an employee has been asked to

From *The Blackwell Encyclopedic Dictionary of Business Ethics*, ed. Patricial H. Werhane and R. Freeman (Malden Mass and Oxford: Blackwell Publishers Ltd., 1997), pp 199–201. Reprinted with permission of Blackwell Publishers Ltd.

break a law or to violate a stated public policy, cases where employees are not allowed to exercise certain constitutional rights such as the right to vote, serve on a jury, or collect worker compensation are all considered wrongful discharges. Employees won 67 percent of their suits on wrongful discharge during a recent three-year period. These suits were won, not on the basis of a rejection of the principle of EAW, but rather because of breach of contract, lack of just cause for dismissal when a company grievance policy was in place, or violations of public policy (Geyelin, 1989, p. B1).

EAW is often justified for one or more of the following reasons:

1. The proprietary rights of employers guarantee that they may employ or dismiss whomever and whenever they wish.
2. EAW defends employee, managerial, and employer rights equally, in particular the right to freedom of contract, because an employee voluntarily contracts to be hired and can quit at any time.
3. In choosing to take a job, an employee voluntarily commits herself to certain responsibilities and company loyalty, including the knowledge that she is an "at will" employee.
4. Extending due-process rights and other employee protections in the workplace often interferes with the efficiency and productivity of the business organization.
5. Legislation and/or regulation of employment relationships further undermine an already over-regulated economy.

On the other side, there are a number of criticisms of EAW. Perhaps the most serious is that while EAW is defended as preserving employer and employee rights equally, it is sometimes interpreted as justifying arbitrary treatment of employees. This is analogous to considering an employee as a piece of property at the disposal of the employer or corporation. When I "fire" a robot, I do not have to give reasons, because a robot is not a rational being; it has no use for reasons. On the other hand, if I fire a person arbitrarily I am making the assumption that she does not need reasons for the decision, a questionable logic. If I have hired persons, then I should treat them as such, with respect throughout the employment process. This does not preclude firing, but it does ask employers to give reasons for their actions, for reasons are appropriate when one is dealing with persons.

There are other grounds for not abusing EAW as part of recognizing equal obligations implied by freedom of contract. Arbitrariness, although not prohibited by EAW, violates the managerial model of rationality and consistency. This ideal is implied by a consistent application of this common-law principle, that EAW protects employees, managers, and employers equally and fairly. We expect managers, in their roles as employers, to act reasonably and consistently in their decision-making. Not giving reasons for employment decisions belies that expectation. Thus, even if EAW itself is justifiable, the practice of EAW, when interpreted as condoning arbitrary employment decisions, is not.

Looking ahead, the signs are clear that the doctrine of EAW will continue to be refined and challenged. Within the corporation new approaches to work and organizational activity are bringing new modes of employee participation that encourage greater employee expression. The challenge for management and employees is to find creative ways to minimize burdensome litigation while at the same time balancing employer and employee rights.

## RESOURCES

Arvanites, D., and B. T. Ward. 1990. "Employment at Will: A Social Concept in Decline." In *Contemporary Issues in Business Ethics.* 2d ed. Edited by J. J. Desjardins and J. J. McCall. Belmont, Calif.: Wadsworth Publishing, pp. 147–54.

Blades, L. E. 1967. "Employment at Will Versus Individual Freedom: On Limiting the Abusive Exercise of Employer Power." *Columbia Law Review*, 67.

Ewing, D. 1983. *Do It My Way or You're Fired!* New York: John Wiley.

Feinman, J. M. 1991. "The Development of the Employment at Will Rule Revisited." *Arizona State Law Journal* 23, pp. 733–40.

Geyelin, M. 1989. Fired Managers Winning more Lawsuits. *Wall Street Journal*, 7 September, B1.

*Hutton* v. *Watters.* 1915. 132 Tenn. 527, S.W. 134.

*Payne* v. *Western.* 1884. 81 Tenn. 507

Summers, C. B. 1980. "Protecting *All* Employees Against Unjust Dismissal." *Harvard Business Review* (January/February).

Werhane, P. H. 1985. *Persons, Rights, and Corporations.* Englewood Cliffs, N.J.: Prentice-Hall.

Wood, H. G. 1887. *A Treatise on the Law of Master and Servant.* Albany, N.Y.: John D. Parsons.

*John J. McCall*

# Just Cause

Just cause is a policy requiring that dismissal of employees be for just or good reason.

A just cause dismissal policy is best understood in contrast to a strict employment at will (EAW) rule which allows employers absolute discretion to fire an employee. The essence of just cause policies, on the other hand, is to limit the employer's authority to discharge. While there may be many different instantiations of just cause policies, all will address the following: reasons, procedures, and remedies.

What constitutes a good or just reason for dismissal is impossible to define exactly in a brief policy or statute. Typically, "just cause" is defined loosely (e.g., as reasonable and job-related grounds for dismissal) and left to arbitrators or labor courts to define more precisely through their decisions. It is, however, clearly understood that union membership, race, sex, personal bias, political opinions, religion, or ethnicity are invalid reasons; theft, fighting on the job, drug use on the job, excessive absenteeism, or substandard performance are acceptable reasons.

There are interesting corollaries of requiring good reasons: (1) If inadequate performance is a valid reason for discharge, then employers must specify what counts as adequate performance. (2) More broadly, a just cause policy must understand "valid reason" as requiring more than an employer's subjective belief, say, that an employee stole or used drugs at work. Some substantial evidence must he available to make such a belief reasonable. Failure to require these things of employers will obviously make a demand for just cause ineffectual in protecting employees from unfair dismissals.

Just cause policies will also require that some procedures be available to review discharge actions. At the very least, some mechanism for

From *The Blackwell Encyclopedic Dictionary of Business Ethics*, ed. Patricial H. Werhane and R. Freeman (Malder, Mass., and Oxford: Blackwell Publishers Ltd. 1997), pp. 352–53. Reprinted with permission of Blackwell Publishers Ltd.

external and independent assessment of the merits of the employer's reasons must be made available to the employee. Arbitrators or labor courts usually fill this role. While not essential, less formal internal pre-termination hearings or appeals mechanisms are consistent with the spirit of just cause in that these will help prevent unfair discharges. Once the employee completes the probationary period required for coverage, most just cause policies also require prior notice of intent to dismiss and written provision of the reasons.

Finally, all just cause policies must include some remedy for those cases where a firing is found to be unjust. Possible remedies include reinstatement and/or monetary damages. In jurisdictions governed by just cause, monetary damages are usually limited by statute to some small multiple of wages.

While most Western industrialized nations have adopted some form of just cause policy, U.S. state laws almost universally represent a modified EAW rule. In the U.S., employer discretion to discharge is no longer absolute, having been limited incrementally by judicial precedents or statutes that identify impermissible grounds for dismissal. However, aside from those enumerated exceptions, U.S. employers may still fire for any or no reason. Exceptions to this are public employees and union workers, both of whom enjoy protections similar to "just cause," and those who work for corporations that have voluntarily adopted a just cause policy.

Since 1980, just cause statutes have been introduced in ten states. The debate over these proposals is in part a moral debate involving issues of fairness, justice, and collective welfare. Proponents of such statutes are moved by the substantial harms that can accompany job loss. In addition to lost income, workers and their families suffer insecurity, depression, loss of self-respect. They argue that it is unfair to impose these costs on the estimated 150,000+ workers a year discharged without just cause and due process.

Opponents of just cause claim that broad employer authority to dismiss is necessary for workplace discipline and motivation. (Implicit in this argument is the belief that job security and work output are inversely related.) They also point to the need for employer flexibility in the competitive global economy. They argue that just cause is not required by fairness since workers and employers have equal ability to terminate the relationship. Finally, they claim that just cause must be inefficient since if it were efficient, the labor market would force employers to provide it.

Defenders of just cause respond to these challenges by arguing that:

(1) The motivator under EAW is fear of job loss and the psychological literature is unanimous on fear being a poor motivator. At most, fear will assure that workers conform to minimum external standards. It will probably also assure workers who lack innovation and who are dispirited. (2) Those who point to drones as the paradigm of workers with job security need to show that is typical under job security, and if it is, that security and not some other variable (e.g., lack of autonomy) is the cause of low productivity. (3) The appeal to needed flexibility in a competitive economy is a red herring since all just cause policies accept layoffs due to economic conditions. (4) While formally equal, individual employees and employers are not often in positions of equal bargaining strength. As a result, it is not surprising that the private labor market does not typically provide job security. It is also not surprising that grievance procedures are one of the first demands of organized workers.

It remains to be seen which set of arguments carries the day in the continuing U.S. debate.

*James Kiersky*

# Due Process

According to *West's Encyclopedia of American Law*, legal due process is defined as a "fundamental constitutional guarantee that all legal proceedings will be fair and that one will be given notice of the proceedings and an opportunity to be heard before the government acts to take away one's life, liberty, or property. Also, the constitutional guarantee that a law shall not be unreasonable, arbitrary, or capricious."[1] *Black's Law Dictionary* reiterates an important feature of this definition, seeing due process as "an orderly proceeding wherein a person is served with notice, actual or constructive, and has an opportunity to be heard and to enforce and protect his rights before a court having power to hear and determine the case."[2] Having a history that predates even the Magna Carta in 1215, legal due process rights are divided traditionally into two different spheres: substantive due process and procedural due process. The former deals with the "what" or content of the law; the latter, with the "how" or process of the law itself. Procedurally, due process offers a method for appealing decisions whereby a person may obtain at least an explanation for that decision and a chance to present his or her side of the case. Substantively, due process is a means for ensuring fair and consistent reasons for that decision. Deriving in United States law from the Fifth and the Fourteenth Amendments, due process protects individual persons and corporations from national and state government encroachments.

In the business realm, although corporations have a legal right to due process, employees do not. So, at this point in time, the question is whether employers should grant due process to their employees. Of course, in many cases they do, often through collective bargaining agreements. However, many employees are not covered by such agreements, and so our question is whether employers should provide due process for such employees.

The arguments against extending procedural due process rights to employees are based primarily on corporate utility. If every employee is entitled to a grievance or arbitration procedure concerning almost any corporate action, an enormous amount of time and money might well be devoted to due process hearings. Again, a large corporation may need to downsize and quickly terminate 20,000 to survive. It would have a very difficult time working through 20,000 due process hearings. At the other end of the corporate spectrum, a small sole proprietor with only a few employees may find it awkward and impractical to implement an internal due process procedure, but expensive to send cases to outside arbitration.

With respect to certain types of employer action, especially termination, fairness considerations can also be employed against extending due process rights to employees. If it is allowed that it is morally acceptable for an employee to simply quit without giving the firm a chance for a hearing on the employee's decision, then fairness seems to dictate that the employer should be able to terminate an employee without granting that employee access to an appeals hearing.

Several arguments based on fairness or utility considerations favor extending due process to employees. Concerning fairness, if we agree with Kant that humans should always be treated as ends in themselves and never as a mere means, then respect for employees is necessary and some form of grievance procedure seems required as an indication of that respect. It would at least preclude an employee being discarded like a used machine or waste product. Second, fairness requires that similar cases be treated similarly. Procedural due process, being allowed a hearing, would help see to it that managerial decisions are not arbitrary or capricious. The checks and balances of substantive due process would help to ensure more rational, objective, and consistent decisions. For example, unfair terminations are more apt to be discovered and remedied when due process is utilized consistently.

Consequentialist reasons are also offered to support extending due process to employees. With respect to the individual being terminated, the consequences are decidedly better if there is a predictable, consistently applied and rational grievance procedure in place that will help to assure that corporate decisions are soundly based. Furthermore, the consequences for other employees would have to be beneficial in the main, for (a) their own job security is not threatened by the unwarranted loss of another employee, (b) employee morale would have to be improved by knowing that there is in place a functioning, well-considered set of procedures to protect them, and (c) even employees who are justifiably terminated would at least know why they were fired and what they need to do in order to keep future jobs they may hold. The consequences for the firm itself seem to favor due process insofar as more people, and people with higher qualifications, will want to work for a firm that respects them and these people will leave employers who do not afford them as much respect. A firm's reputation may be enhanced by having a due process system. And that reputation will help attract or repel quality employees. Furthermore, unjust terminations which are not corrected by a due process procedure will certainly have disutility for the firm.

Because businesses and the contexts in which they operate are so diverse, some businesses should probably have due process for their employees while others should not. If a company adopts a due process system, David Ewing suggests seven general factors it ought to include:

1. It must be a procedure that follows rules. It must not be arbitrary and capricious.
2. It must be visible in the sense of being familiar enough that potential violators of rights as well as victims of abuse know of it and its particulars.
3. It must be predictably effective. Employees need to have confidence that previous decisions in favor of rights will be upheld in the present and future and that equal cases will be treated equally.
4. It must become a part of the institution itself in the sense that it is a relatively permanent and infrequently changeable part of corporate policy that will not suddenly be gone when business exigencies dictate.
5. It must be perceived as equitable by both employers and employees. The standards applied from case to case must be respected by those for whom the system works, from the top of management to the rank and file employee.
6. It must be easy to use, so that fear of procedural complexities will not baffle employees into failing to utilize the system or believing that it will not work.
7. It must apply to all employees.[3]

There will, of course, be a variety of ways that a due process system can be institutionalized, and the best method will be dependent on the size and type of the firm.

# NOTES

1. *West's Encyclopedia of American Law*, vol. 4 (St. Paul, Minn.: West Group, 1998), p. 166.

2. Henry Campbell Black, *Black's Law Dictionary: Definitions of the Terms and Phrases of American and English Jurisprudence, Ancient and Modern*, 6th ed. (St. Paul, Minn.: West Publishing, 1990), p. 500.

3. Ewing, David W. *Freedom Inside the Organization* (New York: E.P. Dutton, 1977), p. 156ff.

# PRIVACY

# Fantenetti Valve Corporation

Fantenetti Valve Corporation, headquartered in Patterson, New Jersey, is a specialty valve manufacturer with 2001 sales of $426 million. Unlike many of its competitors, Fantenetti does not mass produce standard valves, but instead focuses primarily on research and design work; it employs a relatively high percentage of scientific and technical personnel and spends about 6 percent of its annual sales on research. Most of its manufacturing is subcontracted with other firms. Fantenetti is not unionized. We interviewed Rose Mills, personnel manager at Fantenetti Valve Corporation, concerning that company's policies on security.

QUESTION: We hear a lot about security these days Rose; what's Fantenetti's policy?

MILLS: We are a large, technologically based firm, with about 6,000 employees in five states. Our technical data are our lifeblood, and we simply have to minimize risk with respect to trade secrets, formulas, marketing plans, and our growth strategies. Since most of the risk relates to the background and experiences of our employees, we must have data about them. We're in a tough position. We try to be sensitive to people's rights, but managers cannot make rational decisions without data, and this includes data on people—we certainly would be open to criticism if we acted without benefit of information on the people we hire and employ.

QUESTION: How do you get the data you want, and what's included?

MILLS: Well, each person's an individual. What's relevant in one case may not be relevant in another. So, at the time of application we ask the applicant to sign the following authorization:

> I understand that my employment at Fantenetti Valve Corporation is subject to verification of previous employment, data provided in my application, and any related documents, and will be contingent on my submitting to and passing both a physical examination administered by a company appointed physician and whatever tests are authorized by Fantenetti Valve Corporation. I authorize educational institutions, law enforcement authorities, employers, and all organizations and individuals having information relevant to my employment at Fantenetti Valve Corporation, to provide such information. I release all organizations and individuals, including Fantenetti Valve Corporation, from any liability in connection with the release of information about me. I understand that an investigative report may be made by or authorized by and submitted to, Fantenetti Valve Corporation.

This gives us some flexibility on the data we collect about each applicant; what's important in the case of one person may not be with another.

QUESTION: But isn't this just too broad? Doesn't it authorize you to to gather any data in whatever way without incurring any liability at all?

MILLS: Our experience is that you never know where an investigation will lead. So you need a blanket authorization. Of course we don't do anything outside the law. You know that the law today is very strict about what you can and cannot do. We stay strictly within the law. But if we want information that the law permits us to gather, we go after it. And once we hire someone, he's free to inspect his dossier anytime and to insert comments. I suppose we are unfair to some applicants. We do hire professionals to run our tests and background checks. And where we have only a few applicants we may invite in an otherwise promising candidate who has a few bad spots on his record. We sit down, talk about, and maybe clarify the problem. But, you know, in most cases we are swamped with candidates, so we can quickly narrow the list to the cream of the crop, most of whom have no problems with previous employers, school records, credit bureaus, health, and so on. But let me add that we also base our decisions on objective tests that we administer regarding aptitude, intelligence, and personality.

QUESTION: Aren't some of these sorts of tests of doubtful validity, especially personality tests?

MILLS: Let me say that we are an equal opportunity employer. We do some federal work, and we've always met Equal Employment Opportunity Commission (EEOC) and Office of Federal Contract Compliance (OFCC) guidelines. Beyond that, we are a scientific company. We believe in science. We believe that personality traits are measurable. You may have a person with the aptitude and brains for a job, but she has a personality flaw. In our sensitive business it's important that we measure a person's maturity, stability, and compatibility. Personality tests aren't infallible, but they're better than just a hunch about a person. They give us some idea about areas of a person's adequacy and inadequacy. They also help place people, to fit them into the right corporate slot.

QUESTION: Don't some of these tests touch on variables like masculinity/femininity? Are you interested in this sort of adequacy?

MILLS: It might be relevant. You don't know what is relevant until you look at each particular case. By "adequacy" we are looking at two things: (1) Is this person going to fit into the job? We don't want an introvert as a salesman. The tests tell us whether an applicant is an introvert. And (2), is the applicant going to fit into Fantenetti? If an applicant isn't going to mesh with our corporate culture, we don't want her.

QUESTION: Is homosexuality a thing of interest here?

MILLS: It may be; you can't generalize. You have to look at each case as it comes up. If he is gay and going to be disruptive, we don't want him. But, then, we don't want anyone who is disruptive. We have our values, our traditions. We have this all worked out in our mission statement. And we want employees who are totally dedicated to those values. It's very simple: if you have certain measurable personality traits, it's probable that you will be happy at Fantenetti. And if you are happy here, you will probably be productive. So, we use personality tests. But let me stress that we are interested in the person as well as Fantenetti. The person whose values do not mesh with ours will often become frustrated or alienated. He should be someplace else. If we can measure these traits, we are doing some applicants a favor by not hiring them.

QUESTION: But in these cases aren't you faced with an invasion of privacy?

MILLS: Of course, people have a right to privacy. We don't invade a person's home. We don't force people to apply for a job here or force them to take our tests. People sometimes think only employees have rights, but Fantenetti also has rights. We have a right to hire only employees who will avoid doing what we tell them not to do. We have a right to expect loyalty. We have a right to hire people who will act exclusively for Fantenetti's benefit. And we have a right to know what type of person we are hiring. In addition to examining past behavior, we also give each applicant a pencil and paper integrity test. What we are looking at here is the applicant's attitude toward theft; we try to determine whether the prospect is inclined to deviant behavior.

QUESTION: What's this test like?

MILLS: Fantenetti didn't make up the test. It was constructed and is graded by Psytest Systems. We selected this test because a 1991 study by the American Psychological Association indicated that the test's results are validated by academic research. I don't doubt that many such tests are unscientific, but Psytest seems to have passed muster. The test basically is true/false. You mark down "true" or "false" to statements such as:

1. Most work-related accidents can be avoided.
2. There are some people I definitely hate.
3. I always try to do my best at work.
4. I find it difficult to make friends with people.
5. In most cases I insist on doing things my own way.
6. I have never told a lie.

7. Making personal phone calls while at work is not the same as stealing.

8. The typical supervisor generally puts in a full day of hard work.

9. In some cases I try to get even with someone who has hurt me.

10. I would trick someone out of their money if I could definitely get away with it.

11. I have never done anything I felt guilty about.

12. It would be nice to have enough money to not have to work again.

QUESTION: Doesn't this smack of Big Brother? You either take the test or you are not hired. Doesn't the Fifth Amendment say you have a right to remain silent and not incriminate yourself? Doesn't the test amount to an unreasonable search that the Fourth Amendment bars? And isn't it a form of coerced expression that essentially violates the First Amendment?

MILLS: Look, I'm no Constitutional scholar, but these tests are used and there's no law explicitly banning them. The rights you mention are important, but they're not inalienable; they have to be balanced with Fantenetti's right to its property.

QUESTION: Are these tests valid?

MILLS: Of course, these tests are not perfect; no test is. Some honest people get excluded from consideration, and some thieves slip through. Psytest does, however, note that the American Psychological Association's 1991 study said the preponderance of evidence indicates that such tests work, i.e., they help predict which prospective employees may prove undependable or steal. The study concluded: "Despite all our reservations about honesty tests, we do not believe there is any sound basis for prohibiting their development and use. Indeed, to do so would only invite alternative forms of preemployment screening that would be less open, scientific, and controllable."

QUESTION: But one of our strengths in the United States is that we take individual rights seriously. And this procedure reminds me of the frontier judge who, desirous of seeing that the guilty did not escape punishment, sentenced everyone before him to hang.

MILLS: Well, an integrity test will, in some cases, deny a person a job. Yet any selection process culls people. A hundred people apply for a job. A personnel manager can discard ninety for any reason—or no real reason. Maybe one of them would have been the best for the job. Who knows? But the objective tests give one some basis that applies to every applicant and serves as a reasonable basis for rejection.

QUESTION: You say these tests are objective, but are they? It looks like the questions are loaded with ambiguity. Won't the really honest person simply fail the test? He thinks: "Sure, I lied—when I was a boy," or "I make a few calls on company time, say, to check up on a sick child, but I don't think that's theft," or "I don't always give 100 percent; I have bad days." So he fails. The clever liar, however, gives them what they want to hear and gets the job.

MILLS: The tests aren't infallible. But Psytest includes certain questions, such as, "I have never told a lie," that tempt liars to answer 'true," but which are clearly false. Everyone lies sometime. So the test-taker who answers "true" is assumed to be lying. Psytest sprinkles such questions throughout the test to unmask liars.

Psytest has some good evidence that their tests work. A four-year study of employees in a supermarket chain showed that testing reduced inventory loss along with employee terminations due to theft. We asked Psytest for references of firms that used their system, and everyone was satisfied.

QUESTION: How valid are the tests when applied to individuals?

MILLS: The Psytest test has 100 questions. Each applicant scores a particular number. If Joe scores 60, this means 60 percent of the other applicants gave answers that were less honest. Fantenetti itself then sets the score below which we will not consider the applicant.

QUESTION: How accurate is the score, the 60 assigned to Joe?

MILLS: Psytest tells us its test is 85 percent reliable. It is 85 percent sure Joe gave answers that were more honest than 60 percent of all applicants.

QUESTION: Many tests have been found to discriminate. How about integrity tests?

MILLS: Psytest assures us their test is corrected for bias by assigning different weights to questions, depending on whether the test is given to blacks, whites, or Hispanics. To make sure they are being fair, Psytest also scores test-takers against others in their own group in order to balance out differences in schooling, lifestyle, and family background. For the most part, the questions are readily understandable to a person with a sixth-grade level of reading comprehension. So we don't think the tests discriminate.

QUESTION: There are lots of studies that indicate employees today want to be trusted; they want autonomy, respect, responsibility, etc. And some research shows people produce better if they are trusted. But Fantenetti starts out by not trusting its applicants. Isn't this counterproductive?

MILLS: We do want employees we can trust, but an applicant is not an employee. We believe integrity tests give us a higher percentage of employees we can trust than if we didn't use the tests. In business we have to keep our eye on the bottom line, and we think the bottom line looks better when we use these tests.

QUESTION: Does all this data become part of one's permanent file?

MILLS: Yes, but she always has access to it, and can insert comments. We don't try to stereotype people with tests. Files are constantly updated. Everyone is evaluated annually, and the employee sees and signs her evaluation. She may add comments. Other data is constantly added: letters of commendation or warning, relevant memoranda, newspaper clippings, employee suggestions, health insurance information, and so on.

QUESTION: Do you separate job performance data from personal information?

MILLS: No. It's all related to job performance.

QUESTION: Can the employee see anything in his file at any time?

MILLS: There are only two things he cannot see. We have a form that compares workers for merit raises, promotions, and layoffs. Since this data is comparative, and includes personal information on several employees, it is not available. We also have a corporate development plan that contains management's opinion of an individual's potential, any long-range plans the company might have regarding the employee, and a list of possible replacements. This isn't available either. But let me add that we're practically required to keep such files. We have to promote minorities, and so we have to get the data. To compare people and groups we have to have data on everyone.

QUESTION: Who has access to these files?

MILLS: A superior has access to the file of any subordinate responsible to her on the organizational chart. Those people designated "senior manager" have access to the file of anyone below that level. You must have this sort of access to facilitate the information flow. We're a "people" company, and we have to get the right people in the right jobs.

QUESTION: Do you allow outsiders access to your employee files?

MILLS: You have to. The Occupational Safety and Health Administration (OSHA) requires health information. The IRS wants payroll data. The Defense Department examines our security checks. I could go on. The police and the courts can get certain data. We also generally agree to provide data on job title, salary, and length of service to the credit bureaus and investigating agencies that screen our applicants. We don't release any other information unless the employee agrees to it.

## FOR DISCUSSION

Has Rose Mills presented an acceptable defense of Fantenetti's policies regarding employees' records? In what areas is her defense strong? In what areas is it weak? If it were your responsibility to redesign Fantenetti's procedures, would you make any changes? Why?

# LANSCAPE

Clare Valerian is a systems analyst at Califon, Inc., a large distributor of electronic equipment. Her primary responsibility is to make certain that the 127 end-users in Califon's U.S. headquarters can access data, post to accounts, send and receive e-mail, and accomplish all the other duties they need to perform on the corporation's local area network. She describes herself as a facilitator and troubleshooter. She must respond quickly to the users' complaints and needs, and even provide training for novice users. It's a demanding and time-consuming job, and until two weeks ago, Clare was spending up to twelve hours a day one-on-one with her users. She spent much of her time traveling to various sites in the different corporate buildings. The telephone was not much help, because Clare had to see for herself exactly what the users saw on their screens.

Recently, however, a utility program called LANSCAPE has changed her workday completely. The utility program and the telephone at her desk allow her to solve user problems without ever having to go directly to the users' workstations and terminals. The program allows Clare to view and actually take over the activities of network users. Typically, her first task upon arriving at her desk is to check her e-mail messages for trouble spots, print the messages, bring up LANSCAPE, and call each user one at a time.

"John, this is Clare in Systems. You left me a message about a problem with the inventory reorder module. I've got your screen up on my terminal now. Can you get out of the word processor and transfer to the inventory system? . . . Good. I see the main menu. . . . Now, the reorder module. Go ahead and repeat the steps that got you into trouble yesterday. . . . OK, fine . . . oops, I see what you did. The system asks for ENTER and you hit RETURN. What kind of keyboard to you have? . . . That's what I thought. For now,

From Ernest A. Kallman and John P. Grillo, *Ethical Decision Making and Information Technology*, 2d ed. (New York; McGraw-Hill Companies, 1996). Copyright © 1996, The McGraw-Hill Companies. Reprinted with permission of the McGraw-Hill Companies.

remember to hit ENTER. I'll get the maintenance programmer to change the module to accept RETURN, too. Sorry about that. . . . Thanks. Good-bye."

Then Clare goes on to the next call. "Bill, this is Clare in Systems. Your word processor bombed? Why don't you call it up and repeat the . . . oh, I see the problem. You're working with the buggy version, 2.3. I'll delete it from the system. You'll have to remember to use V2.4 from now on. . . . No problem. Good-bye."

Clare is delighted with the LANSCAPE utility. She roves electronically from one troubled user to another, seeing on her screen exactly what the user sees. The amount of time it takes to solve the problems is about the same, but because she can solve them from her desk, she has eliminated the frustrating delays of travel time. In addition, she is at her desk when the users call, and they are pleased with the fast response time.

Clare even has time to scan users' activities without their making a request. Her troubleshooting has become more proactive than reactive. She can scan a number of users without their knowledge, and when she finds one in trouble, she can interrupt and help.

"Harry, this is Clare in Systems. I'm looking at your screen now. . . . I know you didn't call, but I thought I'd beat you to the punch. You can speed up that multiple posting to a single customer by using the TAB key instead of updating the record for each entry. . . . Yes, like that. . . . Glad to be of service."

Last week Clare and her boss, the Director of User Support, met with the Vice President of Information Systems, Art Betony, to evaluate LAN-SCAPE. Clare said, "Without this program, I'd have to control the activities of every user in every system test and move from one building to the other. With LANSCAPE, I can watch over their shoulders without being there. LANSCAPE is inexpensive and easy to use. I fully endorse its continued use and recommend we obtain additional copies and make it available to all support personnel." The three went on to discuss the increase in user satis-faction and productivity that had resulted from the use of LANSCAPE.

Yesterday Art was having his usual Tuesday lunch with his boss, Exec-utive Vice President Alberta Wilson. Art couldn't stop praising LAN-SCAPE.

Alberta seemed especially interested. "You mean you can tell me at any time what people are doing?"

"Not quite," Art answered. "We can only see the screens of the users who are logged in. But of course that's exactly what my people need for their purposes."

"But the people you observe this way . . . do they know their screens are being observed?"

"No, not unless we tell them. The LANSCAPE program doesn't change anything on their screens. Of course, that's a necessary feature of the system because my people have to see exactly what the users see."

"Could you install LANSCAPE on my terminal, in my office?"

"Of course. But what value would that be?"

Alberta leaned forward and whispered, "I shouldn't reveal this outside the Human Resources department, but I think I want to enlist your support. Here at headquarters, we may have one or more persons dealing in drugs. We have suspects but no proof. Somehow these people are taking orders and making deliveries right on the premises. And during company time. I suspect they're using the phone and maybe even the computer to make their deals. We tried various surveillance methods with no success. What I want to do is use LANSCAPE to randomly check on what the suspects are doing. Then, if we catch them red-handed, we'll have our evidence and we can prosecute."

Art frowned and said, "Gee, I don't know if I should give you that software, Alberta. Let me think about it and get back to you."

## FOR DISCUSSION

What should Art do? Why?

# Drug Testing at Explo, Inc.

Explo, Inc. is a leading manufacturer and distributor of blasting powder, blasting caps, nitroglycerine-based explosives, ammonium nitrate, nitric acid, and sulfuric acid. Explo's main plant is located in the southeastern United States and employs approximately 400 nonunion employees, including 40 salaried and 320 hourly workers. In January of 1997 management at Explo decided that the company should investigate the possibility of implementing a drug-testing program for all of its employees. Management's decision was prompted by two noteworthy events. First, in November of 1996 an explosion occurred at a plant owned by one of Explo's main competitors, Acme Powder Company. The accident at Acme killed three employees and destroyed approximately one-third of Acme's manufacturing capacity. The cause of the accident was determined to be carelessness on the part of one of the Acme employees who was killed in the blast. When this employee's body was examined his pocket was found to contain marijuana, and an autopsy indicated that the employee was high on the drug at the time of his death.

Second, approximately two weeks after the Acme disaster, one of the foremen at Explo was arrested by local authorities for selling drugs from his home. This event convinced Explo's management that Explo employees were not immune to drug use, and that the company should take steps to protect its personnel and property from the sort of calamity that occurred at Acme. Having made this decision, management ordered Explo's director of human resources, Mr. T. T. Barnum, to investigate the feasibility of implementing a drug-testing program at Explo.

Barnum knew very little about drug-testing procedures or the legal problems that sometimes arise when companies institute employee drug-screening programs. However, Explo routinely bought raw materials from a local company, Chemico Chemicals, and Barnum knew that Chemico had established a drug-testing program for its employees two or three years earlier. Also, Chemico recently had appointed Ayn Oakley as its new director of personnel, and Barnum was well acquainted with Oakley. Barnum respected Oakley's abilities, and he resolved to call her and seek the benefit of her experience at Chemico before recommending anything to the management at Explo.

When Barnum contacted Oakley she told him that she had inherited Chemico's drug-testing program from her predecessor, and that it had been the source of nothing but problems since its inception. Because of these problems, she had suspended all drug testing at Chemico and was reviewing and re-evaluating every aspect of the program. When pressed by Barnum for details, Oakley described Chemico's testing program and enumerated the various problems spawned by the program's implementation.

According to Oakley, safety considerations prompted Chemico to establish its drug-testing program late in 1994. Development, implementation, and oversight of the program was the responsibility of Oakley's predecessor, Clive Beatty. Beatty anticipated few legal problems when he instituted the program at Chemico, for Chemico was a private employer acting on its own initiative, and Beatty knew that, in general, the constitutionality of drug testing was an issue only when the government served as employer, or testing in the private sector was mandated by the government. In addition, Beatty felt that labor relations issues would be of minor importance, for although substance testing of workers was a mandatory subject of bargaining for unions, Chemico, like Explo, was a nonunion employer.

After considering various alternative drug-testing programs, Beatty convinced Chemico's management that drug testing should be required as a condition of employment, and that testing should be conducted under the following circumstances:

1. All new job applicants would be tested as part of their pre-employment physical examination.
2. An employee would be tested whenever there was a sudden, unexplained and sustained decline in the job performance of that employee.
3. An employee would be tested whenever that employee was involved in an accident, violated a publicized safety precaution, or was reported by a supervisor to have acted in a careless and dangerous manner.
4. Random, company-wide testing would be conducted upon all employees. Names would be randomly selected by computer, and

testing would take place during periodic, company-sponsored physical examinations.

During the initial job interview, all applicants for employment at Chemico were informed verbally that they would have to complete a pre-employment physical that included a drug screen. In addition, written notice of the drug-test requirement was included on the company's job application form, and prospective employees were required to sign the form so as to indicate that they had been informed of the screening mandate.

Employees of Chemico were informed of the drug-testing requirement three months before implementation of the program. Fliers providing a detailed description of the screening program were included in the pay envelopes of all workers, and employees were required to sign a statement indicating that they had received a description of the testing program. Signed statements from all employees were returned to Chemico's personnel office.

Job applicants who tested positive for drugs during the pre-employment process were rejected from consideration for employment. Employees who tested positive were placed on a six-week leave of absence. At the end of this six week period the employee would be retested. If the employee's test results were negative, he/she would return to work and be randomly retested over the next twelve months. Any employee who tested positive on more than one occasion would be discharged.

The mechanics of drug testing at Chemico were complex. Immediately prior to taking a test, subjects signed a drug-test consent form. At the same time, each test subject also provided a list of all prescription and nonprescription drugs which he or she had taken in the preceding month. To guard against employees tampering with their urine samples, the company physician witnessed the sample collection procedure for male workers, while the company nurse witnessed for female employees. After a sample had been obtained, the employee would initial the sample container and watch the container as it was labelled with his/her name. Next, the sample would be sealed in a tamper-proof pouch which the employee also initialed. A courier delivered all samples to a local laboratory. If any pouch showed signs of tampering when it was given to the lab technician, the sample in that pouch would not be tested, and a new sample would be secured.

Urine samples were tested by the Enzyme Immunoassay (EIA) process. This process screens for the presence of amphetamines, barbiturates, benzodiazepines, marijuana, cocaine, methadone, methaqualone, opiates, PCP, and propoxphene. Whenever a sample tested positive, that sample would be retested so as to ensure that the first test was free from error. If the second sample tested negative, the test results would be considered void, and a new sample would be secured from the employee for retest.

When Chemico instituted its drug-screening program, Beatty expected few difficulties. However, just the opposite was true; indeed, testing of new job applicants was about the only aspect of the program that did not cause problems. Random testing produced the greatest controversy. No sooner had the program been announced than workers began to express feelings of oppression, anxiety, and insecurity concerning the testing procedure. Many questioned the accuracy of the EIA process, and others insisted that the program's purpose was not to ensure safety, but rather to rid the corporation of workers whom management felt were malcontents. Over time, those who opposed random testing coalesced to form an organized group of resistance, and members of this group were now at the forefront of a movement to unionize workers at Chemico. Oakley told Barnum that she was convinced that the movement for unionization would never have gotten off the ground if Chemico had not implemented its drug screening program.

In addition to the movement toward unionization, employee opposition to drug testing produced other problems for Chemico. For one thing, Chemico's drug-testing program gave rise to a plethora of lawsuits, most of which were still before the court. Not long after random testing was established, one female employee challenged the procedure by filing a common-law invasion-of-privacy tort. Company lawyers told Oakley that if this employee succeeded in showing that random testing intruded upon her privacy in such a manner that it would be considered "highly offensive" to a "reasonable person," then it was possible that she could be awarded a large sum as recompense for a wrongful intrusion upon her seclusion. The crux of the woman's argument was that drug testing at Chemico was "highly offensive" because, in the absence of any reasonable suspicion that she was a drug user, the procedure forced her to allow the company nurse to witness the collection of her urine sample. The issue was still before the court and Chemico's lawyers were not optimistic about the outcome. They noted that employees of other companies had successfully challenged random testing by bringing invasion-of-privacy torts, and that one such employee had been awarded $485,000 in damages. Further, they stated that whether or not a particular activity counts as a "highly offensive" intrusion upon seclusion is something to be decided by a jury, and that most jury members are employees rather than employers.

Thus, juries are more likely to sympathize with plaintiffs than with defendants in invasion-of-privacy torts.

In addition to the female employee's invasion-of-privacy challenge to random testing, two male employees brought similar suits challenging other aspects of Chemico's drug-screening program. The first of these employees (E1) had been tested immediately after he was involved in a minor accident at the plant's loading dock. Chemico argued that involvement in an accident creates a reasonable assumption of drug use on the part of the worker(s) involved in the accident because approximately 50 percent of all industrial accidents are drug or alcohol related. In response, E1 argued that it was patently obvious that carelessness could not have been a contributing cause of the particular accident in which he was involved, and that forcing him to have a drug test in the absence of reasonable suspicion of individual impairment was a highly offensive intrusion upon his seclusion because it caused fellow workers and members of the community to suspect that he was a drug user. The second employee (E2) made a similar claim. E2 was tested after his job performance declined noticeably and his absenteeism rate increased. E2 claimed that his performance on the job had suffered because he was having problems with his teenage son who was addicted to cocaine and alcohol. Further, E2 argued that testing him for drugs in these circumstances was a highly offensive intrusion upon his privacy because it held him up to ridicule in the eyes of his son, and thus destroyed any ability he had to influence his son's actions.

Common-law invasion-of-privacy torts were not the only court cases spawned by Chemico's drug-screening activities. A class action suit had been brought by a number of minority status employees charging that Chemico was using its drug-testing program to harass minority workers. In addition, another employee (E3) claimed that drug testing in his particular case violated state common law because the testing was motivated by malevolent, non-job-related reasons. E3 had been tested for drugs when his supervisor (S) reported that he had repeatedly violated company safety precautions. E3 claimed that he had violated no safety precautions, and argued that S concocted the false report to punish him when he discovered that E3 was dating his estranged wife.

In addition to the court cases suing Chemico for damages under state common law, a number of employees who had been discharged because they tested positive for drug use sought reinstatement in their jobs. At least three employees went to court seeking such reinstatement. Two claimed that they should be rehired because the test results indicating that they were drug users were inaccurate. Basically, these employees argued that when their urine samples were tested by the EIA procedure, the method produced a false positive result which was replicated when the test was repeated. The employees noted that in addition to the EIA procedure for drug screening there are at least two other methods that can be used to test for drug use, namely, the thin layer chromatography (TLC) procedure, and the gas chromatography/mass spectrometry (GC/MS) test. The employees argued that Chemico should use all three procedures in its drug-screening program, and only discharge employees when they test positive on all three tests.

The third employee who sought reinstatement after being dismissed for positive EIA test results openly admitted to drug use. However, this employee claimed that under state law, dependency on drugs was to be considered a handicap, and that as a result, Chemico had an affirmative duty to make reasonable accommodations on his behalf. Rather than being terminated, this employee argued that he should be allowed to enter a drug rehabilitation center, and then be permitted to return to work once he had completed the program of study at that center.

Finally, Oakley told Barnum that Chemico's drug-screening program had given rise to two disputes concerning eligibility for unemployment benefits. The first case involved a relatively new employee who was discharged when he tested positive on a random drug screen. Rather than seeking reinstatement, this individual filed for unemployment compensation. Chemico protested; however, the state division of employment security refused to disqualify the former employee for receipt of benefits. The division ruled that Chemico had not shown that the employee's discharge was for misconduct, because the company had failed to demonstrate either that the employee had used drugs in the workplace, or that the employee's work performance was below par. Chemico appealed this ruling, and the appeals referee's decision was pending.

Chemico's second case involving unemployment compensation was quite unlike its first. In this instance Chemico opposed the claim of a worker who sought unemployment compensation during the unpaid, six-week leave of absence that he was forced to take after he first tested positive on his drug test. This case had not yet been decided by the state division of employment security.

Oakley told Barnum that her decision to reevaluate the drug-screening program at Chemico was prompted by the many problems engendered by that program. She also said that she had come to the conclusion that the entire program needed to be reworked. Her present thinking on the subject was that the right course of action was to continue testing new job applicants, but to drop the testing of employees, and instead require that these individuals attend a series of drug education seminars. The seminars would be offered on company time and repeated annually. Oakley did not think that the drug education classes would be anywhere near as effective as drug testing in reducing drug use among company personnel. Still, substituting drug education for drug screening would go a long way toward mollifying employee discontent, and at the same time save the corporation a great deal of money.

After listening to Oakley, Barnum felt confused. He knew that at companies where drug testing had been implemented, 8 to 12 percent of the work force was found to have been using illegal drugs. If these figures applied to Explo's employees, Barnum felt that it was only a matter of time until Explo experienced a significant drug-related accident. Given the highly dangerous character of Explo's business, this was something that it was in *everyone's* interest—employer and employees alike—to avoid. On the other hand, Chemico's experience showed that implementing a drug-testing program at Explo could have quite deleterious consequences for the corporation. Further, Barnum was not sure whether he liked Oakley's solution to the problems faced by Chemico. By opting to drop all employee testing she was minimizing present costs for her corporation, for she was avoiding lawsuits, placating disgruntled employees, and reducing the cost of testing (testing cost Chemico $70.00 per employee). However, Oakley acknowledged that testing job applicants and instituting a drug education program would not be as effective as screening employees in reducing the possibility of a drug-related accident at Chemico. In essence, then, Oakley was taking a chance; for if a serious accident did occur at Chemico, losses in terms of lives and property easily could outweigh the benefits derived from the decision not to test employees for drug use.

It did not take Barnum long to see that his options were not limited simply to those of accepting or rejecting the course of action which Oakley had adopted. For one thing, Barnum noted that the drug-testing program established at Chemico lacked any mechanism for rehabilitating workers who were found to have a drug dependency. If Explo implemented a screening program, it could introduce such a mechanism. That is to say, rather than firing workers who were found to be using drugs,

Explo could see that these workers were given counseling and medical help for their problems. Such action would benefit Explo's workers, contribute to the social good, and no doubt help to forestall employee discontent with any drug-testing program which Explo implemented. Still, if 10 percent of Explo's employees were to enter drug rehabilitation programs, health insurance costs at Explo could become prohibitively burdensome. Furthermore, Barnum was not sure that Explo had any duty to benefit society as a whole, or to cure its workers of drug abuse. Also, Barnum suspected that there might be less expensive ways to placate workers and undermine employee opposition to drug testing. In the end, then, Barnum was left uncertain as to what sort of report he should make to management concerning the feasibility of establishing a drug-testing program at Explo.

## FOR DISCUSSION

If you were T. T. Barnum, would you recommend that a drug-testing program be implemented at Explo Inc.? If not, why not? If so, what sort of program would you recommend be instituted, and why?

*John R. Boatright*

# The Right to Privacy

Speaking broadly, the right to privacy is the right to be left alone. We will not discuss this broad characterization of the right to privacy, however, but will concentrate on privacy as the right of a person not to have others spy on his or her private life. In this more narrow sense, the right to privacy can be defined as the right of persons to determine the type and extent of disclosure of information about themselves.[1]

The employee's right to privacy has become particularly vulnerable with the development of recent technologies.[2] Employees who use phones and computers can be legally monitored by their employer, who may wish to check how fast they are working, whether they are engaged in personal or business-related activities, or simply what they are doing. Polygraph, or "lie detector" machines, although generally prohibited by federal law in most industries, are still allowed during internal investigations of suspected employee theft or economic loss and in a number of "exempt" industries. Computerized methods of obtaining, storing, retrieving, collating, and communicating information have made it possible for employers to collect and keep personal information about their employees, such as company medical records, credit histories, criminal and arrest histories, FBI information, and employment histories. Genetic testing, although not yet widely used by many companies, already allows employers to test an employee for about fifty genetic traits that indicate that the employee will be more likely than others to develop certain diseases (such as cystic fibrosis or sickle-cell anemia) or be affected by certain workplace toxins or occupational hazards. It is expected that in the future, genetic tests of workers and job candidates will enable employers to screen out a wide range of workers whose genes indicate that they are likely to add to the company's medical insurance costs or add to the costs of installing workplace protections. Urine tests allow companies to screen out employees who take drugs, drink alcohol, or smoke tobacco at home. Written psychological tests, personality inventory tests, and "honesty" tests make it possible for an employer to uncover a wide range of personal characteristics and tendencies that most persons would rather keep private, such as their level of honesty or their sexual orientation.

Not only have these innovations made a person's privacy more vulnerable, but they have come at a time when managers are particularly anxious to learn more about their employees. Advances in industrial psychology have demonstrated relationships between an employee's private home life or personality traits, and on-the-job performance and productivity.

There are two basic types of privacy: psychological privacy and physical privacy.[3] *Psychological* privacy is privacy with respect to a person's inner life. This includes the person's thoughts and plans, personal beliefs and values, feelings, and wants. These inner aspects of a person are so intimately connected with the person that to invade them is almost an invasion of the very person. *Physical* privacy is privacy with respect to a person's physical activities. Since people's inner lives are revealed by their physical activities and expressions, physical privacy is important in part because it is a means for protecting psychological privacy. However, many of our physical activities are considered "private" apart from their connection to our inner life. A person normally feels degraded, for example, if forced to disrobe publicly or to perform biological or sexual functions in public. Physical privacy, therefore, is also valued for its own sake.

The purpose of rights is to enable the individual to pursue his or her significant interests and to protect these interests from the intrusions of other individuals. To say that persons have a moral right to something is to say at least that they have a vital interest in that "something." Why is privacy considered important enough to surround it with the protection of a right?[4] To begin with, privacy has several *protective* functions. First, privacy ensures that others do not acquire information about us that, if revealed, would expose us to shame, ridicule, embarrassment, blackmail, or other harm. Second, privacy also prevents others from interfering in our plans simply because they do not hold the same values we hold. Our private plans may involve activities that, although harming no one, might be viewed with distaste by other people. Privacy protects us against their intrusions and thereby allows us the freedom to behave in unconventional ways. Third, privacy protects those whom we love from being injured by having their beliefs about us shaken. There may be things about ourselves that, if revealed, might hurt those whom we love. Privacy ensures that such matters are not made public. Fourth, privacy also protects individuals from being led to incriminate themselves. By protecting their privacy, people are protected against involuntarily harming their own reputations.

Privacy is also important because it has several *enabling* functions. First, privacy enables a person to develop ties of friendship, love, and trust. Without intimacy these relationships could not flourish. Intimacy, however, requires both sharing information about oneself that is not shared with everyone and engaging in special activities with others that are not publicly performed. Without privacy, therefore, intimacy would be impossible and relationships of friendship, love, and trust could not exist. Second, privacy enables certain professional relationships to exist. Insofar as the relationships between doctor and patient, lawyer and client, psychiatrist and patient all require trust and confidentiality, they could not exist without privacy. Third, privacy also enables a person to sustain distinct social roles. The executive of a corporation, for example, may want, as a private citizen, to support a cause that is unpopular with his or her firm. Privacy enables the executive to do so without fear of reprisal. Fourth, privacy enables people to determine who they are by giving them control of the way they present themselves to society in general and of the way that society in general looks upon them. At the same time, privacy enables people to present themselves in a special way to those whom they select. In both cases, this self-determination is secured by the right of the individual to determine the nature and extent of disclosure of information about oneself.

It is clear, then, that our interest in privacy is important enough to recognize it as a right. However, this right must be balanced against other individuals' rights and needs. Employers in particular sometimes have a legitimate right to inquire into the activities of employees or prospective employees. The employer is justified in wanting to know, for example, what a job candidate's past work experience has been and whether the candidate has performed satisfactorily on previous jobs. An employer may also be justified in wanting to identify the culprits when the firm finds itself the subject of pilferage or employee theft, and of subjecting employees to on-the-job surveillance in order to discover the source of thefts. How are these rights to be balanced against the right to privacy? Three elements must be considered when collecting information that may threaten the employee's right to privacy: relevance, consent, and method.[5]

*Relevance.* The employer must limit inquiry into the employee's affairs to those areas that are directly relevant to the issue at hand. Although employers have a right to know the person they are employing and to know how the employee is performing, employers are not justified in inquiring into any areas of the employee's life that do not affect the employee's work performance in a direct and serious manner. To investigate an employee's political beliefs or the employee's social life, for example, is an invasion of privacy. Moreover, if a firm acquires information about an employee's personal life in the course of a legitimate investigation, it has an obligation to destroy the information, especially when such data would embarrass or otherwise injure the employee if it were leaked. The dividing lines between justified and unjustified investigation are fairly clear with respect to lower-level employees: There is clearly little justification for investigating the marital problems, political activities, or emotional characteristics of clerical workers, sales workers, or factory laborers. The dividing line between what is and what is not relevant, however, becomes less clear as one moves higher in the firm's management hierarchy. Managers are called on to represent their company before others and the company's reputation can be significantly damaged by a manager's private activities or emotional instability. A vice president's drinking problem or membership in a disreputable association, for example, will affect the vice president's ability to adequately represent the firm. The firm in such cases may be justified in inquiring into an officer's personal life or psychological characteristics.

*Consent.* Employees must be given the opportunity to give or withhold their consent before the private aspects of their lives are investigated. The firm is justified in inquiring into the employee's life only if the employee has a clear understanding that the inquiry is being made and clearly consents to this as part of the job or can freely choose to refuse the job. The same principle holds when an employer undertakes some type of surveillance of employees for the purpose, say, of uncovering or preventing pilferage. Employees should be informed of such surveillance so they can ensure they will not inadvertently reveal their personal lives while under surveillance.

*Methods.* The employer must distinguish between methods of investigation that are both ordinary and reasonable, and methods that are neither. Ordinary methods include the supervisory activities that are normally used to oversee employees' work. Extraordinary methods include devices like hidden microphones, secret cameras, wiretaps, lie detector tests, personality inventory tests, and spies. Extraordinary methods are unreasonable and unjustified unless the circumstances themselves are extraordinary. Extraordinary methods of investigation might be justified if a firm is suffering heavy losses from employee theft that ordinary supervision has failed to stop. Extraordinary devices, however, are not justified merely because the employer hopes to be able to pick up some interesting tidbits about employee loyalties. In general, the use of extraordinary devices is justified only when the following conditions have been met: (1) The firm has a problem that can be solved in no other manner than by employing such extraordinary means; (2) the problem is serious and the firm has well-founded grounds for thinking that the use of extraordinary means will identify the culprits or put an end to the problem; (3) the use of the extraordinary devices is not prolonged beyond the time needed to identify the wrongdoers or after it becomes clear that the devices will not work; (4) all information that is uncovered but that is not directly relevant to the purposes for which the investigation was conducted is disregarded and destroyed; (5) the failure rate of any extraordinary devices employed (such as lie detectors, drug tests, or psychological tests) is taken into account and all information derived from devices with a known failure rate is verified through independent methods that are not subject to the same failure rates.

## NOTES

1. See Charles Fried, *An Anatomy of Values: Problems of Personal and Social Choice* (Cambridge: Harvard University Press, 1970), p. 141.

2. See John Hoerr, "Privacy in the Workplace," *Business Week*, 28 March 1988, pp. 61–65, 68; Susan Dentzer, "Can You Pass the Job Test?" *Newsweek*, 5 May 1986; Sandra N. Hurd, "Genetic Testing: Your Genes and Your Job," *Employee Responsibilities and Rights Journal* 3, no. 4 (1990): 239–52; U.S. Congress, Office of Technology Assessment, *Genetic Monitoring and Screening in the Workplace*, OTA-BA-455 (Washington, D.C.: U.S. Government Printing Office, October 1990); Arthur R. Miller, *The Assault on Privacy: Computers, Data Banks and Dossiers*, (Ann Arbor: University of Michigan Press, 1971).

3. See Garrett, *Business Ethics*, pp. 47–49, who distinguishes these two types of privacy (as well as a third kind, "social" privacy).

4. The analyses in this paragraph and the following are drawn from Fried, *Anatomy of Values*, pp. 137–52; Richard A. Wasserstrom, "Privacy," in Richard A. Wasserstrom, ed., *Today's Moral Problems*, 2d ed. (New York: Macmillan, Inc., 1979); Jeffrey H. Reiman, "Privacy, Intimacy and Personhood," *Philosophy and Public Affairs* 6, no. 1 (1976): 26–44; and James Rachels, "Why Privacy Is Important," *Philosophy and Public Affairs* 4, no. 4 (1975): 295–333.

5. The remarks that follow are based in part on Garrett, *Business Ethics*, pp. 49–53; for a more stringent view which concludes that polygraphs, for example, should not be used at all by employers, see George G. Brenkert, "Privacy, Polygraphs, and Work," *Business and Professional Ethics Journal* 1, no. 1 (fall 1981): 19–35.

# Corporate Policy Statements

*Employee Records.* General Motors believes that its employees' private personal activities are not properly the concern of GM so long as they do not adversely affect attendance, job performance, working relationships with fellow employees, or the public image of the corporation.

General Motors does not consider such procedures as polygraph tests proper in the evaluation of job candidates, nor does the corporation include in personnel records non-business-related information, unless submitted or authorized in writing by the employee. Nonetheless, compliance with government regulations and administration of labor agreements and employee-benefit programs have greatly increased the amount of personal data GM is required to record.

GM policy dictates that such records be treated with the same strict confidentiality accorded to all GM's proprietary information. Any employee may examine his or her own personnel record.

Employees are advised, upon inquiry, of the kinds of files and data which the corporation must maintain concerning them. These may contain personally identifiable information only if it is relevant and necessary to the proper administration of the business or to compliance with the law or government regulation.

All written information about employees is to be recorded and maintained accurately, factually, and objectively. Employees have the opportunity to correct or amend any information concerning themselves, to ensure accuracy and fairness. Furthermore, GM personnel whose job responsibilities legitimately permit them access to such information are directed to protect employee records from unauthorized release, transfer, access, or use.

Personally identifiable information must not be disclosed outside the corporation unless the employee consents, with the following exceptions: the *fact* of employment may be verified for employee credit approval; *dates* of employment may be verified for employment reference checks; an employee's elected bargaining representative may be entitled by labor contract to certain information; and a law or a court order may require disclosure of certain information.

General Motors

IBM has four basic practices concerning the use of personal information about employees: To collect, use and retain only personal information that is required for business or legal reasons; to provide employees with a means of ensuring that their personal information in IBM personnel records is correct; to limit the internal availability of personal information about an individual only to those with a clear business need to know; and to release personal information outside IBM only with approval of the employee affected, except to verify employment or to satisfy legitimate investigatory or legal requirements. But even with these practices, not every case can be covered. What constitutes a legitimate business need for a particular piece of information? Should information about an employee ever be released without his or her knowledge, even if it might be to his or her benefit? Ultimately, you must balance the right of the organization to use information for valid business purposes with the individual's right to privacy. Your own conscience and judgment and the advice of your management and of IBM Personnel all should be considered in this delicate area.

IBM

The nature of the services offered by American Express Company necessitates collection and retention of a substantial amount of personal information about the individuals to whom services are provided. We must avoid any unjustifiable intrusion on an individual's right to privacy. We must strive for a reasonable balance between the operational needs of our businesses and the personal needs of individuals. In an effort to attain such balance we will be guided by the following principles with regard to the collection, custody, and distribution of personal information concerning the individuals to whom we provide services. (1) Obtain only that personal information which is necessary and relevant to the conduct of our business; (2) use only lawful means to collect information; obtain it directly from the individual to the extent practicable; and make reasonable efforts to assure the reliability of information acquired from others; (3) explain the general uses of personal information to all individuals who question the reasons that they provide such information, and refrain from using the information for other purposes without informing the individual; (4) establish appropriate administrative, technical, and physical safeguards to assure that access to records is limited to those who are authorized and that information is disseminated only by and to those with a legitimate business purpose or regulatory function, or where disclosure is required by subpoena or other legal process; (5) provide personal data records with secure storage and ensure that personnel who are involved with custody or maintenance of such records are aware of their responsibility to preserve their confidentiality; (6) promptly notify the individual in the case where records are subpoenaed, unless specifically prohibited from doing so by court order. Respond according to the law, but wait the full length of time allowed by the subpoena before providing the information in order to allow the individual the opportunity to exercise his or her rights; (7) advise the individual of the Company's policy with respect to mailing lists and provide the individual with the opportunity to have his or her name removed from such lists; (8) respond to all individuals who question the reasons that adverse determinations have been made about them, and advise them of the nature of information acted upon, except for information which relates to the investigation of an insurance claim or of a possible criminal offense. This will, of course, be subject to ethical considerations and applicable laws; (9) upon request, except with regard to insurance claims investigations, and within a reasonable period of time, advise an individual of factual data (maintained about that person) such as residence, address, place of employment, etc., and give the individual the opportunity to verify this factual data and to provide corrected or amended information where appropriate; (10) review periodically corporate policy regarding the collection, retention, use, and protection of individually identifiable data to ensure that this policy is in keeping with the shifting needs of both the business and the individual.

American Express Co.

# WORKER SAFETY

# AIDS on the
# Grand Motors Assembly Line

Bill Snelling is a twenty-eight-year-old married father of three who became HIV positive from a blood transfusion two years ago when undergoing surgery in the Glenview General Hospital for a ruptured appendix. For various reasons, Snelling suspected that the blood supply he had used might be contaminated, and had himself tested at the HMO contracted under his health plan with his employer, the Grand Motors Assembly Plant in Glenview. When he was given the news, the HMO promised complete confidentiality.

Snelling, a robust athletic type who jogs and bikes every day after work and does not drink or smoke, decided to continue working on the assembly line at GM because, as he explained to his wife, "I still need to feed a family, and I feel quite healthy." He promised his wife that if he ever got the disease, he would quit when he felt too weak to do the job well. Snelling, incidentally, is one of eight people who are testing HIV positive on the GM assembly line according to the confidential records of the HMO. The director of the HMO promised all of them strict confidentiality but has also recommended informally that they try to seek employment that would not expose them to any risk of cutting themselves in the work-place. One of the problems with working on the assembly line, they were each told, is that there is some minimal risk that workers who become careless will cut themselves occasionally, even when using gloves, while bolting and fitting parts to the chassis. When that occurs the next person on the assembly line may become exposed to the blood and become HIV positive. But, they were also told, the probability of contracting HIV in this manner is extremely low and perhaps even lower than .0003, which is the probability of contracting HIV from a deep needle puncture contaminated with HIV virus. Snelling, like the others on the assembly line who were HIV positive, feels that the probability of anybody becoming HIV positive from contact with his blood, if he should ever cut himself, is so low that it could not be a problem for anybody but himself. So he decides not to follow the advice of the HMO director to seek employment where he could not cut himself.

When asked, the director of the HMO reports to the the the GM management, and the plant manager, Thomas Brown, that there are eight assembly line workers testing positive for HIV at the Glenview plant, that they have been guaranteed confidentiality, and that there is no significant threat to the health of anybody who may come in contact with the blood of any of them, should they cut themselves on the assembly line. However, four days later an unsigned memo was sent to Brown's office with names of the eight HIV employees. Brown read the memo and filed it, but could not track down who sent it. The HMO director denied sending it.

Shortly thereafter, Thomas Brown, the plant manager, is approached by the head of the local AFL-CIO auto workers union who reports that he has heard disturbing news that a number of people on the assembly line are HIV positive and that if that is true, the workers want to know their names. The union leader says the rumor is that Brown knows the names. Brown tells him that there are some people on the line who are HIV positive but that they have been promised confidentiality and, besides, the risk to anybody else on the line is incredibly small—smaller, he says, "than the risk of being run over by a truck while sleeping in your bed." Even so, the union leader demands to know which people on the assembly line are HIV positive. He says, "We need to get them out of the plant, because no matter how small the probability of contracting the HIV virus, any probability at all, given the fatal effects, should be removed from the workplace." He then cites the Occupational Safety and Health Administration's (OSHA's) rule that workers have a right to know of any condition in the workplace that could possibly adversely affect their health. Brown responds that the right in question does not extend to knowing the names of the people who are HIV positive; to which the union leader responds that unless they know the

the names of the people involved they cannot be sure "the problem" will be taken care of in a way that protects the safety and health of the workers. He threatens to go to OSHA and file suit to get the names from either Brown or the HMO, unless Brown voluntarily discloses the information in the morning. The union leader adds that he thinks Brown surely has a moral obligation to protect the workers in his plant and that GM has also promised adequate safety for workers. He says he thinks that GM should consider the health of workers who are totally innocent to be more important than those who have sexually misbehaved. The union leader says he knows Brown can handle this problem and can get back to him in a way that will allow him to verify the names and verify that the problem has been dealt with. If not, he says the rank and file will take it out on him and he in turn will take it out on Brown. He reminded Brown that in addition to the lawsuits he could cause all sorts of work stoppages, and would do so, since his credibility, his ability to get results, was on the line.

Brown said in response that HIV-infected workers were protected by the federal 1990 Americans with Disabilities Act (ADA). The ADA prohibits employers from discriminating against people with disabilities. Title I of the ADA states that disabilities covered by the ADA include "a physical or mental impairment that substantially limits one or more of an individual's major life activities" (42 USC §12102 (2); Interpretive Guidelines § 1630. 2(g)). Those HIV-infected surely qualify, and, in fact Section 1630. 2 (j) expressly provides that "HIV infection" is "inherently substantially limiting." He appealed to the union leader, Stan Rollins, saying: "Stan, we have our jobs because we can take the heat. Now is your time to take some heat."

Rollins replied that his was an elected job, Brown's wasn't. He said he was familiar with the ADA, but added that an employer has a defense against an ADA charge if the worker represents a "direct threat" to the health or safety of himself or others. The union regards the eight workers as direct theats to its workers. He said he intends to press ahead with his lawsuit to get the names and remove the eight from the line, but in the meantime would settle for Brown removing them from the line temporarily to some other position at GM where they could not harm anyone.

Brown said that Rollins was citing only part of the law. He said a company's defenses against a discrimination charge by an HIV-infected employee are that either (1) the person is unable to perform the job, (2) he cannot reasonably be accommodated, or (3) he represents a direct threat to himself or others. But there was no real direct threat by the eight in his opinion, contrary to (3). The eight were all fully capable of doing their jobs at the present time, contrary to (1). And hence, there was no basis for removing the workers from the line, which undercut (2). To reassign them without a good reason would invite a lawsuit of the type that Stan Rollins' union always threatened—reassignment without just cause. Furthermore, GM would have no defense in a due process hearing. So that approach simply invited a lawsuit.

Rollins said he would see to it that the union would just wink at any action Brown took to silently remove them. He said Brown could do it any way he wanted, perhaps promote them, but move them to a place where they counted spare parts. Rollins said this was done all the time and in a big plant would go unnoticed. He asked Brown for a personal favor, and said it would be remembered.

## FOR DISCUSSION

What should Thomas Brown do? Why?

*Robert Almeder*
*J. D. Millar*

# The Moral Right to Know
# in the Workplace

## INTRODUCTION

The complexities involved in explaining the notion of a basic moral right are certainly more than anyone can confront successfully in a short paper. Literally, hundreds of books and lengthy treatises have been written, and are still being written, on the nature of morality and moral rights. Collectively they reflect remarkably different and mutually exclusive basic views on the nature of moral rights and, although there are many thoughtful persons willing to defend what they regard as *the correct view* about the nature and scope of basic moral rights, the awful truth of the matter is that there is no consensus, either public or academic, on just what a moral right is. Accordingly, when it comes to stating the nature of moral rights, anyone taking a clear and dogmatic stand is much like the proverbial fool rushing in where angels fear to tread. Indeed, it almost seems that the most one can do is to adopt a particular view one finds congenial, and then "sallie forth to do battle with the heathen." Even so, a cautious and steadfast refusal to confront honestly and persistently the issue of human moral rights seems like a reprehensible abandonment of the responsibility to promote the public good. In short, woe to those who seek to understand human moral rights, and woe to those who don't.

In spite of these woes, we will outline, and then propose a way to overcome, the major obstacle to constructing an enlightened public policy on the moral right to know in the workplace. If we are correct in what we propose, there should be little doubt about the future general direction

This paper is a revised and expanded version of J. D. Millar's keynote address delivered to the New York Academy of Science and subsequently published in the *Annals of the New York Academy of Sciences* 572 (December 29, 1989).

morally sensitive legislative enactment should take. But first let us examine the major obstacle just mentioned.

## CONSEQUENTIALIST AND NONCONSEQUENTIALIST VIEWS ON MORAL RIGHTS

In examining the moral right to know in the workplace, we must keep in mind that there are two basic and mutually exclusive views about the nature of human rights. The first is the *consequentialist theory of rights*, and the second is the *nonconsequentialist theory of rights*. Under the first theory, a right is an obligation to be treated in a certain way and it exists if recognition of the right produces the best general outcome for all those affected by the exercise of the right. Accordingly, we must look to the consequences of exercising the right, and if the consequences (broadly conceived) prove to promote the best net outcome, given all the available alternatives, then the right exists; otherwise it does not exist. For example, on this view, the question of whether people have a right to life is simply a matter of determining the consequences of allowing people to kill others without a very good reason; and because the consequences of so acting do not produce the best general outcome for all those affected by the behavior, the consequentialist urges that everybody has the right to life—meaning thereby that nobody ought to take anybody else's life without having a very good reason for doing so.[1]

Under the second theory of rights, the nonconsequentialist theory of rights, rights do and can exist even if recognition of them does not produce the best general outcome. On the nonconsequentialist view, for example, even if killing an innocent person could guarantee the survival of a thousand innocent people who would otherwise most surely die, it would still be wrong to kill an innocent person. On the nonconsequentialist theory of rights, there are certain things one ought never do no matter what the consequences. Immanuel Kant, for example, argued that no matter what the consequences, one should never lie, steal, or murder.[2]

Perhaps the best way to capture the difference between these two distinct theories on the nature of human rights is to examine an example moral philosophers sometimes probe when discussing the nature of morality. This is the famous "Commandant Example."[3] It goes like this: Suppose you are an occupant of a P.O.W. camp, and the commandant (who is reliable but wildly insane), approaches you and says, "Either kill one of the innocent babies in this camp, or I will kill 5,000 inmates, including women and children." Assuming that you cannot destroy the commandant, what would be the morally correct course of action? If one kills the innocent baby in order to save a larger number of innocent persons, then one has opted for the consequentialist theory of rights—the baby does not have the right to life, because recognition of the right does not produce the best general outcome. Conversely, if one refuses to kill the innocent baby, then one has opted for the nonconsequentialist theory of rights under which no matter what the consequences, it is never permissible to kill an innocent person. The important point here is that no matter what one's choice, there does not seem to be any effective decision procedure to resolve the dispute over what is the correct moral course of action. By implication, there is no known decision procedure to resolve the dispute over which view about human moral rights is correct.

Consequentialists typically criticize nonconsequentialists on the grounds that anybody who would *not* kill an innocent baby to save a larger number of innocent people is more like a moral fanatic than a committed moral agent acting on moral principle. After all, they say, anybody who is not willing to kill an innocent baby to save the world is surely morally blind. Nonconsequentialists, however, simply see morality as having nothing to do with the consequences of acts and stand in amazement over what they regard as the moral blindness of anybody who would kill an innocent baby to save a larger number of innocent people.[4] They would refuse to kill the innocent baby, and then ascribe responsibility for the death of the 5,000 innocent inmates to the evil commandant. Those who simply *see* morality as a matter promoting consequences productive of the greatest net good for the greatest number cannot help but regard the nonconsequentialist position as one of moral blindness and those who simply *see* morality as a matter of doing certain things no matter what the consequences, are equally convinced of the moral blindness of the consequentialist position. The rest of us see no way of resolving the dispute by appeal to some agreeable principle or reason that would allow us to answer objectively the question of whether, or to what extent, the morality of an act is to be judged in terms of the overall effects of the act viewed as a rule. Consequently, the important point is that no matter which position one accepts on the nature of moral rights, there does not seem to be any viable decision procedure for effectively resolving the dispute over which view of moral rights is the correct one. Those who must make public policy in the presence of such a dilemma may well appreciate the feeling of existential despair.[5]

# IN DEFENSE OF THE CONSEQUENTIALIST

When we turn to the debate about the moral right to know in the work-place, we recognize immediately these two distinct views on the nature of moral rights. On the one hand, there are those who will insist that no matter what the consequences of revealing information about possible harms in the workplace, workers have an absolute right to that informa-tion as an extension of their right to autonomy or even of their right to life.[6] On this latter view, the probable loss of life that results from recog-nizing a worker's right to know is totally irrelevant to the question of whether someone has the right to know about such harms in the work-place. On the other hand, the consequentialist view of the right to know inspires those who insist that a failure to look at the consequences of revealing information about possible harms seems too much like the moral fanaticism of those who insist that no matter what the conse-quences, certain things ought never be done. The problem, of course, is that those who fashion public policy must struggle with the question of whether the right to know in any particular case is a valid right only if revealing the information produces less human harm than withholding it. It is not difficult to refer to a number of instances in which more life was lost or harmed by revealing information about possibly harmful sub-stances than would have been if that information had not been issued.[7] Some aspects of the present public reaction to providing information on AIDS suggest this. After all, a past surgeon general publicly said that "most of the people who are scared to death of contracting AIDS, couldn't catch it if they tried."[8] Typically, however, such cases are the exception; but what they establish is that we should be willing, when the situation demands it, to take a close look at the consequences of revealing infor-mation about possible harms in the workplace. Those who object to such a policy because they adopt a nonconsequentialist theory of rights must recognize that their position on human rights is no more privileged than the consequentialists, however strenuously voiced.

Furthermore, the nonconsequentialist often overlooks the crucial fact that this society has already spoken very strongly in favor of the conse-quentialist view on the moral right to life. Certainly, as a nation, we grant that human life is sacred and that everyone has a fundamental right to life. However, we do not hesitate to endorse an institution which knowingly conscripts and kills a number of innocent persons in the interest of pre-venting the predictable death of a larger number of innocent persons. We refer, of course, to the institution of war. If having a right to life meant that one's life could never be taken no matter what the consequences, then the institution of war would be inescapably and intrinsically evil. The bottom line here is that this society has not chosen, and is unwilling to live with, the principle that no matter what the consequences, one should never take a human life. Why should we act any differently when it comes to the moral right to know, especially when the latter is construed as an extension of the right to autonomy and life itself? Whether we talk about war, or even capital punishment, we stand as a society ready to endorse the view that the right to life means no more than that one must have a very good reason to take another person's life; and that reason may well be the greater harm in terms of loss of life that results from not taking that person's life. It is difficult to see why we should not adopt the same general attitude when it comes to the moral right to know in the workplace.

## IN DEFENSE OF THE NONCONSEQUENTIALIST

Even though it makes sense to examine the consequences of revealing information in order to determine whether the right to know exists, the concern behind the nonconsequentialist posture should by no means be ignored. As we have already noted, the Kantian view that morality has nothing to do with the consequences has commanded the respect of a good number of serious and profound thinkers.

But what precisely is the concern motivating the nonconsequentialist on the right to know in the workplace? To begin with, there is a long-standing and deeply felt suspicion that some industries or corporations are only too willing to be indifferent to the safety and health of the worker if the cost of compassion is even marginally burdensome to the shareholder. Nobody will deny that abuses of this sort have occurred in the past. In the absence of a good watchdog, such abuses are likely to occur in the future. To a considerable extent this concern may be addressed by the remarkable effect of strict liability law and its capacity to engender real fear in the hearts of those who might otherwise have been tempted to play fast and loose with the health and safety of workers. There are those who feel that strict liability law may be quite unfair to employers; but nobody should deny that it places remarkable contraints, although no insuperable constraints, on the degree of indifference an employer can responsibly maintain with respect to the health and safety of employees.

Of itself, however, liability law works only *after* certain harms (including loss of life) have occurred; and while it may allay some of the nonconsequentialist concern, liability law is certainly no substitute for a mechanism that would make an appeal to liability law less likely or necessary.

Second, what often bothers and motivates the nonconsequentialist is the ominous prospect of the life of the worker being measured purely in terms of economic units. Some people, of course, erroneously believe that this prospect is an integral part of any cost-benefit analysis associated with determining the costs incurred in protecting the health and safety of the workers. Certainly, however, the consequentialist theory of rights *does not imply* that the sanctity of human life is to be measured in terms of a certain dollar figure. Any conception of a suitable "cost-benefit analysis" that would ever imply as much is erroneous and doomed to moral extinction. The consequentialist theory of moral rights by no means implies that any worker can, without her enlightened consent, be exposed to certain material harms simply as part of the cost of doing business. If anything, such a policy would, if widely implemented, tend as a rule to produce the greatest amount of harm for all those affected.

And, finally, we can dispel the core concern of the nonconsequentialist simply by adopting the same policy toward the right to know that we, as a society, adopt with regard to the right to life. In other words, although saying that a person *has a moral right to life* is saying that nobody can take his life without a very good reason, those who would take it will need to assume a very heavy burden of proof and will be forced to demonstrate the presence of such a compelling reason if they are to avoid harsh punishment. Society reflects this moral right as primitive by making laws against killing, and in so doing specifies what it believes are suitably strong reasons for not considering particular acts of killing (such as capital punishment or war) legally reprehensible. *Prima facie* there is a law against such behavior and, if the law is willfully broken, then the stated penalty will be imposed in no uncertain terms. In other words, the law exists to protect a *prima facie* moral right, and that moral right we recognize because failure to do so would, as a rule, fail to promote the greatest amount of good for all affected.

Similarly, although saying that a person has a right to know does not *mean* that nobody can withhold relevant information without his permission, it does mean that nobody can withhold such information without having a very good reason which will need to be defended because withholding such information breaks the law. Those who would ostensibly withhold such information need to assume a heavy burden of proof and publicly defend such a procedure in a fully articulated legal context just because the law places such a special value on human life. Where the long-term good of society as a whole renders withholding relevant information demonstrably defensible, it will find its way into the law and public policy as a way of refining our understanding of the value of life. Otherwise, here again, the law prohibits very specifically any failure to disclose information on what is materially harmful to workers in the workplace.[9] Given that we may understand the right to know as a justifiable extension of the right to autonomy and, hence, by implication, the right to life, this sort of reasoning may alleviate somewhat the concerns at the root of the non-consequentialist view on the nature of the right to know in the workplace. Importantly enough, this way of defending and alleviating the nonconsequentialist concern does not require of us that we abandon the consequentialist view of the right to know in the workplace.

Doubtless, there are nonconsequentialists who will insist that *their* concern will be respected only when, no matter what the consequences, nothing could ever possibly count as a reason for anybody's withholding information from the worker on what is possibly harmful in the workplace. As we have just argued, however, while there is no way to meet that concern stated in that way, this society has, as a whole, given special pre-eminence to the right to life by visiting with the harshest of penalties those who break well-defined laws respecting the *prima facie* right to life.

## CONCLUSION

Naturally, there are many other problems or obstacles in fashioning and implementing a broadly agreeable public policy on the right to know in the workplace. There are fine questions involved in determining the nature of certain risks, just as there are important questions associated with determining how much risk of harm needs to be present before a worker's right to know is materially affected. And we have said little here about the legal right to know, or the status of that legal right. We have only sought to confront what we take to be the major obstacle to constructing a morally inspired policy on the right to know in the workplace. That obstacle is reflected in the nonconsequentialist view that, no matter what the consequences, no worker should ever be exposed, without his (or her) enlightened and informed consent, to significant risk to harm. While addressing the concerns that motivate this latter claim, we have, in sum, urged that the *moral* right to know in the workplace is best construed as the consequentialist construes it. This implies, among other things, that the worker has a *prima facie* moral right to know about any materially harmful condition or substance in his (or her) workplace; and this amounts to saying that nobody can morally withhold that information without having a demonstrably very good reason for doing so. Those who would withhold such information need to assume the burden of proof and demonstrate the presence of such a reason—which may be a compelling reason only because revealing the information is certifiably more likely to involve a greater loss of life. At any rate, whether they succeed in so demonstrating the presence of such a reason is incidental to the fact that such behavior is, as things presently stand, illegal.

In the end, makers of public policy cannot avoid profound public controversy over the nature and scope of basic moral rights. Invariably, there are passionate defenders on both sides of the issue. Forging public policy in the absence of a broad public consensus is nothing more than the arbitrary imposition by government of some preferred, but by no means necessarily privileged, moral view. It hardly seems the legitimate role of a democratic government, even in the name of moral leadership, to so impose views that are deeply controversial and incapable of broad-based support by the population at large. It is better by far, for reasons of stable public policy, that we seek the painful path of building a general public consensus among the well-informed and well-meaning citizenry. This involves pleading one's moral intuitions publicly in the interest of promoting as humane a society as we can imagine. If we can achieve no such consensus, then the law will, as a matter of necessity, settle the issue in the interest of an efficient discharge of social functions . . . and, from the viewpoint of evolution at least, that is not a particularly unfortunate outcome.

## NOTES

1. For a general discussion of consequentialist and nonconsequentialist theories of ethics, see William Frankena, *Ethics* (New York: Prentice Hall, 1982), pp. 15–45. See also David Lyons, "Human Rights and the General Welfare," in *Rights*, ed. David Lyons (Belmont, Calif.: Wadsworth Publishing Company, 1979), pp. 187ff. and Bernard Williams and J. J. C. Smart, *Utilitarianism For and Against* (New York: Cambridge University Press, 1976).

2. For a general discussion of Kant's views see Frankena, *Ethics*, pp. 25–29, and Immanuel Kant, *The Foundation of the Metaphysics of Morals* (New York: Liberal Arts Press, 1959). See also, as an example of the nonconsequentialist position, G. E. M. Anscombe, "Modern Moral Philosophy," *Philosophy* (1958): 7.

3. See Williams and Smart, *Utilitarianism For and Against*. The example was initially offered by Williams.

4. See, for example, G. E. M. Anscombe, "Modern Moral Philosophy," *Philosophy* (1958): 7. See also Alan Gewirth, *Moral Philosophy* (Chicago: University of Chicago Press, 1979).

5. The more practical dimensions of this problem occur, for example, when one is asked to devise public policy on matters affecting the permissibility and financing of abortion for various reasons. Another case in point, one more pertinent to the issue of the right to know in the workplace, was recently noted elsewhere by J. D. Millar, who, as Director of NIOSH (National Institute of Occupational Safety and Health), in 1981 consulted respectively (1) the Office of General Counsel of Public Health Service and (2) the Centers for Disease Control Ethics Committee on the question of whether NIOSH should inform some workers who, as a result of a retrospective cohort mortality study, were determined to be at some risk to death as a result of exposure to hazardous materials in the workplace. From the attorneys in the Office of General Counsel he was advised that NIOSH had no legal duty to advise the individuals involved and, moreover, if NIOSH were to so inform the workers, it would incur certain legal liabilites as a result. From the CDC Ethics Committee he was advised that he did have a moral duty to inform the workers as an instance of the general responsibility to ensure that workers have knowledge of their exposure to hazardous material. Because the CDC Ethics Committee was arguing that, regardless of the consequences (in this case the legal consequences as well as the effects on the conduct of business and all that that implies) all workers had a right to know, it was assuming a nonconsequentialist posture on the right to know and the responsibility to disclose.

6. See Ruth R. Faden and Thomas L. Beauchamp, "The Right to Know in the Workplace," *The Canadian Journal of Philosophy*, Suppl. vol. 8 (1982): 199ff. For another interesting discussion on the tension between consequentialist and nonconsequentialist theory as it affects occupational health, see Sherry I. and Paul W. Brant-Rauf, "Occupational Health Ethics: OSHA and the Courts," *Journal of Health Politics, Policy and Law* 5, no. 3 (fall 1980).

7. On this point see Faden and Beauchamp, "The Right to Know in the Workplace," pp. 197–200. The point Faden and Beauchamp make is that one sometimes has a responsibility to beneficence, which may well conflict with the worker's right to autonomy, in which case, depending on the circumstances, we may have good reason to withhold information. There are, for example, cases in which female workers suffer a demonstrably low risk of sterility or fetal damage as a result of certain exposures. To reveal such information is likely to induce behaviors (such as certain types of x-raying) more life threatening than the original exposures.

8. Opening General Session, Annual Meeting of the Association of Military Surgeons of the United States. Las Vegas, Nevada, November 9, 1987.

9. Nobody should think, incidentally, that this paper condones or encourages the view that it is morally permissible to break the current laws pertaining to employer responsibilities to inform employees of what may materially and/or adversely affect them in the workplace. Those laws are, we submit, a product of the consequentialist posture we adopt as a society seeking the general common good. (For a clear statement of those laws, see J. D. Millar, "The Right to Know in the Workplace," *Annals of the New York Academy of Science* 572 [December 1989]). Our basic concern here is to determine how the law and public policy should be written to embody basic moral rights in the presence of what seems to be mutually exclusive views on the basic nature of those rights.

# WHISTLEBLOWING

*Case Study*

# Whistleblowing at Northern Airlines

When Mack Thomas became foreman of Northern Airlines' Bay Six maintenance crew at Chicago's O'Hare Airport, he knew he had his work cut out for him. The crew ranked dead last in productivity over the previous year, and Thomas's manager, Stan Gibbons, said he expected improvement pronto.

Northern ranked each of its mechanics from 1st (top) to 100th (lowest) percentile on the basis of productivity, leadership, and attitude. Thomas noted that, on average, his crew ranked in the 73rd percentile, with no individual higher than 58th and the lowest ranked 97th. He would be working with mechanics, all of whom ranked below average. The lack of leadership ability among the crew, its poor productivity record, and a generally sour attitude toward Northern made for a difficult problem that would not be easily resolved.

Nevertheless, Thomas welcomed the challenge. He had moved his Bay Three crew from fifth to second in productivity among Northern's eight crews in two years. He knew the Bay Six crew was older and set in its ways, but if he could improve its ranking, he thought he would be chosen for the foreman supervisor slot that would be coming open in about two years.

Thomas asked Stan Gibbons if he could bring in two top mechanics from his old Bay Three crew to give him some role models. Gibbons said he didn't want to break up a team that had momentum; he wanted Thomas to see if he could turn the Bay Six crew around. On reflection, Thomas felt that Gibbons had his eye on him for promotion. If he could succeed with the Bay Six crew, he would prove his management abilities.

When he faced the Bay Six crew for the first time, Mack Thomas said:

> The facts show that you guys are dead last. And in case you don't know it, you're the laughing-stock of Northern Airlines. We're going to change that. We're going to be number one in two years. That's our goal. Don't tell me to be patient. Patience is for those with no goals. My goal is to be number one; your goal is to be number one. To reach that goal we're going to do two things: work smarter and work harder.
>
> We're not working hard enough here. In some cases we're not working. Northern's rule is that you get five unexplained sick days per year and you can be late for work six times per year. Now this policy hasn't been enforced with the Bay Six crew. One of you had 16 unexplained sick days last year. And one of you, Pacello, was tardy over 20 times last year—almost once every two weeks. I'm going to fire anyone who violates either rule. No exceptions. No excuses.
>
> We're also going to work smarter. For example, we know we have to write up in the maintenance log every safety problem we encounter. The Federal Aviation Administration requires this, and it's Northern's policy. But I also have a rule here: you must consult with me before entering a problem in the maintenance log. I want to see that those problems are described correctly. When I first started as foreman over at Bay Three a lot of problems were logged that made for a lot of make-work. Guys would inflate a problem on paper, and then sit around in the hangar doing nothing. That won't happen here. We're going to move the metal.

Tony Pacello was a bit apprehensive about being singled out by Mack Thomas. Punctuality was not a real problem. Tony knew he had taken advantage of a lax foreman, but, as a former Air Force mechanic, he knew he could and would get to work on time. Talk about being "Number One" did bother Tony. The ranking system Northern used didn't take safety into account. Pacello had a low ranking of 77, but no person had ever been hospitalized because of a safety problem with a plane he helped maintain. For Pacello, safety was "Number One," and he hoped that legitimate safety concerns would not be labeled "make-work."

For three months Pacello reported on time, took no sick leave, and enjoyed his work. No major problems were encountered; only routine maintenance was required. Morale did seem to be improving in Bay Six. Pacello was a bit irritated with Thomas's temper tantrums and his hyperactive behavior, but he had to admit that the team was pulling together.

Thomas took the team out for a few beers on occasion, and paid for a catered picnic for Bay Six family members.

The first problem Pacello found was a chafed brake hose on a landing gear. He told Thomas it needed to be fixed immediately. Thomas said the replacement would cause a flight delay and inquired whether the problem was serious enough to require immediate attention or could be deferred until the plane's scheduled overhaul in a week. Pacello said it should be fixed. Thomas, a former mechanic, examined the brake, said it wasn't serious, ordered it taped, and told Pacello not to write it up in the FAA log. Instead, he told Pacello to be sure to fix the problem a week later. Pacello objected, saying that all such problems had been reported in the past and resolved immediately. Thomas repeated that the chafing wasn't serious enough to repair or report and said that the Bay Six team had not operated properly in the past. Pacello did not agree that there was no danger, and he knew that FAA rules required him to log a problem for which he had evidence. He mentioned this to Thomas, who boiled over: "I told you there's no problem, Pacello, no chance of a problem. I'm giving you a direct order to certify that plane. Get it? Now get out!" Pacello left and certified the plane for flight. Thereafter, Pacello called Stan Gibbons and reported the incident. Gibbons said he would look into the situation, but never got back to Pacello.

A month later, Pacello and his fellow mechanic Art Necassi reported to Thomas that a plane's engine housing latch had jammed after the engine's inspection and that they hadn't been able to release it. They believed the problem should be logged and resolved, which would mean a flight postponement. Thomas said: "Look, the engine was inspected. It's okay. The jamming you mention means the latch is locked; it just can't be unlocked. A locked latch will not come open. So, there's no problem, no real problem. Move the metal; we will clean it up later." Necassi said he thought the problem should be fixed and logged, but that he wanted to talk with Tyler Morgan, Stan Gibbons's boss, before he logged it. Thomas said he should talk with Gibbons if he talked with anyone, but he added that he wanted to look at the latch first. He did so and pronounced the flight ready to go. He told Necassi to think it over for fifteen minutes before calling anyone. When Necassi called, Morgan told him he had talked with Thomas, who reported that he had seen this problem many times and that it was not reportable. Morgan also said that Thomas told him he had consulted with Gibbons. Morgan told Necassi to listen to Thomas and not let Pacello influence him: "Tony's a nice guy, but he's in the 77th percentile.

We've repeatedly had to lay him off or transfer him. He's spent more time maintaining ground vehicles here than planes. He hasn't spent enough time on aircraft to really know what he's doing." Necassi certified the plane for flight after Pacello refused. When informed of Morgan's comments about him, Pacello said: "Something's gotta give here and it won't be me."

Three weeks later Necassi discovered a broken floor panel in a plane scheduled to fly in two hours. He conferred with Pacello, who said no panels were in inventory. Pacello immediately entered the item in the FAA logbook. A short time later, Thomas confronted Pacello, saying: "Of all the planes we're working, this is the only one with a chance of making the 7 A.M. takeoff, and you shoot it down." After ordering Necassi and Pacello to take a break, Thomas told another mechanic to patch the panel with sheet metal. When Pacello returned to the plane, he felt the panel sink beneath his feet, and had visions of it breaking and interfering with the steering control cables that run under the floor. Since he had filed the log notation, Pacello knew he could be held responsible by the FAA if he was party to a substandard repair. He went for a smoke, and, while there, watched the plane take off. Finally, he went to a phone and called the FAA. Northern was contacted immediately; the plane was located in Minneapolis, with the cables in normal working order; a new panel was shipped in, and after a day's delay, the plane was certified for flight.

When the plane returned to Chicago, Pacello noticed that his logbook entry had been changed; it now indicated the broken panel was in a different location. The log indicated that repairs had been completed. Since falsifying an aircraft logbook is a federal felony, Pacello again called the FAA, which investigated. Pacello said he had no doubt that Thomas did it. Speaking for Northern, Tyler Morgan said it was probable that another mechanic did it to discredit Thomas. The FAA could not decide who was at fault.

Nine days after the incident, Thomas saw Pacello sitting in a first-class seat while Necassi was working on a loose seat behind the one Pacello was in. Thomas immediately suspended Pacello for loafing, though the latter insisted that he was helping by pushing the frame into place with his legs. Necassi supported Pacello's version. Thomas called in Gibbons and Morgan. What happened next is unclear. Thomas, Gibbons, and Morgan claim they told Pacello to return to the hangar the next day to meet and discuss his suspension. Necassi and Pacello say no such meeting was mentioned. After Pacello did not appear for the meeting, he was fired. Pacello was later reinstated through Northern's grievance procedure, although he was demoted to ground vehicle maintenance.

After his reinstatement, Pacello held a news conference in which he alleged that Northern had committed serious unethical and illegal acts. He laid out the specifics regarding the chafed hose, the engine housing latch, and the broken floor panel. He also mentioned the altered logbook, and the fact that Northern's grievance procedure had reinstated him after he had been fired. Pacello said he felt sure Northern would neither investigate the actions of Thomas, Gibbons, and Morgan nor discipline them, and he asked the media to conduct their own investigation.

## For Discussion

How many times did Tony Pacello blow the whistle? Was he justified in blowing the whistle on Northern Airlines? Why or why not? Discuss Northern's responses to Pacello's acts. Were these responses justified? Why or why not? If you were placed in charge of Northern's response to safety issues, would you make any changes? If not, why not? If so, why would you make the specific changes you recommend?

*Alan F. Westin*

# Whistleblowing: Loyalty and Dissent in the Corporation

... [O]ur society needs to rethink the current definitions of loyalty and dissent in corporate life. We must come up with a strategy that will apply a combination of new remedies to increase the protection of legitimate whistleblowing. And, we have to start discussing this issue with some urgency now. ...

Having stated this conclusion, it may seem that this presents a relatively straightforward problem for American law and social policy: just create some new procedure to protect whistleblowers. But the problem is not at all simple. Consider the following factors that have to be taken into account in framing new public policies.

1. *Not all whistleblowers are correct in what they allege to be the facts of management's conduct, and determining the accuracy of whistleblowing charges is not always easy.* If it were possible to collect all the instances of corporate employee whistleblowing charges in the United States in a given year and then determine how often managements were justified in their actions and the employees mistaken, my guess is that employers would deserve to win many of these disputes. This has been the experience under independent labor arbitration, when unionized workers challenge dismissals as not being for "just cause." It is also the experience when government employees have appealed to the courts to vindicate free-expression rights in government whistleblowing cases. Putting the whistle to one's lips does not guarantee that one's facts are correct.

2. *There is always the danger that incompetent or inadequately performing employees will take up the whistle to avoid facing justified per-*

*sonnel sanctions.* Forbidding an employer to dismiss or discipline an employee who protests against illegal or improper conduct by management invites employees to take out "antidismissal insurance" by lodging a whistleblowing complaint. Any new system to protect whistleblowers must find ways to deal with this possibility.

3. *Employees can choose some ways of blowing the whistle that would be unacceptably disruptive, regardless of their protest.* Suppose an employee at a chemical plant takes out an ad in the local newspaper that says, "My company is violating the law by polluting the town reservoir." Or suppose a black employee of the XYZ Corporation comes to work on the assembly line one day wearing a large button that says "XYZ is a Honkie Firm that Practices Racism against its Black Workers." Finally, suppose an automobile design engineer, without raising the issue with his supervisor or upper management, reports to the National Transportation Safety Board that he believes the gas tank of a new model just entering production will pose grave safety problems. These illustrations demonstrate that any system to protect rights of employee expression must consider the time, place, and manner in which an employee voices that dissent.

4. *Some whistleblowers are not protesting unlawful or unsafe behavior but social policies by management that the employee considers unwise.* When this is the case, should an employee be entitled to remain on the job? In considering this, it helps to recall that whistleblowing can come in a wide variety of ideological stripes. Most government and corporate whistleblowers have recently been people who are asserting liberal values when they call for changes in corporate policies. But in the late 1940s and early fifties, the most celebrated whistleblowers were persons leaking information to anti-Communist legislators or the press about allegedly "soft-on-communism" policies by members of the Truman administration or their private employers. It was Senator Richard M. Nixon who proposed legislation in 1951 to protect the jobs of such federal-employee whistleblowers if they revealed classified information about corruption or pro-Communists to congressional committees. At that moment, liberals and civil libertarians defended the need for autonomy and confidentiality in the executive branch, and deplored the totalitarian "informer" mentality being championed by the McCarthyites. This suggests that any policy protecting whistleblowers must reckon with the likelihood of shifting ideological directions among protesting employees, and consider how often society wants social policies to be determined in the private sector through whistleblowing disputes.

5. *The legal definitions of what constitutes a safe product, danger to health, or improper treatment of employees are often far from clear or certain.* It usually takes years and many test cases before the courts and regulatory agencies define just what is required in a given situation. This leaves open a wide range of judgments and choices as to what is proper compliance activity. Until the law becomes clear, shouldn't management have the authority to select compliance strategies, since management bears the legal responsibility for meeting standards? This is especially true since the harsh realities of foreign business competition and rising production expenses create legitimate concerns for management about containing costs, including the cost of complying with government regulations. In addition, the jobs of millions of corporate employees, the well-being of local communities in which companies operate, and the strength of the national economy are all involved in the determination of reasonable risk-to-cost calculations.

6. *The efficiency and flexibility of personnel administration could be threatened by the creation of legal rights to dissent and legalized review systems.* If it becomes legally protected to challenge management policies and procedures and to appeal directives to outside authorities, this could lead to a flood of unjustified and harassing employee complaints. It could require personnel managers to document every action as a defense to possible litigation, and embroil managements in consistent employee litigation. It could also create an "informer ethos" at work that would threaten the spirit of cooperation and trust on which sound working relationships depend.

7. *There can be risks to the desirable autonomy of the private sector in expanding government authority too deeply into internal business policies.* Although democratic societies have a major interest in allowing private organizations to run their own affairs and to make their own personnel decisions, they insist that these private organizations are also subject to obeying the law. Having courts or government tribunals pass on the validity of a wide range of personnel decisions could give the government more authority to define loyalty and disloyalty for 80 million private-sector employees than would be desirable, and could also give government too much authority to control what products are produced and how they are manufactured.

This catalogue of institutional and social problems does *not* mean that we should abandon the effort to install new whistleblower protections in the private sector. It does suggest that we need to be sensitive to the multifaceted aspects of the task, and to recognize that care now could save much regret later over the "unanticipated consequences" of a new policy.

*Ronald F. Duska*

# Whistleblowing

Whistleblowing: A practice in which employees who know that their company is engaged in activities that (a) cause unnecessary harm, (b) are in violation of human rights, (c) are illegal, (d) run counter to the defined purpose of the institution, or (e) are otherwise immoral, inform the public or some governmental agency of those activities. The ethical problem is whether and under what conditions whistleblowing is acceptable behavior and/or morally required behavior. Whistleblowing, if required, would involve a conflict between the obligation of loyalty the individual is presumed to have to the company and the obligation to prevent harm the individual is presumed to have to the public. But the exact nature and demands of these conflicting obligations to the company and the public are disputed.

Most business ethicists claim that employees have some obligation to the company or employer, which is usually characterized as an obligation of loyalty. Whistleblowing violates that obligation. In that context the company is viewed as analogous to a sports team. In sports whistleblowing is the function of neutral, detached referees who are supposed to detect and penalize illicit behavior of opposing teams. It is neither acceptable nor a responsibility of a player to call a foul on one's teammates. If the analogy holds, what is unacceptable in sports is also unacceptable in business. From this perspective whistleblowing is viewed as an act of disloyalty ("finking," "tattle tale") and there is a presumption against it. Consequently, a countervailing obligation to the public would be the only justification for overriding the obligation to the team or company. There is a wide range of views on the issue ranging from the position that whistleblowing as an act of disloyalty is never justified to the opposite position that employees owe no loyalty to a company and given their right to freedom of expression they can ethically disclose whatever they wish

From *The Blackwell Encyclopedic Dictionary of Business Ethics*, ed. Patricia H. Werhane and R. Freeman (Oxford: Blackwell, 1997), pp. 654–56. Reprinted with permission.

about a company, except where their work contract expressly or at least implicitly prohibits it.

Most business ethicists writing on whistleblowing maintain a fiduciary obligation of loyalty that whistleblowing violates, so the burden of proof or justification falls to the whistleblower. However, defenders of whistleblowing maintain that in conditions where companies violate ethical and/or legal constraints, whatever obligation of loyalty an employee has is abrogated, and whistleblowing is not only permissible but may also be morally required, on the grounds that individuals have a responsibility to the general public to prevent harm or illegal activity. Hence the conflict of obligations we mentioned. However, it is possible to argue that even if the illegal or immoral behavior of the company abrogates the responsibility of loyalty, there is no consequent good samaritan obligation to the general public to "blow the whistle."

So two arguments are needed. One to show whistleblowing is permissible, a second to show it is required. This latter argument is quite important, since blowing the whistle can lead to harm to the whistleblower. Under what conditions is one required to do what would likely harm oneself?

The argument for the permissibility of whistleblowing sets down a set of conditions to be met before a whistleblower can justifiably inform on her company.

1. The whistleblowing should be done for the purpose of exposing unnecessary harm, violation of human rights, illegal activity, or conduct counter to the defined purpose of the corporation, and should be done from the appropriate moral motive, that is, not from a desire to get ahead, or out of spite or some such motive. Nevertheless, whether the act of whistleblowing is called for is not determined by the motive of the whistleblower but by the company acting either immorally or illegally.

2. The whistleblower should make certain that his or her belief that inappropriate actions are ordered or have occurred is based on evidence that would persuade a reasonable person.

3. The whistleblower should have acted only after a careful analysis of the danger: (a) how serious is the moral violation? (minor moral matters need not be reported); (b) how immediate is the moral violation? (the greater time before the violation occurs the greater chances that internal mechanisms will prevent the anticipated violation); (c) is the moral violation one that can be specified (general claims about a rapacious company, obscene profits, and actions contrary to public interest simply will not do).

4. Except in special circumstances, the whistleblower should have exhausted all internal channels for dissent before informing the public. The whistleblower's action should be commensurate with one's responsibility for avoiding and/or exposing moral violations. If there are personnel in the company whose obligation it is to monitor and respond to immoral and/or illegal activities, it would be their responsibility to address those issues. Thus, the first obligation of the would-be whistleblower, would be to report the unethical activities to those persons, and only if they do not act, to inform the general public.

5. The whistleblower should have some chance of success. Ought implies can, so if there is no hope in arousing societal or government pressure, then one needlessly exposes oneself and one's loved ones to hardship for no conceivable moral gain.

But these conditions speak mainly to the *permissibility* of blowing the whistle. A further, often overlooked question is under what conditions is it morally required (*obligatory*), if ever, for an employee to blow the whistle? The literature on this subject is sparse, except that there seems to be a good deal of tacit agreement that some sort of good samaritan principle is operative here. Hence if there is an obligation to prevent harm, under conditions where there is a need and the person is capable of preventing the harm without sacrificing something of comparable moral worth and if the person is the last resort, then that obligation would operate in the case of whistleblowing. Conditions 4 and 5 may be read as assuming that there is a responsibility to blow the whistle. But to show that obligation requires showing there is an obligation to the general public to prevent harm.

In the corporate context, the company is seen as a team and expects loyalty. Forsaking the team to function as a detached referee to blow the whistle is seen as disloyal and cause for punitive action. In such a culture, to blow the whistle requires a certain moral heroism. Given the fact that society depends on whistleblowers to protect it from unscrupulous operators, justified whistleblowers need some protection. To assure the existence of necessary whistleblowers (somebody's got to do it), sound legislation is needed to protect the whistleblower.

Finally, whistleblowing is not restricted to the area of business. It occurs in all walks of life. Professionals may be held to the standards of their profession, that sometimes require blowing a whistle. For example, accountants and engineers have a dual obligation to their clients and to the public. Hence, they have a fiduciary responsibility to report certain illegal or potentially harmful activities if they encounter them in the course of their auditing or accounting or constructing. These obligations come from the professional status of the accountants and engineers, just as such obligations extend to all professionals, such as doctors and lawyers, who have obligations to their profession and the public to blow the whistle on colleagues who violate certain canons of appropriate behavior. But beyond the professions, whistleblowing is required in other walks of life: for example, the participants in an honor code have a responsibility to report violations. While such whistleblowing activity is viewed unfavorably, it is a necessary part of human activity.

Enlightened companies, aware that harmful, immoral, or illegal behavior that needs to be reported is likely to occur from time to time, have begun to make provisions for regularizing the monitoring of behavior with ombudspersons or corporate responsibility officers. Such offices provide an outlet for those who feel obliged to report the unseemly behavior of their companies, without the need to go public. These provisions are desirable because they will alleviate the necessity of going public and blowing the whistle on harmful or illegal behavior.

# SELECT BIBLIOGRAPHY

Arvey, R. *Fairness in Selecting Employees.* Reading, Mass.: Addison-Wesley, 1979.

Cohen, M., T. Nagel, and T. Scanlon, eds. *Equality and Preferential Treatment.* Princeton: Princeton University Press, 1977.

Edwards, R. *Rights at Work: Employment Relations in the Post Union Era.* New York: Twentieth Century Fund, 1993.

Elliston, F. et al. *Whistleblowing and Whistleblowing Research.* 2 vols. New York: Praeger, 1985.

Ezorsky, G.,ed. *Moral Rights in the Workplace.* Albany: SUNY Press, 1987.

Gibson, M. *Workers' Rights.* Totowa, N.J.: Roman and Allanheld, 1983.

Gross, B., ed. *Reverse Discrimination.* Amherst, N.Y.: Prometheus Books, 1977.

Hopkins, W. *Ethical Dimensions of Diversity.* Thousand Oaks, Calif.: Sage, 1997.

Morris, C. *Bearing Witness: Sexual Harassment and Beyond—Everywoman's Story.* Boston: Little, Brown & Co., 1994.

Wagner, E. *Sexual Harassment in the Workplace.* New York: Amacom, 1992.

Weiss, J. *Organizational Behavior and Change: Managing Diversity, Cross Cultural Dynamics and Ethics.* Anaheim, Calif.: West, 1995.

Werhane, P. *Persons, Rights, and Corporations.* Englewood Cliffs, N.J.: Prentice-Hall, 1985.

Westin, A., and S. Salisbury, eds. *Individual Rights in the Corporation.* New York: Random House, 1980.

# ELECTRONIC SOURCES

American Civil Liberties Organization   www.aclu.org/issues/worker/campaign.html

Annenberg Privacy Studies   www.annenberg.nwu.edu/pubs/downside

The Carol and Lawrence Zicklin Center for Business Ethics Research   rider.wharton.upenn.edu/~ethics/zicklin/

Centre for Applied Ethics   www.ethics.ubc.ca/resources/

Ethics Officer Association   www.eoa.org/

Ethics Resource Center   www.ethics.org

International Society of Business, Economics and Ethics   www.synethos.org

Occupational Safety and Health Association   www.osha.gov

U.S. Department of Labor   www.dol.gov

U.S. Equal Employment Opportunity Commission (EEOC)   www.eeoc.gov

# 5. ETHICS AND FINANCE

## INTRODUCTION

Finance was at the forefront of ethical concern in the 1980s and 1990s. The collapse and subsequent bailout of a large part of the savings and loan business, the insider trading scandals that shook Wall Street's most prestigious investment banking houses, the wave of hostile corporate takeovers that threatened to gobble up and dismember even America's largest corporations, the corporate compensation packages and "golden parachutes" that seemed grossly extravagant to many, and the number of firms that went bankrupt shortly after receiving an auditor's "clean opinion"—all convinced many observers that Wall Street was consumed by greed.

In this section John Boatright discusses a broad range of ethical issues in finance, while the insider trading scenarios offer the reader an opportunity to examine the morality of several real world situations.

Mohammad Abdolmohammadi and Mark Nixon discuss in some detail the nature of the accounting profession, with particular reference to the American Institute of Certified Public Accountants' Code of Professional Conduct, the profession's enforcement of the code, and controversial issues that arise in the accounting profession.

# Insider Trading Scenarios

In any discussion of finance ethics, insider trading is front and center. There is no question whether insider trading is illegal. Section 10b-5 of the 1934 Securities Exchange Act makes it illegal to defraud or deceive a person in connection with the purchase or sale of a security. Although 10b-5 is nonspecific, courts interpret it as barring corporate insiders possessing material, nonpublic, confidential information from trading in securities of their firms. Although the notion of an "insider" is not clearly specified, it certainly includes those who have a confidential relationship in the conduct of the business. The rule is called the "disclose or abstain" rule, for the insider generally has a choice between trading after the confidential information has been disclosed or refraining from trading until the information becomes public.

Although it is clear that insider trading is illegal in the United States, it is legal in many countries, and many philosophers and economists argue that insider trading is ethically permissible and should be legalized. They argue that such trading makes markets more efficient by helping to move stock prices in the "correct" direction, i.e., toward a level the stock would be at if the information were known. For example, if a stock sells at $10 when insider trading commences, such trading will help move the stock toward the $18 value it will reach when the information is made public. Anyone who buys as the stock moves up will benefit. Furthermore, anyone who sells as the stock moves from $10 to $18 benefits in the sense that he gets a higher price than he would if insider trading had not occurred. So few are harmed by insider trading. Finally, the defenders of insider trading argue that the inventors of valuable information in a firm are probably not compensated adequately for their contribution to the firm, and that permitting insider trading is the best way to compensate them.

Those against insider trading have developed three main arguments. First, they argue that many will definitely be harmed by insider trading, and that defenders of permitting it have not proven it would have overall utility. Second, they argue that financial markets should be fair in the sense that all investors should have a chance to have access to corporate information that would affect a stock's price, but that permitting insider trading gives insiders an unfair informational advantage. Third, they argue that any information one generates when working for a company belongs to the firm, not the employee, and hence the company is entitled to exclusive use of all information generated or acquired by its employees. However, inside traders take this information and use it for their own personal interest. In a sense, then, they are taking corporate property—stealing it— and using it for their own benefit.

The following ten scenarios are based on legal holdings. However, in discussing them we will not focus on the legal aspects of the cases. Instead, your task is to discuss the morality of the acts in each scenario.

1. As CEO of Mover Corp., you are aware of confidential good news that should soon propel Mover's stock above its present value of $6 per share. You sell stock short through a stockbroker who you know will tell his clients you are selling short and that the stock will decline. Mover's stock slips to $4. You cover your short, making $2 per share. You then buy more stock at $4, release the news, and when Mover stock hits $15, you unload.

2. You work for Mine, Inc. as an inventor and have just discovered an additive that seems to increase gas mileage three miles per gallon. Although you are sure of the discovery, your boss wants to wait two months to announce it to be sure the results are triple-checked. You are sixty-five in a month, the mandatory retirement age. Mine, Inc. has no retirement benefits and pays its inventors no bonuses. You take out a home-equity loan, add it to your entire life savings, and buy $250,000 of Mine stock, tripling your investment when the news is announced.

3. You and your golfing partner, both executives at Engulf, Inc., are discussing Engulf's secret plan to acquire Flaccid, Inc. Your caddy overhears your discussion and purchases Flaccid stock. Next week Engulf announces its bid and Flaccid stock doubles, whereupon the caddy sells.

4. You are an upper-level manager with Torpor, Inc. and you know Torpor will announce a disappointing earnings report in a week. You know the present law prohibits you from selling before the news, but you tell your best friend, who calls his stockbroker with the news. Your friend sells Torpor stock short on his broker's advice, and the broker calls all his clients who hold Torpor and advises them to dump Torpor stock.

5. You are having a beer with Ken Moore, attorney for Art Grab, a cor-

porate raider, when Moore leans over and confides: "Grab is going to initiate purchases of Zilch, Inc. next week." You immediately purchase 10,000 shares of Zilch, and cash out in two weeks when the price doubles on public news of the takeover attempt.

6. Upper, Inc. is about to report fantastic earnings. You go to Fax Inc. to fax Upper's earnings to its printer, who will print the quarterly report. The fax operator sees the results and immediately places an order for Upper stock. The fax receiver at the printer also notices the results and buys Upper stock.

7. You write the column "Wall Street Beat" for *Barrens*, the top-ranked financial daily. You know your influence is such that a positive or negative discussion of a stock will cause it to rise or fall 6 percent on average. All of your information comes from your analyses; none comes from insiders of the firms you discuss. When you have particularly strong comments on a stock, you trade in the stock before your column appears. You pass your information on to your friends, who also trade on it.

8. You are working in the mergers and acquisitions department of Kidunot & Co. on a takeover concerning two companies, the details of which are confidential. You sell the information to Evan Booski, a well-known arbitrager, who buys stock in the takeover target, makes $3 million from the transaction, and gives you $400,000 for the information.

9. You work for Golddigger & Co., which has a mergers and acquisitions (M & A) department that advises clients on financing, mergers, and takeovers, and an arbitrage department that trades in the stock of likely takeover targets. You are aware that the law requires there be no leakage of information between the two departments within a firm. You arrange through a counterpart at Kidunot & Co. to trade information between Kidunot's arbitrage and Golddigger's M & A departments, and between Kidunot's M & A and Golddigger's arbitrage departments. By trading on such information Kidunot and Golddigger each gain $30 million per year. You also trade in your own private account on the information passed to Golddigger from Kidunot.

10. As an investment analyst knowledgeable about the banking industry, you have been approached by two bank officials who want you to expose serious wrongdoing at their bank, which will soon bring about a total collapse of the bank's stock. They do not wish to go public themselves, for fear of never working in the industry again. You investigate further and write a critical research report but do not release it until you have called all your clients who own the bank's stock and tell them to sell.

*John R. Boatright*

# Finance Ethics

Although many business ethics problems are common to every functional area, finance involves some distinctive ethical issues that require separate treatment. Because financial activity is closely regulated, these issues are often addressed as matters of law rather than ethics, but the basis of regulation in finance includes some fundamental ethical precepts, such as fairness in financial markets and the duties of fiduciaries. The law is an uncertain regulator, though, and much financial activity presupposes unwritten rules of ethical behavior. People trained in finance enter many different lines of work, and so finance ethics is necessarily diverse; ethical conduct is not the same for bond traders, mutual fund managers, and corporate financial officers, for example. Moreover, finance ethics is concerned not only with individual conduct but also with the operation of financial markets and financial institutions. Finally, the financial management of corporations, with its objective of maximizing shareholder wealth, raises yet different ethical issues.

Despite this complexity, the field of financial ethics can be organized under the three major headings of financial markets, financial services, and financial management.

- *Financial markets* are vulnerable to unfair trading practices (fraud and manipulation), unfair conditions (an unlevel playing field), and contractual difficulties (forming, interpreting, and enforcing contracts). The main aim of federal securities laws and the self-regulation of exchanges is expressed in the phrase "fair and orderly" markets, which reflects the need in financial markets to balance the twin goals of fairness and efficiency.

From *A Companion to Business Ethics*, ed. Robert E. Frederick (Oxford: Blackwell Publishers, 1999), pp. 153–64.

- Many individuals and institutions serve as financial intermediaries, providing *financial services* on behalf of others. Financial intermediaries commonly make decisions as agents for principals in an agency relation, and they often become fiduciaries with fiduciary duties. Agents and fiduciaries have an obligation to act solely in the interests of other parties and, especially, to avoid conflicts of interest. Although financial services providers are often merely sellers in a buyer-seller relation, they still have the obligations of any seller to avoid deceptive and abusive sales practices.

- *Financial Management:* Business firms are legally structured as the financial instruments of shareholders, and officers and directors are agents of firms, and have a fiduciary duty to manage the firms with the objective of maximizing shareholder wealth. Ethical issues in financial management concern the actions that violate the duties of financial managers and the discretion of financial managers to serve the interests of nonshareholder groups, commonly called "stakeholders."

All financial activity takes place in a larger economic, political, and social setting, and so ethical issues arise about the overall impact of financial activity. Although financial decision making is generally limited to the financial factors of risk and return over time, ethics includes a consideration of the ethical treatment of everyone affected by a decision, and the consequences for the whole of society.

## FINANCIAL MARKETS

The fundamental ethical requirement of financial markets is that they be *fair*. Fairness may be defined either *substantively* (when the price of a security reflects the actual value) or *procedurally* (when buyers are enabled to determine the actual value of a security). In the United States, some state securities laws aim at substantive fairness by requiring expert evaluation of new securities (so-called blue-sky laws), but the federal Securities Act of 1933 and the Securities Exchange Act of 1934 attempt to secure fairness procedurally by requiring adequate disclosure. The rationale for mandatory disclosure is that securities transactions are more likely to be fair when material information must be disclosed, and investors have easy access to information.

## Unfair Trading Practices

Fraud, manipulation, and other unfair trading practices lead not only to unfair treatment in securities transactions but to a loss of investor confidence in the integrity of financial markets. Speculative activity also produces excess volatility, which was blamed for the stock market crashes of 1929 and October 1987.

Both fraud and manipulation are defined broadly. Section 17(a) of the 1933 Securities Act and Section 10(b) of the 1934 Securities Exchange Act prohibit anyone involved in the issue or exchange of securities to make a false statement of a material fact, to omit a fact that makes a statement of material facts misleading, or to engage in any practice or scheme that would serve to defraud. Whereas fraud generally involves the disclosure or concealment of information that bears on the value of a security, manipulation consists of trading for the purpose of creating a misleading impression about a security's value.

Fraud is obviously committed by an initial stock offering that inflates the assets of a firm or fails to disclose some of its liabilities. Insider trading has been prosecuted as a fraud on the grounds that nonpublic material information ought to be disclosed before trading. In the 1920s, the stock market was manipulated by traders who bid up the price of stock in order to sell at the peak to unwary investors. In recent years, concern has been expressed about a form of program trading known as index arbitrage, in which traders are able to create volatility in different markets, solely for the purpose of trading on the resulting price differences.

## Fair Conditions

Fairness in financial markets is often expressed by the concept of a level playing field. A playing field may be unlevel because of inequalities in information, bargaining power, resources, processing ability, and special vulnerabilities.

Unequal information, or *information asymmetry*, may refer either to the fact that the parties to a transaction do not possess the same information or that they do not have the same access to information. The possession of different information is a pervasive feature of markets that is not always ethically objectionable. Indeed, investors who invest resources in acquiring superior information are entitled to exploit this advantage, and they perform a service by making markets more efficient. The unequal possession of information is unfair only when the information has not been legitimately acquired or when its use violates some right or obligation. Other arguments against insider trading, for example, are that the information has not been acquired legitimately but has been misappropriated from the rightful owner (the "misappropriation theory") and that an insider who trades on information that has been acquired in a fiduciary relation violates a fiduciary duty. Equal access to information is problematical because accessibility is not a feature of information itself but a function of the investment that is required to obtain information. To the objection that an inside trader is using information that is inherently inaccessible, some reply that anyone can become an insider by devoting enough resources.

Similarly, inequalities in bargaining power, resources, and processing ability—which are pervasive in financial markets—are ethically objectionable only when they are used in violation of some right or obligation and especially when they are used coercively. The main ethical requirement is that people not use any advantage unfairly. For example, American stock markets permit relatively unsophisticated investors with modest resources and processing ability to buy stocks on fair terms, and some changes, such as increased use of program trading or private placements, are criticized for increasing the advantages of institutional investors. (The growth of mutual funds has served to reduce the adverse consequences of inequalities among investors.) Vulnerabilities, such as impulsiveness or overconfidence, create opportunities for exploitation that can be countered by such measures as a "cooling off" period on purchases and loans, and the warning to request and read a prospectus before investing.

## Financial Contracting

Some financial instruments, such as home mortgages and futures options, are contracts which commit the parties to a certain course of action, and many financial relations, such as being a trustee or corporate officer, are contractual in nature. Contracts are often vague, ambiguous, or incomplete, with the result that disagreements arise about what is ethically and legally required.

First, beyond the written words of *express contracts* lie innumerable tacit understandings that constitute *implied contracts*. Financial affairs would be impossible if every detail had to be made explicit. However, whatever is left implicit is subject to differing interpretations, and insofar as implied contracts are not legally enforceable, they may be breached with impunity. Not only financial instruments but the relations of corporations with employees, customers, suppliers, and other stakeholders consist of implied contracts, from which each party receives some value. One objection to hostile takeovers is that raiders are able to finance such deals by capturing the value of the implied contracts that the target firm has made with its stakeholders.

Second, contracts are sometimes imperfect because of limitations in our cognitive ability, especially incomplete knowledge, bounded rationality, and future contingencies. In addition, some situations may be too complex and uncertain to permit careful planning. As a result, the parties may fail to negotiate contracts that produce the maximum benefit for themselves. Disputes in contractual relations also arise over what constitutes a breach of contract and what is an appropriate remedy.

Agency and fiduciary relations are one solution for the problems of imperfect contracting because they replace specific obligations with a general duty to act in another's interests. In particular, the fiduciary relation of managers to shareholders has arisen because of the difficulties of writing contracts for this particular relation. Similarly, supplier relations are not easily reduced to contractual terms. The term *relational contracting* has been coined to describe the building of working relations as an alternative to rigid contracts.

## FINANCIAL SERVICES

The financial services industry—which includes commercial banks, securities and investment firms, mutual and pension funds, insurance companies, and financial planners—provides a vast array of financial services to individuals, businesses, and governments. Financial services firms act primarily as financial *intermediaries*, which is to say that they use their capital to provide services rather than to trade on their own behalf. In providing financial services, these firms sometimes act as agents or fiduciaries with respect to clients; at other times, they act as sellers in a typical buyer-seller relation. Thus, a broker who is authorized to trade for a client's account is an agent, but a broker who makes a cold call to a prospect is merely a salesperson. Many ethical disputes result from misunderstandings about the nature of a financial service provider's role.

## Fiduciaries and Agents

A fiduciary is a person who is entrusted to act in the interests of another. Fiduciary duties are the duties of a fiduciary to act in that other person's interest without gaining any material benefit except with the knowledge and consent of that person. Similar to the fiduciary relation is the relation of *agent* and *principal*, in which one person (the agent) is engaged to act on behalf of another (the principal). Whereas fiduciary relations arise when something of value is entrusted to another person, agency relations are due to the need to rely on others for their specialized knowledge and skill. In both relations, the specific acts to be performed are not fully specified in advance and fiduciaries and agents have wide latitude.

A major source of unethical conduct by fiduciaries and agents is conflict of interest, in which a personal interest of the fiduciary or agent interferes with the ability of the person to act in the interest of the other person. Fiduciaries and agents are called upon to exercise judgment on behalf of others, and their judgment can be compromised if they stand to gain personally by a decision. For example, a conflict of interest is created when a brokerage firm offers a higher commission for selling in-house mutual funds. The conflict arises because the broker has an incentive to sell funds that may not be in a client's best interests. Whether mutual fund managers should be permitted to trade for their own accounts is a controversial question because of the perceived conflict of interest. Fiduciaries and agents also have duties to preserve the confidentiality of information and not to use the information for their own benefit. Thus, "piggyback" trading, in which a broker copies the trades of a savvy client, is a breach of confidentiality.

Agency relations are subject to some well-known difficulties that arise from the inability of principals to monitor agents closely. These difficulties are opportunism, moral hazard, and adverse selection. Opportunism, or shirking, occurs because of the tendency of agents to advance their own interests despite the commitment to act on behalf of another. In agency theory, which is the study of agency relations, whatever a principal loses from opportunism is known as agency loss. The total of the agency loss and expenditures to reduce it are called agency costs. Moral hazard arises when the cost (or risk) of an activity is borne by others, as when a person seeks more medical care because of insurance. Moral hazard can be reduced in insurance by requiring deductibles and copayments, which provide an insured person with an incentive to lower costs. Insurance companies can also seek out better insurance prospects, but this leads to the problem of adverse selection. Adverse selection is the tendency, in insurance, of less suitable prospects to seek more insurance, which increases the risk for insurers who cannot easily identify good and bad insurance prospects. More generally, principals are not always able to judge the suitability of agents, and agents have an incentive to misrepresent themselves.

Many ethical problems, ranging from churning of client accounts by stockbrokers to the empire-building tendencies of CEOs, result from the difficulties inherent in agency relations. These problems can be addressed by closer monitoring and by changes in the structure of the relation. For example, the incentive for brokers to churn could be reduced by basing compensation more on the performance of clients' portfolios and less on the volume of trades. In addition, compensating executives with stock options aligns their interests more closely with those of the shareholders and thus prevents empire building. The most effective solutions for ethical problems in agency relations are twofold: first, there must be a strong sense of professionalism accompanied by professional organizations with codes of ethics; second, a high degree of trust must be present. Trust is essential in the financial services industry, and companies generally pay a heavy price for violating the public's confidence.

## Sales Practices

In the selling of financial products, such as mutual funds, insurance policies, and loans, the ordinary standards for ethical sales practices apply. Thus, the financial services industry, like any business, has an obligation to refrain from deception and to make adequate disclosure of material information. A mutual fund prospectus, for example, is screened by regulatory authorities, but personal sales pitches and mass-media advertising sometimes contain false and misleading claims. For example, figures in an advertisement may exaggerate the fund's past performance or omit sales charges. Whether an advertisement is deceptive is often a matter of dispute. The generally accepted standard for disclosure is materiality, which refers to information about which an average prudent investor ought to be informed or to which a reasonable person would attach importance in making a decision.

For many financial products, the degree of risk is material information that ought to be disclosed. Thus, some clients of investment firms have attributed large losses in derivatives to inadequate disclosure of the risks involved. Brokers and insurance agents have an obligation to recommend only products that are *suitable*. Risk and suitability are closely related because whether an investment is suitable generally depends on the level of risk that is appropriate for an investor. Suitability is often difficult to determine, and investments may be unsuitable for many different reasons. Thus, a security might be unsuitable because it does not offer sufficient diversification or it is not sufficiently liquid, or because it involves inappropriate trading techniques, such as the use of margin.

Financial products are susceptible to abusive sales practices, such as "twisting," in which an insurance agent persuades a client to replace an existing policy merely for the commission, and "flipping," which is the practice of replacing one loan with another in order to generate additional fees. The poor are frequent targets of abuses by loan providers who offer high-interest loans and add on various "options" of little value. Finally, financial products should meet certain standards of integrity. Just as automobiles and houses can be shoddily made, so, too, are there shoddy financial products. The sale of limited partnerships, for example, has been criticized in recent years for dubious valuation of assets and questionable practices by developers.

Victims of fraud or abuse by financial services firms generally have recourse to the courts, but the securities industry in the USA requires most customers (and employees) to sign a predispute arbitration agreement (PDAA) that commits them to binding arbitration of disputes. Mandatory arbitration is spreading to the holders of credit cards, insurance policies, and other financial products. Although arbitration has many advantages over litigation, critics charge that the process is often unfair and denies investors adequate protection. The controversy over compulsory arbitration in the securities industry focuses on three issues: the requirement that investors sign a PDAA as a condition of opening an account, the alleged industry bias of arbitration panels, and the permissibility of punitive damages. In addition, the requirement that employees submit complaints about such matters as discrimination and harassment to arbitration denies them the right to sue in court, a right that employees outside the securities industry take for granted.

## Financial Services Firms

Financial services firms are themselves businesses, and the management of such a business raises some ethical issues, especially in the treatment of institutional clients. For example, underwriters of municipal bonds have been criticized for making political contributions in city elections in order to gain access. Firms as well as individuals encounter conflicts of interest, such as the reluctance of brokerage firms to issue a negative analysis of a client company's stock. In recent years, rogue traders have caused great losses at some firms, including the collapse of a major bank.

The managers of large investment portfolios for mutual funds, insurance companies, pension funds, and private endowments face two important ethical questions.

1. Should they consider social factors in making decisions, such as how a corporation treats its employees or its record on the environment?
2. Should they vote the stock that they hold, and if so, what criteria should they use to evaluate the issues that are submitted to a vote?

Some large institutional investors take a hands-off approach, while others are becoming actively involved as shareholders in a movement known as relationship investing.

## FINANCIAL MANAGEMENT

Financial managers have the task of actively deploying assets rather than investing them. Unlike a portfolio manager who merely buys stocks of corporations for a client, a corporate financial manager is involved in the running of a corporation. Investment decisions in a corporation are concerned not with which securities to hold but with what business opportunities to pursue. These decisions are still made using standard financial criteria, however. Finance theory can be applied to the operation of a corporation by viewing the various components of a business as a portfolio with assets that can be bought and sold. Option pricing theory, in particular, suggests that all of the possibilities for a firm can be regarded as options to buy and sell assets. Bankruptcy, for example, is exercising an option to "sell" the corporation to the debtholders. (However, one critic has called this a "thoroughly immoral view of finance.")

The ethical issues in financial management are twofold.

• Financial managers, as agents and fiduciaries, have an obligation to manage assets prudently and especially to avoid the use of assets for personal benefit. Thus, managers, who have preferential access to information, should not engage in insider trading or self-dealing. For example, management buyouts, in which a group of managers take a public corporation private, raise the question whether people who are paid to mind the store should seek to buy it.

- Financial managers are called upon to make decisions that impact many different groups, and they have an obligation in their decision making to balance some competing interests. For example, should the decision to close a plant be made solely with the shareholders' interests in mind or should the interests of the employees and the local community be taken into account?

## Balancing Competing Interests

In finance theory, the objective of the firm is shareholder wealth maximization (SWM). This objective is reflected in corporate law, according to which officers and directors of corporations are agents of the corporation and have a fiduciary duty to operate the corporation in the interests of the shareholders. Despite the seemingly unequivocal guide of SWM, financial managers still face the need, in some situations, to balance competing interests. In particular, decisions about levels of risk and hostile takeovers reveal some difficulties in the pursuit of SWM.

*The level of risk.* Maximizing shareholder wealth cannot be done without assuming some risk. A critical, often overlooked, task of financial management is determining the appropriate level of risk. Leveraging, for example, increases the riskiness of a firm. The capital asset pricing model suggests that, for properly diversified shareholders, the level of risk for any given firm, called *unique* risk, is irrelevant and that only market or *systemic* risk is important. Finance theory treats bankruptcy as merely an event risk that is worth courting if the returns are high enough. If a firm is in distress, then a high-risk, "bet-the-farm" strategy is especially beneficial to shareholders, because they will reap all the gains of success, while everyone will share the losses of failure (the moral hazard problem). Consequently, a financial manager should seek the highest return adjusted for risk, no matter the actual consequences.

However, a high-risk strategy poses dangers for bondholders, employees, suppliers, and managers themselves, all of whom place a high value on the continued operation of the firm. Employees, in particular, are more vulnerable than shareholders to unique, as opposed to systemic, risk because of their inability to diversify. Is it ethical for financial managers to increase risk in a firm so as to benefit shareholders, at the expense of other corporate constituencies? Does the firm, as an ongoing entity, have value that should be considered in financial decision making? Some have argued that managing purely by financial criteria, without regard for the level of risk, is immoral.

*Hostile takeovers.* Hostile takeovers are often epic battles with winners and losers. For this reason, the rules for acquiring controlling interest should be fair to all parties involved. Managers of target companies feel entitled to a fair chance to defend their jobs; shareholders who sell their shares, and those who do not, have a right to make a decision in a fair and orderly manner; bondholders often lose in takeovers because of the increased debt; and employees and residents of local communities, who usually have no say in the decision, are generally the groups most harmed.

Insofar as a takeover is conducted in a market through the buying and selling of shares, there exists a "market for corporate control." Critics of hostile takeovers question whether such an important decision should be made in the marketplace. Does a market for corporate control provide adequate protection for all of the parties whose interests are affected? Incumbent managers have many defenses. Collectively called "shark repellents," these include poison pills, white knights, lockups, crown jewel options, the Pac-Man defense, golden parachutes, and greenmail. These are frequently criticized for being self-serving and for giving management an undue advantage in thwarting shareholder desires for change.

The directors of a target company, whose approval is often necessary for a successful takeover, have a fiduciary duty to act in the best interests of the firm itself, which may not be identical with the interests of either the preexisting shareholders or those who seek control. A majority of states have adopted so-called other constituency statutes that permit boards of directors to consider other constituencies, such as employees, suppliers, customers, and local communities, in evaluating a takeover bid. Many other laws govern the conduct of raiders and defenders alike, so that the market for corporate control is scarcely a pure market. In general, courts and legislatures have created rules for takeovers that seek both fairness and efficiency.

## *The Financial Theory of the Firm*

The financial argument for SWM, and the legal argument for the fiduciary duties of corporate officers and directors, are each built upon a conception of the business firm as a nexus of contracts between a firm and its constituencies, including shareholders, debtholders, employees, suppliers, and customers. This nexus-of-contracts view of the firm is employed in law and finance as a descriptive model for explaining the legal and financial structure of firms as well as a normative model for justifying fiduciary duties and SWM. The normative adequacy of the nexus-of-contracts view has been challenged, especially by those who contend that corporations have ethical obligations to various nonshareholder constituencies which are not accounted for in the model. Stakeholder theory is offered by some as a more adequate descriptive and normative model of the modern corporation.

Fiduciary duties in corporate law were originally founded on the role of shareholders as the owners of the corporation who had entrusted their assets to management. With the separation of ownership and control in the modern corporation, shareholders ceased to be owners in any meaningful sense, and the fiduciary duties of corporate managers to shareholders are now based on the premise that serving the shareholders' interests maximizes total wealth creation. The aim of corporate governance structures is to restrain managers, who have *de facto* control, from using corporate assets for their own benefit and to give them incentives to apply these assets to their most productive uses. In terms of agency theory, this end can be achieved at the lowest agency cost by imposing a fiduciary duty on managers to maximize shareholder wealth.

In finance theory, shareholders are residual risk bearers, which is to say that they are entitled only to the earnings that remain (the residue) after all other obligations (such as wages to employees and payments to suppliers) are met. The argument, then, is that people with capital would agree to become residual risk bearers only if a firm is operated in their interests. Without this protection, investors would seek other contractual arrangements, such as the guaranteed returns of a bondholder. In the nexus-of-contracts firm, bondholders' returns, employees' wages, and suppliers' payments are assured by fixed-term contracts, but the interests of shareholders can be protected only if management agrees to serve their interests. Furthermore, residual risk bearers have the greatest incentives to ensure that the firm is operated so as to create the maximum amount of wealth. The primacy of shareholder interests thus benefits society as a whole.

## Stockholders vs. Stakeholders

The shareholder-centered financial theory of the firm is criticized for giving inadequate recognition to the rights and interests of nonshareholder constituencies. Critics make four related points concerning ethical standards, externalities, abuses in contracting, and distribution.

*Ethical standards.* Corporations ought to treat all corporate constituencies or stakeholder groups according to certain minimal ethical standards. Agents and fiduciaries do not have a right to advance the interests that they are pledged to serve in ways that violate fundamental rights or inflict wrongful harm. Thus, to expose workers and consumers to hazardous substances, or to exploit labor in lesser-developed countries, is unjustified.

*Externalities.* Business activity imposes great social costs in the form of externalities or spillover effects. When pollution or urban blight, for example, is a direct result of corporate investment decisions, then critics contend that they have an obligation to address these problems.

*Abuses in contracting.* Contracting provides an opportunity for one party to take unfair advantage of the other party. Such advantage-taking occurs in many forms. For example, downsizing may involve breaking an implicit understanding of job security for loyal employees. Some solvent corporations have sought bankruptcy protection so as to avoid paying product liability claims to injured consumers or to renege on collective bargaining agreements. In agency theory, principals are assumed to be vulnerable to shirking by agents, but agents can abuse principals by predatory behavior that has been called "sharking."

*Distribution.* The financial theory of the firm takes no account of the inequalities that result from contracting in the nexus-of-contracts firm. In the United States, the widening gulf between low- and high-wage employees, and the high levels of executive compensation are causes for concern. In general, markets achieve efficiency, not equity, hence the need to attend to the equity/efficiency trade-off.

## Stakeholder Theory

These four sources of ethical problems are acknowledged in the finance literature, and disagreements occur primarily over their solution. Proponents of the financial theory of the firm generally argue that other constituencies should either protect themselves (workers can bargain for safer working conditions, for example) or seek regulatory protection by means of occupational safety and health laws. On the financial theory of the firm, the responsibility for upholding ethical standards, forcing the internalization of costs, and so on, belongs ultimately to government, not to corporate managers. The main argument for this position is that corporate managers have neither the right nor the ability to pursue multiple, nonfinancial goals.

By contrast, stakeholder theory contends that the list of corporate constituencies includes all those who have a legitimate interest in the activities of a firm, regardless of any interest that the firm takes in them. Furthermore, the interests of these stakeholder groups merit consideration for their own sake, not because of their usefulness to the firm. Stakeholder theory has not been developed as a full-fledged alternative to the financial theory, and it is questionable whether it is necessarily incompatible with it. SWM is justified on the financial theory for its benefits to the whole of society, which includes all stakeholder groups. Corporate managers need not consider the interests of all stakeholders as long as these interests are adequately protected by some means, such as government regulation. In addition, managing a corporation with attention to stakeholder interests may be an effective means for maximizing shareholder value. Some very successful companies are driven by philosophies that put employees or customers first.

Finally, the concept of shareholder wealth is problematical. The existence of different kinds of securities blurs the distinction between equity and debt, and creates multiple classes of shareholders with divergent interests. Even holders of ordinary common stock may differ in their risk preferences or time horizons. Some finance research indicates that managing to maximize short-term stock price may not result in maximum shareholder value in the long run. Thus, SWM is not a wholly objective guide for financial managers, and the decisions about the shareholders' interest may themselves involve some value judgments.

# Dilemma of an Accountant

In 1976 Senator Lee Metcalf (D-Mont.) released a report on the public accounting industry which rocked the profession. Despite a decade of revisions in rules and regulations (variously established by the Securities and Exchange Commission, Accounting Principles Board, and Financial Accounting Standards Board), public accounting firms were still perceived by many on Capitol Hill as biased in favor of their clients, incapable of or unwilling to police themselves, and at times participants in coverups of client affairs. Senator Metcalf even went so far as to suggest nationalizing the industry in light of these activities.

Just prior to the Metcalf report, Daniel Potter began working as a staff accountant for Baker Greenleaf, one of the Big Eight accounting firms. In preparation for his CPA examination, Dan had rigorously studied the code of ethics of the American Institute of Certified Public Accountants (AICPA), and had thoroughly familiarized himself with his profession's guidelines for morality. He was aware of ethical situations which might pose practical problems, such as maintaining independence from the client or bearing the responsibility for reporting a client's unlawful or unreasonably misleading activities, and he knew the channels through which a CPA was expected to resolve unethical business policies. Dan had taken the guidelines very seriously: they were not only an integral part of the auditing exam, they also expressed to him the fundamental dignity and calling of the profession—namely, to help sustain the system of checks and balances on which capitalism has been based. Daniel Potter firmly believed that every independent auditor was obligated to maintain professional integrity, if what he believed to be the best economic system in the world was to survive.

Thus, when Senator Metcalf's report was released, Dan was very interested in discussing it with numerous partners in the firm. They responded thoughtfully to the study and were concerned with the possible ramifications of Senator Metcalf's assessment. Dan's discussions at this time and his subsequent experiences during his first year and a half at Baker Greenleaf confirmed his initial impressions that the firm deserved its reputation for excellence in the field.

Dan's own career had been positive. After graduating in Economics from an Ivy League school, he had been accepted into Acorn Business School's accountant training program, and was sponsored by Baker Greenleaf. His enthusiasm and abilities had been clear from the start, and he was rapidly promoted through the ranks and enlisted to help recruit undergraduates to work for the firm. In describing his own professional ethos, Dan endorsed the Protestant work ethic on which he had been raised, and combined this belief with a strong faith in his own worth and responsibility. A strong adherent to the assumptions behind the profession's standards and prepared to defend them as a part of his own self-interest, he backed up his reasoning with an unquestioning belief in loyalty to one's employer and to the clients who helped support his employer. He liked the clear-cut hierarchy of authority and promotion schedule on which Baker Greenleaf was organized, and once had likened his loyalty to his superior to the absolute loyalty which St. Paul advised the slave to have towards his earthly master "out of fear of God" (Col. 3:22). Thus, when he encountered the first situation where both his boss and his client seemed to be departing from the rules of the profession, Dan's moral dilemma was deep-seated and difficult to solve.

The new assignment began as a welcome challenge. A long-standing and important account which Baker had always shared with another Big Eight accounting firm needed a special audit, and Baker had reason to expect that a satisfactory performance might secure it the account exclusively. Baker put its best people on the job, and Dan was elated to be included on the special assignment team; success could lead to an important one-year promotion.

Oliver Freeman, the project senior, assigned Dan to audit a wholly-owned real estate subsidiary (Sub) which had given Baker a lot of headaches in the past. "I want you to solve the problems we're having with this Sub, and come out with a clean opinion (i.e., a confirmation that the client's statements are presented fairly) in one month. I leave it to you to do what you think is necessary."

For the first time Dan was allotted a subordinate, Gene Doherty, to help him. Gene had worked with the project senior several times before on the same client's account, and he was not wholly enthusiastic about Oliver's supervision. "Oliver is completely inflexible about running things his own way—most of the staff accountants hate him. He contributes a 7:00 A.M. to 9:00 P.M. day every day, and expects everyone else to do the same. You've *really* got to put out, on his terms, to get an excellent evaluation from him." Oliver was indeed a strict authoritarian. Several times over the next month Dan and Oliver had petty disagreements over interpretive issues, but when Dan began to realize just how stubborn Oliver was, he regularly deferred to his superior's opinion.

Three days before the audit was due, Dan completed his files and submitted them to Oliver for review. He had uncovered quite a few problems but managed to solve all except one: one of the Sub's largest real estate properties was valued on the balance sheet at $2 million, and Dan's own estimate of its value was no more than $100,000. The property was a run-down structure in an undesirable neighborhood, and had been unoccupied for several years. Dan discussed his proposal to write down the property by $1,900,000 with the Sub's managers, but since they felt there was a good prospect of renting the property shortly, they refused to write down its value. Discussion with the client had broken off at this point, and Dan had to resolve the disagreement on his own. His courses of action were ambiguous, and depended on how he defined the income statement: according to AICPA regulations on materiality, any difference in opinion between the client and the public accountant which affected the income statement by more than 3 percent was considered material and had to be disclosed in the CPA's opinion. The $1,900,000 write-down would have a 7 percent impact on the Sub's net income, but less than 1 percent on the client's consolidated net income. Dan eventually decided that since the report on the Sub would be issued separately (although for the client's internal use only), the writedown did indeed represent a material difference in opinion.

The report which he submitted to Oliver Freeman contained a recommendation that it be filed with a subject-to-opinion proviso, which indicated that all the financial statements were reasonable subject to the $1.9 million adjustment disclosed in the accompanying opinion. After Freeman reviewed Dan's files, he fired back a list of "To Dos," which was the normal procedure at Baker Greenleaf. Included in the list was the following note:

1. Take out the pages in the files where you estimate the value of the real estate property at $100,000.
2. Express an opinion that the real estate properties are correctly evaluated by the Sub.
3. Remove your "subject-to-opinion" designation and substitute a "clean opinion."

Dan immediately wrote back on the list of "To Dos" that he would not alter his assessment since it clearly violated his own reading of accounting regulations. That afternoon Oliver and Dan met behind closed doors.

Oliver first pointed out his own views to Dan:

1. He (Oliver) wanted no problems on this audit. With six years of experience he knew better than Dan how to handle the situation.
2. Dan was responsible for a "clean opinion."
3. Any neglect of his duties would be viewed as an act of irresponsibility.
4. The problem was not material to the client (consolidated) and the Sub's opinion would only be used "in house."
5. No one read or cared about these financial statements anyway.

The exchange became more heated as Dan reasserted his own interpretation of the write-down, which was that it was a material difference to the Sub and a matter of importance from the standpoint of both professional integrity and legality. He posited a situation where Baker issued a clean opinion which the client subsequently used to show prospective buyers of the property in question. Shortly thereafter the buyer might discover the real value of the property and sue for damages. Baker, Oliver, and Dan would be liable. Both men agreed that such a scenario was highly improbable, but Dan continued to question the ethics of issuing a clean opinion. He fully understood the importance of this particular audit and expressed his loyalty to Baker Greenleaf and to Oliver, but nevertheless believed that, in asking him to issue knowingly a false evaluation, Freeman was transgressing the bounds of conventional loyalty. Ultimately a false audit might not benefit Baker Greenleaf or Dan.

Freeman told Dan he was making a mountain out of a molehill and he was jeopardizing the client's account and hence Baker Greenleaf's welfare. Freeman also reminded Dan that his own welfare patently depended on the personal evaluation which he would receive on this project. Dan hotly replied that he would not be threatened, and as he left the room, he asked, "What would Senator Metcalf think?"

A few days later Dan learned that Freeman had pulled Dan's analysis from the files and substituted a clean opinion. He also issued a negative evaluation of Daniel Potter's performance on this audit. Dan knew that he had the right to report the incident to his partner counselor or to the personnel department, but was not terribly satisfied with either approach. He would have preferred to take the issue to an independent review board within the company, but Baker Greenleaf had no such board. However, the negative evaluation would stand, Oliver's arrogance with his junior staff would remain unquestioned, and the files would remain with Dan's name on them unless he raised the incident with someone.

He was not at all sure what he should do. He knew that Oliver's six years with Baker Greenleaf counted for a lot, and he felt a tremendous obligation to trust his superior's judgment and perspective. He also was aware that Oliver was inclined to stick to his own opinions. As Dan weighed the alternatives, the vision of Senator Metcalf calling for nationalization continued to haunt him.

*Mohammad J. Abdolmohammadi*
*Mark R. Nixon*

# Ethics in the Public Accounting Profession

*I know only that what is moral is what you feel good after and
what is immoral is what you feel bad after.*

—Ernest Hemingway

## INTRODUCTION

The American Heritage Dictionary defines profession as "the body of qualified persons in an occupation or field." A major characteristic of a "qualified person" is the specialized knowledge of the profession: medical knowledge for medical doctors, accounting knowledge for certified public accountants (CPAs). Professionals have an ethical responsibility to have acquired the specialized knowledge before offering their professional services. Professionals are also expected to keep abreast of the knowledge enhancements through continuing professional education. Another characteristic of professionals is that they possess the mental attitude of serving the public with the best of their ability so as to earn the public trust. How does a profession enforce these ethical responsibilities? By self-monitoring, supported by a viable code of conduct. In fact, the existence of a code of professional conduct is considered a hallmark of any profession.

The Code of Professional Conduct of the American Institute of Certified Public Accountants (AICPA) is the primary source of guidance for accountants in public practice. Similar codes, issued by the Institute of Management Accountants (IMA) and the Institute of Internal Auditors

From *A Companion to Business Ethics*, ed. Robert E. Frederick (Oxford: Blackwell Publishers Ltd., 1999).

(IIA), govern accountants and auditors in private practice. In recent times, the accounting profession has developed several recognized subspecialties, such as Certified Personal Financial Planner, or Certified Fraud Examiner. Each of the subspecialties have also adopted professional codes of conduct that are consistent with AICPA's Code of Professional Conduct. The focus of this chapter is on professional accountants in public practice. Consequently, we limit our discussion to the CPAs who are obliged to adhere to the Code of Professional Conduct of the AICPA. The AICPA Code (hereafter, the Code) is designed to serve a multitude of purposes:

- A message that the professional CPA has a duty to serve the public (Collins and Schulz, 1995, p. 32)
- A means of conferring legitimacy upon the professional body, i.e., the AICPA (Preston et al., 1995, p. 509)
- Protecting public interest or a client where the professional delivers a specialized service which cannot be easily measured or judged as to its quality (Preston et al., 1995, p. 508; Neale, 1996, p. 223)
- Providing a filtering mechanism to limit the number of professionals to those who are willing and capable of adhering to the Code and unattractive to those who do not abide by it (Neale, 1996, p. 223).

In the remainder of this chapter, first, we briefly discuss the types of services that are provided by CPAs. Of particular importance to the discussion of ethics is ethics audit services as an emerging area of assurance services that major public accounting firms have begun to offer in recent years. Second, we provide a brief discussion of the AICPA's Code of Professional Conduct with a focus on its principles, but also examples of its rules. Third, the elaborate professional ethics enforcement program is discussed, where illustrative cases and descriptive statistics about the AICPA's disciplinary actions over a twenty-year period are provided. The chapter ends with a concluding section where some observations about controversial ethical issues facing the profession are discussed.

## PUBLIC ACCOUNTING SERVICES

The AICPA has approximately 350,000 members, all of whom are CPAs. To be a CPA, most states require that an individual have had some experience in public accounting. The most distinguishing characteristic of a public accounting practice is to provide audit services for financial statements of various businesses. These financial statements are normally used by the CPA's clients to provide information to stockholders, potential investors, creditors, and regulatory agencies. However, not all CPAs remain in public practice. A large number of members of the AICPA are in industry, such as those working in accounting departments of private or public companies. Others are in private practice (provide clients with unaudited financial statements, tax and business consulting), government or education. While there are some minor differences in the ways in which these members keep their AICPA membership in "good standing," they all are required to adhere to the provisions of the Code. (For example, members in public practice are generally subject to more stringent continuing professional education requirements than those in industry or education.) However, due to the importance of the public trust to the profession, those in public practice are scrutinized more closely than others. For this reason, it is important to identify various areas of services provided by the CPAs in public practice with some emphasis on those in ethics audit services.

CPAs in public practice provide these services:

- Audit services
- Compilation and review services
- Attestation services
- Management advisory services, including internal audit services
- Tax services
- Assurance services, including ethics audit services

The purpose of an *audit service* is to add credibility to financial statements of clients by issuing a report on the fair presentation of the financial statements taken as a whole. A vast majority of clients receive a standard three paragraph audit opinion (called an "unqualified" opinion) which is essentially a bill of health. Variations of this opinion indicate that the auditor is either taking some exceptions (called "modified wording" or a "qualified opinion" depending on the extent of the exception), or states that the financial statements are not presented fairly (called an "adverse opinion"). If the auditor finds that he/she is not independent of the client, then a "disclaimer of opinion" is issued. The Auditing Standards Board of the AICPA is responsible for developing the *Statements on Auditing Standards* that must be followed by auditors in the conduct of their audits. It is important to note that the issuance of an independent audit opinion can *only* be made by a CPA. The other services listed below can be provided by individuals that are not CPAs.

A *compilation* is the presentation of financial information, in the form of financial statements, without the CPA expressing any opinion on them. A *review* is where a CPA has conducted only limited procedures and can give only limited assurance that the financial statements require no material modification. Compilation and review services are normally for non-public companies that may not require full audited statements, but do want some limited assurance about the reliability of their financial statements.

The Statement of Standards for Attestation Engagements, *Attestation Standards* (AT Section 100) defines an attest engagement as "one in which a practitioner is engaged to issue or does issue a written communication that expresses a conclusion about the reliability of a written assertion that is the responsibility of another party." If the written communication is about historical financial statements, then the attestation is the same as an audit. However, a client may want an opinion on its representations related to its own internal controls, or investment performance history, or remaining reserves in an oil field. In these types of engagements, the CPA will still be held to the same level of professional standards as if they were auditing financial statements.

*Management advisory services*, including internal audit services, are often referred to as *consulting services*. Most of the consulting is related to the internal operations or planning for a client. A practitioner has developed an expertise in a client's affairs and is probably also an expert in the client's industry. This background makes the practitioner a logical choice to consult on matters related to accounting information systems (including hardware and software choices), inventory planning and flows, executive compensation arrangements, or designing pension and profit-sharing plans.

*Tax services* relate to corporations, other businesses, and individuals. The services can be limited to only the preparation of federal, state, and local tax returns, but frequently include advice on merger and acquisition, tax planning for current tax minimization or estate planning, and representation in tax audits from the Internal Revenue Service. The tax services area is an example where a practitioner is not required to be strictly independent from the client. The practitioner is expected to be an advocate for the client and to minimize the client's total tax liability.

*Assurance services, including ethics audit services* are defined by an AICPA special committee as "independent professional services that improve the quality of information, or its context, for decision makers" (Pallais, 1996, p. 16). Assurance services can include audit and attestation, but also include other nontraditional services. Assurance services are centered on improving the quality of information, and frequently involve situations where one party wants to monitor another, even when both parties work for the same company (Pallais, 1996). Ethics audit services would be an example of the latter service and will be discussed further in a later section.

A recent meeting of the National Association of State Boards of Accountancy concluded that regardless of the type of service provided, CPAs are required to have seven "competencies" (Haberman, 1998, p. 17): four of these competencies are technical in nature (e.g., the ability to assess the achievement of an entity's objectives); one relates to decision making, problem solving, and critical thinking; and another one concerns the ability to communicate the scope of work, findings and conclusions; but the one that is most relevant to ethics is "an understanding of the Code of Professional Conduct." Also, in a National Future Forum held in January 1998, five core values were identified for CPAs: continuing education and lifelong learning, competence, integrity, attunement with broad business issues, and objectivity (CPA Vision Project, 1998). Of particular importance to this chapter are integrity and objectivity that are part of the Code as well. This Code is discussed in the next section.

Among the services identified above, assurance services have gained much attention in recent years as an area of significant growth for the accounting profession. These services are provided to improve the quality of information or its context for decision makers. An example of these assurance services is the CPA *WebTrust*[SM] service by which CPAs assess the reliability of information in company Web sites, and if the information is found to be reliable, the *WebTrust*[SM] seal is stamped on the client's Web site.

The AICPA's Special Committee on Assurance Services (also known as the Elliott Committee after its chairman, Robert Elliott) has proposed many areas of assurance services. Of special interest to ethicists is "assessment of ethics-related risk and vulnerabilities" (Elliott and Pallais, 1997, p. 63). Some accounting firms (e.g., Arthur Andersen, KPMG Peat Marwick) have already begun offering ethics audit services. According to KPMG Peat Marwick, the ethics audit has four components (KPMG, 1997):

- An assessment of the ethical climate of the client encompassing culture, environment, motives, and pressures
- An assessment of performance incentives—the issue is whether the performance incentives provide a motivation to behave outside the moral norm

- The communication of the message about what is acceptable or unacceptable ethical behavior—this communication covers issues of ethical policies, procedures, and training downstream from management to employees; it also covers the nature of upstream communication from employees to management
- Compliance where the policies, procedures, and offices involved in the enforcement of the client's ethics program are assessed.

Although an ethics audit is designed for a company's internal purposes, it is clear that there could be external ramifications. The fact that a company has conducted an ethics audit may have positive implications with outside regulatory agencies, suppliers, customers, or prospective employees.

Ethics audit services are partly governed by *Statements on Auditing Standards* promulgated by the Auditing Standards Board (1997). However, there are significant differences between ethics audits and financial audits. For example, an ethics audit is used to identify a client's areas of vulnerability in comparison with its industry benchmarks. This is different from comparison of a company's ethical performance with absolute ethical philosophies. It is also different from a financial audit where the fairness of financial statements is assessed against generally accepted accounting principles. KPMG Peat Marwick LLP states that an ethics audit is a "positive confirmation of the existence and effective implementation of best ethical practices" (KPMG, 1996).

A concern about the multitude of services provided by CPAs is that conflict of interest may arise from an auditor performing the financial audit as well as other services. This is said to threaten auditor independence. As discussed in the next section, independence is one of the major rules in the Code. In the past, it was not uncommon for auditors to decline engagements or not provide additional services if there was any threat, real or perceived, to their independence. We will return to a discussion of the magnitude of this issue in the final section. Suffice it to say here that, today, it is common for CPAs to avoid this problem by offering various services from separate divisions of the audit firm so as to minimize issues of conflict of interest. In one case, the accounting firm split into two separate entities: Andersen World-wide split into Arthur Andersen to provide audit and tax services and Andersen Consulting to provide management advisory services. Recently, however, Andersen Consulting has alleged that Arthur Andersen is also providing management advisory services to its big clients against the contract that resulted in the split of Andersen in the first place.

## AICPA'S CODE OF PROFESSIONAL CONDUCT

The AICPA's mission statement charges its CPA members with the responsibility to "serve the public interest in performing the highest quality of professional services" (AICPA, 1988, p. vii). The code calls for honorable behavior, even at the sacrifice of personal interest. Various steps are necessary to prepare the CPA for these services. These steps include education, certification, licensing, and practice, but also a mental ability and commitment to discharging one's responsibility with care and diligence. (Note that all states require that CPAs in public practice be licensed. A CPA may choose not to be a member of the AICPA, and thus not subject to the AICPA code. However, most state licensing authorities have adopted the AICPA code as their ethical and professional standards.)

The AICPA's Code of Professional Conduct states, in its preamble, that being a member is voluntary, but by accepting membership one assumes an obligation to the public, clients, and colleagues. To guide behavior, the AICPA has instituted a code that has four components:

- Principles of professional conduct
- Rules of conduct
- Interpretations of rules of conduct
- Rulings by the Professional Ethics Division of the AICPA and its Trial Board

### Table 1. AICPA's Principles of Professional Conduct

| *Principle* | *AICPA Directive* |
| --- | --- |
| 1. Responsibilities | In carrying out their responsibilities as professionals, members should exercise sensitive professional and moral judgments in all their activities. |
| 2. The public interest | Members should accept the obligation to act in a way that will serve the public interest, honor the public trust, and demonstrate commitment to professionalism. |
| 3. Integrity | To maintain and broaden public confidence, members should perform all professional responsibilities with the highest sense of integrity. |
| 4. Objectivity and independence | A member should maintain objectivity and be free of conflicts of interest in discharging professional responsibilities. A member in public practice should be independent in fact and appearance when providing auditing and other attestation services. |

| 5. | Due care | A member should observe the profession's technical and ethical standards, strive continually to improve competence and the quality of services, and discharge professional responsibility to the best of the member's ability. |
| 6. | Scope and nature of services | A member in public should observe the Principles of the Code of Professional Conduct in determining the scope and nature of services to be provided. |

*Source:* AICPA (1988)

There are six principles in the code. These principles and the AICPA directives related to them are listed in table 1. They provide the basic foundation of ethical and professional conduct that is expected of the CPA. However, due to their conceptual nature, these principles are not enforceable. Nevertheless, they point to the importance of public interest (Principles 1 and 2) and the requisite moral characteristics of CPAs in public practice (Principles 3–6).

The Rules of Conduct and the Interpretations of the Rules of Conduct are more specific in nature than the principles, and as such, they are enforceable. A detailed discussion of these rules and their interpretation is beyond the scope of this chapter but may be found in the AICPA publications and standard auditing texts. To show the general tenet of the rules, we provide a summary here:

- Section 100: Independence, Integrity, and Objectivity (e.g., Rule 102-2 prohibiting conflict of interest)
- Section 200: General Standards and Accounting Principles (e.g., Rule 201-1 requiring competence)
- Section 300: Responsibilities to Clients (e.g., Rule 301-1 prohibition of dissemination of any confidential client information obtained during the course of an audit)
- Section 500: Other Responsibilities and Practices (e.g., Rule 501-1 forbidding retention of client records)

Section 400 that related to responsibilities to colleagues no longer has any rules at this time. However, concurrent with the issuance of the new code in 1988, the AICPA also approved a mandatory quality peer review program where CPA firms provide reviews of the quality of practice in other CPA firms and present recommendations for improvement. The AICPA also established a number of practice-monitoring committees to facilitate these peer reviews for CPA firms.

The final component of the code, Rulings by the Professional Ethics Division and the Trial Board of the AICPA, relates to the AICPA's activities to enforce the rules and their interpretations. These issues are discussed in the next section.

## ENFORCEMENT OF THE CODE OF CONDUCT

Violations of the code can be diverse and numerous. A detailed listing and discussion of these violations is beyond the scope of this chapter. Here are several examples:

- A CPA was engaged to prepare the financial statements of a company and then audited those same financial statements—a violation of the rule of independence.
- A practitioner prepared a fraudulent tax return on a client's behalf.
- A practitioner did not have the necessary technical skills to perform required work for an engagement—a violation of competence.
- A CPA did not release documents to a client—a violation of Rule 501-l requirements.

These violations result in disciplinary actions by the AICPA such as admonishment, termination or suspension of membership in the institute. Since 1975, the Joint Trial Board of the AICPA has been the source of disciplinary action with the participation of some state societies. This cooperation has recently been expanded to include virtually all fifty states and has resulted in the establishment of the Joint Ethics Enforcement Program (JEEP) since 1995. JEEP maximizes the resources for investigation and eliminates duplication (News Report, 1995).

Penalties for violation of the code range from a recommendation that a member take remedial or corrective action, to a permanent expulsion from the AICPA. For example, a member who has violated the code may be recommended by the Professional Ethics Division to take a continuing professional education course. If the member does not comply with the recommendation, the Ethics Division may refer him/her to the Trial Board for a hearing. The Trial Board may suspend a member for up to two years or expel him or her for violating the code. In cases where a crime punishable by imprisonment for more than one year has occurred the member is automatically suspended or terminated from AICPA membership. A similar penalty can be imposed for filing a false income tax return on a client's behalf.

The disciplinary actions of the Joint Trial Board are publicized in the AICPA's newsletter, *The CPA Letter*. Generally, this means that a similar action has been taken by the professional state society of CPAs in the state where the violator has membership. (Note that a CPA can have membership in more than one state society. Furthermore, a CPA can get licensing from various state boards of CPA for practice in multiple states.) These state societies have codes of professional conduct for their membership that are identical with, or similar to, the AICPA code (AICPA, 1997, p. 6).

On the surface, the actions taken by the AICPA and/or state societies of CPAs may appear to be insignificant in nature since membership in these associations is voluntary and one can resign at any time. In reality, an action such as termination of membership may indeed tarnish one's reputation as a CPA to the extent that one would voluntarily leave the profession altogether. Also, consider the fact that the practice of public accounting requires licensing by governmental regulatory agencies such as state boards of public accountancy. The AICPA and/or state society actions to terminate or suspend membership may precede or succeed revocation or suspension of practice licenses by state boards of accountancy. Thus, the CPA may be barred from practice, involuntarily, for a period of time or forever, depending on the nature of the violation.

State boards of public accountancy have been set up to enforce state accounting laws. These boards are generally charged with the responsibility of overseeing the accounting profession in their states. Consequently, they have mechanisms by which complaints against CPAs are documented, investigated, and adjudicated. These complaints "can come from a variety of sources, including clients, third parties such as federal, state, and local governments, and other CPAs, especially successor accountants and auditors. The state board must investigate each complaint to assess its merit and, if necessary, determine the appropriate corrective action" (Ruble, 1997).

The disciplinary actions taken by state boards of accountancy and state societies of CPAs may also be the result of court action against a member. For example, a criminal conviction in a court of law may automatically result in suspension or termination of membership in state societies and the AICPA, as well as loss of practice license by the state board of public accountancy.

As stated earlier, violations of the AICPA code may require a hearing by the Ethics Division of the AICPA or its Trial Board. State societies of CPAs have similar mechanisms, and they cooperate closely with the AICPA. Virtually all state boards have joined with the AICPA to create the Joint Ethics Enforcement Program (JEEP). This program has developed a detailed manual for effective and efficient treatment of code violations. According to the AICPA professional standards and the provisions of the JEEP manual (AICPA, 1997), there are two distinct methods of dealing with member violations. The first is suspension or termination of membership without a hearing, i.e., automatic disciplinary action. The second is the AICPA disciplinary action process where provisions are made for a hearing.

The automatic sanctions are generally the result of court actions or other governmental (e.g., Securities and Exchange Commission) actions against CPAs. As soon as notification is received by the secretary of the AICPA, a suspension or termination notice is automatically mailed to the member via registered or certified mail. If the member does not appeal, then the action is viewed as final and publicized in *The CPA Letter*. However, if the member appeals in writing, then the Trial Board forwards the appeal to an *ad hoc* committee for a decision. If the appeal is granted, then the case is forwarded to the Ethics Division for appropriate action. Otherwise, the automatic decision is affirmed and publicized in *The CPA Letter*. The disciplinary action is termination in cases of:

- crime punishable by imprisonment for more than a year;
- willful failure to file an income tax return when required by law;
- filing false or fraudulent income tax return on own or client behalf; and
- willful aid in preparation and presentation of a false and fraudulent income tax return of a client.

Membership will be revoked or suspended without a hearing if the member's practice license is suspended or revoked as a disciplinary action by a governmental agency.

The cases that do not result in automatic suspension or termination of membership are code violations that have been brought to the attention of state societies or the AICPA through complaints made by individuals, clients, or other CPAs. JEEP processes these cases. The member can plead guilty and/or resign from the AICPA and state society membership. In this case, the Trial Board may recommend acceptance of the member's resignation, but require that the member appear for a hearing by the Trial Board at a later date. If the member does not plead guilty or the Trial Board does not accept the member's resignation, a panel is set up by the Trial Board for investigation of the case. The Trial Board may choose not to accept a member's resignation due to the seriousness of a violation. They may feel that, to serve the public interest, the member needs to be publicly expelled. The panel may decide that no action is necessary or may schedule a hearing. The result of the hearing may be that no action is necessary or that the member must be admonished, suspended, terminated, or must perform some activity such as taking $x$ hours of continuing professional education. The member can appeal this decision within thirty days, and if granted, the Trial Board will review the decision and will uphold it, change it, or find the member innocent and inform the member of its decision. If the decision is that a violation had occurred for which disciplinary action is taken, then the decision is publicized in *The CPA Letter*.

## ILLUSTRATIVE DISCIPLINARY ACTIONS

To illustrate the disciplinary actions against CPAs, we first present the facts about an individual who was found to have violated the AICPA code. We will then present descriptive data to show the extent of the disciplinary actions taken over a twenty-year period. This information is extracted from a disciplinary action database we have compiled from an examination of *The CPA Letter* published from 1977 till 1996.

Case 353 occurred in 1990. The individual was found to have violated the AICPA code by having assisted in the preparation of a false tax return and having obstructed justice by lying about it (i.e., perjury). The information came from conviction in the court of law and automatically resulted in termination of AICPA membership.

A summary of the twenty-year data is presented in table 2. The data are classified by the type of disciplinary action (termination, suspension, and other) and by the source of action (automatic or hearing). Also provided are the averages per year. These averages are calculated by dividing the raw numbers by twenty years (1977–1996). Finally, we have divided the average yearly disciplinary actions by the average number of members in the AICPA over the twenty-year period to find the average number of disciplinary actions per 10,000 AICPA members.

Several observations from table 2 are interesting to note. First, a majority of cases were automatic disciplinary actions. Of the 488 terminations, 330 were automatic as compared with 158 that resulted from the

Joint Trial Board hearings. Similarly, . . . of the 250 cases of suspension, 138 were automatic as compared with 112 that resulted from hearings. The exception was "other" cases that resulted in admonishment, censure or other types of disciplinary actions. None of these cases was the result of an automatic disciplinary action. Thus, overall, of the 803 cases, 468 were subjects of automatic action as compared with 335 hearings by the Joint Trial Board.

### Table 2. AICPA's Disciplinary Action Statistics 1977–1996

| Disciplinary action | Source | | | |
|---|---|---|---|---|
| | Automatic | Hearing | Total | Average Per 10,000 |
| Termination | 330 | 158 | 488 | |
| | 16.5 /year) | (7.9/year) | (24.4/year) | 1.1 |
| Suspension | 138 | 112 | 250 | |
| | (6.9/year) | (5.6/year) | (12.5/year) | 0.5 |
| Other (e.g., admonish | 0 | 65 | 65 | |
| or censure) | (0/year) | (3.25/year) | (3.25/year) | 0.1 |
| Total | 468 | 335 | 803 | |
| | (23.4/year) | (16.75/year) | (40.15/year) | 1.7 |
| Average per 10,000 | 1.0 | 0.7 | 1.7 | |
| Membership size: 1977 | 130,331 | | | |
| 1996 | 324,938 | | | |
| Average | 227,634 | | | |

Source: Disciplinary Action Database compiled by the authors from the CPA Letter.

Second, a related observation is that a majority of the cases, automatic or hearing, resulted in the termination of the violator from the AICPA membership. Of the 468 automatic cases, 330 resulted in termination of membership. Similarly, 158 of the 335 hearing cases resulted in termination of the violator. Suspension was next followed by "other" disciplinary actions.

Third, the average per 10,000 membership indicates that overall, only 1.7 persons (1 automatic and 0.7 from hearing) were disciplined per year. Of these, 1.1 were terminated, 0.5 were suspended, and 0.1 were subjected to other disciplinary actions.

A conclusion from this data is that violations of the Code by the AICPA members are rare. The assumption is that all major cases are detected and adjudicated by the AICPA, state boards of accountancy, and state societies of CPAs. There are, of course, unreported or undetected violations of the code as well. Thus, the true level of ethical behavior is not possible to observe. However, it is in the best interest of a self-regulating profession to expose unethical behavior. With this in mind, there are several significant overall ethical controversies facing the profession and these are discussed in the next section.

## CONTROVERSIAL ETHICAL ISSUES IN THE ACCOUNTING PROFESSION

As discussed in the previous sections, the accounting profession has developed a code of conduct and has an elaborate disciplinary program in place to enforce the code. Surveys of CPAs (e.g., Cohen and Pant, 1991) indicate that the code and its enforcement are viewed as effective for the professional body. This does not, however, mean that the profession has been free from criticism. While CPAs, in general, do not believe that unethical behavior leads to success, they do perceive that opportunities exist in the accounting profession to engage in unethical behavior. This is because surveys of CPAs indicate that some clients request fraudulent alteration of tax returns or financial statements (Finn et al., 1988).

Critics allege that these client pressures, causing ethical problems for the profession, are partly due to the professionals having abandoned the legitimacy of ethical character that was the norm in the early 1900s. Critics support this allegation by noting that, in the early 1900s, there were virtually no general auditing or accounting standards, while today there is a large complicated set of standards and rules. Critics claim that today's CPAs rely on "following the rules" rather than focusing on what is the best, fairest or clearest presentation of accounting information. As technical expertise has become the cornerstone of the CPA practice, the legitimacy of technique has replaced the legitimacy of character (Abbott, 1988, p. 190). Even within this technical expertise, critics argue that some CPAs have ignored their clients' creative accounting in which earnings have been manipulated in some cases. For example, Lomas Financial Corporation has filed a $300 million lawsuit against its auditors alleging that two audit partners collaborated with the management of Lomas Financial Corporation to conceal risky financial practices that contributed to the company's failure (MacDonald, 1997).

Similarly, a large potential area of concern for CPA firms is the exposure to lawsuits from consulting engagements. The largest lawsuit yet filed against a CPA firm ($4 billion) was related to a consulting engagement by an accounting firm to develop and implement a "turnaround plan" for Merry-Go-Round Enterprises (MacDonald, 1997). The suit alleges fraud, fraudulent concealment, negligence, and lack of independence. These are issues that are normally raised in an audit engagement lawsuit. William Brewer, an attorney, states "It's an unusual suit. Big Six accounting firms have generally not been sued for their consulting work. However, it's a sign of the times. You'll see many more of these cases in the future as accountants hold themselves out as business consultants" (MacDonald, 1997, p. 312).

In other cases, rapid changes in information technology have brought the CPA's knowledge under question. The new information technology has also changed the public need for CPA services. For example, whereas traditional audited financial statements were issued three or four months after the closing of the client's fiscal year, the new technology has made it possible to provide the information on line and in real time. As mentioned earlier, the profession has responded by developing the *WebTrusts*SM service to respond to this need.

Perhaps the most significant ethical challenge to the profession is the question of independence. It has been alleged that auditors systematically violate the code's independence rule. The code is clear in its direction of the need for independence, not only in fact which is unobservable, but also in appearance which can be observed by third parties. The auditor may, in fact, exercise independence from the client even if he or she has financial interest in the company. However, to assure independence in appearance, the auditor is prohibited from having any direct interest such as stock ownership in the client, or significant indirect interest such as ownership of stocks in the client by the CPA's close relatives.

Critics argue that independence rules must also be addressed in cases of providing conflicting services to the client. For example, how can an auditor be independent of his or her client in conducting a financial audit if the auditor is also the one who had provided advice in the development or purchase of the client's accounting system? Similarly, the profession has been criticized for taking inadequate responsibility for detecting fraudulent financial reporting by clients in situations where the auditor's self interest has been on the line. These allegations have resulted in Congressional investigations of the profession. For example, Senator Metcalf investigated the profession in 1976 (U.S. Senate, 1976) while Senator Moss did the same in 1978 (U.S. Senate, 1978). (A detailed discussion of these investigations and the profession's response to them is beyond the scope of this chapter; they are stated here to show the significance of the issues.)

The profession's response has been to set up commissions to investigate these issues, and to provide recommendations based on which new pronouncements could be issued. For example, in response to Senators Metcalf and Moss investigations, the AICPA established The Commission on Auditors' Responsibilities in the mid-1970s (The Cohen Commission, 1973). The recommendations from this commission led to the establishment of another commission later to investigate fraudulent financial reporting (The Treadway Commission, 1987) and later to yet another commission (COSO, 1992) that made a long list of recommendations. As a result of the recommendations of these commissions, the profession has taken significant steps to enhance its guidance for practitioners by issuing new pronouncements. The revised Code of Conduct issued in 1988 (AICPA, 1988) tightened the code requirements by eliminating some ambiguous and controversial sections. Specifically, the new code allows for advertising by CPAs that was prohibited by the earlier code. In the same year, the Auditing Standards Board issued a package of nine new *Statements on Auditing Standards* (dubbed expectation gap standards) to provide better guidance to the auditors in their conduct of the financial audit. More recently, the Auditing Standards Board responded to the Treadway Commission (1987) and COSO (1992) reports by issuing a new *Statement on Auditing Standards No. 82* that requires auditors to plan the audit so that if fraud exists, it can be detected (Auditing Standards Board, 1997). In the past, the profession steadfastly denied responsibility to plan the audit for the purpose of detecting fraud although it maintained that if fraud was indicated in the course of the normal audit, it would be investigated.

Other contemporary ethical issues confronting the profession include confidentiality, public confidence, and serving the public interest.

## *Confidentiality*

The CPA is entrusted with a large amount of information from the client. The auditor is prohibited to share this information with others, except in response to court order and other exceptional situations. For example, the auditor can provide financial ratios to industry trade groups so long as specific client information is not revealed. However, the auditor cannot use confidential information for self or other financial interests such as trading stocks based on the insider information gathered in the course of the audit.

## Public Confidence

The profession allows CPAs to advertise, but through its ethics rulings limits the type of advertising to those that enhance public confidence. For example, contingent fees and commissions are not allowed for referral of attest function services (i.e., audits, compilation, and reviews), but allowed for management advisory services. Contingent fees and referral commissions were prohibited altogether until 1988 when under pressure from The Federal Trade Commission, the AICPA council voted to change the rule (Mintz, 1990, p. 3). Nevertheless, critics argue that advertising has helped change public accounting from a profession to a business (Mason, 1994).

## Serving the Public Interest

As stated earlier, the profession only recently has begun to accept responsibility for planning the audit for detection of fraud and other illegal acts (Auditing Standards Board, 1997). More needs to be done to clarify the CPA's responsibility to the public. For example, should the CPA engage in whistle-blowing when an illegal act or fraud is detected to have been committed by a client? As critics argue, at the present time, "the resolution of conflicts between an accountant's client, on the one hand, and the general public, on the other, is usually balanced in favor of the client. The legal system supports this outcome, at least for the time being" (Epstein and Spalding, 1993, p. 271). Others argue that the source of this problem is the weight that is placed on confidentiality at the expense of public interest (Collins and Schulz, 1995).

## CONCLUSION

The accounting profession has developed an elaborate Code of Conduct complete with a continuing education and an effective enforcement program. However, more needs to be done to make accountants more responsive to public expectations to enhance public trust. While the profession has been forthcoming in its responses to Congressional hearings and private commission recommendations in the past two decades, more is needed to continue building a more trustworthy profession. This is especially urgent in light of the speedy change that is fostered by the age of information technology.

# REFERENCES

Abbott, A. 1988. *The System of Professions: An Essay on the Division of Expert Labor.* Chicago, Ill.: University of Chicago Press.

AICPA. 1988. *Code of Professional Conduct.* New York: AICPA.

AICPA. 1997. *Joint Ethics Enforcement Program (JEEP): Manual of Procedures.* New York: AICPA.

Auditing Standards Board. 1997. *Statement on Auditing Standards No. 82: Consideration of Fraud in a Financial Statement Audit.* New York: AICPA.

Cohen, J. R., and L. W. Pant. 1991. "Beyond Bean Counting: Establishing High Ethical Standards in the Public Sccounting Profession." *Journal of Business Ethics*, 10, 45–56.

Collins, A., and N. Schulz. 1995. "A Critical Examination of the AICPA Code of Professional Conduct." *Journal of Business Ethics*, 14, 31–41.

COSO (Committee of Sponsoring Organizations of the Treadway Commission). 1992. *Internal Control: Integrated Framework.* Harborside, N.J.: AICPA.

CPA Vision Project. 1998. "CPA Vision Project Identifies Top Five Core Values." *The CPA Letter* 1 (June): 9.

Elliott, R. K., and D. M. Pallais. 1997. "First: Know Your Market." *Journal of Accountancy* (July): 56–63.

Epstein, M. J., and A. D. Spalding. 1993. *The Accountant's Guide to Legal Liability and Ethics.* Boston, Mass.: Irwin.

Finn, D. W., L. B. Chenko, and S. D. Hunt. 1988. "Ethical Problems in Public Accounting: The View from the Top." *Journal of Business Ethics*, 7, 605–15.

Haberman, L. D. 1998. "Regulatory Reform at NASBA." *Journal of Accountancy.* (February): 16–17.

KPMG. 1996. *Innovating Best Ethical Practices.* Montvalle, N.J.: KPMG Peat Marwick LLP.

KPMG. 1997. "Creating the Moral Organization." *KPMG Internet Web Site.* Montvalle, NJ: KPMG Peat Marwick, LLP.

MacDonald, E. 1997. "Trustee Files $4 Billion Lawsuit against Ernst & Young." *The Wall Street Journal*, December 2, 240, B 12.

Mason, E. 1994. "Public Accounting: No Longer a Profession?" *The CPA Journal* 64, no. 6 (July): 34–37.

Mintz, S. 1990. *Cases in Accounting Ethics and Professionalism.* New York: McGraw-Hill.

Neale, A. 1996. "Conduct, Misconduct and Accounting." *Journal of Business Ethics*, 15, 219–26.

News Report. 1995. "New Era in Ethics Enforcement." *Journal of Accountancy*, August 13.

*New York Times*. 27 December 1997, pp. 147, B147.

Pallais, D. 1996. "Assurance Services: Where We Are, Where We're Going." *Journal of Accountancy* 182, no. 3 (September): 16–17.

Preston, A. M., D. J. Cooper, and D. P. Scarbrough. 1995. "Changes in the code of Ethics of the US Accounting Profession. 1917 and 1988: The Continual Quest for Legitimization." *Accounting, Organizations and Society* (August): 507–46.

Ruble, M. R. 1997. "Letter from the State Board: What Should You Do Next?" *Journal of Accountancy* 183 no. 5 (May): 75.

The Cohen Commission. 1978. *Report, Conclusions, and Recommendations*. New York: AICPA.

The Treadway Commission. 1987. *Report of the National Commission on Fraudulent Financial Reporting*. New York: AICPA.

US Senate Subcommittee on Reports, Accounting and Management of the Committee on Governmental Affairs: the Metcalf Committee 1976: *The Accounting Establishment*. Washington, D.C.: U.S. Government Printing Office.

US Senate: the Moss Committee 1978: *Report of the Committee on Auditors' Responsibilities*. Washington, D.C.: U.S. Government Printing Office.

# SELECT BIBLIOGRAPHY

Arganda, A., ed. *The Ethical Dimension of Financial Institutions and Markets.* New York: Springer-Verlag, 1995.

Baker, H., E. Veit, and M. Murphy. *Ethics in the Investment Profession: An International Survey.* Charlottesville, Va.: Institute of Chartered Financial Analysts, 1995.

Bear, L., and R. Maldonado-Bear. *Free Markets, Finance, Ethics, and Law.* Englewood Cliffs, N.J.: Prentice-Hall, 1994.

Boatright, J. *Ethics in Finance.* Oxford: Blackwell, 1999.

Causey, D., and S. Causey. *Duties and Liabilities of Public Accountants.* Mississippi State, Miss.: Accountants Press, 1995.

Collins, A., and N. Schultz. "A Critical Examination of the AICPA Code of Professional Conduct." *Journal of Business Ethics* 14 (1995): 31–41.

Collins, D. *Ethical Dilemmas in Accounting.* Belmont, Calif.: South-Western, ITP, 1994.

Dobson, J., ed. *Finance Ethics: The Rationality of Virtue.* Lanham, Md.: Rowman and Littlefield, 1997.

Edwards, J., and R. Hermanson. *Essentials of Financial Accounting with Ethics Cases.* Burr Ridge, Ill.: Irwin, 1993.

——. *Essentials of Managerial Accounting with Ethics Cases.* Burr Ridge, Ill.: Irwin, 1993.

Epstein, M., and A. Spalding. *The Accountant's Guide to Legal Liability and Ethics.* Boston, Mass.: Irwin, 1993.

Hoffman, W., J. Kamm, and R. Frederick, eds. *The Ethics of Accounting and Finance: Trust, Responsibility and Control.* Westport, Conn.: Quorum Books, 1996.

Loeb, S., ed. *Ethics in the Accounting Profession,* Santa Barbara: Wiley, 1978.

Lynch, J. *Banking and Finance: Managing the Moral Dimension.* New York: American Educational Systems, 1994.

Manne, H. *Insider Trading and the Stock Market.* New York: Free Press, 1966.

Mintz, S. *Cases in Accounting Ethics and Professionalism.* New York: McGraw-Hill, 1990.

Parks, R. *The Witch Doctor of Wall Street.* Amherst, N.Y.: Prometheus Books, 1996.

Prindl, A., and B. Prodhan, eds. *Ethical Conflicts in Finance: The ACT Guide.* Oxford: Blackwell, 1994.

Twentieth Century Fund. *Abuse on Wall Street: Conflicts of Interest in the Securities Markets.* Westport, Conn.: Quorum Books, 1990.

Veit, E., and M. Murphy. *Ethics in the Investment Profession: A Survey.* Charlottesville, Va.: Institute of Chartered Financial Analysts, 1992.

Williams, O., F. Reilly, and J. Houck, eds. *Ethics and the Investment Industry.* Lanham, Md.: Rowman and Littlefield, 1989.

## ELECTRONIC SOURCES

The Institute of Internal Auditors   www3.theiia.org
AICPA Code of Professional Conduct   www.aicpa.org/about/code/index.htm

# 6. BUSINESS AND THE CONSUMER

## INTRODUCTION

In producing and marketing goods and services, the firm incurs moral and legal obligations to the consumer. The consumer also has responsibilities with regard to the use of a product. This chapter discusses three key issues in the relationship between business and consumers: product safety, advertising, and selling.

Until 1916 a manufacturer was not legally liable for an injury to a consumer unless there was privity (private knowledge) of contract between manufacturer and consumer, i.e., purchasers could sue only those who sold an item directly to them. Since few manufacturers sold goods directly to the public, most were immune from suit. Recent times have seen a legal shift from *caveat emptor* (let the buyer beware) to *caveat venditor* (let the seller beware). Strict liability, the dominant product liability theory at present, only requires that a consumer prove the product was defective and caused the injury. Strict liability is grounded in part in utilitarian considerations; it encourages manufacturers to make safer products, which results in fewer accidents. George Brenkert argues that strict liability is also consistent with and, indeed, rests upon, the foundations of the free market. Robert Malott suggests a variety of problems with the strict liability doctrine and argues for a set of constraints on strict liability that he believes would make the law more reasonable and fair. In contrast, Beverly Moore argues that strict liability does not adequately protect consumers; he advocates the theory of absolute liability, i.e., the producer should be liable for any injury, regardless of fault.

Advertising has been subject to perhaps more criticism than any other business practice; the section on advertising discusses the central criticisms. John Z. Miller, following Galbraith, argues that advertisements create desires which the producer of the advertised product then satisfies. He claims that advertising actually undercuts the free market, which assumes the producer merely satisfies antecedently existing desires.

Miller also argues that advertising is bad because it is so pervasive and promotes materialistic values exclusively. Finally, Miller argues that advertising is often deceptive, misleading, or simply provides no information to consumers. In response, Charles Collins argues that advertising is a form of speech, and hence producers have a right to advertise their products. He argues that all advertising provides consumers with some information, and that many advertisements labeled by critics as "deceptive" are not properly classified. Collins claims, against Galbraith and Miller, that advertising does not create desires; he also argues that advertising cannot be said to control consumer behavior.

Although most business schools do not include a course on selling, more graduates probably start in sales than in any other area of business. David Holley accepts the basic framework of the free market and then describes three features that must be met in sales practices for the successful functioning of the free market. The case study presents five scenarios that we will all face as buyers or sellers.

# PRODUCT SAFETY

*Case Study*

# *Biss* v. *Tenneco, Inc.*

Robert Biss was injured when a loader he was operating went off the road, collided with a telephone pole, and pinned him between the loader and the pole. Shortly before he died, Biss told witnesses that he lost control of the loader. Mrs. Biss brought suit against Tenneco, the loader's manufacturer, based on an alleged design defect in the loader since it was not equipped with a rollover protection structure, known as a ROPS.

The action involved a so-called second collision issue; that is, the claim was not that the loader itself had a design defect, thus causing the accident, but that there was a design defect that caused or enhanced the injuries arising from the accident. Tenneco, it was claimed, should have provided a ROPS as standard, rather than optional, equipment, and its failure to do so constituted a design defect that caused or enhanced Biss's injuries arising from the accident. The New York Supreme Court considered the following to be the applicable rule of law:

> A manufacturer is obligated to exercise that degree of care in his plan or design so as to avoid any unreasonable risk of harm to anyone who is likely to be exposed to the danger when the product is used in the manner for which the product was intended, as well as unintended yet reasonably foreseeable use.

409 N.Y.S. 2d 874 (A.D. 1978)

The court reasoned that manufacturers are not obligated to provide accident-proof merchandise but they are required to exercise reasonable care. There was no defect in the loader itself, and a ROPS was available to the purchaser, Vincent Centers, for whom Biss worked. Accordingly, the court ruled:

> That being so, defendants had fulfilled their duty to exercise reasonable skill and care in designing the product as a matter of law when they advised the purchaser that an appropriate safety structure for the loader was available.

The court pointed out that injury from a rollover accident is posed by the use of construction equipment, but noted that the danger varies according to the job and site for which the equipment is used:

> It is not a danger inherent in a properly constructed loader. Neither is it a danger which the manufacturer alone may discover or one which he is more favorably positioned to discover. If knowledge of the available safety options is brought home to the purchaser (Vincent Centers) the duty to exercise reasonable care in selecting those appropriate to the intended use rests upon him. He is the party in the best position to exercise an intelligent judgment to make the trade-off between cost and function, and it is he who should bear the responsibility if the decision on optional safety equipment presents an unreasonable risk to users. To hold otherwise casts the manufacturer and supplier in the role of insurers answerable to injured parties in any event, because the purchaser of the equipment for his own reasons, economic or otherwise, elects not to purchase available options to ensure safety.

Mrs. Biss's suit against Tenneco was dismissed, 3–0.

## FOR DISCUSSION

What theory of product liability has the court applied in this case? Do you agree with this theory? Why or why not? Do you agree with the court's decision in this particular case? Why or why not? If Mrs. Biss sued Vincent Centers, rather the Tenneco, do you believe she should (legally and morally) win? Why or why not?

# *Austin* v. *Ford Motor Co.*

A variation of the second collision issue was presented in the case of Barbara Austin, who died in a one-car accident. A motorist testified that Ms. Austin passed him when he was traveling at a speed of 65 to 70 mph. The Austin auto, a Ford, was estimated to have been going 20 to 25 mph faster than the vehicle she passed—a speed of approximately 90 mph—when her car left the road, rolled over twice, and landed on its top. Ms. Austin was thrown from her car and killed. A state police officer found a portion of Austin's seat belt on the ground and a portion still attached to the front seat.

The plaintiffs, Ms. Austin's children, produced two witnesses who provided evidence that she was wearing a seat belt, and that a defective belt was a cause of death. According to the testimony of a state police technician, a microscopic examination of the belt showed that the webbing had been irregularly cut through. He said that a sharp instrument was needed to cut the belt, that the cut portion was not normally visible, and that nothing in the auto could have caused the cut. An engineer testified to the probable causal connection between the seat belt's breaking and Austin's death. Ford countered that it was probable that the impact of the accident was of sufficient force to cause Austin's death.

The court's opinion focused on the issue of causation:

> The accident was a grievous one and the facts support a finding of negligent driving by the decedent. But the heart of the case is causation, not of the accident but of the death. In an action such as this, is it a permissible inference or conclusion that decedent's negligent driving was a cause of her death? . . . The court is persuaded to the conclusion that it is not.

The court distinguished the cause of the accident from the cause of Austin's death. Ms. Austin's negligence caused the accident, but, since seat belts are designed to protect the wearer in the event of a collision,

273 N.W. 2d 233 (1979)

including a collision that is caused by the driver's own negligence, the court regarded Austin's negligent driving as an irrelevant factor in assessing the cause of her death. The court reasoned that Austin would have survived the accident had the seat belt not been dangerously defective, and hence the defective seat belt was a cause of death.

> . . . Ford's negligence in furnishing an unsafe and defective seat belt was found to be a cause of the death of Barbara Austin and there is no evidence to show that Barbara Austin's own negligence contributed to her death. . . .

Judge Coffey dissented from the majority's opinion:

> The jury found that her (Austin's) excessive speed was the cause of her injuries. How can it be said that her negligence in driving 90 mph, which caused the accident, was not a cause of her death? The answer of the majority is that seat belts are designed to protect the wearer from injuries suffered in an accident which may be the wearer's fault. . . . As a policy matter, the majority has decided in this case that negligence as the cause of the accident (and therefore the injuries) of the deceased will not be compared with the product liability imposed on the manufacturer for the failure of the seat belt. I have reservations about the wisdom of this policy. When applied to the theory that an injury would have been prevented if the injured party had worn a seat belt, its corollary will result in re-introducing a form of assumption of risk into Wisconsin law.

## For Discussion

What theory of product liability has the court applied in this case? Do you agree with this theory? Why or why not? Do you agree with the majority or the dissenting opinion in this case? Why do you agree with one opinion and disagree with the other?

# *Griggs* v. *BIC Corp.*

On October 10, 1985, a three-year-old child removed a BIC lighter from his stepfather's pants pocket in the early hours of the morning and set fire with it to the bedding on which his eleven-month-old stepbrother, Zachary Griggs, slept. Zachary sustained serious burn injuries. In the preceding six months the parents were aware of two incidents in which the three year old attempted to light matches or a lighter, and for which the child was disciplined. Prior to Zachary's injuries, his mother had seen warnings BIC placed on the packaging of its lighters telling people to keep them away from children. The mother also conceded that independent of the BIC warning she was aware these lighters should be kept away from children. The parents sued BIC Corporation in Pennsylvania, claiming the lighter was defective under strict liability theory and that BIC was negligent (*Griggs* v. *BIC Corp.* 981 F. 2d 1429 [3rd Cir. 1992]).

Pennsylvania laws say that strict liability requires two elements of proof: (1) the product was defective, and (2) the defect caused the plaintiff's injuries. The plaintiffs in *Griggs* did not claim the lighter was defective because it failed to perform as it was intended to perform, but that it was defective because it was not childproof. In deciding this issue, the court held that:

> . . . the existence of a defect is intimately related to the product's intended use because the product is defective only if it left the supplier's control lacking any element necessary to make it safe for its intended use or possessing any feature that renders it unsafe for the intended use . . . . [accordingly] a product may not be deemed defective unless it is unreasonably dangerous to intended users (1433).

The court held that in Pennsylvania a manufacturer does not have a duty under strict liability law to guard against foreseeable use by unintended users. Because BIC's lighter was safe for its intended use, the lighter was not defective, and hence, under strict liability law, BIC was not liable.

The Griggs's also alleged that BIC was negligent in producing the lighter. Under Pennsylvania law, the elements of negligence are: (1) a duty or obligation recognized by the law, requiring the actor to conform to a certain standard of conduct for the protection of others against unreasonable risks; (2) a failure to conform to the standard required; (3) a causal connection between the conduct and the resulting injury; and (4) actual loss or damage resulting to the interests of another (1434). The Pennsylvania Supreme Court stated that the test of negligence is whether the wrongdoer could have anticipated and foreseen the likelihood of harm to the injured person resulting from his act (1435). The "duty" in (1) above is specified by the risk that should reasonably be perceived by the actor (or manufacturer). The court noted:

> In strict liability, the focus is on a defect in the product . . . and that defect is determined in relation to . . . the intended user, who puts the product to its intended use. In negligence, the focus is on the reasonableness of a defendant's conduct . . . and this reasonableness is determined [by] . . . anyone who foreseeably may be subject to an unreasonable risk of foreseeable harm (1438).

In the *Griggs* case, then, the issue was whether the foreseeable risks were unreasonable. To establish this the court relied on a risk-utility analysis which compared the consequences to BIC in terms of the economic costs to childproof its lighter to the consequences in terms of fires started by children using lighters. The court noted:

> Residential fires started by children playing with lighters are estimated to have taken an average of 120 lives each year. . . . [O]n average at least 750 persons were injured each year in residential fires started by children playing with lighters. . . . The annual cost of childplay lighter fires [is] $300–$375 million or 60–75 cents per lighter sold (1436).

The court concluded that the risk of harm was unreasonable. Accordingly, BIC was held to be negligent.

## FOR DISCUSSION

Do you agree with the court's opinion on strict liability in this case? Why or why not? Do you agree with the court's finding of negligence in this case? Why or why not?

# The DES Daughters

The drug diethylstilbestrol (DES), first produced in 1937, was not patented and was available for production by any pharmaceutical company. It was used to treat a variety of illnesses, and in 1947 several drug companies asked the Food and Drug Administration (FDA) for approval to use DES as a miscarriage preventative based on studies in medical journals which said DES was safe and effective for pregnant women to use. The FDA approved DES for this purpose, and in 1952 the FDA declared DES to be safe for general use, meaning that any drug manufacturer could produce and market DES without submitting additional safety and efficacy tests to the FDA. By 1971 about 300 companies had manufactured DES.

In 1971, two medical papers suggested there was a link between a form of cancer in young women and the ingestion of DES by their mothers during pregnancy. The FDA then banned the marketing of DES for use by pregnant women. Subsequently, hundreds of lawsuits were filed against DES manufacturers by the daughters of women who had taken DES during pregnancy. These plaintiffs were often referred to as the "DES daughters."

Although states employ different definitions of "strict liability," the basic idea is that a manufacturer (M) of a product that is defective, the defect of which causes harm to a user, can be held legally responsible for the harm caused. So a DES daughter who could establish that her illness was caused by her mother's DES use would have to prove that M produced the DES her mother used in order to establish her strict liability case against M. The problem for many DES daughters is that the effects do not occur for some time, during which physicians' records have often been lost or discarded. Moreover, the 300 DES manufacturers were only required to keep records for five years. So many DES daughters have been unable to establish exactly which manufacturer made the DES their mothers used, and hence have been unable to establish strict liability claims.

Some states have extended strict liability theory by adopting what is called "market share liability" theory. In *Sindell* v. *Abbott Laboratories*

(1980, 26 Cal. 3d 588, 607 P. 2d 924. 163 Cal. Rptr. 132), the California Supreme Court held that a DES plaintiff must: (1) charge various manufacturers of a substantial share of the DES which her mother may have used, and (2) prove all the elements of a strict liability case except identification of the actual manufacturer of the DES her mother used. Then the burden of proof shifts to the manufacturers charged to individually prove that they did not make the DES that caused the injury, and, if a defendant fails to prove it did not make the DES which caused the injury, it joins a pool of like firms, with each liable for a percentage of the judgment represented by its share of the market from among those charged. Variations of the market share liability theory were adopted in New York, Washington, and Wisconsin.

In *Sindell*, the court gave three general reasons for adopting the theory of market share liability. First, the plaintiffs in such cases are innocent and the manufacturers sued have all produced a defective product. Of the two, the manufacturers of the defective product should bear the cost. Second, manufacturers in general are better able to bear the cost involved in such injuries. Third, because the manufacturers are in the best position to recognize and guard against defects in the products they produce, holding manufacturers liable for defects provides an incentive for them to make safer products. In *Sindell*, the court believed that by using this theory the plaintiffs would be compensated and each manufacturer's liability would be approximately equal to the damages caused by the DES it produced.

Several state courts have rejected market share liability, notably, Iowa, Missouri, and Illinois (*Smith* v. *Eli Lilly & Co.* 560 N.E. 2d 324 [Ill. 1990]), claiming that in *Sindell* "substantial share" was left unspecified (i.e., local, state, national, etc.). More general criticisms are: (1) because there is a relatively high probablility the actual wrongdoer is not before the court, and the theory exposes those who were sued to a greater liability than they were responsible for (since only a "substantial share" of manufacturers need be named in the suit), the theory is unfair; and (2) the theory has disutility because it discourages research while adding little incentive to manufacture safer products, since every company in an industry faces potential liability regardless of its safety efforts.

# FOR DISCUSSION

Setting aside the legal issues, discuss the morality of having courts adopt the theory of market share liability for cases like the DES case.

*George G. Brenkert*

# Strict Products Liability and Compensatory Justice

Strict products liability is the doctrine that the seller of a product has legal responsibilities to compensate the user of that product for injuries suffered because of a defective aspect of the product, even when the seller has not been negligent in permitting that defect to occur.[1] Thus, even though a manufacturer, for example, has reasonably applied the existing techniques of manufacture and has anticipated and cared for nonintended use of the product, he may still be held liable for injuries a product user suffers if it can be shown that the product was defective when it left the manufacturer's hands.

To say that there is a crisis today concerning this doctrine would be to utter a commonplace which few in the business community would deny. The development of the doctrine of strict products liability, according to most business people, threatens many businesses financially. Furthermore, strict products liability is said to be a morally questionable doctrine, since the manufacturer or seller has not been negligent in permitting the injury-causing defect to occur. On the other hand, victims of defective products complain that they deserve full compensation for injuries sustained in using a defective product whether or not the seller is at fault. Medical expenses and time lost from one's job are costs no individual should have to bear by himself. It is only fair that the seller share such burdens.

In general, discussions of this crisis focus on the limits to which a business ought to be held responsible. Much less frequently, discussions of strict products liability consider the underlying question of whether the doctrine of strict products liability is rationally justifiable. But unless this question is answered it would seem premature to seek to determine the

From *Business Ethics: Readings and Cases in Corporate Morality*, ed. Michael Hoffmann and Jennifer Mill Moore (New York: McGraw-Hill, 1984), pp. 344–55. Copyright © 1984 by George G. Brenkert. Reprinted by permission of the author.

limits to which businesses ought to be held liable in such cases. In the following paper I discuss this underlying philosophical question and argue that there is a rational justification for strict products liability which links it to the very nature of the free enterprise system.

To begin with, it is crucial to remember that what we have to consider is the relationship between an entity doing business and an individual. The strict liability attributed to business would not be attributed to an individual who happened to sell some product he had made to his neighbor or a stranger. If Peter sold an article he had made to Paul and Paul hurt himself because the article had a defect which occurred through no negligence of Peter's, we would not normally hold Peter morally responsible to pay for Paul's injuries.

It is different for businesses. They have been held to be legally and morally obliged to pay the victim for his injuries. Why? What is the difference? The difference is that when Paul is hurt by a defective product from corporation X, he is hurt by something produced in a socioeconomic system purportedly embodying free enterprise. In other words, among other things:

1. Each business and/or corporation produces articles or services it sells for profit.
2. Each member of this system competes with members of the system in trying to do as well as it can for itself not simply in each exchange, but through each exchange for its other values and desires.
3. Competition is to be "open and free, without deception or fraud."
4. Exchanges are voluntary and undertaken when each party believes it can benefit thereby. One party provides the means for another party's ends if the other party will provide the first party the means to its ends.[2]
5. The acquisition and disposition of ownership rights—that is, of private property—is permitted in such exchanges.
6. No market or series of markets constitutes the whole of a society.
7. Law, morality, and government play a role in setting acceptable limits to the nature and kinds of exchange in which people may engage.[3]

What is it about such a system which would justify claims of strict products liability against businesses? . . . In the free enterprise system, each person and/or business is obligated to follow the rules and understandings which define this socioeconomic system. Following the rules is expected to channel competition among individuals and businesses to socially positive results. In providing the means to fulfill the needs of others, one's own ends also get fulfilled.

Though this does not happen in every case, it is supposed to happen most of the time. Those who fail in their competition with others may be the object of charity, but not of other duties. Those who succeed, qua members of this socioeconomic system, do not have moral duties to aid those who fail. Analogously, the team which loses the game may receive our sympathy but the winning team is not obligated to help it to win the next game or even to play it better. Those who violate the rules, however, may be punished or penalized, whether or not the violation was intentional and whether or not it redounded to the benefit of the violator. Thus, a team may be assessed a penalty for something that a team member did unintentionally to a member of the other team but which injured the other team's chances of competition in the game by violating the rules.

This point may be emphasized by another instance involving a game that brings us closer to strict products liability. Imagine that you are playing table tennis with another person in his newly constructed table tennis room. You are both avid table tennis players and the game means a lot to both of you. Suppose that after play has begun, you are suddenly and quite obviously blinded by the light over the table—the light shade has a hole in it which, when it turned in your direction, sent a shaft of light unexpectedly into your eyes. You lose a crucial point as a result. Surely it would be unfair of your opponent to seek to maintain his point because he was faultless—after all, he had not intended to blind you when he installed that light shade. You would correctly object that he had gained the point unfairly, that you should not have to give up the point lost, and that the light shade should be modified so that the game can continue on a fair basis. It is only fair that the point be played over.

Businesses and their customers in a free enterprise system are also engaged in competition with each other. The competition here, however, is multifaceted as each tries to gain the best agreement he can from the other with regard to the buying and selling of raw materials, products, services, and labor. Such agreements must be voluntary. The competition which leads to them cannot involve coercion. In addition, such competition must be fair and ultimately result in the benefit of the entire society through the operation of the proverbial invisible hand.

Crucial to the notion of fairness of competition are not simply the demands that the competition be open, free, and honest, but also that each person in a society be given an equal opportunity to participate in the system in order to fulfill his or her own particular ends. Friedman formulates this notion in the following manner:

> . . . the priority given to equality of opportunity in the hierarchy of values . . . is manifested particularly in economic policy. The catchwords were free enterprise, competition, laissez-faire. Everyone was to be free to go into any business, follow any occupation, buy any property, subject only to the agreement of the other parties to the transaction. Each was to have the opportunity to reap the benefits if he succeeded, to suffer the costs if he failed. There were to be no arbitrary obstacles. Performance, not birth, religion, or nationality, was the touchstone.[4]

What is obvious in Friedman's comments is that he is thinking primarily of a person as a producer. Equality of opportunity requires that one not be prevented by arbitrary obstacles from participating (by engaging in a productive role of some kind or other) in the system of free enterprise, competition, and so on in order to fulfill one's own ends ("reap the benefits"). Accordingly, monopolies are restricted, discriminatory hiring policies have been condemned, and price collusion is forbidden.

However, each person participates in the system of free enterprise *both* as a worker/producer *and* as a consumer. The two roles interact; if the person could not consume he would not be able to work, and if there were no consumers there would be no work to be done. Even if a particular individual is only (what is ordinarily considered) a consumer, he or she plays a theoretically significant role in the competitive free enterprise system. The fairness of the system depends upon what access he or she has to information about goods and services on the market, the lack of coercion imposed on that person to buy goods, and the lack of arbitrary restrictions imposed by the market and/or government on his or her behavior.

In short, equality of opportunity is a doctrine with two sides which applies both to producers and to consumers. If, then, a person as a consumer or a producer is injured by a defective product—which is one way his activities might arbitarily be restricted by the action of (one of the members of) the market system—surely his free and voluntary participation in the system of free enterprise will be seriously affected. Specifically, his equal opportunity to participate in the system in order to fulfill his own ends will be diminished.

Here is where strict products liability enters the picture. In cases of strict liability the manufacturer does not intend for a certain aspect of his product to injure someone. Nevertheless, the person is injured. As a result, he is at a disadvantage both as a consumer and as a producer. He cannot continue to play either role as he might wish. Therefore, he is denied that equality of opportunity which is basic to the economic system in question just as surely as he would be if he were excluded from employment by various unintended consequences of the economic system which nevertheless had racially or sexually prejudicial implications. Accordingly, it is fair for the manufacturer to compensate the person for his losses before proceeding with business as usual. That is, the user of a manufacturer's product may justifiably demand compensation from the manufacturer when its product can be shown to be defective and has injured him and harmed his chances of participation in the system of free enterprise.

Hence, strict liability finds a basis in the notion of equality of opportunity which plays a central role in the notion of a free enterprise system. That is why a business which does *not* have to pay for the injuries an individual suffers in the use of a defective article made by that business is felt to be unfair to its customers. Its situation is analogous to that of a player's unintentional violation of a game rule which is intended to foster equality of competitive opportunity.

A soccer player, for example, may unintentionally trip an opposing player. He did not mean to do it; perhaps he himself had stumbled. Still, he has to be penalized. If the referee looked the other way, the tripped player would rightfully object that he had been treated unfairly. Similarly, the manufacturer of a product may be held strictly liable for a product of his which injures a person who uses that product. Even if he is faultless, a consequence of his activities is to render the user of his product less capable of equal participation in the socioeconomic system. The manufacturer should be penalized by way of compensating the victim. Thus, the basis upon which manufacturers are held strictly liable is compensatory justice.

In a society which refuses to resort to paternalism or to central direction of the economy and which turns, instead, to competition in order to allocate scarce positions and resources, compensatory justice requires that the competition be fair and losers be protected.[5] Specifically, no one who loses should be left so destitute that he cannot reenter the competition. Furthermore, those who suffer injuries traceable to defective merchandise or services which restrict their participation in the competitive system should also be compensated.

Compensatory justice does not presuppose negligence or evil intentions on the part of those to whom the injuries might ultimately be traced. It is not perplexed or incapacitated by the relative innocence of all parties involved. Rather, it is concerned with correcting the disadvantaged situation an individual experiences due to accidents or failures which occur in the normal working of that competitive system. It is on this basis that other compensatory programs which alleviate the disabilities of various minority groups are founded. Strict products liability is also founded on compensatory justice.

An implication of the preceding argument is that business is not morally obliged to pay, as such, for the physical injury a person suffers. Rather, it must pay for the loss of equal competitive opportunity—even though it usually is the case that it is because of a (physical) injury that there is a loss of equal opportunity. Actual legal cases in which the injury which prevents a person from going about his or her daily activities is emotional or mental, as well as physical, support this thesis. If a person were neither mentally nor physically harmed, but still rendered less capable of participating competitively because of a defective aspect of a product, there would still be grounds for holding the company liable.

For example, suppose I purchased and used a cosmetic product guaranteed to last a month. When used by most people it is odorless. On me, however, it has a terrible smell. I can stand the smell, but my coworkers and most other people find it intolerable. My employer sends me home from work until it wears off. The product has not harmed me physically or mentally. Still, on the above argument, I would have reason to hold the manufacturer liable. Any cosmetic product with this result is defective. As a consequence my opportunity to participate in the socioeconomic system is curbed. I should be compensated.

There is another way of arriving at the same conclusion about the basis of strict products liability. To speak of business or the free enterprise system, it was noted above, is to speak of the voluntary exchanges between producer and customer which take place when each party believes he has an opportunity to benefit. Surely customers and producers may miscalculate their benefits; something they voluntarily agreed to buy or sell may turn out not to be to their benefit. The successful person does not have any moral responsibilities to the unsuccessful person—at least as a member of this economic system. If, however, fraud is the reason one person does not benefit, the system is, in principle, undermined. If such fraud were universalized, the system would collapse. Accordingly, the person committing the fraud does have a responsibility to make reparations to the one mistreated.

Consider once again the instance of a person who is harmed by a product he bought or used, a product that can reasonably be said to be defective. Has the nature of the free enterprise system also been undermined or corrupted in this instance? Producer and consumer have exchanged the product but it has not been to their mutual benefit; the manufacturer may have benefited, but the customer has suffered because of the defect. Furthermore, if such exchanges were universalized, the system would also be undone.

Suppose that whenever people bought products from manufacturers the products turned out to be defective and the customers were always injured, even though the manufacturers could not be held negligent. Though one party to such exchanges might benefit, the other party always suffered. If the rationale for this economic system—the reason it was adopted and is defended—were that in the end both parties share the equal opportunity to gain, surely it would collapse with the above consequences. Consequently, as with fraud, an economic system of free enterprise requires that injuries which result from defective products be compensated. The question is: Who is to pay for the compensation?

There are three possibilities. The injured party could pay for his own injuries. However, this is implausible since what is called for is compensation and not merely payment for injuries. If the injured party had simply injured himself, if he had been negligent or careless, then it is plausible that he should pay for his own injuries. No compensation is at stake here. But in the present case the injury stems from the actions of a particular manufacturer who, albeit unwittingly, placed the defective product on the market and stands to gain through its sale.

The rationale of the free enterprise system would be undermined, we have seen, if such actions were universalized, for then the product user's equal opportunity to benefit from the system would be denied. Accordingly, since the rationale and motivation for an individual to be part of this socioeconomic system is his opportunity to gain from participation in it, justice requires that the injured product user receive compensation for his injuries. Since the individual can hardly compensate himself, he must receive compensation from some other source.

Second, some third party—such as government—could compensate the injured person. This is not wholly implausible if one is prepared to modify the structure of the free enterprise system. And, indeed, in the long run this may be the most plausible course of action. However, if one accepts the structure of the free enterprise system, this alternative must be rejected because it permits the interference of government into individual affairs.

Third, we are left with the manufacturer. Suppose a manufacturer's product, even though the manufacturer wasn't negligent, always turned out to be defective and injured those using his products. We might sympathize with his plight, but he would either have to stop manufacturing altogether (no one would buy such products) or else compensate the victims for their losses. (Some people might buy and use his products under these conditions.) If he forced people to buy and use his products he would corrupt the free enterprise system. If he did not compensate the injured users, they would not buy and he would not be able to sell his products. Hence, he would partake of the free enterprise system—that is, sell his products—only if he compensated his user/victims. Accordingly, the sale of this hypothetical line of defective products would be voluntarily accepted as just or fair only if compensation were paid the user/victims of such products by the manufacturer.

The same conclusion follows even if we consider a single defective product. The manufacturer put the defective product on the market. Because of his actions others who seek the opportunity to participate on an equal basis in this system in order to benefit therefrom are unable to do so. Thus, a result of his actions, even though unintended, is to undermine the system's character and dignity. Accordingly, when a person is injured in his attempt to participate in this system, he is owed compensation by the manufacturer. The seller of the defective article must not jeopardize the equal opportunity of the product user to benefit from the system. The seller need not guarantee that the buyer/user will benefit from the purchase of the product; after all, the buyer may miscalculate or be careless in the use of a nondefective product. But if he is not careless or has not miscalculated, his opportunity to benefit from the system is illegitimately harmed if he is injured in its use because of the product's defectiveness. He deserves compensation.

It follows from the arguments in this and the preceding section that strict products liability is not only compatible with the system of free enterprise but that if it were not attributed to the manufacturer the system itself would be morally defective. And the justification for requiring manufacturers to pay compensation when people are injured by defective products is that the demands of compensatory justice are met.[6]

# NOTES

1. This characterization of strict products liability is adapted from Alvin S. Weinstein et al., *Products Liability and the Reasonably Safe Product* (New York: John Wiley & Sons, 1978), chap. 1. I understand the seller to include the manufacturer, the retailer, distributors, and wholesalers. For the sake of convenience, I will generally refer simply to the manufacturer.

2. F. A. Hayek emphasizes this point in "The Moral Element in Free Enterprise," in *Studies in Philosophy, Politics, and Economics* (New York: Simon and Schuster, 1967), p. 229.

3. Several of these characteristics have been drawn from Milton Friedman and Rose Friedman, *Free to Choose* (New York: Avon Books, 1980).

4. Ibid., pp. 123–24.

5. I have drawn heavily, in this paragraph, on the fine article by Bernard Boxhill, "The Morality of Reparation," reprinted in *Reverse Discrimination*, ed. Barry R. Gross (Amherst, N.Y.: Prometheus Books, 1977), pp. 270–78.

6. I would like to thank the following for providing helpful comments on earlier versions of this paper: Betsy Postow, Jerry Phillips, Bruce Fisher, John Hardwig, and Sheldon Cohen.

*Robert H. Malott*

# Let's Restore Balance to Product Liability Law

When I began my business career thirty years ago, the liability of manufacturers and distributors for injuries suffered by a product user was limited and easily understood: businesses could be held responsible if their actions or conduct were negligent. During the past three decades, however, product liability law has changed dramatically, creating confusion among manufacturers and distributors as to what exactly constitutes liability. The focus has shifted from the conduct of product makers and sellers to the condition of the product itself. Liability can now result if a court or jury determines that a product's design, its construction, or its operating instructions and safety warnings make it unreasonably dangerous or hazardous to use.

These changes have produced a tremendous expansion in the scope of product-related injuries for which manufacturers and distributors are now held accountable. The most graphic evidence of this escalating exposure is the rapid growth in the number of product liability suits being filed and in the amounts of damages awarded. Between 1974 and 1981, for example, the number of product liability suits filed in federal district courts grew at an average annual rate of 28 percent, nearly three-and-a-half times faster than the average annual increase in civil suits filed in federal courts.[1]

For some, the changes of the past three decades represent merely a redressing of the balance of product liability law, which for too long was viewed as favoring product makers at the expense of product users. Other observers, however, are increasingly concerned that the pendulum has swung too far in favor of the injured product user, imposing on manufac-

From Robert H. Mallott, "Let's Restore Balance to Product Liability Law," *Harvard Business Review* 61, no. 3 (May-June 1983): 67–74. Copyright © 1983 by the President and Fellows of Harvard College. All rights reserved. Reprinted by permission of *Harvard Business Review*.

turers and distributors enormous and inequitable costs that are ultimately passed on to society as a whole.

## CHANGING FOCUS OF TORT LAW

Although the changes in product liability law of the 1960s and 1970s appeared to sweep onto the national scene with little forewarning, legal scholars note that the changes were, in fact, part of a continuous but quiet trend dating from the turn of the century.

Prior to about 1900, tort law, as a branch of the common law, had for several hundred years tended to limit liability to cases of "fault," or moral responsibility. In product liability cases, this meant that a buyer had no ground for recovering damages for injuries incurred while using a product, unless he or she could prove that the product's maker or seller had been negligent in its construction or sale.

The legal standards for determining liability on negligence grounds were clear: the court or jury had only to determine that the product maker or seller had failed to act reasonably and prudently. Despite the seeming vagueness of the terms *reasonable* and *prudent* as standards of conduct, the common law included a well-developed body of case law which enabled judges to instruct juries on the determination of *negligent conduct*.

For particular kinds of torts, such as damages caused by wild animals or illnesses caused by unwholesome food, the common law did, however, permit injured parties to recover damages without requiring that they prove the defendant guilty of negligent conduct. Because foodstuffs could become spoiled or impure through no fault of the producer or seller, and because wild animals pose unusual hazards or dangers, the law allowed courts and juries to assign liability even though there was no fault or lapse of conduct. This concept of liability without fault is known as *strict liability*.

Around the turn of the century, portions of the legal community began arguing that a concept of liability based solely on fault was inadequate to protect product users and consumers from the dangers of modern civilization. The advent of larger and more complicated machinery in the workplace and the introduction of labor-saving appliances into the home dramatically increased productivity and improved the standards of living. The new technologies, however, also exposed workers on the job and product users at home to greater hazards of injury than earlier generations faced.

As products and manufacturing processes became more and more complex, a negligence-based concept of liability posed an onerous burden on an injured victim seeking compensation: he or she was required to identify what part of a product failed or to prove that the failure or accident could be explained only by the manufacturer's or seller's negligence. Moreover, mass production techniques introduced the possibility that defective products could be produced and offered for sale, despite manufacturers' quality checks and testing.

Yet, a negligence-based liability doctrine precluded recovery by an injured consumer because the manufacturer had not acted negligently. Thus, there was a need—concerned lawyers, judges, and scholars agreed—for legal grounds other than negligence on which injured individuals could recover damages for injuries or loss.

In response, lawyers and judges expanded the concept of strict liability to products that have manufacturing defects. In so doing, they overturned the doctrine of "no liability without fault." Instead, as tort law expert William L. Prosser noted:

"In some cases the defendant may be liable, although he is not only charged with no moral wrongdoing, but has not even departed in any way from a reasonable standard of intent or care."[2]

By applying strict liability to product injury cases, the courts were, in one sense, simply expanding the common law, as they had been for hundreds of years. At a more fundamental level, however, the courts were engaged in judicial legislation, making sweeping changes in the relationship between producers and consumers. As Prosser also noted:

"The basis of this policy is a social philosophy which places the burden of the more or less inevitable losses due to a complex civilization upon those best able to bear them or to shift them to society at large."[3]

The liability was assigned to the manufacturer or distributor, according to Prosser, because business "is in a better position to administer the unusual risk by passing it on to the public than is the innocent victim."[4]

The application of the strict liability doctrine to product liability cases gained a stamp of legitimacy with its acceptance by the California Supreme Court in the 1963 decision in a case in which a man was injured while using a combination power tool in his home workshop.[5] The concept was further boosted a year later by its inclusion in the 1964 Restatement of Torts, a summary of tort law by the prestigious American Law Institute. By the early 1970s, strict liability had been accepted virtually nationwide.

## QUESTIONABLE ISSUES

Now, the question is no longer "Whose fault is it?" Rather, "Is there a condition of the product that creates an unnecessary hazard or danger?"

Answering the product condition question, with respect to an alleged manufacturing defect, is easy: defective manufacturing is obvious because the product does not conform to the maker's design specifications. Had the extension of the strict liability doctrine been limited to injuries caused by manufacturing defects, liability exposure, although broader than it was under the negligence doctrine, would be clear and comprehensible.

Unfortunately, however, strict liability has been extended to product conditions other than manufacturing. In particular, some courts have determined that product designs may create hazardous conditions of use or that products may be sold without sufficient warning of hidden risks.

For an injured consumer, extending strict liability to design and warning "defects" was a logical next step in expanding the scope of damage recovery. To the manufacturers and sellers of those products, the step from manufacturing defects to design and warning defects was dramatic. Unlike the test for manufacturing defects, there are no standards to guide judicial decisions on the adequacy of a product's warnings or design.

Not surprisingly, each state has developed its own definition of strict liability for design and warnings. For instance, California deems a design defective if the product "fails to perform as safely as an ordinary consumer would expect it to when used in an intended or reasonably foreseeable manner." In Pennsylvania, on the other hand, a product's design is defective if it left the supplier's control "lacking any element to make it safe for its intended use or possessing any feature that renders it unsafe for the intended use."

Further complicating matters, phrases such as "intended use," "when used in a reasonably foreseeable manner," or "performs as safely as an ordinary consumer would expect" have no agreed-on meaning—and no common understanding based on case law built up over many years—to guide their application by the courts.

By making manufacturers liable for any aspect of a product's condition that causes it to be unreasonably dangerous, the strict liability doctrine has made design safety an issue to be decided by judges and juries. Because there are no judicial standards that define minimum safety requirements, the courts have enormous latitude in deciding cases. In practice, they have tended to come down on the side of the product user. Consider the following case.

In 1974 a Pennsauken, New Jersey, police officer, responding to a burglar alarm, was severely injured when the Dodge Monaco police car he was driving spun off a rain-soaked highway. While moving backward, the car struck a steel pole 15 inches in diameter on the driver's side behind the front door. The police officer, Richard Dawson, sued the car's manufacturer, Chrysler Corporation, on the ground that the Monaco's design was unreasonably dangerous because it did not specify a rigid steel body, which would have prevented penetration of the passenger compartment.

In its defense Chrysler argued that the Monaco was designed with a flexible body to maximize passenger protection in front- or rear-end collisions, by far the most numerous types of accidents. A flexible frame absorbs the impact of these collisions by crumpling up. Moreover, Chrysler argued, a rigid side body construction would add about 250 pounds to the weight of the car, reducing its fuel efficiency and increasing its operating costs as well as price. Chrysler, faced with federal regulations both on fuel economy standards and front-end collision survivability, contended that the Monaco's design was optimal, given the infrequency of side collisions compared with front and rear accidents. The jury accepted the plaintiff's argument and awarded him damages of more than $2 million. On appeal, the federal appeals court upheld the trial court's verdict.[6]

This decision, and decisions in other cases like it, lead to the following conclusion: if a product's design will not prevent all accidents, then juries may choose to consider it inadequately safe. The result has been an almost unfathomable expansion of the scope of product liability, with exorbitant costs to society.

Manufacturers simply cannot design products that will prevent harm or injuries from all possible accidents. In creating a product, they must choose a design that affords the most practicable protection from injuries in the most frequent types of accidents. If a manufacturer can show, as Chrysler did, that its design was chosen to minimize the injuries from the types of accidents that are most likely to occur, is it reasonable to make the company liable simply because it did not use an alternative design that might have prevented injuries from a type of accident that occurs much less frequently?

Judges and juries have also been given the power to determine the adequacy of safety warnings and operating instructions under the strict liability doctrine. Again, the lack of any judicial standards has expanded the scope of liability. The lack of a warning specifically directed to any hazard that results in an accident or injury has been sufficient ground for courts and juries to judge the manufacturer liable. For an assessment of liability against the manufacturer, experience has taught that it does not matter whether the product is to be used only by skilled operators, not the general public, or how obvious the hazard is.

My own company, FMC Corporation, was sued in 1971 by a laborer injured when a crane operator maneuvered the boom of an FMC-built crane into high voltage electrical transmission lines. The plaintiff argued that FMC should be liable for his injuries because (1) the company had not posted warnings on the crane or in its cab of the dangers of operating the crane near high power lines, and (2) because it had not installed safety devices that, in the opinion of witnesses called by the plaintiff, could have alerted the operator to potential contact with electrical power lines.

In its defense, FMC argued that it had not put a warning in the crane's cab because the crane was intended to be used by trained heavy equipment operators thoroughly familiar with the hazards of working around electrical power lines. The company also noted that its engineers had concluded that proximity warning devices available at the time the crane was built (in 1957) did not operate with sufficient reliability to justify their use. An unreliable proximity warning device could pose a safety hazard of its own, in that workers who relied on it could be injured if they assumed that the device would protect them. Nonetheless, the court decided in the plaintiff's favor and awarded a judgment of $2.5 million.[7]

The doctrine of strict liability makes manufacturers liable for injuries if a product does not perform safely when used in "an intended" or "reasonably foreseeable manner." Again, it is up to the courts to determine what constitutes intended or reasonably foreseeable use. Recent cases have extended the boundaries of what may be construed as foreseeable use, with enormous implications for the liability exposure of manufacturers.

In one case, American Home Products, the makers of Pam, an aerosol which is sprayed on pots and pans to prevent food from sticking during cooking, was sued in 1979 by the mother of a fourteen-year-old boy who died after internally inhaling the freon propellant from a can of Pam. At the time of the youth's death, the can bore the following warning: "Avoid direct inhalation of concentrated vapor. Keep out of the reach of children." The boy's mother charged that the company should be held accountable because this warning was inadequate, particularly because the company had knowledge of forty-five deaths, prior to her son's, involving teenagers concentrating the fumes and inhaling them in order to produce a tingling sensation in the lungs. The jury awarded her $585,000 in damages.[8]

The decision in this case disturbs me for two reasons. First, it is unreasonable to suppose that there is any kind of warning a manufacturer could use to prevent an individual from deliberately misusing a product. And second, the individual, not the manufacturer, should be responsible for the consequences of his or her own actions, particularly in cases of intentional misuse.

Should manufacturers be liable for hazards posed by their products that may result in injuries many years later, but which scientific knowledge cannot detect at the time a product is marketed? The answer courts give to this very difficult question will have extraordinary implications for the liability exposure of manufacturers of pharmaceuticals, toxic materials, and chemical products that may have harmful effects that take many years to develop.

The asbestos controversy has highlighted this issue in recent years. Prolonged exposure to significant amounts of asbestos in its fibrous form can cause asbestosis, a restrictive lung disease characterized by scarring of the tissues. It is also associated with the development of some cancers. Fibrous asbestos, however, has been widely used as a flame-retardant, fire-resistant insulating material. In particular, the U.S. Navy and the Maritime Commission required the use of asbestos in the construction of warships and cargo vessels during World War II to protect seamen against the spread of fire on board battle-damaged ships.

Today, asbestos makers face thousands of claims for damages from workers exposed to asbestos, half of which were filed by those exposed to asbestos in shipyards during and after World War II. In August 1982, Manville Corporation filed for bankruptcy, maintaining that although it was still solvent, the 16,500 pending asbestos claims, combined with a potential 30,000 additional claims, would exhaust its assets.

A recent New Jersey Supreme Court decision may extend the liability exposure of asbestos makers even further. In *Beshada, et al.* v. *Johns-Manville Products Corporation, et al.*, the court struck down the state-of-the-art defense used by asbestos makers. The companies argued that they should not be liable for failing to warn of the dangers of asbestos exposure because they were unaware of the danger at the time the product was marketed and because such dangers could not have been detected with the scientific techniques then available.

In its ruling the court differentiated between the defenses that are applicable in a suit based on negligence and one based on strict liability. A manufacturer may use the state-of-the-art defense only when it is being sued for negligence: a company is not acting negligently by offering a product for sale that to its knowledge—given the state of scientific techniques—does not pose a hazard. In a strict liability suit, however, the state-of-the-art defense is not admissible because the product's condition—not the manufacturer's actions and what it knew or could not have known—is the focus of the action.

By holding manufacturers liable for injuries that may be incurred from products whose hazards cannot now be foreseen, this ruling may threaten the future viability of many companies or even of entire industries.

## CONSEQUENCES OF IMBALANCE

The lack of clear and discernible standards means that the verdicts reached in product liability suits today are often inequitable and inconsistent.

This imbalance is not surprising, because courts and juries today are asked to make judgments that they are not well equipped to make. Strict liability has moved determinations of liability from the realm of the mainly objective to that of the substantially subjective. Judges and juries are required to determine what constitutes a hazardous design or an inadequate warning—matters in which they are invariably not experts. They are required to render an evaluation—through hindsight—of decisions made by manufacturer's engineers and experts after extensive study during the design process.

Another source of inconsistency in product liability verdicts today is the varying interpretations of liability from state to state. These cause different results in different jurisdictions, out of cases based on essentially the same facts. For instance, shortly after the Illinois court's judgment against FMC in the crane case, courts in New Mexico and Minnesota ruled in similar cases that the manufacturer was not liable because the hazard of driving a steel boom into high power lines was obvious.

Strict liability has dramatically increased the costs of product liability. The old negligence-based tort law, which assigned damages to the responsible party, has been converted into a business-financed "social insurance system" for product injury victims. Under this system the size and number of product liability awards have increased greatly, and they give every indication of continuing to grow at astronomical rates.

It is therefore entirely appropriate to ask whether the costs imposed by current interpretations of product liability law are reasonable in relationship to the damages incurred, just as it is necessary to ask who will pay these costs.

Ultimately, of course, the costs are borne by consumers as the costs of liability insurance premiums and liability judgments are passed through to them. These costs can be quite high: one small machine tool manufacturer has reported that its cost of liability insurance went from $200 per machine in 1970 to $11,000 per machine in 1982.[9]

The defenders of the current state of product liability law often claim that manufacturers, aware of their potential liability, make better products than they would otherwise. Our experience suggests that exactly the opposite may also occur: companies may hesitate to introduce new products or expand into new markets because of the potential liability.

For example, FMC's former Power Transmission Group produced high-quality commercial bearings for use as components in machines and equipment built by other manufacturers. As a component manufacturer, FMC had no control over the design of the products into which bearings were placed. Yet, in the event of a failure, a claimant could sue the component manufacturer as well as the product manufacturer. In 1971 we concluded that the potential product liability exposure from the use of FMC bearings in helicopter rotors was too great, given the small share of our market that such use constituted. We therefore issued a directive stating that no orders for bearings would knowingly be accepted for use in manufacturing in-flight aircraft controls.

I should also point out that injured parties are poorly served by the adversary process of settling product liability suits. As much or more money is being paid to adjudicate a claim as is being paid to compensate victims. There is some indication that the contingency fee basis on which most plaintiffs' lawyers are engaged tends to escalate damage claims. James A. Henderson Jr. of Boston University's School of Law has estimated that:

"Out of every dollar paid by consumers to cover the relevant liability costs, less than fifty cents—estimates vary downward from forty-five cents to thirty cents—are returned to the consumers in benefits. Most of the rest—between fifty-five and seventy cents out of every premium dollar—goes to pay the lawyers, adjusters, and the like. If I were a cynic, I would say that if this is a social insurance scheme, it is being run primarily to benefit the trial bar."[10]

## REDRESSING THE BALANCE

If one accepts the conclusion that today's product liability system based on strict liability produces inequitable, inconsistent, and excessively costly judgments against manufacturers, then one ought to ask what can be done to reestablish reasonableness and fairness in liability decisions.

The answer—establishment of clear and precise standards of liability—seems simple enough. The challenge is to ensure standards that are understandable by manufacturers, equitable to product makers and users alike, and uniformly interpreted by courts and juries nationwide (thus ensuring consistency of results). Among the standards needed are:

### 1. A Negligence-Based Standard for Judging the Adequacy of Product Design and the Appropriateness of Warnings.

The basic question in design and warning cases should be refocused on the manufacturer's conduct. Did the manufacturer use reasonable and prudent care in designing the product or providing warnings of hidden risks? Plaintiffs will almost always be able to show, as the plaintiff did in *Dawson* v. *Chrysler*, that an alternative design may, in the opinion of an expert chosen by the plaintiff, have prevented a particular accident.

Instead of making manufacturers liable because they cannot design a product in such a way as to prevent all accidents, would it not be more reasonable to focus on the degree of care taken by the manufacturer in designing the product?

### 2. A Standard Creating a Presumption that a Product Conforming to Goverment Safety Requirements is Reasonably Safe.

Currently, an injured product user may buttress his or her suit against a manufacturer by citing a product's failure to conform to government safety standards as evidence of inadequate design. The reverse, however, is not true. In many states, manufacturers are not permitted to cite the fact that a product meets or exceeds all applicable government standards as evidence of the adequacy of a product's design.

It would be more equitable (1) to allow compliance with government standards to create a presumption that a product is reasonably safe, and (2) to allow plaintiffs to rebut that presumption if they can show that the manufacturer knew that governmentally established standards were inadequate for a normal or intended use of the product.

### 3. A Standard Requiring Assignment of Liability and Damages on the Basis of Comparative Responsibility.

Frequently, injury from a product has several causes. For example, a person who misuses or alters a product may be responsible to some degree for his own or someone else's injury. In such cases, the courts should allocate liability among all responsible parties, and defendants should pay damages only in proportion to their share of the liability.

To require manufacturers to absorb the cost of someone else's carelessness creates an inequitable financial burden, a burden which the manufacturer must pass on to the consumer in the form of higher prices.

### 4. A Standard Limiting Liability for Manufacturing or Design Defects to a Specific Period of Time.

Products that have served their purpose without evidence of harm for a prolonged period should not be reexamined with regard to the manufacturer's liability for the adequacy of design and warning at a later date. No company should be forced to defend the adequacy of the design and safety warnings on a product that has operated safely for decades. In one egregious example, the Oliver Machinery Company was sued in the 1970s by a man who was injured while using a table saw manufactured by the company in 1942—more than thirty years before the accident!

At some point in time a manufacturer's responsibility should end. Appropriate allowances should be made, of course, when setting such limits, for chemical products or other toxic substances that may cause illness or damage only after prolonged exposure.

## NOTES

1. Data compiled from the *Annual Report of the Director of the Administrative Office of the United States Courts, 1974–1981* (Washington, D.C.: U.S. Government Printing Office).

2. William L. Prosser, *Handbook of the Law Torts* (St. Paul, Minn.: West Publishing Company, 1955), p. 317.

3. Ibid., p. 315.

4. Ibid., p. 318.

5. *Greenman* v. *Yuba Power Products*, California Supreme Court, January 24, 1963.

6. *Dawson* v. *Chrysler Corporation*, U.S. Court of Appeals, Third Circuit, September 11, 1980.

7. *Burke* v. *Illinois Power Company, FMC Corporation, et al.*, Illinois Appellate Court, January 18, 1978.

8. *Harless* v. *Boyle-Midway Division, American Home Products Company*, U.S. District Court, Northern District of Florida, February 22, 1980.

9. Statement of Herbert W. Goetz, manager of product safety, Cincinnati Incorporated, on behalf of the National Product Liability Council, before the Subcommittee on Consumer, Committee on Commerce and Transportation, U.S. Senate (March 12, 1982).

10. Statement of James A. Henderson Jr. before the Subcommittee on Consumer, Committee on Commerce and Transportation, U.S. Senate (March 9, 1982).

*Beverly C. Moore Jr.*

# Product Safety:
# Who Should Absorb the Cost?

Product safety will be an important concern of the consumer movement until effective steps are taken to reduce the cost of accidents. Cost estimates for 1970 for three major categories of accidents are $5.5 billion for household product accidents (National Commission on Product Safety), $8 billion for work-related accidents (National Safety Council), and $16.2 billion for automobile accidents (Insurance Information Institute). The $30 billion total, encompassing 105,000 deaths and 390,000 permanent disabilities, is a substantial understatement.

In addition to significant underreporting, particularly of work-related accidents, such intangible damages as pain and suffering and the noneconomic value of lives lost are excluded. The comprehensive total cost of accidents in the United States may be in the vicinity of $50 billion, excluding the cost of administering a compensation system.

Presumably there will continue to be accident costs as long as there are accident prevention costs which are greater. These prevention costs are generally of two kinds:

One, *human carefulness*, in addition to having a relatively finite potential for further perfectibility, appears to be becoming more costly to exercise in a world which is increasingly complex, full of gadgets, warnings, directions, and distractions.

The other, *product* design, has quite the opposite potential. Its perfectibility—ultimately in preventing negligent, even intentionally caused accidents—and the cost of its perfectibility, is dependent solely on the progress of technology. Judging from the recent past, one can expect that technological progress, given the proper incentives, will be steady and dramatic.

---

Reprinted by permission from *Trial* magazine (January/February 1972). The Association of Trial Lawyers of America.

It can be reliably forecast, therefore, that primarily through improvements in product design, accident prevention costs, and thus the net cost of accidents, will be reduced over time.

The pace at which that development unfolds depends upon what external pressures are brought to bear upon the corporations which design products (or employ workers or perform services).

Competition—the external force upon which we generally rely to spur product improvements and cost-saving technologies—is not always or even usually effective in forcing product safety improvements. Competition can work to the extent that the safety improvement is substantial enough to be noticed by a significant number of consumers who will pay the higher cost necessitated by the improvement in order to avoid a cognizable accident risk. Examples could be cited where this has occurred, but generally the consumer lacks the information to evaluate such particularized criteria.

While the problem could be ameliorated somewhat by mandatory disclosure of accident risk information at point of purchase, a further problem remains: Accident-prone products are often produced by oligopolistic firms which compete sluggishly, if at all, in safety improvements.

With a single adjustment, however, competition could be harnessed as the prime lever of cost-effective safety improvements—irrespective of consumer ignorance of accident risks, irrespective of the general absence of competition within oligopolistic industries.

The adjustment is to transfer the entire cost of a product's accidents from its victims to the producer, regardless of fault. By forcing corporations to internalize their social costs—i.e., treating them as ordinary business expenses—the price mechanism will force the adoption of cost-effective safety improvements.

Suppose, for example, that the auto industry was saddled with $20 billion annually for accident costs, not to mention an additional $10 billion liability for air pollution damage and other externalities. The average price of an automobile would increase by $2,000. Sales would drop dramatically as consumers would resort to mass transit and other less costly means of transportation. This state of affairs would persist until the industry developed a car safe enough to reduce its damage liability to the point at which prices could be lowered sufficiently to generate a profitable sales volume.

One suspects that safer cars would soon be on the market. The continuing solvency of General Motors would depend upon that. And if, perchance, the industry is unable to reduce net accident costs sufficiently to stay in business, then it will have been demonstrated that automobiles have been economically feasible instrumentalities only by virtue of their costs being subsidized by their accident victims.

From the accident victim's viewpoint, this "enterprise liability" concept differs markedly from present and proposed compensation systems.

- It differs from the fault system in that not 42 percent, but 100 percent, of accident victims' economic losses are compensated.
- It differs from workmen's compensation formulas in that there is no schedule of maximum benefits preventing the victim from recovering his full economic and intangible losses.
- It differs from strict products liability doctrine in that no defect need be established.

Enterprise liability goes beyond no-fault in two important aspects:

First, except for very small or new firms, the producers of accident-prone products would be prohibited from resorting to liability insurance to spread their accident-damage risks. In light of the ultimate objective, these corporations cannot be permitted to avoid the safety competition touched off when an individual firm lowers its price after implementing a damage-reducing product design change.

Second, enterprise liability would not tolerate any exceptions to no-fault principles, such as denial of compensation to drunk drivers.

There is no attempt here to be solicitous of accident victims generally or of drunk drivers in particular, or to impute "blame" to the auto industry. From society's perspective, any benefits to victims are purely incidental to the overriding purpose (which compensation serves)—preventing accidents so that there will ultimately be no victims to compensate.

This is accomplished by imposing the cost of any general category of accidents upon the party (i.e., producer or victim) who is best able to prevent that class of accidents. We have assumed that the producer will usually be that party.

In the case of automobile accidents, one is initially impressed with the argument that the fear of the accident itself is a sufficient deterrent to negligent driving even if the driver is assured of compensation for his own negligence. Likewise, there is no good reason for supposing that placing the loss upon the drunk driver will deter drunk driving to a greater extent than placing it upon the manufacturer according to the general rule. After all, the drunk driver persists, notwithstanding our having held him liable before.

It seems much more promising to encourage the industry to develop devices which will render intoxicated persons unable to operate a parked motor vehicle. Nor is this to say that additional measures, such as traffic fines and license suspensions, should not continue to act as a deterrent to individual carelessness.

Although the concept of internalizing social costs has been advocated by economists as a means of solving our pollution problems, it has not been seriously proposed, even by consumer advocates, as a means of reducing accident costs.

(There has been considerable academic discussion. *See* G. Calabresi, *The Costs of Accidents* (1970); Reviewed in 80 *Yale Law Journal* 647 (1971), 84 *Harvard Law Review* 1322 (1971); Coase, "The Problem of Social Cost," 3 *Journal of Law & Economics* 1 (1960).)

The traditional approach, advocated by the Product Safety Commission and already incorporated into federal auto safety legislation, has instead been to authorize a government agency to promulgate and enforce standards.

These may bring about a reduction in accident costs. But the cost-internalization alternative will generally bring about an even greater accident-cost reduction, and it will accomplish this result with a minimum of prevention costs.

The reasons for the superiority of cost internalization are not difficult to discern. At worst the government agency will become the captive of its regulatees. Congressional appropriations will be minimal, and sanction-less "voluntary compliance" will become the enforcement mode. At best, agency standard setting will be cumbersome and crude.

The basic dilemma is that regulators must operate in a milieu of static technology. Even if the standard that is promulgated—the air bag, for example—is or appears to be the most cost-effective means of reducing accidents at the time of its adoption, a more advanced technology may be developed shortly thereafter. Even if the agency is vigilant to replace the old standard with the new, there will always be some lag.

Also under cost internalization, the pressure to develop new technology is on the industry, where the greatest expertise presumably resides. Under the standards approach, however, this onus is placed upon the agency, which is likely to adopt a standard which either prevents too few accidents or is more costly than necessary with respect to the accidents it does prevent.

Under cost internalization, the industry has an incentive to do neither, but rather to follow the course which will reduce its damage liability at least cost to the consumer.

This is not to say that government standards can play no desirable role. Standards may complement cost internalization in cases where the accident damage cannot be measured with sufficient precision or where there is a small but real possibility of planetwide disaster—if the polar ice caps were to melt on account of increased atmospheric carbon dioxide levels attributable to fuel combustion, for example.

A relatively sure and simple legal apparatus can be fashioned to internalize accident costs without reliance upon government discretion.

A product safety commission would be established with a mandate to gather accident data to be used as evidence in private class-action lawsuits. These actions would seek recovery from the corporate defendants of a lump sum damage fund (plus attorneys' fees and claims administration costs) on behalf of the class as an entity. Individual accident victims would then file claims against the fund, just as they would against a fire insurance company. In the likelihood that not all individual claims will be filed, the remainder of the damage fund will revert in trust "to the benefit of accident victims generally," to be disbursed under court supervision.

The data-collecting agency would be empowered to order corporations, doctors and hospitals to comply with accident reporting procedures. If the agency failed to gather the data necessary to establish class-action damages, any private citizen could file suit to compel the agency to act. If the citizen suit was successful, the agency would be ordered to pay the plaintiff's attorney's fees and expenses, plus a cash bonus to reward his initiative as a private attorney general.

No doubt it will be argued that the higher product costs resulting from cost internalization would be "regressive." This objection is really that *all* prices are regressive—for bread, postage stamps, whatever. To allocate resources most efficiently, prices should reflect costs. The costs of product accidents, pollution, and other externalities are no less "costs" than are the costs of labor, land, and capital.

Nor must one resign himself to the inevitability of disproportionately burdening the poor with the cost of accidents. The reason why it is desirable to internalize those costs is that a net economic gain is thereby produced which can be directly transferred to the poor.

To illustrate, suppose that the total annual cost of accidents is $60 billion including pain and suffering, other intangibles and administration of a compensation system. Suppose further that two-thirds, or $40 billion, of that cost could be eliminated at a prevention cost of $20 billion, leaving a net gain of $20 billion. Through a negative income tax device this sum could then be used to supplement the incomes of low-income persons to an extent which would far outweigh the regressive impact of higher product prices.

# ADVERTISING

# *FTC* v. *Colgate-Palmolive Co.*

Colgate-Palmolive engaged the Ted Bates advertising agency to develop an advertising campaign based on the slogan "Rapid Shave outshaves them all." The result was a series of three one-minute commercials in which it was claimed that Rapid Shave could soften even the toughness of sandpaper. The test showed Rapid Shave being applied to what was claimed to be sandpaper. The ad used these words: "To prove Rapid Shave's super-moisturizing power, we put it right from the can onto this tough, dry sandpaper. It was apply, soak, and off in a stroke." Simultaneously, the viewer saw a razor shave the surface, leaving it completely smooth. But the actual surface was not sandpaper, rather, Plexiglas to which sand had been applied, because, it was claimed, sandpaper looks like ordinary colored paper when shown on television. Evidence brought to the attention of the Federal Trade Commission (FTC) also showed that, although Rapid Shave could actually shave the sand from real sandpaper, it could do so only after a soaking period of about eighty minutes, rather than the few moments shown on television.

In 1960 the FTC issued a complaint against Colgate and Bates claiming the commercials were false and deceptive. The hearing examiner dismissed the complaint, reasoning that neither misrepresentation—concerning moistening time or the identity of the shaved surface—would mis-

---

U.S. Sp. Ct., 1965. 380 U.S. 374, 85 S. Ct. 1035, 13 L. Ed. 2d 904.

lead the public. In 1961 the FTC reversed the hearing examiner, claiming that since Rapid Shave could not shave actual sandpaper in the time depicted in the ads, the product's moisturizing power had been misrepresented. The commission also held that undisclosed use of a Plexiglas substitute was deceptive.

In 1962 the First Circuit Court of Appeals twice upheld the FTC order against misrepresentation relating to the time factor, and Colgate conceded this issue. But the Appeals Court refused to allow enforcement of the FTC's claim of misrepresentation regarding the Plexiglas substitution. The issue facing the Supreme Court then was whether a commercial (portraying tests that supposedly confirm the claims made for a product) may use simulated props and devices that differ from materials the defendants originally claimed to be using in the tests.

A majority of the Supreme Court decided against Colgate. Television commercials that include a test were ruled deceptive if the test uses materials other than those which it purports to use. The majority argued mainly by analogy. Similar cases established that it is deceptive: (1) to state falsely that a product ordinarily sells for an inflated price but that it is being offered at a reduced price, even if the offered price represents the product's actual value; (2) to conceal that a product has been reprocessed even though it is as good as new; and (3) for a seller to misrepresent to the public that he is in a certain line of business, even though the misstatement in no way affects the quality of a product. Speaking for the majority, Chief Justice Warren went on to say:

> Respondents . . . insist that the present case is not like any of the above, but is more like a case in which a celebrity or independent testing agency has in fact submitted a written verification of an experiment actually observed, but, because of the inability of the camera to transmit accurately an impression of the paper on which the testimonial is written, the seller reproduces it on another substance so that it can be seen by the viewing audience. This analogy ignores the finding of the commission that in the present case the seller misrepresented to the public that it was being given objective proof of a product claim. In respondents' hypothetical the objective proof of the product claim that is offered, the word of the celebrity or agency that the experiment was actually conducted, does exist; while in the case before us the objective proof offered, the viewer's own perception of an actual experiment, does not exist. . . .
>
> The Court of Appeals has criticized the reference in the commission's order to "test, experiment or demonstration" as not being capable of practical interpretation. It could find no difference between the Rapid

Shave commercial and a commercial which extolled the goodness of ice cream while giving viewers a picture of a scoop of mashed potatoes appearing to be ice cream. We do not understand this difficulty. In the ice cream case the mashed potato prop is not being used for additional proof of the product claim, while the purpose of the Rapid Shave commercial is to give the reviewer objective proof of the claim made. If in the ice cream hypothetical the focus of the commercial becomes the undisclosed potato prop and the viewer is invited, explicitly or by implication, to see for himself the truth of the claims about the ice cream's rich texture and full color, and perhaps compare it to a "rival product," then the commercial has become similar to the one now before us. Clearly, however, a commercial which depicts happy actors delightedly eating ice cream that is in fact mashed potatoes . . . is not covered by the present order.

Justice Harlan spoke for the minority, and in favor of Colgate, in the 7–2 decision:

The only question here is what techniques the advertiser may use to convey essential truth to the television viewer. If the claim is true and valid, then the technique for projecting that claim, within broad boundaries, falls purely within the advertiser's art. The warrant to the Federal Trade Commission is to police the verity of the claim itself. . . .

I do not see how such a commercial can be said to be "deceptive" in any legally acceptable use of that term. The Court attempts to distinguish the case where a "celebrity" has written a testimonial endorsing some product, but the original testimonial cannot be seen over television and a copy is shown over the air by the manufacturer. . . . But in both cases the viewer is told to "see for himself " in the one case that the celebrity has endorsed the product; in the other, that the product can shave sandpaper; in neither case is the viewer actually seeing the proof and in both cases the objective proof does exist, be it in the original testimonial or the sandpaper test actually conducted by the manufacturer. In neither case, however, is there a material misrepresentation, because what the viewer sees *is* an accurate image of the objective proof. . . .

It is commonly known that television presents certain distortions in transmission for which the broadcasting industry must compensate. Thus, a white towel will look a dingy gray over television, but a blue towel will look a sparkling white. On the Court's analysis, an advertiser must achieve accuracy in the studio even though it results in an inaccurate image being projected on the home screen. . . . Would it be proper for respondent Colgate, in advertising a laundry detergent, to "demonstrate" the effectiveness of a major competitor's detergent in washing white sheets; and then "before the viewer's eyes," to wash a white (not a blue) sheet with the competitor's detergent? The studio test would accurately show the quality of the product, but the image on the screen would look as though the sheet had been washed with an ineffective detergent. All that had happened here is the converse: a demonstration has been altered in the studio to compensate for the distortions of the television medium, but in this instance in order to present an accurate picture to the television viewer.

## FOR DISCUSSION

Analyze carefully the reasoning of Justices Warren and Harlan. In your opinion which Justice presents the best argument? Why? Pay attention to their uses of "misrepresentation" and "deception." Do you yourself believe Colgate's advertisement was deceptive? If so, what aspects were deceptive, and why were they deceptive? If you believe the advertisement was not deceptive, what is the basis for your claim? What additional arguments can you provide for your view beyond the arguments presented by the justices?

# Natural Cereals

Breakfast Foods, Inc. (BFI) is a national manufacturer of food products with three dry cereal divisions—children's, family, and natural. BFI also sells frozen breakfast entrees such as waffles and pancakes.

BFI's marketing department has just hired three assistant branch managers. One of these, Sally Thompson, received her MBA from a major midwestern university. Before joining BFI, Sally spent two years with the marketing group of a large food manufacturer. Although her experience at the former firm was educational, Sally often felt frustrated by the lack of responsibility.

Moving to BFI was good for Sally. BFI is a decentralized, progressive company, and management believes in giving people significant responsibility as soon as possible. Sally learned early that BFI management is quick to reward success but does not tolerate those who do not accept responsibility and its ramifications.

## THE ASSIGNMENT

Sally's first major project is to improve market share in the adult cereal market through advertising and labeling strategies. Her charge is to suggest a new or modified marketing campaign for the Natural Cereals Division. Natural Cereals' brands are Fiber Rich, Bran Breakfast Flakes, Natural Bran, and Bran Bits. Sally is excited. This project allows her to work with two of the marketing department's best professionals, Tom Miller and Joe Bradley.

This case was developed by Norman E. Bowie and Patrick E. Murphy of the Arthur Andersen & Co. Business Ethics Program. Reprinted by permission of Arthur Anderson & Co. SC.

Tom Miller, a group product manager for the Natural Cereals Division, is a twenty-year veteran of BFI and has greatly influenced company policy. Tom is well-known throughout BFI as a fair, yet demanding, manager with a high degree of integrity. He transferred from the Family Cereals Division five years ago, having made his reputation as the product manager for Winkies, the number-two brand in the company. Since Tom's time is limited, he assigned Joe Bradley to informally supervise Sally on this project.

Joe, recently promoted to product manager, has been with BFI for four and one-half years, most of which were spent in the Family Cereals Division. His best-known campaign was for Sparkles, a children's cereal. Joe joined forces with a well-known toy manufacturer to give away a miniature character toy with each box of Sparkles. The box also contained an order form so parents could purchase the remaining set of characters directly from the manufacturer. This campaign increased market share of Sparkles by 10 percent. Sally knows she can learn a lot from Joe. She also knows he is Tom's friend and protégé. Sally suspects Joe will one day take Tom's position.

Another reason this is the perfect project for Sally is the fact that she is extremely health conscious. She believes too many cereals contain excessive amounts of sugar, which can encourage unhealthy eating habits in children and adults. An avid reader of health food literature, she has seen a number of scientific studies showing a correlation between high fiber and cancer reduction. For example, people who have a diet rich in fiber tend to have a significantly lower incidence of colon cancer.

Sally is well aware of the public's fear of cancer and has faced the trauma of cancer herself. She had a lump removed from a breast only a year ago. Fortunately, it was benign. Her father was not so lucky. Three years ago he succumbed to lung cancer. Sally believes cancer shortens lives and, given the agonizing deaths it causes, leaves severe emotional scars on surviving family members. She has such scars, as well as considerable anxiety about her own fate. She is committed to doing whatever she can in the war against cancer.

## COMPETITIVE/MARKET ANALYSIS

After consulting Joe, Sally examines a file of articles compiled by her predecessor about competitors in the cereal industry. The articles point out that intense industry competition is due to strong brands and high levels of advertising. Competitors spend $75,000,000 on advertising, two-thirds of which goes for television commercials. The good news is that adult ready-to-eat bran/fiber cereals grew twice as fast as the market, and sales increased over 20 percent last year.

In 1984, one competitor launched the first health claims advertising campaign for any food product—its high-fiber bran cereal. The company included information from the National Cancer Institute (NCI) on its packages and its advertising copy, which it had worked out in advance with NCI. The claims linked a specific product with the prevention of a particular disease—cancer. Although the Food and Drug Administration (FDA), which has jurisdiction over health claims, was not completely happy with this ad campaign, they did not block the ads. The following statement appeared on the back of the company's cereal box:

> The National Cancer Institute believes eating the right foods may reduce your risk of some kinds of cancer. Research evidence indicates high fiber foods are important to good health. High fiber foods, like bran cereal, are considered to be part of a healthy diet. Bran cereals are one of the best sources of fiber.

Also, this competitor's television ads made the following claim:

> Cancer! It doesn't worry me as much since I learned that I can fight back by a healthy diet. The National Cancer institute believes a high-fiber, low-fat diet may reduce your risk of some kinds of cancer. High fiber is important to a healthy diet, just like training is important to an athlete. I run, bike, and swim regularly. But that isn't enough. They say it's a matter of eating right, too. My health is really important, so I made some changes, like eating foods high in fiber.

This campaign proved quite effective. Annual sales of the company's cereals grew from $2,100,000 in 1983 to $2,800,000 in 1985. Sally found a study in *Public Health Reports*[1] that examined the effect of this campaign on sales. The article showed that in the twenty-four weeks following the start of the health claim campaign, there was a sharp increase in sales of this competitor's high fiber cereal. Its share of the total cereal market rose from 0.99 to 1.46 percent, a relative increase of 47 percent.

This competitor followed up its initial campaign with other campaigns that made health claims for its other high fiber cereals. Since 1984, the competitor has increased its advertising by one-third and introduced six new brands aimed at adults. These ads using the cancer preventative message were rather controversial. Certain people objected to the ads because they did not say what kinds of cancer they were referring to and how much of the cereal you had to eat. This statement by Dr. Timothy Johnson (medical director for a major television network) on a *Nightline* program raised several additional questions.

> [W]hen it comes specifically to diet and cancer connection, there is considerable uncertainty. I spent several months this past year looking very carefully at this hypothesis and talking literally to cancer experts all over the world, and found that opinion was divided and that the studies were inconsistent. Now, the language of the . . . ad is really quite accurate. It says, "Some studies suggest that it may. . . ." Problem is, there are other studies that suggest it may not. And the evidence is there for inconsistency. Now, you might say, so what? It's a diet that won't hurt, it may help, why not hedge our bets? And I really don't have any problem with that approach, but I do have two further concerns. One is that we may squander our scientific credibility in suggesting certainty where it does not exist, and then when we come to the public and really need to talk to them, they may not believe us. And I worry about what may happen on the fringes, not so much with the . . . ad but in health food stores or in other ways in which products and pills and books are promoted as a sure-fire answer to cancer with a particular diet program.[2]

Another competitor has also jumped on the fiber bandwagon by introducing four new high-fiber products. It has promoted its brands with a health claim using a variation of the initial NCI message on the back panel of its bran cereal package. Although this strategy did not increase total sales, the company was able to hold its market share position.

In studying company and trade data, Sally finds that Breakfast Foods, Inc., has lost two percentage points since 1985 and that its overall cereal market share is currently 14 percent. This is far behind the 40 percent share of the market leader and somewhat lower than its main competitor, which holds 20 percent. The data confirm the company has been losing market share to competitors that make a connection between high-fiber cereals and a possible reduction in the risk of getting certain kinds of cancer.

Prepared with these facts and figures, Sally schedules a meeting with Joe. She knows the approach she wants to take but decides it would be best to get Joe's advice before developing her preliminary ad campaign.

## PRELIMINARY AD CAMPAIGN

As Sally enters Joe's office, he holds up her analysis summary. "Good work, Sally! Your analysis makes the picture clear. We've got to move before our market share drops any lower, and a health-oriented campaign is the way to go." Joe leans back in his chair, clasps his hands behind his head, and motions for Sally to have a seat.

Sally, pleased by Joe's support, replies, "I think the best approach is to follow our competitors' general strategy. People simply don't know enough about their health. Cancer isn't something to take lightly. People need to become more aware of . . ."

"You're right," Joe interrupts. "A hard-hitting health campaign is what we need. We've probably benefited from the bran-cancer connection indirectly. Making it official with a clear, powerful message should benefit us even more. What we don't want to do, though, is waste our efforts. Tom just sent this memo to us." Joe slides an open trade report across his desk.

Sally picks up the report and reads the part circled in red:

> It costs just as much to run a lousy commercial as a good one. More than most products, cereal is "marketing sensitive"; that is, dollars spent on mediocre marketing simply fall into the void, while the same amount spent on a well-aimed pitch can dramatically increase sales.[3]

"This is what it's all about, Sally. We have to come up with a blockbuster campaign for Natural Cereals. Otherwise, we're going to lose our shirts. Let's meet with Tom to get his input. I know he'll support our approach 100 percent."

## THE MEETING

Fortunately, Sally and Joe were able to schedule a meeting with Tom for that afternoon. As they walk into Tom's office, Sally feels a little uneasy. She remembers Tom's comments over lunch last week. He had made it very clear he feels marketing and advertising must be truthful as well as persuasive. Sally wonders whether Tom will be concerned by the objections to the competitor's campaign she had read during her analysis.

"Well, this was quick work!" Tom says. "I'm glad to see you've come up with some ideas already. You got my note, I assume. This is going to be one tough campaign—we have to make it count."

"Yeah," says Joe, "Sally has worked around the clock on this. I think you will be pleased with what we've done." Joe smiles and turns to Sally.

Tentatively, Sally begins. "I've read a lot about bran cereals, and it looks like our major competitor has been quite successful. We can build on the health claims they've started. We really wouldn't be providing a new message, but it seems clear health claims will sell."

Tom leans back in his chair, closes his eyes and pauses. After what seems like an eternity to Sally, he says, "I don't know. That's an interesting approach, but it isn't the only one. I'm pretty hesitant about all this new emphasis on health claims. I'm not sure our competitors are presenting the whole picture."

Joe jumps in. "I agree, Tom. I spent a lot of time pondering this issue. But Sally convinced me. I think a carefully developed health campaign is the way to go."

"Well, Sally," says Tom, "I'm not saying no. You've obviously done your homework. But I want to make sure you consider the implications. You know the FDA has been looking into this matter and has issued a directive." Tom rummages through his file drawer, hands Sally a folder, and continues. "Take it and read it. Then come back next Monday with several campaign options. You've put a lot of effort into this so far. Now let's just take some time to consider the alternatives."

## CAMPAIGN OPTIONS

Sally goes to work immediately. From the information Tom gave her, she finds that in November 1987 the FDA proposed regulations allowing manufacturers to print messages on food labels about the health benefits of their products. Specifically, the FDA listed four criteria for evaluating health related claims and information on food labeling:

1. Information on the labeling must be truthful and not misleading to the consumer.
2. Information should be based on and be consistent with valid, reliable scientific evidence that is publicly available.
3. Available information regarding the relationship between nutrition and health shows that good nutrition is a function of total diet over time, not of specific foods.
4. The use of health-related information constitutes a nutritional claim that triggers the requirements of FDA's regulations regarding nutrition labeling.

The next morning, Sally makes a copy of the criteria and heads for Joe's office to get his thoughts.

After reading over them, Joe is silent. He shakes his head slightly and says, "I'm not sure these criteria will have any impact on our plans."

"Well," says Sally, "I think we might want to tone down our approach a little, don't you?"

"Not really," Joe smiles. "I did a little research myself last night and I learned the Federal Trade Commission, which regulates advertising, is pretty sympathetic to our competitors' ads. They believe the claim that some people might actually avoid cancer of the colon or rectum by eating their cereals is generally accurate. I think the FTC would allow advertising claims based on this labeling information."

"I don't know how seriously we should take the FDA's position, Joe. But I do know we should stick with the health orientation. Let me think of some specific options and I'll get back to you."

"Okay, it's your show. But," says Joe, "keep in mind we can't blow this campaign. It's got to have an impact."

Sally feels uneasy as she leaves Joe's office. She knows Joe is right. Her career is at stake. This is a highly visible campaign. Yet, she knows Tom is right, too. She starts to think of ideas for her marketing campaign. The FDA proposal would allow her to coordinate packaging and advertising, and that would give consumers a consistent message.

## ADVERTISING AND PACKAGING OPTIONS

To determine the best approach, Sally plans to develop several advertising and packaging alternatives for the natural product line. She will take the alternatives to Joe to see what he thinks. She just received from the research department the cereal's side panel containing nutritional and ingredient information (see Exhibit 1). Now she has to work on the marketing options.

Besides the ad linking high-fiber cereals with cancer risk reduction she reviewed earlier, she found a recent ad for another product noting it was high in vitamin B and provided an energy boost. As the first option, she thought of a possible hard-hitting strategy using the statement "Vitamin Enriched" on packaging and in advertising.

The report she recently received from BFI's research department indicated that Natural brands contained thirteen essential vitamins and minerals. She would feel comfortable putting this on the package and in advertising. In closely investigating the side panel listing nutritional information, she finds that Natural Bran Cereal, by itself, contains no fat. She knows a large part of the market is conscious of the levels of fat in foods. This could be another good claim to make.

But there are problems. Sally knows that the vitamin content is similar in all bran cereals. She also knows from internal company documents that most Americans are not deficient in B vitamins, nor does the amount of B vitamins contained in the cereal give one instant energy.

The second option she thinks of focuses exclusively on the appeal of bran and fiber as possible preventatives to cancer. She learns from company records that the amount of bran in Natural Cereals has increased by 40 percent in the last two years. One label alternative is: "With 40 Percent More Bran." Sally also knows this amount is equal to the most bran in any cereal. Therefore, another label or ad option is: "Containing the Highest Level of Fiber—Help prevent cancer by eating high fiber foods." She could place these statements in large boldface print on the package label and use them in advertising. This would reiterate the competition's strategy of linking cancer reduction with bran.

EXHIBIT 1: EACH SERVING CONTAINS 10 GRAMS OF DIETARY FIBER

**Nutrition Information Per Serving**
Serving Size: 1 oz. (About $^2/_3$ Cup) (28.35 g)
Servings Per Package: 20

|  | 1 oz. (28.15 g) Cereal | With $^1/_2$ Cup (118 ml) Vitamin D Fortified Whole Milk |
|---|---|---|
| Calories | 90 | 160 |
| Protein | 3 g | 7 g |
| Carbohydrate | 28 g | 34 g |
| Fat | 0 | 4 g |
| Sodium | 230 mg | 290 mg |

## Percentages of U.S. Recommended Daily Allowances (U.S. RDA)

| | | |
|---|---|---|
| Protein | 4% | 10% |
| Vitamin A | 25% | 30% |
| Vitamin C | ** | ** |
| Thiamine | 25% | 30% |
| Riboflavin | 25% | 35% |
| Niacin | 25% | 25% |
| Calcium | ** | 15% |
| Iron | 45% | 45% |
| Vitamin D | 10% | 25% |
| Vitamin $B_6$ | 25% | 30% |
| Folic Acid | 25% | 25% |
| Vitamin $B_{12}$ | 25% | 30% |
| Phosphorus | 15% | 25% |
| Magnesium | 15% | 20% |
| Zinc | 10% | 15% |
| Copper | 10% | 10% |

**Contains less than 2% of the U.S. RDA of these nutrients

Ingredients: Whole Wheat, Wheat Bran, Sugar, Natural Flavoring, Salt and Corn Syrup. Vitamins and Minerals: Iron, Vitamin A, Palmitate, Niacinamide, Zinc Oxide (Source of Zinc), Vitamin $B_6$, Riboflavin (Vitamin $B_2$), Thiamine Mononitrate (Vitamin $B_1$), Vitamin $B_{12}$, Folic Acid, and Vitamin D.

## Carbohydrate information

| | 1 oz. Cereal | With $1/_2$ Cup Whole Milk |
|---|---|---|
| Starch and Related Carbohydrates | 13g | 13g |
| Sucrose and Other Sugars | 5g | 11g |
| Dietary Fiber | 10g | 10g |
| Total Carbohydrate | 28g | 34g |

Another label she considers as part of this second option uses "natural" in the title for Bran Breakfast Flakes or Bran Bits. The slogan "Fiber for Health" is also a possible package label and advertising tag line.

Although these two options would probably be most effective, the FDA criteria keep running through her mind. As a result, she develops a third option downplaying health claims.

Option Three would point out that her product is a high-fiber, low-fat natural food. The label and the ads would feature energetic, healthy young people eating her breakfast cereals before an early morning tennis match. However, other traditional selling devices would be used, and the link to cancer reduction would not appear. From a marketing standpoint, she believes coupons on the back of the package might appeal to a broader market. She could also promote BFI's new "Resealable Pack," which allows the inside bag to be resealed for freshness. Other possibilities include discounts on a T-shirt and a cookbook featuring recipes using Natural's cereals. All of this would add up to a broad-based marketing appeal without relying totally on fiber and health claims. She thinks Tom might like this approach.

Sally knows these ideas are somewhat sketchy, but she wants Joe's input. She schedules a meeting for the following morning. She grabs a quick sandwich at the cafeteria and goes back to her desk to review her notes and reasoning for the meeting.

## EVALUATING THE OPTIONS

Joe listens quietly to Sally's options. As she describes each, he jots down a few notes. When she finishes, he simply says, "Combine Options One and Two."

"But I'm not sure that's the best way," Sally begins. "They are persuasive, but I think we should consider the implications."

Joe shakes his head. "The implication is that you need to increase market share and increase it quickly. Option Three won't do it. Options One and Two will. Everything we put on the package and the ads will be the truth. We could simply say 'Vitamin Enriched and Contains Vitamin B.' We don't need to say anything about vitamin B and an energy boost. Plus, we know the FTC won't object to cancer-reduction claims.

"There is nothing wrong with this approach. Besides, as you said yourself, we're doing people a favor. It isn't our responsibility to make people health experts. That's not our job, but selling cereal is."

Sally frowns. "What do you think Tom will say?"

"Look," Joe responds, "I talked with Tom about this over dinner. He said, basically, what I decide goes. Even if he doesn't agree totally, he won't overrule me. Tom is an excellent manager but doesn't have to concern himself with the details. The bottom line is that if we don't go with a hard-hitting campaign, we're going to lose our shirts. I've made my reputation around here, Sally. Now it's your turn. I want you to develop a full campaign combining Options One and Two."

Sally walks out of Joe's office. The project she wanted so badly isn't turning out the way she expected. She knows that, technically, Joe is supposed to just advise her, but could she realistically ignore his request? Besides, maybe he is right. What he said makes sense. Options One and Two are literally true. And is it her responsibility to make people health experts?

She sits down at her desk and begins to clear her mail. An envelope there from Tom contains a note and list of questions:

SALLY/JOE:

Here are a list of questions I use to evaluate the legal and ethical impact of advertising I have done. Please look them over. We do not want any legal or pressure group problems!

- Are your claims accurate?
- Do you have competent and reliable evidence to support your claims? It should be evidence that the scientific or medical community is willing to support.
- Have you disclosed important limitations or qualifications to the claims you have made about your product?
- Have you misrepresented or cited out of context the contents of a report or scientific study? Have you suggested there is a consensus of medical opinion on an issue when there is not?
- Have you suggested that a report is government sponsored when it is not?
- Is your advertising inconsistent with information on the label? Has FDA found the food ingredient in your product to be ineffective for your advertising purpose?[4]

Sally quickly scans the list. Exasperated, she phones Joe and blurts out, "Have you read the note from Tom?"

"Yes, Sally, I did," sighs Joe. "I read it this morning, and my position is the same. We can answer yes to each question." Sally slowly replaces the receiver and thinks aloud, "Now what?"

## FOR DISCUSSON

What is the problem Sally Thompson faces? What should Sally do? Why?

## NOTES

1.  Alan S. Levy and Raymond C. Stokes, "Effects of Health Promotion Advertising on Sales of Ready-To-Eat Cereals," *Public Health Reports* (July-August 1987): 398–403.

2.  ABC News, transcript of *Nightline*, program 1181, 2 December 1985.

3.  Quoted in Pamela Sherrid, "Fighting Back at Breakfast," *Forbes*, 7 October 1985, p. 127.

4.  Dianne L. Taylor, "Health-Related Food Advertising: 'The Time Is Ripe for Change,' " *Food Engineering* (December 1984): 21.

# The Advertising Code of American Business

We hold that advertising has a responsibility to inform and serve the American public and to further the economic life of this nation. Believing this, the following principles are hereby affirmed.

## 1. Truth

Advertising shall tell the truth, and shall reveal material facts, the concealment of which might mislead the public.

## 2. Responsibility

Advertising agencies and advertisers shall be willing to provide substantiation of claims made.

## 3. Taste and Decency

Advertising shall be free of statements, illustrations, or implications which are offensive to good taste or public decency.

## 4. Disparagement

Advertising shall offer merchandise or service on its merits, and refrain from attacking competitors or disparaging their products, services, or methods of doing business.

## 5. Bait Advertising

Advertising shall be bona fide and the merchandise or service offered shall be readily available for purchase at the advertised price.

## 6. Guarantees and Warranties

Advertising of guarantees and warranties shall be explicit. Advertising of any guarantee or warranty shall clearly and conspicuously disclose its nature and extent, the manner in which the guarantor or warrantor will perform and the identity of the guarantor or warrantor.

## 7. Price Claims

Advertising shall avoid price or savings claims which are unsupported by facts or which do not offer bona fide bargains or savings.

## 8. Unprovable Claims

Advertising shall avoid the use of exaggerated or unprovable claims.

## 9. Testimonials

Advertising containing testimonials shall be limited to those of competent witnesses who are reflecting a real and honest choice.

*John Z. Miller*

# Ethics and Advertising

I don't intend to state anything original. Instead, I want to remind you of criticisms of advertising that indicate that all is not well in Adland. Of course, we all realize that our industry is enormously successful; we are a $100 billion a year industry, with over seven thousand competing firms. We are coming off a decade of unprecedented growth. But commercial success does not imply ethical behavior, and it is quite clear that the American public is concerned about advertising. There are deep reasons for this distrust.

Although we all know what the free market is, let's highlight a couple of its features in order to better see what is ethically problematic about advertising. First, economists all assume people have certain wants and are free to choose products based on those wants. The consumer is said to be king; producers merely satisfy preexisting wants. Ads provide information about products; consumers are then free to try products and see whether they satisfy their wants. Second, for the market to work well, both consumers and producers need reasonably complete transaction information. Advertising enters here, for it supposedly supplies the bulk of such information. To make a long story short, one moral defense of the free market is that it gives consumers what they want more efficiently than other economic systems. And advertising is central to this efficiency because it informs people about products that may satisfy their wants.

The claim that the consumer is king is seriously questioned by John Kenneth Galbraith. In *The Affluent Society* he showed that advertising does not simply satisfy antecedently specified consumer wants; instead, ads create wants. Everyone has seen the graph that shows cigarette consumption maps directly onto ad expenditures, and everyone knows that cigarette ads associating smoking with glamour and sex in some cases created the desire to smoke. To those of you who claim that it cannot be proven that ads even influenced people to smoke I say: get real. Many of today's kids want to avoid smoke altogether, in large part because of negative advertising. In the early 1970s Lee Iacocca was fond of saying, "Safety

491

doesn't sell," implying that consumers didn't want safe autos. That may well have been true at the time. Clearly, however, ads which for decades showed acceleration, speed, and power mixed with sex, and which omitted any reference to the dangers of speed, etc., were a big factor in determining what the public wanted. In some cases ads take rather indefinitely specified wants and give them a specific shape. Everyone needs a sense of self-esteem, a feeling of confidence and satisfaction with oneself. Advertising did not create that need or want. In the 1950s, however, Americans wanted large autos, and they wanted large autos because they were convinced that large autos were necessary for self-esteem and they were so convinced largely by advertising and by the auto producers who offered them only large autos. Fashion provides another example. Annually, designers and producers make clothes that are distinct from the previous year's clothes. Marketers then create a desire for the new line of clothes, which retailers then stock. Advertisers do not create a desire for clothing, but it is clear they create a desire for a line of clothes that is already produced and for which consumers had no desire before the ad campaign began.

Galbraith's point is that over a large domain of products the producer is king. He creates desires in consumers, which he then satisfies through production. And this is ethically troublesome on two accounts. First, we take it that autonomy is valuable and that anything that undercuts it is bad. The free-market model assumes wants are antecedent to ads and that consumers are autonomous agents. Yet, if producers via ads create and shape desires, then the consumer is not entirely autonomous. Second, the standard defense of the free market, namely, that it satisfies more wants better than other economic systems, is undercut if advertising creates the wants it satisfies. If we agree that the American market with its heavy advertising creates and satisfies wants, it doesn't follow that the consumer is better off having the wants the advertiser has created. If a drug pusher creates a desire for cocaine in you, he expands your range of wants but you are not better off for having that want. Consumers have an ethical concern here; after all, the producer will market anything that will legally make him a profit.

Advertising in America also influences wants negatively because of the materialism and sameness of the products it promotes and because of its pervasiveness. The wants ads influence are directed at beer, gasoline, diamonds, trucks, moisturizers, furs, fried chicken, foundation garments, watches, tissues, money, autos, tacos, cigarettes, chocolates, refrigerators, toys, nylons, electricity, shaving cream, batteries, and mouthwash. Although some of these products are unobjectionable, the idea that assaults us unrelentingly is that our problems are eliminable by an object. Success, happiness, joy—all are depicted as produced by an external consumable thing, and not the result of years of hard work, learning, and commitment. I am not claiming that advertising is the sole or even the primary cause of American materialism, but that it is a significant partial cause is obvious.

In part because they focus almost entirely on material consumables, ads are also deadeningly similar. Ads stereotype people, primarily as consumers, but also by addressing concocted psychological inadequacies and by portraying the American ideal as young, successful, white, and suburban. All of these negative effects are compounded by advertising's pervasiveness. Television, radio, newspapers, magazines, the roadways—all are saturated with ads hawking commercial products. On average, each of us sees 1,600 ads per day. Children watch television six hours a day and talk with their parents for fifteen minutes; they are in school six hours a day for twelve years, but are bombarded by ads throughout their lives.

Finally, although some ads are amusing, they generally deaden taste. Ads are repeated endlessly, are often intentionally irritating, and appeal to the lowest level of cognitive ability. It is often said that the fact that ads are unaesthetic does not mean they are unethical. In a deep sense, however, our moral capacity depends on our ability to reason, assess facts, exercise our imagination, and empathize with others. A practice, then, is ethical to the extent that it exercises and improves our cognitive, imaginative and affective capacities. In this sense, much of education is ethical while advertising fails the test.

It is sometimes claimed that ads control people; subliminal ads are often cited. Yet, even if subliminal ads do cause people to act in certain ways, it is difficult to see how this could be true of the typical ad. "Bud Light: Everything Else Is Just A Light." Cute, but it is hard to see how the ad could totally preclude choice, which is what "control" implies. Yet, even if such ads do not control a viewer as a brainwasher controls his victim, the viewer is in a subtle sense manipulated by the ads. A clean-cut, handsome young man is shown enjoying a beer, and then pictured in the presence of an attractive, scantily clad young lady. Now the person who buys that brand of beer may well say he is buying it because he likes it or prefers its taste, but the ad works by linking the brand with his unconscious desire for sex, and the link is established between the brand and the fulfillment of that desire in the ad. So the real reason he buys the brand is the link set up between the brand and his unconscious desire, and he is not consciously aware of this link or the desire. In this way we are manipulated, if not controlled, by advertising.

As I see it, although no ad controls us, it is very difficult in America to avoid being heavily influenced or manipulated by the aim of advertisers, which is to get us to consume things, and by the pervasiveness and numbing sameness of the messages. The freedom to choose between this material object and that material object, between beer and pop, doesn't amount to much. We are perhaps truly free to the extent that we can step back, critically assess, and significantly change our entire way of living our lives. Advertising, however, mainly offers us beer or pop. This massive lifestyle conditioning is the threat advertising poses; it grinds down one's ability to entertain alternative lifestyles. Think of the bumperstickers you see. (1) "Born to Shop." Advertising's conditioning is so relentless that the consumer believes that shopping (for advertised products) is innate, natural, inevitable. (2) "A Woman's Place Is in the Mall." It is not the use of the advertised product that is significant or worthwhile, no, the *purchasing* of things gives women significance; their place is where things can be bought. (3) "When the Going Gets Tough, the Tough Go Shopping." Our deepest problems are solved by buying things advertised—typically on soap operas. (4) "Shop Till You Drop." Shopping is an all-consuming activity worth pursuing until you and your credit line are exhausted. While in some cases used as spoofs, it is sad that these slogans often reflect Americans' lives, and inescapably true that advertising must bear some responsibility for this sorry state of affairs.

Having shown that in many cases it is the producer via advertising who is king, and not the consumer, we can now examine the other primary prop of advertising, namely, that for the free market to work well both consumers and producers need reasonably complete market information and that ads supply the information. The indictment is that the "information" ads provide is often deceptive, misleading, or simply absent. Before we develop these charges we must examine the claim that ads are essentially lies.

Now, of course, very few advertisers sanction outright lying. The liar makes a claim that he believes is false with the intent to get his hearer to accept the claim as true. Both conditions must be met in order to label a claim a lie. This enables the advertiser to say with a straight face: "Everybody's talking about the new Starfire [automobile]." This isn't a lie because nobody believes that everybody is talking about the new Starfire. Hence, the second condition for lying is not met; since the advertiser knows nobody will accept the claim as true, he has not lied. He is engaged in mere "puffery." Although there isn't much outright lying in advertising, at least among large firms, the industry's standards are supposed to be much higher than the mere avoidance of lying. The advertising industry itself has a brief code of ethics that admonishes advertisers to tell the truth and not mislead consumers, and it says ads should avoid exaggerated or unprovable claims. Furthermore, the FTC is legally responsible for seeing that ads are not false. But it is false that everybody is talking about the new Starfire; the claim is certainly unprovable. In too many cases the industry and FTC are all too content to let a false claim slip by with the rationalization that at least it isn't a lie.

Although a liar asserts what he believes is false, ads can be deceptive without making false statements. An ad is deceptive if it causes consumers to have false beliefs about a product. Deceptive ads are unethical because the consumer who purchases based on false beliefs will not match products adequately with his interests. Since its founding in 1914, the FTC has sought to ban deceptive ads, but it must be admitted that deception is still rampant. Let's look at a few examples.

Volvo's ads have always stressed safety and chassis strength. In 1989 it ran an ad showing a six-ton truck being lowered onto a Volvo auto, which did not sag at all under the truck's weight. The ad was similar to Volvo ads from the early 1970s, which showed a Volvo holding up six other Volvos, again without sagging.

Now many viewers undoubtedly believed that the suspension and tires of the Volvo must be extraordinary to support such weight. In fact, however, in the 1989 ad jacks were hidden behind the tires and used to prop up the auto. Viewers saw the Volvo holding up the truck but did not see the jacks. After the ads were questioned, a Volvo spokesperson said the ads would not have looked the same without the jacks: "The tires would have exploded, and the springs would have compressed."

Volvo claimed the ads were not deceptive, because they were intended to exhibit the strength of Volvo's bodies and roofs, not the suspension or tires. However, the print version of Volvo's ad did not refer to body and roof strength; it simply said: "What you see here is exactly what you think you see here." Now, I'm not going to accuse Volvo or its advertisers of lying, but surely many readers believed that the Volvo has extraordinary suspension and tire strength. Certainly many readers believed the Volvo had suspension and tire strength sufficient to support a truck. But these are false beliefs produced by the ad. The TV ad that showed the truck being lowered onto the Volvo said "How well does your car stand up to heavy traffic?" Undoubtedly, many drivers of makes with suspension systems better than or equal to the Volvo's formed the belief that their make does not have a suspension system as good as Volvo's, and this false belief was produced by the ad. So these ads were deceptive.

In 1990 Volvo ran a TV ad that showed a pickup with huge tires being repeatedly driven over a line of autos, all of which were crushed except the Volvo. However, the Volvo's roof was reinforced with steel that viewers could not see and the other cars' roof support systems were cut through or weakened. No statements were made, so no false claims were made, yet clearly viewers would believe falsely that the Volvo's body strength was superior. Such ads are deceptive and unethical.

A 1990 ad showed an Oldsmobile dropped by parachute from a cargo plane. It hits the ground and drives away. But two Olds 98s are involved. The one dropped is an empty shell. The verbal part of the ad discusses Oldsmobile's customer satisfaction program. The company says the parachute represents the security provided by the program. Since the ad didn't mention anything about the car's performance and didn't claim that the car could be driven away after a parachute drop, Oldsmobile claimed the ad wasn't deceptive. But even though no performance claims are made, the visual focus of the ad is on the parachute drop. Many viewers falsely believe the Olds can be dropped and driven off, somewhat akin to the tanks we see dropped and then driven off in Airborne ads. Such an ad is deceptive even though it makes no false claims.

Since children are highly impressionable, advertisers have particular obligations to them, obligations that are often not met. A notorious case in point was Hudson Pharmaceutical Corporation's ads for "Spiderman" vitamins. Hudson's TV ads, aimed at preteens, featured Spiderman, an agile cartoon hero of immense strength. The ads depicted Spiderman gobbling a handful of Spiderman vitamins and then dispatching a bunch of bad guys, just like in the cartoons. However, children find it difficult to distinguish programming from advertisements, and the Spiderman of the cartoons looked like the Spiderman of the ads. So it was easy for viewers to falsely believe that eating a handful of vitamins will enable one to demonstrate incredible feats of strength. These ads were clearly deceptive. Furthermore, tests revealed that some of the Spiderman vitamins were very harmful when ingested in large amounts. The FTC ordered Hudson to stop the ads, but that the government had to intervene is an embarrassment to the advertising industry.

Of course, many advertisements do provide quite useful information. A picture may show you what a desk looks like, list its dimensions, and indicate its price, all of which will be informative. In such cases it will generally pay the advertiser to be truthful, for the consumer can verify whether the object has the features advertised. Still, there will be many cases in which ads convey only truthful information but are immoral. An ad may state all the beneficial features of a product but simply omit all negative features. It tells the truth, but only a half-truth. An advertisement will mention all the good features of a refrigerator, while overlooking all the defects and shortcomings that you can find if you read *Consumer Reports*. Now, clearly the producer and/or advertiser know their product's defects and shortcomings, but they present an ad which implies that the product has only good points. The consumer wants a product that satisfies his interests. If he believes that the product has only the advertised qualities but it actually has negative qualities that are unadvertised, then his interests will not be satisfied. Selling based on such advertised half-truths is unfair to the consumer.

I am not claiming that advertisers should be required to list *all* the positive and negative features of products. Ads would become prohibitively lengthy and confusing. But if not mentioning a feature clearly encourages consumers to buy a product for a use for which it was not intended and will not work, then it is ethical to mention it even though sales will be lost. And if not mentioning a negative feature will probably result in serious harm, then that feature should be mentioned. For example, it seems entirely appropriate to require advertisers of salt substitutes (which contain potassium) to state that the product is not appropriate for those on potassium-restricted diets, even though the salt substitute package itself lists potassium as an ingredient.

Many ballyhooed ads don't really provide any information. Coca-Cola ads are always right at the top of the "most memorable" ad list, but what information is conveyed by "Coke Is the Real Thing" or "Coke Adds Life"? Such ads contain no factual information. To show Coca-Cola being used by a bunch of joyful, jumping juveniles associates the product with a stereotyped "good life," but no information is conveyed. Let's not pretend that such ads facilitate the free market by providing reasonably complete transaction information. The aim here is to sell pop by persuasion based on psychological association. The ads are repeated relentlessly as a form of psychological conditioning. Now there is nothing unethical about selling products, and nothing intrinsically wrong about persuasion. We can persuade by providing information or by other (mainly psychological) means. Again, there is nothing intrinsically wrong with the latter. But let's not pretend that ads which provide no information are somehow vital to satisfying a condition that free-market theorists regard as necessary to such a market, namely, that market transactions should rest on consumers' knowledge of the qualities of products they are purchasing.

For an efficient market, consumers as well as producers need reasonably complete market information. Ads, along with sources like *Consumer Reports*, can provide such information. In all too many cases, however, ads are deceptive, convey misleading half-truths, or simply don't present any information at all.

Advertisers have taken full advantage of the 1990s, the decade of the "me" generation and lax regulation. At some point the pendulum will swing toward tighter regulation because so much of advertising is ethically suspect. We need to help move advertising more toward the status of a profession, with a balanced commitment to the public as well as our clients. We need a more developed and better enforced code of ethics. We need a stronger commitment to provide consumers with more and better information, while also cleaning up the ad clutter that is so deadening today. We can and ought to discipline ourselves for the benefit of the common good.

*Charles Collins*

# In Defense of Advertising

Advertising never has had much appeal to the cognoscenti. It doesn't have an abstract foundation that would enable it to find a niche within the theoretical tidiness of economics, and for those in the humanities who appeal to the "higher" values, advertising is too tied to mammon. Critics of advertising, ranging from philosophers, who contend that the market is "unfair," to economists, such as Galbraith, who decry the market's bad effects, used to have socialism on which to fall back. In the new age, philosopher-kings would determine production and distribution; advertising would be eliminated. And, in fact, as socialism was practiced advertisements were not needed; in socialist utopias such as the former USSR, Albania, Cuba, and North Korea it turned out that there were no goods to distribute. Socialism did satisfy the philosophers' demand for fairness; everyone shared equally in nothing. Since socialism, through its own internal contradictions, is reducing itself to absurdity, we are left with the market, messy as it may be. In fact, critics of advertising never had much of a case. Let's see why this is so.

Advertising's critics typically focus just on its negative aspects, of which admittedly there are some. However, if this sort of evidence is used to argue that advertising should be banned, the evidence is woefully insufficient for two reasons. First, advertising may well have benefits that outweigh its negative aspects. Second, to conclude that we should adopt some other method of conveying market information to consumers requires critics to propose and defend a method superior to advertising. This they have not done. Let us examine these two points.

Let's admit that in some cases advertising contributes to oligopoly, as in beer and cereals. Let's admit that in some cases it raises the cost of products to consumers, who pay for the cost of advertising. So what? In other cases advertising enables a company to gain market entry, which fosters competition. In many cases advertising increases sales, thereby lowering unit costs, which leads to lower prices. So the benefits of advertising must be discussed as well as its drawbacks, and no good empirical evidence exists to show that overall the negatives outweigh the positives as regards the issues of anticompetitiveness and prices.

Second, to show that advertising in some cases has some bad aspects does nothing to establish that there is some other method better at doing what advertising does. Of course, there is considerable controversy over what advertising does or should do. Yet if the suggestion is that we should ban advertising and replace it with, say, direct selling, this is just nonsense in a complex society such as ours. If the suggestion is that we replace advertising with a government controlled operation that would put out a product like *Consumer Reports*, then the burden is on those who make the proposal to show that such a system would be better than advertising. Of course, free-market defenders have no quarrel with *Consumer Reports* as it exists today; there is room in a free society both for *Consumer Reports* and commercial advertising.

Those who would ban advertising also need to recognize that businesses have a right to advertise, a right based on the right to free speech. The general benefits of free speech are well known. It promotes the independence and autonomy of speaker and hearer. It encourages criticism and reasoned deliberation, both important aspects of human development. Finally, free speech and the competition of ideas tend to help us establish the truth about issues. Since advertising is a form of speech, producers have a right to advertise. In some areas, such as political speech, the right to freedom of speech is almost unqualified; politicians can lie about their opponents and still avoid prosecution. Those of us who advocate a right to commercial speech recognize that the right is qualified. In the United States we require advertisers to tell the truth, and there is a good justification for prosecuting advertisers who make false claims. Advertising performs its function by providing information to the consumer, it cannot do so by making false claims. Nevertheless, within certain constraints companies do have a right to advertise.

Although there do not appear to be good reasons for banning advertising altogether, critics argue that regulation of advertising should be tightened considerably. One line of reasoning often voiced is inconsistent. Liberals often argue that freedom of speech in the political arena should not be restricted, on the assumption that the American public is sophisticated enough to filter the lies, falsehoods, misleading claims, and deceptive tactics that politicians employ. But they also argue that the American public is not sophisticated enough to filter out exaggeration and deception in advertising, even though advertisers cannot by law lie or make false claims. Although liberals often have blinders on when it comes to governmental paternalism, it should be clear that they cannot consistently maintain both positions.

Some critics object that advertisements often fail to provide informational content. So, it might be granted that advertising's function is to inform consumers, but then claimed that advertisements often do not inform. However, Phillip Nelson has recently developed arguments to the strong conclusion that all advertising is informative.[1] Clearly, some advertisements are informative, e.g., they state a product's function, size, cost, and so on. Generally, it will be in the producer's interest to state these features truthfully. The size and cost of a suit, for example, can be directly verified by a consumer prior to purchase. And it will generally pay to advertise a product's function truthfully; the producer who advertises an analgesic as a laxative will not get many repeat purchases. Accordingly, much advertising is informative. But what of advertisements such as "It's Miller Time" or "Coca-Cola Classic Is the Real Thing"? Nelson argues that even if the message is not informative the fact that the product is advertised is informative. It pays to advertise those products that do satisfy consumers' wants; it does not pay to advertise products that fail to satisfy consumers' wants. Since repeat purchasing by consumers will typically increase the advertising budget, the amount of advertising provides consumers with information about what brands satisfy consumer wants. So advertising can provide valuable information to consumers even though it is as empty as "Coca-Cola Classic Is the Real Thing."

Much of the critics' fire has been directed at "deceptive" advertising. Let's begin by differentiating lying from deception. A lie is a statement by a person who, knowing the statement is false, intends that his listeners will take the statement as true. To deceive a person is to cause him to have false beliefs. An advertisement, then, lies if it makes a false statement and the producer/advertiser intends that the consumer will take the statement to be true. An advertisement is deceptive if it causes a consumer to have false beliefs about the product advertised. Some refinement of the definition of "deception" will be required, but we can start here in order to see the difference between these concepts.

According to these definitions, an advertisement that lies involves a false claim, but a deceptive advertisement may not contain any false claims. It may tell the truth, yet still cause the consumer to have a false belief. So some deceptive advertisements are not lies. Furthermore, although all lies involve making a false claim, some false claims are not deceptive. If I lie in poker, you may not believe me, i.e., you are not deceived. So, some lies do not involve deception. One may say that a liar attempts to deceive his hearer; he does not always succeed. A person who is deceived by an advertisement does actually have a false belief as a result of the advertisement, irrespective of whether the deceiver makes a false claim.

Lying is not a major concern in advertising. For one thing, it is illegal. The 1937 Wheeler Amendment prohibits unfair or deceptive advertising, and explicitly says that a false advertisement is unfair or deceptive. Since a lie must contain a false statement, advertisements can neither make false claims nor lie. The advertising profession also explicitly bans lying because it prohibits false claims. It does so by insisting that advertisements contain true claims. The Advertising Code of the American Advertising Federation says: "Advertising shall tell the truth . . . be willing to provide substantiation of claims made . . . and avoid the use of unprovable claims." The profession monitors and polices advertisements, and believe me, if an advertisement makes a false claim, competitors let everyone in the professional body and at the FTC know about it. The FTC acts quickly to prohibit false advertisements. Accordingly, consumers need not worry that advertisements lie; they need not even worry that they contain false claims:

So far we have argued that all advertisements provide some information to consumers and that an overwhelming percentage of advertisements not only do not lie, they do not contain false claims. Are some advertisements, nonetheless, deceptive? According to our initial definition, many advertisements will be deceptive. We said that an advertisement is deceptive if it causes a consumer to have false beliefs about the product advertised. Judging from surveys which indicate that a rather high percentage of Americans believe that the Abominable Snowman exists, we could probably find some consumer whose false belief that the Jolly Green Giant exists and eats beans was caused by Pillsbury's advertisements. Such an advertisement would be deceptive on this definition of "deception."

From a legal standpoint, we know that the 1937 Wheeler Amendment broadened the FTC's powers to include the prohibition of deceptive advertising. So the issue is whether the FTC should adopt the above definition of deception. Ivan Preston has called the above definition the basis of the "ignorant man" standard, the idea being that the law should protect even the most ignorant person against "deceptive" advertising.[2] Preston points out that the FTC placed a strong emphasis on the ignorant man standard from roughly 1919 to 1963, but his tracing out of cases reveals a reduction to absurdity of the standard. The FTC, for example, outlawed Charles of the Ritz's use of "Rejuvenescence" as a facial cream name because it might cause consumers to falsely believe that it would literally restore youth and the appearance of youth. The FTC banned Clairol from saying that its dye would "color hair permanently" because one witness said she thought that someone might be caused to falsely believe that all the hair a person grows over a lifetime would be colored, even though the witness admitted that she would not be so fooled. The court itself said that it didn't see how anyone would be deceived, but had to admit that someone could be deceived, which seemed to preclude use of the advertisement by the ignorant man standard. The court sided with the FTC. The point is that any advertisement, no matter how truthful, will probably cause some ignoramus to have some false belief about a product. The FTC recognized the reduction to absurdity in 1963: "An advertiser cannot be charged with liability in respect of every conceivable misconception, however outlandish, to which his representations might be subject among the foolish or feeble-minded. . . . A representation does not become 'false and deceptive' merely because it will be unreasonably misunderstood by an insignificant and unrepresentative segment of the class of persons to whom the representation is addressed."[3]

If pressed to its logical conclusion, the ignorant man standard precludes or severely restricts advertising. Of course, many of advertising's critics desire that result. Again, however, no such proposal can be seriously entertained unless the legislation's costs are weighed against advertising's benefits. Furthermore, the burden is on the critics to show that the harm of advertising as presently practiced outweighs its benefits. Now we know that: (1) all advertising provides some information; (2) the law requires that advertisements not make false claims; (3) severely restricting advertising would increase consumers' search costs; (4) the cost of ignoramus-based litigation would be high; and (5) a basic assumption of democratic society is that individuals are able to detect and deflect the attempt to deceive. All this suggests that instead of banning or severely restricting advertising based on the ignorant man standard we should reject the concept of deception on which it rests.

Let us say, then, that an advertisement is deceptive if a reasonable person to whom the advertisement is directed would have false beliefs about the product advertised as a result of the advertisement. This was the standard employed in common law prior to establishment of the FTC in 1914, and it has been the standard followed in recent years by the FTC, roughly since 1963. This standard would permit Charles of the Ritz to use "Rejuvenescence" as the name of a facial cream and allow Clairol to claim that a dye "colors hair permanently." It would also allow "Coca-Cola

Classic Is the Real Thing"; this metaphor is outside the true/false domain. No reasonable person would be deceived by it. The reasonable man standard also permits the "half-truths" that critics find so disturbing about advertising. To tell the whole truth about whether a product is the best for a consumer to buy, the advertiser would have to list all of a product's features and compare those with all competing products—an impossible task in an advertisement. But every reasonable consumer knows that advertisers will present only those features favoring their products, so he is not deceived.

We should, in no uncertain terms, prohibit deceptive advertising, since advertising cannot fulfill its function of providing information to the consumer if the consumer is deceived about advertised products. And some advertisements are unquestionably deceptive. The recent Volvo advertisement, showing a pickup with monster tires being driven over the roofs of a row of automobiles with only the Volvo's roof holding up while the other automobiles' roofs caved in, was deceptive. Volvo had reinforced the roof of its automobile, but had cut the roof supports of the other automobiles. Clearly, the reasonable consumer could not know these facts, and probably would be deceived; it would be reasonable to form the false belief that the Volvo's roof support system is much better that its competitors'. However, you will note that this advertisement had a very short run; it was quickly fingered as deceptive and withdrawn. The upshot is that the advertising profession should work hard to prevent deceptive advertising and should take quick action to remove it when it occurs. But to inform the consumer adequately we need the reasonable man definition of "deception" rather than the ignorant man standard.

Let us now turn from the issues of truth and deception to advertising's effects. We consider two aspects of this issue: whether advertising creates desires and whether it controls consumers.

The traditional view of the market is that consumers have desires and producers make products to satisfy those desires. However, Galbraith argues that producers create certain desires through advertising, which they then satisfy through production.[4] So the producer is actually sovereign, not the consumer. Galbraith calls this the "dependence effect." Of course, certain desires, e.g., the desire for food, sex, and shelter are not created; they are basic or "original" to consumers in the sense that they are wired into people at birth. But other desires, e.g., for mouthwash, off-road vehicles, earrings, soda pop, and air conditioners, are nonbasic; they are, in Galbraith's term, "contrived," largely by advertising. Galbraith believes that as a capitalist society becomes more affluent desires are increasingly created by the very process by which they are satisfied, primarily by advertisers hired by those who produce the products.

According to Galbraith, the dependence effect has two bad consequences. To continuously increase production and make increasing profits, producers must create ever more desires, which puts consumers on a squirrel-wheel of materialistic consumption. Second, our preoccupation with our own consumption, constantly reinforced by advertising, leads to a neglect of public goods, such as schools, environmental quality, and mass transit. We have too much perfume and not enough parks.

Galbraith doesn't precisely detail which desires advertising creates, but he is mistaken in thinking that it creates any desires. Of course, people didn't desire the automobile before it was invented. However, they did desire mobility, and once the automobile was invented many thought it was a good means to mobility. People couldn't have desired a Fedders air conditioner prior to the invention of air conditioning, but they did desire comfort, and when the air conditioner was invented many thought the Fedders that they saw advertised was a good means to achieve comfort. So they tried it out. Men couldn't have desired Aramis before that scent was concocted, but they desired to attract women, and when Aramis became available many thought Aramis was a good means to attract women. Advertising may have persuaded them to give Aramis a try, but it certainly didn't create the desire. Critics castigate advertising for creating the desire to smoke, but overlook the popularity of marijuana, heroin, and cocaine, none of which is advertised. In general, then, advertising does not create desires; given a certain desire, the advertiser brings to the consumer's attention a product that may satisfy that desire. If the consumer chooses to try the product, it may or may not satisfy the desire. If it does, he may purchase the product again; if it doesn't, he probably won't buy it again.

Advertising simply doesn't have the power Galbraith attributes to it. Thousands of new products are introduced annually, many of which are heavily advertised. The vast majority fail to gain a market niche and are withdrawn. It is true that those products heavily advertised succeed more often than those not advertised. However, this is due to the fact that producers advertise those products they have good reason (via test marketing) to believe will satisfy consumers' desires, and not because they believe advertising can create desires.

Galbraith draws a loosely specified distinction between basic/original/ real desires on the one hand and nonbasic/derived/contrived desires on the other. The latter are said to be less worthy of satisfaction or less important than the former. But, as critics such as von Hayek have noted, all of the arts fall into the latter category.[5] We may be born with the desire for food, but the desire for Mozart is no less contrived than the desire for air conditioning—on the assumption that desires are contrived. A veritable army of educators is engaged in the task of contriving a desire for Mozart, Shakespeare, and Rembrandt. Are these desires, contrived by the producer (the educational system), unimportant or in some sense unworthy of satisfaction? Clearly, Galbraith would say no. So the overall dilemma for Galbraith is that either desires are not created, or, if some are, the mere fact that they are created does not mean they are unworthy of satisfaction.

It is precisely here that Galbraith's socialism becomes manifest. Among the set of contrived desires, some, contrived by Big Brother and intellectuals like Galbraith, are worthy of satisfaction, while others, contrived by advertising, are unimportant. Control advertising and you curb unimportant desires. Socialism, having failed totally to solve the problem of the production and distribution of goods, reemerges in new guise by telling us that most goods are unnecessary and that Big Brother and the professors will determine for us what goods are important or unimportant.

The remaining major criticism of advertising is that it in some sense "controls" consumers. Typically, it is assumed that some advertising, notably subliminal advertising, does control consumers. So, it is assumed that if "eat" is flashed on a theater screen in a way that is below the threshold of conscious recognition of the term, moviegoers will stream out to buy popcorn or candy. It is then argued that other forms of advertising analogously control consumers.

One problem is that there is simply no evidence that subliminal advertising works. For example, Moore argues that theoretical considerations are inconsistent with the claim that subliminal advertising can get a person to do anything,[6] and McDaniel, et al., point out that empirical research fails to support the claim that purchasing behavior is influenced by subliminal stimuli.[7] Ever since Wilson Key wrote *Subliminal Seduction*, he has made a nice living by going from campus to campus pointing out hidden sexual symbolism in just about any advertisement.[8] He intimates to kids who desperately want to be free that that devil, the advertiser, can manipulate them into buying just about anything via subliminal messages. But, as with an inkblot, there is no telling what a viewer will see in an advertisement. It is perhaps curious and amusing that Key sees sex in a Sunkist orange, but, even if some advertisements do contain subliminal messages, there is no theoretical or empirical basis for his assertion that such messages control or even influence consumers.

Once the claim that subliminal advertising works is undercut, it is difficult to see how advertising could be said to "control" consumer behavior. In one sense I control your behavior if I can actually get you to do what I want you to do. The advertiser wants you to purchase the advertised product, but he certainly cannot ensure that you will do so. Again, advertising simply does not have the power critics attribute to it.

It is also claimed that some advertising controls consumers by linking a product with certain "unconscious" desires.[9] For example, after watching a beer commercial that portrays a young man drinking a Budweiser and then cozying up to an attractive young lady, I may subsequently purchase a Budweiser and, when asked, say I purchased it because I like that brand of beer. But, say the critics, the real reason I bought the Bud is that the commercial linked that brand with my unconscious sexual desire. The problem here is that the desire is not "unconscious." Of course I desire sex. I am also aware that I desire sex. I believe that sex is desirable, and am aware I have this belief. Furthermore, I think that Budweiser sometimes works as a means to sex (although I know from experience that Colt-45 does not "work every time"). In certain cases it doesn't; one has to experiment. Finally, I am aware I like Budweiser. So, all of this is within the orbit of my conscious awareness. I choose; I am not controlled.

It has been argued that the consumer only rarely understands the full range of the object's features, what it will do, and what the consequences of using it will be; hence, advertising can cause consumers to make irrational choices, i.e., choices they would not make if they knew all the relevant facts. As Arrington has recently argued, however, if we require every fact about a product to be known before we can be said to rationally desire the product, then, since this is impossible, no desire will be rational. On the other hand, if we require only knowledge of the relevant information to label the desire rational, then prior desires establish the relevance of information.[10] Now it is precisely advertising that enables us to fulfill those prior desires. It does so by providing information to the consumer and by laying out an array of means that may enable the consumer to satisfy such desires. A consideration of a variety of means to realize a given desire is certainly a prime instance of what we regard as rational behavior. So advertising cannot be convicted of causing irrational desires.

So the claim that advertising controls consumers' behavior is indefensible. Nobody really believes that an automobile advertisement linking, as most do, the twin desires of mobility and sex, could control a consumer. In fact, most automobile advertisers explicitly tell their clients that their advertisement will not sell the automobile; at best it persuades the consumer to go to a dealer's showroom to see and try the product. The advertisement cannot, and should not be expected to, list all the automobile's features or compare it to all competing automobiles. The consumer must drive this and other automobiles and read automotive magazines to get that information.

If we put aside the professors' theorizing, do we find *any* evidence that advertising in *any* sense "controls" consumers? No, we don't. No empirical studies show this. Information Resources, Inc., recently released the results of an exhaustive six-year study of 30,000 households' television viewing and reading patterns and their purchasing behavior.[11] The study was unique in that it focused on individuals rather than on aggregate behavior patterns. The firm knew, for example, what television commercials a subject viewed, what products he purchased with what coupons, even what he ate for lunch. The detailed study promised to indicate whether advertising works, and, if so, point to or explain how it works. What were the results? Well, the study concluded that there is no "simple correspondence" between more advertising and higher sales, that new brands need to be advertised more heavily when they are introduced, and that it is better to advertise during prime-time than other times. Ho hum. Interestingly, one of the advertisers' stock assumptions was shot down. Advertisers often test an advertisement on a sample of consumers to see whether they can recall it. But Information Resources' research reveals that the relation between high recall and increased sales is "tenuous at best." This study certainly explodes the myth that advertising controls behavior; for X to control Y there must be at least a correlation between X and Y, but even that seems questionable in the case of advertising and sales.

In conclusion, advertising is defensible. Since advertising is a form of speech, producers have a right to advertise unless they harm consumers or deny them certain rights. But advertising does not violate consumers' rights. It does not manipulate them by creating desires, and it cannot be said to control consumers' behavior. Instead, it simply presents choices to consumers; in total, advertising presents a wide variety of means to satisfy consumers' desires. Whether the consumer tries the product is his free choice. Whether the product satisfies the consumer's desire is up to the consumer to decide. If it does, he may repurchase the product; if not, he will try something else. Advertising should provide information to consumers, and all advertising does so. We have in place professional and governmental mechanisms to prevent or quickly withdraw advertisements that lie or make false claims. We do need to protect consumers against deceptive advertising, but to do so we should continue to employ the "reasonable" man standard rather than the "ignorant" man standard. Although this standard permits puffery and half-truths, such practices are permissible, since reasonable people are not deceived by them. Undoubtedly, advertising has some bad effects, but it certainly has not been shown that they outweigh its numerous good effects. To ban or severely restrict advertising, critics will have to provide consumers with product information. Such an alternative will have to be compatible with the free market, for the socialist option has recently been consigned to the dustbin of history.

## NOTES

1. Phillip Nelson, "Advertising and Ethics," in *Ethics, Free Enterprise, and Public Policy*, ed. Richard T. De George and Joseph A. Pichler (New York: Oxford University Press, 1978), pp. 187–98.

2. Ivan Preston, *The Great American Blow-up: Puffery in Advertising and Selling* (Madison: University of Wisconsin Press, 1975).

3. Heinz W. Kirchner, 63 FTC 1282 (1963).

4. John Kenneth Galbraith, *The Affluent Society* (Boston: Houghton Mifflin Co., 1958).

5. F. A. von Hayek, "The Non Sequitur of the 'Dependence Effect,' " *Southern Economic Journal* 27 (1961): 346–48.

6. Timothy E. Moore, "Subliminal Advertising: What You See Is What You Get," *Journal of Marketing* 46 (spring 1982): 38–47.

7. Stephen McDaniel, Sandra Hart, and James McNeal, "Subliminal Stimulation as a Marketing Tool," *The Mid-Atlantic Journal of Business* 20 (1983): 41–48.

8. Wilson Key, *Subliminal Seduction* (New York: New American Library, 1973).

9. Roger Crisp, "Persuasive Advertising, Autonomy, and the Creation of Desire," *Journal of Business Ethics* 6 (1987): 413–18.

10. Robert L. Arrington, "Advertising and Behavior Control," *Journal of Business Ethics* 1 (1982): 3–12.

11. *Wall Street Journal*, 4 November 1991, pp. B1, 6.

*Case Study*

*George Rainbolt*

# Linking Databases at ClickThrough

In 1996, four friends, Niquitta Funes, Hassan Knight, Scott Sayar, and
Geoff Steenblik, started ClickThrough, Inc. immediately after they
received their bachelor's degrees from the University of Michigan. Click-
Through purchases banner space on the Web pages of various Web sites,
and then contracts with various companies to develop banner ads and
place them on those Web pages. ClickThrough was one of the first Internet
advertising companies and the four friends were excited to be working at
a dot-com on the cutting edge of marketing and technology. They awarded
themselves nice salaries, but the real hope was to make money in stock
which, should ClickThrough successfully go public and do well, might be
worth millions. Funes was VP for Production, in charge of making the ads
and cookies. Knight was VP for Sales and he was in charge of buying and
selling banner space. Sayers was VP for Finance, charged with keeping
track of the money and making sure employees were paid. Steenblik was
President and CEO. Shares in the company were distributed according to
the initial financial investment made by the four friends. Steenblik held 55
percent of the shares and Funes, Knight, and Sayers each held 15 percent.

In order to set its ad rates, ClickThrough makes extensive use of
"cookies." Cookies are very small computer programs which are placed on
the hard drive of the computer which views a web page. When someone
first looks at a page on which ClickThrough has banner space, one of
ClickThrough's cookies is placed on that hard drive. If that computer is
later used to view another page on which ClickThrough has a banner ad,
the cookie originally placed on the hard drive is read and updated. In this
way, ClickThrough could develop a "clickstream," a record of the web
pages which have been visited by a particular computer. Cookies cannot,
however, identify the person using a particular computer. A clickstream is
valuable information because it allows ClickThrough to target its ads to

the interests of the person(s) using the computer. For example, a computer used to visit several sites related to classic cars might see banner ads for companies which sold parts for classic cars while a computer used to visit several sites related to cooking would instead see ads for cooking equipment. This information allows an Internet advertiser to increase the "clickthrough rate," the rate at which individuals seeing a banner ad click on it to get more information. The higher the clickthrough rate, the more ClickThrough can charge for the ad.

ClickThrough, although not profitable, grew quickly and therefore rapidly hired a team of programmers, sales associates, and clerical staff. In 1999, Steenblik proposed that ClickThrough buy Direct Mail Marketing Systems (DMMS), an old-fashioned direct marketing firm which was in the business of postal mail marketing. By this time, ClickThrough had developed a large clickstream database. These clickstreams, however, were still not identified by the name of the person who used the computer. Instead, computers were tracked using a globally unique identifier (GUID). GUIDs are unique to each computer, not to the individual using the computer. DMMS, on the other hand, had a large database with the names and addresses of individuals. Each of these names was associated with a customer profile. The customer profiles were lists of the products customers had purchased by mail and they were used by DMMS to direct its catalogs to individuals likely to buy the products in those catalogs. Steenblik proposed buying DMMS and combining its database with ClickThrough's. In this way, ClickThrough would be able to associate names and addresses with particular clickstreams. It would then be possible to develop a targeted and unified marketing scheme to a particular individual. This marketing plan could include banner ads, unsolicited e-mail (aka spam), and direct mail. ClickThrough could offer these unified marketing plans to various organizations. For example, a charitable organization working to cure a disease could purchase a marketing campaign using the names, postal addresses, and e-mail addresses of people who had visited pages which contained information about that disease.

In addition, Steenblik thought that many organizations would be willing to pay large sums of money for the combined database. Health insurance companies would be willing to pay for this kind of information because they could use it to avoid selling insurance to people who might have diseases which are expensive to treat. Employers would pay for this information to screen out a possible employee because the person's clickstream indicated possible illegal behaviors (for example, visiting drug paraphernalia sites) or health problems which would raise the company's health insurance costs. Other companies could either pay ClickThrough to send information to those in the combined database or buy all or part of the database from ClickThrough. (In the *later* case, they could resell the database.)

ClickThrough brought in a team of consultants to consider whether it should purchase DMMS. The consultants reported that the purchase of DMMS and the proposed use of its database was perfectly legal. The consultants pointed out that purchasing DMMS raised some serious public relations issues. As a closely held company, ClickThrough would not have to worry about the objections of stockholders, but the public at large might react adversely to ClickThrough's plan. The consultants suggested that a broad-based and strong negative public reaction might lead to a great deal of bad publicity and even to legislative action to ban the proposed use of the DMMS database. On the other hand, the consultants agreed with Steenblik's view that DMMS would be a significant asset to ClickThrough. In addition to the points raised by Steenblik, the consultants noted that DMMS had a history of solid, although less-than-spectacular, profits. The combination of DMMS and ClickThrough would, therefore, be significantly more attractive to investors when ClickThrough's shares were offered to the public. The consultants' view was that buying DMMS and using its database had a high probability of being very profitable for the four friends. They could well be millionaires. On the other hand, the consultants also reported that, because of the possible public relations problems, there was a relatively small probability that the purchase of DMMS would be a disaster of such proportions as to threaten the viability of ClickThrough.

## For Discussion

In your opinion, is it ethical for ClickThrough to buy DMMS and use the databases in the way Steenblik suggests? Why or why not? Would it be ethical for ClickThrough to buy DMMS and not combine the databases? If ClickThrough bought DMMS, can you think of other possible uses of the combined database? Do these possible uses raise ethical problems? Why or why not?

*George Rainbolt*

# The Internet and Consumer Privacy

Recent technological innovations have dramatically increased the ability of companies to gather and process information. The increasing powers of computers coupled with the development of the World Wide Web allow information to be gathered and analyzed much more quickly and at much lower cost than ever before. Instead of keeping records on pieces of paper, which are difficult to store and even more difficult to search, computers keep electronic records which are easy to store and search. Fifty years ago, for example, keeping a large database of consumers' past purchasing habits in order to direct catalog mailings was technologically impossible. Today it is routine. This raises the following question: what are the moral limits of a company's use of information about its customers? When, if ever, does a company's use of information about consumers violate their privacy rights?

The development of computers in the 1960s led to the creation of consumer databases. These databases could be searched to make marketing efforts, principally catalogs and phone solicitations, more effective. Over time, the records from individual companies were sometimes combined and other sorts of records (for example, motor vehicle records, telephone records, lists gathered from individuals who return rebate or warranty cards, and survey records) were added to these databases.

In 1995 the creation of the Web dramatically increased the power and scope of consumer databases. The Web allows individuals to search for information. Much of this information is related, directly or indirectly, to the purchase of products and services. Apart from the purchase of products and services on the Web, individuals search for information about possible purchases. They buy books and read book reviews. They buy cars and read crash-test data. They buy stereo equipment and chat with people who have recently purchased stereo equipment.

---

Companies can and do track how people use the Web. The essential tools in this tracking are "cookies," very small computer programs which are placed on the hard drive of the computer which views a Web page. If a computer is used to visit a particular Web page, that page can place a cookie on that computer. If that computer is again used to visit that Web page, the computer which produces the Web page can read the cookie. Cookies can store a wide variety of information. They can, for example, store information about past purchases made from a particular computer, about Web pages visited since the cookie was last read, or about new programs installed since the cookie was last read. Data from cookies can be combined to form a "clickstream," a record of the Web pages which have been visited by a particular computer. Some cookies merely provide a clickstream within a particular site (for example, the clickstream of a computer at a site that sells books) while others provide a clickstream across sites. In theory, a clickstream could be a complete record of absolutely everything done on a computer, every key typed, every file saved, every Web page visited. In practice, however, such detailed information is rarely useful. Clickstreams can be anonymous or identified. An anonymous clickstream is one which is merely associated with a particular computer, not with a person. An identified clickstream is a clickstream associated with a particular person. The easiest way to identify a clickstream is to search the clickstream itself to see if the owner has typed in a name. For example, the clickstream might contain the name, address, phone number, and credit card number given by the user to make a purchase.

Using cookies, companies can and do compile large databases of information about consumers. The moral issues raised by these databases can, initially, be broken into two categories. First, people worry about illegal uses of this information. The main cause for concern here is that unethical individuals will hack into a company's database to gain information to make illegal purchases. For example, a hacker might use credit card numbers to make purchases. Second, people worry about the legal use of the information in consumer databases. Some companies sell information to individuals who are trying to find other individuals. For example, residency information might be sold to a lawyer attempting to find a father who has ceased to make child-support payments. Companies sell information to other companies for use in marketing efforts. A political party might, for example, buy the subscriber list of a magazine whose subscribers are likely to support that party. This list would then be used to solicit donations. Companies also sell information to other companies for use in hiring decisions. For example, a company might buy the list of those who have used a bail bond service in order to avoid hiring people who have been arrested.

In general, and with some important exceptions to be discussed below, the law holds that the information in a company's database is that company's property. It may be analyzed, bought, and sold. Some companies have privacy policies. These policies explain how the company uses the information in its databases. The courts have generally, if not universally, held that these privacy polices are part of a contract between the companies who sell via the Web and the people who buy things from these companies. Therefore, if a company has a privacy policy and violates that policy, this would constitute fraud and would therefore be illegal. However, it is important to note that a company need not have a privacy policy. In addition, if company X's Web site has a banner ad from company Y, the information that company Y collects is not covered by X's privacy policy. Furthermore, if company X, following its own privacy policy, sells information to company Z, Z's use of that information is not covered by X's privacy policy.

Turning to the exceptions noted above, in specific areas the law places limits on how companies may use consumer databases in addition to those which may be found in privacy policies. The complete list of such exceptions would be long, but three examples may serve as illustrations. The Fair Credit Reporting Act of 1970 prohibits disclosure of credit reports to anyone besides authorized customers and requires that consumers be given access to records and allowed to correct inaccuracies. The Family Educational Rights and Privacy Act of 1974 limits the disclosure of educational records to third parties and requires that students be given access to records and allowed to correct inaccuracies. The Right to Financial Privacy Act of 1978 provides for 4th-Amendment-like protection for bank records.

Companies have collected information about consumers for centuries. The way that companies use information about consumers is not fundamentally changed by the Web and increased computing power. But these new technologies have caused a dramatic difference in degree. Companies can now collect and analyze much more information than in the past. The fundamental philosophical issues have not changed but their importance has increased dramatically. Philosophical discussion of the moral limits of a company's use of information about its customers must begin with an analysis of the concept of privacy.[1] Loss of privacy is the primary fear raised by the existence of consumer databases. A fact is private to the degree that knowledge of it is restricted. A fact is completely private when only one person knows it. A fact is completely non-private when everyone knows it. The privacy of a fact is a matter of degree depending on the number of people who know it. The more people who know some fact, the less private it is. How private a fact is needs to be distinguished from how important that fact is. A trivial fact can be very private or hardly private at all. An important fact can be very private or hardly private at all. A private person is a person who does not reveal many facts about herself to others. A place is a private place to the degree that one can engage in activities in that place without others knowing facts about what one is doing. My windowless basement is more private than my bedroom with its many windows overlooking the apartments across the street. My bedroom, however, is more private than the town square.

A person has privacy to the extent to which facts about her are not known by others. There are four variables to consider when evaluating how much privacy a person has. First, one must consider the number of facts about her that are known by others. Second, one must consider how many other people know these facts. Third, one must consider how important these facts are. The revelation of a few important facts about a person may do much more to lessen a person's privacy than the revelation of a large number of trivial facts. Fourth, in general, the more specific information is, the more the revelation of it lessens a person's privacy. The fact that a particular man has sexual fantasies about women is hardly news. A specific description of these fantasies, on the other hand, would probably significantly lessen his privacy.

Notice that false information about a person does not diminish his privacy. Instead, it misleads others. False information can be very damaging to a person (if, for example, one is falsely believed to have committed a crime) but the damage is not a loss of privacy. Furthermore, notice that privacy is not a matter of the degree of control which one has over who knows facts about oneself. Suppose that, after calm and deliberate reflection, a movie star gives an extremely revealing interview. She reveals many facts about herself, facts which most of us would prefer not to share with others. She does all of this voluntarily. She has very good control over who knows these facts. If she had not spoken, others would not have known them. If one holds that privacy is a matter of the degree of control which one has over who knows facts about oneself, then one is forced to conclude that the movie star did not lose any privacy in giving the interview. This is incorrect. She voluntarily gave up some of her privacy. That she voluntarily gave it up does not mean that she did not give it up.[2]

Why do people value privacy? Privacy can be valued in two ways: intrinsically or instrumentally. One values something intrinsically when one values it for its own sake. One values something instrumentally when one values it as a means to some end. It is beyond dispute that privacy is instrumentally valued and that it is instrumentally valued in a number of different ways. First, it allows one to attempt difficult tasks without others viewing one's mistakes. I prefer to practice the guitar in private because practicing in public would open me to the ridicule of those who heard my poor attempts at playing. In this way privacy encourages people to take risks, to be creative, to be innovative.[3] Second and relatedly, privacy allows one to consider different opinions before displaying them in public.[4] I might argue for a particular unpopular political view with a friend in private because, if it turns out that I am unconvinced by my own arguments, I avoid the ridicule of adopting an unpopular view. In this way, privacy encourages informed deliberation and well-formed argument. Third, as James Rachels has noted, privacy is valuable because it allows us to adopt different roles in different contexts.[5] One can be the mad lover in one place and the dignified manager in another place. Fourth, it allows one to hide things that one must hide to make relationships possible. For example, a wife might think that her husband is much too thin. She might also know that he is extremely sensitive about his weight and would be horribly upset if he knew that she thought he was too thin. For this reason, she keeps her opinion to herself. While openness is often needed in a relationship, withholding information is also sometimes important. Fifth, privacy is valued because knowing facts brings power. This is most obvious in commercial transactions. If a woman knows that a man is desperate to sell his house, then she might offer to buy it at a lower price than she would if she did not know this fact. Therefore, he has reason to keep his feelings about the house private. Even more obviously, those who have done something wrong generally try to keep this information private in order to escape punishment.

In addition to the undisputed instrumental value of privacy, many people seem to value it intrinsically, for its own sake. People, even setting aside the instrumental value of privacy, just seem to prefer that certain facts about them not be known. Many, for example, keep private diaries full of information which is not compromising and which is of very little interest to others. The intrinsic value of privacy for many is also illustrated by those individuals who seek to prevent others from knowing facts which would bring them praise. I know someone who gives over $10,000 a year to charities but she has told only four or five people of her practice.

Privacy is one thing that people value. But it is not the only thing that people value and other values can conflict with privacy. One value which often conflicts with privacy is security. Those who seek to injure, defraud, steal and do other things to damage the security of others, obviously wish to keep their actions and intentions private. On the Web, this tension can be seen in discussions of privacy in on-line buying. Some wish more privacy while others point out that such privacy would make it harder to detect and capture those who commit on-line fraud. The debate over encryption of e-mail is another example of this tension. Some argue that strong encryption should be allowed to protect privacy while law enforcement officials worry that strong encryption will allow a great deal of crime to go undetected.

Another value which often conflicts with privacy is freedom of information. People wish to know that those in positions of authority are ethical people making ethical decisions. When evaluating a manager for potential promotion, a vice president might, for example, wish to verify that the manager's recent vacation trip to Paris was not paid for by a supplier. The vice president wants to be sure that the manager is buying supplies from the best supplier, not the one who pays for his trips to Paris. But the manager might well regard investigation into how he paid for the vacation as a violation of his privacy rights. This issue also arises with respect to elected officials. Some feel that certain well-qualified individuals decide not to run for political office because recent changes in the law require that elected officials reveal much about their lives.

Efficiency is another value which may conflict with privacy. More information can lead to better products, fewer annoying e-mails, less junk mail, and a generally more efficient society. Suppose that W.W., Inc. makes widgets. It sells widgets by catalog and knows that many people would like to have a widget or two. However, W.W. does not know precisely which people want widgets and which don't. It must send offers to a large group of people, some of whom want widgets and some of whom do not. Those who do not want widgets regard the offer as junk mail. W.W.'s costs would be lower and widgets would be cheaper if it knew exactly who wanted widgets and who didn't. So W.W. might purchase a clickstream database and analyze it for positive comments about widgets. It could then send offers only to those who wanted widgets. In addition, firms developing products often have questions about what kind of products people want. Privacy restrictions make it more expensive for firms to develop products that meet people's needs because firms must spend money to find out what people want. Accordingly, a firm might buy a database of clickstreams to look for complaints about a type of product. It could then use this information to redesign products to avoid these problems.

In light of this discussion of the nature and value of privacy, what are the moral limits of a company's use of information about its customers? How should one balance the value of privacy against other values? Some, such as Richard Posner, give very little weight to privacy.[6] Posner argues that, just as it is wrong for a seller to conceal facts about a product, it is wrong for people to conceal facts about themselves. Posner thinks that it is wrong for a seller to conceal facts about a product. If I am buying a car and the seller fails to tell me it has a bad axle, then it seems that the seller has done something wrong. Posner argues that it is similarly wrong for people to conceal facts about themselves. In order for others to make good decisions about whom to hire, whom to marry, and whom to befriend, it is best that people not be allowed to conceal information. On this view, the facts in a company's consumer database are to be treated as the company's property to do with as the company sees fit. If your address and record of recent purchases are as much company property as are the company's buildings, then the company should not be required to seek your permission to sell this information about you any more than it should be required to seek your permission to sell its buildings.

Posner's argument seems weak. First, he fails to note the distinction between saying things that are false and saying nothing at all. There seems to be a difference between a seller who fails to say that a car has a bad axle and one who (falsely) says that it has a good axle. It is not so clear that a seller who openly sells a product as is and says nothing about it at all has done anything wrong. Following Posner's analogy, this would lead us to conclude that while people should not make false statements about themselves, they have, in general, no obligation to reveal all. Second, Posner explicitly assumes that the facts which people seek to keep private are discreditable facts. This assumption is called into question once one notes that people may value privacy intrinsically. Moreover, the instrumental importance of privacy for creativity, opinion-formation, and relationships seems to speak against Posner's assumption. Finally, Posner assumes that there is one agreed upon view of discreditable facts. However, in many cases, there is disagreement about what is discreditable. For example, some think that homosexual behavior is discreditable, but others disagree. Those who think it is not discreditable may be correct. If they are, then some people may wish to keep their sexual preference private, not because it is discreditable, but because others mistakenly believe that it is discreditable.

At the other end of the spectrum regarding the value of privacy, some argue that consumers have the right that information about them not be sold or given to others without their consent.[7] Defenders of this view often argue that the information about a person in a company's database should be treated as the property of the person, not the property of the company. Companies would presumably have to pay people for the right to sell information about them to others.

There seem to be serious objections to this view. First, some argue that there is at least one important difference between facts about people and more typical cases of property. Property generally involves the more or less exclusive use of something. My pickup truck is my property. At least part of what this means is that I may use the pickup when I please and you may not. We would hardly call the pickup my property if anyone could use it whenever they wished. However, facts, unlike pickup trucks, are not things that only one person can use at a time. My knowledge of a fact does not mean that you cannot know that same fact at the same time I do. Many people know that the moon orbits the earth. If I am driving a pickup truck, on the other hand, then, at least at that moment, you cannot be driving it. Defenders of the view that information about a person should be treated as the property of that person need to consider this dissimilarity between facts and typical property. Second, they need to offer a clear and coherent theory of what it means for a fact to be *about* someone. When is a fact about one person and not about another? Is the fact that a man's wife is cheating on him a fact about him, a fact about his wife, or a fact about both of them? Is the fact that my second cousin is a felon a fact about him, about me, or about both of us? This is a crucial question for the defenders of the view that people have a right that information *about* them not be sold or given to others without their consent. If, for example, it is held that the fact that my second cousin is a felon is about both my cousin and myself, then someone would need the consent of both of us to transfer this information to another.

Others reject both Posner's view and the view that people have a general right that information about them not be transferred without their consent. They argue that the analogy between privacy and property is unhelpful. Instead, they hold that we should develop a set of rules for the use of consumer databases. Different commentators have defended different sets of rules. Some suggest that there is no value to the false information contained in a database. Any large database will inevitably contain false information. The preservation of false information has little to recommend it. It does not serve efficiency; indeed, efficiency is promoted by the correction of false information. It does not improve security or freedom of information. Therefore, on this view, one moral restriction on the use of consumer databases is that consumers should have access to their own records to check for and correct inaccuracies. It might be argued that allowing this sort of access would be too costly. This argument, however, is undermined by our experience with the Fair Credit Reporting Act of 1970. As noted above, this law requires that credit agencies give consumers access to their credit reports. They are allowed to charge a small fee to cover the cost of providing these reports. There seems to be no practical barrier to extending this model to other databases, including those developed using the Web.

Another rule often proposed is that the owners of a consumer database have an obligation to take reasonable measures to insure that the database does not fall into the hands of criminals. It would be unethical, it is argued, for a company to store consumer information on a computer to which everyone with an internet connection has free access. Here the interests of consumers and the database owners are very similar. The value of a database diminishes if others have free access to it. Therefore, protecting the database from unauthorized use not only protects the privacy of consumers but the value of the database itself.

Rather than requiring that companies get permission before selling information in a consumer database, some argue that it is more efficient to require that those who collect information tell consumers that they are collecting information and what they will do with the information and then offer consumers a chance to opt out. For example, a Web site selling books might post a note on its main page telling consumers that any clicks beyond this page will be recorded and might be used to send them promotional offers or sold to other companies. Those who do not wish to reveal information about themselves would need only leave the Web page. Of course, they would thereby give up the chance to buy books from that Web retailer.

These three different positions illustrate the wide diversity of opinion that the issue of consumer privacy raises. The Web and increased computing power dramatically increase the potential for conflict regarding consumer privacy and require the legal system to choose from the many positions discussed in this article.

# NOTES

1. The analysis of privacy offered here is my own. It is substantially different from the analyses offered by others. For example, some do not think that privacy is a matter of degree but I hold the view that it is. For different analyses of privacy see Alan Westin, *Privacy and Freedom* (New York: Atheneum Press, 1967), J. Roland Pennock and John W. Chapman, eds., *Nomos XIII: Privacy* (New York, Atherton Press, 1971), Ruth Gavison, "Privacy and the Limits of Law," *Yale Law Journal* 89 (1980): 421–71, James Rachels, "Why Privacy Is Important," *Philosophy and Public Affairs* 4 (1975): 323–33, and Ferdinand Schoeman, *Privacy and Social Freedom* (Cambridge: Cambridge University Press, 1992).

2. This analysis leaves a number of questions unanswered. First, there are technical issues concerning the individuation of facts. Is the fact that I have two hands one fact or two? Second, much could be said about what makes facts trivial or important. Third, one must note the distinction between propositional and sensory knowledge. Sensory knowledge, actually hearing or seeing someone do something, may be a greater loss of privacy than, for example, reading about someone.

3. See Gavison, "Privacy and the Limits of Law."

4. Ibid.

5. See Rachels, "Why Privacy Is Important."

6. Richard Posner, "The Right of Privacy," *Georgia Law Review* 12 (1978): 393–422 and "Privacy, Secrecy, and Reputation," *Buffalo Law Review* 28 (1979): 1–55.

7. Larry Hunter, "Public Image," *Whole Earth Review* (January 1986): 32–36.

# SELLING

*Case Study*

*Clinton L. Oaks*

# Roger Hixon: Let the Buyer Beware

What obligation, if any, does a vendor have to point out to a prospective buyer the flaws or defects in his product? Roger Hixon, a former executive with a national firm and now a teacher of business policy at a western college, raised this question with respect to the remarks of a guest speaker in a previous class period. The speaker had talked about various levels of business ethics among the salesmen for companies with whom he dealt regularly. He had concluded that while some companies had a very strict policy calling for honesty and complete disclosure, many did not.

During the ensuing discussion, one student commented, "I hear all these platitudes being mouthed about how 'complete disclosure is always good business practice.' How many of you practice complete disclosure in your personal business dealings? I am sure I don't." At this point, just as the discussion was beginning to get a little heated, the instructor noted that the class period was nearly over. He invited several of those who were participating most actively in the discussion to write up a specific incident for discussion the next time the class met.

---

## JOAN STULLARD

"My parents, who live in a small college town in the northern part of the state, decided a year ago last spring to try to sell their home and move into a condominium. Since my father is pretty close to retirement, they tried to sell the place themselves rather than going through a real estate agent. The real estate market up there, unlike that in many urban areas, was quite slow. By late August, they had only had one potential buyer who had shown enough interest to come back several times.

"One of the nicest features of our home was its large backyard. A huge cottonwood tree standing in one corner of the yard provided the entire house and yard with shade against the late afternoon sun. The tree was very large—its trunk had a circumference of nearly fifteen feet. The only problem with it was that it was dying. While it looked healthy and green from our house, our neighbors behind the tree could see many dead and potentially dangerous branches. A violent storm would often litter their yards and prompt them to call us and demand that we cut down the tree.

"The prospective buyer who had shown the greatest interest in the place was standing on the patio one afternoon with my father. 'That sure is a nice, big tree,' he said. I was standing at the door, and overheard his remark. His comment wasn't one that required an answer. I found myself wondering what, if anything, my father would say."

## MARK BASCOM

"My brother is working as a used car salesman at Clark Motors. He tells me that the manager of the used car lot keeps a folder on every car in stock. Everything that is known about the car is recorded in the folder. This would include information about the previous owner, any major body or engine repairs, the mechanic's evaluation at the time the car came on the lot, etc.

"Before school started, my brother got permission to borrow a Buick Estate Wagon for several days to take a short vacation. He said he and his wife really enjoyed the car but they were appalled at the gas mileage—less than eight miles per gallon on the open road. When he returned the car, he made a note of this in the car's folder. He also talked to one of the mechanics about it. 'I'm not surprised,' the mechanic commented. 'As you know, we clean the carburetor, put in new plugs and points, adjust the timing and so forth whenever we get a car—but that particular model always was a gas hog.'

"A few days later a young couple who were looking at cars on the lot expressed a great deal of interest in this car. They asked my brother a lot of questions and he, having had some personal experience with the car, was able to answer them in greater detail than was normally the case. He was also able to point out some of the features of the car that might have otherwise been overlooked. The longer they talked, the more enthusiastic the couple became. Almost the only question they didn't ask was about the car's mileage. They had to leave at 4:30 to pick up their child at the babysitter's but made an appointment to come back at 9:30 the next morning to work out the details of the sale.

"That night my brother came over to talk about a deal we were working on together. While he was there he told me about what had happened and said, 'As you know, things have been really tight for Jean and me since we took that trip, and the commission on this sale would really help us right now. I have always tried, as a matter of policy, to answer honestly any question that a prospective buyer raises. If I were to tell this couple about the gas mileage on that car, however, I'm pretty sure they would back out of the sale. I don't intend to try to deceive them, but do I have any obligation to tell them about it if they don't ask?' "

JEFF MOYER

"My wife and I live approximately thirty-five miles away from the university. She teaches school in a district that is also about thirty miles from where we live, but in the opposite direction. As you can imagine, transportation is a big item in our budget. Neither of us has been successful in finding a car pool. Fortunately, my wife's parents have graciously allowed us to continue to use the car my wife drove before we were married. We own an older car, and with the two cars we have been able to get by up to now.

"When my wife accepted the teaching position we knew the travel involved would be both time consuming and expensive. However, our projections on costs were painfully underestimated. Not only have gas and oil prices increased sharply, but we hadn't realized that both cars would need new tires. Because we drive as far as we do, we have had to have tune-ups on both cars more frequently than anticipated. In addition to all this, we have had to have work done on our own car's distributor, muffler, and lights—all of which has cost us well over four hundred dollars. Just recently we had more trouble requiring a mechanic's examination. His diagnosis was 'You need a valve job.'

"While I was trying to figure out where I could borrow the projected $800 for the valve job, the mechanic said, 'The engine block is pitted and needs to be ground down. If you are going to do that you might as well overhaul the whole engine.'

" 'How much will that be over the $800?' I asked, bracing for the shock.

" 'About $1,200,' the mechanic replied.

"Fighting the churning feeling in my stomach, I asked what would happen if he didn't grind down the block. I was told that the engine head and block might not seal when put back together after the work was done on the valves. 'Just try to get it to seal,' I told him, knowing our budget was already dripping with red ink.

"The mechanic put the engine back together and I crossed my fingers. Evidently it sealed because the car is running now. I suspect that with all the miles that it travels weekly it may need the overhaul before long. I can't begin to afford that. Both my father and father-in-law have given me the same advice. 'Get rid of the car while it is still running.'

"I checked on the Blue Book value of this model and it ranged from $3,600 to $4,300. I was pretty sure that if I were to tell the buyer about the engine block, I would have more difficulty in selling it and I would probably have to knock $1,000 to $1,200 off the going price.

"I try to think of myself as an honest person, and I don't think I could lie about it if someone asked me whether or not the car engine needed an overhaul. But suppose they didn't ask? Am I obligated to tell them anyway?

"Suppose I were to trade in the car on another car at an auto dealership. A dealer will almost always have a mechanic check out the car before he makes you an offer. Do I need to say anything in a situation like that? If I said anything I am sure it would lower the offer the dealer would make to me, but I am not at all sure, based upon my past experience, that the dealer would pass this information and a lower price on to another customer. In such a transaction isn't there almost a mutual understanding that everyone is governed by the old merchant's law of 'Let the buyer beware'?

"Having decided not to keep the car, I felt my choices were: (1) tell whoever buys the car about the engine; (2) tell whoever buys the car about the engine only if he or she asks if I know of any mechanical flaws; (3) tell about the engine only if I sell the car myself instead of trading it in; and (4) don't tell anyone about the engine even if asked. What should I have done?"

DON CASE

"Just after I turned sixteen, I spent a summer working with my best friend on his dad's used car lot. Our job was to 'clean-up' and 'recondition' cars before they were put on the sales lot. We were to make them presentable so they could be shown to prospective buyers.

"Some of the things we had to do were what you might expect. We washed and waxed the body, scrubbed the seats and door interiors and shampooed the rugs. We also tightened any loose screws and repositioned the carpet, tightening down the carpet edges.

"My friend's dad taught us how to do a lot of other things as well. We were to use a powerful grease cutting detergent to wash the engine and eliminate the dirt, oil, and grease that had accumulated on it. 'A buyer is always impressed with a clean engine,' he told us, 'and besides he won't be alarmed by any evidence that oil is leaking from the engine.' We were also shown how to use a spray shellac on all the rubber hoses so that they would look like they were new.

"If the car was burning any oil, we were to add a can of STP. If the blue smoke coming out of the back end was heavy we would add two cans and sometimes three.

"Rust had often eaten through the steel from the wheel well and would show around the fenders. With the help of a steel brush and a can of spray paint this was easily hidden and the rust would not show through the paint again for at least a month.

"Sometimes the carpets were too stained with grease and dirt to be cleaned. A coat of dark spray coloring hid the stains and would make the carpets look nice for at least a week or two after the car was purchased.

"I was young enough at the time and grateful enough to have a job that I don't ever remember even questioning the rightness or wrongness of the things we did. My friend's dad's conscience must have troubled him a little, however, because he was always telling us that there wasn't anything wrong or illegal about what we were doing. He told us that every used car lot did the same thing and he had to do it to remain competitive. 'We never turn back an odometer,' he said. 'That is illegal. The buyer expects that a used car lot will do everything possible to make a used car look good— and part of his job as a buyer is to check out anything that might be wrong.'

"Two or three years later, I had a used car of my own to sell. Without thinking much about it, I gave it the same treatment we used to give cars on the lot, including the addition of two cans of STP. I put a "For Sale" sign in the window and parked it on our curb. The next night, a girl about my age who evidently didn't know much about cars, came by to ask me how much I was asking for it. After I told her, she asked, 'Is the car in good condition? Do you know of any problems that I am likely to have with it?' What should I have said?"

NED OSBORNE

"At the end of last spring semester, one of my roommates transferred to a school down in Texas. Before he left, he turned over to me two pairs of skis, both virtually new. He said, 'There isn't any market for these right now but they should be easy to sell in the fall. Why don't you keep them for me until then?'

"Knowing that he wasn't much of a skier, I asked him, 'Where did you get them?' He replied, 'One of the guys I run around with gave them to me. I don't know for sure but I wouldn't be surprised if he picked them up off an unlocked ski rack on a car parked in front of the motel where he used to work. At any event there aren't any identifying marks on them. I checked in the local ski shops around here and both pairs retail for around $500. Sell them for whatever you can get and you keep half of it.' Before I had any chance to protest, he took off.

"Those skis stood in my closet for nearly six months. Late in the fall, we got a little cramped for room and I decided I had better do something with them. I was half tempted to just turn them over to campus security and tell them they had been left in my apartment and I didn't know whose they were.

"One day when I was trying to rearrange some of the things in the closet, I had both pairs of skis out on my bed. A friend of another roommate saw them and said, 'You wouldn't like to sell a pair of skis, would you? I am really in the market and they look just like what I have been looking for.'

"Without stopping to think about it, I asked, 'What will you give me?' He said, 'I'll give you $250.00 for the pair on the right.'

"What should I have done? My textbooks that fall had cost me about twice what I had estimated and I was really strapped for cash. I hadn't stolen the skis—in fact I didn't know for sure they had been stolen. I could truthfully say that a roommate had left them with me to sell and let it go at that. Was I obligated to tell a prospective purchaser that they might have been stolen? I can imagine what effect that might have had on the reputation of those of us living in the apartment.

"If the skis were stolen, it was extremely unlikely that the rightful owners could ever be located. In view of this, what difference did it make whether or not they had been stolen? If I turned them over to campus security, they would probably just keep them for a while and then sell them at an auction. If the end result would be the same—that is, that the skis would end up with some third party who didn't know who the original owner was and who could care less—why shouldn't I pick up a few dollars to cover my 'costs of handling'?"

## For Discussion

Joan Stullard

Should Joan's father disclose to prospective buyers the status of the cottonwood tree?

Mark Bascom

How should Mark respond to his brother?

Jeff Moyer

Which of Jeff's four strategies should he adopt?

Don Case

How should Don respond? Does the fact that an action is a customary industry practice make a moral difference?

Ned Oborne

Should Ned sell the skis?

*David M. Holley*

# A Moral Evaluation
# of Sales Practices

A relatively neglected area in recent literature on business ethics is the ethics of sales practices. Discussions of the moral dimensions of marketing have tended to concentrate almost exclusively on obligations of advertisers or on the moral acceptability of the advertising system. By contrast, little attention has been given to the activities of individual salespersons.[1]

This neglect is surprising on several counts. First, efforts to sell a product occupy a good deal of the time of many people in business. Developing an advertising campaign may be a more glamorous kind of activity, but it is sales on the individual level that provides the revenue, and for most businesses the number of persons devoted to selling will far exceed the number devoted to advertising. Second, the activity of selling something is of intrinsic philosophical significance. It furnishes a paradigm case of persuasive communication, raising such issues as deception, individual autonomy, and the social value of a marketing-oriented system for distributing goods and services. While the practice of advertising raises these same issues, the potential for manipulation of vulnerable consumers comes into much sharper focus at the level of individual sales.

In this paper I will attempt to develop a framework for evaluating the morality of various sales practices. Although I recognize that much of the salesforce in companies is occupied exclusively or primarily with sales to other businesses, my discussion will focus on sales to the individual consumer. Most of what I say should apply to any type of sales activity, but the moral issues arise most clearly in cases in which a consumer may or may not be very sophisticated in evaluating and responding to a sales presentation.

Originally published in *Business and Professional Ethics* 5, no. 1 (fall 1987). This edited version appeared in *Ethical Theory and Business*, 3d ed., ed. Tom Beauchamp and Norman E. Bowie (Englewood Cliffs, N.J.: Prentice Hall, 1988), pp. 448–57. Copyright © 1987 by David M. Holley. Reprinted by permission of the author.

My approach will be to consider first the context of sales activities, a market system of production and distribution. Since such a system is generally justified on teleological grounds, I describe several conditions for its successful achievement of key goals. Immoral sales practices are analyzed as attempts to undermine these conditions.

# I

The primary justification for a market system is that it provides an efficient procedure for meeting people's needs and desires for goods and services.[2] This appeal to economic benefits can be elaborated in great detail, but at root it involves the claim that people will efficiently serve each other's needs if they are allowed to engage in voluntary exchanges.

A crucial feature of this argument is the condition that the exchange be voluntary. Assuming that individuals know best how to benefit themselves and that they will act to achieve such benefits, voluntary exchange can be expected to serve both parties. On the other hand, if the exchanges are not made voluntarily, we have no basis for expecting mutually beneficial results. To the extent that mutual benefit does not occur, the system will lack efficiency as a means for the satisfaction of needs and desires. Hence, this justification presupposes that conditions necessary for the occurrence of voluntary exchange are ordinarily met.

What are these conditions? For simplicity's sake, let us deal only with the kind of exchange involving a payment of money for some product or service. We can call the person providing the product the *seller* and the person making the monetary payment the *buyer*. I suggest that voluntary exchange occurs only if the following conditions are met:

1. Both buyer and seller understand what they are giving up and what they are receiving in return.
2. Neither buyer nor seller is compelled to enter into the exchange as a result of coercion, severely restricted alternatives, or other constraints on the ability to choose.
3. Both buyer and seller are able at the time of the exchange to make rational judgments about its costs and benefits.

I will refer to these three conditions as the knowledge, noncompulsion, and rationality conditions, respectively.[3] If the parties are uninformed, it is possible that an exchange might accidentally turn out to benefit them. But given the lack of information, they would not be in a position to make a rational judgment about their benefit, and we cannot reasonably expect beneficial results as a matter of course in such circumstances. Similarly, if the exchange is made under compulsion, then the judgment of personal benefit is not the basis of the exchange. It is possible for someone to be forced or manipulated into an arrangement that is in fact beneficial. But there is little reason to think that typical or likely.[4]

It should be clear that all three conditions are subject to degrees of fulfillment. For example, the parties may understand certain things about the exchange but not others. Let us posit a theoretical situation in which both parties are fully informed, fully rational, and enter into the exchange entirely of their own volition. I will call this an *ideal exchange*. In actual practice there is virtually always some divergence from the ideal. Knowledge can be more or less adequate. Individuals can be subject to various irrational influences. There can be borderline cases of external constraints. Nevertheless, we can often judge when a particular exchange was adequately informed, rational, and free from compulsion. Even when conditions are not ideal, we may still have an *acceptable exchange*.

With these concepts in mind, let us consider the obligations of sales personnel. I suggest that the primary duty of salespeople to customers is to avoid undermining the conditions of acceptable exchange. It is possible by act or omission to create a situation in which the customer is not sufficiently knowledgeable about what the exchange involves. It is also possible to influence the customer in ways that short-circuit the rational decision-making process. To behave in such ways is to undermine the conditions that are presupposed in teleological justifications of the market system. But the moral acceptability of the system may become questionable if the conditions of acceptable exchange are widely abused. The individual who attempts to gain personally by undermining these conditions does that which, if commonly practiced, would produce a very different system from the one that supposedly provides moral legitimacy to that individual's activities.

# II

If a mutually beneficial exchange is to be expected, the parties involved must be adequately informed about what they are giving up and what they are receiving. In most cases this should create no great problem for the seller[5], but what about the buyer? How is she to obtain the information needed? One answer is that the buyer is responsible for doing whatever investigation is necessary to acquire the information. The medieval principle of *caveat emptor* encouraged buyers to take responsibility for examining a purchase thoroughly to determine whether it had any hidden flaws. If the buyer failed to find defects, that meant that due caution had not been exercised.

If it were always relatively easy to discover defects by examination, then this principle might be an efficient method of guaranteeing mutual satisfaction. Sometimes, however, even lengthy investigation would not disclose what the buyer wants to know. With products of great complexity, the expertise needed for an adequate examination may be beyond what could reasonably be expected of most consumers. Even relatively simple products can have hidden flaws that most people would not discover until after the purchase, and to have the responsibility for closely examining every purchase would involve a considerable amount of a highly treasured modern commodity, the buyer's time. Furthermore, many exchange situations in our context involve products that cannot be examined in this way—goods that will be delivered at a later time or sent through the mail, for example. Finally, even if we assume that most buyers, by exercising enough caution, can protect their interests, the system of *caveat emptor* would take advantage of those least able to watch out for themselves. It would in effect justify mistreatment of a few for a rather questionable benefit.

In practice the buyer almost always relies on the seller for some information, and if mutually beneficial exchanges are to be expected, the information needs to meet certain standards of both quality and quantity. With regard to quality, the information provided should not be deceptive. This would include not only direct lies but also truths that are intended to mislead the buyer. Consider the following examples:

1. An aluminum siding salesperson tells customers that they will receive "bargain factory prices" for letting their homes be used as models in a new advertising campaign. Prospective customers will be brought to view the houses, and a commission of $100 will be paid for each sale that results. In fact, the price paid is well above market rates, the workmanship and materials are substandard, and no one is ever brought by to see the houses.[6]
2. A used car salesperson turns back the odometer reading on auto-

mobiles by an average of 25,000 to 30,000 miles per car. If customers ask whether the reading is correct, the salesperson replies that it is illegal to alter odometer readings.

3. A salesperson at a piano store tells an interested customer that the "special sale" will be good only through that evening. She neglects to mention that another "special sale" will begin the next day.

4. A telephone salesperson tells people who answer the phone that they have been selected to receive a free gift, a brand new freezer. All they have to do is buy a year's subscription to a food plan.

5. A salesperson for a diet system proclaims that under this revolutionary new plan the pounds will melt right off. The system is described as a scientific advance that makes dieting easy. In fact, the system is a low-calorie diet composed of foods and liquids that are packaged under the company name but are no different from standard grocery store items.

The possibilities are endless, and whether or not a lie is involved, each case illustrates a salesperson's attempt to get a customer to believe something that is false in order to make the sale. It might be pointed out that these kinds of practices would not deceive a sophisticated consumer. Perhaps so, but whether they are always successful deceptions is not the issue. They are attempts to mislead the customer, and given that the consumer must often rely on information furnished by the salesperson, they are attempts to subvert the conditions under which mutually beneficial exchange can be expected. The salesperson attempts to use misinformation as a basis for customer judgment rather than allowing that judgment to be based on accurate beliefs. Furthermore, if these kinds of practices were not successful fairly often, they would probably not be used.

In the aluminum siding case, the customer is led to believe that there will be a discount in exchange for a kind of service, allowing the house to be viewed by prospective customers. This leaves the impression both that the job done will be of high quality and that the price paid will be offset by commissions. The car salesperson alters the product in order to suggest false information about the extent of its use. With such information, the customer is not able to judge accurately the value of the car. The misleading reply to inquiries is not substantially different from a direct lie. The piano salesperson deceives the customer about how long the product will be obtainable at a discount price. In this case the deception occurs through an omission. The telephone solicitor tries to give the impression that there has been a contest of some sort and that the freezer is a prize. In this way, the nature of the exchange is obscured.

The new diet-system case raises questions about how to distinguish legitimate "puffery" from deception. Obviously, the matter will depend to some extent on how gullible we conceive the customer to be. As described, the case surely involves an attempt to get the customer to believe that dieting will be easier under this system and that what is being promoted is the result of some new scientific discovery. If there were no prospect that a customer would be likely to believe this, we would probably not think the technique deceptive. But in fact a number of individuals are deceived by claims of this type.

Some writers have defended the use of deceptive practices in business contexts on the grounds that there are specific rules applying to those contexts that differ from the standards appropriate in other contexts. It is argued, for example, that deception is standard practice, understood by all participants as something to be expected and, therefore, harmless, or that it is a means of self-defense justified by pressures of the competitive context.[7] To the extent that the claims about widespread practice are true, people who know what is going on may be able to minimize personal losses, but that is hardly a justification of the practice. If I know that many people have installed devices in their cars that can come out and puncture the tires of the car next to them, that may help keep me from falling victim, but it does not make the practice harmless. Even if no one is victimized, it becomes necessary to take extra precautions, introducing a significant disutility into driving conditions. Analogously, widespread deception in business debases the currency of language, making business communication less efficient and more cumbersome.

More importantly, however, people are victimized by deceptive practices, and the fact that some may be shrewd enough to see through clouds of misinformation does not alter the deceptive intent. Whatever may be said with regard to appropriate behavior among people who "know the rules," it is clear that many buyers are not aware of having entered into some special domain where deception is allowed. Even if this is naive, it does not provide a moral justification for subverting those individuals' capacity for making a reasoned choice.

Only a few people would defend the moral justifiability of deceptive sales practices. However, there may be room for much more disagreement with regard to how much information a salesperson is obligated to provide. In rejecting the principle of caveat emptor, I have suggested that there are pragmatic reasons for expecting the seller to communicate some information about the product. But how much? When is it morally culpable to withhold information? Consider the following cases:

1. An automobile dealer has bought a number of cars from another state. Although they appear to be new or slightly used, these cars have been involved in a major flood and were sold by the previous dealer at a discount. The salesperson knows the history of the cars and does not mention it to customers.
2. A salesperson for an encyclopedia company never mentions the total price of a set unless he has to. Instead he emphasizes the low monthly payment involved.
3. A real estate agent knows that one reason the couple selling a house with her company wants to move is that the neighbors often have loud parties and neighborhood children have committed minor acts of vandalism. The agent makes no mention of this to prospective customers.
4. An admissions officer for a private college speaks enthusiastically about the advantages of the school. He does not mention the fact that the school is not accredited.
5. A prospective retirement home resident is under the impression that a particular retirement home is affiliated with a certain church. He makes it known that this is one of the features he finds attractive about the home. Though the belief is false, the recruiters for the home make no attempt to correct the misunderstanding.

In all these cases the prospective buyer lacks some piece of knowledge that might be relevant to the decision to buy. The conditions for ideal exchange are not met. Perhaps, however, there can be an acceptable exchange. Whether or not this is the case depends on whether the buyer has adequate information to decide if purchase would be beneficial. In the case of the flood-damaged autos, there is information relevant to evaluating the worth of the car that the customer could not be expected to know unless informed by the seller. If this information is not revealed, the buyer win not have adequate knowledge to make a reasonable judgment. Determining exactly how much information needs to be provided is not always clear-cut. We must in general rely on our assessments of what a reasonable person would want to know. As a practical guide, a salesperson might consider, "What would I want to know if I were considering buying this product?"

Surely a reasonable person would want to know the total price of a product. Hence the encyclopedia salesperson who omits this total is not providing adequate information. The salesperson may object that this information could be inferred from other information about the monthly payment, length of term, and interest rate. But if the intention is not to have the customer act without knowing the full price, then why shouldn't it be provided directly? The admissions officer's failure to mention that the school is unaccredited also seems unacceptable when we consider what a reasonable person would want to know. There are some people who would consider this a plus, since they are suspicious about accrediting agencies imposing some alien standards (e.g., standards that conflict with religious views). But regardless of how one evaluates the fact, most people would judge it to be important for making a decision.

The real estate case is more puzzling. Most real estate agents would not reveal the kind of information described, and would not feel they had violated any moral duties in failing to do so. Clearly, many prospective customers would want to be informed about such problems. However, in most cases failing to know these facts would not be of crucial importance. We have a case of borderline information. It would be known by all parties to an ideal exchange, but we can have an acceptable exchange even if the buyer is unaware of it. Failure to inform the customer of these facts is not like failing to inform the customer that the house is on the site of a hazardous waste dump or that a major freeway will soon be adjacent to the property.

It is possible to alter the case in such a way that the information should be revealed or at least the buyer should be directed another way. Suppose the buyer makes it clear that his primary goal is to live in a quiet neighborhood where he will be undisturbed. The "borderline" information now becomes more central to the customer's decision. Notice that thinking in these terms moves us away from the general standard of what a reasonable person would want to know to the more specific standard of what is relevant given the criteria of this individual. In most cases, however, I think that a salesperson would be justified in operating under general "reasonable person" standards until particular deviations become apparent.[8]

The case of the prospective retirement home resident is a good example of how the particular criteria of the customer might assume great importance. If the recruiters, knowing what they know about this man's religious preferences, allow him to make his decision on the basis of a false assumption they will have failed to support the conditions of acceptable exchange. It doesn't really matter that the misunderstanding was not caused by the salespeople. Their allowing it to be part of the basis for a decision borders on deception. If the misunderstanding was not on a matter of central importance to the individual's evaluation, they might have had no obligation to correct it. But the case described is not of that sort.

Besides providing nondeceptive and relatively complete information, sales people may be obligated to make sure that their communications are understandable. Sales presentations containing technical information that is likely to be misunderstood are morally questionable. However, it would be unrealistic to expect all presentations to be immune to misunderstanding. The salesperson is probably justified in developing presentations that would be intelligible to the average consumer of the product he or she is selling and making adjustments in cases where it is clear that misunderstanding has occurred.

# III

The condition of uncompelled exchange distinguishes business dealings from other kinds of exchanges. In the standard business arrangement, neither party is forced to enter the negotiations. A threat of harm would transform the situation to something other than a purely business arrangement. Coercion is not the only kind of compulsion, however. Suppose I have access to only one producer of food. I arrange to buy food from this producer, but given my great need for food and the absence of alternatives, the seller is able to dictate the terms. In one sense I choose to make the deal, but the voluntariness of my choice is limited by the absence of alternatives.

Ordinarily, the individual salesperson will not have the power to take away the buyer's alternatives. However, a clever salesperson can sometimes make it seem as if options are very limited and can use the customer's ignorance to produce the same effect. For example, imagine an individual who begins to look for a particular item at a local store. The salesperson extolls the line carried by his store, warns of the deficiencies of alternative brands, and warns about the dishonesty of competitors, in contrast to his store's reliability. With a convincing presentation, a customer might easily perceive the options to be very limited. Whether or not the technique is questionable may depend on the accuracy of the perception. If the salesperson is attempting to take away a legitimate alternative, that is an attempt to undermine the customer's voluntary choice.

Another way the condition of uncompelled choice might be subverted is by involving a customer in a purchase without allowing her to notice what is happening. This would include opening techniques that disguise the purpose of the encounter so there can be no immediate refusal. The customer is led to believe that the interview is about a contest or a survey or an opportunity to make money. Not until the end does it become apparent that this is an attempt to sell something, and occasionally if the presentation is smooth enough, some buyers can be virtually unaware that they have bought anything. Obviously, there can be degrees of revelation, and not every approach that involves initial disguise of certain elements that might provoke an immediate rejection is morally questionable. But there are enough clear cases in which the intention is to get around, as much as possible, the voluntary choice of the customer. Consider the following examples:

1. A seller of children's books gains entrance to houses by claiming to be conducting an educational survey. He does indeed ask several "survey" questions, but he uses these to qualify potential customers for his product.
2. A salesperson alludes to recent accidents involving explosions of furnaces and, leaving the impression of having some official government status, offers to do a free inspection. She almost always discovers a "major problem" and offers to sell a replacement furnace.
3. A man receives a number of unsolicited books and magazines through the mail. Then he is sent a bill and later letters warning of damage to his credit rating if he does not pay.

These are examples of the many variations on attempts to involve customers in exchanges without letting them know what is happening. The first two cases involve deceptions about the purpose of the encounter. Though they resemble cases discussed earlier that involved deception about the nature or price of a product, here the salesperson uses misinformation as a means of limiting the customers' range of choice. The customer does not consciously choose to listen to a sales presentation but finds that this is what is happening. Some psychological research suggests that when people do something that appears to commit them to a course of action, even without consciously choosing to do so, they will tend to act as if such a choice had been made in order to minimize cognitive dissonance. Hence, if a salesperson successfully involves the customer in considering a purchase, the customer may feel committed to give serious thought to the matter. The third case is an attempt to get the customer to believe that an obligation has been incurred. In variations on this technique, merchandise is mailed to a deceased person to make relatives believe that some payment is owed. In each case, an effort is made to force the consumer to choose from an excessively limited range of options.

# IV

How can a salesperson subvert the rationality condition? Perhaps the most common way is to appeal to emotional reactions that cloud an individual's perception of relevant considerations. Consider the following cases:

1. A man's wife has recently died in a tragic accident. The funeral director plays upon the husband's love for his wife and to some extent his guilt about her death to get him to purchase a very expensive funeral.
2. A socially insecure young woman has bought a series of dance lessons from a local studio. During the lessons, an attractive male instructor constantly compliments her on her poise and natural ability and tries to persuade her to sign up for more lessons.[9]
3. A life insurance salesperson emphasizes to a prospect the importance of providing for his family in the event of his death. The salesperson tells several stories about people who put off this kind of preparation.
4. A dress salesperson typically tells customers how fashionable they look in a certain dress. Her stock comments also include pointing out that a dress is slimming or sexy or "looks great on you."
5. A furniture salesperson regularly tells customers that a piece of furniture is the last one in stock and that another customer recently showed great interest in it. He sometimes adds that it may not be possible to get any more like it from the factory.

These cases remind us that emotions can be important motivators. It is not surprising that salespeople appeal to them in attempting to get the customer to make a purchase. In certain cases the appeal seems perfectly legitimate. When the life insurance salesperson tries to arouse the customer's fear and urges preparation, it may be a legitimate way to get the customer to consider something that is worth considering. Of course, the fact that the fear is aroused by one who sells life insurance may obscure to the customer the range of alternative possibilities in preparing financially for the future. But the fact that an emotion is aroused need not make the appeal morally objectionable.

If the appeal of the dress salesperson seems more questionable, this is probably because we are not as convinced of the objective importance of appearing fashionable, or perhaps because repeated observations of this kind are often insincere. But if we assume that the salesperson is giving an honest opinion about how the dress looks on a customer, it may provide some input for the individual who has a desire to achieve a particular effect. The fact that such remarks appeal to one's vanity or ambition does not in itself make the appeal unacceptable.

The furniture person's warnings are clearly calculated to create some anxiety about the prospect of losing the chance to buy a particular item unless immediate action is taken. If the warnings are factually based, they would not be irrelevant to the decision to buy. Clearly, one might act impulsively or hastily when under the spell of such thoughts, but the salesperson cannot be faulted for pointing out relevant considerations.

The case of the funeral director is somewhat different. Here there is a real question of what benefit is to be gained by choosing a more expensive funeral package. For most people, minimizing what is spent on the funeral would be a rational choice, but at a time of emotional vulnerability it can be made to look as if this means depriving the loved one or the family of some great benefit. Even if the funeral director makes nothing but true statements, they can be put into a form designed to arouse emotions that will lessen the possibility of a rational decision being reached.

The dance studio case is similar in that a weakness is being played upon. The woman's insecurity makes her vulnerable to flattery and attention, and this creates the kind of situations in which others can take advantage of her. Perhaps the dance lessons fulfill some need, but the appeal to her vanity easily becomes a tool to manipulate her into doing what the instructor wants.

The key to distinguishing between legitimate and illegitimate emotional appeals lies in whether the appeal clouds one's ability to make a decision based on genuine satisfaction of needs and desires. Our judgment about whether this happens in a particular case will depend in part on whether we think the purchase likely to benefit the customer. The more questionable the benefits, the more an emotional appeal looks like manipulation rather than persuasion. When questionable benefits are combined with some special vulnerability on the part of the consumer, the use of the emotional appeal appears even more suspect.

In considering benefits, we should not forget to consider costs as well. Whether a purchase is beneficial may depend on its effects on the family budget. Ordinarily it is not the responsibility of a salesperson to inquire into such matters, but if it becomes clear that financial resources are limited, the use of emotional appeals to get the customer to buy more than she can afford becomes morally questionable. Occasionally we hear about extreme cases in which a salesperson finds out the amount of life insurance received by a widow and talks her into an unnecessary purchase for that amount, or in which the salesperson persuades some poor family to make an unwise purchase on credit requiring them to cut back on necessities. The salesperson is not responsible for making a rational calculation for the customer, but when a salesperson knowingly urges an action that is not beneficial to the consumer, that is in effect trying to get the consumer to make an irrational judgment. Any techniques used to achieve this end would be attempts to subvert the conditions of mutually beneficial exchange.

For obvious reasons, salespeople want as many customers as possible to make purchases, and therefore they try to put the decision to purchase in the best possible light. It is not the job of a salesperson to present all the facts as objectively as possible. But if playing on a customer's emotions is calculated to obscure the customer's ability to make rational judgments about whether a purchase is in her best interest, then it is morally objectionable.

# V

I have attempted to provide a framework for evaluating the morality of a number of different types of sales practices. The framework is based on conditions for mutually beneficial exchange and ultimately for an efficient satisfaction of economic needs and desires. An inevitable question is whether this kind of evaluation is of any practical importance.

If we set before ourselves the ideal of a knowledgeable, unforced, and rational decision on the part of a customer, it is not difficult to see how some types of practices would interfere with this process. We must, of course, be careful not to set the standards too high. A customer may be partially but adequately informed to judge a purchase's potential benefits. A decision may be affected by nonrational and even irrational factors and yet still be rational enough in terms of being plausibly related to the individual's desires and needs. There may be borderline cases in which it is not clear whether acting in a particular way would be morally required or simply overscrupulous, but that is not an objection to this approach, only a recognition of a feature of morality itself.

# NOTES

1. In a survey of the major textbooks in the field of business ethics, I discovered only one with a chapter on sales practices: David Braybrooke's *Ethics in the World of Business*, chap. 4 (Totowa, N.J.: Rowman and Allanheld, 1983). That chapter contains only a brief discussion of the issue; most of the chapter is devoted to excerpts from court cases and the quotation of a code of ethics for a direct-mail marketing association.

2. The classic statement of the argument from economic benefits is found in Adam Smith, *The Wealth of Nations* (1776) (London: Methusen and Co. Ltd., 1930). Modern proponents of this argument include Ludwig von Mises, Friedrich von Hayek, and Milton Friedman.

3. One very clear analysis of voluntariness making use of these conditions may be found in John Hospers's *Human Conduct: Problems of Ethics*, 2d ed. (New York: Harcourt Brace Jovanovich, 1982), pp. 385–88.

4. I will refer to the three conditions indifferently as conditions for voluntary exchange or conditions for mutually beneficial exchange. By the latter designation I do not mean to suggest that they are either necessary or sufficient conditions for the occurrence of mutual benefit, but that they are conditions for the reasonable expectation of mutual benefit.

5. There are cases, however, in which the buyer knows more about a product than the seller. For example, suppose Cornell has found out that land Fredonia owns contains minerals that make it twice as valuable as Fredonia thinks. The symmetry of my conditions would lead me to conclude that Cornell should give Fredonia the relevant information unless perhaps Fredonia's failure to know was the result of some culpable negligence.

6. This case is described in Warren Magnuson and Jean Carper, *The Dark Side of the Marketplace* (Englewood Cliffs, N.J.: Prentice Hall, 1968), pp. 3–4.

7. Albert Carr, "Is Business Bluffing Ethical?" *Harvard Business Review* 46 (January-February 1968): 143–53. See also Thomas L. Carson, Richard E. Wokutch, and Kent F. Murrmann, "Bluffing in Labor Negotiations: Legal and Ethical Issues," *Journal of Business Ethics* 1 (1982): 13–22.

8. My reference to a reasonable person standard should not be confused with

the issue facing the FTC of whether to evaluate advertising by the reasonable consumer or ignorant consumer standard as described in Ivan Preston, "Reasonable Consumer or Ignorant Consumer. How the FTC Decides," *Journal of Consumer Affairs* 8 (winter 1974): 131–43. There the primary issue is with regard to whom the government should protect from claims that might be misunderstood. My concern here is with determining what amount of information is necessary for informed judgment. In general I suggest that a salesperson should begin with the assumption that information a reasonable consumer would regard as important needs to be revealed and that when special interests and concerns of the consumer come to light they may make further revelations necessary. This approach parallels the one taken by Tom Beauchamp and James Childress regarding the information that a physician needs to provide to obtain informed consent. See their *Principles of Biomedical Ethics*, 2d ed. (New York: Oxford University Press, 1983), pp. 74–79.

9. This is adapted from a court case quoted in Braybrooke, pp. 68–70.

# SELECT BIBLIOGRAPHY

Arrington, R. "Advertising and Behavior Control." *Journal of Business Ethics* 1 (1982): 3–12.

Beauchamp, T., and N. Bowie. *Ethical Theory and Business.* 5th ed. Upper Saddle River, N.J.: Prentice-Hall, 1997, chaps. 4, 7.

Brobeck, S. *The Modern Consumer Movement.* Boston: G.K. Hall & Co., 1990.

Chonko, L. *Ethical Decision-Making in Marketing.* Thousand Oaks, Calif.: Sage, 1995.

Crisp, R. "Persuasive Advertising, Autonomy, and the Creation of Desire." *Journal of Business Ethics* 6 (1987): 413–18.

Fletcher, G. "Fairness and Utility in Tort Theory." *Harvard Law Review* 85 (1972): 537–73.

Holley, D. "Information Disclosure in Sales." *Journal of Business Ethics* 17 (1998): 631–41.

Huber, P. *Liability: The Legal Revolution and Its Consequences.* New York: Basic Books, 1988.

Laczniack, G., and P. Murphy, eds. *Marketing Ethics.* Lexington: Lexington Books, 1987.

Mayer, R. *The Consumer Movement.* Boston: Twayne Publishers, 1989.

Moskin, J. R., ed. *The Case for Advertising.* New York: American Association of Advertising Agencies, 1973.

Oakes, G. *The Soul of the Salesman.* Amherst, N.Y.: Humanity Books, 1990.

Posner, R. "Strict Liability: A Comment." *The Journal of Legal Studies* 2 (1973): 205–21.

Schlegelmilch, B. *Marketing Ethics: An International Perspective.* Boston: International Thompson, 1998.

Schudson, M. *Advertising, the Uneasy Persuasion.* New York: Basic Books, 1984.

Smith, N., and J. Quelch. *Ethics in Marketing.* Burr Ridge, Ill.: Richard D. Irwin, 1994.

Velasquez, M. *Business Ethics.* 4th ed. Upper Saddle River, N.J.: Prentice-Hall, 1998, chap. 6.

Weinstein, A., et. al. *Products Liability and the Reasonably Safe Product.* New York: John Wiley and Sons, 1978.

# ELECTRONIC SOURCES

Cata Law   www.catalaw.com

Consumer Law   www.consumerlawpage.com

Consumer Product Safety Commission   www.cpsc.gov

Federal Trade Commission   www.ftc.gov

Privacy International   www.privacy.org

# 7. Business and the Environment

## Introduction

Most of us favor economic growth. We also are interested in a clean environment. These interests often clash: nuclear power, oil and chemical spills, ozone depletion, automobile exhaust, pesticides, fertilizers, timber cutting, hydroelectricity, resource depletion, landfills, toxic waste, acid rain, strip mining, global warming, commercial fishing and netting, wetlands drainage—all illustrate contests between commercial interests and environmentalists. In this chapter we examine the ethical responsibilities of business in the environmental arena.

One view on this issue is the economic approach represented in William F. Baxter's *People or Penguins*, according to which environmental issues are essentially resource allocation issues. Hence, the best way to handle them is by the free market. Baxter's view is that there is an optimal level of pollution, just as there is an optimal level of resource consumption, and this level is determined by the market, not political factors.

Others argue that the political arena is more appropriate for dealing with environmental issues than economics. William Blackstone approaches the environmental issue from a rights perspective, claiming that a livable environment is not only desirable but a human right. We have a human (or moral) right to a decent environment because such a state is necessary if people are to fulfill their human capacities. Because we have a human right to a livable environment, business and society have obligations not to interfere with that right; accordingly, Blackstone argues we should incorporate this right into our legal system, even though doing so will restrict businesses' economic and property rights.

Traditional ethical approaches to the environment all stress *human* values; for example, Blackstone's concern is with a human right to a clean environment, and utilitarians standardly focus on utility for humans. Many of today's environmentalists take sharp issue with the view that nature should be protected only if doing so promotes human interests or rights.

Manuel G. Velasquez points out that the new field of ecological ethics claims that some nonhumans have value in themselves, a value independent of their use for humans.

Given the present level of environmental concern in America, how should corporations act? Norman Bowie claims that business has no special responsibility to protect the environment beyond what the law and ordinary moral obilgations require. In contrast, the Lovinses and Paul Hawken argue that businesses have more extensive environmental responsibilities. They argue for what they call "natural capitalism," a set of practices they claim will lead to both sustained profitability and a sustainable environment.

# ENVIRONMENTAL RESPONSIBILITY

*Case Study*

# Macklin Mining Company

The 1972 Federal Water Pollution Act aims to eliminate discharges of pollutants into the nation's waters. Although the act leaves the primary prevention and enforcement responsibilities to the states, it establishes broad guidelines to which states must conform. It requires industries that discharge pollutants to use the "best available" technology to eliminate them. In establishing the best available technology, consideration is to be given to the cost of control, the age of the industrial facility, the control process used, and the overall environmental impact of the controls. The law also authorizes loans to help small businesses meet water-pollution control requirements. In addition, it sets water quality standards and requires states to set daily load limits for pollutants that will not impair propagation of fish and wildlife. With respect to enforcement, the law requires polluters to keep proper records, to install and use monitoring equipment, and to sample their discharges. States, upon approval of the Federal Environmental Protection Agency (EPA), are authorized to enter and inspect any polluting facility. Penalties for violating the law range from $2,500 to $25,000 per day and up to one year in prison for the first offense, and up to $50,000 a day and two years in prison for subsequent violations.

Macklin Mining Company is primarily a coal mining company that operates three mines in Tennessee. Macklin's is a marginal operation, with revenue/net income over the last four years of: 1996, $10.2 million/$35 thousand; 1995, $10.4 million/$42 thousand; 1994, $10.9 million/$31 thousand; 1993, $10.1 million/$7 thousand. The company operates the Macklin mine in Bone County, Tennessee, where it employs fifty-two people. The mine is situated in a low area near Talk Creek, which flows into the Bone River, four miles downstream.

Because of its setting, Macklin has always had a drainage problem with its Talk Creek mine. Prior to 1990, it dumped mine drainage directly into Talk Creek. In 1990 the Tennessee Pollution Control Administration (TPCA) ordered Macklin to cease dumping into Talk Creek. After two years of negotiation, the company proposed to build a settling pond for drainage adjacent to the mouth of the mine and Talk Creek. The pond was finished in 1993 at a cost of $42,000. By 1994 the river was relatively free of contaminants, and residents reported the return of fish to Talk Creek.

In late 1996, however, the TPCA received reports that Talk Creek was again being polluted, and on February 29, 1997, the TPCA filed a complaint against Macklin, claiming that discharge from the firm's settling pond was responsible for extensive pollution of Talk Creek. Macklin responded, claiming that it was not in violation of the Tennessee statute that prohibits discharge of contaminants into state waters.

The TPCA's complaint was filed with the Tennessee Environmental Council (TEC), which hears such cases and, if the charged party is in violation of law, fixes a penalty. The TEC has broad responsibilities and can assess any combination of the following penalties: (1) a maximum penalty of $50,000 for a violation of the State Pollution Control Act, (2) a maximum penalty of $2,500 for each day the violation continues, (3) institution of a program to bring the violator into compliance with the law, and/or (4) an injunction shutting down the firm until compliance is effected.

A hearing before the TEC was held on August 3, 1997. John Benn, regional manager for the TPCA, presented the state's case. He said that the TPCA initially investigated the complaint of nearby residents, who thought Talk Creek was again being polluted. The initial investigation was delayed by a heavy case load, but on November 29, 1996, Benn said, a TPCA inspector found that, although Talk Creek was of relatively clear appearance above the Macklin mine, it was a dark, reddish color below the firm's settling pond. Photographs showing this were submitted. Subsequent water analysis showed the water above the pond to have a slightly alkaline pH of 7.1, whereas below the pond the pH was a somewhat acidic 6.8. Analysis indicated that the dissolved mineral content (mainly iron) below the pond was 132 percent greater than above it. The suspended solids count was 267 percent higher below the pond than above it. Analysis also revealed that the water below the pond had a very low dissolved oxygen content, much lower than above the pond. There were also increased sulphate, chloride, bromide, and phosphate concentrations below the pond. Benn stated that the TPCA repeated these experiments on December 14, 1996, again on January 2, 1997, and a third time on January 8, 1997, with very similar results. Benn testified that on January 14, 1997 a Tennessee State biologist sampled Talk Creek and found that, although there was an abundance of organic life and numerous fish above the Macklin mine, there were no fish discovered in shocking experiments just below the settling pond or at four 1,000-yard intervals below the pond. His investigators and scientists concluded that the absence of dissolved oxygen caused the fish to die.

Benn stated that although inspectors could not directly observe a concentrated flow at any one point, an aerial photograph indicated general seepage along the 170 yards that the settling pond fronts Talk Creek. He concluded by saying that in his opinion the environmental damage was extensive, that it had effectively eradicated life in lower Talk Creek.

Speaking for twelve families who live along lower Talk Creek, Jim Clance said they all worried about their drinking water. He said he had read that once water quality goes down it never seems to go back up. He added that the Macklins "only know money" and that the TEC should "shut 'em down or fine 'em to the gills."

Jim Kelly spoke on behalf of the local sportsmen's association. He said that although he was no expert on environmental matters, his association was very concerned with Macklin's pollution of a very fine fishing stream and he wanted to point out certain aspects of the 1972 Federal Water Pollution Act Amendments (FWPAA). According to these amendments "States must establish the total maximum daily load of pollutants . . . that will not impair propagation of fish and wildlife." Since all fish were killed in Talk Creek, Kelly pointed out that Macklin clearly violated the FWPAA, whatever standards the state set. He also pointed out the FWPAA's provision that "Any citizen or group of citizens whose interests may be adversely affected has the right to take court action against anyone violating an effluent standard or limitation or an order issued by EPA or a State, under the law." Kelly said his association had retained a lawyer and would take legal action against Macklin if the state failed to act. Finally, he noted the FWPAA provision that "A State's permit program is subject to revocation by EPA, after a public hearing, if the State fails to implement the law adequately." He indicated that his association would also pursue this course of action if the state failed to act.

Sharon Smith, who described herself as a "local environmental watchdog," said that the Federal Water Pollution Control Act of 1972 stated its objective was to "restore and maintain the chemical, physical, and biological integrity of the Nation's waters." She said the TPCA had clearly shown that the mine had negatively affected the chemical and biological integrity of Talk Creek. And she said that one of the goals of the 1977 Clean Water Act was that of achieving water quality sufficient for the protection and propagation of fish, shellfish, and wildlife and for recreation in and on the water. Macklin clearly was in violation, she said, since it had again eradicated all life in the stream. She said the state needed to deal harshly with Macklin because it was a chronic polluter. Up to 1990, she stated, Macklin had gotten away with direct dumping into Talk Creek, which effectively destroyed it. She noted that this was eighteen years after the federal government declared such dumping illegal. She pointed out that the 1972 Water Pollution Control Act required companies to use the "best practicable technology" (i.e., technology actually used by the least polluting mines) to reduce pollution by 1977. And she said the 1977 Clean Water Act required companies to eliminate discharge wastes by the best available technology by 1984. Her belief was that Macklin knew the law but just ignored it for eighteen years until he was apprehended in 1990, and the state just didn't bother to enforce the law. She noted that John Macklin was Chairman of the Bone County Democratic Party from 1974–76 and 1982–86, and still was a member of the statewide Tennessee Democratic Council, a politically powerful group with close ties to the state's most influential politicians. She said Macklin intentionally violated the law for eighteen years. Then, when the TPCA caught him in 1990, he stalled for three more years. Then, three years later he destroyed the creek again. She said Macklin would ask for leniency, but did not deserve it.

Ms. Smith said it was ironic that the 1996 Safe Drinking Water Act provided $7.6 billion to ensure safe drinking water, when Macklin was allowed to pollute Talk Creek for all these years. She also said the EPA had not yet tested the Bone River, but it was also undoubtedly polluted by the Talk Creek discharge. She thought that people did not seem to understand the consequences of allowing this sort of thing to continue, but noted that the polluted water went west to the Mississipi River and in the Gulf of Mexico there is an area about sixty feet deep and the size of New Jersey that is practically without life—no crabs, no shrimp, no fish. Why? No oxygen—the same as Talk Creek.

As for the penalty, Ms. Smith said she could see how an unintentional first-time violator should just be warned and forced to comply with the law. However, she said Macklin knew what he was doing and knew it was illegal for the better part of twenty five years. She felt that Macklin should be fined maximally or he would just continue to laugh at the law.

Jim Robbis, manager of the Talk Creek mine, testified for Macklin. He said there was no health hazard: "The state itself indicated it is an iron problem; nobody ever died from rust in their water. And people don't obtain their oxygen by taking in water."

Robbis said that Macklin installed the settling pond in 1993, that it was built to comply with stringent TPCA specifications, that the TPCA approved it upon completion, and that the company had maintained the pond to state standards. He said that Macklin employed Environmental Monitors, an independent firm, to test the site, and that on September 16, 1996, that firm reported to Macklin and the TPCA that Macklin was in full compliance with the law. He noted that Environmental Monitors had tested the site triannually, as required by law, since 1993, and that it had always been in compliance, except for one period during 1994 when heavy rains caused a small spillover of the settling pond. Robbis added that although Environmental Monitors was scheduled at the site during the third week of January 1997, an equipment breakdown caused the testing firm to delay its check until mid-February. By that time the TPCA had filed its complaint.

Robbis said that he noticed some water discoloration in the creek in mid-October 1996, but he recalled that it extended above the mine and thought it was caused by heavy rains. He added that pockets of iron leech out above the mine periodically, and he didn't think anything of the light red tinge.

John Macklin, president of the firm, then spoke. He said this was all very painful for him, that he had never been in court before today, but that he would do his best to defend his honor and that of his family, his company and its employees.

He began by saying that he would not apologize for the fact that his father knew Franklin Delano Roosevelt and had helped bring federal government money to Bone Country during the great depression, nor would he apologize for knowing John Fitzgerald Kennedy, with whom he worked to get federal funds for the Bone County library and also the rerouting of the freeway so that it went through the county. Politics, he thought, was noble as long as it served the public interest. He said he never benefitted one iota from his political work, not one dime.

Mr. Macklin said it was distressing to him that Talk Creek had become polluted. But he did not believe his mine was the cause. He said the TPCA had not proven its case, and that he could back up 100 percent Jim Robbis' claim that there was discoloration in Talk Creek above the mine sometime in mid-October 1996. Jim had mentioned it to him about a week after the occurrence, on October 23, 1996, but when the two of them looked at the creek that morning, it looked clear, and Robbis had said to him at that time that it was probably caused by rain leaching out iron above the mine in the previous week, an event over which Macklin had no control. He said that Robbis had told him on that same date, 10/23/96, that Environmental Monitors had said Macklin was in compliance with the law as of September 16, 1996. Mr. Macklin submitted his calendar, which showed that he had a meeting scheduled with Mr. Robbis at 10:00 A.M. on October 23, 1996. He said he did not dispute the EPA's tests run between 11/96 and 1/97, but that in all likelihood the discharge above the mine in mid-October, 1996 was responsible for the EPA's findings.

Mr. Macklin said the words of some of the residents pained him deeply because he too considered himself an environmentalist. He noted he had donated twelve acres on Talk Creek in 1985 for a park called Macklin Park, used frequently by some of the locals who now criticized him. He said he avoided strip mining because it was environmentally unsound, and that above his underground mines he purposefully kept the areas forested. No logging, he noted, was permitted, even though it would have helped the bottom line during many lean years.

He said the record would show that he had never broken the law. He claimed his Talk Creek mine had never had a major accident. He said that as far as he knew, based on his lawyers' advice, he never was in any violation of the law from 1972 to 1990 because there was only iron, dissolved iron, in Talk Creek. He said he hoped everyone understood Jim Robbis's remarks on this iron issue. Iron, he said, is not bad for people; in fact, it is necessary, and most Americans do not get enough of it. Since there was no real harm, he had been advised at the time that he had done nothing illegal. He said that Macklin agreed to a settling pond in 1992 not because it felt it was acting illegally, but because he was told that the cost of litigation would be greater than the cost of just going ahead and building the settling pond.

Mr. Macklin said that he had lived in Bone County all his life and that he knew every person working at the Talk Creek mine as well as almost every member of their families. He said he was proud they had good homes and some of them could send their children on to college. The Talk Creek mine, he pointed out, was Bone County's third largest employer—after Wal-Mart and the county itself. He noted the unemployment rate of over 11 percent in Bone County, that his firm's annual wages totaled over $1.9 million in 1996, and said he was especially concerned about six of his employees who were close to pension eligibility. In fact, he said he sometimes kept on unproductive workers so that members of their families who were ill could continue to have insurance benefits.

Mr. Macklin said that although coal has a bright future, the past four years had been difficult: profits were higher ten years ago than at present. Compliance with Occupational Safety and Health Administration and environmental legislation had made the Talk Creek operation marginal. In fact, building the settling pond in 1993 had negated the entire year's profit. He said that profits during the last four years were so minimal that he would have made more money by selling his mines, putting his money in bank certificates of deposit, and just relaxing. A full fine of $25,000, he noted, would nearly wipe out one year's profit. Fines of $2,500 per day would probably mean bankruptcy for the entire firm. He pointed out that the pricing situation in the coal industry was improving, and he believed profits would increase substantially in the next year. An injunction shutting down the mine until compliance could be effected would not only penalize employees, it would wipe out Macklin's chance for the profit necessary to keep the mine open. He could agree to a more extensive test procedure to see if the pond was really responsible for the discharge. If so, there was only one reasonable alternative. A new pond would be constructed south of the present one. The present mine and pond would continue as is until the drainage could be shifted to the new pond in a year or so. This was the only way that Macklin could cover the cost of the new pond. This would mean the discharge into Talk Creek would continue, but the creek had snapped back before and would do so again. Even then, he said that on this alternative it would be a close call; if the price of coal turned down, the only option might be to shut the mine. He didn't want to do that, but said he wasn't running a charity.

Mr. Macklin closed by saying he had worked his entire life to benefit the people of Bone County and that if his company was found innocent he would just like to get back to that task.

## FOR DISCUSSION

If you were the TEC judge, what judgment would you reach in this case? Why? If you believe Macklin is guilty, what penalty would you assess? Why? What factors must be weighed in making your decision?

*William F. Baxter*

# People or Penguins:
# The Case for Optimal Pollution

I start with the modest proposition that, in dealing with pollution, or indeed with any problem, it is helpful to know what one is attempting to accomplish. Agreement on how and whether to pursue a particular objective, such as pollution control, is not possible unless some more general objective has been identified and stated with reasonable precision. We talk loosely of having clean air and clean water, of preserving our wilderness areas, and so forth. But none of these is a sufficiently general objective: each is more accurately viewed as a means rather than as an end.

With regard to clean air, for example, one may ask, "How clean?" and "What does clean mean?" It is even reasonable to ask, "Why have clean air?" Each of these questions is an implicit demand that a more general community goal be stated—a goal sufficiently general in its scope and enjoying sufficiently general assent among the community of actors that such "why" questions no longer seem admissible with respect to that goal.

If, for example, one states as a goal the proposition that "every person should be free to do whatever he wishes in contexts where his actions do not interfere with the interests of other human beings," the speaker is unlikely to be met with a response of "why." The goal may be criticized as uncertain in its implications or difficult to implement, but it is so basic a tenet of our civilization—it reflects a cultural value so broadly shared, at least in the abstract—that the question "why" is seen as impertinent or imponderable or both.

I do not mean to suggest that everyone would agree with the "spheres of freedom" objective just stated. Still less do I mean to suggest that a society could subscribe to four or five such general objectives that would be adequate in their coverage to serve as testing criteria by which all other

From William F. Baxter, *People or Penguins: The Case For Optimal Pollution* (Columbia University Press, 1974).

disagreements might be measured. One difficulty in the attempt to construct such a list is that each new goal added will conflict, in certain applications, with each prior goal listed; and thus each goal serves as a limited qualification on prior goals.

Without any expectation of obtaining unanimous consent to them, let me set forth four goals that I generally use as ultimate testing criteria in attempting to frame solutions to problems of human organization. My position regarding pollution stems from these four criteria. If the criteria appeal to you and any part of what appears hereafter does not, our disagreement will have a helpful focus: which of us is correct, analytically, in supposing that his position on pollution would better serve these general goals. If the criteria do not seem acceptable to you, then it is to be expected that our more particular judgments will differ, and the task will then be yours to identify the basic set of criteria upon which your particular judgments rest.

My criteria are as follows:

1. The spheres of freedom criterion stated above.
2. Waste is a bad thing. The dominant feature of human existence is scarcity—our available resources, our aggregate labors, and our skill in employing both have always been, and will continue for some time to be, inadequate to yield to every man all the tangible and intangible satisfactions he would like to have. Hence, none of those resources, or labors, or skills, should be wasted—that is, employed so as to yield less than they might yield in human satisfactions.
3. Every human being should be regarded as an end rather than as a means to be used for the betterment of another. Each should be afforded dignity and regarded as having an absolute claim to an evenhanded application of such rules as the community may adopt for its governance.
4. Both the incentive and the opportunity to improve his share of satisfactions should be preserved to every individual. Preservation of incentive is dictated by the "no-waste" criterion and enjoins against the continuous, totally egalitarian redistribution of satisfactions, or wealth, but subject to that constraint, everyone should receive, by continuous redistribution if necessary, some minimal share of aggregate wealth so as to avoid a level of privation from which the opportunity to improve his situation becomes illusory.

The relationship of these highly general goals to the more specific environmental issues at hand may not be readily apparent, and I am not yet ready to demonstrate their pervasive implications. But let me give one indication of their implications. Recently scientists have informed us that use of DDT in food production is causing damage to the penguin population. For the present purposes let us accept that assertion as an indisputable scientific fact. The scientific fact is often asserted as if the correct implication—that we must stop agricultural use of DDT—followed from the mere statement of the fact of penguin damage. But plainly it does not follow if my criteria are employed.

My criteria are oriented to people, not penguins. Damage to penguins, or sugar pines, or geological marvels is, without more, simply irrelevant. One must go further, by my criteria, and say: Penguins are important because people enjoy seeing them walk about rocks; and furthermore, the well-being of people would be less impaired by halting use of DDT than by giving up penguins. In short, my observations about environmental problems will be people-oriented, as are my criteria. I have no interest in preserving penguins for their own sake.

It may be said by way of objection to this position, that it is very selfish of people to act as if each person represented one unit of importance and nothing else was of any importance. It is undeniably selfish. Nevertheless I think it is the only tenable starting place for analysis for several reasons. First, no other position corresponds to the way most people really think and act—i.e., corresponds to reality.

Second, this attitude does not portend any massive destruction of nonhuman flora and fauna, for people depend on them in many obvious ways, and they will be preserved because and to the degree that humans do depend on them.

Third, what is good for humans is, in many respects, good for penguins and pine trees—clean air, for example. So that humans are, in these respects, surrogates for plant and animal life.

Fourth, I do not know how we could administer any other system. Our decisions are either private or collective. Insofar as Mr. Jones is free to act privately, he may give such preferences as he wishes to other forms of life: he may feed birds in winter and do with less himself, and he may even decline to resist an advancing polar bear on the ground that the bear's appetite is more important than those portions of himself that the bear may choose to eat. In short my basic premise does not rule out private altruism to competing life-forms. It does rule out, however, Mr. Jones's inclination to feed Mr. Smith to the bear, however hungry the bear, however despicable Mr. Smith.

Insofar as we act collectively on the other hand, only humans can be afforded an opportunity to participate in the collective decisions. Penguins cannot vote now and are unlikely subjects for the franchise—pine trees more unlikely still. Again each individual is free to cast his vote so as to benefit sugar pines if that is his inclination. But many of the more extreme assertions that one hears from some conservationists amount to tacit assertions that they are specially appointed representatives of sugar pines, and hence that their preferences should be weighted more heavily than the preferences of other humans who do not enjoy equal rapport with "nature." The simplistic assertion that agricultural use of DDT must stop at once because it is harmful to penguins is of that type.

Fifth, if polar bears or pine trees or penguins, like men, are to be regarded as ends rather than means, if they are to count in our calculus of social organization, someone must tell me how much each one counts, and someone must tell me how these life-forms are to be permitted to express their preferences, for I do not know either answer. If the answer is that certain people are to hold their proxies, then I want to know how those proxy-holders are to be selected: self-appointment does not seem workable to me.

Sixth, and by way of summary of all the foregoing, let me point out that the set of environmental issues under discussion—although they raise very complex technical questions of how to achieve any objective—ultimately raise a normative question: what *ought* we to do. Questions of *ought* are unique to the human mind and world—they are meaningless as applied to a nonhuman situation.

I reject the proposition that we ought to respect the "balance of nature" or to "preserve the environment" unless the reason for doing so, express or implied, is the benefit of man.

I reject the idea that there is a "right" or "morally correct" state of nature to which we should return. The word "nature" has no normative connotation. Was it "right" or "wrong" for the earth's crust to heave in contortion and create mountains and seas? Was it "right" for the first amphibian to crawl up out of the primordial ooze? Was it "wrong" for plants to reproduce themselves and alter the atmospheric composition in favor of oxygen? For animals to alter the atmosphere in favor of carbon dioxide both by breathing oxygen and eating plants? No answers can be given to these questions because they are meaningless questions.

All this may seem obvious to the point of being tedious, but much of the present controversy over environment and pollution rests on tacit normative assumptions about just such nonnormative phenomena: that it is "wrong" to impair penguins with DDT, but not to slaughter cattle for prime rib roasts. That it is wrong to kill stands of sugar pines with industrial fumes, but not to cut sugar pines and build housing for the poor. Every man is entitled to his own preferred definition of Walden Pond, but there is no definition that has any moral superiority over another, except by reference to the selfish needs of the human race.

From the fact that there is no normative definition of the natural state, it follows that there is no normative definition of clean air or pure water—hence no definition of polluted air—or of pollution—except by reference to the needs of man. The "right" composition of the atmosphere is one which has some dust in it and some lead in it and some hydrogen sulfide in it—just those amounts that attend a sensibly organized society thoughtfully and knowledgeably pursuing the greatest possible satisfaction for its human members.

The first and most fundamental step toward solution of our environmental problems is a clear recognition that our objective is not pure air or water but rather some optimal state of pollution. That step immediately suggests the question: How do we define and attain the level of pollution that will yield the maximum possible amount of human satisfaction?

Low levels of pollution contribute to human satisfaction but so do food and shelter and education and music. To attain ever lower levels of pollution, we must pay the cost of having less of these other things. I contrast that view of the cost of pollution control with the more popular statement that pollution control will "cost" very large numbers of dollars. The popular statement is true in some senses, false in others; sorting out the true and false senses is of some importance. The first step in that sorting process is to achieve a clear understanding of the difference between dollars and resources. Resources are the wealth of our nation; dollars are merely claim checks upon those resources. Resources are of vital importance; dollars are comparatively trivial.

Four categories of resources are sufficient for our purposes. At any given time a nation, or a planet if you prefer, has a stock of labor, of technological skill, of capital goods, and of natural resources (such as mineral deposits, timber, water, land, etc.). These resources can be used in various combinations to yield goods and services of all kinds—in some limited quantity. The quantity will be larger if they are combined efficiently, smaller if combined inefficiently. But in either event the resource stock is limited, the goods and services that they can be made to yield are limited; even the most efficient use of them will yield less than our population, in the aggregate, would like to have.

If one considers building a new dam, it is appropriate to say that it will be costly in the sense that it will require $x$ hours of labor, $y$ tons of steel and concrete, and $z$ amount of capital goods. If these resources are devoted to the dam, then they cannot be used to build hospitals, fishing rods, schools, or electric can openers. That is the meaningful sense in which the dam is costly.

Quite apart from the very important question of how wisely we can combine our resources to produce goods and services, is the very different question of how they get distributed—who gets how many goods? Dollars constitute the claim checks which are distributed among people and which control their share of national output. Dollars are nearly valueless pieces of paper except to the extent that they do represent claim checks to some fraction of the output of goods and services. Viewed as claim checks, all the dollars outstanding during any period of time are worth, in the aggregate, the goods and services that are available to be claimed with them during that period—neither more nor less.

It is far easier to increase the supply of dollars than to increase the production of goods and services—printing dollars is easy. But printing more dollars doesn't help because each dollar then simply becomes a claim to fewer goods, i.e., becomes worth less.

The point is this: many people fall into error upon hearing the statement that the decision to build a dam, or to clean up a river, will cost $X million. It is regrettably easy to say: "It's only money. This is a wealthy country, and we have lots of money." But you cannot build a dam or clean a river with $X million—unless you also have a match, you can't even make a fire. One builds a dam or cleans a river by diverting labor and steel and trucks and factories from making one kind of goods to making another. The cost in dollars is merely a shorthand way of describing the extent of the diversion necessary. If we build a dam for $X million, then we must recognize that we will have $X million less housing and food and medical care and electric can openers as a result.

Similarly, the costs of controlling pollution are best expressed in terms of the other goods we will have to give up to do the job. This is not to say the job should not be done. Badly as we need more housing, more medical care, and more can openers, and more symphony orchestras, we could do with somewhat less of them, in my judgment at least, in exchange for somewhat cleaner air and rivers. But that is the nature of the trade-off, and analysis of the problem is advanced if that unpleasant reality is kept in mind. Once the trade-off relationship is clearly perceived, it is possible to state in a very general way what the optimal level of pollution is. I would state it as follows:

People enjoy watching penguins. They enjoy relatively clean air and smog-free vistas. Their health is improved by relatively clean water and air. Each of these benefits is a type of good or service. As a society we would be well advised to give up one washing machine if the resources that would have gone into that washing machine can yield greater human satisfaction when diverted into pollution control. We should give up one hospital if the resources thereby freed, would yield more human satisfaction when devoted to elimination of noise in our cities. And so on, trade-off by trade-off, we should divert our productive capacities from the production of existing goods and services to the production of a cleaner, quieter, more pastoral nation up to—and no further than—the point at which we value more highly the next washing machine or hospital that we would have to do without than we value the next unit of environmental improvement that the diverted resources would create.

Now this proposition seems to me unassailable but so general and abstract as to be unhelpful—at least unadministerable in the form stated. It assumes we can measure in some way the incremental units of human satisfaction yielded by very different types of goods. The proposition must remain a pious abstraction until I can explain how this measurement process can occur. In subsequent chapters I will attempt to show that we can do this—in some contexts with great precision and in other contexts only by rough approximation. But I insist that the proposition stated describes the result for which we should be striving—and again, that it is always useful to know what your target is even if your weapons are too crude to score a bull's eye.

*William T. Blackstone*

# Ethics and Ecology

## THE RIGHT TO A LIVABLE ENVIRONMENT AS A HUMAN RIGHT

Let us first ask whether the right to a livable environment can properly be considered to be a human right. For the purposes of this paper, however, I want to avoid raising the more general question of whether there are any human rights at all. Some philosophers do deny that any human rights exist.[1] In two recent papers I have argued that human rights do exist (even though such rights may properly be overridden on occasion by other morally relevant reasons) and that they are universal and inalienable (although the actual exercise of such rights on a given occasion is alienable).[2] My argument for the existence of universal human rights rests, in the final analysis, on a theory of what it means to be human, which specifies the capacities for rationality and freedom as essential, and on the fact that there are no relevant grounds for excluding any human from the opportunity to develop and fulfill his capacities (rationality and freedom) as a human. This is not to deny that there are criteria which justify according human rights in quite different ways or with quite different modes of treatment for different persons, depending upon the nature and degree of such capacities and the existing historical and environmental circumstances.

If the right to a livable environment were seen as a basic and inalienable human right this could be a valuable tool (both inside and outside of legalistic frameworks) for solving some of our environmental problems, both on a national and on an international basis. Are there any philosophical and conceptual difficulties in treating this right as an inalienable

From William T. Blackstone, *Philosophy and Environmental Crisis* (Athens, Ga.: The University of Georgia Press, 1974), pp. 30–42. Reprinted with the permission of the publisher.

human right? Traditionally we have not looked upon the right to a decent environment as a human right or as an inalienable right. Rather, inalienable human or natural rights have been conceived in somewhat different terms: equality, liberty, happiness, life, and property. However, might it not be possible to view the right to a livable environment as being entailed by, or as constitutive of, these basic human or natural rights recognized in our political tradition? If human rights, in other words, are those rights which each human possesses in virtue of the fact that he is human and in virtue of the fact that those rights are essential in permitting him to live a human life (that is, in permitting him to fulfill his capacities as a rational and free being), then might not the right to a decent environment be properly categorized as such a human right? Might it not be conceived as a right which has emerged as a result of changing environmental conditions and the impact of those conditions on the very possibility of human life and on the possibility of the realization of other rights such as liberty and equality? Let us explore how this might be the case.

Given man's great and increasing ability to manipulate the environment, and the devastating effect this is having, it is plain that new social institutions and new regulative agencies and procedures must be initiated on both national and international levels to make sure that the manipulation is in the public interest. It will be necessary, in other words, to restrict or stop some practices and the freedom to engage in those practices. Some look upon such additional state planning, whether national or international, as unnecessary further intrusion on man's freedom. Freedom is, of course, one of our basic values, and few would deny that excessive state control of human action is to be avoided. But such restrictions on individual freedom now appear to be necessary in the interest of overall human welfare and the rights and freedoms of *all* men. Even John Locke with his stress on freedom as an inalienable right recognized that this right must be construed so that it is consistent with the equal right to freedom of others. The whole point of the state is to restrict unlicensed freedom and to provide the conditions for equality of rights for all. Thus it seems to be perfectly consistent with Locke's view and, in general, with the views of the founding fathers of this country to restrict certain rights or freedoms when it can be shown that such restriction is necessary to insure the equal rights of others. If this is so, it has very important implications for the rights to freedom and to property. These rights, perhaps properly seen as inalienable (though this is a controversial philosophical question), are not properly seen as unlimited or unrestricted. When values which we hold dear conflict (for example, individual or group freedom and the freedom of all, individual or group rights and the rights of all, and individual or group welfare and the welfare of the general public) something has to give; some priority must be established. In the case of the abuse and waste of environmental resources, less individual freedom and fewer individual rights for the sake of greater public welfare and equality of rights seem justified. What in the past had been properly regarded as freedoms and rights (given what seemed to be unlimited natural resources and no serious pollution problems) can no longer be so construed, at least not without additional restrictions. We must recognize both the need for such restrictions and the fact that none of our rights can be realized without a livable environment. Both public welfare and equality of rights now require that natural resources not be used simply according to the whim and caprice of individuals or simply for personal profit. This is not to say that all property rights must be denied and that the state must own all productive property, as the Marxist argues. It is to insist that those rights be qualified or restricted in the light of new ecological data and in the interest of the freedom, rights, and welfare of all.

The answer then to the question, Is the right to a livable environment a human right? is yes. Each person has this right qua being human and because a livable environment is essential for one to fulfill his human capacities. And given the danger to our environment today and hence the danger to the very possibility of human existence, access to a livable environment must be conceived as a right which imposes upon everyone a correlative moral obligation to respect.

A good case can be made for the view that not all moral or human rights should be legal rights and that not all moral rules should be legal rules. It may be argued that any society which covers the whole spectrum of man's activities with legally enforceable rules minimizes his freedom and approaches totalitarianism. There is this danger. But just as we argued that certain traditional rights and freedoms are properly restricted in order to insure the equal rights and welfare of all, so also it can plausibly he argued that the human right to a livable environment should become a legal one in order to assure that it is properly respected. Given the magnitude of the present dangers to the environment and to the welfare of all humans, and the ingrained habits and rules, or lack of rules, which permit continued waste, pollution, and destruction of our environmental resources, the legalized status of the right to a livable environment seems both desirable and necessary.

Such a legal right would provide a tool for pressing environmental transgressions in the courts. At the present the right to a livable environment, even if recognized as a human right, is not generally recognized as a legal one. One cannot sue individuals or corporations for polluting the environment, if the pollution harms equally every member of a community. One can sue such individuals or corporations if they damage one's private property but not if they damage the public environment.

The history of government, in this country and elsewhere, has been that of the gradual demise of a laissez-faire philosophy of government. Few deny that there are areas of our lives where government should not and must not intrude. In fact, what we mean by a totalitarian government is one which exceeds its proper bounds and attempts to control nearly all human activities. But in some areas of human life, it has been seen that the "keep-government-out-of-it" attitude just will not work. The entire quality of life in a society is determined by the availability and distribution of goods and services in such vital areas as education, housing, medical treatment, legal treatment, and so on. In the field of education, for example, we have seen the need for compulsory education and, more recently, for unitary school systems in order to provide equality of educational opportunity.

In the same way, it is essential that government step in to prevent the potentially dire consequences of industrial pollution and the waste of environmental resources. Such government regulations need not mean the death of the free enterprise system. The right to private property can be made compatible with the right to a livable environment, for if uniform antipollution laws were applied to all industries, then both competition and private ownership could surely continue. But they would continue within a quite different set of rules and attitudes toward the environment. This extension of government would not be equivalent to totalitarianism. In fact it is necessary to insure equality of rights and freedom, which is essential to a democracy.

## ECOLOGY AND ECONOMIC RIGHTS

We suggested above that it is necessary to qualify or restrict economic or property rights in the light of new ecological data and in the interest of the freedom, rights, and welfare of all. In part, this suggested restriction is predicated on the assumption that we cannot expect private business to provide solutions to the multiple pollution problems for which they themselves are responsible. Some companies have taken measures to limit the polluting effect of their operations, and this is an important move. But we are deluding ourselves if we think that private business can function as its own pollution police. This is so for several reasons: the primary objective of private business is economic profit. Stockholders do not ask of a company, "Have you polluted the environment and lowered the quality of the environment for the general public and for future generations?" Rather they ask, "How high is the annual dividend and how much higher is it than the year before?" One can hardly expect organizations whose basic norm is economic profit to be concerned in any great depth with the long-range effects of their operations upon society and future generations or concerned with the hidden cost of their operations in terms of environmental quality to society as a whole. Second, within a free enterprise system companies compete to produce what the public wants at the lowest possible cost. Such competition would preclude the spending of adequate funds to prevent environmental pollution, since this would add tremendously to the cost of the product—unless all other companies would also conform to such antipollution policies. But in a free enterprise economy such policies are not likely to be self-imposed by businessmen. Third, the basic response of the free enterprise system to our economic problems is that we must have greater economic growth or an increase in gross national product. But such growth many ecologists look upon with great alarm, for it can have devastating long-range effects upon our environment. Many of the products of uncontrolled growth are based on artificial needs and actually detract from, rather than contribute to, the quality of our lives. A stationary economy, some economists and ecologists suggest, may well be best for the quality of man's environment and of his life in the long run. Higher GNP does not automatically result in an increase in social well-being, and it should not be used as a measuring rod for assessing economic welfare. This becomes clear when one realizes that the GNP

aggregates the dollar value of all goods and services produced—the cigarettes as well as the medical treatment of lung cancer, the petroleum from offshore wells as well as the detergents required to clean up after oil spills, the electrical energy produced and the medical and cleaning bills resulting from the air-pollution fuel used for generating the electricity. The GNP allows no deduction for negative production, such as lives lost from unsafe cars or environmental destruction perpetrated by telephone, electric and gas utilities, lumber companies, and speculative builders.[3]

To many persons, of course, this kind of talk is not only blasphemy but subversive. This is especially true when it is extended in the direction of additional controls over corporate capitalism. The fact of the matter is that the ecological attitude forces one to reconsider a host of values which have been held dear in the past, and it forces one to reconsider the appropriateness of the social and economic systems which embodied and implemented those values. Given the crisis of our environment, there must be certain fundamental changes in attitudes toward nature, man's use of nature, and man himself. Such changes in attitudes undoubtedly will have far-reaching implications for the institutions of private property and private enterprise and the values embodied in these institutions. Given that crisis we can no longer look upon water and air as free commodities to be exploited at will. Nor can the private ownership of land be seen as a lease to use that land in any way which conforms merely to the personal desires of the owner. In other words, the environmental crisis is forcing us to challenge what had in the past been taken to be certain basic rights of man or at least to restrict those rights. And it is forcing us to challenge institutions which embodied those rights.

Much has been said about the conflict between these kinds of rights, and the possible conflict between them is itself a topic for an extensive paper. Depending upon how property rights are formulated, the substantive content of those rights, it seems plain to me, can directly conflict with what we characterize as human rights. In fact our moral and legal history demonstrate exactly that kind of conflict. There was a time in the recent past when property rights embodied the right to hold human beings in slavery. This has now been rejected, almost universally. Under nearly any interpretation of the substantive content of human rights, slavery is incompatible with those rights.

The analogous question about rights which is now being raised by the data uncovered by the ecologist and by the gradual advancement of the ecological attitude is whether the notion of property rights should be even further restricted to preclude the destruction and pollution of our environmental resources upon which the welfare and the very lives of all of us and of future generations depend. Should our social and legal system embrace property rights or other rights which permit the kind of environmental exploitation which operates to the detriment of the majority of mankind? I do not think so. The fact that a certain right exists in a social or legal system does not mean that it ought to exist. I would not go so far as to suggest that all rights are merely rule-utilitarian devices to be

adopted or discarded whenever it can be shown that the best consequences thereby follow.[4] But if a right or set of rights systematically violates the public welfare, this is prima facie evidence that it ought not to
exist. And this certainly seems to be the case with the exercise of certain
property rights today.

In response to this problem, there is today at least talk of "a new economy of resources," one in which new considerations and values play an important role along with property rights and the interplay of market forces. Economist Nathaniel Wollman argues that "the economic past of 'optimizing'
resource use consists of bringing into an appropriate relationship the ordering of preferences for various experiences and the costs of acquiring those
experiences. Preferences reflect physiological-psychological responses to
experience or anticipated experience, individually or collectively revealed,
and are accepted as data by the economist. A broad range of noneconomic
investigations is called for to supply the necessary information."[5]

Note that Wollman says that noneconomic investigations are called
for. In other words the price system does not adequately account for a
number of value factors which should be included in an assessment. "It
does not account for benefits or costs that are enjoyed or suffered by
people who were not parties to the transaction."[6] In a system which
emphasizes simply the interplay of market forces as a criterion, these factors (such as sights, smells, and other aesthetic factors, justice, and
human rights—factors which are important to the well-being of humans)
are not even considered. Since they have no direct monetary value, the
market places no value whatsoever on them. Can we assume, then, that
purely economic or market evaluations provide us with data which will
permit us to maximize welfare, if the very process of evaluation and the
normative criteria employed exclude a host of values and considerations
on which human welfare depends? The answer to this question is plain.
We cannot make this assumption. We cannot rely merely upon the interplay of market forces or upon the sovereignty of the consumer. The concept of human welfare and consequently the notion of maximizing that
welfare requires a much broader perspective than the norms offered by
the traditional economic perspective. A great many things have value and
use which have no economic value and use. Consequently we must
broaden our evaluational perspective to include the entire range of values
which are essential not only to the welfare of man but also to the welfare
of other living things and to the environment which sustains all of life. And
this must include a reassessment of rights.

## ETHICS AND TECHNOLOGY

I have been discussing the relationship of ecology to ethics and to a theory of rights. Up to this point I have not specifically discussed the relation of technology to ethics, although it is plain that technology and its development is responsible for most of our pollution problems. This topic deserves separate treatment, but I do want to briefly relate it to the thesis of this work.

We tend too readily to assume that new technological developments will always solve man's problems. But this is simply not the case. One technological innovation often seems to breed a half-dozen additional ones which themselves create more environmental problems. We certainly do not solve pollution problems, for example, by changing from power plants fueled by coal to power plants fueled by nuclear energy, if radioactive waste from the latter is worse than pollution from the former. Perhaps part of the answer to pollution problems is less technology. There is surely no real hope of returning to nature (whatever that means) or of stopping *all* technological and scientific development, as some advocate. Even if it could be done, this would be too extreme a move. The answer is not to stop technology, but to guide it toward proper ends, and to set up standards of antipollution to which all technological devices must conform. Technology has been and can be used to destroy and pollute an environment, but it can also be used to save and beautify it. What is called for is purposeful environmental engineering, and this engineering calls for a mass of information about our environment, about the needs of persons, and about basic norms and values which are acceptable to civilized men. It also calls for priorities on goals and for compromises where there are competing and conflicting values and objectives. Human rights and their fulfillment should constitute at least some of those basic norms, and technology can be used to implement those rights and the public welfare.

# NOTES

1. See Kai Nielsen's "Skepticism and Human Rights," *Monist* 52, no. 4 (1968): 571–94.

2. See my "Equality and Human Rights," *Monist* 52, no. 4 (1968): 619–39 and my "Human Rights and Human Dignity," in *Human Dignity*, ed. Rubin Gotesky and Laszlo Ervin (New York: Gordar and Breach, 1970).

3. See Melville J. Ulmer, "More Than Marxist," *New Republic*, 26 December 1970, p. 14.

4. Some rights, I would argue, are inalienable, and are not based merely on a contract (implicit or explicit) or merely upon the norm of maximizing good consequences. (See David Braybrooke's *The Test for Democracy: Personal Rights, Human Welfare, Collective Preference* [New York: Random House, 1968], which holds such a rule-utilitarian theory of rights, and my "Human Rights and Human Dignity" for a rebuttal.)

5. Nathaniel Wollman, "The New Economics of Resources," *Daedalus* 96, no. 2 (fall 1967): 1100.

6. Ibid.

*Manuel G. Velasquez*

# Ecological Ethics

The problem of pollution (and of environmental issues in general) is seen by some researchers as a problem that can best be framed in terms of our duty to recognize and preserve the "ecological systems" within which we live.[1] An ecological system is an interrelated and interdependent set of organisms and environments, such as a lake—in which the fish depend on small aquatic organisms, which in turn live off of decaying plant and fish waste products.[2] Because the various parts of an ecological system are interrelated, the activities of one of its parts will affect all the other parts. Because the various parts are interdependent, the survival of each part depends on the survival of the other parts. Now business firms (and all other social institutions) are parts of a larger ecological system, "spaceship earth."[3] Business firms depend upon the natural environment for their energy, material resources, and waste disposal and that environment in turn is affected by the commercial activities of business firms. The activities of eighteenth-century European manufacturers of beaver hats, for example, led to the wholesale destruction of beavers in the United States, which in turn led to the drying up of the innumerable swamp lands that had been created by beaver dams.[4] Unless businesses recognize the interrelationships and interdependencies of the ecological systems within which they operate, and unless they ensure that their activities will not seriously injure these systems, we cannot hope to deal with the problem of pollution.

The fact that we are only a part of a larger ecological system has led many writers to insist that we should recognize our moral duty to protect the welfare not only of human beings, but also of other *nonhuman parts* of this system.[5] This insistence on what is sometimes called *ecological ethics* or "deep ecology" is not based on the idea that the environment should be protected for the sake of human beings. Instead, ecological

From Manuel G. Velasquez, *Business Ethics: Concepts and Cases*, 4th ed. (Upper Saddle River, N.J.: Prentice-Hall, Inc., 1998), pp. 270–73.

573

ethics are based on the idea that nonhuman parts of the environment deserve to be preserved *for their own sake*, regardless of whether this benefits human beings. Several supporters of this approach have formulated their views in a "platform" consisting of the following statements:

1. The well-being and flourishing of human and nonhuman life on Earth have value in themselves. . . . These values are independent of the usefulness of the nonhuman world for human purposes.
2. Richness and diversity of life forms contribute to the realization of these values and are also values in themselves.
3. Humans have no right to reduce this richness and diversity except to satisfy vital needs.
4. The flourishing of human life and cultures is compatible with a substantial decrease of the human population. The flourishing of nonhuman life requires such a decrease.
5. Present human interference with the nonhuman world is excessive and the situation is rapidly worsening.
6. Policies must therefore be changed. The changes in policies affect basic economic, technological, and ideological structures. The resulting state of affairs will be deeply different from the present.
7. The ideological change is mainly that of appreciating life quality . . . rather than adhering to an increasingly higher standard of living.
8. Those who subscribe to the foregoing points have an obligation directly or indirectly to participate in the attempt to implement the necessary changes.[6]

An "ecological ethic" is thus an ethic that claims that the welfare of at least some nonhumans is intrinsically valuable and that because of this intrinsic value, we humans have a duty to respect and preserve them. These ethical claims have significant implications for those business activities that affect the environment. In June 1990, for example, environmentalists successfully petitioned the U.S. Fish and Wildlife Service to bar the timber industry from logging potentially lucrative old-growth forests of northern California in order to save the habitat of the spotted owl, an endangered species.[7] The move was estimated to have cost the timber industry millions of dollars, to have cost workers as many as 36,000 lumber jobs, and to have raised the costs of consumer prices for fine wood products such as furniture and musical instruments. Throughout the 1980s members of the Sea Shepherd Conservation Society sabotaged whale processing plants, sunk several ships, and otherwise imposed costs on the whaling industry.[8] Members of Earth First! have driven nails into randomly selected trees of forest areas scheduled to be logged so that power logging saws are destroyed when they bite into the spiked trees. Supporters of the view that animals have intrinsic value have also imposed substantial costs on cattle ranchers, slaughterhouses, chicken farms, fur companies, and pharmaceutical and cosmetic corporations that use animals to test chemicals.

There are several varieties of ecological ethics, some more radical and far-reaching than others. Perhaps the most popular version claims that in addition to human beings, other animals have intrinsic value and are deserving of our respect and protection. Some utilitarians have claimed, for example, that pain is an evil whether it is inflicted on humans or on members of other animal species. The pain of an animal must be considered as equal to the comparable pain of a human and it is a form of "specist" prejudice (akin to racist or sexist bias against members of another race or sex) to think that the duty to avoid inflicting pain on members of other species is not equal to our duty to avoid inflicting comparable pain on members of our own species.[9]

Certain nonutilitarians have reached similar conclusions by a different route. They have claimed that the life of every animal "itself has value" apart from the interests of human beings. Because of the intrinsic value of its life each animal has certain "moral rights," in particular the right to be treated with respect.[10] Humans have a duty to respect this right, although in some cases a human's right might override an animal's right.

Both the utilitarian and the rights arguments in support of human duties toward animals imply that it is wrong to raise animals for food in the crowded and painful circumstances in which agricultural business enterprises currently raise cows, pigs, and chickens; they also imply that it is wrong to use animals in painful test procedures as they are currently used in some businesses—for example, to test the toxicity of cosmetics.[11]

Broader versions of ecological ethics would extend our duties beyond the animal world to include plants. Thus, some ethicists have claimed that it is "arbitrary" and "hedonistic" to confine our duties to creatures that can feel pain. Instead, they urge, we should acknowledge that all living things including plants have "an interest in remaining alive" and that consequently they deserve moral consideration for their own sakes.[12] Other authors have claimed that not only living things but even a natural species, a lake, a wild river, a mountain, and even the entire "biotic community" has a right to have its "integrity, stability, and beauty" preserved.[13] If correct, these views would have important implications for businesses engaged in strip-mining or logging operations.

Some versions of ecological ethics have turned away from talk of "duties" and "obligations" and have instead urged an approach toward nature that is more closely linked to notions of virtue and character. An early version of such an approach was fashioned by Albert Schweitzer who wrote that when traveling on a river in Africa, "at the very moment when, at sunset, we were making our way through a herd of hippopotamuses, there flashed upon my mind, unforeseen and unsought, the phrase, "Reverence for Life."[14] As he later articulated it, to be a person who has reverence for life is to see life itself, in all its forms, as having inherent worth, a worth that inspires an unwillingness to destroy and a desire to preserve:

> The man who has become a thinking being feels a compulsion to give to every will-to-live the same reverence for life that he gives to his own. He experiences that other life in his own. He accepts as being good: to preserve life, to promote life, to raise to its highest value life which is capable of development; and as being evil: to destroy life, to injure life, to repress life which is capable of development. This is the absolute, fundamental principle of the moral.[15]

More recently, the philosopher Paul Taylor has urged a similar approach, writing that "character traits are morally good in virtue of their expressing or embodying a certain ultimate moral attitude, which I call respect for nature."[16] This respect for nature, Taylor argues, is based on the fact that each living thing seeks its own good and so is a "teleological center of a life": "To say it is a teleological center of a life is to say that its internal functioning as well as its external activities are all goal-oriented, having the constant tendency to maintain the organism's existence through time and to enable it successfully to perform those biological operations whereby it reproduces its kind and continually adapts to changing environmental events and conditions."[17] The goal-oriented nature of all living things, Taylor argues, implies that all living things have an inherent "good of their own" that should be respected. Such respect is the only attitude consistent with a "biocentric outlook" that realizes that we ourselves are living members of earth's community of life, that we are part of a system of interdependence with other living things, that living things have their own good, and that we are not inherently superior to other living things within that system.

But these attempts to extend moral rights to nonhumans or to claim that an attitude of respect for all nature is morally demanded, are highly controversial, and some authors have labeled them "incredible."[18] It is difficult, for example, to see why the *fact* that something *is* alive implies that it *should* be alive and that we therefore have a *duty* to keep it alive or to express respect or even reverence for it, and it is difficult to see why the fact that a river or a mountain exists, implies that it should exist and that we have a duty to keep it in existence or revere it. Facts do not imply values in this easy way.[19] It is also controversial whether we can claim that animals have rights or intrinsic value.[20]

# NOTES

1. Barry Commoner, *The Closing Circle* (New York: Alfred A. Knopf, Inc., 1971), chap. 2.

2. See Kenneth E. F. Watt, *Understanding the Environment* (Boston: Allyn & Bacon, Inc., 1982).

3. Matthew Edel, *Economics and the Environment* (Englewood Cliffs, N.J.: Prentice Hall, 1973); for the term "spaceship earth," see Kenneth Boulding, "The Economics of the Coming Spaceship Earth," in *Environmental Quality in a Growing Economy*, ed. Henry Jarret (Baltimore: Johns Hopkins Press for Resources for the Future, 1966).

4. George Perkins, *Man and Nature* (Cambridge: Harvard University Press, 1965), p. 76.

5. For discussions favoring this view as well as criticisms see the essays collected in *Ethics and the Environment*, ed. Donald Scherer and Thomas Attig (Englewood Cliffs, N.J.: Prentice Hall, 1983); see also W. K. Frankena, "Ethics and the Environment," in *Ethics and Problems of the 21st Century*, ed. K. E. Goodpaster and K. M. Sayre (Notre Dame, Ind.: University of Notre Dame Press, 1979), pp. 3–20; William T. Blackstone, "The Search for an Environmental Ethic," in *Matters of Life and Death*, ed. Tom Regan (New York: Random House, Inc., 1980), pp. 299–335; an excellent and extensive annotated bibliography is provided by Mary Anglemyer, et al., *A Search for Environmental Ethics, An Initial Bibliography* (Washington, D.C.: Smithsonian Institution Press, 1980).

6. Quoted in Bill Devall, *Simple in Means, Rich in Ends, Practicing Deep Ecology* (Salt Lake City, Utah: Peregrine Smith Books, 1988), pp. 14–15.

7. Ted Gup, "Owl vs. Man," *Time*, 25 June 1990, pp. 56–62; Catherine Caufield, "A Reporter at Large: The Ancient Forest," *New Yorker*, 14 May 1990, pp. 46–84.

8. Devall, *Simple in Means, Rich in Ends*, p. 138.

9. Peter Singer, *Animal Liberation* (New York: Random House, Inc., 1975).

10. Tom Regan, *The Case for Animal Rights* (Berkeley, Calif.: University of California Press, 1983); in a similar vein, Joel Feinberg argues that animals have interests and consequently have rights in "The Rights of Animals and Unborn Generations," in *Philosophy and Environmental Crisis*, ed. William T. Blackstone (Athens, Ga.: University of Georgia Press, 1974).

11. See William Aiken, "Ethical Issues in Agriculture," in *Earthbound: New Introductory Essays in Environmental Ethics*, ed. Tom Regan (New York: Random House, Inc., 1984), pp. 247–88.

12. Kenneth Goodpaster, "On Being Morally Considerable," *Journal of Philosophy* 75 (1978): 308–25; see also Paul Taylor, "The Ethics of Respect for Nature," *Environmental Ethics* 3 (1981): 197–218; Robin Attfield, "The Good of Trees," *The Journal of Value Inquiry* 15 (1981): 35–54; and Christopher D. Stone, *Should Trees Have Standing? Toward Legal Rights for Natural Objects* (Boston: Houghton Mifflin, 1978).

13. Aldo Leopold, "The Land Ethic," in *A Sand County Almanac* (New York: Oxford University Press, 1949), pp. 201–26; see also J. Baird Callicott, "Animal Liberation: A Triangular Affair," *Environmental Ethics* 2, no. 4 (winter 1980): 311–38; John Rodman, "The Liberation of Nature?" *Inquiry* 20 (1977): 83–131; K. Goodpaster argues that the "biosphere" as a whole has moral value in "On Being Morally Considerable"; Holmes Rolston III holds a similar position in "Is There an Ecological Ethic?" *Ethics* 85 (1975): 93–109; for a variety of views on this issue see Bryan G. Norton, ed., *The Preservation of Species* (Princeton, N.J.: Princeton University Press, 1986).

14. Albert Schweitzer, *Out Of My Life and Thought*, trans. A. B. Lemke (New York: Holt, 1990), p. 130.

15. Ibid., p. 131.

16. Paul Taylor, *Respect for Nature* (Princeton, N.J.: Princeton University Press, 1986), p. 80.

17. Ibid., pp. 121–22.

18. W. K. Frankena, "Ethics and the Environment," in *Ethics and Problems of the 21st Century*, ed. K. E. Goodpaster and K. M. Sayre (Notre Dame, Ind.: University of Notre Dame Press, 1979), pp. 3–20.

19. For other criticisms of these arguments see Edward Johnson, "Treating the Dirt: Environmental Ethics and Moral Theory," in *Earthbound: New Introductory Essays in Environmental Ethics*, ed. Tom Regan (New York: Random House, 1984), pp. 336–65; see also the discussion between Goodpaster and Hunt in W. Murray Hunt, "Are *Mere Things* Morally Considerable?" *Environmental Ethics* 2 (1980): 59–65, and Kenneth Goodpaster, "On Stopping at Everything: A Reply to W. M. Hunt," *Environmental Ethics* 2 (1980): 281–84.

20. See, for example, R. G. Frey, *Interests and Rights: The Case Against Animals* (Oxford: Clarendon Press, 1980), and Martin Benjamin, "Ethics and Animal Consciousness," in *Ethics: Theory and Practice*, ed. Manuel Velasquez and Cynthia Rostankowski (Englewood Cliffs, N.J.: Prentice Hall, 1985).

*Norman E. Bowie*

# Morality, Money, and Motor Cars

Environmentalists frequently argue that business has special obligations to protect the environment. Although I agree with the environmentalists on this point, I do not agree with them as to where the obligations lie. Business does not have an obligation to protect the environment over and above what is required by law; however, it does have a moral obligation to avoid intervening in the political arena in order to defeat or weaken environmental legislation. In developing this thesis, several points are in order. First, many businesses have violated important moral obligations, and the violation has had a severe negative impact on the environment. For example, toxic waste haulers have illegally dumped hazardous material, and the environment has been harmed as a result. One might argue that those toxic waste haulers who have illegally dumped have violated a special obligation to the environment. Isn't it more accurate to say that these toxic waste haulers have violated their obligation to obey the law and that in this case the law that has been broken is one pertaining to the environment? Businesses have an obligation to obey the law—environmental laws and all others. Since there are many well-publicized cases of business having broken environmental laws, it is easy to think that business has violated some special obligations to the environment. In fact, what business has done is to disobey the law. Environmentalists do not need a special obligation to the environment to protect the environment against illegal business activity; they need only insist that business obey the laws.

Business has broken other obligations beside the obligation to obey the law and has harmed the environment as a result. Consider the grounding of the Exxon oil tanker *Valdez* in Alaska. That grounding was allegedly caused by the fact that an inadequately trained crewman was piloting the tanker while the captain was below deck and had been drinking. What needs to be determined is whether Exxon's policies and

From *Ethics and the Environment: The Public Policy Debate,* ed. W. Michael Hoffman, Robert Frederick, and Edward Petry Jr. (New York: Quorum Books, 1990), pp. 89–97.

procedures were sufficiently lax so that it could be said Exxon was morally at fault. It might be that Exxon is legally responsible for the accident under the doctrine of respondent superior, but Exxon is not thereby morally responsible. Suppose, however, that Exxon's policies were so lax that the company could be characterized as morally negligent. In such a case, the company would violate its moral obligation to use due care and avoid negligence. Although its negligence was disastrous to the environment, Exxon would have violated no special obligation to the environment. It would have been morally negligent.

A similar analysis could be given to the environmentalists' charges that Exxon's cleanup procedures were inadequate. If the charge is true, either Exxon was morally at fault or not. If the procedures had not been implemented properly by Exxon employees, then Exxon is legally culpable, but not morally culpable. On the other hand, if Exxon lied to government officials by saying that its policies were in accord with regulations and/or were ready for emergencies of this type, then Exxon violated its moral obligation to tell the truth. Exxon's immoral conduct would have harmed the environment, but it violated no special obligation to the environment. More important, none is needed. Environmentalists, like government officials, employees, and stockholders, expect that business firms and officials have moral obligations to obey the law, avoid negligent behavior, and tell the truth. In sum, although many business decisions have harmed the environment, these decisions violated no environmental moral obligations. If a corporation is negligent in providing for worker safety, we do not say the corporation violated a special obligation to employees; we say that it violated its obligation to avoid negligent behavior.

The crucial issues concerning business obligations to the environment focus on the excess use of natural resources (the dwindling supply of oil and gas, for instance) and the externalities of production (pollution, for instance). The critics of business want to claim that business has some special obligation to mitigate or solve these problems. I believe this claim is largely mistaken. If business does have a special obligation to help solve the environmental crisis, that obligation results from the special knowledge that business firms have. If they have greater expertise than other constituent groups in society, then it can be argued that, other things being equal, business's responsibilities to mitigate the environmental crisis are somewhat greater. Absent this condition, business's responsibility is no greater than and may be less than that of other social groups. What leads me to think that the critics of business are mistaken?

William Frankena distinguished obligations in an ascending order of the difficulty in carrying them out: avoiding harm, preventing harm, and doing good.[1] The most stringent requirement, to avoid harm, insists no one has a right to render harm on another unless there is a compelling, overriding moral reason to do so. Some writers have referred to this obligation as the moral minimum. A corporation's behavior is consistent with the moral minimum if it causes no avoidable harm to others.

Preventing harm is a less stringent obligation, but sometimes the obligation to prevent harm may be nearly as strict as the obligation to avoid harm. Suppose you are the only person passing a two-foot-deep working pool where a young child is drowning. There is no one else in the vicinity. Don't you have a strong moral obligation to prevent the child's death? Our obligation to prevent harm is not unlimited, however. Under what conditions must we be good samaritans? Some have argued that four conditions must exist before one is obligated to prevent harm: capability, need, proximity, and last resort.[2] These conditions are all met with the case of the drowning child. There is obviously a need that you can meet since you are both in the vicinity and have the resources to prevent the drowning with little effort; you are also the last resort.

The least strict moral obligation is to do good—to make contributions to society or to help solve problems (inadequate primary schooling in the inner cities, for example). Although corporations may have some minimum obligation in this regard based on an argument from corporate citizenship, the obligations of the corporation to do good cannot be expanded without limit. An injunction to assist in solving societal problems makes impossible demands on a corporation because at the practical level, it ignores the impact that such activities have on profit.

It might seem that even if this descending order of strictness of obligations were accepted, obligations toward the environment would fall into the moral minimum category. After all, the depletion of natural resources and pollution surely harm the environment. If so, wouldn't the obligations business has to the environment be among the strictest obligations a business can have?

Suppose, however, that a businessperson argues that the phrase "avoid harm" usually applies to human beings. Polluting a lake is not like injuring a human with a faulty product. Those who coined the phrase *moral minimum* for use in the business context defined harm as "particularly including activities which violate or frustrate the enforcement of rules of domestic or institutional law intended to protect individuals against prevention of health, safety or basic freedom."[3] Even if we do not insist that the violations be violations of a rule of law, polluting a lake would not count as a harm under this definition. The environmentalists would respond that it would. Polluting the lake may be injuring people who might swim in or eat fish from it. Certainly it would be depriving people of the freedom to enjoy the lake. Although the environmentalist is correct, especially if we grant the legitimacy of a human right to a clean environment, the success of this reply is not enough to establish the general argument.

Consider the harm that results from the production of automobiles. We know statistically that about 50,000 persons per year will die and that nearly 250,000 others will be seriously injured in automobile accidents in the United States alone. Such death and injury, which is harmful, is avoidable. If that is the case, doesn't the avoid-harm criterion require that the production of automobiles for profit cease? Not really. What such arguments point out is that some refinement of the moral minimum standard needs to take place. Take the automobile example. The automobile is itself a good-producing instrument. Because of the advantages of automobiles, society accepts the possible risks that go in using them. Society also accepts many other types of avoidable harm. We take certain risks—ride in planes, build bridges, and mine coal—to pursue advantageous goals. It seems that the high benefits of some activities justify the resulting harms. As long as the risks are known, it is not wrong that some avoidable harm be permitted so that other social and individual goals can be achieved. The avoidable-harm criterion needs some sharpening.

Using the automobile as a paradigm, let us consider the necessary refinements for the avoid-harm criterion. It is a fundamental principle of ethics that "ought" implies "can." That expression means that you can be held morally responsible only for events within your power. In the ought-implies-can principle, the overwhelming majority of highway deaths and injuries is not the responsibility of the automaker. Only those deaths and injuries attributable to unsafe automobile design can be attributed to the automaker. The ought-implies-can principle can also be used to absolve the auto companies of responsibility for death and injury from safety defects that the automakers could not reasonably know existed. The company could not be expected to do anything about them.

Does this mean that a company has an obligation to build a car as safe as it knows how? No. The standards for safety must leave the product's cost within the price range of the consumer ("ought implies can" again). Comments about engineering and equipment capability are obvious enough. But for a business, capability is also a function of profitability. A company that builds a maximally safe car at a cost that puts it at a competitive disadvantage and hence threatens its survival is building a safe car that lies beyond the capability of the company.

Critics of the automobile industry will express horror at these remarks, for by making capability a function of profitability, society will continue to have avoidable deaths and injuries; however, the situation is not as dire as the critics imagine. Certainly capability should not be sacrificed completely so that profits can be maximized. The decision to build products that are cheaper in cost but are not maximally safe is a social decision that has widespread support. The arguments occur over the line between safety and cost. What we have is a classical tradeoff situation. What is desired is some appropriate mix between engineering safety and consumer demand. To say there must be some mix between engineering safety and consumer demand is not to justify all the decisions made by the automobile companies. Ford Motor Company made a morally incorrect choice in placing Pinto gas tanks where it did. Consumers were uninformed, the record of the Pinto in rear-end collisions was worse than that of competitors, and Ford fought government regulations.

Let us apply the analysis of the automobile industry to the issue before us. That analysis shows that an automobile company does not violate its obligation to avoid harm and hence is not in violation of the moral minimum if the trade-off between potential harm and the utility of the products rests on social consensus and competitive realities.

As long as business obeys the environmental laws and honors other standard moral obligations, most harm done to the environment by business has been accepted by society. Through their decisions in the marketplace, we can see that most consumers are unwilling to pay extra for products that are more environmentally friendly than less friendly competitive products. Nor is there much evidence that consumers are willing to conserve resources, recycle, or tax themselves for environmental causes.

Consider the following instances reported in the *Wall Street Journal*.[4] The restaurant chain Wendy's tried to replace foam plates and cups with paper, but customers in the test markets balked. Procter and Gamble offered Downey fabric softener in concentrated form that requires less packaging than ready-to-use products; however the concentrate version is less convenient because it has to be mixed with water. Sales have been poor. Procter and Gamble manufactures Vizir and Lenor brands of detergents in concentrate form, which the customer mixes at home in reusable bottles. Europeans will take the trouble; Americans will not. Kodak tried to eliminate its yellow film boxes but met customer resistance. McDonald's has been testing mini-incinerators that convert trash into energy but often meets opposition from community groups that fear the incinerators will pollute the air. A McDonald's spokesperson points out that the emissions are mostly carbon dioxide and water vapor and are "less offensive than a barbecue." Exxon spent approximately $9,200,000 to "save" 230 otters ($40,000 for each otter). Otters in captivity cost $800. Fishermen in Alaska are permitted to shoot otters as pests.[5] Given these facts, doesn't business have every right to assume that public tolerance for environmental damage is quite high, and hence current legal activities by corporations that harm the environment do not violate the avoid-harm criterion?

Recently environmentalists have pointed out the environmental damage caused by the widespread use of disposable diapers. Are Americans ready to give them up and go back to cloth diapers and the diaper pail? Most observers think not. Procter and Gamble is not violating the avoid-harm criterion by manufacturing Pampers. Moreover, if the public wants cloth diapers, business certainly will produce them. If environmentalists want business to produce products that are friendlier to the environment, they must convince Americans to purchase them. Business will respond to the market. It is the consuming public that has the obligation to make the trade-off between cost and environmental integrity.

Data and arguments of the sort described should give environmental critics of business pause. Nonetheless, these critics are not without counterresponses. For example, they might respond that public attitudes are changing. Indeed, they point out, during the Reagan deregulation era, the one area where the public supported government regulations was in the area of environmental law. In addition, *Fortune* predicted environmental integrity as the primary demand of society on business in the 1990s.[6]

More important, they might argue that environmentally friendly products are at a disadvantage in the marketplace because they have public good characteristics. After all, the best situation for the individual is one where most other people use environmentally friendly products but he or she does not, hence reaping the benefit of lower cost and convenience. Since everyone reasons this way, the real demand for environmentally friendly products cannot be registered in the market. Everyone is understating the value of his or her preference for environmentally friendly products. Hence, companies cannot conclude from market behavior that the environmentally unfriendly products are preferred.

Suppose the environmental critics are right that the public goods characteristic of environmentally friendly products creates a market failure. Does that mean the companies are obligated to stop producing these environmentally unfriendly products? I think not, and I propose that we use the four conditions attached to the prevent-harm obligation to show why not. There is a need, and certainly corporations that cause environmental problems are in proximity. However, environmentally clean firms, if there are any, are not in proximity at all, and most business firms are not in proximity with respect to most environmental problems. In other words, the environmental critic must limit his or her argument to the environmental damage a business actually causes. The environmentalist might argue that Procter and Gamble ought to do something about Pampers; I do not see how an environmentalist can use the avoid-harm criterion to argue that Procter and Gamble should do something about acid rain. But even narrowing the obligation to damage actually caused will not be sufficient to establish an obligation to pull a product from the market because it damages the environment or even to go beyond what is legally required to protect the environment. Even for damage actually done, both the high cost of protecting the environment and the competitive pressures of business make further action to protect the environment beyond the capability of business. This conclusion would be more serious if business were the last resort, but it is not.

Traditionally it is the function of the government to correct for market failure. If the market cannot register the true desires of consumers, let them register their preferences in the political arena. Even fairly conservative economic thinkers allow government a legitimate role in correcting market failure. Perhaps the responsibility for energy conservation and pollution control belongs with the government.

Although I think consumers bear a far greater responsibility for preserving and protecting the environment than they have actually exercised, let us assume that the basic responsibility rests with the government. Does that let business off the hook? No. Most of business's unethical conduct regarding the environment occurs in the political arena.

Far too many corporations try to have their cake and eat it, too. They argue that it is the job of government to correct for market failure and then use their influence and money to defeat or water down regulations designed to conserve and protect the environment.[7] They argue that consumers should decide how much conservation and protection the environment should have, and then they try to interfere with the exercise of that choice in the political arena. Such behavior is inconsistent and ethically inappropriate. Business has an obligation to avoid intervention in the political process for the purpose of defeating and weakening environmental regulations. Moreover, this is a special obligation to the environment since business does not have a general obligation to avoid pursuing its own parochial interests in the political arena. Business need do nothing wrong when it seeks to influence tariffs, labor policy, or monetary policy. Business does do something wrong when it interferes with the passage of environmental legislation. Why?

First, such a noninterventionist policy is dictated by the logic of the business's argument to avoid a special obligation to protect the environment. Put more formally:

1. Business argues that it escapes special obligations to the environment because it is willing to respond to consumer preferences in this matter.
2. Because of externalities and public goods considerations, consumers cannot express their preferences in the market.
3. The only other viable forum for consumers to express their preferences is in the political arena.
4. Business intervention interferes with the expression of these preferences.
5. Since point 4 is inconsistent with point 1, business should not intervene in the political process.

The importance of this obligation in business is even more important when we see that environmental legislation has special disadvantages in the political arena. Public choice reminds us that the primary interest of politicians is being reelected. Government policy will be skewed in favor of policies that provide benefits to an influential minority as long as the greater costs are widely dispersed. Politicians will also favor projects where benefits are immediate and where costs can be postponed to the future. Such strategies increase the likelihood that a politician will be reelected.

What is frightening about the environmental crisis is that both the conservation of scarce resources and pollution abatement require policies that go contrary to a politician's self-interest. The costs of cleaning up the environment are immediate and huge, yet the benefits are relatively long range (many of them exceedingly long range). Moreover, a situation where the benefits are widely dispersed and the costs are large presents a two-fold problem. The costs are large enough so that all voters will likely notice them and in certain cases are catastrophic for individuals (e.g., for those who lose their jobs in a plant shutdown).

Given these facts and the political realities they entail, business opposition to environmental legislation makes a very bad situation much worse. Even if consumers could be persuaded to take environmental issues more seriously, the externalities, opportunities to free ride, and public goods characteristics of the environment make it difficult for even enlightened consumers to express their true preference for the environment in the market. The fact that most environmental legislation trades immediate costs for future benefits makes it difficult for politicians concerned about reelection to support it. Hence it is also difficult for enlightened consumers to have their preferences for a better environment honored in the political arena. Since lack of business intervention seems necessary, and might even be sufficient, for adequate environmental legislation, it seems business has an obligation not to intervene. Nonintervention would prevent the harm of not having the true preferences of consumers for a clean environment revealed. Given business's commitment to satisfying preferences, opposition to having these preferences expressed seems inconsistent as well.

The extent of this obligation to avoid intervening in the political process needs considerable discussion by ethicists and other interested parties. Businesspeople will surely object that if they are not permitted to play a role, Congress and state legislators will make decisions that will put them at a severe competitive disadvantage. For example, if the United States develops stricter environmental controls than other countries do, foreign imports will have a competitive advantage over domestic products. Shouldn't business be permitted to point that out? Moreover, any legislation that places costs on one industry rather than another confers advantages on other industries. The cost to the electric utilities from regulations designed to reduce the pollution that causes acid rain will give advantages to natural gas and perhaps even solar energy. Shouldn't the electric utility industry be permitted to point that out?

These questions pose difficult questions, and my answer to them should be considered highly tentative. I believe the answer to the first question is "yes" and the answer to the second is "no." Business does have a right to insist that the regulations apply to all those in the industry. Anything else would seem to violate norms of fairness. Such issues of fairness do not arise in the second case. Since natural gas and solar do not contribute to acid rain and since the costs of acid rain cannot be fully captured in the market, government intervention through regulation is simply correcting a market failure. With respect to acid rain, the electric utilities do have an advantage they do not deserve. Hence they have no right to try to protect it.

Legislative bodies and regulatory agencies need to expand their staffs to include technical experts, economists, and engineers so that the political process can be both neutral and highly informed about environmental matters. To gain the respect of business and the public, its performance needs to improve. Much more needs to be said to make any contention that business ought to stay out of the political debate theoretically and practically possible. Perhaps these suggestions point the way for future discussion.

Ironically business might best improve its situation in the political arena by taking on an additional obligation to the environment. Businesspersons often have more knowledge about environmental harms and the costs of cleaning them up. They may often have special knowledge about how to prevent environmental harm in the first place. Perhaps business has a special duty to educate the public and to promote environmentally responsible behavior.

Business has no reticence about leading consumer preferences in other areas. Advertising is a billion-dollar industry. Rather than blaming consumers for not purchasing environmentally friendly products, perhaps some businesses might make a commitment to capture the environmental niche. I have not seen much imagination on the part of business in this area. Far too many advertisements with an environmental message are reactive and public relations driven. Recall those by oil companies showing fish swimming about the legs of oil rigs. An educational campaign that encourages consumers to make environmentally friendly decisions in the marketplace would limit the necessity for business activity in the political arena. Voluntary behavior that is environmentally friendly is morally preferable to coerced behavior. If business took greater responsibility for educating the public, the government's responsibility would be lessened. An educational campaign aimed at consumers would likely enable many businesses to do good while simultaneously doing very well.

Hence business does have obligations to the environment, although these obligations are not found where the critics of business place them. Business has no special obligation to conserve natural resources or to stop polluting over and above its legal obligations. It does have an obligation to avoid intervening in the political arena to oppose environmental regulations, and it has a positive obligation to educate consumers. The benefits of honoring these obligations should not be underestimated.

## NOTES

The title for this chapter was suggested by Susan Bernick, a graduate student in the University of Minnesota philosophy department.

1. William Frankena, *Ethics*, 2d ed. (Englewood Cliffs, N.J.: Prentice-Hall, 1973), p. 47. Actually Frankena has four principles of prima facie duty under the principle of beneficence: one ought not to inflict evil or harm; one ought to prevent evil or harm; one ought to remove evil; and one ought to do or promote good.

2. John G. Simon, Charles W. Powers, and Jon P. Gunneman, *The Ethical Investor: Universities and Corporate Responsibility* (New Haven, Conn.: Yale University Press, 1972), pp. 22–25.

3. Ibid., p. 21.

4. Alicia Swasy, "For Consumers, Ecology Comes Second," *Wall Street Journal*, 23 August 1988, p. B1.

5. Jerry Alder, "Alaska after Exxon," *Newsweek*, 18 September 1989, p. 53.

6. Andrew Kupfer, "Managing Now for the 1990s," *Fortune*, 26 September 1988, pp. 46–47.

7. I owe this point to Gordon Rands, a Ph.D. student in the Carlson School of Management. Indeed the tone of the chapter has shifted considerably as a result of his helpful comments.

*Amory B. Lovins*
*L. Hunter Lovins*
*Paul Hawken*

# A Road Map for Natural Capitalism

This article puts forward a new approach not only for protecting the biosphere but also for improving profits and competitiveness. Some very simple changes to the way we run our businesses, built on advanced techniques for making resources more productive, can yield startling benefits both for today's shareholders and for future generations.

This approach is called *natural capitalism* because it's what capitalism might become if its largest category of capital—the "natural capital" of ecosystem services—were properly valued. The journey to natural capitalism involves four major shifts in business practices, all vitally interlinked:

- *Dramatically increase the productivity of natural resources.* Reducing the wasteful and destructive flow of resources from depletion to pollution represents a major business opportunity. Through fundamental changes in both production design and technology, far-sighted companies are developing ways to make natural resources—energy, minerals, water, forests—stretch 5, 10, even 100 times further than they do today. These major resource savings often yield higher profits than small resource savings do—or even saving no resources at all would—and not only pay for themselves over time but in many cases reduce initial capital investments.

- *Shift to biologically inspired production models.* Natural capitalism seeks not merely to reduce waste but to eliminate the very concept of waste. In closed-loop production systems, modeled on nature's designs, every output either is returned harmlessly to the ecosystem as a nutrient, like compost, or becomes an input for

From *Harvard Business Review* 77, no. 3 (May–June, 1999): 145–58.

manufacturing another product. Such systems can often be designed to eliminate the use of toxic materials, which can hamper nature's ability to reprocess materials.

- *Move to a solutions-based business model.* The business model of traditional manufacturing rests on the sale of goods. In the new model, value is instead delivered as a flow of services—providing illumination, for example, rather than selling lightbulbs. This model entails a new perception of value, a move from the acquisition of goods as a measure of affluence to one where well-being is measured by the continuous satisfaction of changing expectations for quality, utility, and performance. The new relationship aligns the interests of providers and customers in ways that reward them for implementing the first two innovations of natural capitalism—resource productivity and closed-loop manufacturing.

- *Reinvest in natural capital.* Ultimately, business must restore, sustain, and expand the planet's ecosystems so that they can produce their vital services and biological resources even more abundantly. Pressures to do so are mounting as human needs expand, the costs engendered by deteriorating ecosystems rise, and the environmental awareness of consumers increases. Fortunately, these pressures all create business value.

Natural capitalism is not motivated by a current scarcity of natural resources. Indeed, although many biological resources, like fish, are becoming scarce, most mined resources, such as copper and oil, seem ever more abundant. Indices of average commodity prices are at twenty-eight-year lows, thanks partly to powerful extractive technologies, which are often subsidized and whose damage to natural capital remains unaccounted for. Yet even despite these artificially low prices, using resources manyfold more productively can now be so profitable that pioneering companies—large and small—have already embarked on the journey toward natural capitalism.[1] . . . Let's map the route toward natural capitalism.

## DRAMATICALLY INCREASE THE PRODUCTIVITY OF NATURAL RESOURCES

In the first stage of a company's journey toward natural capitalism, it strives to wring out the waste of energy, water, materials, and other resources throughout its production systems and other operations. There are two main ways companies can do this at a profit. First, they can adopt a fresh approach to design that considers industrial systems as a whole rather than part by part. Second, companies can replace old industrial technologies with new ones, particularly with those based on natural processes and materials.

*Implementing Whole-System Design.* Inventor Edwin Land once remarked that "people who seem to have had a new idea have often simply stopped having an old idea." This is particularly true when designing for resource savings. The old idea is one of diminishing returns—the greater the resource saving, the higher the cost. But that old idea is giving way to the new idea that bigger savings can cost less—that saving a large fraction of resources can actually cost less than saving a small fraction of resources. This is the concept of expanding returns, and it governs much of the revolutionary thinking behind whole-system design. Lean manufacturing is an example of whole-system thinking that has helped many companies dramatically reduce such forms of waste as lead times, defect rates, and inventory. Applying whole-system thinking to the productivity of natural resources can achieve even more.

Consider Interface Corporation, a leading maker of materials for commercial interiors. In its new Shanghai carpet factory, a liquid had to be circulated through a standard pumping loop similar to those used in nearly all industries. A top European company designed the system to use pumps requiring a total of 95 horsepower. But before construction began, Interface's engineer, Jan Schilham, realized that two embarrassingly simple design changes would cut that power requirement to only 7 horsepower—a 92 percent reduction. His redesigned system cost less to build, involved no new technology, and worked better in all respects.

This small example has big implications for two reasons. First, pumping is the largest application of motors, and motors use three-quarters of all industrial electricity. Second, the lessons are very widely relevant. Interface's pumping loop shows how simple changes in design mentality can yield huge resource savings and returns on investment. This isn't rocket science; often it's just a rediscovery of good Victorian engineering principles that have been lost because of specialization.

Whole-system thinking can help managers find small changes that lead to big savings that are cheap, free, or even better than free (because they make the whole system cheaper to build). They can do this because often the right investment in one part of the system can produce multiple benefits throughout the system. For example, companies would gain eighteen distinct economic benefits—of which direct energy savings is only one—if they switched from ordinary motors to premium-efficiency motors or from ordinary lighting ballasts (the transformerlike boxes that control fluorescent lamps) to electronic ballasts that automatically dim the lamps to match available daylight. If everyone in America integrated these and other selected technologies into all existing motor and lighting systems in an optimal way, the nation's $220-billion-a-year electric bill would be cut in half The after-tax return on investing in these changes would in most cases exceed 100 percent per year.

*Adopting Innovative Technologies.* Implementing whole-system design goes hand in hand with introducing alternative, environmentally friendly technologies. Many of these are already available and profitable but not widely known. Some, like the "designer catalysts" that are transforming the chemical industry, are already runaway successes. Others are still making their way to market, delayed by cultural rather than by economic or technical barriers.

The automobile industry is particularly ripe for technological change. After a century of development, motorcar technology is showing signs of age. Only 1 percent of the energy consumed by today's cars is actually used to move the driver: only 15 percent to 20 percent of the power generated by burning gasoline reaches the wheels (the rest is lost in the engine and drivetrain) and 95 percent of the resulting propulsion moves the car, not the driver. The industry's infrastructure is hugely expensive and inefficient. Its convergent products compete for narrow niches in saturated core markets at commoditylike prices. Auto making is capital intensive, and product cycles are long. It is profitable in good years but subject to large losses in bad years. Like the typewriter industry just before the advent of personal computers, it is vulnerable to displacement by something completely different.

Enter the Hypercar. Since 1993, when Rocky Mountain Institute placed this automotive concept in the public domain, several dozen current and potential auto manufacturers have committed billions of dollars to its development and commercialization. The Hypercar integrates the best existing technologies to reduce the consumption of fuel as much as 85 percent and the amount of materials used up to 90 percent by introducing four main innovations.

First, making the vehicle out of advanced polymer composites, chiefly carbon fiber, reduces its weight by two-thirds while maintaining crashworthiness. Second, aerodynamic design and better tires reduce air resistance by as much as 70 percent and rolling resistance by up to 80 percent. Together, these innovations save about two-thirds of the fuel. Third, 30 percent to 50 percent of the remaining fuel is saved by using a "hybrid-electric" drive. In such a system, the wheels are turned by electric motors whose power is made onboard by a small engine or turbine, or even more efficiently by a fuel cell. The fuel cell generates electricity directly by chemically combining stored hydrogen with oxygen, producing pure hot water as its only by-product. Interactions between the small, clean, efficient power source and the ultralight, low-drag auto body then further reduce the weight, cost, and complexity of both. Fourth, much of the traditional hardware—from transmissions and differentials to gauges and certain parts of the suspension—can be replaced by electronics controlled with highly integrated, customizable, and upgradable software.

These technologies make it feasible to manufacture pollution-free, high-performance cars, sport utilities, pickup trucks, and vans that get 80 to 200 miles per gallon (or its energy equivalent in other fuels). These improvements will not require any compromise in quality or utility.

In the long term, the Hypercar will transform industries other than automobiles. It will displace about an eighth of the steel market directly and most of the rest eventually, as carbon fiber becomes far cheaper. Hypercars and their cousins could ultimately save as much oil as OPEC now sells. Indeed, oil may well become uncompetitive as a fuel long before it becomes scarce and costly. Similar challenges face the coal and electricity industries because the development of the Hypercar is likely to accelerate greatly the commercialization of inexpensive hydrogen fuel cells. These fuel cells will help shift power production from centralized coal-fired and nuclear power stations to networks of decentralized, small-scale generators. In fact, fuel cell–powered Hypercars could themselves be part of these networks. They'd be, in effect, 20-kilowatt power plants on wheels. Given that cars are left parked—that is, unused—more than 95 percent of the time, these Hypercars could be plugged into a grid and could then sell back enough electricity to repay as much as half the predicted cost of leasing them. A national Hypercar fleet could ultimately have five to ten times the generating capacity of the national electric grid.

# REDESIGN PRODUCTION
# ACCORDING TO BIOLOGICAL MODELS

In the second stage on the journey to natural capitalism, companies use closed-loop manufacturing to create new products and processes that can totally prevent waste. This plus more efficient production processes could cut companies' long-term materials requirements by more than 90% in most sectors.

The central principle of closed-loop manufacturing, as architect Paul Bierman-Lytle of the engineering firm CH2M Hill puts it, is "waste equals food." Every output of manufacturing should be either composted into natural nutrients or remanufactured into technical nutrients—that is, it should be returned to the ecosystem or recycled for further production. Closed-loop production systems are designed to eliminate any materials that incur disposal costs, especially toxic ones, because the alternative—isolating them to prevent harm to natural systems—tends to be costly and risky. Indeed, meeting EPA and OSHA standards by eliminating harmful materials often makes a manufacturing process cost less than the hazardous process it replaced.

Interface is leading the way to this next frontier of industrial ecology. While its competitors are "down cycling" nylon- and PVC-based carpet into less valuable carpet backing, Interface has invented a new floor-covering material called Solenium, which can be completely remanufactured into identical new product. This fundamental innovation emerged from a clean-sheet redesign. Executives at Interface didn't ask how they could sell more carpet of the familiar kind; they asked how they could create a dream product that would best meet their customers' needs while protecting and nourishing natural capital.

Solenium lasts four times longer and uses 40 percent less material than ordinary carpets—an 86 percent reduction in materials intensity. What's more, Solenium is free of chlorine and other toxic materials, is virtually stainproof, doesn't grow mildew, can easily be cleaned with water, and offers aesthetic advantages over traditional carpets. It's so superior in every respect that Interface doesn't market it as an environmental product—just a better one.

Solenium is only one part of Interface's drive to eliminate every form of waste. Chairman Ray C. Anderson defines waste as "any measurable input that does not produce customer value," and he considers all inputs to be waste until shown otherwise. Between 1994 and 1998, this zero-waste approach led to a systematic treasure hunt that helped to keep resource inputs constant while revenues rose by $200 million. Indeed, $67 million of the revenue increase can be directly attributed to the company's 60 percent reduction in landfill waste.

Subsequently, president Charlie Eitel expanded the definition of waste to include all fossil fuel inputs, and now many customers are eager to buy products from the company's recently opened solar-powered carpet factory. Interface's green strategy has not only won plaudits from environmentalists, it has also proved a remarkably successful business strategy. Between 1993 and 1998, revenue has more than doubled, profits have more than tripled, and the number of employees has increased by 73 percent.

## CHANGE THE BUSINESS MODEL

In addition to its drive to eliminate waste, Interface has made a fundamental shift in its business model—the third stage on the journey toward natural capitalism. The company has realized that clients want to walk on and look at carpets—but not necessarily to own them. Traditionally, broadloom carpets in office buildings are replaced every decade because some portions look worn out. When that happens, companies suffer the disruption of shutting down their offices and removing their furniture. Billions of pounds of carpets are removed each year and sent to landfills, where they will last up to 20,000 years. To escape this unproductive and wasteful cycle, Interface is transforming itself from a company that sells and fits carpets into one that provides floor covering services.

Under its Evergreen Lease, Interface no longer sells carpets but rather leases a floor-covering service for a monthly fee, accepting responsibility for keeping the carpet fresh and clean. Monthly inspections detect and replace worn carpet tiles. Since at most 20 percent of an area typically shows at least 80 percent of the wear, replacing only the worn parts reduces the consumption of carpeting material by about 80 percent. It also minimizes the disruption that customers experience—worn tiles are seldom found under furniture. Finally, for the customer, leasing carpets can provide a tax advantage by turning a capital expenditure into a tax-deductible expense. The result: the customer gets cheaper and better services that cost the supplier far less to produce. Indeed, the energy saved from not producing a whole new carpet is in itself enough to produce all the carpeting that the new business model requires. Taken together, the five-fold savings in carpeting material that Interface achieves through the Evergreen Lease and the seven-fold materials savings achieved through the use of Solenium deliver a stunning 35-fold reduction in the flow of materials needed to sustain a superior floor-covering service. Remanufacturing, and even making carpet initially from renewable materials, can then reduce the extraction of virgin resources essentially to the company's goal of zero.

Interface's shift to a service-leasing business reflects a fundamental change from the basic model of most manufacturing companies, which still look on their businesses as machines for producing and selling products. The more products sold, the better—at least for the company, if not always for the customer or the earth. But any model that wastes natural resources also wastes money. Ultimately, that model will be unable to compete with a service model that emphasizes solving problems and building long-term relationships with customers rather than making and selling products. The shift to what James Womack of the Lean Enterprise Institute calls a "solutions economy" will almost always improve customer value *and* providers' bottom lines because it aligns both parties' interests, offering rewards for doing more and better with less.

The shift to a service business model promises benefits not just to participating businesses but to the entire economy as well. Womack points out that by helping customers reduce their need for capital goods such as carpets, and by rewarding suppliers for extending and maximizing asset values rather than for churning them, adoption of the service model will reduce the volatility in the turnover of capital goods that lies at the heart of the business cycle. That would significantly reduce the overall volatility of the world's economy. At present, the producers of capital goods face feast or famine because the buying decisions of households and corporations are extremely sensitive to fluctuating income. But in a continuous-flow-of-services economy, those swings would be greatly reduced, bringing a welcome stability to businesses. Excess capacity—another form of waste and source of risk—need no longer be retained for meeting peak demand. The result of adopting the new model would be an economy in which we grow and get richer by using less and become stronger by being leaner and more stable.

# REINVEST IN NATURAL CAPITAL

The foundation of textbook capitalism is the prudent reinvestment of earnings in productive capital. Natural capitalists who have dramatically raised their resource productivity, closed their loops, and shifted to a solutions-based business model have one key task remaining. They must reinvest in restoring, sustaining, and expanding the most important form of capital—their own natural habitat and biological resource base.

The pioneering corporations that have made reinvestments in natural capital are starting to see some interesting paybacks. The independent power producer AES, for example, has long pursued a policy of planting trees to offset the carbon emissions of its power plants. That ethical stance, once thought quixotic, now looks like a smart investment because a dozen brokers are now starting to create markets in carbon reduction. Similarly, certification by the Forest Stewardship Council of certain sustainably grown and harvested products has given Collins Pine the extra profit margins that enabled its U.S. manufacturing operations to survive brutal competition. Taking an even longer view, Swiss Re and other European reinsurers are seeking to cut their storm-damage losses by pressing for international public policy to protect the climate and by investing in climate-safe technologies that also promise good profits. Yet most companies still do not realize that a vibrant ecological web underpins their survival and their business success. Enriching natural capital is not just a public good—it is vital to every company's longevity.

It turns out that changing industrial processes so that they actually replenish and magnify the stock of natural capital can prove especially profitable because nature does the production; people need just step back and let life flourish. Industries that directly harvest living resources, such as forestry, farming, and fishing, offer the most suggestive examples. Here are [two]:

- Allan Savory of the Center for Holistic Management in Albuquerque, New Mexico, has redesigned cattle ranching to raise the carrying capacity of rangelands, which have often been degraded not by overgrazing but by undergrazing and grazing the wrong way. Savory's solution is to keep the cattle moving from place to place, grazing intensively but briefly at each site, so that they mimic the dense but constantly moving herds of native grazing animals that coevolved with grasslands. Thousands of ranchers are estimated to be applying this approach, improving both their range and their profits. This "management-intensive rotational grazing" method, long standard in New Zealand, yields such clearly superior returns that over 15 percent of Wisconsin's dairy farms have adopted it in the past few years.

- The California Rice Industry Association has discovered that letting nature's diversity flourish can be more profitable than forcing it to produce a single product. By flooding 150,000 to 200,000 acres of Sacramento valley rice fields—about 30 percent of California's rice-growing area—after harvest, farmers are able to create seasonal wetlands that support millions of wildfowl, replenish groundwater, improve fertility, and yield other valuable benefits. In addition, the farmers bale and sell the rice straw, whose high silica content—formerly an air-pollution hazard when the straw was burned—adds insect resistance and hence value as a construction material when it's resold instead.

Although such practices are still evolving, the broad lessons they teach are clear. In almost all climates, soils, and societies, working with nature is more productive than working against it. Reinvesting in nature allows farmers, fishermen, and forest managers to match or exceed the high yields and profits sustained by traditional input-intensive, chemically driven practices. Although much of mainstream business is still headed the other way, the profitability of sustainable, nature-emulating practices is already being proven. In the future, many industries that don't now consider themselves dependent on a biological resource base will become more so as they shift their raw materials and production processes more to biological ones. There is evidence that many business leaders are starting to think this way. The consulting firm Arthur D. Little surveyed a group of North American and European business leaders and found that 83 percent of them already believe that they can derive "real business value [from implementing a] sustainable-development approach to strategy and operations."

# A BROKEN COMPASS?

If the road ahead is this clear, why are so many companies straying or falling by the wayside? We believe the reason is that the instruments companies use to set their targets, measure their performance, and hand out rewards are faulty. In other words, the markets are full of distortions and perverse incentives. Of the more than sixty specific forms of misdirection that we have identified,[2] the most obvious involve the ways companies allocate capital and the way governments set policy and impose taxes. Merely correcting these defective practices would uncover huge opportunities for profit.

Consider how companies make purchasing decisions. Decisions to buy small items are typically based on their initial cost rather than their full lifecycle cost, a practice that can add up to major wastage. Distribution transformers that supply electricity to buildings and factories, for example, are a minor item at just $320 apiece, and most companies try to save a quick buck by buying the lowest-price models. Yet nearly all the nation's electricity must flow through transformers, and using the cheaper but less efficient models wastes $1 billion a year.

Many executives pay too little attention to saving resources because they are often a small percentage of total costs (energy costs run to about 2 percent in most industries). But those resource savings drop straight to the bottom line and so represent a far greater percentage of profits. Many executives also think they already "did" efficiency in the 1970s, when the oil shock forced them to rethink old habits. They're forgetting that with today's far better technologies, it's profitable to start all over again.

If corporate practices obscure the benefits of natural capitalism, government policy positively undermines it. In nearly every country on the planet, tax laws penalize what we want more of—jobs and income—while subsidizing what we want less of—resource depletion and pollution. In every state but Oregon, regulated utilities are rewarded for selling more energy, water, and other resources, and penalized for selling less, even if increased production would cost more than improved customer efficiency. In most of America's arid western states, use-it-or-lose-it water laws encourage inefficient water consumption. Additionally, in many towns, inefficient use of land is enforced through outdated regulations, such as guidelines for ultrawide suburban streets recommended by 1950s civil-defense planners to accommodate the heavy equipment needed to clear up rubble after a nuclear attack.

. . . If the U.S. government and private industry could redirect the dollars currently earmarked for remedial costs toward reinvestment in natural and human capital, they could bring about a genuine improvement in the nation's welfare. Companies, too, are finding that wasting resources also means wasting money and people. Those intertwined forms of waste have equally intertwined solutions. Firing the unproductive tons, gallons, and kilowatt-hours often makes it possible to keep the people, who will have more and better work to do.

## RECOGNIZING THE SCARCITY SHIFT

In the end, the real trouble with our economic compass is that it points in exactly the wrong direction. Most businesses are behaving as if people were still scarce and nature still abundant—the conditions that helped to fuel the first Industrial Revolution. At that time, people were relatively scarce compared with the present-day population. The rapid mechanization of the textile industries caused explosive economic growth that created labor shortages in the factory and the field. The Industrial Revolution, responding to those shortages and mechanizing one industry after another, made people a hundred times more productive than they had ever been.

The logic of economizing on the scarcest resource, because it limits progress, remains correct. But the pattern of scarcity is shifting: now people aren't scarce but nature is. This shows up first in industries that depend directly on ecological health. Here, production is increasingly constrained by fish rather than by boats and nets, by forests rather than by chain saws, by fertile topsoil rather than by plows. Moreover, unlike the traditional factors of industrial production—capital and labor—the biological limiting factors cannot be substituted for one other. In the industrial system, we can easily exchange machinery for labor. But no technology or amount of money can substitute for a stable climate and a productive biosphere. Even proper pricing can't replace the priceless.

Natural capitalism addresses those problems by reintegrating ecological with economic goals. Because it is both necessary and profitable, it will subsume traditional industrialism within a new economy and a new paradigm of production, just as industrialism previously subsumed agrarianism. The companies that first make the changes we have described will have a competitive edge. Those that don't make that effort won't be a problem because ultimately they won't be around. In making that choice, as Henry Ford said, "Whether you believe you can, or whether you believe you can't, you're absolutely right."

## NOTES

1. Our book, *Natural Capitalism*, provides hundreds of examples of how companies of almost every type and size, often through modest shifts in business logic and practice, have dramatically improved their bottom lines.

2. Summarized in the report "Climate: Making Sense and Making Money" at http://www.rmi.org/catalog/climate.htm.

# SELECT BIBLIOGRAPHY

Buchholz, R. *Principles of Environmental Management.* Englewood Cliffs, N.J.: Prentice-Hall, 1993.

Callicott, J., ed. *In Defense of the Land Ethic.* Albany, N.Y.: State University of New York Press, 1989.

Des Jardins, J. *Environmental Ethics.* Belmont, Calif.: Wadsworth, 1993.

Engel, J., et al., eds. *Ethics of Environment and Development.* Tucson: University of Arizona Press, 1991.

Gibson, M. *To Breathe Freely: Risk, Consent, and Air.* Totowa, N.J.: Rowman and Allanheld, 1985.

Grayson, L., et al., *Business and Environmental Accountability.* Mahwah, N.J.: Erlbaum, 1993.

Hardin, G., and J. Baden. *Managing the Commons.* San Francisco: W. H. Freeman, 1977.

Hoffman, W., et al., eds. *Business Ethics and the Environment.* New York: Quorum Books, 1990.

Regan, T., ed. *Earthbound: New Introductory Essays in Environmental Ethics.* New York: Random House, 1984.

Rolston, H. *Environmental Ethics.* Philadelphia: Temple University Press, 1988.

Rolston, H. *Philosophy Gone Wild: Environmental Ethics.* Amherst, N.Y.: Prometheus Books, 1991.

Sagoff, M. *The Economy of the Earth.* New York: Cambridge University Press, 1990.

Smith, D. *Business and the Environment.* New York: St. Martin's Press, 1993.

Taylor, P. *Respect for Nature.* Princeton, N.J.: Princeton University Press, 1986.

Tietenberg, T. *Environmental and Natural Resource Economics.* Glenview, Ill.: Scott, Foresman & Co., 1984.

Zimmerman, M., et al., eds. *Environmental Philosophy.* Englewood Cliffs, N.J.: Prentice-Hall, 1993.

# ELECTRONIC SOURCES

Communications for a Sustainable Future    http://csf.colorado.edu
Consumer Law    www.consumerlawpage.com
Environmental Protection Agency    www.epa.gov
Essential Organization    http://www.essential.org
Ethics Resource Center    www.ethics.org
Greenmoney    http://www.greenmoney.com
United Nations Environment Programme    www.unep.ch

# 8. MULTINATIONAL CORPORATIONS

## INTRODUCTION

Multinational corporations, those that produce and/or market goods in more than one country, pose a host of ethical problems. Should a multinational have one conflict of interest policy and one employee rights policy applicable transnationally, or should these be tailored to the business climate in different countries? How much profit should be repatriated to the country where the firm is headquartered, and how much should be reinvested in the host country? Should products sold be uniform across national boundaries, e.g., should drugs be marketed abroad that do not meet Food and Drug Administration (FDA) safety standards in the United States? Should American firms be allowed to operate in countries that are ruled by repressive governments?

Discussion of these issues is complicated by the fact that there is no effective organization for policing multinational operations. In any specific country, laws can be passed to curb practices judged to be immoral and detrimental to society, but critics charge that the absence of a transnational legal body and enforcement mechanism invites multinationals to sidestep moral issues and operate in a purely egoistic fashion.

James Kiersky's article discusses the numerous ethical complexities facing multinational managers, complexities illustrated in the the two case studies in this section. Articles by Richard T. DeGeorge and John R. Boatright provide ethical guidance for organizations facing the complex issues in the international realm that Kiersky notes.

*Case Study*

*Norman E. Bowie*
*Stefanie Ann Lenway*

# H. B. Fuller in Honduras: Street Children and Substance Abuse

In the summer of 1985 the following news story was brought to the attention of an official of the H. B. Fuller Company in St. Paul, Minnesota.

### Glue Sniffing Among Honduran Street Children in Honduras: Children Sniffing Their Lives Away

AN INTER PRESS SERVICE FEATURE

BY PETER FORD

Tegucigalpa July 16, 1985 (IPS)—They lie senseless on doorsteps and pavements, grimy and loose limbed, like discarded rag dolls.

Some are just five or six years old. Others are already young adults, and all are addicted to sniffing a commonly sold glue that is doing them irreversible brain damage.

Roger, 21, has been sniffing "Resistol" for eight years. Today, even when he is not high, Roger walks with a stagger, his motor control wrecked. His scarred face puckers with concentration, his right foot taps nervously, incessantly, as he talks.

Since he was 11, when he ran away from the aunt who raised him, Roger's home has been the streets of the capital of Honduras, the second poorest nation in the western hemisphere after Haiti.

Roger spends his time begging, shining shoes, washing car windows, scratching together a few pesos a day, and sleeping in doorways at night.

---

From *Ethical Issues in Business: A Philosophical Approach*, 5th ed., ed. Thomas Donaldson and Patricia H. Werhane (Prentice-Hall, Upper Saddle River, N.J., 1996). This case was prepared by Norman E. Bowie and Stefanie Ann Lenway, University of Minnesota. All rights reserved by Graduate School of Business, Columbia University. Reprinted by permission.

Sniffing glue, he says, "makes me feel happy, makes me feel big. What do I care if my family does not love me? I know it's doing me damage, but it's a habit I have got, and a habit's a habit. I cannot give it up, even though I want to."

No one knows how many of Tegucigalpa's street urchins seek escape from the squalor and misery of their daily existence through the hallucinogenic fumes of "Resistol." No one has spent the time and money needed to study the question.

But one thing is clear, according to Dr. Rosalio Zavala, Head of the Health Ministry's Mental Health Department, "these children come from the poorest slums of the big cities. They have grown up as illegal squatters in very disturbed states of mental health, tense, depressed, aggressive.

"Some turn that aggression on society, and start stealing. Others turn it on themselves, and adopt self destructive behavior. . . ."

But, he understands the attraction of the glue, whose solvent, toluene, produces feelings of elation. "It gives you delusions of grandeur, you feel powerful, and that compensates these kids for reality, where they feel completely worthless, like nobodies."

From the sketchy research he has conducted, Dr. Zavala believes that most boys discover Resistol for the first time when they are about 11, though some children as young as five are on their way to becoming addicts.

Of a small sample group of children interviewed in reform schools here, 56 percent told Zavala that friends introduced them to the glue, but it is easy to find on the streets for oneself.

Resistol is a contact cement glue, widely used by shoe repairers, and available at household goods stores everywhere. . . .

In some states of the United States, glue containing addictive narcotics such as toluene must also contain oil of mustard—the chemical used to produce poisonous mustard gas—which makes sniffing the glue so painful it is impossible to tolerate. There is no federal U.S. law on the use of oil of mustard, however. . . .

But even for Dr. Zavala, change is far more than a matter of just including a chemical compound, such as oil of mustard, in a contact cement.

"This is a social problem," he acknowledges. "What we need is a change in philosophy, a change in social organization."

Resistol is manufactured by H. B. Fuller S. A., a subsidiary of Kativo Chemical Industries S. A., which in turn is a wholly owned subsidiary of the H. B. Fuller Company of St. Paul, Minnesota.[1] Kativo sells more than a dozen different adhesives under the Resistol brand name in several countries in Latin America for a variety of industrial and commercial applications. In Honduras the Resistol products have a strong market position.

Three of the Resistol products are solvent-based adhesives designed with certain properties that are not possible to attain with a water-based formula. These properties include rapid set, strong adhesion, and water resistance. These products are similar to airplane glue or rubber cement and are primarily intended for use in shoe manufacturing and repair, leatherwork, and carpentry.

Even though the street children of each Central American country may have a different choice of a drug for substance abuse, and even though Resistol is not the only glue that Honduran street children use as an inhalant, the term "Resistolero" stuck and has become synonymous with all street children, whether they use inhalants or not. In Honduras Resistol is identified as the abused substance.

Edward Sheehan writes in *Agony in the Garden*:

> Resistol. I had heard about Resistol. It was a glue, the angel dust of Honduran orphans. . . . In Tegucigalpa, their addiction had become so common they were known as los Resistoleros. (p. 32)

# HONDURAS[2]

The social problems that contribute to widespread inhalant abuse among street children can be attributed to the depth of poverty in Honduras. In 1989, 65 percent of all households and 40 percent of urban households in Honduras were living in poverty, making it one of the poorest countries in Latin America. Between 1950 and 1988, the increase in the Honduran gross domestic product (GDP) was 3.8 percent, only slightly greater than the average yearly increase in population growth. In 1986, the Honduran GDP was about U.S. $740 per capita and has only grown slightly since. Infant and child mortality rates are high, life expectancy for adults is sixty-four years, and the adult literacy rate is estimated to be about 60 percent.

Honduras has faced several economic obstacles in its efforts to industrialize. First, it lacks abundant natural resources. The mountainous terrain has restricted agricultural productivity and growth. In addition, the small domestic market and competition from more industrially advanced countries has prevented the manufacturing sector from progressing much beyond textiles, food processing, and assembly operations.

The key to the growth of the Honduran economy has been the production and export of two commodities—bananas and coffee. Both the vagaries in the weather and the volatility of commodity markets had made the foreign exchange earned from these products very unstable. Without consistently strong export sales, Honduras has not been able to buy sufficient fuel and other productive input to allow the growth of its manufacturing sector. It also had to import basic grains (corn and rice) because the country's traditional staples are produced inefficiently by small farmers using traditional technologies with poor soil.

In the 1970s the Honduran government relied on external financing to invest in physical and social infrastructures and to implement development programs intended to diversify the economy. Government spending increased 10.4 percent a year from 1973. By 1981, the failure of many of these development projects led the government to stop financing state-owned industrial projects. The public sector failures were attributed to wasteful administration, mismanagement, and corruption. Left with little increase in productivity to show for these investments, Honduras continues to face massive budgetary deficits and unprecedented levels of external borrowing.

The government deficit was further exacerbated in the early 1980s by increasing levels of unemployment. By 1983, unemployment reached 20 to 30 percent of the economically active population, with an additional 40 percent of the population underemployed, primarily in agriculture. The rising unemployment, falling real wages, and low level of existing social infrastructure in education and health care contributed to the low level of labor productivity. Unemployment benefits were very limited and only about 7.3 percent of the population was covered by social security.

Rural-to-urban migration has been a major contributor to urban growth in Honduras. In the 1970s the urban population grew at more than twice as fast a rate as the rural population. This migration has increased in part as a result of a high birth rate among the rural population, along with a move by large landholders to convert forest and fallow land, driving off subsistence farmers to use the land for big-scale cotton and beef farming. As more and more land was enclosed, an increasing number of landless sought the cities for a better life.

Tegucigalpa, the capital, has had one of the fastest population increases among Central American cities, growing by 178,000 between 1970 and 1980, with a projected population of 975,000 by the year 2000. Honduras' second largest city, San Pedro Sula, is projected to have a population of 650,000 by 2000.

The slow growth in the industrial and commercial sectors has not been adequate to provide jobs for those moving to the city. The migrants to the urban areas typically move first to cuarterias (rows) of connected rooms. The rooms are generally constructed of wood with dirt floors, and they are usually windowless. The average household contains about seven persons, who live together in a single room. For those living in the rooms facing an alley, the narrow passageway between buildings serves both as sewage and waste disposal area and as a courtyard for as many as 150 persons.

Although more than 70 percent of the families living in these cuarte-rias had one member with a permanent salaried job, few could survive on that income alone. For stable extended families, salaried income is supplemented by entrepreneurial activities, such as selling tortillas. Given migratory labor, high unemployment, and income insecurity, many family relationships are unstable. Often the support of children is left to mothers. Children are frequently forced to leave school, helping support the family through shining shoes, selling newspapers, or guarding cars; such help often is essential income. If a lone mother has become sick or dies, her children may be abandoned to the streets.

# KATIVO CHEMICAL INDUSTRIES S.A.[3]

Kativo celebrated its fortieth anniversary in 1989. It is now one of the 500 largest private corporations in Latin America. In 1989, improved sales in most of Central America were partially offset by a reduction of its sales in Honduras.

Walter Kissling, chairman of Kativo's board and senior vice president for H. B. Fuller's international operations, has the reputation of giving the company's local managers a high degree of autonomy. Local managers often have to respond quickly because of unexpected currency fluctuations. He comments that, "In Latin America, if you know what you are doing, you can make more money managing your balance sheet than by selling products." The emphasis on managing the balance sheet in countries with high rates of inflation has led Kativo managers to develop a distinctive competence in finance.

In spite of the competitive challenge of operating under unstable political and economic conditions Kativo managers emphasized in the annual report the importance of going beyond the bottom line:

> Kativo is an organization with a profound philosophy and ethical conduct, worthy of the most advanced firms. It carries out business with the utmost respect for ethical and legal principles and its orientation is not solely directed to the customer, who has the highest priority, but also to the shareholders, and communities where it operates.

In the early 1980s the managers of Kativo, which was primarily a paint company, decided to enter the adhesive market in Latin America. Their strategy was to combine their marketing experience with H. B. Fuller's products. Kativo found the adhesive market potentially profitable in Latin America because it lacked strong competitors. Kativo's initial concern was to win market share. Resistol was the brand name for all adhesive products including the water-based school glue.

## KATIVO AND THE STREET CHILDREN

In 1983, Honduran newspapers carried articles about police arrests of "Resistoleros"—street children drugging themselves by sniffing glue. In response to these newspaper articles, Kativo's Honduras advertising agency, Calderon Publicidad, informed the newspapers that Resistol was not the only substance abused by street children and that the image of the manufacturer was being damaged by using a prestigious trademark as a synonym for drug abusers. Moreover glue sniffing was not caused by something inherent in the product but was a social problem. For example, on one occasion the company complained to the editor, requesting that he "make the necessary effort to recommend to the editorial staff that they abstain from using the brand name Resistol as a synonym for the drug, and the adjective Resistolero as a synonym for the drug addict."

The man on the spot was Kativo's vice president, Humberto Larach ("Beto"), a Honduran, who headed Kativo's North Adhesives Division. Managers in nine countries including all of Central America, Mexico, the Caribbean and two South American countries, Ecuador and Colombia, reported to him. He had become manager of the adhesive division after demonstrating his entrepreneurial talents managing Kativo's paint business in Honduras.

Beto had proven his courage and his business creativity when he was among 105 taken hostage in the Chamber of Commerce building in downtown San Pedro Sula by guerrillas from the Communist Popular Liberation Front. Despite fire fights between the guerrillas and government troops, threats of execution, and being used as a human shield, Beto had sold his product to two clients (fellow hostages) who had previously been buying products from Kativo's chief competitor! Beto also has a reputation for emphasizing the importance of "Making the bottom line," as a part of Kativo corporate culture.

By summer 1985, more than corporate image was at stake. As a solution to the glue sniffing problem social activists working with street children suggested that oil of mustard, allyl isothiocyanate, could be added to the product to prevent its abuse. They argued that a person attempting to sniff glue with oil of mustard added would find it too powerful to tolerate. Sniffing it has been described like getting an "overdose of horseradish." An attempt to legislate the addition of oil of mustard received a boost when Honduran Peace Corps volunteer, Timothy Bicknell, convinced a local group called the "Committee for the Prevention of Drugs at the National Level," of the necessity of adding oil of mustard to Resistol. All members of the committee were prominent members of Honduran society.

Beto, in response to the growing publicity about the "Resistoleros," requested staff members of H. B. Fuller's U.S. headquarters to look into the viability of oil of mustard as a solution with special attention to side effects and whether it was required or used in the United States. H. B. Fuller's corporate industrial hygiene staff found 1983 toxicology reports that oil of mustard was a cancer-causing agent in tests run with rats. A 1986 toxicology report from the Aldrich Chemical Company described the health hazard data of allyl isothiocyanate as:

**Acute Effects**

May be fatal if inhaled, swallowed, or absorbed through skin.
Carcinogen.
Causes burns.
Material is extremely destructive to tissue of the mucous membranes and upper respiratory tract, eyes and skin.

**Prolonged Contact Can Cause:**

Nausea, dizziness, and headache.
Severe irritation or burns.
Lung irritation, chest pain and edema which may be fatal.
Repeated exposure may cause asthma.

In addition the product had a maximum shelf-life of six months.

To the best of our knowledge, the chemical, physical, and toxicological properties have not been thoroughly investigated.

In 1986, Beto contacted Hugh Young, president of Solvent Abuse Foundation for Education (SAFE), and gathered information on programs SAFE had developed in Mexico. Young, who believed that there was no effective deterrent, took the position that the only viable approach to substance abuse was education, not product modification. He argued that reformulating the product was an exercise in futility because "nothing is available in the solvent area that is not abusable." With these reports in hand, Beto attempted to persuade Resistol's critics, relief agencies, and government officials that adding oil of mustard to Resistol was not the solution to the glue sniffing problem.

During the summer of 1986 Beto had his first success in changing the mind of one journalist. Earlier in the year Marie Kawas, an independent writer, wrote an article sympathetic to the position of Timothy Bicknell and the Committee for the Prevention of Drugs in Honduras. In June, Beto met with her and explained how both SAFE and Kativo sought a solution that was not product-oriented but that was directed at changing human behavior. She was also informed of the research on the dangers of oil of mustard (about which additional information had been obtained). Kawas then wrote an article:

### Education Is the Solution for Drug Addiction
LA CEIBA
BY MARIE J. KAWAS

A lot of people have been interested in combating drug addiction among youths and children, but few have sought solutions, and almost no one looks into the feasibility of the alternatives that are so desperately proposed. . . .

Oil of mustard (allyl isothiocyanate) may well have been an irresponsible solution in the United States of America during the sixties and seventies, and the Hondurans want to adopt this as a panacea without realizing that their information sources are out of date. Through scientific progress, it has been found that the inclusion of oil of mustard in products which contain solvents, in order to prevent their perversion into use as an addictive drug, only causes greater harm to the consumers and workers involved in their manufacture. . . .

Education is a primordial instrument for destroying a social cancer. An effort of this magnitude requires the cooperation of different individuals and organizations. . . .

Future generations of Hondurans will be in danger of turning into human parasites, without a clear awareness of what is harmful to them. But if drugs and ignorance are to blame, it is even more harmful to sin by indifference before those very beings who are growing up in an environment without the basic advantages for a healthy physical and mental existence. Who will be the standard bearer in the philanthropic activities which will provide Honduras with the education necessary to combat drug addiction? Who will be remiss in their duty in the face of the nation's altruism?

At first, Beto did not have much success at the governmental level. In September 1986, Dr. Rosalio Zavala, Head of the Mental Health Division of the Honduran Ministry of Health, wrote an article attacking the improper use of Resistol by youth. Beto was unsuccessful in his attempt to contact Dr. Zavala. He had better luck with Mrs. Norma Castro, Governor of the State of Cortes, who after a conversation with Beto became convinced that oil of mustard had serious dangers and that glue sniffing was a social problem.

Beto's efforts continued into the new year. Early in 1987, Kativo began to establish Community Affairs Councils, as a planned expansion of the world-wide company's philosophy of community involvement. These employee committees had already been in place in the United States since 1978.

A company document gave the purpose of Community Affairs Councils:

> To educate employees about community issues.
> To develop understanding of, and be responsive to the communities near our facilities.
> To contribute to Kativo/H. B. Fuller's corporate presence in the neighborhoods and communities we are a part of.
> To encourage and support employee involvement in the community.
> To spark a true interest in the concerns of the communities in which we live and work.

The document goes on to state, "We want to be more than just bricks, mortar, machines and people. We want to be a company with recognized values, demonstrating involvement, and commitment to the betterment of the communities we are a part of." Later that year, the Honduran community affairs committees went on to make contributions to several organizations working with street children.

In May 1987, Beto visited Jose Oqueli, Vice-Minister of Public Health, to explain the philosophy behind H. B. Fuller's Community Affairs program. He also informed him of the health hazards of oil of mustard; they discussed the cultural, family and economic roots of the problem of glue-sniffing among street children.

In June 1987, Parents Resource Institute for Drug Education (PRIDE) set up an office in San Pedro Sula. PRIDE'S philosophy was that through adequate parental education on the drug problem, it would be possible to deal with the problems of inhalant use. PRIDE was a North American organization that had taken international Nancy Reagan's "just say no" approach to inhalant abuse. Like SAFE, PRIDE took the position that oil of mustard was not the solution to glue sniffing.

Through PRIDE, Beto was introduced to Wilfredo Alvarado, the new Head of the Mental Health Division in the Ministry of Health. Dr. Alvarado, an advisor to the Congressional Committee on Health, was in charge of preparing draft legislation and evaluating legislation received by Congress. Together with Dr. Alvarado, the Kativo staff worked to prepare draft legislation addressing the problem of inhalant addicted children. At the same time, five Congressmen drafted a proposed law that required the use of oil of mustard in locally produced or imported solvent based adhesives.

In June 1988, Dr. Alvarado asked the Congressional Committee on Health to reject the legislation proposed by the five congressmen. Alvarado was given sixty days to present a complete draft of legislation. In August 1988, however, he retired from his position and Kativo lost its primary communication channel with the Committee. This was critical because Beto was relying on Alvarado to help insure that the legislation reflected the technical information that he had collected.

The company did not have an active lobbying or government monitoring function in Tegucigalpa, the capital, which tends to be isolated from the rest of the country. (In fact, the company's philosophy has generally been not to lobby on behalf of its own narrow self-interest.) Beto, located in San Pedro Sula, had no staff support to help him monitor political developments. Monitoring, unfortunately, was an addition to his regular, daily responsibilities. His ability to keep track of political developments was made more difficult by the fact that he traveled about 45 percent of the time outside of Honduras. It took over two months for Beto to learn of Alvarado's departure from government. When the legislation was passed in March, he was completely absorbed in reviewing strategic plans for the nine country divisions which report to him.

On March 30, 1989, the Honduran Congress approved the legislation drafted by the five congressmen.

After the law's passage Beto spoke to the press about the problems with the legislation. He argued:

> This type of cement is utilized in industry, in crafts, in the home, schools, and other places where it has become indispensable; thus by altering the product, he said, not only will the drug addiction problem not be solved, but rather, the country's development would be slowed.
>
> In order to put an end to the inhalation of Resistol by dozens of people, various products which are daily necessities would have to be eliminated from the marketplace. This is impossible, he added, since it would mean a serious setback to industry at several levels . . .
>
> There are studies that show that the problem is not the glue itself,

but rather the individual. The mere removal of this substance would immediately be substituted by some other, to play the same hallucinogenic trip for the person who was sniffing it.

# H. B. FULLER: THE CORPORATE RESPONSE

In late April 1986, Elmer Andersen, H. B. Fuller Chairman of the Board, received the following letter:

4/21/86

Elmer L. Andersen
H. B. Fuller Co.

Dear Mr. Andersen

I heard part of your talk on public radio recently, and was favorably impressed with your philosophy that business should not be primarily for profit. This was consistent with my previous impression of H. B. Fuller Co. since I am a public health nurse and have been aware of your benevolence to the nursing profession.

However, on a recent trip to Honduras, I spent some time at a new home for chemically dependent "street boys" who are addicted to glue sniffing. It was estimated that there are 600 of these children still on the streets in San Pedro Sula alone. The glue is sold for repairing *tennis shoes* and I am told it is made by H. B. Fuller in *Costa Rica*. These children also suffer toxic effects of liver and brain damage from the glue. . . .

Hearing you on the radio, I immediately wondered how this condemnation of H. B. Fuller Company could be consistent with the company as I knew it before and with your business philosophy.

Are you aware of this problem in Honduras, and, if so, how are you dealing with it?

That a stockholder should write the seventy-six-year-old Chairman of the Board directly is significant. Elmer Andersen is a legendary figure in Minnesota. He is responsible for the financial success of H. B. Fuller from 1941 to 1971 and his values reflected in his actions as CEO are embodied in H. B. Fuller's mission statement.

### H. B. Fuller Mission Statement

The H. B. Fuller corporate mission is to be a leading and profitable worldwide formulator, manufacturer, and marketer of quality specialty chemicals, emphasizing service to customers and managed in accordance with a strategic plan.

H. B. Fuller Company is committed to its responsibilities, in order of priority, to its customers, employees and shareholders. H. B. Fuller will conduct business legally and ethically, support the activities of its employees in their communities, and be a responsible corporate citizen.

It was also Elmer Andersen who, as president and CEO, made the decision that foreign acquisitions should be managed by locals. Concerning the 1967 acquisition of Kativo Chemical Industries Ltd. Elmer Andersen said:

> We had two objectives in mind. One was directly business related and one was altruistic. Just as we had expanded in America, our international business strategy was to pursue markets where our competitors were not active. We were convinced that we had something to offer Latin America that the region did not have locally. In our own small way, we also wanted to be of help to that part of the world. We believed that by producing adhesives in Latin America and by employing only local people, we would create new jobs and help elevate the standard of living. We were convinced that the way to aid world peace was to help Latin America become more prosperous.

Three years later a stockholder dramatically raised the Resistol issue for a second time directly by a stockholder. On June 7, 1989, Vice President for Corporate Relations Dick Johnson received a call from a stockholder whose daughter was in the Peace Corps in Honduras. She asked, "How can a company like H. B. Fuller claim to have a social conscience and continue to sell Resistol which is 'literally burning out the brains' of children in Latin America?"

Johnson was galvanized into action. This complaint was of special concern because he was about to meet with a national group of socially responsible investors who were considering including H. B. Fuller's stock in their portfolio. Fortunately Karen Muller, Director of Community Affairs, had been keeping a file on the glue sniffing problem. Within twenty-four hours of receiving the call, Dick had written a memo to CEO Tony Andersen.

In that memo he set forth the basic values to be considered as H. B. Fuller wrestled with the problem. Among them were the following:

1. H. B. Fuller's explicitly stated public concern about substance abuse.
2. H. B. Fuller's "Concern for Youth" focus in its community affairs projects.

3. H. B. Fuller's reputation as a socially responsible company.
4. H. B. Fuller's history of ethical conduct.
5. H. B. Fuller's commitment to the intrinsic value of each individual.

Whatever "solution" was ultimately adopted would have to be consistent with these values. In addition, Dick suggested a number of options including the company's withdrawal from the market or perhaps altering the formula to make Resistol a water-based product, eliminating sniffing as an issue.

Tony responded by suggesting that Dick create a task force to find a solution and a plan to implement it. Dick decided to accept Beto's invitation to travel to Honduras to view the situation first hand. He understood that the problem crossed functional and divisional responsibilities. Given H. B. Fuller's high visibility as a socially responsible corporation, the glue sniffing problem had the potential for becoming a public relations nightmare. The brand name of one of H. B. Fuller's products had become synonymous with a serious social problem. Additionally, Dick understood that there was an issue larger than product misuse involved, and it had social and community ramifications. The issue was substance abuse by children, whether the substance is a H. B. Fuller product or not. As a part of the solution, a community relations response was required. Therefore, he invited Karen to join him on his trip to Honduras.

Karen recalled a memo she had written about a year earlier directed to Beto. In it she had suggested a community relations approach rather than Beto's government relations approach. In that memo Karen wrote:

> This community relations process involves developing a community-wide coalition from all those with a vested interest in solving the community issue—those providing services in dealing with the street children and drug users, other businesses, and the government. It does require leadership over the long-term both with a clear set of objectives and a commitment on the part of each group represented to share in the solution. . . .

In support of the community relations approach Karen argued that:

1. It takes the focus and pressure off H. B. Fuller as one individual company.
2. It can educate the broader community and focus on the best solution, not just the easiest ones.
3. It holds everyone responsible, the government, educators, H. B. Fuller's customers, legitimate consumers of our product, social service workers, and agencies.
4. It provides H. B. Fuller with an expanded good image as a company

that cares and will stay with the problem—that we are willing to go the second mile.

5. It can de-politicize the issue.
6. It offers the opportunity to counterbalance the negative impact of the use of our product named Resistol by re-identifying the problem.

Karen and Dick left on a four-day trip to Honduras September 18. Upon arriving they were joined by Beto, Oscar Sahuri, General Manager for Kativo's adhesives business in Honduras, and Jorge Walter Bolanos, Vice President Director of Finance, Kativo. Karen had also asked Mark Connelly, a health consultant from an international agency working with street children, to join the group. They began the process of looking at all aspects of the situation. Visits to two different small shoe manufacturing shops and a shoe supply distributor helped to clarify the issues around pricing, sales, distribution, and the packaging of the product.

A visit to a well-run shelter for street children provided them with some insight into the dynamics of substance abuse among this vulnerable population in the streets of Tegucigalpa and San Pedro Sula. At a meeting with the officials at the Ministry of Health, they reviewed the issue of implementing the oil-of-mustard law, and the Kativo managers offered to assist the committee as it reviewed the details of the law. In both Tegucigalpa and San Pedro Sula, the National Commission for Technical Assistance to Children in Irregular Situations (CONATNSI), a country-wide association of private and public agencies working with street children, organized meetings of its members at which the Kativo managers offered an explanation of the company's philosophy and the hazards involved in the use of oil of mustard.

As they returned from their trip to Honduras, Karen and Dick had the opportunity to reflect on what they had learned. They agreed that removing Resistol from the market would not resolve the problem. However, the problem was extremely complex. The use of inhalants by street children was a symptom of Honduras' underlying economic problems—problems with social, cultural, and political aspects as well as economic dimensions.

Honduran street children come from many different circumstances. Some are true orphans, while others are abandoned. Some are runaways, while others are working the streets to help support their parents. Children working at street jobs or begging usually earn more than the minimum wage. Nevertheless, they are often punished if they bring home too little. This creates a vicious circle; they would rather be on the street than take punishment at home—a situation that increases the likelihood they will fall victim to drug addiction. The street children's problems are exacerbated by the general lack of opportunities and a lack of enforcement of school attendance laws. In addition, the police sometimes abuse street children.

Karen and Dick realized that Resistol appeared to be the drug of choice for young street children, and children were able to obtain it in a number of different ways. There was no clear pattern, and hence the solution could not be found in simply changing some features of the distribution system. Children might obtain the glue from legitimate customers, small shoe repair stalls, by theft, from "illegal" dealers, or from third parties who purchased it from legitimate stores and then sold it to children. For some sellers the sale of Resistol to children could be profitable. The glue was available in small packages which made it more affordable, but the economic circumstances of the typical legitimate customer made packaging in small packages economically sensible.

The government had long been unstable. As a result there was a tendency for people working with the government to hope that new policy initiatives would fade away within a few months. Moreover there was a large continuing turnover of government, so that any knowledge of H. B. Fuller and its corporate philosophy soon disappeared. Government officials usually had to settle for a quick fix, for they were seldom around long enough to manage any other kind of policy. Although it was on the books for six months by the time of their trip, the oil-of-mustard law had not yet been implemented, and national elections were to be held in three months. During meetings with government officials, it appeared to Karen and Dick that no further actions would be taken as current officials waited for the election outcome.

Kativo company officers, Jorge Walter Bolanos and Humberto Larach, discussed continuing the government relations strategy hoping that the law might be repealed or modified. They were also concerned with the damage done to H. B. Fuller's image. Karen and Dick thought the focus should be on community relations. From their perspective, efforts directed toward changing the law seemed important but would do nothing to help with the long-term solution to the problems of the street children who abused glue.

Much of the concern for street children was found in private agencies. The chief coordinating association was CONATNSI, created as a result of a seminar sponsored by UNICEF in 1987. CONATNSI was under the direction of a Board of Directors elected by the General Assembly. It began its work in 1988; its objectives included (a) improving the quality of services,

(b) promoting interchange of experiences, (c) coordinating human and material resources, (d) offering technical support, and (e) promoting research. Karen and others believe that CONATNSI had a shortage of both financial and human resources, but it appeared to be well-organized and was a potential intermediary for the company.

As a result of their trip, they knew that a community relations strategy would be complex and risky. H. B. Fuller was committed to a community relations approach, but what would a community relations solution look like in Honduras? The mission statement did not provide a complete answer. It indicated the company had responsibilities to its Honduran customers and employees, but exactly what kind? Were there other responsibilities beyond that directly involving its product? What effect can a single company have in solving an intractable social problem? How should the differing emphases in perspective of Kativo and its parent, H. B. Fuller, be handled? What does corporate citizenship require in situations like this?

## NOTES

1. The Subsidiaries of the North Adhesives Division of Kativo Chemical Industries S. A. go by the name "H. B. Fuller (Country of Operation)," e.g., H. B. Fuller S. A. Honduras. To prevent confusion with the parent company we will refer to H. B. Fuller S. A. Honduras by the name of its parent, "Kativo."

2. The following discussion is based on *Honduras: A Country Study*, 2d ed., ed. James D. Rudolph (Washington, D.C.: Department of the Army, 1984).

3. Unless otherwise indicated all references and quotations regarding H. B. Fuller and its subsidiary Kativo Chemical Industries S. A. are from company documents.

## SOURCES

Acker, Alison. *The Making of a Banana Republic.* Boston: South End Press, 1988.

H. B. Fuller Company. *A Fuller Life: The Story of H. B. Fuller Company: 1887–1987* St. Paul: H. B. Fuller Company, 1986.

Rudolph, James D. ed. *Honduras: A Country Study.* 2d ed. Washington, D.C.: Department of the Army, 1984.

Schine, Eric. "Preparing for Banana Republic U.S." *Corporate Finance.* December, 1987.

Sheehan, Edward. *Agony in the Garden: A Stranger in Central America.* Boston: Houghton Mifflin, 1989.

# What Price Safety?

This case takes place in 1995 in Nambu, an Asian nation with a centuries-old philosophical and ethical tradition emphasizing duty and harmony in all human relationships. In 1969 Motorola formed a joint venture (JV) partnership with a Nambunese multinational company to produce microelectronic products at a new facility in the city of Anzen, Nambu. Motorola's ownership share was 60 percent; the local partner company's, 40 percent. Many of the Anzen Facility's key managerial personnel were Motorolans, while the lower-level associates were Nambunese citizens and employees of the partner company.

From its very beginning, the Anzen Facility developed a strong tradition of safety consciousness. Even the most casual visitor to the Anzen plant would notice numerous signs and displays, in both Nambunese and English, urging associates to "Think and Act Safely," "Wear Protective Eyeglasses," "Report Dangerous Situations," etc.

Motorola also had other operations in Nambu. In charge of Human Resources for all these operations, including the Anzen joint venture, was Canadian Stan Stark, forty-seven. Stan was based at Motorola headquarters, 300 kilometers north of Anzen. Since first assuming his position five years ago, Stan had made safety one of his top priorities. He took pride in the fact that during this period he had further reduced the Anzen Facility's already-low rate of accidents and lost workdays.

Sharing in this pride was a Motorolan of Dutch nationality, Henk Van Dyke, thirty-eight. Henk had been at Anzen for three years, assigned by Motorola to serve as the Human Resources manager for the entire JV facility. He enjoyed working in Nambu, but was somewhat handicapped because he did not speak Nambunese. Henk reported to Stan.

One of the operations at the Anzen Facility was "Final Test Assembly,"

From *Uncompromising Integrity: Motorola's Global Challenge*, R. S. Moorthy, Richard T. DeGeorge, Thomas Donaldson, William J. Ellos, S. J., Robert C. Soloman, and Robert B. Textor (Schaumburg Ill., Motorola University Press, 1998).

carried out by three eight-person teams on each daily shift. These team members were all Nambunese employees of the partner company.

The employee relations manager for the Anzen Facility was Willard Wa. Willard, an employee of the partner company, was born fifty-four years ago in a small village in northern Nambu, and had been assigned to the JV partnership since its very first day of operation. Willard reported to Henk.

The manufacturing manager for the Final Test Assembly operation was a Nambunese Motorolan named Victor Min, forty-nine, whom Motorola had assigned to the JV partnership for this purpose. To all who knew him, Victor personified a deep dedication to traditional Nambunese cultural values of duty and obedience.

One of the most respected of the Final Test Assembly teams was Team Three, nicknamed the "Morning Glory" team. Members of this team were intensely proud of their performance in both productivity and safety, which was among the best in the entire facility. Morning Glory team members viewed this performance as the result not only of exceptional skill, but equally important, of an unusual degree of harmony and cooperation within their team.

When Victor took over management of the Final Test Assembly operation in 1994, he made an effort to get acquainted with everyone under his supervision. He soon felt comfortable with all the Morning Glory team members except one, namely Tommy Tang, thirty-one. Tommy had been hired by the partner company only two years earlier, after having spent several years as a mountaineering guide. Compared with most Nambunese, Tommy's values leaned a bit more toward freedom and a bit less toward duty. He hated to wear the protective eyeglasses that all Final Test Assembly associates were required to wear on duty. When his teammates would urge him to put on his safety glasses, he would give a variety of reasons why he couldn't.

On several occasions Victor spotted Tommy in the Final Test Assembly Area *without* his protective eyeglasses. Each time he would counsel Tommy on the need to wear them. The last time he shouted, "Tommy, this is the last time I will see you here without your safety glasses. From now on, you will either wear them or else!"

Then, four weeks later, a terrible event occurred. Victor entered the Final Test Assembly Area and noticed Tommy working closely with his Morning Glory teammates. All of them were wearing their protective eyeglasses *except* Tommy. Suddenly Victor lost control of his temper. He jumped at Tommy and slapped him several times on both sides of the head, screaming, "This will teach you!" Tommy doubled over in pain, holding his ears. Then, despite his pain, he apologized over and over to Victor for not having complied with safety regulations. After two or three minutes of apology, Tommy went to see the facility's nurse.

The other seven Morning Glory members stood in shocked silence. Nothing like this had ever happened before at Anzen. None of them reported the incident. Nonetheless, rumors about it, both accurate and otherwise, spread instantly throughout the entire facility.

That night Victor had trouble sleeping. The following morning he went directly to see Tommy in the Final Test Assembly Area. He noted that Tommy was wearing the required eyeglasses. In the presence of several Morning Glory team members, Victor apologized and presented Tommy with a red envelope inside of which he had placed a substantial amount of his own money. Tommy accepted the envelope and the apology. The two men then shook hands and parted amicably.

Then, a few days later came some shocking news from the facility's doctor: Tommy had suffered permanent partial loss of his hearing as a result of the slaps he received from Victor. As a matter of standard procedure, the doctor reported this finding to both Stan Stark and Henk Van Dyke.

Stan was stunned. He sat silently for a moment. Then he placed a conference call to Henk and Willard, and questioned them about the incident and the doctor's report. Then Stan decided: "Both of you know that no Motorolan is *ever* allowed to physically assault a fellow associate. Could each of you please investigate this incident, and give me your recommendations within 48 hours."

Willard proceeded immediately to conduct the most thorough investigation he could. The first thing he discovered was that neither Tommy nor any of his teammates wanted to discuss the matter at all. They all felt that their team's harmony would be best served by treating the entire matter as if it had never happened. After all, Victor had apologized, Tommy had accepted the apology, and Tommy was now complying with all safety regulations. So, the only really important thing was to get on with the team's heavy workload.

But Willard persisted. Finally he got some solid facts:

- Several Morning Glory members stated categorically that Victor had never before struck a subordinate or threatened to.
- These team members believed that Victor's outburst of temper was unique, and they considered any repetition unlikely. "Victor has

learned his lesson," said one, "and from now on he will handle his stress better. We will help him."

- Victor's personnel file revealed nothing to suggest he was prone to losing his temper or "acting out" violently.
- Tommy, despite his impaired hearing, could still function effectively with his Morning Glory teammates.

Two days later Willard phoned Stan with his recommendations. "Frankly," said Willard, "I think the solution is pretty simple. I recommend that the JV partnership cover all of Tommy's medical costs and then quietly, without any ceremony, make a reasonable indemnification payment to him with our apologies. Beyond that, I recommend that we do nothing—except, of course, to keep monitoring the situation carefully. In my opinion as a former manufacturing associate, this would be the best solution, because it is now clear to me that the Morning Glory team is functioning well, and continuing to accept Victor's leadership."

A few minutes later, Stan got a call from Henk. "Well," said Henk, "I recommend that we terminate Victor right away. Victor is a Motorolan, and knows very well that he is not supposed to strike an associate. That would be a violation of the basic dignity to which every Motorolan is entitled, and to which I believe all JV partnership employees are also entitled. We cannot allow a Motorolan to enforce regulations for our associates' safety by violating that safety! That just doesn't make any sense at all. And while we are at it, we should pay Tommy's medical bills and terminate him, too."

Next Stan walked down the hall to consult Cuthbert Kim, senior counsel in the Motorola Law Department for Nambu. Stan carefully explained the facts of the case and then asked, "Cuthbert, what's the procedure if I decide to terminate Victor and Tommy?"

"Well, I'm afraid there is no such procedure," replied Cuthbert. "While it is true that under Nambunese law striking a subordinate is grounds for termination, it is also true that once an apology has been offered and accepted, the law determines that life can and should go on again, and that termination is not legally justified. So, you *can't* terminate him. And you can't terminate Tommy, either. But of course you could *separate* them from the company, provided you could manage to negotiate buyout agreements that they would accept."

Stan found this hard to believe, but when he checked with an external Nambunese consulting attorney, he received essentially the same answer.

The next day, Stan asked Cuthbert to do some research and find out how much it would cost to buy the two associates out. Soon Cuthbert came back with the answer: "Since Victor still has about 11 years before he is due to retire from Motorola, he could probably bargain hard. My estimate is that the JV partnership would probably have to pay him about five years' worth of salary plus benefits and fringes. For Tommy, it might be three years' worth, because he is a relatively new employee."

"That's a huge amount of money," gasped Stan. "On the other hand, the behavior that both Victor and Tommy have modeled is certainly not the kind of behavior I want at Anzen. I'll think about it and then let you know my decision."

## FOR DISCUSSION

What should Stan do? Why?

*James Kiersky*

# Ethical Complexities Involving Multinational Corporations

By no means a new phenomenon on the business scene, multinational corporations (MNCs) present a number of distinctive ethical problems peculiar to their organizational format. These problems are not simply a function of MNCs' size, for many localized national corporations (LNCs) are larger in terms of financial net worth, number of shareholders, gross sales, or number of employees.

The first and most obvious set of conditions that gives rise to ethical problems grows out of the fact that MNCs function in three domains: (A) a home base of operation where the MNC is headquartered and chartered, (B) a foreign base of operation in a host country, and (C) additional foreign markets beyond both (A) and (B). Each of these domains has a unique web of ethical beliefs and principles which often conflicts with those of the other domains. A major problem, peculiar to MNCs, concerns one of venue: when a situation arises involving conflicting claims among the different domains of (A), (B), and/or (C), where is the appropriate place to adjudicate the conflict legally or ethically—the parent company's national court system, the host country's courts, the place where the problems occurred, a neutral site, a place most likely to render a "just" verdict, or a mutually agreed upon location?

What seems to create this particular niche of ethical complexities for the international business community are the permutations and combinations of factors already present in most business operations of any size. In other words, for most businesses the following identifiable "players" are involved:

1. Managers—who make the decisions
2. Employees—who carry out those decisions
3. Shareholders—who finance those decisions and expect to profit from them

4. Consumers—who utilize the fruits of those decisions
5. Environmental community—which is affected by those decisions
6. Governments—who regulate those decisions
7. Competitors—who must contend with those decisions

Of course, there are other "players," for example, lending institutions, who do not fit neatly into any one of these main categories. The list is not meant to be complete; it merely identifies the range of concerns at play. While there are invariably conflicting interests and different values motivating each of these "players," the MNC not only involves all seven of them, but creates interesting sub-alliances by virtue of the fact that each domain of the MNC—(A), (B), and (C) above—has its own set of the seven players. With each issue that emerges, the sub-alliances seem to change team members.

In order to illustrate more concretely the general complexities being characterized, consider a few scenarios. For example, in the hopes of being able to meet foreign competition the chief executive officer of a manufacturing MNC wishes to move production plants to a host country (B) where the labor market is significantly cheaper than in the home country (A). While many stockholders of that MNC (which would include A-3, B-3, and C-3 above) may applaud such a move, along with labor unions, prospective employees, and the government in the host country (B-2 and B-6), there is likely to be an outcry of betrayal from the home labor market (A-2), the home government (A-6), the general populace of the home country (A-4 and A-5), as well as from foreign competitors (C-7), and possibly competitors in the host nation (B-7).

A second, rather different sort of scenario involves an MNC home-based in a nation (A) which is committed to human rights, egalitarianism, and/or affirmative action programs but which has overseas affiliates operating in a host nation (B) committed to programs which are dictatorial and openly racist. The conflict of values which may take shape in this case will depend upon what actions are taken or contemplated. For instance, hiring and termination practices in affiliates in the host country will have different repercussions not only in the different domains of (A), (B), and (C), but within one and the same domain. A minority of citizens and consumers in (B) may vehemently oppose the same practices strongly endorsed by a majority of citizens and consumers in (B), or in (A) or (C) for that matter. The consequences of business activities proposed as well as undertaken are likely to have further effects in all three domains which may not have been foreseen.

A third type of situation is likely to find its way into newsprint in the 2000s. An MNC home-based in (A) has been operating in country (B) for many years. Country (B) has recently upgraded its environmental legislation and now decides to press civil claims against that MNC for long-term damage to its waterways, soil, air, and its citizenry. The entire host affiliate of that MNC in country (B) is not even financially equivalent to the amount of the claims, so that the MNC in country (A) decides to sue its own insurance company, itself an MNC, headquartered in country (C). Who is to be held responsible, both ethically and legally and, furthermore, which set of ethical and legal standards is the appropriate one to decide such an issue? The same questions are similarly applicable to product liability issues, or industrial "accidents."

In many of the cases of the types mentioned a need seems to be indicated to at least examine the feasibility of establishing an "international marketplace" with "internationally acceptable rules of the game" and "international court and enforcement mechanisms." Just how these could be established and financed, what would be the chief obstacles and sources of opposition as well as support are questions that should be explored.

*Richard T. De George*

# Ethical Dilemmas for Multinational Enterprise: A Philosophical Overview

First World multinational corporations (MNCs) are both the hope of the Third World and the scourge of the Third World. The working out of this paradox poses moral dilemmas for many MNCs. I shall focus on some of the moral dilemmas that many American MNCs face.

Third World countries frequently seek to attract American multinationals for the jobs they provide and for the technological transfers they promise. Yet when American MNCs locate in Third World countries, many Americans condemn them for exploiting the resources and workers of the Third World. While MNCs are a means for improving the standard of living of the underdeveloped countries, MNC are blamed for the poverty and starvation such countries suffer. Although MNCs provide jobs in the Third World, many criticize them for transferring these jobs from the United States. American MNCs usually pay at least as high wages as local industries, yet critics blame them for paying the workers in underdeveloped countries less than they pay American workers for comparable work. When American MNCs pay higher than local wages, local companies criticize them for skimming off all the best workers and for creating an internal brain-drain. Multinationals are presently the most effective vehicle available for the development of the Third World. At the same time, critics complain that the MNCs are destroying the local cultures and substituting for them the tinsel of American life and the worst aspects of its culture. American MNCs seek to protect the interests of their shareholders by locating in an environment in which their enterprise will be safe from destruction by revolutions and confiscation by socialist regimes.

From *Ethics and the Multinational Enterprise*, ed. W. Michael Hoffman, Ann E. Lange, and David Fedo (Lanham, Md.: University Press of America, 1986).

When they do so, critics complain that the MNCs thrive in countries with strong, often right-wing, governments.[1]

The dilemmas the American MNCs face arise from conflicting demands made from opposing, often ideologically based, points of view. Not all of the demands that lead to these dilemmas are equally justifiable, nor are they all morally mandatory.

We can separate the MNCs that behave immorally and reprehensibly from those that do not by clarifying the true moral responsibility of MNCs in the Third World. To help do so, I shall state and briefly defend five theses.

THESIS I: MANY OF THE MORAL DILEMMAS MNCS FACE ARE FALSE DILEMMAS WHICH ARISE FROM EQUATING UNITED STATES STAN-DARDS WITH MORALLY NECESSARY STANDARDS.

Many American critics argue that American multinationals should live up to and implement the same standards abroad that they do in the United States and that United States mandated norms should be followed.[2] This broad claim confuses morally necessary ways of conducting a firm with United States government regulations. The FDA sets high standards that may be admirable. But they are not necessarily morally required. OSHA specifies a large number of rules which in general have as their aim the protection of the worker. However, these should not be equated with morally mandatory rules. United States wages are the highest in the world. These also should not be thought to be the morally necessary norms for the whole world or for United States firms abroad. Morally mandatory standards that no corporation—United States or other—should violate, and moral minima below which no firm can morally go, should not be confused either with standards appropriate to the United States or with standards set by the United States government. Some of the dilemmas of United States multinationals come from critics making such false equations.

This is true with respect to drugs and FDA standards, with respect to hazardous occupations and OSHA standards, with respect to pay, with respect to internalizing the costs of externalities, and with respect to foreign corrupt practices. By using United States standards as moral standards, critics pose false dilemmas for American MNCs. These false dilemmas in turn obfuscate the real moral responsibilities of MNCs.

THESIS II: DESPITE DIFFERENCES AMONG NATIONS IN CULTURE AND VALUES, WHICH SHOULD BE RESPECTED,THERE ARE MORAL NORMS THAT CAN BE APPLIED TO MULTINATIONALS.

I shall suggest seven moral guidelines that apply in general to any multinational operating in Third World countries and that can be used in morally evaluating the actions of MNCs. MNCs that respect these moral norms would escape the legitimate criticisms contained in the dilemmas they are said to face.

1. *MNCs should do no intentional direct harm.* This injunction is clearly not peculiar to multinational corporations. Yet it is a basic norm that can be usefully applied in evaluating the conduct of MNCs. Any company that does produce intentional direct harm clearly violates a basic moral norm.

2. *MNCs should produce more good than bad for the host country.* This is an implementation of a general utilitarian principle. But this norm restricts the extent of that principle by the corollary that, in general, more good will be done by helping those in most need, rather than by helping those in less need at the expense of those in greater need. Thus the utilitarian analysis in this case does not consider that more harm than good might justifiably be done to the host country if the harm is offset by greater benefits to others in developed countries. MNCs will do more good only if they help the host country more than they harm it.

3. *MNCs should contribute by their activities to the host country's development.* If the presence of an MNC does not help the host country's development, the MNC can be correctly charged with exploitation, or using the host country for its own purposes at the expense of the host country.

4. *MNCs should respect the human rights of its employees.* MNCs should do so whether or not local companies respect those rights. This injunction will preclude gross exploitation of workers, set minimum standards for pay, and prescribe minimum standards for health and safety measures.

5. *MNCs should pay their fair share of taxes.* Transfer pricing has as its aim taking advantage of different tax laws in different countries. To the extent that it involves deception, it is itself immoral. To the extent that it is engaged in to avoid legitimate taxes, it exploits the host country, and the MNC does not bear its fair share of the burden of operating in that country.

6. *To the extent that local culture does not violate moral norms, MNCs should respect the local culture and work with it, not*

*against it.* MNCs cannot help but produce some changes in the cultures in which they operate. Yet, rather than simply transferring American ways into other lands, they can consider changes in operating procedures, plant planning, and the like, which take into account local needs and customs.

7. *MNCs should cooperate with the local government in the development and enforcement of just background institutions.* Instead of fighting a tax system that aims at appropriate redistribution of incomes, instead of preventing the organization of labor, and instead of resisting attempts at improving the health and safety standards of the host country, MNCs should be supportive of such measures.

THESIS III: WHOLESALE ATTACKS ON MULTINATIONALS ARE MOST OFTEN OVERGENERALIZATIONS. VALID MORAL EVALUATIONS CAN BE BEST MADE BY USING THE ABOVE MORAL CRITERIA FOR CONTEXT-AND-CORPORATION-SPECIFIC STUDIES AND ANALYSIS.

Broadside claims, such that all multinationals exploit underdeveloped countries or destroy their culture, are too vague to determine their accuracy. United States multinationals have in the past engaged—and some continue to engage—in immoral practices. A case by case study is the fairest way to make moral assessments. Yet we can distinguish five types of business operations that raise very different sorts of moral issues: (1) banks and financial institutions, (2) agricultural enterprises, (3) drug companies and hazardous industries, (4) extractive industries, and (5) other manufacturing and service industries.

If we were to apply our seven general criteria in each type of case, we would see some of the differences among them. Financial institutions do not generally employ many people. Their function is to provide loans for various types of development. Financial institutions can help and have helped development tremendously. Yet the servicing of debts that many Third World countries face condemns them to impoverishment for the foreseeable future. The role of financial institutions in this situation is crucial and raises special and difficult moral problems, if not dilemmas.

Agricultural enterprises face other demands. If agricultural multinationals buy the best lands and use them for export crops while insufficient arable land is left for the local population to grow enough to feed itself, then MNCs do more harm than good to the host country—a violation of one of the norms I suggested above.

Drug companies and dangerous industries pose different and special problems. I have suggested that FDA standards are not morally mandatory standards. This should not he taken to mean that drug companies are bound only by local laws, for the local laws may require less than morality requires in the way of supplying adequate information and of not producing intentional, direct harm.[3] The same type of observation applies to hazardous industries. While an asbestos company will probably not be morally required to take all the measures mandated by OSHA regulations, it cannot morally leave its workers completely unprotected.[4]

Extractive industries, such as mining, which remove minerals from a country, are correctly open to the charge of exploitation unless they can show that they do more good than harm to the host country and that they do not benefit only either themselves or a repressive elite in the host country.

Other manufacturing industries vary greatly, but as a group they have come in for sustained charges of exploitation of workers and the undermining of the host country's culture. The above guidelines can serve as a means of sifting the valid from the invalid charges.

THESIS IV: ON THE INTERNATIONAL LEVEL AND ON THE NATIONAL LEVEL IN MANY THIRD WORLD COUNTRIES THE LACK OF ADEQUATE JUST BACKGROUND INSTITUTIONS MAKES THE USE OF CLEAR MORAL NORMS ALL THE MORE NECESSARY.

American multinational corporations operating in Germany and Japan, and German and Japanese multinational corporations operating in the United States, pose no special moral problems. Nor do the operations of Brazilian multinational corporations in the United States or Germany. Yet First World multinationals operating in Third World countries have come in for serious and sustained moral criticism. Why?

A major reason is that in the Third World the First World's MNCs operate without the types of constraints and in societies that do not have the same kinds of redistributive mechanisms as in the developed countries. There is no special difficulty in United States multinationals operating in other First World countries because in general these countries *do* have appropriate background institutions.[5]

More and more Third World countries are developing controls on multinationals that insure the companies do more good for the country than harm.[6] Authoritarian regimes that care more for their own wealth than for the good of their people pose difficult moral conditions under which to operate. In such instances, the guidelines above may prove helpful.

Just as in the nations of the developed, industrial world the labor movement serves as a counter to the dominance of big business, consumerism serves as a watchdog on practices harmful to the consumer, and big government serves as a restraint on each of the vested interest groups, so international structures are necessary to provide the proper background constraints on international corporations.

The existence of MNCs is a step forward in the unification of mankind and in the formation of a global community. They provide the economic base and substructure on which true international cooperation can be built. Because of their special position and the special opportunities they enjoy, they have a special responsibility to promote the cooperation that only they are able to accomplish in the present world.

Just background institutions would preclude any company's gaining a competitive advantage by engaging in immoral practices. This suggests that MNCs have more to gain than to lose by helping formulate voluntary, UN (such as the code governing infant formulae),[7] and similar codes governing the conduct of all multinationals. A case can also be made that they have the moral obligation to do so.

THESIS V: THE MORAL BURDEN OF MNCs DO NOT EXONERATE LOCAL GOVERNMENTS FROM RESPONSIBILITY FOR WHAT HAPPENS IN AND TO THEIR COUNTRY. SINCE RESPONSIBILITY IS LINKED TO OWNERSHIP, GOVERNMENTS THAT INSIST ON PART OR MAJORITY OWNERSHIP INCUR PART OR MAJORITY RESPONSIBILITY.

The attempts by many underdeveloped countries to limit multinationals have shown that at least some governments have come to see that they can use multinationals to their own advantage. This may be done by restricting entry to those companies that produce only for local consumption, or that bring desired technology transfers with them. Some countries demand majority control and restrict the export of money from the country. Nonetheless, many MNCs have found it profitable to engage in production under the terms specified by the host country.

What host countries cannot expect is that they can demand control without accepting correlative responsibility. In general, majority control implies majority responsibility. An American MNC, such as Union Carbide, which had majority ownership of its Indian Bhopal plant, should have had primary control of the plant. Union Carbide, Inc. can be held liable for the damage the Bhopal plant caused because Union Carbide, Inc. did have majority ownership.[8] If Union Carbide did not have effective control, it is not relieved of its responsibility. If it could not exercise the control that its responsibility demanded, it should have withdrawn or sold off part of its holdings in that plant. If India had had majority ownership, then it would have had primary responsibility for the safe operation of the plant.

This is compatible with maintaining that if a company builds a hazardous plant, it has an obligation to make sure that the plant is safe and that those who run it are properly trained to run it safely. MNCs cannot simply transfer dangerous technologies without consideration of the people who will run them, the local culture, and similar factors. Unless MNCs can be reasonably sure that the plants they build will be run safely, they cannot morally build them. To do so would be to will intentional, direct harm.

The theses and guidelines that I have proposed are not a panacea. But they suggest how moral norms can be brought to bear on the dilemmas American multinationals face and they suggest ways out of apparent or false dilemmas. If MNCs observed those norms, they could properly avoid the moral sting of their critics' charges, even if their critics continued to level charges against them.

## NOTES

1. The literature attacking American MNCs is extensive. Many of the charges mentioned in this paper are found in Richard J. Barnet and Ronald E. Muller, *Global Reach: The Power of the Multinational Corporations* (New York: Simon & Schuster, 1974), and in Pierre Jalee, *The Pillage of the Third World*, translated from the French by Mary Klopper (New York and London: Modern Reader Paperbacks, 1968).

2. The position I advocate does not entail moral relativism, as my third thesis shows. The point is that although moral norms apply uniformly across cultures, U.S. standards are not the same as moral standards, should themselves be morally evaluated, and are relative to American conditions, standard of living, interests, and history.

3. For a fuller discussion of multinational drug companies see Richard T. De George, *Business Ethics*, 2d ed. (New York: Macmillan, 1986), pp. 363–67.

4. For a more detailed analysis of the morality of exporting hazardous industries, see my *Business Ethics*, pp. 367–72.

5. This position is consistent with that developed by John Rawls in his *A Theory of Justice* (Cambridge, Mass.: Harvard University Press, 1971), even though Rawls does not extend his analysis to the international realm. The thesis

does not deny that United States, German, or Japanese policies on trade restrictions, tariff levels, and the like can be morally evaluated.

6. See, for example, Theodore H. Moran, "Multinational Corporations: A Survey of Ten Years' Evidence," Georgetown School of Foreign Service, 1984.

7. For a general discussion of UN codes, see Wolfgang Fikentscher, "United Nations Codes of Conduct: New Paths in International Law," *The American Journal of Comparative Law* 30 (1980): 577–604.

8. The official Indian Government report on the Bhopal tragedy has not yet appeared. The Union Carbide report was partially reprinted in the *New York Times*, 21 March 1985, p. 48. The major *New York Times* reports appeared on December 9, 1984, January 28, 30, and 31, and February 3, 1985.

*John R. Boatright*

# Ethics in International Business

Transnational corporations [face a quandry,] namely, deciding which standards of ethics to follow. Should TNCs be bound by the laws and prevailing morality of the home country and, in the case of American corporations, act everywhere as they do in the United States? Should they follow the practices of the host country and adopt the adage "When in Rome, do as the Romans do?" Or are there special ethical standards that apply when business is conducted across national boundaries? And if so, what are the standards appropriate for international business?

Unfortunately, there are no easy answers to these questions. In some cases, the standards contained in American law and morality ought to be observed beyond our borders; in other cases, there is no moral obligation to do so. Similarly, it is morally permissible for managers of TNCs to follow local practice and "do as the Romans do" in some situations but not others. And even if there are special ethical standards for international business, they cannot be applied without taking into account differences in cultures and value systems, the levels of economic development, and the social and political structures of the foreign countries in which TNCs operate. The existence of special standards, in other words, does not require us to act in the same way in all parts of the world, regardless of the situation. Local circumstances must always be taken into consideration in conducting business abroad.

## "No Double Standards!"

Let us consider, first, the position taken by some critics of TNCs: that business ought to be conducted in the same way the world over with no

From John R. Boatright, *Ethics and the Conduct of Business*, 2d ed., (Upper Saddle River, N.J.: Prentice-Hall, Inc., 1997).

double standards. In particular, U.S. corporations ought to observe domestic law and a single code of conduct in their dealings everywhere. This position might be expressed as, "When in Rome or anywhere else, do as you would at home."[1] A little reflection suffices to show that this high level of conduct is not morally required of TNCs in all instances and that they should not be faulted for every departure from home country standards in doing business abroad. Good reasons can be advanced to show that different practices in different parts of the world are, in some instances, morally justified.

First, the conditions prevailing in other parts of the world are different in some morally relevant respects from those in the United States and other developed countries. If Rome is a significantly different place, then standards that are appropriate at home do not necessarily apply there. Drug laws in the developed world, for example, are very stringent, reflecting greater affluence and better overall health. The standards embodied in these laws are not always appropriate in poorer, less developed countries with fewer medical resources and more severe health problems.

In the United States, the risk of prescribing an antidiarrheal drug such as Lomotil to children is not worth taking. But a physician in Central America, where children frequently die of untreated diarrhea, might evaluate the risk differently. Similarly, the effectiveness of Chloromycetin for massive infections might offset the possibility of aplastic anemia in a country where some people would die without the drug. A missionary in Bolivia who spoke with doctors about the extensive use of chloramphenicol (the generic name for Chloromycetin) reported: "The response was that in the States, because of our better state of general health, we could afford to have the luxury of saving that drug for rare cases. Here, the people's general health is so poor that one must make an all out attack on illness."[2]

Second, some aspects of American law and practice reflect incidental features of our situation, so that not all U.S. standards express universal moral requirements.[3] The fact that a drug has not been approved in the home country of a transnational or has been withdrawn from the market does not automatically mean that it is unsafe or ineffective. A drug for a tropical disease might never have been submitted for approval, since there is no market for it in the country where it is manufactured. Other drugs might not be approved because of concerns that are unfounded or open to question.

The FDA acted conservatively in initially refusing approval for Depo-Provera, for example; many countries of Western Europe and Canada, with equally strict drug-testing requirements, permitted the use of this drug as a last-resort contraceptive. In borderline cases, there is room for legitimate debate between competent, well-intentioned persons about the correctness of FDA decisions. Also, the approval of drugs in the United States is a lengthy process. Companies convinced of the safety of a drug might be justified in rushing it to market in countries where it is legally permitted, while waiting for approval at home, especially if there is a pressing need abroad. Finally, some critics charge that the long delay in the FDA's approval of Depo-Provera was based on political considerations arising from the opposition of some groups to birth control.

Third, many factors in other countries, especially in the Third World, are beyond the control of TNCs, and they often have little choice but to adapt to local conditions—if they are going to do business at all. This position can perhaps be expressed as, "We do not entirely agree with the Romans, but we sometimes find it necessary to do things their way." For example, physicians in the third world often prefer to prescribe multiple drugs for a single ailment. Hence, the demand for combination antibiotics. Although this practice is disapproved by the American medical community, extending the U.S. ban on such drugs to the rest of the world is unlikely to bring about any significant change. If combination antibiotics were not sold, many doctors would continue to issue prescriptions for several different drugs to be taken simultaneously, very possibly in the wrong proportions.

As another example, consider the ethics of marketing prescription drugs directly to consumers. Deep opposition to this practice exists in the United States, and drug companies are severely criticized for ad campaigns that appeal to patients over the heads of physicians. In much of the Third World, however, self-medication is a deeply ingrained practice, since many people are too poor to consult a doctor, if, indeed, one is available. And many drugs that are available only by prescription in the United States are freely dispensed by pharmacists in the third world—and even by street corner vendors. Under these conditions, drug companies contend that advertising cannot be effective if it is aimed only at physicians. Drug companies are accused, however, of encouraging self-medication and inducing the population to spend scarce resources on pills, tonics, and other medications when they have so many more pressing needs.

# "WHEN IN ROME . . ."

The opposite extreme—that the only guide for business conduct abroad is what is legally and morally accepted in any given country where a TNC operates—is equally untenable. "When in Rome do as the Romans do" cannot be followed without exception. In order to see this, however, we need to distinguish at least three different arguments that are used to support this position. These correspond to the objections to the first position just examined and can be sketched briefly as follows:

1. *There really are morally relevant differences.* The justification for holding a double standard and marketing a drug in a host country that is not approved at home, for example, is that the conditions that prevail in the country are different in morally relevant respects.

2. *The people affected have a right to decide.* Where different standards exist, the right of a host country to determine which to apply should be respected. The primary responsibility for setting standards properly rests on the government and the people of the country in which business is being conducted.

3. *There is no other way of doing business.* Where local conditions require that corporations engage in certain practices as a condition of doing business, then those practices are justified. This is a version of the argument "We do not entirely agree with the Romans, but we sometimes find it necessary to do things their way."

The first argument presupposes the existence of general principles of justification, such as the utilitarian principle that justifies practices in terms of their consequences for benefit and harm. As a result, it is possible that no ultimate conflict exists in some cases of apparent double standards; whatever principles are employed simply justify different practices when conditions are different in morally relevant respects. Many of the criticisms directed against TNCs fail to recognize the extent to which the practices in host countries are capable of being justified by the same principles that justify different practices at home. We have already noted some of the relevant differences that might justify different marketing practices for prescription drugs, but there are many other cases that illustrate the point.

Consider whether a double standard is involved, for example, when TNCs pay wages in less developed countries that are a fraction of those in the developed world. One possible position is that although there are vast differences in the actual wages paid by a TNC in the United States and, say, Mexico, the disparity is not unjust *if the same mechanism for setting wages is employed in both cases*. Thus, the wage paid to a worker in the Third World must provide a decent standard of living in that country and be arrived at by a process of fair bargaining that fully respects workers as human beings. In order for these conditions to be satisfied, unions might also be necessary to ensure that workers are adequately represented.[4] What is morally objectionable about the wages paid by many TNCs in the Third World, then, is not that they are lower than those in the home country but that they are imposed on workers in violation of their rights.

How far this argument is able to justify the use of different standards in host and home countries is a matter for speculation. Although a few of the marketing practices for which the pharmaceutical industry is criticized can perhaps be justified in this manner, it is difficult to believe that the differences between countries are sufficient to justify extensive double standards. A serious effort by TNCs to apply the ethical principles underlying home country standards to the varying conditions they encounter in different parts of the world would be a welcome development—and one that would result, most likely, in many changes in current marketing practices.

## ABIDING BY LOCAL STANDARDS

The argument "The people affected have a right to decide" is not a form of ethical relativism. Just because physicians in some less developed countries routinely sell free samples does not make the practice right. Even when the practice is legal in the country in question and condoned by the local medical community, the indirect payment provided by the sale of free samples that makes it possible for drug companies to bribe physicians can still be branded as morally wrong. The argument is rather an expression of respect for the right of people to govern their own affairs. Imposing the standards of a developed, first world country in the Third World is criticized by some as a form of "ethical imperialism."[5]

Although there is some merit in this argument, it cannot be accepted without considerable qualification. A respect for the right of people to set their own standards does not automatically justify corporations in inflicting grave harm on innocent people, for example, or violating basic human rights. In deciding whether to employ a practice that is regarded as wrong at home but is legal and apparently approved in a host country, a number of factors must be considered.

First, some countries, especially those in the Third World, lack the capacity to regulate effectively the activities of transnational corporations within their own borders. The governments of these countries are, in many instances, no less committed than those in the United States and Western Europe to protecting their people against harm from prescription and over-the-counter drugs, but they do not always have the resources— the money, skilled personnel, and institutions—to accomplish the task.

The law in Nigeria, for example, prohibits the marketing of any drug in a way that is "false, or misleading, or is likely to create a wrong impression as to its quality, character, value, composition, merit, or safety."[6] Such a law cannot be effective, however, without an agency such as the FDA to acquire information about the vast number of drugs that enter the country and issue detailed guidelines for their use. Such steps can also be thwarted by powerful transnationals. One Nigerian has complained:

> . . . [W]e have a proposed new drug reviewed by a committee of experts—many of them highly competent people trained in England, Canada, and the United States. They review all the evidence, both that submitted by the company and that published in the best scientific journals. They may decide that the proposed drug is not safe or not effective enough, and they reject the application. But then the company goes to court with all its expensive legal talent. It files suit. And sometimes our recommendation is overruled.[7]

Second, some countries with the capacity to regulate transnationals lack the necessary *will*. Often, the local medical community and powerful segments of the population benefit from the unethical marketing practices of the giant drug companies and willingly permit and even encourage their use. TNCs, through the exercise of economic power, including payments to government officials, frequently are able to influence regulatory measures. Third World governments also have to be cautious about offending powerful economic interests in countries of the developed world on which they depend for aid. The absence of laws against unethical marketing practices is sometimes part of a pattern of oppression that exists within the country itself. Drug companies are taking advantage of the immorality of others, therefore, when they use certain practices in third world countries with corrupt governments and elites.

In order for the argument "The people affected have a right to decide" to justify the adoption of different standards, it is necessary to ask whether the standard in a host country, if it is lower than that at home, truly represents the considered judgment of the people in question. Does it reflect the decision that they would make if they had both the capacity to protect their own interests effectively and the means for expressing their collective will? A genuine respect for the right of people to determine which standards to apply in their own country requires a careful and sympathetic consideration of what people would do under certain hypothetical conditions rather than what is actually expressed in the law, conventional morality, and commonly accepted practices.

As in the case of the first argument, it is difficult to speculate on the consequences of applying this one to the broad range of situations faced by TNCs. There is little reason to believe, however, that people in less developed countries, if consulted, would approve the marketing of drugs with more indications and fewer warnings than are provided in the United States, or that they would approve the dumping of drugs that are not permitted to be prescribed in the United States, and so on. The common contention that bribery and other forms of corruption are accepted in the third world often proves to be unfounded. Although common in some countries, these practices are, nevertheless, deeply resented by the bulk of the population and often regretted even by many who stand to benefit. Revelations of official corruption have led to the downfall of more than one government, thus indicating that bribery is not approved in those countries.

## THE NEED TO "GO ALONG"

The final argument, "There is no other way of doing business," like the other two, has some merit. As long as they have a right to operate abroad, corporations ought to be permitted to do what is necessary for the conduct of business—within limits, of course. American firms with contracts for projects in the Middle East, for example, have complied in many instances with requests not to station women and Jewish employees in those countries. Although discrimination of this kind is morally repugnant, it is (arguably) morally permissible when the alternative is to risk losing business in the Arab world. Attempts have been made to justify the practice on the ground that American corporations are forced to go along.

A more complicated case is provided by the Arab boycott of Israel, which was begun by the countries of the Arab League in 1945.[8] In order to avoid blacklisting that would bar them from doing business with participating Arab countries, many prominent American transnationals cooperated by avoiding investment in Israel. Other U.S. corporations, however, refused to cooperate with the boycott for ethical reasons. An executive of RCA, which is now part of General Electric, declared:

> We're a worldwide communications company that has done business with China and Romania, and we'd like to do business with the Arabs. But we are not going to end relations with Israel to get an Arab contract. This is a moral issue that we feel strongly about.[9]

(The position taken by RCA is now required by law. An amendment to the Export Administration Act, signed into law in June 1977 over vigorous objections by segments of the business community, prohibits American corporations from cooperating with the Arab boycott against Israel.)

As with the other arguments, "There is no other way of doing business" cannot be accepted without some qualifications. First, the alternative is seldom to cease doing business; rather, the claim that a practice is "necessary" often means merely that it is the most profitable way of doing business. Drug companies might lose some business by refusing to market combination antibiotics, for example, but the amount is not likely to be substantial, especially if the changeover is accompanied by a promotional effort to educate doctors about the proper use of drugs. Similarly, direct marketing is less likely to be objectionable if advertising is used to educate consumers about drugs in a way that genuinely contributes to their well-being instead of the profit of the transnationals. The Arab embargo against Israel greatly complicated the problems of doing business in the Middle East, but some companies were able to avoid cooperating with the boycott and still have business relations with Arab countries.

Second, there are some situations in which a company is morally obligated to withdraw if there is no other way to do business. At one time, any company with plants and other production facilities in South Africa was required by law to observe the rigid segregation imposed by apartheid. Some critics held at the time that if the only alternative to participating in racial oppression is to cease all operations there, then the latter is the morally preferable course of action. Subsequently, the South African government allowed U.S. subsidiaries to integrate their work force and abide by the so-called Sullivan Code, which bars discrimination in employment. However, the Sullivan Code does not address the charge that American firms were still contributing by their presence to the survival of a country that systematically violated the rights of its own people. Also, critics charge that some of the products sold in South Africa contributed to the maintenance of apartheid. Several computer companies in the United States, including IBM, for example, were accused of selling equipment that enabled the South African police to enforce the hated passbook and to keep track of dissidents. American banks have also been criticized for making loans that helped to preserve the economic stability of the white regime. These critics contend that such involvement in an immoral system cannot be justified and that the only moral course was to cease doing business there.

Defenders point out in reply that American companies provided high-paying jobs for blacks in South Africa and that their presence encouraged a gradual process of liberalization. If they had withdrawn, the condition of the oppressed majority would, most likely, not have improved and pressure on the government to make reforms would have been eased. The main consequence would probably have been that other foreign investors and white South Africans would take the place of the departing American firms with worse consequences.

The difficulty with both of the qualifications just discussed lies in finding the appropriate cutoff points. When is conforming to the local way of doing things absolutely necessary and when is it a matter of convenience or mere profitability? When is it morally permissible for a corporation to remain in a country such as South Africa under apartheid and when is a corporation morally obligated to withdraw? Answering these questions requires a careful consideration of the hard realities of the situation and the possibility of justifying each practice. The argument "There is no other way of doing business," therefore, does not settle the matter in any given case but only serves as a starting point for further ethical inquiry.

## SPECIAL STANDARDS FOR INTERNATIONAL BUSINESS

Our results so far have been largely negative. The two extreme positions—"When in Rome, do as the Romans do" and "When in Rome or anywhere else, do as you would at home"—are both inadequate guides in international business. However, the discussion of these positions suggests some principles that can be used to make decisions in difficult cases. These principles recognize that the world of the TNC requires a slightly different approach to issues than the one appropriate to a corporation operating wholly within a single nation-state. This is so for several reasons besides those already mentioned.

First, some of the conditions that create a social responsibility for corporations in a country such as the United States are absent elsewhere. The basis for many of the obligations of American corporations to employees, consumers, and the public at large lies in the extensive powers and privileges that we have conferred upon them. Their responsibility to society rests, in other words, on an implicit "social contract," and that contract does not exist to the same degree when corporations operate abroad. The role of TNCs is often limited to marketing goods produced elsewhere, participating in joint ventures with local companies, and so on. Thus, they are not full-fledged "corporate citizens" of a host country, so to speak, but are more like guests. Hence, they have less reason to exhibit the good citizenship that we expect of domestic corporations, although they should still be good "corporate guests."

Second, the lack of effective international law with comprehensive multinational agreements, codes of conduct, and the like creates a less regulated, more competitive environment for international business. One benefit of a legal system is a uniform system of enforceable rules that provides a level playing field for all firms. Business competition within a single country with an extensive set of laws is thus like an athletic competition. International business, by contrast, is more akin to war, which cannot be conducted by the detailed rules of a boxing match, for example. Even war is bound by moral limits, however, such as the concept of a just war and rules such as the Geneva Convention.

Because of these features of international business, it is not appropriate to hold that TNCs have all the same obligations abroad that they have at home and to use the same principles of justification to determine the extent of their obligations in foreign operations. Still, there is a minimal set of obligations that every corporation is morally bound to observe no matter where the activity takes place. An ethical framework for international business consists in part, then, of the moral minimum for corporations operating abroad.

## MINIMAL AND MAXIMAL DUTIES

Thomas Donaldson suggests that we distinguish the minimal and maximal duties of corporations and come to some agreement about the former. A maximal duty or obligation, he says, is one whose fulfillment would be "praiseworthy but not absolutely mandatory," whereas a minimal duty is one such that "the persistent failure to observe [it] would deprive the corporation of its moral right to exist."[10] The requests of third world countries for help in improving living conditions and developing the local economy, although often expressed as demands for justice, are, in Donaldson's view, pleas for a kind of "corporate philanthropy" that is, at best, a maximal duty and not a moral minimum.[11] Further impoverishing a people or violating a fundamental human right, such as employing child labor, is, by contrast, a failure to observe minimal obligations that apply to all business enterprises.

What principles might serve to justify the minimal duties or obligations of corporations engaged in international business? Two have been proposed. One is the principle of *negative harm*, which holds that in their dealings abroad, corporations have an obligation not to add substantially to the deprivation and suffering of people.[12] The utilitarian injunction to produce the greatest possible benefit to people creates a set of maximal obligations of TNCs, but a concern with consequences can take a number of progressively weaker forms that include preventing harm and merely avoiding the infliction of harm. William K. Frankena distinguishes four versions of an obligation of beneficence: (1) One ought not to inflict evil or harm, (2) one ought to prevent evil or harm, (3) one ought to remove evil, and (4) one ought to do or promote good.[13] The negative-harm principle, which is the weakest form, is (arguably) a moral minimum, so that regardless of what other obligations corporations have in foreign operations, they have this one. The only morally justified exceptions to the obligation not to inflict substantial harm on a people are to avoid violating an important right of some kind or to produce a greater benefit in the long run.

A second principle, proposed by Thomas Donaldson, is that corporations have an obligation to respect certain rights; namely, those that ought to be recognized as *fundamental international rights*.[14] TNCs are not obligated to extend all the rights of U.S. citizens to people everywhere in the world, but there are certain basic rights that no person or institution, including a corporation, is morally permitted to violate. Fundamental international rights are roughly the same as *natural* or *human* rights, and some of these are given explicit recognition in documents ranging from general statements, such as the United Nations Universal Declaration of Human Rights, to the very specific, such as the World Health Organization (WHO) Code of Marketing Breast Milk Substitutes.

Of course, the main problem with a principle to respect fundamental international rights (or fundamental rights, for short) is specifying the rights in question. Even undeniable human rights that create an obligation for some person or institution, such as the government of a country, are not always relevant to a transnational corporation. Everyone has a right to subsistence, for example, but TNCs may be under no obligation to feed the hungry in a country where it operates. It has an obligation, however, not to contribute directly to starvation by, say, converting cultivated land to the production of an export crop. To deal with these complications, Donaldson says that a right must meet the following conditions:

1. The right must protect something of very great importance.
2. The right must be subject to substantial and recurrent threats.
3. The obligations and burdens imposed by the right must be (a) affordable and (b) distributed fairly.[15]

The "fairness-affordability" criterion, expressed in condition 3, serves to relieve corporations of an obligation to do what is beyond its resources and more than its fair share. Although a more extensive list could perhaps be justified by Donaldson's conditions, he suggests the following as a moral minimum:

1. The right to freedom of physical movement.
2. The right to ownership of property.
3. The right to freedom from torture.
4. The right to a fair trial.
5. The right to nondiscriminatory treatment.
6. The right to physical security.
7. The right to freedom of speech and association.
8. The right to minimal education.
9. The right to political participation.
10. The right to subsistence.[16]

Sample applications of these rights, according to Donaldson, include: failing to provide safety equipment, such as goggles, to protect employees from obvious hazards (the right to physical security); using coercive tactics to prevent workers from organizing (the right to freedom of speech and association); employing child labor (the right to minimal education); and bribing government officials to violate their duty or seeking to overthrow democratically elected governments.[17]

## NOTES

1. Norman E. Bowie, "The Moral Obligations of Multinational Corporations," in *Problems of International Justice*, ed. Steven Luper-Foy (Boulder, Colo.: Westview Press, 1987), p. 97.

2. Quoted in Ledogar, *Hungry for Profits*, pp. 46–47.

3. This point is made by Richard T. DeGeorge, "Ethical Dilemmas for Multinational Enterprise," in *Ethics and the Multinational Enterprise* ed. W. Michael Hoffman, Ann E. Lange, and David A. Fedo (Lanham, Md.: University Press of America, 1986), p. 40.

4. For an argument of this kind, see Henry Shue, "Transnational Transgressions," in Tom Regan, *Just Business: New Introductory Essays in Business Ethics* (New York: Random House, 1984), pp. 271–91.

5. See, for example, Jack Berman, "Should Companies Export Ethics?" *New York Times*, 2 September 1973, sec. 3, p. 12.

6. Silverman, Lee, and Lydecker, *Prescriptions for Death*, 116.

7. Ibid., p. 111.

8. For a history of the Arab boycott, see Dan S. Chill, *The Arab Boycott of Israel* (New York: Praeger, 1976).

9. Walter Guzzardi Jr., "That Curious Barrier on the Arab Frontier," *Fortune* (July 1975): 170.

10. Thomas Donaldson, *The Ethics of International Business* (NewYork: Oxford University Press, 1989), p. 62.

11. Ibid., p. 63.

12. For an application of the negative-harm principle to business in South Africa, see Patricia H. Werhane, "Moral Justifications for Doing Business in South Africa," in Hoffman, Lange, and Fedo, *Ethics and the Multinational Enterprise*, pp. 435–42. The principle is applied to hazardous wastes and technology in Henry Shue, "Exporting Hazards," in *Boundaries: National Autonomy and Its Limits* ed. Peter G. Brown and Henry Shue (Totowa, N.J.: Rowman and Littlefield, 1981), pp. 107–45.

13. William K. Frankena, *Ethics*, 2d ed. (Englewood Cliffs, N.J.: Prentice Hall, 1973), p. 47.

14. Donaldson, *The Ethics of International Business*, chap. 5.

15. Ibid., pp. 75–76.

16. Ibid., p 81.

17. Ibid., pp. 87–89.

# SELECT BIBLIOGRAPHY

Brady, F. *Ethical Universals in International Business.* New York: Springer-Verlag, 1997.

De George, R. *Competing With Integrity in International Business.* New York: Oxford University Press, 1993.

Dixon, C., et. al., eds. *Multinational Corporations and the Third World.* London: Croom Helm, 1986.

Donaldson, T. *The Ethics of International Business.* New York: Oxford University Press, 1989.

Elfstrom, G. *Moral Issues and Multinational Corporations.* New York: St. Martin's Press, 1991.

Fisher, B., and J. Turner, eds. *Regulating the Multinational Enterprise.* Westport, Conn.: Quorum, 1985.

Ghosh, P., ed. *Multinational Corporations and Third World Development.* Westport, Conn.: Greenwood Press, 1984.

Harvey, B., ed. *Business Ethics: A European Approach.* Upper Saddle River, N.J.: Prentice-Hall, 1994.

Hoffman, M., et al., eds. *Emerging Global Business Ethics.* Westport, Conn.: Greenwood Press, 1993.

———. *Ethics and the Multinational Enterprise.* Lanham, Md.: University Press of America, 1986.

Lange, H., et. al. *Working Across Cultures.* Norwell, Mass.: Kluwer, 1997.

Madden, C. ed. *The Case for the Multinational Corporation.* New York: Praeger, 1977.

Minus, P. *The Ethics of Business in a Global Economy.* Norwell, Mass.: Kluwer, 1993.

Rubner, A. *The Might of the Multinationals.* Westport, Conn.: Praeger, 1990.

Schlegelmilch, B. *Marketing Ethics: An International Perspective.* Boston: International Thomson, 1998.

Tavis, L., ed. *Multinational Managers and Poverty in the Third World.* Notre Dame, Ind.: Notre Dame University Press, 1982.

# ELECTRONIC SOURCES

CIBERWEB   http://ciber.centers.purdue.edu

Communications for a Sustainable Future   http://csf.colorado.edu

Essential Organization   http://www. essential.org

International Labour Organization   www.ilo.org

The North-South Institute   www.nsi-ins.ca

United States Trade Representative   www.ustr.gov